UNIVERSAL TELEVISION:

The Studio and Its Programs, 1950-1980

by
JEB H. PERRY

The Scarecrow Press, Inc.
Metuchen, N.J., & London
1983

Research Associate: STEVE EBERLY

Library of Congress Cataloging in Publication Data

Perry, Jeb H., 1958-
  Universal Television.

  Includes index.
  1. Universal Television (Firm) I. Title.
PN1992.92.U5P47   1983   791.45'75   83-4269
ISBN 0-8108-1628-8

Copyright © 1983 by Jeb H. Perry

Manufactured in the United States of America

For

H. D. C.

An Acknowledgment to

THE TELEVISION INFORMATION OFFICE

I am greatly indebted to New York City's Television Information Office (TIO), whose extensive collection of program data and extremely helpful staff are an invaluable resource to anyone engaged in television research. This volume could not have been completed without their assistance.

TIO was established in October 1959 to provide "a two-way bridge of understanding between the television industry and its many publics." It is supported by the three major television networks (ABC, CBS, NBC), individual commercial stations and groups, educational stations and the National Association of Broadcasters.

For over two decades, TIO has been providing an outstanding information service to educators, students, the press, and the general public, as well as broadcasters.

I am most grateful to the following TIO staff members for their generous assistance: Leslie Slocum, James B. Poteat, Bert Briller and Edona McCaffery.

I would also like to thank Iris Gelt, "Higgins," Richard P. Longobardi, MCA Television Limited, James Robert Parish, and Jo Swerling, Jr. for many kind favors.

My special thanks to Lamont Johnson and Roy Huggins for their encouragement, and to Steve Eberly, my research associate.

CONTENTS

Preface	vii
Introduction	xi
Foreword, by Roy Huggins	xxi
The Series	1
The Telefeatures	115
The Pilots	245
The Specials	255
The Emmy Awards: Nominees and Winners	267
Appendix I: Theatrical Films Edited from Series Episodes	295
Appendix II: Theatrical Films Based on Series	299
Index	301
About Jeb H. Perry and Roy Huggins	443

PREFACE

As the first book to be written on the output of a TV studio, UNIVERSAL TELEVISION presented its author with a number of research challenges. Chief among them was the initial and time-consuming task of determining which programs were the product of Universal Television and its predecessor, Revue Productions, Inc. No one could provide a complete list-- not even the studio itself.

After searching, cross-referring and re-searching numerous sources, I was finally able to compile what I believe to be a complete list of Universal Television's output from 1950 to 1980--an overwhelming catalog of more than 200 series, 250 telefeatures, 20 pilots and 20 specials. This comprises, in all, an astounding total of over 8,400 individual shows and 7,300 hours of programming which, if run continuously, would take over 10 months to view.

Armed with the program list, I was ready to accept my next challenge: the compilation of production data on the seemingly endless product of the world's most prolific television studio.

My major resource was New York City's Television Information Office (TIO) where a dedicated and friendly young librarian turned over her voluminous program files and reference books to the enthusiastic and, I'm sure she must have thought, slightly deranged author.

During the next eight months I visited TIO daily, filling several notebooks with facts and figures, scribbing data on countless index cards and putting thousands of miles on TIO's hapless photocopier. By the second month of my stay at TIO I had become such a familiar sight that one day an employee inquired of me, "Do you work here?" If I had any sense, I thought to myself, I would, but I had dedicated myself--at least for the time being--to the world of television research and had come to accept its paltry economic rewards and the looks of disbelief at my answer to the cocktail-party query "And what do you do?"

How could I give up all that for a normal existence? How could I give up sorting and annotating fact sheets and newspaper articles while riding the train? How could I give up watching hours of Universal TV shows when I got home from work? How could I give up filling file drawer after file drawer with the reams of printed material I had collected? Very easily, and I would have if it weren't for the support and encouragement of friends, relatives and a certain librarian who, when I returned two years later to do additional research for this project, must have had her suspicions about my lack of sanity confirmed.

Most of the cast and credit listings in this volume were obtained from material compiled by the studio and the television networks. Nearly all of the cast listings are complete, as are most producers' credits. Though additional production credits are extensive in many cases, there are an equal number of instances in which they only scratch the surface. This situation is due to the haphazard record-keeping of the studio and the television networks which compiled a great deal of data on some programs and very little on others. The reader is assured that the author has made every effort to expand in-

Preface / ix

complete studio and network credit listings through additional research.

The most elusive production credits were those of sound mixers, makeup artists, costume designers and other less-visible personnel. Equally difficult to locate were the credits of directors and writers of series episodes as they were rarely included in network program data. The TV series is, after all, a producer's medium, in which it is all but impossible to distinguish the work of one individual director or writer from another, so it is not surprising that their contributions are rarely cited in program records.

This is the first book on television to list all available credits of production personnel--from cinematographers, art directors and film editors to hair stylists, title designers and makeup artists--and it is hoped that this initial effort to document the contributions of the TV craftsperson will inspire further detailed research of television programs and their creators. Though such documentation has long been a hallmark of film research, it has not been employed in a book on television until now.

In addition to the cast and credit listings for each program, this volume includes an index which lists the individual credits of approximately 3,500 actors, producers, directors, writers, cinematographers, composers, art directors, film editors and other production personnel. Also included are selected Universal Television executives and the production companies that have produced programs in association with the studio.

Though the lists of actors' and producers' credits are essentially complete, those of production personnel are, for the most part, only representative. This is because, as mentioned above, credit listings are extensive for some programs but incomplete for others. Therefore, a craftsperson who worked on a dozen programs may have only a few of them listed in program records and, thus, in the index. While this situation is regrettable--and galling to the researcher-- it is also unavoidable.

Despite such flaws, I hope that the reader will find this volume to be a useful and innovative piece of television research.

February 1982   J. H. P.

INTRODUCTION

The company that was to become the colossus of Universal Television, for years the most prolific supplier of small-screen programming, began as Revue Productions, Inc., the TV division of the talent agency MCA (Music Corporation of America). Revue, along with its sister company MCA Television Limited, which co-produced and later distributed the programs in syndication, was incorporated in 1950 and, by the mid-1950s, was responsible for such now-classic entries as Alfred Hitchcock Presents, General Electric Theatre and Leave It to Beaver.

Music Corporation of America was the brainchild of Chicago ophthalmologist Jules Caesar Stein, who founded the company in 1924 with his partner, musician William R. Goodhart, Jr., to book dance bands into nightclubs. Eventually the company took on other acts and by 1941, when it acquired the CBS Artist Bureau, was the largest talent agency in the world.

The phenomenal success of television impressed Lew Wasserman, president of MCA since 1946, and he wasted no time in getting his company into the quickly expanding field.

MCA obtained space at the old Republic Studios (4024 N. Radford Avenue in North Hollywood, California), today the CBS Studio Center, and set up Revue Productions. Before long they were churning out dozens of series, including The Restless Gun, Biff Baker, U.S.A., Tales of Wells Fargo and The Deputy starring Henry Fonda. Most of the programs were licensed to the networks, but several, like State Trooper,

The Man Behind the Badge, and Soldiers of Fortune, were sold directly to local stations and MCA Television Limited soon became the leading telefilm syndication firm.

In 1959, with $11,250,000 it had made from Revue Productions, MCA purchased the mammoth, 410-acre lot of Universal Pictures (founded in 1912 by producer Carl Laemmle) on Lankershim Boulevard in Universal City, California and dubbed it Revue Studios. Universal Pictures had hit on hard times with the shutdown of its once-prosperous B-picture unit and cutbacks in the production of feature films--all due to the impact of television--so its owners were happy to sell their grossly underused lot and soundstages, even if the buyer was their enemy--a TV company.

By 1962, MCA was in the unusual position of both selling (via the agency) and buying (via Revue) talent. The Justice Department also found this unusual--if not illegal--and so ordered MCA to divest itself of either its TV holdings or its agency. MCA chose the latter, as its potential for success in the new telefilm industry seemed unlimited. (Revue Productions earned $72,600,000 in 1961, as opposed to the $8,400,000 brought in by MCA Artists Limited, the talent agency.)

The divestiture allowed MCA to go ahead with two major projects: the acquisition of Universal Pictures itself (including the company's entire catalog of motion pictures) and a merger with Decca Records (which became Universal City Records and is now known as MCA Records).

In 1964, Revue Studios was renamed Universal City Studios, Inc. and Revue Productions became Universal Television. The name MCA Television Limited continued to be used for the telefilm syndication company. The name Revue survived through the early 1970s as the monicker for a subsidiary label of Universal City Records.

Throughout its history, Revue/Universal Television has been responsible for many programming innovations. In 1962, it premiered television's first 90-minute Western, The Virginian. The following season it expanded Wagon Train to 90 minutes and added another series of the same length, Arrest and Trial.

In 1964, the studio made its first attempt at an "umbrella" concept, tying together three separate situation comedies (Harris Against the World, Karen and Tom, Dick and Mary) under the title 90 Bristol Court. The gimmick was that the stars of the shows all lived in the same apartment complex. The concept was not a success.

The year 1964 also saw the debut of Project 120, the first series of 120-minute movies made especially for television. The initial production, The Killers, was deemed too violent for the home screen and was diverted to theatrical release. The other two, See How They Run and The Hanged Man, were broadcast on NBC Wednesday Night at the Movies.

In 1966, Universal Television introduced its World Premiere movie series on NBC-TV. These films, made especially for television like the Project 120 entries, became a huge success and hundreds were churned out, often as pilots for series, as was the initial effort, Fame Is the Name of the Game.

In 1968, Universal Television brought another innovation to TV: a 90-minute series with three rotating characters (one appeared each week) connected by a common place of employment. The result was The Name of the Game (based on the TV-movie Fame Is the Name of the Game), a program about the owner and reporters of a publishing empire.

The year 1969 saw the premiere of The Bold Ones, which was the umbrella title for three rotating series (The Doctors, The Lawyers and The Protectors) dealing with aspects of contemporary American society. In the program's second season The Protectors was dropped and a new element, The Senator, took its place.

In 1970, the studio brought together four series with divergent themes under the umbrella title of Four-in-One. The programs (McCloud, Rod Serling's Night Gallery, The Psychiatrist and San Francisco International Airport) ran for six consecutive weeks each and were ostensibly the first mini-series.

The following season, Universal Television unveiled the NBC Mystery Movie, a series of 90-minute rotating programs in the detective genre. One week viewers tuned in to Columbo, the next week to McCloud and the following to McMillan and Wife. The format was very popular and the next season Hec Ramsey was added to the line-up and a separate series, NBC Wednesday Mystery Movie (Banacek, Cool Million and Madigan), premiered. In later seasons other programs were introduced while unsuccessful ones were dropped, and the show continued through the 1976-77 season.

In 1971, the studio had another "first": the presentation of a two-part, four-hour made-for-TV movie (Vanished). It was a substantial success and paved the way for the long-form drama, or the "mini-series."

The year 1976 was an important one for Universal Television. It marked the premiere of the studio's first genuine mini-series, Rich Man, Poor Man. Although the mini-series format had been around for three years on American television, or for six years if one counts the Four-in-One entries as mini-series, Rich Man, Poor Man was the program that made the genre immensely popular and set the stage for the success of the studio's NBC's Best Sellers, the first of which was Captains and the Kings in 1976.

Introduction / xv

The other highlight of 1976 was the creation by a group of independent TV stations and MCA Television Limited of Operation Prime Time (OPT), a sort of "fourth network" which broadcast high-budget mini-series via film prints placed with each of the 95 stations in the consortium. The stations pooled their resources to finance the project and, as was hoped, got their investment back on the first run with five additional showings allotted to them.

The first OPT program was <u>Testimony of Two Men</u>, broadcast in May 1977. It was followed by <u>The Immigrants</u> and the American Bicentennial trilogy of <u>The Bastard</u>, <u>The Rebels</u>, and <u>The Seekers</u>. Each was an appreciable success.

In 1978-79, NBC broadcast Universal Television's biggest project in its 28-year history: the mini-series of James A. Michener's massive novel <u>Centennial</u>. At a running time of 26 hours, it was the longest mini-series ever. At a cost of $25,000,000 it was the most expensive show in TV history. The cast included 74 major speaking parts, and it took six producers, four directors, and four photographers to bring it to the screen. This, the latest of Universal Television's innovations, is sure to be followed by others, as the ever-changing TV industry demands more variations on creative programming.

MCA, Inc. today, in addition to Universal Television, MCA Television Limited, Universal Pictures, and MCA Records, also owns the Universal City Studios Tour and Amphitheatre, the G.P. Putnam's Sons publishing house, Colorado's Columbia Savings and Loan Association, Spencer Gifts (retail stores), Mid Continent Computer Services, Yosemite Park & Curry Company (amusement facility), Universal 8 and Universal 16 (home movie distributors), MCA DiscoVision (video discs), MCA Merchandising, MCA Music (publishing) and MCA New Ventures (business investments), among other companies. In 1978, MCA, Inc. grossed $1,120,644,000.

These days, Universal Television usually holds its own as the major supplier of TV shows to the networks, although in recent years it has been challenged--and sometimes beaten --by independent producers.

During its 30-year history, Universal Television and its predecessor, Revue Productions, Inc., gained a reputation for quantity at the expense of quality. One detractor claimed in the late 1950s that Revue was like a giant "sausage factory," grinding out an overwhelming, and often undistinguished, amount of product. While this observation is in part verified by a sampling of the critical appraisals of the studio's productions in trade papers, it would be unfair not to mention that a number of Revue/Universal Television's programs were fine examples of the best that could be achieved in an industrialized/commercialized medium.

In addition to the aforementioned Alfred Hitchcock Presents, General Electric Theatre, Leave It to Beaver, Wagon Train, The Virginian, Arrest and Trial, The Name of the Game, Columbo, Rich Man, Poor Man, and Centennial, there were such high-quality entries as The Alfred Hitchcock Hour, Startime, Alcoa Premiere, Thriller, Kraft Suspense Theatre, Bob Hope Presents the Chrysler Theatre, The Jack Benny Show, 87th Precinct, Run for Your Life, Ironside, It Takes a Thief, Rod Serling's Night Gallery, The Lawyers, The Protectors, The Doctors, The Senator, McMillan and Wife, Banacek, Tenafly, The Snoop Sisters, The Man and the City, The Law, The Rockford Files, The Family Holvak, Toma, Baretta, Kojak, The Night Stalker, and Quincy, M.E.

In the telefeature department, Universal Television produced such socially conscious and sensitive dramas as A

Clear and Present Danger, The Whole World Is Watching, A Case of Rape, Deadlock!, Farewell to Manzanar, The Gun, The Law, The Marcus-Nelson Murders, Sarah T.--Portrait of a Teenage Alcoholic, Tail Gunner Joe, and director Lamont Johnson's outstanding collaborations with writers Richard Levinson and William Link (My Sweet Charlie, That Certain Summer, and The Execution of Private Slovik). In addition, there were such entertainments as director Steven Spielberg's Duel, Prescription: Murder, and Ransom for a Dead Man with Peter Falk as Columbo, director Don Siegel's Stranger on the Run with Henry Fonda, Fear No Evil with Louis Jourdan and Frankenstein: The True Story with James Mason heading an all-star cast.

In the specials category, Universal Television has also had its shining hours with Applause, The Adventures of Don Quixote, The Red Pony, Hamlet, The Man Who Came to Dinner, The Snow Goose, and the Portrait entries.

In addition to its large catalog of programs, Universal Television was responsible for developing one of the most impressive stables of creative producers in the industry. Among those who worked for the studio at one time or another were Alfred Hitchcock (Alfred Hitchcock Presents, Startime), Roy Huggins (The Lawyers, The Rockford Files), Hubbell Robinson (Startime, Thriller), Joe Connelly and Bob Mosher (Leave It to Beaver, The Munsters), Robert Altman (Kraft Suspense Theatre), Norman Lloyd (Alfred Hitchcock Presents, The Name of the Game), William Frye (The Deputy, Thriller), Richard Berg (Alcoa Premiere, Bob Hope Presents the Chrysler Theatre), Edward J. Montagne (Man Against Crime, McHale's Navy), David Levinson (The Doctors, The Senator), Leslie Stevens (The Name of the Game, McCloud), George Eckstein (The Name of the Game, Banacek), Jack Laird (Rod

Serling's Night Gallery, Kojak), William Sackheim (The Senator, The Law), Jo Swerling, Jr. (The Lawyers, Baretta), Leonard B. Stern (McMillan and Wife, The Snoop Sisters), Richard Irving (The Name of the Game, The Virginian), Glen A. Larson (It Takes a Thief, Quincy, M.E.), Cy Chermak (Ironside, The Night Stalker), David Victor (Marcus Welby, M.D., Owen Marshall, Counselor at Law), David J. O'Connell (Marcus Welby, M.D., Lanigan's Rabbi), Roland Kibbee and Dean Hargrove (Columbo, The Family Holvak), Jack Webb (Dragnet 1967-1970, Adam-12), Jon Epstein (Owen Marshall, Counselor at Law, Rich Man, Poor Man), Frank Price (The Virginian, Alias Smith and Jones), Robert A. Cinader (Adam-12, Emergency!), Howie Horwitz (Banacek, Baretta), Harve Bennett (The Six Million Dollar Man, Rich Man, Poor Man), Richard Levinson and William Link (Columbo and numerous telefeatures), Barbara Schultz (Wide World Mystery, ABC Afternoon Playbreak), Robert F. O'Neill (Gemini Man, The Invisible Man), Stephen J. Cannell (The Rockford Files, Baa Baa Black Sheep), Steven Bochco (Delvecchio, The Invisible Man), Kenneth Johnson (The Incredible Hulk, The Bionic Woman), and John Wilder (Centennial).

A number of directors who are today known for their theatrical motion pictures did their earlier work in TV at Universal. Among them were Lamont Johnson (The Name of the Game episode), Steven Spielberg (The Psychiatrist episode), Jeannot Szwarc (Toma episode), Randal Kleiser (Marcus Welby, M.D. episode), Frank A. Pierson (The Neon Ceiling telefeature), Sidney Pollack (Bob Hope Presents the Crysler Theater episode), Michael Ritchie (The Sound of Anger telefeature), and John Badham (The Law telefeature).

Directors are not the only ones who have gone from doing television programs at Universal to working on theatrical films. The talents who have achieved the cross-over range from cinematographer Vilmos Zsigmond to composer John Williams.

But the talented people who worked at Universal Television were not limited to those who later went into motion pictures. The studio cultivated its own dedicated production personnel, a number of whom were associated with the company for many years--people like directors Don Weis, Boris Sagal, Douglas Heyes, Buzz Kulik, Lou Antonio, Herschel Daugherty, Alan Crosland, Jr., Daryl Duke, Gordon Hessler, William A. Graham, Alf Kjellin, Jerry London, Russ Mayberry, Leo Penn, Jack Smight, Richard A. Colla, Walter Doniger, and Robert Day; cinematographers Lionel Lindon, Benjamin H. Kline, John L. Russell, Ray Rennahan, Bud Thackery, Enzo A. Martinelli, Jack A. Marta, Lloyd Ahern, Ben Colman, Alric Edens, Andrew Jackson, Jacques R. Marquette, Gene Polito, Walter Strenge, Bill Butler, Gerald Perry Finnerman, Vilis Lapenieks, William Margulies, John F. Warren, and Harry L. Wolf; composers Stanley Wilson, Lyn Murray, Pete Rugolo, Richard Clements, Melvyn Lenard, Leonard Rosenman, Elmer Bernstein, John Addison, Mike Post, Pete Carpenter, Dick De Benedictis, Gil Melle, Oliver Nelson, Billy Goldenberg, Lalo Schifrin, Dave Grusin, and Hal Mooney; art directors John J. Lloyd, Howard E. Johnson, John E. Chilberg II, Joseph Alves, Jr., Raymond Beal, George Webb, John Meehan, Loyd S. Papez, William H. Tuntke, Henry Bumstead, William D. DeCinces, Russell Kimball, and George Patrick; film editors Richard G. Wray, Sam E. Waxman, Robert Watts, David J. O'Connell, Edward Haire, Richard Belding, Douglas Stewart, Edward A. Biery, Edward M. Abroms, Larry Lester, Robert F. Shugrue, Budd Small, Richard Bracken, Frank E. Morriss, Robert L. Kimble, xx / Introduction

and John Kaufman, Jr.; set decorators John McCarthy, James S. Redd, Joseph J. Stone, Ralph Sylos, Lowell Chambers, and Jerry Adams; makeup artists Bud Westmore and Jack Barron; costume designers Vincent Dee, Grady Hunt, Burton Miller, and Charles Waldo; hair stylists Florence Bush and Larry Germain; sound mixers Lyle Cain, Earl N. Crain, Jr., David H. Moriarty, and Melvin M. Metcalfe, Sr.; main title designers Wayne Fitzgerald and Jack Cole; and many others. (While many of the above have worked in films, most are best known for their work at Revue/Universal Television).

Universal Television also had its share of talent in the "front office." Among the people who looked after the business end of the company were presidents like Taft Schreiber, Sidney Sheinberg, Frank Price, and Donald Sipes and vice-presidents like Howard Christie, Richard Lewis, Richard Irving, Roy Huggins, Stuart Erwin, Jr., and Jennings Lang.

Throughout its history, Universal has been a driving and trend-setting force in the television industry. This book is a tribute to its people and its product.

FOREWORD

by Roy Huggins

The time to write a history of almost anything, from people and places to abstract ideas, is the time at which those ideas, people, or places have taken form, preferably at a point of stasis. A history written too soon is a prologue to someone else's history, and a history written too late is an addendum.

Jeb H. Perry has chosen the perfect moment to write this history, and he has chosen the company, Universal, that is the paradigm of television production companies. When did the central, possibly even the "golden," period in television begin? In 1951 when the coaxial cable was at last completed? In 1952, when the federal government's freeze on television outlets was lifted? The date can be fixed only arbitrarily, by agreement among historians, but there is little doubt that the date will be fixed somewhere between 1951 and 1955. It was in the latter year that the first one-hour filmed drama series appeared on network television. Before that time television had been radio with pictures, dominated by the advertising companies that had dominated radio. The one-hour filmed show broke both the radio pattern and sponsor domination. Television had found its own identity.

Twenty-five years later another change began to take place in television, a change so great that it could be said to mark the end of an era that had lasted for a quarter of a century. In the mid-seventies the prime-time audience for network programming did something it had never done before: it began to decline. Since 1975 the audience has declined from over 90 percent of the viewers available to less than 80 percent, and the networks themselves acknowledge that the percentage will probably drop below 70 percent in the next five to seven years.

The reasons for the decline are two-fold: technology and aesthetics. The technological developments are obvious. There are now more than 40 cable television services in operation. Also how many households are using their television sets to watch pre-recorded disks and cassettes is not known with any degree of accuracy. Equally unknown is the number pre-empting the television set to play electronic games. What is known with absolute certainty is that the number of households switching off prime-time television is growing rapidly.

American households today are more apt to be without bathtubs and telephones than without television sets. That saturation point was a long time coming, and its progress brought about a constant but slow change in the "class" makeup of the audience. Television sets have always been relatively expensive, and in the early years the audience tended to be "upper middle class." By the end of the 1950's the audience was comfortably middle class. Since that time the whole economic spectrum has slowly come to be represented in the television audience, and as that occurred programming changed in response, and the "upper" segments of the audience began to watch television less and less frequently. Changes in the style of programming were only partly responsible for the defection. People who could afford it began to find less passive ways to enjoy their leisure.

In 1970 the FCC adopted stringent regulative measures that put the fear of God and the stockholders into the hearts of network managers. The new regulations encouraged the emergence of independent producers, who began taking a scary share of the market. This development, along with such others as the continued acceleration of costs, led to a heightening of competition between the three networks that makes the competition between General Motors, Ford, and Chrysler look like child's play. Suddenly a half point on the Nielsen scale became a matter of life or death. The cost of a half minute of prime time is based on the Nielsen numbers, and today those numbers alone determine the fate of a show. Throughout the sixties the networks tended to cancel shows for a variety of reasons, frequently casual, sometimes arcane. The Fugitive, for example, was cancelled at the end of its fourth season despite continued ratings strength. In today's television world the cancellation of a show with the ratings and demographics of The Fugitive would be unthinkable. Today the quality of a show may become an embarrassment to a network, but if the ratings stay up, the show stays on.

The so-called "Golden Age" of television may not have been as golden as its devotees claim, but there were few if any one-hour shows whose source was comic-books. Today the comic-book era is upon us like a plague, and for the first time in television's history large numbers of viewers are declaring themselves disenchanted with the medium. A recent study commissioned by the National Association of Broadcasters brought forth that surprising (to them) message. Said John Bowen, one of the authors of the study, "From the mid-1970's, and continuing into the present day, viewers have become increasingly evaluative, judgmental and critical of the programming offered to them by the three commercial television networks." Viewers declare that they are watching less television because they are dissatisfied with programming. In 1977, 72 percent of those surveyed thought television was "more realistic." In the 1983 survey, that figure had dropped to 59 percent. Whether or not these findings are supported by Nielsen's estimate of the number of hours television sets are turned on, the fact remains that this is the first such "friendly" survey to turn up a wide range of negative opinion.

Jeb Perry's timing for his history of Universal Television could not, therefore, have been more opportune. The history of that studio now has a beginning, a middle, and an end. I do not mean to imply that Universal Television is on its way out, but the story of that company from 1980 on will not much resemble the story that Mr. Perry tells in this exhaustive, interesting, and important book. It is a story that required telling, and Mr. Perry has done so superbly.

THE SERIES

Note

As this book is only concerned with the productions of Universal Television and its predecessor, Revue, it does not include "pickups," i.e., series which were not produced by Revue/Universal but which were acquired for distribution by its sister company, MCA Television Limited. (Such programs include Follow That Man produced by R. J. Reynolds/Pathescope and Love That Bob produced by McCadden Corporation.)

See APPENDIX I for a list of theatrical films edited from series episodes and APPENDIX II for a list of theatrical films based on Universal Television series.

ABC AFTERNOON PLAYBREAK/ABC MATINEE TODAY

ABC Television Network, October 30, 1973-May 20, 1976; 4 episodes in color on tape produced by Universal Television; 90 minutes.

A dramatic anthology. See THE SPECIALS: Alone with Terror, The Mask of Love, My Secret Mother, and A Special Act of Love for details.

ABC WIDE WORLD OF ENTERTAINMENT

ABC Television Network, January 8, 1973-January 10, 1976; 10 episodes in color on tape produced by Universal Television; 90 minutes.

Wide World Mystery segments. See THE TELEFEATURES: The Book of Murder, Death Is a Bad Trip, The House of Evil, A Little Bit Like Murder, Murder by Proxy, Murder Works Overtime, Night Life, The Nightmare Step, A Prowler in the Heart, and The Suicide Club for details.

ADAM-12

NBC Television Network, September 21, 1968-August 26, 1975; 174 episodes in color on film; 30 minutes.

2 / Series

A police drama chronicling the adventures of Officers Pete Malloy and Jim Reed of the Los Angeles Police Department.

Cast: Officer Pete Malloy (Martin Milner), Officer Jim Reed (Kent McCord), Sgt. MacDonald (William Boyett), Officer Ed Wells (Gary Crosby), Officer Woods (Fred Stamsoe).

Credits: Executive Producers: Jack Webb, Herman S. Saunders; Producers: Herman S. Saunders, Tom Williams, James Doherty, Jerry Stanley, R. A. Cinader; Created by: R. A. Cinader, Jack Webb; Directors: Bruce Kessler, Joseph Pevney, Jack Webb, Robert Douglas, James Doherty, Stan Crosland, Dennis Donnelly, Alan Crosland, Jr., Jean Yarbrough, Phil Rawlins, Hollingsworth Morse, Harry Morgan, others; Writers: Jack Webb, Michael Donovan, Jack Hawn, Joseph Michael Calvelli, Robert I. Holt, Preston Wood, John Randolph, James Doherty, Guerdon Trueblood, Robert Hamner, Richard Neil Morgan, Don Ingalls, others; Associate Producers: Carl Vitale, William Stark, Tom Williams; Story Editors: David H. Vowell, Stephen J. Cannell; Executive Story Consultant: John T. Dugan; Music: Frank Comstock; Directors of Photography: F. Bud Mautino, Jerry Sims; Art Director: Lester L. Green; Set Decorations: A. C. Montenaro, John Sturtevant; Assistant Director: Warren Smith; Unit Manager: Mel A. Bishop; Film Editors: Robert Richards, A.C.E., Sam E. Waxman, A.C.E., James Nownes; Assistant to the Producer: Tom Williams; Sound: Phil Mitchell; Color by: Technicolor; Titles & Optical Effects: Universal Title; Editorial Supervision: Richard Belding; Music Supervision: Stanley Wilson, Hal Mooney; Production Assistant: Tracy Webb; Costume Supervisor: Vincent Dee; Makeup Artist: Bud Westmore; Hair Stylist: Larry Germain; Technical Advisors: Chief Edward M. Davis, L.A.P.D., Ed Walker, Sgt. Frank Whitman, L.A.P.D.; Produced by: Mark VII Limited, Adam-12 Productions, in association with Universal Television and NBC-TV; Exclusive Distributor: MCA Television Limited.

THE ADVENTURES OF KIT CARSON

Distributed by MCA Television Limited, 1953-1954; 53 episodes in black & white on film; 30 minutes.

A western based on the adventures of frontier scout Kit Carson and his south-of-the-border chum El Toro.

Cast: Kit Carson (Bill Williams), El Toro (Don Diamond).

Credits: Produced by: Revue Productions, Inc.; Exclusive Distributor: MCA Television Limited.

ALCOA PREMIERE/PREMIERE

ABC Television Network, October 10, 1961-September 12, 1963; 56

episodes in black & white on film; 60 minutes. Sponsor and Agency for Alcoa Premiere: Aluminum Company of America through Fuller, Smith & Ross, Inc. Sponsors and Agencies for Premiere: Armour and Company through Foote, Cone & Belding, Inc.; Mead Johnson & Company through Kenyon & Eckhard, Inc.; Mobil Oil Co., Inc. through Ted Bates and Company, Inc.; North American Philips Co., Inc. through C. J. LaRoche and Co., Inc.; Ovaltine Food Products Co., Division of the Wander Company through Tatham-Laird, Inc.; Polaroid Corp. through Doyle Dane Bernbach, Inc.; R. J. Reynolds Tobacco Co. through William Esty & Company, Inc.; Sunbeam Corporation through Perrin & Associates.

A dramatic anthology hosted by Fred Astaire. Guest stars included James Stewart, George Gobel, Ralph Bellamy, Suzanne Pleshette, Charlton Heston, Telly Savalas, Richard Conte, Ricardo Montalban, Mickey Rooney, Fred Astaire, Cliff Robertson, Tommy Sands, Shelley Winters, Edward Asner, and Lee Marvin. Syndicated as Fred Astaire Presents. The episode entitled "Seven Against the Sea" (April 3, 1962), in which Ernest Borgnine played the commander of a PT boat in World War II, was the inspiration for the comedy series McHale's Navy (which see). Eight episodes of Alcoa Premiere were rebroadcast on Kraft Mystery Theatre (which see).

Cast: Host, Fred Astaire.

Credits: Executive Producer: Richard Lewis; Producers: Richard Berg, George Schaefer, Everett Freeman, Peter Tewksbury, Alfred Hitchcock, Alex Segal, Eric Ambler, others; Directors: John Ford, Alex Segal, Coby Ruskin, Robert Ellis Miller, Lawrence Dobkin, Dennis Sanders, Alan Crosland, Jr., Bernard Girard, Robert Florey, Ted Post, Peter Tewksbury, others; Writers: Jameson Brewer, Howard Leeds, Elton Packard, Henry F. Greenberg, Ray Bradbury, David Karp, Don Stanford, Henry Cecil, Ernest Kinoy, Peter Tewksbury, Peggy & Lou Shaw, Oscar Millard, James Gunn, others; Associate Producer: Frank Baur; Art Directors: Martin Obzina, Alex Mayer, others; Directors of Photography: William H. Clothier, John F. Warren, A.S.C., Benjamin H. Kline, A.S.C., others; Film Editors: Richard Belding, Tony Martinelli, Howard Epstein, others; Set Decorators: John McCarthy, Martin C. Bradfield, others; Music Supervision: Stanley Wilson; Music by: Johnny Williams; Main Title Design: Saul Bass; Produced by: Avasta Productions, Revue Productions, Inc.; Exclusive Distributor: MCA Television Limited.

THE ALFRED HITCHCOCK HOUR

CBS Television Network, September 20, 1962-September 6, 1965; 93 episodes in black & white on film; 60 minutes.

A mystery/suspense anthology hosted by Alfred Hitchcock. Guest stars included Robert Redford, Dean Stockwell, James Mason, Joan Fontaine, Lillian Gish, Bob Newhart, Gena Rowlands, John Cassavetes, Darren McGavin, Bruce Dern, Elsa Lanchester, Angie

4 / Series

Dickinson, Franchot Tone, Vera Miles and John Gavin. Alfred Hitchcock directed one episode.

Cast: Host, Alfred Hitchcock.

Credits: Executive Producer: Alfred Hitchcock; Producers: Joan Harrison, Norman Lloyd; Associate Producer: Gordon Hessler; Directors: Alfred Hitchcock, Bernard Girard, Alf Kjellin, Jack Smight, others; Writers: Alfred Hayes, Robert Bloch, Henry Slesar, James Bridges, others; Film Editors: Edward W. Williams, A.C.E., Douglas Stewart; Music Score: Lyn Murray; Music Supervision: Stanley Wilson; Theme music based on the "Funeral March of Two Marionettes," by Charles François Gounod; Produced by: Shamley Productions, Inc, Revue Productions, Inc.; Exclusive Distributor: MCA Television Limited.

ALFRED HITCHCOCK PRESENTS

CBS Television Network, October 2, 1955-June 26, 1960; NBC Television Network, September 27, 1960-June 26, 1962; 265 episodes in black & white on film; 30 minutes.

A mystery/suspense anthology hosted by Alfred Hitchcock. Guest stars included Gene Barry, Sir Cedric Hardwicke, Phyllis Thaxter, Dennis Day, William Shatner, Claude Rains, Fay Wray, Art Carney, Roger Moore, Barbara Baxley, Dick Van Dyke, Burt Reynolds, Peter Falk, Edward Asner and Peggy Ann Garner. Alfred Hitchcock directed 17 episodes. His introductory and closing remarks were written by James Allardyce.

Cast: Host, Alfred Hitchcock.

Credits: Executive Producer: Alfred Hitchcock; Produced by: Joan Harrison; Directors: Alfred Hitchcock, Alan Crosland, Jr., Bretaigne Windust, Paul Henreid, Robert Stevens, Ida Lupino, John Brahm, Don Weis, Boris Sagal, Herschel Daugherty, others; Writers: Ray Bradbury, Francis Cockrell, Albert E. Lewin, Burt Styler, others; Director of Photography: John L. Russell, A.S.C.; Associate Producer: Norman Lloyd; Art Director: John J. Lloyd; Editorial Supervisor: Richard G. Wray, A.C.E.; Film Editor: Edward W. Williams, A.C.E.; Music Supervisor: Frederick Herbert; Music by: Stanley Wilson, Lyn Murray; Theme music based on the "Funeral March of Two Marionettes" by Charles Francois Gounod; Set Decorator: Mac Mulcahy; Assistant Director: Ronnie Rondell; Sound: John C. Grubb; Costume Supervisor: Vincent Dee; Makeup: Leo Lotito, Jr.; Hair Stylist: Florence Bush; Sound Recording: RCA; Produced by: Shamley Productions, Inc., Revue Productions, Inc.; Exclusive Distributor: MCA Television Limited.

ALIAS SMITH AND JONES

ABC Television Network, January 21, 1971-January 13, 1973; 48

episodes in color on film; 60 minutes.

A Western about the adventures of Jed "Kid" Curry and Hannibal Heyes, two outlaws who suddenly decided to go straight. Guest stars included Burl Ives, James Drury, Earl Holliman, Susan Saint James, Dick Cavett, Walter Brennan, Ann Sothern, Michele Lee and Neville Brand.

Cast: Hannibal Heyes alias Joshua Smith (Peter Deuel, Roger Davis), Jed "Kid" Curry alias Thaddeus Jones (Ben Murphy), Clementine Hale (Sally Field).

Credits: Executive Producer: Roy Huggins; Associate Executive Producer: Jo Swerling, Jr.; Executive In Charge of Production: Frank Price; Produced and Created by: Glen A. Larson; Directors: Gene Levitt, Jack Arnold, Mel Ferber, Barry Shear, Jeffrey Hayden, others; Writers: Glen A. Larson, John Thomas James, Dick Nelson, Sy Salkowitz, Irv Pearlberg, Matthew Howard, others; Associate Producers: Steve Heilpern, Nick Baehr; Music: Bob Prince, John Andrew Tartaglia; Theme Music: Billy Goldenberg; Directors of Photography: Gene Polito, William Cronjager, John M. Stephen; Art Directors: Robert E. Smith, Phil Bennett; Set Decorations: Joseph Stone, Bert F. Allen; Unit Managers: Bud Brill, Ben Bishop; Sound: Robert Strand, Earl N. Crane, Jr.; Assistant Directors: Jack Doran, Warren Smith; Editorial Supervisor: Richard Belding; Film Editors: John Dumas, Richard Bracken; Costume Supervisor: Vincent Dee; Color by: Technicolor; Titles & Optical Effects: Universal Title; Produced by: Universal Television; Exclusive Distributor: MCA Television Limited.

AMERICAN FLYER

Distributed by MCA Television Limited, 1977; 6 episodes in color on tape; 90 minutes.

A musical/variety program.

Cast: Hosts, Dan Rowan, Michele Lee, Tom Hallick.

Credits: Produced by: Universal Television; Exclusive Distributor: MCA Television Limited.

AMY PRENTISS (NBC SUNDAY MYSTERY MOVIE)

NBC Television Network, December 1, 1974-July 6, 1975; 3 episodes in color on film; 90 minutes and 120 minutes.

A crime drama revolving around Amy Prentiss, the chief of detectives of the San Francisco Police Department. The character was introduced in the Ironside episode "Amy Prentiss, AKA The Chief."

Cast: Amy Prentiss (Jessica Walter), Detective Rod Pena (Art

Metrano), Detective Tony Russell (Steve Sandor), Detective Contreras (Johnny Seven), Joan (Gwenn Mitchell), Jill Prentiss (Helen Hunt).

Credits: Produced by: Cy Chermak; Mystery Movie Theme: Henry Mancini; Color by: Technicolor; Titles & Optical Effects: Universal Title; Produced by: Universal Television; Exclusive Distributor: MCA Television Limited.

ARREST AND TRIAL

ABC Television Network, September 15, 1963-September 6, 1964; 30 episodes in black & white on film; 90 minutes. Sponsors and Agency: Libby, McNeill & Libby and Liggett & Myers through J. Walter Thompson Company.

A combination police show and courtroom drama in which the suspects were apprehended in the first part and brought to trial in the second. The arrests were made by Detective Sgt. Nick Anderson and the suspects were defended by Attorney John Egan.

Cast: Detective Sgt. Nick Anderson (Ben Gazzara), Defense Attorney John Egan (Chuck Connors), Deputy D.A. Jerry Miller (John Larch), Assistant Deputy D.A. Barry Pine (John Kerr), Detective Sgt. Dan Kirby (Roger Perry), Lt. Bone (Noah Keen), Mitchell Harris (Don Galloway), Jake Shakespeare (Joe Higgins), Janet Okada (Jo Anne Miya).

Credits: Executive Producer: Frank P. Rosenberg; Directors: John Brahm, others; Writers: Herb Meadow, Paul Mason, others; Film Editors: Danny Landres, Milton Shifman, Richard G. Wray; Produced by: Revue Productions, Inc.; Exclusive Distributor: MCA Television Limited.

ASPEN (NBC'S BEST SELLERS)

NBC Television Network, November 5-7, 1977; 3 episodes in color; 120 minutes (total: 6 hours).

A drama about illicit love, corruption and a sensational murder trial at a Colorado ski resort in the 1960s. Rebroadcast as The Innocent and the Damned.

Cast: Lee Bishop (Perry King), Tom Keating (Sam Elliott), Carl Osborne (Gene Barry), Joan Carolinian (Martine Beswicke), Horton Paine (Joseph Cotten), Max Kendrick (Roger Davis), Sam Dinehart (Lee deBroux), Abe Singer (George DiCenzo), Alex Budde (Tony Franciosa), Kit Pepe (Jessica Harper), Jon Osborne (Doug Heyes, Jr.), Budd Townsend (Bob Hopkins), Joseph Drummond (John Houseman), Owen Keating (John McIntire), Gloria Osborne (Michelle Phillips), Judge Kendrick (William Prince), Angela Morelli (Debi Richter), Vanessa Faye (Stephanie Blackmore).

Credits: Executive Producer: Michael G. Klein; Produced by: Jo Swerling, Jr.; Directed by: Douglas Heyes; Written for Television by: Douglas Heyes; Based on the Book "The Adversary" by: Bart Spicer; Based on the Novel "Aspen" by: Burt Hirschfeld; Associate Producer: Dorothy J. Bailey; Director of Photography: Isidore Mankofsky; Music: Tom Scott, Michael Melvoin; Art Director: John W. Corso; Film Editors: Edwin F. England, Larry Lester, Lawrence Vallario; Set Decorations: Jerry Adams; Assistant Director: Wayne Farlow; Unit Manager: Ray Taylor; Sound: Chuck Haggin; Color by: Technicolor; Titles & Optical Effects: Universal Title; Sound Effects Editor: John Stacy; Music Editor: Walter Ulric Elliott; Costume Designer: Charles Waldo; Produced by: Roy Huggins-Public Arts Productions; In Association With: Universal Television; Exclusive Distributor: MCA Television Limited.

BAA BAA BLACK SHEEP

NBC Television Network, September 21, 1976-August 30, 1977; 22 episodes in color on film; 60 minutes.

A war drama based on the adventures of fighter pilot Maj. Gregory "Pappy" Boyington in World War II. Revived as Black Sheep Squadron (which see).

Cast: Maj. Gregory "Pappy" Boyington (Robert Conrad), General Moore (Simon Oakland), Col. Lard (Dana Elcar), Capt. Gutterman (James Whitmore, Jr.), Lt. Jerry Bragg (Dirk Blocker), Lt. Larry Casey (W. K. Stratton), Lt. T. J. Wiley (Robert Ginty), Lt. Bob Anderson (John Larroquette), Lt. Hutch (Joey Aresco), Lt. Don French (Jeff MacKay), Lt. Bob Doyle (Larry Manetti, Jake Mitchell), Sgt. Andrew Micklin (Red West).

Credits: Executive Producer: Stephen J. Cannell; Produced by: Philip DeGuere; Created by: Stephen J. Cannell; Directed by: Larry Doheny, Russ Mayberry, Edward Dein, Ivan Dixon, Jackie Cooper, others; Written by: Philip DeGuere, Ken Pettus, Stephen J. Cannell, Milt Rosen, others; Director of Photography: Edward R. Plante; Music by: Mike Post, Pete Carpenter; Color by: Technicolor; Titles & Optical Effects: Universal Title; Technical Advisor: Maj. Gregory "Pappy" Boyington; Produced by: Stephen J. Cannell Productions, Universal Television; Exclusive Distributor: MCA Television Limited.

BACHELOR FATHER

CBS Television Network, September 15, 1957-June 11, 1958; NBC Television Network, June 18, 1958-September 19, 1961; ABC Television Network, October 3, 1961-September 25, 1962; 157 episodes in black & white on film; 30 minutes. Sponsors and Agencies: The American Tobacco Co. through Lawrence C. Gumbinner Advertising Agency, Inc.; Armour and Company through Foote, Cone & Belding, Inc.; Whitehall Laboratories; American Home Products.

8 / Series

A situation comedy about distinguished attorney Bentley Gregg raising his niece Kelly.

Cast: Bentley Gregg (John Forsythe), Kelly Gregg (Noreen Corcoran), Peter Tong (Sammee Tong), Howard Meechim (Jimmy Boyd), Ginger Farrell/Ginger Loomis/Ginger Mitchell (Bernadette Withers), Adelaide Mitchell (Evelyn Scott), Elaine Meechim (Joan Vohs), Cal Mitchell (Del Moore), Vickie (Alice Backus), Kitty Deveraux (Shirley Mitchell), Charlie Fong (Victor Sen Yung), Kitty Marsh (Sue Ane Langdon), Suzanne Collins (Jeanne Bal), Connie (Sally Mansfield), Warren Dawson (Aron Kincaid).

Credits: Produced by: Everett Freeman, Harry Ackerman, Robert Sparks; Directed by: Earl Bellamy, Abby Berlin, John Newland, Stanley Z. Cherry, others; Written by: Dan Beaumont, others; Director of Photography: Benjamin H. Kline, A.S.C.; Art Director: George Patrick; Film Editor: Richard G. Wray, A.C.E.; Music Supervision: Stanley Wilson; Music Score: Conrad Salinger, Johnny Williams; Produced by: Bachelor Productions, Revue Productions, Inc.; Exclusive Director: MCA Television Limited.

BANACEK (NBC WEDNESDAY MYSTERY MOVIE)

NBC Television Network, September 13, 1972-September 3, 1974; 16 episodes in color on film; 90 minutes.

A detective drama about Thomas Banacek, a Polish free-lance insurance investigator based in Boston. Based on the telefeature Banacek (which see).

Cast: Thomas Banacek (George Peppard), Carlie Kirkland (Christine Belford), Felix Mulholland (Murray Matheson), Jay Drury (Ralph Manza).

Credits: Executive Producer: George Eckstein; Produced by: Howie Horwitz; Created by: Anthony Wilson; Directors: Jack Smight, Daryl Duke, Dick Heffron, others; Writers: Del Reisman, Stephen Lord, Robert Presnell, Jr., George Sheldon Smith, Lee Stanley, Robert Van Scoyk, others; Executive Story Consultant: Paul Playdon; Story Consultant: Robert Van Scoyk; Director of Photography: Sam Leavitt, A.S.C.; Music by: Billy Goldenberg, Jack Elliot, Allyn Ferguson; Art Director: George Webb; Film Editors: Bill Brame, A.C.E., Robert Watts; Set Decorations: Jerry Adams; Sound: John Carter; Assistant Director: Foster H. Phinnet; Unit Manager: Jim Hogan; Editorial Supervision: Richard Belding; Music Supervision: Hal Mooney; Costumes: Grady Hunt; Main Title Design: Wayne Fitzgerald; Titles & Optical Effects: Universal Title; Color by: Technicolor; Executive in Charge of Production: George Santoro; Produced by: Universal Television; Exclusive Distributor: MCA Television Limited.

BARETTA

ABC Television Network, January 17, 1975-June 1, 1978; 82 episodes in color on film; 60 minutes.

A police drama detailing the undercover work of Det. Tony Baretta. Based on the series Toma (which see).

Cast: Det. Tony Baretta (Robert Blake), Inspector Schiller (Dana Elcar), Billy Truman (Tom Ewell), Lt. Hal Brubaker (Ed Grover), Rooster (Michael D. Roberts).

Credits: Executive Producers: Bernard L. Kowalski, Jo Swerling, Jr., Anthony Spinner, Leigh Vance; Supervising Producer: Ed Waters; Producers: Charles E. Dismukes, Alan Godfrey, Robert Harris, Robert Lewin, Howie Horwitz; Directors: Bernard L. Kowalski, Robert Douglas, Vincent Sherman, John Ward, Douglas Heyes, Don Medford, Bruce Kessler, others; Created by: Stephen J. Cannell; Executive Story Consultant: Sidney Ellis; Music Score: Tom Scott; Theme Music: Dave Grusin; Baretta Theme "Keep Your Eye on the Sparrow" Sung by: Sammy Davis, Jr.; Lyrics: Morgan Ames; Music: Dave Grusin; Associate Producers: William F. Phillips, Joseph D'Agosta; Directors of Photography: Sherman Kunkel, Harry L. Wolf, A.S.C.; Art Director: John P. Bruce; Set Decorations: Charles Rutherford, Ed Baer; Assistant Directors: Larry Powell, Ron Martinez; Unit Managers: Les Berke, Charles E. Dismukes; Film Editor: Gloryette Clark; Sound: Andrew Gilmore; Color by: Technicolor; Titles & Optical Effects: Universal Title; Sound Effects Editor: Marvin Walowitz; Music Editor: Herbert D. Woods; Women's Costumes by: Darryl Martell; Produced by: Roy Huggins-Public Arts Productions; In Association With: Universal Television; Exclusive Distributor: MCA Television Limited.

THE BASTARD

Distributed by MCA Television Limited for Operation Prime Time, May 1978; 2 episodes in color on film; 120 minutes (total: 4 hours).

An historical drama about the adventures of Phillipe Charboneau, the illegitimate son of an English nobleman and a French actress, who set out to claim his inheritance. His search led him to the new land--America--where he became involved with the revolutionaries--Samuel Adams, Paul Revere, Dr. Joseph Ware. Followed by the sequels The Rebels (which see) and The Seekers (which see).

Cast: Phillipe Charboneau/Philip Kent (Andrew Stevens), Marie Charboneau (Patricia Neal), Dan O'Brien (Noah Beery, Jr.), Girard (Peter Bonerz), Benjamin Franklin (Tom Bosley), Anne Ware (Kim Cattrall), Samuel Adams (William Daniels), Benjamin Edes (Buddy Ebsen), Bishop Francis (Lorne Greene), Will Campbell (James Gregory), Alicia (Olivia Hussey), Captain Plummer (Cameron

Mitchell), Captain Caleb (Harry Morgan), Lady Amberly (Eleanor Parker), Solomon Sholto (Donald Pleasence), Abraham Ware (Barry Sullivan), Paul Revere (William Shatner), John Malcolm (Keenan Wynn), Roger Amberly (Mark Neely), Emma Sholto (Elizabeth Shepherd), Lucas (Herb Jefferson, Jr.), Lord North (John Colicos), Daisy (Carol Tru Foster), Lumden (Charles Haid), Narrated by (Raymond Burr).

Credits: Executive Producer: John Wilder; Produced by: Joe Byrne; Directed by: Lee H. Katzin; Written by: Guerdon Trueblood; Based on the Novel by: John Jakes; Director of Photography: Michel Hugo; Music by: John Addison; Art Director: Loyd S. Papez; Film Editors: Robert F. Shugrue, Michael Murphy; Set Decorations: Richard Friedman; Costumes by: Jean-Pierre Dorleac; Color by: Technicolor; Titles & Optical Effects: Universal Title; Produced by: Universal Television; Exclusive Distributor: MCA Television Limited.

BATTLESTAR: GALACTICA

ABC Television Network, September 17, 1978-April 29, 1979; 22 episodes in color on film; 60 minutes.

A science fiction adventure about the crew of the "battlestar" Galactica who fled from the malevolent Count Baltar, a man who was intent on destroying the human race. They hoped to find refuge on a mysterious, far-away planet called Earth. A theatrical film entitled Battlestar: Galactica which was the pilot episode of this series was released in 1979 by Universal Pictures.

Cast: Captain Apollo (Richard Hatch), Lt. Starbuck (Dirk Benedict), Commander Adama (Lorne Greene), Lt. Boomer (Herbert Jefferson, Jr.), Count Baltar (John Colicos), Athena (Maren Jensen), Boxey (Noah Hathaway), Cassiopea (Laurette Spang), Col. Tigh (Terry Carter), Flight Sgt. Jolly (Tony Swartz), Lucifer (Bobby Porter), Itself (Muffit).

Credits: Executive Producer: Glen A. Larson; Supervising Producer: Donald Bellisario; Producers: John Dykstra, Leslie Stevens, David J. O'Connell; Created by: Glen A. Larson; Directors: Richard A. Colla, others; Writers: Glen A. Larson, others; Associate Producers: Gary B. Winter, David G. Phinney; Music Score: Stu Phillips; Theme Music: Glen A. Larson; Theme Music Performed by: The Los Angeles Philharmonic Orchestra; Director of Photography: Frank Thackery; Photographic Effects: John Dykstra; Production and Special Effects Consultants: David W. Garber, Wayne Smith; Art Director: Mary Weaver Dodson; Set Decorations: Lowell Chambers; Casting: Patti Hayes; Test and Display Equipment: Tektronix; Film Editors: George R. Potter, Leon Ortiz-Gil; Sound: John Dignan; Color by: Technicolor; Titles & Optical Effects: Universal Title; Unit Production Manager: Harker Wade; 1st Assistant Director: Britt Lomond; 2nd Assistant Director: Chuck

Lowry; Sound Effects Editor: Dick Wahrman; Music Editor: Herbert D. Woods; Costume Designer: Jean-Pierre Dorleac; Costume Supervisor: Mark Peterson; Produced by: Glen A. Larson Productions; In Association with: Universal Television And ABC-TV; Exclusive Distributor: MCA Television Limited.

BEGGARMAN, THIEF

NBC Television Network, November 26, 1979 and November 27, 1979; 2 episodes in color on film; 120 minutes (total: 4 hours).

A drama about the tempestuous Jordaches, a family consumed by greed. This sequel to the series Rich Man, Poor Man (which see) followed the adventures of Gretchen Jordache Burke, a guilt-ridden widow attempting a Hollywood directorial career; her estranged son Billy, an Army sergeant involved in the black market; and Billy's cousin Wesley Jordache, who went to France to avenge the death of his father.

Cast: Gretchen Jordache Burke (Jean Simmons), Monika Wolner (Tovah Feldshuh), David Donnelly (Glenn Ford), Kate Jordache (Lynn Redgrave), Billy Abbott (Andrew Stevens), Delacroix (Jean-Pierre Aumont), Bunny Dwyer (Bo Hopkins), Wesley Jordache (Tom Nolan), Evans (Alex Cord), Ida (Susan Strasberg), Col. Day (Robert Sterling), Teresa (Anne Francis), Egon (Norbert Weissel), Charboneau (Christian Marquand).

Credits: Directed by: Gordon Hessler; Written by: Art Eisenson; Based on the Novel by: Irwin Shaw; Color by: Technicolor; Titles & Optical Effects: Universal Title; Produced by: Universal Television; Exclusive Distributor: MCA Television Limited.

BELL SYSTEM FAMILY THEATRE

NBC Television Network, March 18, 1973 and October 21, 1974; 2 episodes in color on film produced by Universal Television; 120 minutes and 60 minutes.

A dramatic anthology. See THE SPECIALS: The Cay and The Red Pony for details.

BIFF BAKER, U.S.A.

CBS Television Network, November 13, 1952-March 26, 1953; 26 episodes in black & white on film; 30 minutes. Sponsor: Lucky Strike Cigarettes.

An adventure program about the travels of Biff and Louise Baker, a couple with a successful importing business who performed espionage for the United States.

Cast: Biff Baker (Alan Hale, Jr.), Louise Baker (Randy Stewart).

Credits: Produced by: Revue Productions, Inc.; Exclusive Distributor: MCA Television Limited.

BIG THREE GOLF

Distributed by MCA Television Limited, 1966; 4 episodes in color on film; 60 minutes.

A sports program which covered two matches in Akron and two matches in Palm Desert in 1966.

Credits: Produced by: Uni-World Productions; Exclusive Distributor: MCA Television Limited.

THE BIONIC WOMAN

ABC Television Network, January 14, 1976-May 4, 1977; NBC Television Network, September 10, 1977-September 2, 1978; 58 episodes in color on film; 60 minutes.

The adventures of Jaime Sommers who had a double life: one as a teacher working at a California air force base school and one in which she took on special high-risk government missions, using her tremendous "bionic" powers. A spin-off from The Six Million Dollar Man (which see).

Cast: Jaime Sommers (Lindsay Wagner), Oscar Goldman (Richard Anderson), Dr. Rudy Wells (Martin E. Brooks), Jim Elgin (Ford Rainey), Helen Elgin (Martha Scott).

Credits: Executive Producer: Harve Bennett; Supervising Producer: Kenneth Johnson; Producers: Kenneth Johnson, Arthur Rowe, James D. Parriott; Created by: Kenneth Johnson; Directors: Alan Levi, Michael Preece, Alan Crosland, Jr., Barry Crane, Ken Gilbert, Leo Penn, others; Writers: Dan Kibbie, Arthur Rowe, James D. Parriott, Harve Bennett; Music by: Joe Harnell; Based on the Novel "Cyborg" by: Martin Caidin; Color by: Technicolor; Titles & Optical Effects: Universal Title; Produced by: Harve Bennett Productions; In Association With: Universal Television; Exclusive Distributor: MCA Television Limited.

BJ AND THE BEAR

NBC Television Network, February 10, 1979-   ; 35 episodes in color on film; 60 minutes.

A comedy-adventure series about independent trucker BJ McKay, who hauled anything for a small fee--no questions asked--and his traveling companion, a chimp named Bear.

BJ and the Bear / 13

Cast: BJ McKay (Greg Evigan), Bear (Sam the Chimp).

Credits: Executive Producers: Glen A. Larson, Michael Sloan; Produced by: Joe Boston, Lester Wm. Berke; Co-Producer: Richard Lindheim; Created by: Glen A. Larson, Christopher Crowe; Directors: Bruce Bilson, others; Writers: Christopher Crowe, Michael Sloan, Glen A. Larson, Richard Lindheim, others; Associate Producers: Gilbert Bettman, Jr., Roy Watts; Executive Story Consultant: Sidney Ellis; Music Score: William Broughton; BJ and the Bear Theme by: Glen A. Larson; Sung by: Greg Evigan; Directors of Photography: William Cronjager, A.S.C., Frank P. Beascoechea; Art Director: George Renne; Set Decorations: Joseph J. Stone; Casting by: Patti Hayes; Film Editor: Lawrence J. Gleason; Sound: Edwin J. Somers, Jr.; Color by: Technicolor; Titles & Optical Effects: Universal Title; Unit Production Manager: Mike Frankovich, Jr.; 1st Assistant Director: Len Bram; 2nd Assistant Director: John Liberti; Sound Effects Editor: Joseph B. Divitale; Music Editor: Jerry Cohen; Costume Designer: Yvonne Wood; Animal Supervision: Marvin Downey; Produced in Association With: Glen A. Larson Productions; And Universal Television; Exclusive Distributor: MCA Television Limited.

BLACK BEAUTY

NBC Television Network, January 31, 1978-February 4, 1978; 5 episodes in color on film; 60 minutes (total: 5 hours).

The saga of the Gray family and their horse Black Beauty in late 19th-century Maryland.

Cast: Tom Gray (Martin Milner), Annie Gray (Eileen Brennan), Luke Gray (Ike Eisenmann), Henry Gordon (Cameron Mitchell), Amelia (Diane Ladd), John Manly (William Devane), James Howard (Daniel Tamm), Ruth Manly (Jenny O'Hara), George Gordon (Michael Odom), Bond (Harry Carey, Jr.), Dr. Trumbull (Stuart Silbar), Carmichael (Brock Peters), Joe Green (Dennis Dimster), Dr. Halvorson (Peter Breck), Thomas Green (Luke Sickle), Enos Sutton (Farley Granger), Reuben Smith (Clu Gulager), Elizabeth Sutton (Diana Muldaur), Mr. York (Forrest Tucker), Anne Sutton (Simone Griffith), Peter Blantyre (Christopher Stone), Susan Smith (Sandra Walker), Luke Gray (as a man) (Kristoffer Tabori), Lewis Barry (Edward Albert), Jonas McBride (Jack Elam), Phyllis Carpenter (Glynnis O'Connor), Michael Dexter (John de Lancie), Samuel Livingston (Lonny Chapman), Jerry Barker (Warren Oates), Polly Barker (Zohra Lampert), Jennifer Charles (Jane Actman), Dowling (David Wayne), Harry Barker (Chris Gardner), Dinah Brown (Lee Ann Fahey), Nicholas Skinner (Mel Ferrer), Martin Tremaine (Don De Fore), Horace Tompkins (Van Johnson), Howard Jakes (Ken Curtis), Edgar (Benny Medina), Dobson (Garrison True), Narrated by (David Wayne).

Credits: Executive Producer: Peter S. Fischer; Produced by: Ben Bishop; Directed by: Daniel Haller; Written by: Peter S.

Fischer; Based on the Novel by: Anna Sewell; Associate Producer: Norman Fox; Directors of Photography: John J. Jones, Terry K. Meade; Music by: John Addison; Art Director: Loyd S. Papez; Film Editors: Skip Lusk, Michael S. Murphy; Color by: Technicolor; Titles & Optical Effects: Universal Title; Produced by: Universal Television; Exclusive Distributor: MCA Television Limited.

BLACK SHEEP SQUADRON

NBC Television Network, December 14, 1977-September 1, 1978; 13 episodes in color on film; 60 minutes.

A war drama based on the adventures of fighter pilot Maj. Gregory "Pappy" Boyington in World War II. A revival of Baa Baa Black Sheep (which see).

Cast: Maj. Gregory "Pappy" Boyington (Robert Conrad), General Moore (Simon Oakland), Col. Lard (Dana Elcar), Capt. Gutterman (James Whitmore, Jr.), Lt. Jerry Bragg (Dirk Blocker), Lt. Larry Casey (W. K. Stratton), Lt. T. J. Wiley (Robert Ginty), Lt. Hutch (Joey Aresco), Lt. Bob Anderson (John Larroquette), Lt. Don French (Jeff MacKay), Lt. Bob Doyle (Larry Manetti), Lt. Jeb Pruitt (Jeb Adams), Sgt. Andrew Micklin (Red West), Daniels (Steve Richmond), Nurse Samantha Green (Denise DuBarry), Nurse Nancy (Nancy Conrad), Nurse Ellie (Kathy McCullem), Capt. Dottie Dixon (Katherine Cannon), Nurse Susan (Brianne Leary).

Credits: Executive Producer: Stephen J. Cannell; Supervising Producers: Philip DeGuere, Don Bellisario; Produced by: Alex Beaton; Created by: Stephen J. Cannell; Directors: Larry Doheny, Robert Conrad, others; Writers: Don Bellisario, Stephen J. Cannell, others; Associate Producer: Chuck Bowman; Creative Consultant: Milt Rosen; Director of Photography: Edward R. Plante; Music by: Mike Post, Pete Carpenter; Color by: Technicolor; Titles & Optical Effects: Universal Title; Technical Advisor: Maj. Gregory "Pappy" Boyington; Produced by: Stephen J. Cannell Productions, Universal Television; Exclusive Distributor: MCA Television Limited.

THE BOB CUMMINGS SHOW

CBS Television Network, October 5, 1961-March 1, 1962; 22 episodes in black & white on film; 30 minutes. Sponsors and Agencies: The Kellogg Company through Leo Burnett Co., Inc.; Brown and Williamson Tobacco Company through Ted Bates & Co.

A comedy-adventure about Bob Carson, a high-living, free-spending adventurer who flew his own plane on trouble-shooting assignments. This series is not to be confused with the earlier The Bob Cummings Show (a.k.a. Love That Bob) which was about a commercial photographer and was produced by McCadden Corporation.

The Bob Cummings Show / 15

Cast: Bob Carson (Bob Cummings), Luscious Lionel (Murvyn Vye), Hank Geogerty (Roberta Shore).

Credits: Produced by: William Frye, Robert Finkel; Directed by: Don Weis, others; Written by: Mel Sharp, Mel Diamond, Roland Kibbee, others; Created by: Roland Kibbee; Associate Producer: Eddie Rubin; Story Consultant: Mel Diamond; Director of Photography: Neil Beckner; Music by: Juan Esquivel; Film Editor: Sam Waxman; Art Director: Alex Mayer; Produced by: Revue Productions, Inc.; Exclusive Distributor: MCA Television Limited.

BOB HOPE PRESENTS THE CHRYSLER THEATRE

NBC Television Network, September 27, 1963-September 6, 1967; 114 episodes in color on film; 60 minutes. Sponsor and Agency: Chrysler Corporation through Young & Rubicam Company, Inc.

A dramatic anthology hosted by Bob Hope. Guest stars included Angie Dickinson, Jeffrey Hunter, Milton Berle, Mel Ferrer, Fred Astaire, Louis Jourdan, Peter Falk, Jack Klugman, Mickey Rooney, Julie Harris, Robert Wagner, Bing Crosby, Claire Bloom, Telly Savalas and Sal Mineo. Every fourth week Chrysler Presents a Bob Hope Special was telecast (16 episodes in color on tape and film; 60 minutes and 90 minutes). Bob Hope Presents the Chrysler Theatre was syndicated as Universal Star Time and Theatre of Stars.

Cast: Host, Bob Hope.

Credits: Executive In Charge of Production: Gordon Oliver; Executive Producers: Dick Berg, Alan J. Miller; Producers: Hal Kanter, Jack Laird, Ron Roth, Stanley Chase, Gordon Hessler, Dick Berg, Jess Oppenheimer, Bert Mulligan, Clarence Green, David Lowell Rich, Russell House; Directors: Robert Stevens, Douglas Heyes, David Lowell Rich, Jess Oppenheimer, Alex Singer, Stuart Rosenberg, Josef Leytes, S. Lee Pogostin, James Goldstone, Frank Corsaro, Sydney Pollack, others; Writers: Leslie Stevens, Raphael David Blau, William Wood, S. Lee Pogostin, Alvin Sapinsley, George Lefferts, Rod Serling, Edward Anhalt, others; Associate Producer: Ron Roth; Executive Story Consultant: Robert Kirsch; Directors of Photography: John L. Russell, A.S.C., Benjamin H. Kline, A.S.C., others; Theme Music by: Alex North; Music: Jerry Goldsmith, Bernard Herrmann, others; Color by: Pathé; Produced by: Hovue Productions, Hope Productions, Morpics, Revue Productions, Inc., Universal Television; Exclusive Distributor: MCA Television Limited.

THE BOLD ONES

NBC Television Network, September 14, 1969-June 22, 1973; 85 episodes in color on film.

16 / Series

The umbrella title for four rotating series and a pilot film. See The Doctors, The Lawyers, The Protectors, The Senator and Hernandez: Houston P. D. for details.

BRINGING UP BUDDY

CBS Television Network, October 10, 1960-September 25, 1961; 34 episodes in black & white on film; 30 minutes.

A situation comedy about investment counselor Buddy Flower who lived with his maiden aunts Iris and Violet.

Cast: Violet Flower (Enid Markey), Iris Flower (Doro Merande), Buddy Flower (Frank Aletter).

Credits: Produced and Created by: Joe Connelly, Bob Mosher; Produced by: Kayro Productions, Revue Productions, Inc.; Exclusive Distributor: MCA Television Limited.

BROADSIDE

ABC Television Network, September 20, 1964-September 5, 1965; 32 episodes in black & white on film; 30 minutes. Sponsors and Agencies: Armour & Company through Foote, Cone & Belding, Inc.; Consolidated Cigar Sales Co., Inc. through Papert, Koenig, Lois, Inc.; E. I. Dupont de Nemours & Company, Inc. through N. W. Ayer & Son, Inc.; Menley & James Laboratories through Foote, Cone & Belding, Inc.; Plymouth Division of Chrysler Corporation through N. W. Ayer & Son, Inc.; Remington Rand Division of Sperry Rand Corp. through Young & Rubicam, Inc.

A situation comedy about four U.S. Navy Waves surrounded by thousands of sailors at a Navy supply depot on a South Pacific island during World War II.

Cast: Lt. (jg) Anne Morgan (Kathleen Nolan), Comdr. Roger Adrian (Edward Andrews), Lt. Maxwell Trotter (Dick Sargent), Machinist's Mate Selma Kowalski (Sheila James), Machinist's Mate Molly McGuire (Lois Roberts), Machinist's Mate Roberta Love (Joan Stanley), Machinist's Mate Marion Botnik (Jimmy Boyd), Seaman Nicky D'Angelo (Don Edmonds).

Credits: Executive Producer: Edward J. Montagne; Directed by: Edward J. Montagne, others; Writers: Si Rose, Barry Blitzer, Ray Brenner, Frank Gill, Jr., G. Carleton Brown, others; Director of Photography: Russell Metty, A.S.C.; Music Score: Jerry Fielding; Music Supervision: Stanley Wilson; Film Editor: Sam E. Waxman; Art Director: Russell Kimball; Produced by: Revue Productions, Inc., Universal Television; Exclusive Distributor: MCA Television Limited.

BUCK ROGERS IN THE 25th CENTURY

NBC Television Network, September 27, 1979- ; 22 episodes in color on film; 60 minutes.

A science fiction adventure about the legendary space hero Buck Rogers set in the year 2491. A theatrical motion picture entitled Buck Rogers in the 25th Century which was actually the pilot for this series was released in 1979 by Universal Pictures.

Cast: Buck Rogers (Gil Gerard), Col. Wilma Deering (Erin Gray), Dr. Goodfellow (Wilfrid Hyde-White), Hawk (Thom Christopher), Admiral Asimov (Jay Garner), Twiki (Felix Silla), The Voice of Twiki (Mel Blanc).

Credits: Executive Producer: Bruce Lansbury; Produced by: John Gaynor, David J. O'Connell; Developed for Television by: Glen A. Larson; Directors: Sigmund Neufeld, Jr., others; Associate Producers: David G. Phinney, Medora Heilbron; Story Editor: Robert W. Gilmer; Music Score: Herbert Woods; Theme Music: Glen A. Larson; Director of Photography: Ben Colman; Art Directors: Fred Luff, Bill Camden; Set Decorations: Joanne C. MacDougall; Casting by: Simon Ayer; Titles & Optical Effects: Universal Title; Film Editor: George R. Potter; Sound: Earl N. Crain; Color by: Technicolor; Some Visual Effects Furnished by: Ramtex Corporation; Special Photographic Effects: Universal Hartland; Unit Production Manager: Harker Wade; 1st Assistant Director: Frank Crawford; 2nd Assistant Director: Gerald T. Olson; Sound Effects Editor: Dick R. Wahrman; Music Editor: Herbert Woods; Costume Designer: Al Lehman; Gil Gerard's Costumes Supervised by: Barry Downing; Miniature Effects by: David M. Garber, Wayne Smith; Buck Rogers Characters by Courtesy of: Leisure Concepts, Inc., Robert C. Dille; Produced In Association With: Glen A. Larson Productions And Bruce Lansbury Productions, Ltd. And Universal Television; Exclusive Distributor: MCA Television Limited.

BUCKSKIN

NBC Television Network, July 3, 1958-September 1959; 39 episodes in black & white on film; 30 minutes.

A western about the adventures of Jody O'Connell, a boy living in the small frontier town of Buckskin, Montana with his mother in the 1880s.

Cast: Jody O'Connell (Tommy Nolan), Annie O'Connell (Sallie Brophy), Marshal Tom Sellers (Michael Road).

Credits: Music by: Stanley Wilson, Mort Green; Produced by: Betford Productions, Revue Productions, Inc.; Exclusive Distributor: MCA Television Limited.

18 / Series

CALVIN AND THE COLONEL

ABC Television Network, October 3, 1961-September 22, 1962; 26 episodes in black & white on film; 30 minutes.

An animated cartoon comedy about the big city adventures of a pair of humanized animal cronies from the piney woods of Dixie: a bear named Calvin and the Colonel, a fox. They were joined by Maggie Belle, the Colonel's wife, her sister Sue, lawyer Oliver Wendell Clutch, a weasel, and Gloria, Calvin's poodle sweetie.

Voices: Calvin (Charles Correll), The Colonel (Freeman Gosden), Maggie Belle (Virginia Gregg), Sue, Maggie's Sister (Beatrice Kay), Oliver Wendell Clutch (Paul Frees), Gloria (Gloria Blondell).

Credits: Produced by: Joe Connelly, Bob Mosher; Created by: Freeman Gosden, Charles Correll; Produced by: Kayro Productions, Inc., Creston Productions, Revue Productions, Inc.; Exclusive Distributor: MCA Television Limited.

CAPTAINS AND THE KINGS (NBC'S BEST SELLERS)

NBC Television Network, September 30, 1976-November 25, 1976; 9 episodes in color on film; 60 minutes and 120 minutes (total: 11 hours).

Joseph Armagh, a strong-willed Irish immigrant, found the road to success in mid 19th-century America paved with prejudice, uneasy alliances and shady deals.

Cast: Joseph Armagh (Richard Jordan), Ed Healey (Charles Durning), Katherine Hennessey (Joanna Pettet), Tom Hennessey (Vic Morrow), Martinique (Barbara Parkins), Haroun "Harry" Zeff (Harvey Jason), Mrs. Finch (Ann Sothern), Sister Angela (Celeste Holm), Clair Montrose (Peter Donat), Miss Emmy (Beverly D'Angelo), Strickland (Joe Kapp), Braithwaite (Pernell Roberts), Elizabeth Healey (Blair Brown), Charles Desmond (Robert Vaughn), Bernadette (Patty Duke Astin), Sean Armagh (David Huffman), Mary Armagh (Katherine Crawford), Abraham Lincoln (Ford Rainey), James Spaulding (Kermit Murdock), Governor Hackett (Alan Hewitt), Rory Armagh (Perry King), Courtney (Terry Kiser), Old Syrup (Burl Ives), Marjorie (Jane Seymour), Roger Mace (Rod Hasse), Kevin (Douglas Heyes, Jr.), Anne-Marie (Ann Dusenberry), Judge Chisholm (John Houseman), Claudia Desmond (Cynthia Sikes), Teddy Roosevelt (Lee Jones), Brian Armagh (Cliff De Young), Governor Skerritt (Clifton James), Governor Proctor (Laurence Haddon), William Jennings Bryan (Byron Webster), Father Hale (John Carradine), Sen. Enfield Bassett (Henry Fonda), O'Herlihy (Neville Brand), Jay Regan (William Prince), Foreign Gentleman (Giorgio Tozzi).

Credits: Executive In Charge of Production: Charles Engel; Executive Producer: Roy Huggins; Produced by: Jo Swerling, Jr.;

Directors: Douglas Heyes, Allen Reisner; Written by: Douglas Heyes; Adapted by: Stephen Karpf, Elinor Karpf; Based on the Novel by: Taylor Caldwell; Directors of Photography: Isidore Mankofsky, Vilis Lapenieks, Ric Waite; Music by: Elmer Bernstein; NBC's Best Sellers Theme by: Elmer Bernstein; Art Directors: John W. Corso, Joseph J. Jennings; Film Editors: Edwin F. England, Larry Lester, Christopher Nelson, Lawrence J. Vallario; Set Decorations: Jerry Adams; Color by: Technicolor; Titles & Optical Effects: Universal Title; Produced by: Universal Television; Exclusive Distributor: MCA Television Limited.

CENTENNIAL

NBC Television Network, October 1, 1978-February 4, 1979; 12 episodes in color on film; 120 minutes and 3 hours (total: 26 hours).

A drama based on James Michener's 1,100-page novel about Indians, trappers, traders, gold seekers, homesteaders and ranchers in Colorado from the 1750s to the present.

Cast: Jim Lloyd (William Atherton), Herman Bockweiss (Raymond Burr), Clay Basket (Barbara Carrera), Alexander McKeag (Richard Chamberlain), Pasquinel (Robert Conrad), Col. Frank Skimmerhorn (Richard Crenna), Oliver Seccombe (Timothy Dalton), John Skimmerhorn (Cliff De Young), Capt. Maxwell Mercy (Chad Everett), Prof. Lewis Venor (Andy Griffith), Levi Zendt (Gregory Harrison), Paul Garrett/Narrator (David Janssen), Hans Brumbaugh (Alex Karras), Sheriff Axel Dumire (Brian Keith), Lise Bockweiss (Sally Kellerman), Jacques Pasquinel (Stephen McHattie), Maude Wendell (Lois Nettleton), Samuel Purchase (Donald Pleasence), Lucinda McKeag Zendt (Cristina Raines), Charlotte Buckland (Lynn Redgrave), Morgan Wendell (Robert Vaughn), R. J. Poteet (Dennis Weaver), Mervin Wendell (Anthony Zerbe), Dr. Richard Butler (Robert Walden), Blue Leaf (Maria Potts), Rude Water (Robert Tessier), Bean (Clint Walker), Gray Wolf (Ivan Naranjo), Jim Bridger (Reb Brown), Old Sioux (Chief Dan George), Mike Pasquinel (Kario Salem), Sergeant Lykes (Richard Jaeckel), Broken Thumb (Jorge Rivero), Lisette (Karen Carlson), John McIntosh (Mark Harmon), General Asher (Pernell Roberts), Spade Larkin (James Sloyan), Private Clark (Steve Burns), General Wade (Morgan Woodward), Lost Eagle (Nick Ramus), Abel Tanner (Barney McFadden), Nate Person (Glynn Turman), Nacho (Rafael Campos), Gompert (Robby Weaver), Savage (Damon Douglas), Ragland (Ralph Davies Lewis), Amos Calendar (Jesse Vint), Bufe (Les Lannom), Buck (Dennis Fimple), Canby (Greg Mullavey), Lasater (Scott Hylands), Jim Lloyd (Michael Le Clair), Christian (Timothy Patrick Murphy), Mrs. Brumbaugh (Gloria McMillan), Finlay Perkin (Clive Revill), Clemma (Adrienne La Russa), Muerice (Art Metrano), Reverend Holly (Robert Phalen), Philip (Doug McKeon), Philip (as a man) (Morgan Paull), Tranquilino (A Martinez), Serafina (Silvana Gallardo), Alice Grebe (Julie Sommars), Earl Grebe (Claude Jarman), Beeley Garrett (Alan Vint),

Magnes Volkema (Bo Brundin), Vesta Volkema (Lynn Borden), Sheriff Bogardus (Geoffrey Lewis), Cisco Calendar (Merle Haggard), Sidney Endermann (Sharon Gless), Flor Marquez (Karmin Murcelo), Nate Person III (Robert DoQui), Manolo Marquez (Rene Enriquez), Floyd Calendar (Ed Bakey).

Credits: Executive Producer: John Wilder; Supervising Producer: Richard Caffey; Producers: Alex Beaton, Howard Alston, Malcolm R. Harding, George E. Crosby; Directors: Virgil W. Vogel, Paul Krasny, Harry Falk, Bernard McEveety; Written for Television by: John Wilder, Jerry Ziegman, Charles Larson; Based on the Novel by: James A. Michener; Associate Producers: George E. Crosby, Susan Lichtwardt; Directors of Photography: Ronald W. Browne, Duke Callaghan, Jacques R. Marquette, Charles W. Short; Music: John Addison; Production Designer: Jack Senter; Art Directors: John P. Bruce, Mark Mansbridge, Seymour Klate, Lou Montejano, Sherman Loudermilk, John Corso, Loyd S. Papez; Film Editors: Bill Parker, Robert Watts, Robert F. Shugrue, Ralph Schoenfeld, Howard Deane, John Elias; Set Decorations: Joseph J. Stone, Victoria Hugo, John M. Dwyer, Robert G. Freer; Sound: Edwin J. Somers; Casting by: Mary Petterson; Titles & Optical Effects: Universal Title; Unit Production Manager: Les Berke; 1st Assistant Director: Ron Grow; 2nd Assistant Director: Beau Marks; Sound Effects Editor: Brian Courcier; Music Editor: Dave Kahn; Costume Designer: Helen Colvig; Costume Supervisor: Robert Ellsworth; Color by: Technicolor; Produced by: John Wilder Productions; In Association with: Universal Television; Exclusive Distributor: MCA Television Limited.

CHALLENGE GOLF

Distributed by MCA Television Limited, 1963-1970; 91 episodes in color on film; 60 minutes.

A sports program which featured Arnold Palmer and Gary Player in match play against top professional golfers. The program was filmed before a gallery and there was a prize for thirteen matches.

Cast: Hosts, Arnold Palmer, Gary Player.

Credits: Produced by: Fairway Productions, Revue Productions, Inc.; Exclusive Distributor: MCA Television Limited.

CHANNING

ABC Television Network, September 18, 1963-April 8, 1964; 26 episodes in black & white on film; 60 minutes.

A drama about Channing--a midwest college, a town, students and teachers and their problems, passions and ambitions.

Cast: Dean Fred Baker (Henry Jones), Associate Professor Joseph Howe (Jason Evers). With: Herb Vigran and Ed Nelson.

Credits: Producers: Jack Laird, Stanley Rubin, Jack Guss; Produced by: Betford Productions, Revue Productions, Inc.; Exclusive Distributor: MCA Television Limited.

CHASE

NBC Television Network, September 11, 1973-August 28, 1974; 24 episodes in color on film; 60 minutes.

A police drama about officers who operated in a quasi-official capacity as an out-of-uniform unit which tried to solve major crimes that other Los Angeles Police divisions could not. Forced, on occasion, to investigate without official sanction or appropriations, the unit sometimes had to reach outside the law to operate. Based on the telefeature Chase (which see).

Cast: Capt. Chase Reddick (Mitchell Ryan), Sgt. MacCray (Wayne Maunder), Chief of Detectives Frank Dawson (Albert Reed), Officer Ed Rice (Gary Crosby), Officer Steve Baker (Michael Richardson), Officer Fred Sing (Brian Fong), Officer Norm Hamilton (Reid Smith), Officer Tom Wilson (Craig Gardner).

Credits: Executive Producer: Robert A. Cinader; Produced by: James Schermer; Directors: David Friedkin, Alan Crosland, Jr., others; Writers: Stephen J. Cannell, Michael Donovan, James Schermer, others; Music by: Oliver Nelson; Color by: Technicolor; Titles & Optical Effects: Universal Title; Produced by: Mark VII Limited And Universal Television; In Association with: NBC-TV; Exclusive Distributor: MCA Television Limited.

CHECKMATE

CBS Television Network, September 17, 1960-September 19, 1962; 70 episodes in black & white on film; 60 minutes. Sponsors and Agencies: Lever Bros. Co. through J. Walter Thompson Co.; Kimberly-Clark Corp. through Foote, Cone & Belding; Brown & Williamson Tobacco Corp. through Ted Bates & Co.; Liggett & Myers Tobacco Co. through J. Walter Thompson Co.; Colgate-Palmolive Co. through Ted Bates & Co.

A detective drama about a San Francisco investigative firm, Checkmate, Inc., owned and operated by Don Corey and Jed Sills. The primary mission of the organization was to thwart crimes and to checkmate death.

Cast: Don Corey (Anthony George), Jed Sills (Doug McClure), Carl Hyatt (Sebastian Cabot).

Credits: Producers: Dick Berg, Herb Coleman, Maxwell Shane; Created by: Eric Ambler; Directors: Elliot Silverstein, others; Writers: Richard Fielder, others; Associate Producer: John Rubichan; Directors of Photography: Dale Deverman, others; Art Director: John J. Lloyd; Film Editor: Richard Belding; Music Supervision: Stanley Wilson; Original Music by: Johnny Williams; Produced by: J & M Productions, Revue Productions, Inc.; Exclusive Distributor: MCA Television Limited.

CIMARRON CITY

NBC Television Network, October 11, 1958-September 26, 1959; 26 episodes in black & white on film; 60 minutes.

A Western about Cimarron City, Oklahoma, its mayor, Matthew Rockford, and its deputy sheriff and blacksmith, Lane Temple.

Cast: Mayor Matthew Rockford/Narrator (George Montgomery), Beth Purcell (Audrey Totter), Deputy Sheriff Lane Temple (John Smith), Art Sampson (Stuart Randall), Burt Purdy (Fred Sherman), Alice Purdy (Claire Carleton), Martin Kingsley (Addison Richards), Jesse Williams (George Dunn), Tiny Budinger (Dan Blocker), Dody Hamer (Pete Dunn), Jed Fame (Wally Brown), Silas Perry (Tom Fadden).

Credits: Executive Producer: Richard Lewis; Producers: Felix Jackson, Boris Ingster, Richard Bartlett, Norman Jolley; Directors: Jules Bricken, others; Writers: Gene L. Coon, Fenton Earnshaw, others; Produced by: Mont Productions, Revue Productions, Inc.; Exclusive Distributor: MCA Television Limited.

CITY DETECTIVE

Distributed by MCA Television Limited, 1953-1955; 65 episodes in black & white on film; 30 minutes.

A crime drama about the cases of Bart Grant and his battle against metropolitan crime.

Cast: Bart Grant (Rod Cameron).

Credits: Produced by: Revue Productions, Inc.; Exclusive Distributor: MCA Television Limited.

CITY OF ANGELS

NBC Television Network, February 3, 1976-August 10, 1976; 13 episodes in color on film; 60 minutes.

A detective drama about Jake Axminster, a free-wheeling private investigator who operated in the Los Angeles area during the 1930s.

Cast: Jake Axminster (Wayne Rogers), Marsha (Elaine Joyce), Lt. Quint (Clifton James), Michael Brimm (Philip Sterling).

Credits: Executive Producer: Jo Swerling, Jr.; Created by: Roy Huggins, Stephen J. Cannell; Directors: Don Medford, Douglas Heyes, Sigmund Neufeld, Jr., Robert Douglas, Barry Shear, others; Writers: Stephen J. Cannell, Roy Huggins; Music by: Nelson Riddle; Music Supervision: Hal Mooney; Color by: Technicolor; Titles & Optical Effects: Universal Title; Produced by: Roy Huggins-Public Arts Productions; In Association with: Universal Television And NBC-TV; Exclusive Distributor: MCA Television Limited.

CLIFFHANGERS

NBC Television Network, February 27, 1979-May 22, 1979; 13 episodes in color on film; 60 minutes.

A program comprised of three separate serials in which the hero or heroine was left on the verge of disaster each week. "Stop Susan Williams" was about a globe-trotting newspaper photographer investigating the untimely death of her brother. "The Secret Empire" was about Marshal Jim Donner, a lawman of the 1880s who discovered a secret futuristic kingdom ruled by an evil baron and a princess. "The Curse of Dracula" was about a vampire obsessed with thwarting attempts by an anthropologist and his young partner to destroy him.

"Stop Susan Williams"
Cast: Susan Williams (Susan Anton), Bob Richard (Ray Walston), Jack Schoengarth (Michael Swan).

"The Secret Empire"
Cast: Marshal Jim Donner (Geoffrey Scott), Millie (Carlene Watkins), Billy (Tiger Williams).

"The Curse of Dracula"
Cast: Count Dracula (Michael Nouri), Kurt Von Helsing (Stephen Johnson), Mary Gibbons (Carol Baxter).

Credits: Written and Directed by: Kenneth Johnson; Color by: Technicolor; Titles & Optical Effects: Universal Title; Produced by: Universal Television; In Association With: NBC-TV; Exclusive Distributor: MCA Television Limited.

COLDITZ

BBC-1, Britain, 1972-1973; 13 episodes in color on film; 60 minutes.

An escape saga based on the true story of the impregnable and supposedly escape-proof Colditz castle which was used as a POW

24 / Series

camp by the Nazis during World War II. Inspired by the 1957 film The Colditz Story.

Cast: Robert Wagner, David McCallum, Jack Hedley, Edward Hardwicke, Christopher Neame, Bernard Hepton.

Credits: Produced by: Gerard Glaister; Directed by: Michael Ferguson; Written by: N. J. Crisp; Produced by: BBC-TV; In Association with: Universal Television; Exclusive Distributor: MCA Television Limited.

COLUMBO (NBC SUNDAY MYSTERY MOVIE/NBC WEDNESDAY MYSTERY MOVIE)

NBC Television Network, September 15, 1971-September 4, 1977; 43 episodes in color on film; 90 minutes and 120 minutes.

A police drama about the cases of Lt. Detective Columbo who hid a razor-sharp mind behind an unprepossessing facade and a rumpled raincoat. Based on the telefeatures Prescription: Murder (which see) and Ransom for a Dead Man (which see).

Cast: Lt. Detective Columbo (Peter Falk).

Credits: Executive Producers: Roland Kibbee, Dean Hargrove; Executive in Charge of Production: Richard Irving; Producers: Edward K. Dodds, Everett Chambers, Dean Hargrove, Richard Alan Simmons; Created by: Richard Levinson, William Link; Directors: Steven Spielberg, Patrick McGoohan, Alf Kjellin, Bernard Kowalski, Harvey Hart, Robert Douglas, Richard Quine, Edward M. Abroms, others; Writers: Peter S. Fischer, Larry Cohen, Jackson Gillis, Richard Levinson, William Link, others; Executive Story Consultants: Peter S. Fischer, Jackson Gillis; Directors of Photography: William Cronjager, A.S.C., Richard C. Glouner, A.S.C., Harry Wolf, A.S.C., Lloyd Ahern, A.S.C.; Associate Producer: Edward K. Dodds; Music Score: Dick De Benedictis, Billy Goldenberg, Bernardo Segall, Oliver Nelson, Jeff Alexander; Sunday Mystery Movie Theme: Henry Mancini; Art Directors: John W. Corso, Arch Bacon, Seymour Klate; Set Decorations: William McLaughlin, John McCarthy, Joseph J. Stone; Assistant Directors: Ray Taylor, Kevin Donnelly, David M. Dowell; Unit Managers: Maurie M. Suess, Ray Taylor, Kenny Williams, Ralph Sariego; Film Editors: Bob Kagey, Edward M. Abroms, Larry Lester, Robert Kimble, A.C.E.; Sound: John Kearn, Edwin S. Hall, Jerry Smith; Lenses and Panaflex Camera by: Panavision; Color by: Technicolor; Titles & Optical Effects: Universal Title; Editorial Supervision: Richard Belding; Music Supervision: Hal Mooney; Costumes by: Grady Hunt; Women's Costumes by: Burton Miller; Main Title Design: Wayne Fitzgerald; Produced by: Universal Television; Exclusive Distributor: MCA Television Limited.

CONDOMINIUM

Distributed by MCA Television Limited for Operation Prime Time, November 1980; 2 episodes in color on film; 120 minutes (total: 4 hours).

A suspense drama about a poorly-constructed high-rise on the Gulf Coast of Florida which threatened to topple in the midst of a killer hurricane.

Cast: Gus Garver (Steve Forrest), Sam Harrison (Dan Haggerty), Barbara Messenger (Barbara Eden), Lee Messenger (Ralph Bellamy), Marty Liss (Stuart Whitman), Dru Byrne (Pamela Hensley), Cole Kimber (Jack Jones), Churchbridge (Richard Anderson), Thelma Messenkoff (Ana Alicia), Carlotta (Linda Christian), Julian (Larry Bishop), Lorrie (Mimi Maynard).

Credits: Based on the Novel by: John D. MacDonald; Color by: Technicolor; Titles & Optical Effects: Universal Title; Produced by: Universal Television; Exclusive Distributor: MCA Television Limited.

CONVOY

NBC Television Network, September 17, 1965-December 10, 1965; 13 episodes in black & white on film; 60 minutes.

A war drama based on incidents occurring during the early part of World War II in the North Atlantic when ships carried supplies and troops to the European front. The stories revolved around the Navy destroyer Escort DD 181, guided by Commander Dan Talbot, and the freighter flagship, captained by Ben Foster.

Cast: Naval Commander Dan Talbot (John Gavin), Merchant Marine Captain Ben Foster (John Larch), Chief Officer Steve Kirkland (Linden Chiles), Lt. Dick O'Connor (James Callahan).

Credits: Executive Producer: Frank Price; Producers: Don Siegel, Gordon Hessler, Cy Chermak, others; Directors: Don Siegel, others; Writers: Calvin Clements, others; Created by: Frank Price; Associate Producer: Don Devlin; Music by: Bernard Herrmann; Wardrobe: Vincent Dee; Technical Advisor: Commander John J. Phillips, USN (Ret.); Produced by: Universal Television; In Association With: NBC-TV; Exclusive Distributor: MCA Television Limited.

COOL MILLION (NBC WEDNESDAY MYSTERY MOVIE)

NBC Television Network, October 25, 1972-July 11, 1973; 4 episodes in color on film; 90 minutes.

26 / Series

A detective drama about Jefferson Keyes, an American abroad, who had an international reputation for solving problems--for a fee of one million dollars. Cool and dedicated, Keyes relished the adventure inherent in assignments that whisked him in and out of danger, all over the globe. Based on the telefeature Cool Million (which see).

Cast: Jefferson Keyes (James Farentino), Elena (Adele Mara), Tony (Ed Bernard).

Credits: Executive Producer: Roy Huggins; Produced by: Jo Swerling, Jr., Gene Levitt; Directors: Gene Levitt, others; Writers: Gene Levitt, others; Editorial Supervision: Richard Belding; Music Supervision: Hal Mooney; Color by: Technicolor; Titles & Optical Effects: Universal Title; Produced by: Universal Television; Exclusive Distributor: MCA Television Limited.

CORONADO 9

Distributed by MCA Television Limited, 1959-1960; 39 episodes in black & white on film; 30 minutes.

A detective drama about Dan Adams, a former Naval Intelligence officer who became a private investigator with headquarters on the Coronoda Peninsula in San Diego, California. His telephone exchange was Coronado 9.

Cast: Dan Adams (Rod Cameron).

Credits: Produced by: Revue Productions, Inc.; Exclusive Distributor: MCA Television Limited.

COURT MARTIAL

ABC Television Network, April 8, 1966-September 2, 1966; 26 episodes in black & white on film; 60 minutes.

A World War II adventure drama in which officer-attorneys Capt. David Young and Maj. Frank Whitaker of the Judge Advocate General's department in Europe dealt with military personnel and civilians in various countries as they sought the truth in crimes committed under the stress of war. Based on "The Case Against Paul Ryker," an episode of Kraft Suspense Theatre released theatrically as Sergeant Ryker (1968).

Cast: Capt. David Young (Bradford Dillman), Maj. Frank Whitaker (Peter Graves), Sgt. John MacCaskey (Kenneth J. Warren), Sgt. Wendy (Diane Clare).

Credits: Executive Producer: Richard Irving; Producers: Bill Hill, others; Directors: Harvey Hart, others; Writers: John T.

Dugan, others; Director of Photography: Kenneth Hodges, B.S.C.; Produced by: Roncom Productions, Inc., Independent Television Corporation, Universal Television; Exclusive Distributor: MCA Television Limited; Filmed at: Pinewood Studios, England.

THE CRUSADER

CBS Television Network, October 7, 1955-December 28, 1956; 52 episodes in black & white on film; 30 minutes.

An adventure program about Matt Anders, a crusading writer who waged a one man war against oppression and treachery around the world.

Cast: Matt Anders (Brian Keith).

Credits: Executive Producer: Richard Lewis; Music by: Edmund Wilson; Produced by: Richard Lewis Productions, Revue Productions, Inc.; Exclusive Distributor: MCA Television Limited.

THE D.A.

NBC Television Network, September 17, 1971-January 7, 1972; 13 episodes in color on film; 30 minutes.

A courtroom drama revolving around the deputy district attorney of Los Angeles County. Guest stars included Martin Milner and Kent McCord in their Adam-12 roles of Officers Pete Malloy and Jim Reed. Based on the telefeatures The D.A.: Murder One (which see) and The D.A.: Conspiracy to Kill (which see).

Cast: Deputy D.A. Paul Ryan (Robert Conrad), Chief Deputy D.A. H.M. Stafford (Harry Morgan), D.A. Investigator Bob Ramirez (Ned Romero), Public Defender Katherine Benson (Julie Cobb).

Credits: Executive Producer: Jack Webb; Produced by: Robert H. Forward; Directors: Harry Harris, Alex Nicol, Hollingsworth Morse, Alan Crosland, Jr., others; Writers: Sid Morse, Stephen J. Cannell, Robert C. Dennis, others; Executive Story Consultant: Robert A. Cinader; Theme Music: Nelson Riddle; Music Score: Nelson Riddle, Frank Comstock; Film Editor: Sam G. Waxman; Color by: Technicolor; Titles & Optical Effects: Universal Title; Produced by: Mark VII Limited; In Association With: Universal Television And NBC-TV; Exclusive Distributor: MCA Television Limited.

DELTA HOUSE

ABC Television Network, January 18, 1979-April 28, 1979; 13 episodes in color on film; 30 minutes.

A situation comedy based on the film National Lampoon's Animal House. The program featured the adventures of Jim "Blotto" Blutarski, the younger brother of Bluto from the motion picture. Set on the Faber College campus.

Cast: Jim "Blotto" Blutarski (Josh Mostel), Dean Wormer (John R. Vernon), Flounder (Stephen Furst), D-Day (Bruce McGill), Hoover (Jamie Widdoes), Otter (Peter Fox), Doug Niedermayer (Gary Cookson), Pinto (Richard Seer), Mandy (Susanna Dalton), Muffy (Wendy Goldman), Greg Marmalard (Brian Patrick Clarke). With: Michele Pfeiffer, Lee Wilkof and Peter Kastner.

Credits: Executive Producers: Matty Simmons, Ivan Reitman; Associate Producer: Michael Stotter; Story Editors: Michael Tolkin, Stephen Tolkin; Music Score: Richard Clements; Delta House Theme Composed, Arranged & Recording Supervised by: Jim Steinman; Lyrics: Sean Kelly, Tony Hendra; Sung by: Michael Simmons; Director of Photography: Lester Shorr, A. S. C.; Art Director: Mary Weaver Dodson; Set Decorations: Edward M. Parker; Casting by: Joe Reich; Film Editor: Bob Kagey; Sound: John C. Dignan; Color by: Technicolor; Titles & Optical Effects: Universal Title; Unit Production Manager: Sam Freedle; 1st Assistant Director: Charles Norton; 2nd Assistant Director: Jerry Markus; Sound Effects Editor: Wes Wolfe; Music Editor: Rick Gleitsman; Costume Designer: Kent Warner; Produced by: Matty Simmons-Ivan Reitman Productions; In Association With: Universal Television; Exclusive Distributor: MCA Television Limited.

DELVECCHIO

CBS Television Network, September 9, 1976-July 17, 1977; 22 episodes in color on film; 60 minutes.

A police drama about Sgt. Dominick Delvecchio, a street-wise, outspoken, big city detective with a law school background. Set at the Washington Heights Division of the Los Angeles Police Department.

Cast: Sgt. Dominick Delvecchio (Judd Hirsch), Det. Paul Shonski (Charles Haid), Lt. Macavan (Michael Conrad), Tomaso Delvecchio (Mario Gallo), Sgt. Rivera (Jay Varela).

Credits: Executive Producer: William Sackheim; Producers: Steven Bochco, Michael Rhodes; Created by: Joseph Polizzi, Sam Rolfe; Directors: Walter Doniger, Jerry London, others; Writers: Joseph Polizzi, Sam Rolfe, Burton Armus, Joel Oliansky, others; Director of Photography: Russell Metty; Theme Music by: Billy Goldenberg; Music Score: Richard Clements; Art Director: John E. Chilberg II; Set Decorations: Morrie Hoffman; Film Editor: Howard S. Dean; Camera Operator: John Penner; Color by: Technicolor; Titles & Optical Effects: Universal Title; Produced by: Crescendo Productions, Inc.; In Association With: Universal Television; Exclusive Distributor: MCA Television Limited.

THE DEPUTY

NBC Television Network, September 12, 1959-September 16, 1961; 76 episodes in black & white on film; 30 minutes. Sponsors and Agencies: The Kellogg Company through Leo Burnett Company, Inc.; General Cigar Company through Young & Rubicam, Inc.

A Western about the adventures of Chief Marshal Simon Fry, a dedicated law man, and his deputy, Clay McCord, an expert marksman who hated violence and killing. Set in the Arizona Territory of the 1880s.

Cast: Chief Marshal Simon Fry (Henry Fonda), Deputy Clay McCord (Allen Case), Fran McCord (Betty Lou Keim), Herk Lamson (Wallace Ford), Sgt. Hapgood Tasker (Read Morgan).

Credits: Executive Producer: William Frye; Produced by: Michael Kraike; Created by: Roland Kibbee, Norman Lear; Music by: Jack Marshall; Director of Photography: Ellsworth Fredericks; Art Director: Martin Obzina; Editorial Supervision: Richard G. Wray; Film Editor: James D. Ballas; Music Supervision: Stanley Wilson; Sound: John K. Kean; Makeup: Jack Barron; Set Decorations: William Tapp; Costume Supervisor: Vincent Dee; Hair Stylist: Florence Bush; Produced by: Top Gun Productions; Filmed by: Revue Productions, Inc.; Exclusive Distributor: MCA Television Limited.

DESTRY

ABC Television Network, February 14, 1964-September 11, 1964; 13 episodes in black & white on film; 60 minutes.

A lighthearted Western concerning Harrison Destry and his unsuccessful attempts to avoid trouble while searching for the man who framed him on a robbery charge for which Destry served a prison term.

Cast: Harrison Destry (John Gavin).

Credits: Producers: Frank Telford, Howard Browne; Directors: Donald Siegel, others; Writers: Robert Guy Barrows, others; Associate Producer: Carter de Haven III; Directors of Photography: Lionel Lindon, A.S.C., others; Film Editor: Richard M. Sprague; Art Director: Raymond Beal; Music Supervision: Stanley Wilson; Produced by: Universal Television; Exclusive Distributor: MCA Television Limited.

THE DOCTORS (THE BOLD ONES)

NBC Television Network, September 14, 1969-June 23, 1973; 43 episodes in color on film; 60 minutes.

A medical drama about doctors who were preparing the world for the space age of medicine through their work at the David Craig Institute of New Medicine.

Cast: Dr. David Craig (E. G. Marshall), Dr. Paul Hunter (David Hartman), Dr. Ted Stuart (John Saxon), Dr. Martin Cohen (Robert Walden).

Credits: Executive Producers: Herbert Hirschman, Cy Chermak, David Levinson; Produced by: Joel Rogosin; Directors: Don McDougall, Walter Doniger, Jeffrey Hayden, others; Writers: Cy Chermak, Irv Pearlberg, Gustave Field, Robert Van Scoyk, Phyllis White, Robert White, Joel Rogosin, Sandy Stern, Reuben Bercovitch, Nathaniel Tanchuck, Sy Salkowitz; Associate Producer: Jay Benson; Music Score: Bob Prince, Richard Clements; Director of Photography: Gerald Perry Finnerman, A. S. C.; Story Editor: Lionel Siegel; Art Directors: John J. Lloyd, Jack Chilberg; Set Decorations: Mickey S. Michaels; Film Editors: Albert J. Zuniga, others; Unit Manager: Frank Lossee; Sound: Frank H. Wilkinson, Lyle Cain; Makeup: Bud Westmore; Editorial Supervision: Richard Belding; Music Supervision: Stanley Wilson; Costumes: Charles Waldo; Special Production Advisor: Byron Bloch; Color Coordinator: Robert Brower; Color by: Technicolor; Titles & Opticals Effects: Universal Title; Executive in Charge of Production: Stuart Erwin; Produced by: Harbour Productions Unlimited, Universal Television; In Association With: NBC-TV; Exclusive Distributor: MCA Television Limited.

DOCTORS' HOSPITAL

NBC Television Network, September 10, 1975-January 14, 1976; 13 episodes in color on film; 60 minutes.

A medical drama revolving around Dr. Jake Goodwin, head of Neurological Surgery at Lowell Memorial Hospital. Based on the telefeature One of Our Own (which see).

Cast: Dr. Jake Goodwin (George Peppard), Dr. Norah Purcell (Zohra Lampert), Dr. Felipe Ortega (Victor Campos), Janos Varga (Albert Paulsen), Scotty (Maxine Stuart).

Credits: Executive Producer: Matthew Rapf; Produced by: Jack Laird; Created by: James E. Moser; Directors: Vincent Sherman, Edward Abroms, Robert Abrams, Leo Penn, others; Executive Story Editor: Barry Oringer; Music by: Don Ellis; Color by: Technicolor; Titles & Optical Effects: Universal Title; Produced by: Universal Television; In Association With: NBC-TV; Exclusive Distributor: MCA Television Limited.

DON ADAMS' SCREEN TEST

Distributed by MCA Television Limited, 1975-1976; 24 episodes in

Don Adams' Screen Test / 31

color on tape; 30 minutes.

A game show in which contestants were coupled with guest stars to re-create well-known movie sequences after viewing clips from the original films. Guest stars included Sally Struthers, Milton Berle, Don Rickles, William Shatner, James Caan, Connie Stevens, Patty Duke Astin and Jason Miller. Film scenes used included On the Waterfront, The Plainsman, Tarzan the Ape Man, Casablanca, The Public Enemy and The Hurricane.

Cast: Host, Don Adams.

Credits: Executive Producer: Don Adams; Produced and Directed by: Marty Masetta; Writers: Dee Caruso, Gerald Gardner; Created by: Don Adams; Music Supervision: Hal Mooney; Produced by: Stacy Productions, Universal Television; Exclusive Distributor: MCA Television Limited.

DRAGNET 1967-1970

NBC Television Network, January 12, 1967-September 10, 1970; 98 episodes in color on film; 30 minutes. Sponsors and Agencies: R. J. Reynolds Tobacco Company through William Esty Company; Lever Brothers Company through J. Walter Thompson Company.

A law enforcement drama based on true cases of Los Angeles Police Department officers, depicting the work of two detectives, Sgt. Joe Friday and Officer Bill Gannon. Based on the original series (NBC Television Network, January 3, 1952-September 6, 1959) and the telefeature Dragnet 1966 (which see). The pilot for Adam-12 was an episode of this series.

Cast: Sgt. Joe Friday (Jack Webb), Officer Bill Gannon (Harry Morgan).

Credits: Executive Producer: Jack Webb; Produced by: Jack Webb; Created by: Jack Webb; Directed by: Jack Webb; Writers: Michael Donovan, Richard L. Breen, others; Associate Producers: Robert A. Cinader, William Stark; Directors of Photography: Andrew Jackson, A.S.C., Benjamin H. Kline; Theme Song "Dragnet March" by: Walter Schumann; Music Composed & Conducted by: Lyn Murray, Frank Comstock; Set Decorations: John McCarthy, John Sturtevant; Costume Supervisor: Vincent Dee; Makeup: Bud Westmore; Hair Stylist: Larry Germain; Unit Manager: Edward K. Dodds; Music Supervision: Stanley Wilson; Technical Advisors: The Office of the Chief, Los Angeles Police Department; Color by: Technicolor; Titles & Optical Effects: Universal Title; Produced by: Dragnet Productions, Mark VII Limited; In Association With: Universal Television And NBC-TV; Exclusive Distributor: MCA Television Limited.

32 / Series

THE DUKE

NBC Television Network, April 5, 1979-May 18, 1979; 4 episodes in color on film; 60 minutes and 120 minutes.

A detective drama about Duke Ramsey, a prize fighter who turned private investigator after his manager and mentor was slain, following what turned out to be the Duke's last pro fight.

Cast: Duke Ramsey (Robert Conrad), Joe Cadillac (Larry Manetti), Det. Sgt. Mick O'Brien (Red West).

Credits: Executive Producer: Stephen J. Cannell; Producers: Alex Beaton, Don Carlos Dunaway; Directors: Larry Doheny, Tony LoBianco, Robert Conrad; Writers: Stephen J. Cannell, Shel Willens; Color by: Technicolor; Titles & Optical Effects: Universal Title; Produced by: Stephen J. Cannell Productions, Universal Television; Exclusive Distributor: MCA Television Limited.

THE EDDIE CAPRA MYSTERIES

NBC Television Network, September 8, 1978-January 12, 1979; 13 episodes in color on film; 60 minutes.

A detective drama in the traditional whodunit format which featured the adventures of Eddie Capra, a non-traditional young attorney who preferred the active, investigative side of criminal law rather than courtroom theatrics.

Cast: Eddie Capra (Vincent Baggetta), Lacey Brown (Wendy Phillips), J. J. Devlin (Ken Swofford), Harvey Winchell (Michael Horton), Jennie Brown (Seven Ann McDonald).

Credits: Executive Producer: Peter S. Fischer; Produced by: James McAdams; Created by: Peter S. Fischer; Directors: William Wiard, others; Writers: Peter S. Fischer, others; Executive Story Consultant: Peter Allan Fields; Associate Producer: Stuart Cohen; Music Score: John Cacavas; Theme Music: John Addison; Director of Photography: Mario DiLeo; Art Director: William H. Tuntke; Set Decorations: Jackie J. Carr; Casting by: Patti Hayes; Film Editor: Donald Douglas; Sound: Nick Gaffey; Technical Advisor: Tobey H. Shaffer; Color by: Technicolor; Titles & Optical Effects: Universal Title; Unit Production Manager: Brad Aronson; 1st Assistant Director: Larry Powell; 2nd Assistant Director: Stan Zabka; Sound Effects Editor: Anthony Magro; Music Editor: Robert Mayer; Costume Designer: Charles Waldo; Produced by: Universal Television; Exclusive Distributor: MCA Television Limited.

87th PRECINCT

NBC Television Network, September 25, 1961-September 10, 1962; 30 episodes in black & white on film; 60 minutes.

A mystery-suspense program based on the best-selling novels of Ed McBain (Evan Hunter). Set at New York City's 87th Precinct, the show detailed the action-packed cases, the painstaking police procedures and the behind-the-scenes drama of people involved in the prevention of crime in a large metropolitan city.

Cast: Det. Steve Carella (Robert Lansing), Det. Bert Kling (Ron Harper), Det. Roger Havilland (Gregory Walcott), Det. Meyer Meyer (Norman Fell), Teddy Carella (Gena Rowlands).

Credits: Executive Producer: Hubbell Robinson; Producers: Boris D. Kaplan, Winston Miller; Based on the Inner Sanctum 87th Precinct Novels by: Ed McBain (Evan Hunter); Theme Music and Score by: Morton Stevens; Coordinator: Jo Swerling, Jr.; Costume Supervisor: Vincent Dee; Makeup: Jack Barron; Hair Stylist: Florence Bush; Produced by: Hubbell Robinson Productions, Inc.; In Association With: NBC-TV And Revue Productions, Inc.; Exclusive Distributor: MCA Television Limited.

ELLERY QUEEN

NBC Television Network, September 11, 1975-September 5, 1976; 21 episodes in color on film; 60 minutes.

A detective drama based on characters created by Manfred B. Lee and Frederic Dannay. Set in New York City in the 1940s. Based on the telefeature Ellery Queen (which see).

Cast: Ellery Queen (Jim Hutton), Inspector Richard Queen (David Wayne), Sgt. Velie (Tom Reese).

Credits: Executive Producers: Richard Levinson, William Link; Producers: Peter S. Fischer, Michael Rhodes; Directors: Peter H. Hunt, Seymour Robbie, David Greene, Jack Arnold, Charles S. Dubin, James Sheldon, others; Writers: Peter S. Fischer, others; Story Editor: Robert Van Scoyk; Music by: Elmer Bernstein, Dana Kaproff; Music Supervision: Hal Mooney; Art Directors: William Campbell, John Floyd; Set Decorations: John McCarthy; Color by: Technicolor; Titles & Optical Effects: Universal Title; Produced by: Fairmount/Foxcroft Productions; In Association With: Universal Television And NBC-TV; Exclusive Distributor: MCA Television Limited.

EMERGENCY!

NBC Television Network, January 22, 1972-September 3, 1977; 124 episodes in color on film; 60 minutes. NBC Television Network, 1977-79; 8 specials in color on film; 120 minutes.

A drama program dealing with Squad 51 of the Los Angeles County Fire Department's Paramedical Rescue Service and the doctors and nurses at the emergency ward of Rampart Hospital. Based on the telefeature Emergency! (which see). A Saturday morning animated spin-off was entitled Emergency Plus Four (which see).

Cast: Dr. Kelly Brackett (Robert Fuller), Nurse Dixie McCall (Julie London), Dr. Joe Early (Bobby Troup), Paramedic Roy DeSoto (Kevin Tighe), Paramedic John Gage (Randolph Mantooth), Dr. Morton (Ron Pinkhard), Captain Stanley (Michael Norell), Fireman Chet Kelly (Tim Donnelly), Fireman Lopez (Marco Lopez), Fireman Stoker (Mike Stoker).

Credits: Executive Producers: Jack Webb, Robert A. Cinader; Producers: Robert A. Cinader, Edwin Self; Created by: Harold Jack Bloom, R. A. Cinader; Directors: George Fenady, Christian Nyby, Dennis Donnelly, Lawrence Dobkin, others; Writers: Preston Wood, Kenneth Dorward, others; Associate Producers: William Stark, Gino Grimaldi; Music by: Nelson Riddle, Bill May; Directors of Photography: Bud Thackery, A. S. C., William Margulies, A. S. C.; Art Directors: John J. Lloyd, George Renne; Film Editors: Howard Epstein, Howard Terrill, Warren Adams, A. C. E.; Set Decorations: Mickey Michaels; Assistant Director: Dennis Donnelly; Unit Manager: James M. Walters, Jr.; Editorial Supervisor: Richard Belding; Music Supervision: Hal Mooney; Color by: Technicolor; Titles & Optical Effects: Universal Title; Filmed With The Cooperation of: The Board of Supervisors, The Fire Department and The Department of Hospitals of Los Angeles County; Produced by: Mark VII Limited; In Association With: Universal Television And NBC-TV; Exclusive Distributor: MCA Television Limited.

EMERGENCY PLUS FOUR

NBC Television Network, September 8, 1973-September 4, 1976; 84 episodes in color on film; 30 minutes.

A Saturday morning animated cartoon version of the series Emergency! (which see) based on the activities of the Los Angeles County Paramedic Rescue Service's Squad 51. DeSoto and Gage were joined by four children who were training in rescue techniques. Also based on the telefeature Emergency! (which see).

Voices: Paramedic Roy DeSoto (Kevin Tighe), Paramedic John Gage (Randolph Mantooth), Matt (Matthew Harper), Jason (Jason Phillips), Carol (Carol Harper), Randy (Randy Alrich).

Credits: Executive Producers: Fred Calvert, Michael Caffrey; Produced by: Fred Calvert; Directed by: Fred Calvert; Music by: The Sound Track Music Company; Produced by: Mark VII Limited, Fred Calvert Productions; In Association With: Universal Television And NBC-TV; Exclusive Distributor: MCA Television Limited.

Escape / 35

ESCAPE

NBC Television Network, February 11, 1973-September 9, 1973; 4 episodes in color on film; 30 minutes.

An adventure drama about man's struggle to survive and his ability to cope with life-or-death situations. Guest stars included Bernie Hamilton, Scott Walker, Norman Fell, Cameron Mitchell, Glenn Corbett and Ed Nelson.

Cast: Narrator (Jack Webb).

Credits: Executive Producer: R. A. Cinader; Produced by: Jerry Stanley; Directors: Christian Nyby, Daniel Haller, Gene Nelson, others; Writers: Stephen J. Cannell, Robert C. Dennis; Associate Producer: John Choy; Director of Photography: Emil Oster; Art Director: Joseph Alves, Jr.; Film Editor: Edward Haire, A. C. E.; Set Decorations: Ira Bates; Sound: Don Sharpless; Unit Manager: Frank Lossee; Editorial Supervision: Richard Belding; Color by: Technicolor; Titles & Optical Effects: Universal Title; Produced by: Mark VII Limited; In Association With: Universal Television And NBC-TV; Exclusive Distributor: MCA Television Limited.

EVENING IN BYZANTIUM

Distributed by MCA Television Limited for Operation Prime Time; August 1978; 2 episodes in color on film; 120 minutes (total: 4 hours).

A drama about a washed-up producer named Jesse Craig who came to the Cannes Film Festival in hopes of selling a script about a terrorist plot. Among those interested in the property was Bret Easton, actor and political activist, who was secretly involved in a plot similar to the one detailed in Craig's screenplay.

Cast: Jesse Craig (Glenn Ford), Bret Easton (Vince Edwards), Constance Dobson (Shirley Jones), Gail McKinnon (Erin Gray), Brian Murphy (Eddie Albert), Ian Wadleigh (Patrick Macnee), Inspector Le Dioux (Marcel Hillaire), Fabricio (Gregory Sierra), Inspector DuBois (Christian Marquand), Klein (Simon Oakland), Sonia Murphy (Gloria DeHaven), Danny (Michael Cole), Leonardo (Len Birman), Roger Tory (George Lazenby), Monsieur Carroll (Lee Bergere), Jack Conrad (James Booth), Jerry Olson (Harry Guardino).

Credits: Executive Producer: Glen A. Larson; Supervising Producer: Michael Sloan; Produced by: Robert F. O'Neill; Directed by: Jerry London; Written by: Glen A. Larson, Michael Sloan; Based on the Novel by: Irwin Shaw; Director of Photography: Michael Margulies; Music by: Stu Phillips; Art Director: Loyd S. Papez; Film Editor: Buford Hayes; Color by: Technicolor; Titles & Optical Effects: Universal Title; Produced by: Universal Television; Exclusive Distributor: MCA Television Limited.

36 / Series

THE FAMILY HOLVAK

NBC Television Network, September 7, 1975-October 27, 1975; 13 episodes in color on film; 60 minutes.

A drama about a poverty-stricken preacher in the rural South in the early 1930s and his relationship with a young son, daughter and wife as he struggled to raise his children. Based on the telefeature The Greatest Gift (which see).

Cast: Rev. Thomas Holvak (Glenn Ford), Elizabeth Holvak (Julie Harris), Ramey Holvak (Lance Kerwin), Julie Mae Holvak (Elizabeth Cheshire).

Credits: Executive Producers: Dean Hargrove, Roland Kibbee; Produced by: Richard Collins; Directors: Vincent Sherman, Alf Kjellin, Corey Allen, John Newland, Ralph Senensky, others; Based on the Novel "Ramey" by: Jack Farris; Associate Producer: Edward K. Dodds; Music by: Dick De Benedictis, Lee Holdridge; Theme "Look How Far We've Come" Sung by: Denny Brooks; Music Supervision: Hal Mooney; Costume Designer: Yvonne Wood; Color by: Technicolor; Titles & Optical Effects: Universal Title; Produced by: Universal Television; Exclusive Distributor: MCA Television Limited.

FARADAY AND COMPANY (NBC TUESDAY MYSTERY MOVIE, NBC WEDNESDAY MYSTERY MOVIE)

NBC Television Network, September 26, 1973-August 13, 1974; 6 episodes in color on film; 90 minutes.

An action-drama about a private detective wrongly imprisoned for 28 years who returned to Los Angeles to go into business with his son. He tried to cope with a whole new world of TV, mini-skirts and space travel.

Cast: Frank Faraday (Dan Dailey), Steve Faraday (James Naughton), Holly Barrett (Sharon Gless), Lou Carson (Geraldine Brooks).

Credits: Executive Producer: Leonard B. Stern; Producers: Tony Barrett, Stanley Kallis; Created by: Leonard B. Stern, Ken Pettus, Burt Prelutsky; Directors: Gary Nelson, others; Writers: Leonard B. Stern, Ken Pettus, Burt Prelutsky; Music by: Jerry Fielding; Director of Photography: Ronald Morgan; Film Editor: Richard C. Meyer; Color by: Technicolor; Titles & Optical Effects: Universal Title; Produced by: Talent Associates-Norton Simon, Inc.; In Association With: Universal Television And NBC-TV; Exclusive Distributor: MCA Television Limited.

FAY

NBC Television Network, September 4, 1975-June 2, 1976; 13

episodes in color on film; 30 minutes.

A situation comedy focusing on the renewed life of a 43-year-old woman looking for her identity after leaving an unhappy marriage behind her.

Cast: Fay Stewart (Lee Grant), Lillian (Andrea Lindley), Jack Stewart (Joe Silver), Linda (Margaret Willock), Elliott (Stewart Moss), Danny Cassidy (Bill Gerber), Letty (Lillian Lehman), Al Messina (Norman Alden).

Credits: Executive Producer: Danny Thomas; Producers: Paul Junger Witt, Jerry Mayer, Tony Thomas; Created by: Susan Harris; Directors: Alan Arkin, Richard Kinon, James Burrows, others; Associate Producer: Tony Thomas; Production Executive: Ronald Jacobs; Theme Song by: George Aliceson Tipton; Lyrics by: Stuart Margolin, Elayne Heilveil; Sung by: Jaye P. Morgan; Color by: Technicolor; Titles & Optical Effects: Universal Title; Produced by: Danny Thomas Productions, Universal Television; Exclusive Distributor: MCA Television Limited.

FIRESIDE THEATRE/JANE WYMAN'S FIRESIDE THEATRE

NBC Television Network, August 30, 1955-June 1957; 55 episodes in black & white on film; 30 minutes. Sponsored by Procter & Gamble.

A dramatic anthology. Guest stars included Marjorie Lord, Imogene Coca and Gene Barry. The series was continued as The Jane Wyman Theatre (which see). (An earlier edition of Fireside Theatre was produced by Hal Roach Productions and broadcast on the NBC Television Network, 1949-1955. Revue was not involved with the earlier version.)

Cast: Hostess, Jane Wyman.

Credits: Executive Producer: Edward Lewis; Produced by: Lewman Limited, Revue Productions, Inc.; Exclusive Distributor: MCA Television Limited.

FOUR-IN-ONE

NBC Television Network, September 16, 1970-September 8, 1971; 24 episodes in color on film; 60 minutes.

The umbrella title for four rotating series. See McCloud, The Psychiatrist, Rod Serling's Night Gallery and San Francisco International Airport for details.

38 / Series

FRONTIER CIRCUS

CBS Television Network, October 5, 1961-September 20, 1962; 26 episodes in black & white on film; 60 minutes.

A Western about a traveling circus on the frontier in the 1800s.

Cast: Col. Casey Thompson (Chill Wills), Ben Travis (John Derek), Tony Gentry (Richard Jaeckel).

Credits: Executive Producer: Richard Irving; Produced by: Samuel A. Peeples; Created by: Samuel A. Peeples; Directors: Richard Irving, others; Writers: Samuel A. Peeples, others; Story Editor: Samuel A. Peeples; Associate Producer: Frank Price; Directors of Photography: Benjamin H. Kline, A.S.C., others; Film Editor: Lee Huntington, A.C.E.; Original Music: David Buttolph, Jeff Alexander; Music Supervision: Stanley Wilson; Produced by: Calliope Productions, Inc., Revue Productions, Inc.; Exclusive Distributor: MCA Television Limited.

GALACTICA 1980

ABC Television Network, January 27, 1980-May 4, 1980; 7 episodes in color on film; 60 minutes.

A revival of Battlestar: Galactica (which see).

Cast: Commander Adama (Lorne Greene), Troy (Kent McCord), Dillon (Barry van Dyke), Jamie (Robyn Douglas).

Credits: Executive Producer: Glen A. Larson; Music Score: Stu Phillips; Theme Music: Stu Phillips, Glen A. Larson; Director of Photography: Frank Beascoechea; Art Director: Fred T. Tuch; Set Decorations: Leslie McCarthy; 2nd Unit Director: Joe Bralver; Casting by: Mark Mack; Film Editor: Bill Parker; Sound: James F. Rogers; Color by: Technicolor; Titles & Optical Effects: Universal Title; Educational Advisors: University of Southern California, Department of Physics-History, Department of Cinema-Television; Unit Production Manager: John C. Chulay; 1st Assistant Director: Pat Duffy; 2nd Assistant Director: Doug Metzger; Sound Effects Editor: Dick R. Wahrman; Music Editor: Ted Roberts; Costume Designer: Al Lehman; Miniatures and Special Effects Photographed by: Universal Hartland; Produced In Association With: Glen A. Larson Productions And Universal Television; Exclusive Distributor: MCA Television Limited.

GEMINI MAN

NBC Television Network, September 23, 1976-October 28, 1976; 13 episodes in color on film; 60 minutes.

An adventure program about Sam Casey, a special agent for a world-wide, international security "think tank," who had the power of invisibility. Based on the telefeature Gemini Man (which see).

Cast: Sam Casey (Ben Murphy), Abby Lawrence (Katherine Crawford), Leonard Driscoll (William Sylvester).

Credits: Executive Producer: Harve Bennett; Producers: Leslie Stevens, Robert F. O'Neill, Frank Telford; Directors: Charles R. Rondeau, Michael Caffey, others; Music by: Mark Snow, Lee Holdridge; Color by: Technicolor; Titles & Optical Effects: Universal Title; Produced by: Harve Bennett Productions, Inc., Universal Television; Exclusive Distributor: MCA Television Limited.

GENERAL ELECTRIC THEATRE

CBS Television Network, February 1, 1953-September 16, 1962; 190 episodes in black & white on film; 10 episodes in black & white on tape; 30 minutes. Sponsor and Agency: General Electric Company through Batten, Barton, Durstine & Osborn, Inc.

A dramatic anthology hosted by Ronald Reagan. Broadcast live 1953-54, and produced on film and tape by Revue Productions 1954-62. Guest stars included Raymond Massey, Harry Belafonte, Cloris Leachman, Edward Everett Horton, Jack Benny, Walter Matthau, Myrna Loy, Imogene Coca, Fred Astaire, Claudette Colbert, Lou Costello, Ernie Kovacs and the Marx Brothers in their final appearance together (in "The Incredible Jewel Robbery"). Certain episodes of General Electric Theatre were rebroadcast on Moment of Fear (which see).

Cast: Host, Ronald Reagan.

Credits: Executive Producers: Stanley Rubin, Norman Felton; Producers: Stanley Rubin, Peter Kortner, S. Mark Smith, Marshall Jamison, Albert Lamorisse; Program Supervisor: Ronald Reagan; Directors: Herschel Daugherty, Sherman Marks, David Greene, James Neilson, Ida Lupino, Norman Campbell, Charles Haas, Albert Lamorisse, others; Writers: James Allardice, Mayo Simon, Samuel Taylor, Louis Pelletier, Robert Dozier, Ken Kolb, Guy de Maupassant, Budd Schulberg, William Faulkner, Jessamyn West, Sidney Carroll, Max Ehrlich, Albert Lamorisse, William Cox, William Inge, A. E. Hotchner, Stirling Silliphant, Ken Kolb, Harold Swanton, Stanley Rubin, others; Associate Producers: Ethel Winant, William Morwood, Joseph Gantman; Story Editor: A. J. Carothers; Directors of Photography: Ray Cory, A.S.C., Robert W. Pittack, Paul Ivano, John L. Russell, others; Art Directors: Martin Obzina, John Randolph Lloyd, John J. Lloyd, George Patrick, John Meehan, Craig Smith, Russell Kimball; Music by: Jerry Goldsmith, Lyn Murray, Conrad Salinger; Set Decorations: John McCarthy, Perry Murdock; Film Editors: Michael R. McAdam, Dan Landres; Assistant Director: Jack Orbison; Production Supervisor: William Larsen; Produced by: Revue Productions, Inc.; Exclusive Distributor: MCA Television Limited.

GET CHRISTIE LOVE!

ABC Television Network, September 11, 1974-July 18, 1975; 22 episodes in color on film; 60 minutes. Major Sponsor and Agency: American Home Products Corp. through John F. Murray Advertising Agency, Inc.

A police drama about the undercover cases of the sexy Det. Christie Love of the Special Investigations Division of the Los Angeles Police Department. Based on the telefeature Get Christie Love! produced by Wolper Productions.

Cast: Det. Christie Love (Teresa Graves), Lt. Matt Reardon (Charles Cioffi), Capt. Arthur P. Ryan (Jack Kelly), Det. Steve Belmont (Dennis Rucker), Det. Joe Caruso (Andy Romano), Det. Valencia (Scott Peters), Sgt. Pete Gallagher (Michael Pataki).

Credits: Executive Producer: David L. Wolper; Produced by: Paul Mason; Developed for Television by: Peter Nelson, George Kirgo; Directors: Gene Nelson, others; Writers: Calvin Clements, Rudy Borchert, Olga Ford; Based on the Novel "The Ledger" by: Dorothy Uhnak; Music by: Jack Elliott, Allyn Ferguson, Luchi de Jesus; Produced by: Wolper Productions; In Association With: Universal Television; Exclusive Distributor: MCA Television Limited.

GOING MY WAY

ABC Television Network, October 3, 1962-September 11, 1963; 39 episodes in black & white on film; 60 minutes. Sponsors and Agencies: The American Tobacco Co. through Sullivan, Stauffer, Colwell & Bayles, Inc.; John H. Breck, Inc. through N. W. Ayer & Son, Inc.; Edward Dalton Division of Mead Johnson & Company through Kenyon & Eckhardt, Inc.; Dodge Division, Chrysler Corp. through Batten, Barton, Durstine & Osborn, Inc.; Miles Laboratories through Wade Advertising, Inc.

A drama with strong comedy emphasis which depicted the adventures of a pair of Manhattan parish priests from St. Dominick's Church and their friend who directed a community center in the parish neighborhood. Based on the 1944 film Going My Way.

Cast: Father Chuck O'Malley (Gene Kelly), Tom Colwell (Dick York), Father Fitzgibbon (Leo G. Carroll), Mrs. Featherstone (Nydia Westman).

Credits: Produced by: Joe Connelly; Directors: Joe Pevney, Allen Reisner, others; Writers: Joe Connelly, Emmet Lavery, Juanita

Vaughn, William Fay, Mark Weingart, Robert Hardy Andrews, others; Director of Photography: Jack Warren; Art Director: Frank Arrigo; Supervising Film Editor: Dann Cahn, A.C.E.; Produced by: Kerry Productions, My Way Co., Revue Productions, Inc.; Exclusive Distributor: MCA Television Limited.

GRIFF

ABC Television Network, September 29, 1973-January 5, 1974; 12 episodes in color on film; 60 minutes. Major Sponsors and Agencies: J. C. Penney through McCaffrey & McCall, Inc.; Bristol-Myers through Boclaro.

A detective drama about Wade Griffin, a private investigator whose 30 years' experience on the police force made him a legend in his own time. He and colleague S. Michael (Mike) Murdoch handled only important cases, operating from Wade Griffin Investigation offices in Westwood, California. Based on the telefeature Man on the Outside (which see).

Cast: Wade Griffin (Lorne Greene), S. Michael (Mike) Murdoch (Ben Murphy), Gracie Newcombe (Patricia Stich), Capt. Barney Marcus (Vic Tayback).

Credits: Executive Producer: David Victor; Produced by: Steven Bochco; Created by: Larry Cohen; Directors: Louis Antonio, Kenneth Johnson, Russ Mayberry, Walter Doniger, others; Writers: Kenneth Johnson, Peter S. Fischer, William Driskill, others; Production Executive: Robert F. O'Neill; Director of Photography: Enzo A. Martinelli, A.S.C.; Music by: Eliot Kaplan, Mike Post, Pete Carpenter; Art Director: William H. Tuntke; Film Editor: Fabien Tordjmann; Color by: Technicolor; Titles & Optical Effects: Universal Title; Produced by: Groverton Productions, Ltd.; In Association With: Universal Television; Exclusive Distributor: MCA Television Limited.

HALLMARK HALL OF FAME

NBC Television Network, December 24, 1951-   ; 3 episodes in color produced by Universal Television; 120 minutes, 90 minutes and 60 minutes.

A dramatic anthology. See THE SPECIALS: Hamlet, The Man Who Came to Dinner and The Snow Goose for details.

THE HARDY BOYS MYSTERIES

ABC Television Network, January 30, 1977-January 14, 1979; 28 episodes in color on film; 60 minutes.

42 / Series

A mystery-adventure program about Frank and Joe Hardy, teenage sons of the world famous detective Fenton Hardy, whose enthusiasm for their father's cases led them into exciting and often hair-raising situations. This series alternated with The Nancy Drew Mysteries (which see). In addition to the episodes listed above, there were 8 segments of the combined The Hardy Boys/Nancy Drew Mysteries.

Cast: Joe Hardy (Shaun Cassidy), Frank Hardy (Parker Stevenson), Fenton Hardy (Edmund Gilbert), Aunt Gertrude (Edith Atwater), Callie Shaw (Lisa Eilbacher), Chet Morton (Gary Springer), Nancy Drew (Pamela Sue Martin, Janet Louise Johnson), Carson Drew (William Schallert), George Fayne (Susan Buckner), Bess (Ruth Cox), Harry Gibbon (Phillip R. Allen).

Credits: Executive Producer: Glen A. Larson; Supervising Producers: B. W. Sandefur, Michael Sloan, Herman Groves; Producers: Ben Kadish, Joe Boston, Arlene Sidaris, Joyce Brotman, Christopher Crowe; Co-Producers: Arlene Sidaris, Joyce Brotman; Developed for Television by: Glen A. Larson; Based on the "Hardy Boys" Books by: Franklin W. Dixon; Directors: Joseph Pevney, Glen A. Larson, Vincent Edwards, Michael Caffey, Stuart Margolin, Steve Stern, Ivan Dixon, Dennis Donnelly, others; Writers: Glen A. Larson, Michael Sloan, Gregory S. Dinallo, Robert Pirosh, B. W. Sandefur, James Henerson, Christopher Crowe, others; Associate Producer: Andrew Mirisch; Story Editors: James Menzies, Christopher Crowe; Music Score: Stu Phillips; Theme Music: Glen A. Larson; Directors of Photography: Sy Hoffberg, Don M. Birnkrant, Jack Woolf, Enzo A. Martinelli, A. S. C.; Art Director: Roy Steffensen; Set Decorations: Sam Gross, Ed Baer; Casting by: Joseph Z. Reich; Film Editors: Harry Keramidas, Buford F. Hayes, John Dumas; Sound: Albert D. Cuesta; Color by: Technicolor; Titles & Optical Effects: Universal Title; Unit Production Manager: Les Berke; 1st Assistant Directors: Michael Messinger, Richard Hashimoto; 2nd Assistant Director: Louis Muscate; Sound Effects Editor: Tom McMullen; Music Editor: Fred Prior; Costume Designers: Brienne Von Glyttov, George R. Whittaker; Produced In Association With: Glen A. Larson Productions And Universal Television; Exclusive Distributor: MCA Television Limited.

HAROLD ROBBINS' 'THE SURVIVORS'

ABC Television Network, September 29, 1969-September 17, 1970; 15 episodes in color on film; 60 minutes. Major Sponsors and Agencies: The American Tobacco Company, Inc. through Batten, Barton, Durstine & Osborn, Inc.; R. J. Reynolds Tobacco Co. through William Esty Co., Inc.; Calgon Corp. through Needham, Harper & Steers, Inc.; Beecham Products, Inc. through Kenyon & Eckhardt; The Gillette Company through Batten, Barton, Durstine & Osborn, Inc.; Colgate-Palmolive Co. through Ted Bates & Co., Inc.

A drama program about people who were rich, colorful and exciting

Harold Robbins' 'The Survivors' / 43

--members of the jet set who sought sensation and whose words and actions made headlines.

Cast: Tracy Carlyle Hastings (Lana Turner), Philip Hastings (Kevin McCarthy), Duncan Carlyle (George Hamilton), Baylor Carlyle (Ralph Bellamy), Jeffrey Hastings (Michael Vincent [Jan-Michael Vincent]), Belle (Diana Muldaur), Jonathan (Louis Hayward), Antaeus Riakos (Rossano Brazzi), Jean Vale (Louise Sorel), Miguel Santerra (Robert Viharo), Shelia (Kathy Cannon), Marguerita (Donna Baccala), Tom (Robert Lipton), Eleanor Carlyle (Natalie Schafer).

Credits: Executive Producer: Walter Doniger; Produced by: Richard Caffey, Michael Gleason, Gordon Oliver; Directors: Marc Daniels, John Newland, Lee Philips, Lewis Allen, Paul Henreid, Michael Caffey, Josef Leytes, Walter Doniger, Harvey Hart, Curtis Harrington, George Fenady, Don Weis; Writers: Norman Katkov, Yale M. Udoff, Ellis Kadison, Richard Bluel, John Wilder, Michael Gleason, Walter Michaeljohn, Richard Caffey, Harry Kronman, Walter Doniger, William Robert Yates, others; Color by: Technicolor; Titles & Optical Effects: Universal Title; Produced by: Harold Robbins Co., Universal Television; Exclusive Distributor: MCA Television Limited.

HARRIS AGAINST THE WORLD (90 BRISTOL COURT)

NBC Television Network, October 5, 1964-January 4, 1965; 13 episodes in black & white on film; 30 minutes.

A situation comedy about the plant superintendent of a movie studio and his efforts to resist conformity, mechanization and bankruptcy. He lived with his wife and three children at 90 Bristol Court, a balconied modern multi-unit apartment motel with eight bungalows and a swimming pool, located on the Los Angeles-Beverly Hills line. The other residents of the Court were featured in Karen (which see) and Tom, Dick and Mary (which see).

Cast: Alan Harris (Jack Klugman), Kate Harris (Patricia Barry), Deedee Harris (Claire Wilcox), Billy Harris (David Macklin).

Credits: Executive Producer: Joe Connelly; Produced by: Revue Productions, Inc.; Exclusive Distributor: MCA Television Limited.

HARRIS AND COMPANY

NBC Television Network, March 15, 1979-April 5, 1979; 4 episodes in color on film; 60 minutes.

A drama about Mike Harris, the widowered father of five children who moved his family from Detroit to California in search of a new life.

44 / Series

Cast: Mike Harris (Bernie Casey), J. P. Harris (Lia Jackson), David Harris (David Hubbard), Liz Harris (Renee Brown), Richard Allen Harris (Dain Turner), Tommy Harris (Eddie Singleton), Uncle Charlie (Stu Gilliam), Angie (Carol Tillery Banks).

Credits: Produced by: Universal Television; Exclusive Distributor: MCA Television Limited.

HEC RAMSEY (NBC SUNDAY MYSTERY MOVIE)

NBC Television Network, October 8, 1972-August 25, 1974; 10 episodes in color on film; 120 minutes and 90 minutes.

A Western adventure-mystery about a gunfighter turned lawman who favored investigative criminology over the fast draw. Set in turn-of-the-century Oklahoma Territory.

Cast: Hec Ramsey (Richard Boone), Sheriff Oliver B. Stamp (Rick Lenz), Doc Amos Coogan (Harry Morgan), Arne Tornquist (Dennis Rucker).

Credits: Executive Producer: Jack Webb; Producers: William Finnegan, Douglas Benton, Harold Jack Bloom; Directors: George Marshall, Daniel Petrie, Douglas Benton, others; Writers: Shimon Wincelberg, Harold Jack Bloom, William R. Cox, Douglas Benton; Director of Photography: Robert B. House; Music: Fred Steiner, Lee Holdridge; Film Editor: Edward A. Biery, A.C.E.; Color by: Technicolor; Titles & Optical Effects: Universal Title; NBC Sunday Mystery Movie Theme by: Henry Mancini; Editorial Supervision: Richard Belding; Music Supervision: Hal Mooney; Produced by: Mark VII Limited; In Association With: Universal Television And NBC-TV; Exclusive Distributor: MCA Television Limited.

HEINZ STUDIO 57

DuMont Television Network, September 21, 1954-September 6, 1955; 54 episodes in black & white on film; 30 minutes. Sponsored by Heinz Food Products.

A dramatic anthology. Certain episodes of this series were rebroadcast on Moment of Fear (which see).

Credits: Produced by: Revue Productions, Inc.; Exclusive Distributor: MCA Television Limited.

HERNANDEZ: HOUSTON P.D. (THE BOLD ONES)

NBC Television Network, January 16, 1973; 1 episode in color on film; 60 minutes.

A police drama revolving around the work of Houston, Texas Police Department Det. Ramon Hernandez. Filmed on location. A pilot for an unsold series. Episode title: "The Night Crawler."

Cast: Det. Ramon Hernandez (Henry Darrow), Mamacita (Amapola Del Vando), Tomas (Fabian Gregory).

Credits: Executive Producer: David Levinson; Directed by: Richard Donner; Written by: Robert Van Scoyk; Director of Photography: Bill Butler; Art Director: John E. Chilberg II; Editorial Supervision: Richard Belding; Color by: Technicolor; Titles & Optical Effects: Universal Title; Produced by: Universal Television; In Association With: NBC-TV; Exclusive Distributor: MCA Television Limited.

HOLIDAY LODGE

CBS Television Network, June 25, 1961-October 8, 1961; 13 episodes in black & white on film; 30 minutes.

A situation comedy about Johnny Miller and Frank Boone, social directors at a summer resort called Holiday Lodge. A summer replacement series for The Jack Benny Show (which see).

Cast: Johnny Miller (Johnny Wayne), Frank Boone (Frank Shuster), Dorothy Jackson (Maureen Arthur), Woodrow (Charles Smith), J. W. Harrington (Justice Watson).

Credits: Produced by: J & M Productions, Revue Productions, Inc.; Exclusive Distributor: MCA Television Limited.

HOLMES AND YOYO

ABC Television Network, September 25, 1976-December 11, 1976; 13 episodes in color on film; 30 minutes.

A situation comedy about Alexander Holmes, a detective for the police department, and his partner Gregory "Yoyo" Yoyonovich, a robot.

Cast: Det. Alexander Holmes (Richard B. Shull), Gregory "Yoyo" Yoyonovich (John Schuck), Capt. Harry Sedford (Bruce Kirby); Officer Maxine Moon (Andrea Howard).

Credits: Executive Producer: Leonard B. Stern; Produced by: Arne Sultan; Created by: Jack Sher, Lee Hewitt; Directors: John Astin, Jack Arnold, Leonard B. Stern, Reza S. Badiyi, others; Music by: Leonard Rosenman, Dick Halligan; Color by: Technicolor; Titles & Optical Effects: Universal Title; Produced by: Universal Television; In Association With: Heyday Productions; Exclusive Distributor: MCA Television Limited.

HOUSE CALLS

CBS Television Network, December 17, 1979-   ; 11 episodes in color on film; 30 minutes.

A situation comedy about the zany goings-on in the private and professional life of Dr. Charley Michaels. Based on the 1978 film of the same title.

Cast: Dr. Charley Michaels (Wayne Rogers), Ann Anderson (Lynn Redgrave), Dr. Amos Weatherby (David Wayne), Dr. Norman Solomon (Raymond Buktenica), Conrad Peckler (Mark L. Taylor), Mrs. Phipps (Deedy Peters), Head Nurse Bradley (Aneta Corsaut).

Credits: Executive Producers: Arthur U. Gregory, Jerome Davis; Supervising Producers: Kathy Greer, Bill Greer; Created by: Max Shulman, Julius J. Epstein; Directors: Alan Bergman, Ray Austin, Wayne Rogers, others; Writers: Erik Tarloff, Kathy Greer, Bill Greer, others; Art Director: Sherman Loudermilk; Color by: Technicolor; Titles & Optical Effects: Universal Title; Produced by: Alex Winitsky-Arlene Sellers Productions; In Association with: Universal Television; Exclusive Distributor: MCA Television Limited.

ICHABOD AND ME

CBS Television Network, September 26, 1961-September 18, 1962; 36 episodes in black & white on film; 30 minutes. Sponsor and Agency: Quaker Oats Co. through J. Walter Thompson Co.

A situation comedy about Robert Major, an accomplished New York newspaperman who left the rat race of the big city to buy a newspaper in the quiet country village of Phippsboro.

Cast: Robert Major (Robert Sterling), Ichabod Adams (George Chandler), Abigail Adams (Christine White), Benjie Major (Jimmy Mathers), Aunt Lavinia (Reta Shaw).

Credits: Executive Producers: Joe Connelly, Bob Mosher; Directed by: Sidney Lanfield; Writers: Joe Connelly, Bob Mosher; Director of Photography: Jack MacKenzie; Music by: Frank Morris, Pete Rugolo; Film Editor: Bud Isaacs; Art Director: John Meehan; Produced by: Kayro, Inc.; Filmed by: Revue Productions, Inc.

THE IMMIGRANTS

Distributed by MCA Television Limited for Operation Prime Time, November 1978; 2 episodes in color on film; 120 minutes (total: 4 hours).

A drama chronicling the rise and fall of hard-driven shipping magnate Daniel Lavetta, son of Italian immigrants who settled in San Francisco at the turn of the century.

Cast: Daniel Lavetta (Stephen Macht), Jean Sheldon (Sharon Gless), Joseph Lavetta (Aharon Ipale), Anna Lavetta (Michele Marsh), Thomas Seldon (Richard Anderson), Mark Levy (Michael Durrell), Sarah Levy (Susan Strasberg), Anthony Cassala (Pernell Roberts), Maria Cassala (Ina Balin), Feng Wo (Yuki Shimoda), May Ling (Aimee Eccles), Joseph (Shane Sinutko), Alan Brocker (John Saxon), So-Toy (Beulah Quo), Chris Noel (Lloyd Bochner), Gregory Pastore (Joe Bennett), Pete Lomas (Kevin Dobson), Calvin Braderman (Roddy McDowall), Mary Seldon (Kathleen Nolan), Grant Whittier (Barry Sullivan).

Credits: Executive Producer: Robert A. Cinader; Producers: Gino Grimaldi, Hannah Shearer; Directed by: Alan J. Levi; Written by: Richard Collins; Based on the Novel by: Howard Fast; Director of Photography: Frank Thackery; Music by: Gerald Fried; Art Director: George Renne; Film Editors: Ed Williams, Albert Zuniga; Color by: Technicolor; Titles & Optical Effects: Universal Title; Produced by: Universal Television; Exclusive Distributor: MCA Television Limited.

THE INCREDIBLE HULK

CBS Television Network, March 10, 1978- ; 57 episodes in color on film; 120 minutes and 60 minutes.

An adventure program about the extraordinary transformation of passionately dedicated scientist Dr. David Banner into a primitive man-beast of superhuman strength known as "The Hulk." Based on the telefeature The Incredible Hulk (which see).

Cast: Dr. David Banner (Bill Bixby), Jack McGee (Jack Colvin), The Hulk (Lou Ferrigno), Elaina (Susan Sullivan).

Credits: Executive Producer: Kenneth Johnson; Supervising Producer: Chuck Bowman; Producers: James G. Hirsch; Nicholas Corea; James D. Parriott; Charles Bowman; Developed for Television by: Kenneth Johnson; Directors: Kenneth Johnson, Kenneth Gilbert, Harvey Laidman, others; Writers: Kenneth Johnson, Nicholas Corea, James G. Hirsch, Jim Tisdale, Migdia Varela, others; Story Editors: Karen Harris, Jill Sherman, Andrew Schneider; Associate Producers: Stephen P. Caldwell, Alan Cassidy; Music by: Joseph Harnell; Director of Photography: John McPherson; Art Directors: David Marshall, Lou Montejano, Chuck Davis, Seymour Klate; Set Decorations: Robert Wingo, Joe Mitchell; Casting by: Phil Benjamin, Ron Stephenson; Film Editors: Robert K. Richard, A.C.E., George Ohanian, A.C.E., Jack Schoengarth; Sound: Claude Riggins; Consultant: Stan Lee; Color by: Technicolor; Titles & Optical Effects: Universal Title; Unit Production Managers: Robert B. Steinhauer, Mark A. Burley; 1st

Assistant Director: Wolfgang E. Marum; 2nd Assistant Director: Richard J. Forrest; Sound Effects Editors: Bernard F. Pincus, Patrick Somerset; Music Editors: Walter Ulric Elliott, Celia L. Weiner; Costume Designer: Brienne Von Glyttov; Produced by: Universal Television; Exclusive Distributor: MCA Television Limited.

THE INVESTIGATORS

CBS Television Network, October 5, 1961-December 28, 1961; 13 episodes in black & white on film; 60 minutes.

A detective drama about an insurance investigating team that untangled puzzling insurance claims.

Cast: Russ Andrews (James Franciscus), Steve Banks (James Philbrook), Maggie Peters (Mary Murphy), Bill Davis (Al Austin).

Credits: Produced by: Revue Productions, Inc.; Exclusive Distributor: MCA Television Limited.

THE INVISIBLE MAN

NBC Television Network, September 8, 1975-January 19, 1976; 13 episodes in color on film; 60 minutes.

An adventure program about Dr. Daniel Westin, a scientist with the power of invisibility. Based on the story by H. G. Wells and the telefeature The Invisible Man (which see).

Cast: Dr. Daniel Westin (David McCallum), Walter Carlson (Craig Stevens), Dr. Kate Westin (Melinda Fee).

Credits: Executive Producer: Harve Bennett; Producers: Leslie Stevens, Steve Bochco, Robert F. O'Neill; Directors: Sigmund Neufeld, Jr., Leslie Stevens, Robert Lewis, Alan J. Levi, others; Music by: Henry Mancini, Pete Rugolo, Richard Clements; Music Supervision: Hal Mooney; Color by: Technicolor; Titles & Optical Effects: Universal Title; Produced by: Harve Bennett Productions; In Association With: Universal Television; Exclusive Distributor: MCA Television Limited.

IRONSIDE

NBC Television Network, September 14, 1967-January 16, 1975; 198 episodes in color on film; 120 minutes and 60 minutes.

A police drama about the activities of former Chief of Detectives Robert T. Ironside, as he acted as consultant to the San Francisco Police Department. The veteran law officer was wheel-chair ridden

Ironside / 49

with a spinal injury, the result of an attack by a would-be assassin. Based on the telefeature Ironside (which see). The series Amy Prentiss (which see) was based on the episode "Amy Prentiss, AKA The Chief."

Cast: Chief Robert T. Ironside (Raymond Burr), Det. Sgt. Ed Brown (Don Galloway), Eve Whitfield (Barbara Anderson), Fran Belding (Elizabeth Baur), Mark Sanger (Don Mitchell), Commissioner Randall (Gene Lyons).

Credits: Executive Producers: Cy Chermak, Joel Rogosin, Collier Young, Frank Price; Producers: Norman Jolley, Albert Aley, Lou Morheim, Collier Young, Douglas Benton, Winston Miller, Joel Rogosin, James D. McAdams; Created by: Collier Young; Directors: Boris Sagal, Russ Mayberry, Don Weis, Leo Penn, Don McDougall, Abner Biberman, Richard Colla, Daniel Haller, Allen Reisner, Michael Caffey, others; Writers: William Gordon, James Doherty, Francine Carroll, Don M. Mankiewicz, Christopher Trumbo, Michael Philip Butler, William Douglas Lansford, Sy Salkowitz, Norman Jolley, Lou Morheim, Cy Chermak, Ken Kolb, Lane Slate, others; Associate Producers: James D. McAdams, Jeannot Szwarc; Story Editors: Albert Aley, Norman Jolley; Director of Photography: Bud Thackery, A.S.C.; Theme Music by: Quincy Jones; Music by: Quincy Jones, Oliver Nelson, Marty Paich; Costumes: Grady Hunt; Makeup: Bud Westmore; Color by: Technicolor; Titles & Optical Effects: Universal Title; Production Executive: Robert Beneveds; Supervising Executive: George Santoro; Produced by: Harbour Productions, Universal Television; Exclusive Distributor: MCA Television Limited.

IT TAKES A THIEF

ABC Television Network, January 9, 1968-September 14, 1970; 65 episodes in color on film; 60 minutes. Major Sponsors and Agencies: Colgate-Palmolive Company through Ted Bates & Company; R. J. Reynolds Tobacco Co. through William Esty Company, Inc.; Sterling Drug, Inc. through Dancer-Fitzgerald-Sample, Inc.; Liggett & Myers Tobacco Co. through J. Walter Thompson Company; International Latex Corporation through Ted Bates & Company, Inc.; Bristol-Myers Company through Foote, Cone & Belding, Inc.; Union Carbide Corporation through William Esty Company, Inc.; American Home Products Corporation through the John F. Murray Advertising Agency, Inc.

An adventure series which featured the exploits of Alexander Mundy, a debonair master thief who was paroled from prison to exercise his talents exclusively for the SIA, a U.S. intelligence agency. Based on the telefeature It Takes a Thief (which see).

Cast: Alexander Mundy (Robert Wagner), Noah Bain (Malachi Throne), Wallie Powers (Edward Binns), Alistair Mundy (Fred Astaire).

50 / Series

Credits: Executive Producers: Gordon Oliver, Jack Arnold; Producers: Gene L. Coon, Leonard Horn, Frank Price, Glen A. Larson; Created by: Roland Kibbee; Directors: Don Weis, Leslie Stevens, Jack Arnold, others; Writers: Roland Kibbee, Leslie Stevens, Alan Caillou, Stephen Kandel; Associate Producers: Mort Zarcoff, Glen A. Larson; Theme Music: Dave Grusin; Music by: Ernest Freeman, Benny Golson, Ralph Ferraro; Directors of Photography: Ralph Woolsey, A.S.C., William Margulies, Enzo Serafin; Art Directors: Aurelio Crugnola, Alexander A. Mayer; Film Editors: Tony Martinelli, Frank E. Morriss, Gabrio Astori; Editorial Supervision: Richard Belding; Music Supervision: Stanley Wilson; Production Managers: Danilo Sabatini, James M. Walters, Jr.; Costumes: Burton Miller; Color by: Technicolor; Titles & Optical Effects: Universal Title; Produced by: Universal Television; Exclusive Distributor: MCA Television Limited.

IT'S A MAN'S WORLD

NBC Television Network, September 17, 1962-January 28, 1963; 19 episodes in black & white on film; 60 minutes.

A situation comedy about four boys who lived on the Elephant, a houseboat moored at a dock in the small Midwest college town of Cordella, Ohio.

Cast: Wes Macauley (Glenn Corbett), Howie Macauley (Mike Burns), Tom-Tom DeWitt (Ted Bessell), Vern Hodges (Randy Boone), Houghton Stott (Harry Harvey), Irene Hoff (Jan Norris).

Credits: Produced by: Peter Tewksbury; Directors: Peter Tewksbury, others; Writers: Peter Tewksbury, Jim Leighton, John McGreevey, James Allardice, Ben Masselink, others; Created by: Peter Tewksbury; Associate Producer: Jim Leighton; Story Editor: James Menzies; Music by: Jack Marshall; Director of Photography: Ray Flin; Art Directors: Raymond Beal, John J. Lloyd; Supervising Film Editor: David O'Connell; Film Editor: Danford Greene; Set Decorations: Perry Murdock; Produced by: Revue Productions, Inc.; Exclusive Distributor: MCA Television Limited.

THE JACK BENNY SHOW

NBC Television Network, September 25, 1964-September 10, 1965; 39 episodes in black & white on film; 30 minutes. Sponsors and Agencies: State Farm Mutual Automobile Insurance Co. through Needham, Louis & Brorby, Inc.; Jell-O through Young & Rubicam, Inc.

A situation comedy about the adventures of comedian Jack Benny, his aide "Rochester," and his friends Don Wilson (also the show's announcer) and singer Dennis Day. (An earlier edition of this program was broadcast by the CBS Television Network, 1950-1964. It was not produced by Revue.)

The Jack Benny Show / 51

Cast: Jack Benny, Eddie "Rochester" Anderson, Don Wilson, Dennis Day.

Credits: Executive Producer: Irving A. Fein; Producers: Seymour Burns, Fred de Cordova; Directed by: Fred de Cordova; Writers: Sam Perrin, George Balzer, Hal Goldman, Al Gordon; Music Director: Mahlon Merrick; Production Supervisor: Herman Glazer; Art Director: Frank Arrigo; Film Editor: J. R. Wittridge, A. C. E.; Assistant Director: Charles S. Gould; Produced by: J & M Productions, Revue Productions, Inc.; Exclusive Distributor: MCA Television Limited.

THE JANE WYMAN THEATRE

NBC Television Network, September 26, 1957-May 1958; 29 episodes in black & white on film; 30 minutes.

A dramatic anthology and continuation of Fireside Theatre/Jane Wyman's Fireside Theatre (which see).

Cast: Hostess, Jane Wyman.

Credits: Executive Producer: Edward Lewis; Produced by: Lewman Limited, Revue Productions, Inc.; Exclusive Distributor: MCA Television Limited.

THE JEAN ARTHUR SHOW

CBS Television Network, September 12, 1966-December 5, 1966; 12 episodes in color on film; 30 minutes.

A situation comedy about Patricia Marshall, a successful, irrepressible attorney with a flair and a zest for life who practiced law with her son, Paul.

Cast: Patricia Marshall (Jean Arthur), Paul Marshall (Ron Harper), Mr. Morton (Leonard Stone).

Credits: Music by: Johnny Keating; Produced by: Universal Television; Exclusive Distributor: MCA Television Limited.

JIGSAW (THE MEN)

ABC Television Network, September 21, 1972-August 11, 1973; 8 episodes in color on film; 60 minutes. Major Sponsor and Agency: Chevrolet Motor Division, General Motors Corporation through Campbell-Ewald.

A police drama about Lt. Frank Dain, a special investigator in the State Bureau of Missing Persons who worked independently, travel-

52 / Series

ing anywhere his cases took him and often put his own life on the line when another life was in jeopardy. Based on the telefeature Jigsaw (which see). This series rotated with Assignment: Vienna (produced by MGM Television) and The Delphi Bureau (produced by Warner Bros. Television).

Cast: Lt. Frank Dain (James Wainwright).

Credits: Produced by: Stanley Kallis; Created by: Robert Thompson; Directors: Walter Doniger, David Friedkin, others; Writers: Calvin J. Clements, Sr., Dan Ullman, others; Executive Story Consultant: Mark Rodgers; Director of Photography: Mike Margulies; Music by: Robert Drasnin, Harper McKay; Art Director: Syd Litwack; Film Editors: Howard Epstein, Jack Kirschner; Color by: Technicolor; Titles & Optical Effects: Universal Title; Produced by: Universal Television; Exclusive Distributor: MCA Television Limited.

THE JOHN FORSYTHE SHOW

NBC Television Network, September 13, 1965-August 29, 1966; 30 episodes in color on film; 30 minutes. Sponsor and Agency: Colgate-Palmolive Company through Norman, Craig & Kummell, Inc.

A situation comedy about John Foster, an Air Force major and bachelor who inherited and became headmaster of an exclusive San Francisco school for girls. Based on the pilot film The Mr. and the Misses.

Cast: Major John Foster (John Forsythe), Miss Culver (Elsa Lanchester), Miss Wilson (Ann B. Davis), Sgt. Ed Robbins (Guy Marks), Joanna (Peggy Lipton), Kathy (Darleen Carr), Susan (Tracy Stratford), Pamela (Pamelyn Ferdin), Marcia (Page Forsythe), Norma Jean (Brooke Forsythe).

Credits: Producers: Peter Kortner, Dick Wesson; Directors: Dick Wesson, others; Writers: Joel Kane, others; Associate Producer: Joel Kane; Director of Photography: Ray Rennahan, A.S.C.; Art Director: Alexander Mayer; Film Editor: Richard G. Wray, A.C.E.; Set Decorations: John McCarthy, Audrey Blasdell; Makeup Supervision: Bud Westmore; Costume Supervision: Vincent Dee; Music Supervision: Stanley Wilson; Produced by: Forsythe Productions, Universal Television; In Association With: NBC-TV; Exclusive Distributor: MCA Television Limited.

JOHNNY MIDNIGHT

Distributed by MCA Television Limited, 1959-1960; 39 episodes in black & white on film; 30 minutes.

Johnny Midnight / 53

A drama about Johnny Midnight, an actor-turned-detective who operated in the Times Square area of New York City.

Cast: Johnny Midnight (Edmond O'Brien), Sgt. Sam Olivera (Arthur Batanides), Lt. Geller (Barney Phillips), Aki (Yuki Shemoda).

Credits: Produced by: Jack Chertok; Music by: Joe Bushkin; Music Supervision: Stanley Wilson; Produced by: Jack Chertok TV, Inc., Revue Productions, Inc.; Exclusive Distributor: MCA Television Limited.

JOHNNY STACCATO

NBC Television Network, September 10, 1959-March 24, 1960; 27 episodes in black & white on film; 30 minutes.

An adventure-mystery about a jazz-loving, piano-playing private investigator with a hand for music and a nose for trouble. Set in New York City.

Cast: Johnny Staccato (John Cassavetes), Waldo (Eduardo Ciannelli).

Credits: Executive Producer: William Frye; Produced by: Everett Chambers; Directors: Joseph Pevney, others; Writers: Richard Berg, others; Music by: Elmer Bernstein; Music Supervision: Stanley Wilson; Produced by: Revue Productions, Inc.; Exclusive Distributor: MCA Television Limited.

KAREN (90 BRISTOL COURT)

NBC Television Network, October 5, 1964-August 30, 1965; 28 episodes in black & white on film; 30 minutes.

A situation comedy about 16-year-old Karen Scott and her relationship with her family and friends. Karen lived at 90 Bristol Court, a balconied modern multi-unit apartment motel with eight bungalows and a swimming pool, located on the Los Angeles-Beverly Hills line. The other residents of the Court were featured in Harris Against the World (which see) and Tom, Dick and Mary (which see).

Cast: Karen Scott (Debbie Watson), Steve Scott (Richard Denning), Barbara Scott (Mary LaRoche), Mimi Scott (Gina Gillespie).

Credits: Executive Producer: Joe Connelly; Produced by: Revue Productions, Inc.; Exclusive Distributor: MCA Television Limited.

KINGSTON: CONFIDENTIAL

NBC Television Network, March 23, 1977-August 10, 1977; 13 episodes in color on film; 60 minutes.

An action-adventure drama about R. B. Kingston, the editor-in-chief of a huge news media group who was often called upon to apply his investigative reporting techniques to contemporary, relevant situations. Based on the telefeature Kingston: The Power Play (which see).

Cast: R. B. Kingston (Raymond Burr), Beth Kelly (Pamela Hensley), Tony Marino (Art Hindle), Jessica Frazier (Nancy Olson).

Credits: Executive Producer: David Victor; Producers: Don Ingalls, Joe L. Cramer, James Hirsch, Don Nicholl; Directors: Don McDougall, Chris Nyby, Michael Caffey, Richard Moder, Don Weis, others; Writers: Larry Alexander, Richard Fielder, others; Music by: Richard Shores, Pete Rugolo, Henry Mancini; Color by: Technicolor; Titles & Optical Effects: Universal Title; Produced by: R. B. Productions, Universal Television; Exclusive Distributor: MCA Television Limited.

KOJAK

CBS Television Network, October 24, 1973-April 15, 1978; 118 episodes in color on film; 60 minutes. Sponsors and Agencies: Buick through McCann-Erickson, Inc.; Pontiac through D'Arcy, MacManus, Intermarco, Inc.; American Home Products Corporation through John F. Murray; Johnson & Johnson through Young & Rubicam, Inc.; British Leyland through Bozell & Jacobs.

A police drama that focused on the cases assigned to New York Police Detective Theo Kojak, a veteran cop with no false illusions about his job--a cop's cop. Stubborn and tenacious, he possessed a deep concern for people and keeping justice in an even balance. Based on the telefeature The Marcus-Nelson Murders (which see).

Cast: Lt. Theo Kojak (Telly Savalas), Capt. Frank McNeil (Dan Frazer), Lt. Bobby Crocker (Kevin Dobson), Det. Stavros (Demosthenes [George Savalas]), Det. Saperstein (Mark Russell), Det. Rizzo (Vince Conti).

Credits: Executive Producers: Abby Mann, Matthew Rapf; Supervising Producers: Jack Laird, Matthew Rapf, James McAdams; Producers: James McAdams, Chester Krumholz, Gene Kearney; Created by: Abby Mann; Directors: Russ Mayberry, Jerry London, Charles S. Dubin, David Friedkin, Daniel Haller, Richard Donner, Sigmund Neufeld, Jr., Telly Savalas, others; Writers: Joseph Polizzi, Chester Krumholz, others; Music Score: John Cacavas; Theme Music: Billy Goldenberg; Directors of Photography: Gerald Perry Finnerman, A.S.C., Sol Negrin, A.S.C., Charles Correll, Vilis Lapenieks; Art Directors: Edward Burbrudge, John J. Lloyd, Bill Tuntke, Peter Dohanos; Set Decorations: Philip Smith, John Dwyer, Richard B. Goddard; Assistant Director: Steve Barnett; Unit Managers: David Golden, Mel A. Bishop; Film Editors: Robert O. Lovett, Sidney Katz, A.C.E.; Sound: James T. Sabat; Color by:

Technicolor; Titles & Optical Effects: Universal Title; Mr. Savalas' Wardrobe Furnished by: Botany 500; Technical Advisor: Burton Armus; Sound Effects Editor: Ron Kalish; Music Editor: Robert Mayer; Suggested by the Book "Justice in the Backroom" by: Selwyn Raab; Produced by: Universal Television; Exclusive Distributor: MCA Television Limited.

KRAFT MYSTERY THEATRE

NBC Television Network, June 19, 1963-September 25, 1963; 14 episodes in black & white on film; 60 minutes. Sponsor and Agency: Kraft Foods Division, National Dairy Products through J. Walter Thompson Company.

A mystery anthology comprised of six original episodes and eight episodes first telecast on Alcoa Premiere (which see). (An earlier edition of Kraft Mystery Theatre (1961-62) was made up of episodes originally produced for British television and shows filmed by Desilu Productions, Inc. Revue was not involved in this original version of the program.)

Credits: Produced by: Revue Productions, Inc.; Exclusive Distributor: MCA Television Limited.

KRAFT SUSPENSE THEATRE

NBC Television Network, October 10, 1963-September 9, 1965; 53 episodes in color on film; 60 minutes. Sponsor and Agency: Kraft Foods Division, National Dairy Products through J. Walter Thompson Company.

A dramatic anthology. Guest stars included Peter Lorre, Ida Lupino, Gloria Swanson, Lloyd Bridges, Dean Stockwell, Eddie Albert, Julie Harris, Jeffrey Hunter, Milton Berle, Arthur Kennedy, Louis Jourdan, Tippi Hedren and Telly Savalas. The first episode, "The Case Against Paul Ryker," was released theatrically as Sergeant Ryker by Universal Pictures in 1968. It was the basis for the series Court Martial (which see). Another episode, "In Darkness Waiting," was released theatrically as Strategy of Terror by Universal Pictures in 1969. The "Rapture at Two-Forty" episode of Kraft Suspense Theatre (April 15, 1965) was the pilot for the series Run for Your Life (which see).

Credits: Executive In Charge of Production: Roy Huggins; Executive Producer: Frank P. Rosenberg; Producers: Robert Altman, Robert Blees, Frank Telford, Arthur H. Nadel; Directors: Buzz Kulik, Jack Smight, Robert Altman, others; Writers: Seeleg Lester, William D. Gordon, Robert Altman, John D. F. Black, Andy Lewis, Dean Hargrove, David Moessinger, Gordon Russell, Robert L. Joseph, others; Associate Producers: Jo Swerling, Jr., Joel Rogosin; Directors of Photography: Walter Strenge, A.S.C., Lionel Lindon,

Ellis F. Thackery; Theme Music: Johnny Williams; Music Score: Lyn Murray; Art Director: John J. Lloyd; Film Editor: Robert B. Warwick; Sound: William Lynch; Assistant Director: John Clarke Bowman; Set Decorators: John McCarthy, Robert C. Bradfield; Costume Supervisor: Vincent Dee; Makeup: Jack Barron; Hair Stylist: Florence Bush; Music Supervision: Stanley Wilson; Produced by: Roncom Productions, Inc., Revue Productions, Inc.; Exclusive Distributor: MCA Television Limited.

LANIGAN'S RABBI (NBC SUNDAY MYSTERY MOVIE)

NBC Television Network, January 30, 1977-July 3, 1977; 4 episodes in color on film; 90 minutes.

A mystery-drama about Police Chief Paul Lanigan and Rabbi David Small. Together they solved baffling crime puzzles that occurred in their town and that involved members of Rabbi Small's congregation. Based on the telefeature Lanigan's Rabbi (which see).

Cast: Chief Paul Lanigan (Art Carney), Rabbi David Small (Bruce Solomon), Mrs. Kate Lanigan (Janis Paige), Miriam Small (Janet Margolin), Bobbie Whittaker (Barbara Carney), Lt. Osgood (Robert Doyle).

Credits: Executive Producer: Leonard B. Stern; Producers: Don Mankiewicz, Gordon Cotler, David J. O'Connell; Directors: Joseph Pevney, Leonard B. Stern, others; Music by: Don Costa; Sunday Mystery Movie Theme by: Henry Mancini; Editorial Supervision: Richard Belding; Music Supervision: Hal Mooney; Color by: Technicolor; Titles & Optical Effects: Universal Title; Main Title Design: Wayne Fitzgerald; Produced by: Heyday Productions; In Association with: Universal Television And NBC-TV; Exclusive Distributor: MCA Television Limited.

LARAMIE

NBC Television Network, September 15, 1959-September 17, 1963; 93 episodes in black & white on film; 31 episodes in color on film; 60 minutes.

A Western about the trials and tribulations of two men, a woman, and a boy in a wild corner of Wyoming in the years after the Civil War.

Cast: Slim Sherman (John Smith), Jess Harper (Robert Fuller), Jonesy (Hoagy Carmichael), Andy Sherman (Bobby Crawford, Jr.), Daisy Cooper (Spring Byington), Mike Williams (Dennis Holmes), Mort Corey (Stuart Randall).

Credits: Produced by: John Champion; Directors: Joe Kane, Lesley Selander; Associate Producer: Dan Ullman; Director of Photography: Ray Rennahan; Theme Music by: Cyril Mockridge; Music by: Hans Salter, Richard Sendry; Art Director: Alexander A. Mayer; Film Editor: Ray C. de Vally, Sr.; Set Decorations: John McCarthy; Sound: Earl Crain, Jr.; Color Consultant: Alex Quigora; Costume Supervision: Vincent Dee; Makeup: Jack Barron; Hair Stylist: Florence Bush; Music Supervision: Stanley Wilson; Produced by: Revue Productions, Inc.; Exclusive Distributor: MCA Television Limited.

LAREDO

NBC Television Network, September 16, 1965-September 1, 1967; 56 episodes in color on film; 60 minutes.

A Western with comic overtones about the exploits of the Texas Rangers during the 1870-85 era. The base of operations was Laredo, Texas and the Rangers were the men of Company B. The program spotlighted four men of the company and their captain. The pilot for this series was the The Virginian episode "We've Lost a Train" (NBC Television Network, April 21, 1965), an expanded version of which was released theatrically as Backtrack by Universal Pictures in 1969. Another theatrical release, Three Guns for Texas (1968), was edited from the Laredo episodes "Yahoo," "Jinx" and "No Bugles, One Drum" telecast on the NBC Television Network September 30, 1965, December 2, 1965 and February 24, 1966, respectively.

Cast: Reese Bennett (Neville Brand), Chad Cooper (Peter Brown), Joe Riley (William Smith), Capt. Edward Parmalee (Philip Carey), Erik Hunter (Robert Wolders).

Credits: Executive Producers: Howard Christie, Richard Irving; Produced by: Frederick Shorr; Directors: David Lowell Rich, Earl Bellamy, Paul Stanley, others; Writers: John D. F. Black, others; Director of Photography: Andrew Jackson; Theme Music and Score by: Russ Garcia; Assistant Directors: Les Berke, Jack Doran, Frank Losee; Music Supervision: Stanley Wilson; Produced by: Universal Television; Exclusive Distributor: MCA Television Limited.

THE LAST CONVERTIBLE

NBC Television Network, September 24, 1979, September 25, 1979 and September 26, 1979; 3 episodes in color on film; 120 minutes (total: 6 hours).

A drama about the lives of five close-knit Harvard classmates from 1941 to 1969 and "the last convertible," a spiffy 1939 Packard which passed through each of their hands over the years.

Cast: George Virdon (Bruce Boxleitner), Russ Currier (Perry King), Jean des Barres (Michael Nouri), Terry Garrigan (John Shea), Ron

58 / Series

Dalrymple (Edward Albert), Chris Farris (Deborah Raffin), Kay Haddon (Sharon Gless), Ann Rowan (Kim Darby), Denise (Jeanna Michaels), Nancy (Caroline Smith), Sheila Garrigan (Stacey Nelkin), Mel (Sam Weisman), Liz (Tracy Brooks Swope), Paul McCreed (Fred McCarren), Col. Elkhart (Stuart Whitman), Chief Lonborg (Vic Morrow), Sgt. Drabics (Martin Milner), Maj. Goodman (Pat Harrington), Rosamond Ardley (Lisa Pelikan), Dr. Wetherell (John Houseman).

Credits: Based on the Novel by: Anton Myrer; Color by: Technicolor; Titles & Optical Effects: Universal Title; Produced by: Universal Television; Exclusive Distributor: MCA Television Limited.

THE LAW

NBC Television Network, March 19, 1975-April 16, 1975; 3 episodes in color on film; 60 minutes.

A drama program about public defender Murray Stone. Based on the telefeature The Law (which see).

Cast: Attorney Murray Stone (Judd Hirsch), Van Lorn (Alex Nicol), Michael (Fiona Guinness).

Credits: Color by: Technicolor; Titles & Optical Effects: Universal Title; Produced by: Universal Television; Exclusive Distributor: MCA Television Limited.

THE LAWYERS (THE BOLD ONES)

NBC Television Network, September 21, 1969-September 10, 1972; 27 episodes in color on film; 60 minutes.

A drama about three modern day attorneys who took the stand against unreason, and the demands of a burgeoning society. Based on the telefeatures The Sound of Anger (which see) and The Whole World Is Watching (which see).

Cast: Walter Nichols (Burl Ives), Brian Darrell (Joseph Campanella), Neil Darrell (James Farentino).

Credits: Executive Producer: Roy Huggins; Producers: Jo Swerling, Jr., Steve Heilpern; Directors: Alexander Singer, Dick Heffron, others; Writers: John Thomas James, Jack B. Sowards, Bret Huggins, Dick Nelson, others; Director of Photography: Gene Polito; Art Director: Robert Smith; Set Decorations: John McCarthy; Makeup: Bud Westmore; Hair Stylist: Larry Germain; Costumes: Charles Waldo; Editorial Supervision: Richard Belding; Color by: Technicolor; Titles & Optical Effects: Universal Title; Produced by: Roy Huggins-Public Arts Productions, Universal

Television; In Association With: NBC-TV; Exclusive Distributor: MCA Television Limited.

LEAVE IT TO BEAVER

CBS Television Network, October 4, 1957-September 26, 1958; ABC Television Network, October 3, 1958-September 12, 1963; 234 episodes in black & white on film; 30 minutes. Sponsors and Agencies: The American Motors Corporation through Geyer, Morey, Madden & Ballard, Inc.; Derby Foods through M-E Productions, McCann-Erickson, Inc.; General Foods Corporation through Ogilvy, Benson & Mather, Inc.; General Mills, Inc. through Dancer-Fitzgerald-Sample, Inc.; H. C. Moores Company Division, M & R Dietetic Laboratories, Inc. through Benton & Bowles, Inc.; North American Philips Co., Inc. through C. J. LaRoche Co., Inc.; Ovaltine Food Products Co., Division of the Wander Company through Tatham-Laird, Inc.; Pepsi-Cola Company through Batten, Barton, Durstine & Osborn, Inc.; Polaroid Corporation through Doyle, Dane & Bernbach, Inc.; Mars, Inc. through Needham, Louis & Brorby, Inc.; Peter Paul, Inc. through Dancer-Fitzgerald-Sample, Inc.; Ralston Purina Co. through Gardner Advertising Co. and Guild, Bascom & Bonfigli, Inc.

A situation comedy about the trials and adventures of Theodore "Beaver" Cleaver and his brother Wally, and their harassed yet understanding parents, Ward and June.

Cast: June Cleaver (Barbara Billingsley), Ward Cleaver (Hugh Beaumont), Wally Cleaver (Tony Dow), Theodore "Beaver" Cleaver (Jerry Mathers), Eddie Haskel (Ken Osmond), Larry (Rusty Stevens), "Lumpy" Rutherford (Frank Bank), Whitey (Stanley Fafara), Miss Landers (Sue Randall), Fred Rutherford (Richard Deacon), Gilbert (Stephen Talbot).

Credits: Executive Producer: Harry Ackerman; Produced and Created by: Joe Connelly, Bob Mosher; Directors: Norman Abbott, Norman Tokar, Hugh Beaumont; Writers: Raphael Blau, Joe Connelly, Bob Mosher, Katherine Unson, Dale Unson, others; Directors of Photography: Mack Stengler, A.S.C., Ray Rennahan, A.S.C., Jack MacKenzie, A.S.C., William A. Sickner, A.S.C.; Art Directors: Alexander A. Mayer, John Meehan; Editorial Supervisors: David J. O'Connell, Richard G. Wray, A.C.E.; Film Editors: Robert Seiter, Richard Belding, Edward Haire, A.C.E.; Music Supervisor: Jack B. Wadsworth; Music by: Melvyn Lenard, Michael F. Johnson; Theme Music by: Dave Kahn, Melvyn Lenard, Mort Greene; Sound: William Lynch; Sound Effects Editor: Samuel Caylor; Assistant Director: Dolph M. Zimmer; Set Decorators: John McCarthy, Ralph Sylos; Costume Supervisor: Vincent Dee; Makeup: Jack Barron, Robert Dawn; Hair Stylist: Florence Bush; Produced by: Gomalco Productions, Inc., Revue Productions, Inc.; Exclusive Distributor: MCA Television Limited.

LITTLE WOMEN

NBC Television Network, February 8, 1979-March 8, 1979; 4 episodes in color on film; 60 minutes.

A drama about the lives of the March sisters: their conflicts, joys and heartbreaks. Based on Louisa May Alcott's novel of 19th-century manners and mores and the telefeature Little Women (which see).

Cast: Jo March (Jessica Harper), Meg March (Susan Walden), Amy March (Ann Dusenberry), Cousin Melissa (Eve Plumb), Mr. Lawrence (Robert Young), Mother March (Dorothy McGuire), Father March (William Schallert), Aunt March (Mildred Natwick), Professor Bhaer (David Ackroyd), Laurie (Richard Gilliland), Brooke (Cliff Potts), Godfrey (William Sylvester).

Credits: Executive Producer: David Victor; Based on the Novel by: Louisa May Alcott; Color by: Technicolor; Titles & Optical Effects: Universal Title; Produced by: Groverton Productions, Ltd.; In Association with: Universal Television; Exclusive Distributor: MCA Television Limited.

LOOSE CHANGE (NBC'S BEST SELLERS)

NBC Television Network, February 26, 1978-February 28, 1978; 3 episodes in color on film; 120 minutes (total: 6 hours).

The 1960s adventures of three young women: journalist Kate Evans, artist Tanya Berenson and civil-rights activist Jenny Reston.

Cast: Kate Evans (Cristina Raines), Tanya Berenson (Season Hubley), Jenny Reston (Laurie Heineman), Joe Norman (Ben Masters), Hank Okrun (Gregg Henry), Rob Kagan (Guy Boyd), John Campbell (John Getz), Irene Evans (June Lockhart), Sol Berenson (Joshua Shelley), Ed Thomas (Carl Franklin), Roxanne (Paula Wagner), Peter Lane (Stephen Macht), Mark Stewart (Michael Tolan), Tom Feiffer (Theodore Bikel), Hilda (Kate Reid), Bob O'Brian (James Blendick), Dr. Moe Sinden (David Wayne), George (Gary Swanson), Rosemary (Alice Hirson), Dave Goodwin (Robert Symonds).

Credits: Executive Producer: Jules Irving; Produced by: Michael Rhodes; Directed by: Jules Irving; Written by: Corinne Jacker, Charles E. Israel, Jennifer Miller; Based on the Novel by: Sara Davidson; Directors of Photography: John Elsenbach, Harry L. Wolf; Music by: Don Costa; Art Director: William Campbell; Film Editors: Gene Foster, John Elias, John F. Schreyer; Color by: Technicolor; Titles & Optical Effects: Universal Title; Produced by: Universal Television; Exclusive Distributor: MCA Television Limited.

LUCAS TANNER

NBC Television Network, September 11, 1974-August 20, 1975; 24 episodes in color on film; 60 minutes.

A drama set in Webster Groves, Missouri, about a high school teacher and his relationship with his students. Lucas Tanner loved kids and teaching. Untraditional in his methods, his main concern was instilling in his students a better understanding of themselves as people, preparing them to face the realities of today's world. Based on the telefeature Lucas Tanner (which see).

Cast: Lucas Tanner (David Hartman), Margaret Blumenthal (Rosemary Murphy), Glendon Farrell (Robbie Rist), Jaytee Drumm (Alan Abelew), Cindy Damon (Trish Soodik), Terry Klitsner (Kimberly Beck), Wally Moore (Michael Dwight-Smith), John Hamilton (John Randolph).

Credits: Executive Producer: David Victor; Producers: Jay Benson, Charles S. Dubin; Directors: Alexander Singer, Leo Penn, others; Music by: David Shire; Color by: Technicolor; Titles & Optical Effects: Universal Title; Produced by: Groverton Productions, Ltd.; In Association With: Universal Television; Exclusive Distributor: MCA Television Limited.

LUX PLAYHOUSE

CBS Television Network, October 3, 1958-September 18, 1959; 15 episodes in black & white on film; 30 minutes. Sponsored by Lux Products.

A dramatic anthology which rotated with Schlitz Playhouse of Stars (which see). Certain episodes of this series were re-broadcast on Moment of Fear (which see).

Credits: Executive Producer: Edward Lewis; Produced by: Lewman, Inc., Revue Productions, Inc.; Exclusive Distributor: MCA Television Limited.

M SQUAD

NBC Television Network, September 20, 1957-September 13, 1960; 117 episodes in black & white on film; 30 minutes.

A police drama about Det. Lt. Frank Ballinger, the top man of Chicago's elite M Squad, a unit that tracked down suspected criminals.

Cast: Lt. Frank Ballinger (Lee Marvin), Capt. Grey (Paul Newlan).

Credits: Executive Producer: Richard Lewis; Produced by: John Larkin; Theme Music: Count Basie; Music Supervision: Stanley Wilson; Produced by: Latimer Productions, Revue Productions, Inc.; Exclusive Distributor: MCA Television Limited.

MADIGAN (NBC TUESDAY MYSTERY MOVIE, NBC WEDNESDAY MYSTERY MOVIE)

NBC Television Network, September 20, 1972-February 28, 1973; 6 episodes in color on film; 90 minutes.

A drama about Sgt. Dan Madigan, a tough, experienced detective of the New York Police Department who took on special, solo assignments all over the globe, as well as in his home city. Based on the theatrical film Madigan (1968) produced by Universal Pictures.

Cast: Sgt. Dan Madigan (Richard Widmark).

Credits: Executive Producer: Dean Hargrove; Produced by: Roland Kibbee; Directors: Boris Sagal, others; Writers: Roland Kibbee, Stephen Lord, others; Associate Producer: Edward K. Dodds; Story Consultant: Oliver Crawford; Director of Photography: Jack Priestley; Art Director: Aurelio Crugnola; Film Editor: Sam E. Waxman, A.C.E.; Sound: Aldo DeMartini; Assistant Directors: Joe Pollini, Fred Gallo; Unit Managers: Wallace Worsley, Luciano Piperno; Editorial Supervision: Richard Belding; Music Supervision: Hal Mooney; Main Title Design: Wayne Fitzgerald; Titles & Optical Effects: Universal Title; Color by: Technicolor; Produced by: Universal Television; Exclusive Distributor: MCA Television Limited.

THE MAN AND THE CITY

ABC Television Network, September 15, 1971-January 5, 1972; 13 episodes in color on film; 60 minutes. Sponsors and Agencies: American Home Products Corporation through John F. Murray Advertising Agency, Inc.; S. C. Johnson & Son, Inc. through Benton & Bowles, Inc.; Colgate-Palmolive Co. through Ted Bates & Co., Inc.; Procter & Gamble Co. through Grey Advertising, Inc.

A drama about Mayor Thomas Jefferson Alcala, a compassionate yet politically shrewd veteran of 16 years in office in a large southwestern city. Alcala put his career on the line to become personally involved in problems of individual citizens of the city that he loved and wanted to safeguard environmentally. Filmed on location in Albuquerque, New Mexico. Based on the telefeature The City (which see).

Cast: Mayor Thomas Jefferson Alcala (Anthony Quinn), Andy Hays (Mike Farrell), Marian Crane (Mala Powers).

The Man and the City / 63

Credits: Executive Producer: David Victor; Produced by: Stanley Rubin; Created by: Howard Rodman, Dean Riesner; Directors: Daniel Petrie, Paul Henreid, others; Writers: Bess Boyle, David Moessinger, others; Associate Producer: Joe Cavalier; Executive Story Consultant: Del Reisman; Director of Photography: Enzo A. Martinelli; Music by: Alex North; Art Director: Howard E. Johnson; Film Editor: Bill Mosher, A. C. E. ; Set Decorations: John McCarthy; Sound: John Kean; Editorial Supervision: Richard Belding; Costumes by: Richard Hopper; Main Title Design: Attila de Lado; Color by: Technicolor; Titles & Optical Effects: Universal Title; Produced by: Groverton Productions, Ltd. ; In Association With: Universal Television; Exclusive Distributor: MCA Television Limited.

THE MAN BEHIND THE BADGE

Distributed by MCA Television Limited, 1955; 38 episodes in black & white on film; 30 minutes. Sponsored by Bristol-Myers.

A dramatic anthology based on the files of law enforcement agencies. Originally broadcast as a live series on the CBS Television Network, October 11, 1953-October 3, 1954 (not produced by MCA Television Limited).

Cast: Host/Narrator, Charles Bickford.

Credits: Producers: Bernard Prockter, Jerry Robertson; Produced by: Prockter Television Enterprises; And MCA Television Limited.

MARCUS WELBY, M. D.

ABC Television Network, September 23, 1969-May 11, 1976; 172 episodes in color on film; 60 minutes. Sponsors and Agencies: Colgate-Palmolive Co. through Ted Bates, Inc.; Hunt Foods & Industries, Inc. through William Esty Company, Inc.; Warner-Lambert Pharmaceutical Company, Inc. through J. Walter Thompson Company; Sterling Drug, Inc. through Dancer-Fitzgerald-Sample, Inc.; Bristol-Myers Co. through Boclaro; Gillette Safety Razor Company through Batten, Barton, Durstine & Osborn, Inc.; Procter & Gamble through Leo Burnett Co. , Inc. ; Brown & Williamson Tobacco Company through Ted Bates & Co. , Inc. ; Miles Laboratories, Inc. through Jack Tinker & Partners, Inc.

A medical drama about situations arising from the practice of general medicine in Santa Monica, California by Dr. Marcus Welby, whose dedication led to involvement in the lives of his patients, and his young associate, Dr. Steven Kiley, who contracted to work with Dr. Welby for a year, after which time he intended to resume training as a neurologist. Filmed on location in Santa Monica, California. Based on the telefeature Marcus Welby, M. D. (which see).

Cast: Dr. Marcus Welby (Robert Young), Dr. Steven Kiley (James Brolin), Consuelo Lopez (Elena Verdugo), Myra Sherwood (Anne Baxter), Sandy Porter (Ann Schedeen), Kathleen Faverty (Sharon Gless), Phil Porter (Gavin Brendan), Janet Blake (Pamela Hensley).

Credits: Executive Producer: David Victor; Produced by: David J. O'Connell; Created by: David Victor; Directors: David Lowell Rich, Harry Falk, Marc Daniels, Leo Penn, Richard Learman, Randal Kleiser, Hollingsworth Morse, Jerry London, Richard Lawrence Milton, David Alexander, others; Writers: Edward DeBlasio, Margaret Schneider, Paul Schneider, Jerry McNeely, Judy Burns, Jerry De Bono, Robert Malcolm Young, Richard Fielder, Hesper Anderson, others; Executive Story Consultant: Nina Laemmle; Executive Story Editor: Earl Booth; Directors of Photography: Walter Strenge, A.S.C., Sy Hoffberg; Art Directors: George Patrick, Russell C. Forrest, Howard E. Johnson; Music by: Leonard Rosenman; Film Editors: Michael R. McAdam, A.C.E., Robert Watts, A.C.E., Richard G. Wray, A.C.E., Sam E. Waxman, A.C.E., Edward A. Biery, A.C.E.; Set Decorations: Joseph Reith, John McCarthy, James S. Redd; Editorial Supervision: Richard Belding; Color by: Technicolor; Titles & Optical Effects: Universal Title; Produced by: Groverton Productions, Ltd.; In Association With: Universal Television; Exclusive Distributor: MCA Television Limited.

MARKHAM

CBS Television Network, May 2, 1959-September 22, 1960; 60 episodes in black & white on film; 30 minutes.

A crime drama about globe-trotting private investigator Roy Markham.

Cast: Roy Markham (Ray Milland), John Riggs (Simon Scott).

Credits: Producers: Warren Duff, Joe Sistiam; Music Supervision: Stanley Wilson; Produced by: Markham Productions, Revue Productions, Inc.; Exclusive Distributor: MCA Television Limited.

MATT LINCOLN

ABC Television Network, September 24, 1970-January 14, 1971; 16 episodes in color on film; 60 minutes. Major Sponsors and Agencies: P. Lorillard Company through Lemen & Newell, Inc.; Chas. Pfizer & Company through LaRoche, McCaffrey & McCall, Inc.; Plough, Inc. through Lake-Spiro-Shurman, Inc.; Warner-Lambert Pharmaceutical Company through J. Walter Thompson Company; Beecham Products, Inc. through Kenyon & Eckhardt, Inc.; Noxell Corporation through Sullivan, Stauffer, Colwell & Bayles, Inc.; Hunt-Wesson through William Esty Company.

Matt Lincoln / 65

A drama about a strong, compassionate community psychiatrist, Matt Lincoln, M.D., one of the new breed in psychiatry whose practice took him anywhere in the city his professional skills were needed. Based on the telefeature Dial: Hot Line (which see).

Cast: Dr. Matt Lincoln (Vince Edwards), Tag (Chelsea Brown), Kevin (Michael Larrain), Jimmy (Felton Perry), Ann (June Harding).

Credits: Executive Producer: Frank Price; Produced by: Irving Elman; Created by: Don Ingalls; Directors: Allen Reisner, Ralph Senensky, others; Writers: Charles Israel, Edward J. Lasko, others; Director of Photography: Jack Woolf; Music by: Oliver Nelson; Film Editor: Larry Lester; Technical Advisor: D. F. Muhich, M.D.; Art Director: Howard E. Johnson; Editorial Supervision: Richard Belding; Color by: Technicolor; Titles & Optical Effects: Universal Title; Produced by: Vincent Edwards Productions, Inc. And Universal Television; Exclusive Distributor: MCA Television Limited.

McCLOUD (FOUR-IN-ONE, NBC SUNDAY MYSTERY MOVIE, NBC WEDNESDAY MYSTERY MOVIE)

As an element of Four-In-One: NBC Television Network, September 16, 1970-October 21, 1970; 6 episodes in color on film; 60 minutes. As an element of NBC Wednesday Mystery Movie: September 22, 1971-February 23, 1972; 7 episodes in color on film; 90 minutes. As an element of NBC Sunday Mystery Movie: October 1, 1972-August 28, 1977; 30 episodes in color on film; 120 minutes and 90 minutes.

An adventure-suspense program about Taos, New Mexico Deputy Marshal Sam McCloud on assignment with the New York City Police Department to learn the latest and most sophisticated investigative techniques. Based on the telefeature McCloud: Who Killed Miss U.S.A.? (which see).

Cast: Deputy Marshal Sam McCloud (Dennis Weaver), Peter J. Clifford (J. D. Cannon), Sgt. Joe Broadhurst (Terry Carter), Chris Coughlin (Diana Muldaur).

Credits: Executive Producers: Leslie Stevens, Glen A. Larson; Supervising Producer: Ronald Gilbert Satlof; Producers: Glen A. Larson, Michael Gleason, Lou Shaw, Ronald Gilbert Satlof; Executive In Charge of Production: Richard Irving; Created by: Herman Miller; Directors: Douglas Heyes, Hy Averback, Richard Fielder, Fielder Cook, Nicholas Colasanto, Harry Falk, Russ Mayberry, others; Writers: Douglas Heyes, Millard Lampel, Lonnie Elder, Glen A. Larson, Michael Gleason, others; Associate Producer: Winrich Kolbe; Music Score and McCloud Theme: Stu Phillips; Additional Music by: David Shire; Mystery Movie Theme Music: Henry Mancini; Directors of Photography: Ronald W. Browne, Ben

66 / Series

Colman, A.S.C., Sol Negrin, A.S.C., John M. Stephens; Art Directors: Alexander A. Mayer, George Webb; Set Decorations: Claire P. Brown, Joseph Stone; Assistant Directors: Ron Martinez, James A. Westman, Ralph Ferrin; Unit Managers: Harker Wade, Joseph E. Kenny; Film Editors: Gene E. Ranney, Chuck McClelland, Bob Kagey; Sound: Robert Miller, L. Ralph Zerbe, Edwin S. Hall; Color by: Technicolor; Titles & Optical Effects: Universal Title; Editorial Supervision: Richard Belding; Music Supervision: Hal Mooney; Costumes: Burton Miller, Richard Hopper; Makeup: Bud Westmore; Hair Stylist: Larry Germain; Main Title Design: Wayne Fitzgerald; Produced In Association With: Glen A. Larson Productions And Universal Television; Exclusive Distributor: MCA Television Limited.

McCOY (NBC SUNDAY MYSTERY MOVIE)

NBC Television Network, October 5, 1975-March 28, 1976; 4 episodes in color on film; 120 minutes.

An adventure program about McCoy, a charming con man who made his living by cheating cheaters. Based on the telefeature The Big Ripoff (which see).

Cast: McCoy (Tony Curtis), Gideon Gibbs (Roscoe Lee Browne).

Credits: Executive Producers and Creators: Roland Kibbee, Dean Hargrove; Associate Producer: Edward K. Dodds; Music by: Billy Goldenberg, Dick De Benedictis; Editorial Supervision: Richard Belding; Music Supervision: Hal Mooney; Mystery Movie Theme Music: Henry Mancini; Color by: Technicolor; Titles & Optical Effects: Universal Title; Main Title Design: Wayne Fitzgerald; Produced by: Universal Television; Exclusive Distributor: MCA Television Limited.

McHALE'S NAVY

ABC Television Network, October 11, 1962-August 30, 1966; 138 episodes in black & white on film; 30 minutes. Sponsors and Agencies: Kellogg Company through Leo Burnett Company, Inc.; R. J. Reynolds Tobacco Co. through William Esty Company, Inc.; Oldsmobile Division, General Motors Corporation through D. P. Brother & Company; Warner-Lambert Pharmaceutical Company through J. Walter Thompson Company; American Motors Corporation through Geyer, Morey, Madden & Ballard, Inc.; Bristol-Myers Company through Young & Rubicam, Inc.; Chesebrough-Ponds, Inc. through Norman, Craig & Kummel, Inc.; Dodge Division, Chrysler Corporation through Batten, Barton, Durstine & Osborn, Inc.; The Goodyear Tire & Rubber Company through Young & Rubicam, Inc.; Shulton, Inc. through The Wesley Associates, Inc.

A situation comedy about the crew of PT 73, commanded by Lt. Cmdr. Quinton McHale, who were brave in action and ingenious at circumventing the punishments and restrictions of Capt. Binghamton. Their operations originated in the South Pacific and were later shifted to Italy. Two theatrical features based on the series were produced by Universal Pictures: McHale's Navy (1964) and McHale's Navy Joins the Air Force (1965). The series was inspired by the Alcoa Premiere (which see) episode "Seven Against the Sea," a drama in which Ernest Borgnine played the commander of a PT boat in World War II.

Cast: Lt. Commander Quinton McHale (Ernest Borgnine), Capt. Wallace Burton Binghamton (Joe Flynn), Ensign Charles Parker (Tim Conway), Torpedoman Lester Gruber (Carl Ballantine), Lt. Elroy Carpenter (Bob Hastings), Quartermaster George "Christy" Christopher (Gary Vinson), Machinist's Mate Harrison "Tinker" Bell (Billy Sands), Gunner's Mate Virgil Edwards (Edson Stroll), Radioman Willy Moss (John Wright), Takeo "Fuji" Fujiwara (Yoshio Yoda), Seaman Joseph "Happy" Haines (Gavin MacLeod), Col. Harrington (Henry Beckman), Mayor Mario Lugatto (Jay Novello), Rosa Giovanni (Peggy Mondo), General Bronson (Simon Scott).

Credits: Executive Producer: Edward J. Montagne; Produced by: Si Rose; Associate Producer and Script Consultant: Si Rose; Directors: Hollingsworth Morse, Earl Bellamy, Edward J. Montagne, others; Writers: Frank Gill, Jr., G. Carleton Brown, William Raynor, Miles Wilder, Gene L. Coon, others; Music Score: Axel Stordahl; Directors of Photography: Benjamin H. Kline, A.S.C., Ray Finn, John L. Russell, William Margulies, A.S.C.; Art Directors: Russell Kimball, Alexander A. Mayer; Film Editors: Sam E. Waxman, A.C.E., Edwin H. Bryant, A.C.E.; Editorial Department Head: David J. O'Connell; Musical Supervision: Stanley Wilson; Set Decorator: John McCarthy; Sound: Earl Crain, Jr.; Casting by: Jere Henshaw; Costume Supervisor: Vincent Dee; Hair Stylist: Florence Bush; Produced by: Sto-Rev Co.; Filmed at: Revue Productions, Inc., Universal Television; Exclusive Distributor: MCA Television Limited.

McMILLAN (NBC SUNDAY MYSTERY MOVIE)

NBC Television Network, December 5, 1976-August 21, 1977; 6 episodes in color on film; 90 minutes.

A mystery-drama, with comic overtones, about widowed San Francisco police commissioner Stewart McMillan. A continuation of McMillan and Wife (which see). Based on the original series and the telefeature Once Upon a Dead Man (which see).

Cast: Commissioner Stewart McMillan (Rock Hudson), Agatha Thornton (Martha Raye), Sgt. Steve DiMaggio (Richard Gilliland), Maggie (Gloria Strook).

Credits: Executive Producer: Leonard B. Stern; Produced by: Jon Epstein; Directors: James Sheldon, Jackie Cooper, others;

68 / Series

Music by: Jerry Fielding; Mystery Movie Theme Music: Henry Mancini; Editorial Supervision: Richard Belding; Music Supervision: Hal Mooney; Color by: Technicolor; Titles & Optical Effects: Universal Title; Main Title Design: Wayne Fitzgerald; Produced by: Talent Associates-Norton Simon, Inc. And Universal Television; Exclusive Distributor: MCA Television Limited.

McMILLAN AND WIFE (NBC SUNDAY MYSTERY MOVIE)

NBC Television Network, September 29, 1971-August 15, 1976; 39 episodes in color on film; 120 minutes and 90 minutes.

A mystery-drama, with comic overtones, about San Francisco police commissioner Stewart McMillan and his wife Sally. Based on the telefeature Once Upon a Dead Man (which see). Continued as McMillan (which see).

Cast: Commissioner Stewart McMillan (Rock Hudson), Sally McMillan (Susan Saint James), Sgt. Charles Enright (John Schuck), Mildred (Nancy Walker).

Credits: Executive In Charge of Production: Richard Irving; Executive Producer: Leonard B. Stern; Producers: Paul Mason, Jon Epstein; Created by: Leonard B. Stern; Directors: Roy Winston, Harry Falk, Lee H. Katzin, Lou Antonio, others; Writers: Gloria Goldsmith, others; Executive Story Consultants: Oliver Hailey, Robert Lewin; Associate Producer: Ted Rich; Music Score: Jerry Fielding; Sunday Mystery Movie Theme Music: Henry Mancini; Directors of Photography: Milton R. Krasner, A.S.C., Robert Hauser; Art Director: Kenneth A. Reid; Film Editors: Jack McSweeney, A.C.E., George Ohanian, Les Green; Set Decorations: Don Sullivan; Assistant Director: George Bisk; Sound: John Carter; Unit Manager: Donald Gold; Editorial Supervision: Richard Belding; Music Supervision: Hal Mooney; Costumes by: Burton Miller; Special Photographic Effects: Albert Whitlock; Main Title Design: Wayne Fitzgerald; Titles & Optical Effects: Universal Title; Color by: Technicolor; Produced in Association With: Talent Associates-Norton Simon, Inc. And Universal Television; Exclusive Distributor: MCA Television Limited.

McNAUGHTON'S DAUGHTER

NBC Television Network, March 24, 1976-April 7, 1976; 3 episodes in color on film; 60 minutes.

A crime drama about Deputy D. A. Laurel McNaughton and her cases against murderers. Based on the telefeature McNaughton's Daughter (which see).

Cast: Deputy D.A. Laurel McNaughton (Susan Clark), Lou Farragut (James Callahan), D.A. Charles Quintero (Ricardo Montalban), Ed Hughes (John Elerick).

Credits: Executive Producer: David Victor; Produced by: Harold Gast; Directors: Jack Arnold, Daniel Haller, Gene Nelson; Music by: George Romanis; Editorial Supervision: Richard Belding; Music Supervision: Hal Mooney; Color by: Technicolor; Titles & Optical Effects: Universal Title; Produced by: Groverton Productions, Ltd.; In Association With: Universal Television; Exclusive Distributor: MCA Television Limited.

MEET MR. McNUTLEY

CBS Television Network, September 17, 1953-July 15, 1954; 38 episodes in black & white on film; 30 minutes.

A situation comedy about Prof. Ray McNutley, head of the English Department at an elite women's college. This program was continued as The Ray Milland Show (which see) in which the professor became the drama teacher at another university and had his last name changed to McNulty.

Cast: Prof. Ray McNutley (Ray Milland), Peggy McNutley (Phyllis Avery), Dean Josephine Bradley (Minerva Urecal), Pete Thompson (Gordon Jones).

Credits: Produced by: Revue Productions, Inc.; Exclusive Distributor: MCA Television Limited.

THE MEN

ABC Television Network, September 21, 1972-August 11, 1973; 24 episodes in color on film; 60 minutes.

The umbrella title for three rotating series: Assignment: Vienna produced by MGM Television, The Delphi Bureau produced by Warner Bros. Television and Jigsaw produced by Universal Television (which see).

THE MEN FROM SHILOH

NBC Television Network, September 16, 1970-September 8, 1971; 24 episodes in color on film; 90 minutes.

A Western set at the Shiloh Ranch outside Medicine Bow, Wyoming during the mid-1890s. A continuation of The Virginian (which see), based on the novel by Owen Wister and the 1929 film.

Cast: The Virginian (James Drury), Col. Alan MacKenzie (Stewart Granger), Trampas (Doug McClure), Roy Tate (Lee Majors), Parker (John McLiam).

Credits: Executive Producer for Lee Majors: Herbert Hirschman; Executive Producer for James Drury: Norman Macdonnell; Execu-

70 / Series

tive Producer for Doug McClure: Leslie Stevens; Production Supervisor: Frank Price; Based on the Novel "The Virginian" by: Owen Wister; Directors: Murray Golden, Herbert Hirschman, Russ Mayberry, others; Writers: Leslie Stevens, Jean Holloway, others; Director of Photography: William Margulies; Music by: Leonard Rosenman; Costume Supervisor: Vincent Dee; Makeup: Bud Westmore; Hair Stylist: Larry Germain; Color by: Technicolor; Titles & Optical Effects: Universal Title; Produced by: Universal Television; In Association with: NBC-TV; Exclusive Distributor: MCA Television Limited.

MICKEY SPILLANE'S MIKE HAMMER

CBS Television Network, January 28, 1958-1959; 78 episodes in black & white on film; 30 minutes.

A drama about private investigator Mike Hammer. Based on the novels by Mickey Spillane.

Cast: Mike Hammer (Darren McGavin).

Credits: Based on Characters Created by: Mickey Spillane; Music by: David Kahn, Melvyn Lenard; Produced by: Revue Productions, Inc.; Exclusive Distributor: MCA Television Limited.

THE MISADVENTURES OF SHERIFF LOBO (LOBO)

NBC Television Network, September 18, 1979-   ; 22 episodes in color on film; 60 minutes.

A comedy-adventure program about the high-spirited Sheriff Lobo. A spin-off from BJ and the Bear (which see).

Cast: Sheriff Lobo (Claude Akins), Perkins (Mills Watson), Birdie (Brian Kerwin).

Credits: Executive Producers: Glen A. Larson, William P. D'Angelo; Executive Story Consultant: Lloyd Turner; Story Editors: Stephen Miller, Robert Wolterstorff, Paul M. Belous, Mark Fink; Associate Producers: Gary B. Winter, Stephen L. Brain; Music Score: Jimmie Haskell; The Ballad of Sheriff Lobo Sung by: Frankie Laine; Words and Music: Glen A. Larson; Director of Photography: John M. Nickolaus, A.S.C.; Art Director: John Leimanis; Set Decorations: Leslie McCarthy; Casting by: Patti Hayes; Film Editor: Charles D. Cranford; Sound: John C. Dignan; Color by: Technicolor; Titles & Optical Effects: Universal Title; Unit Production Manager: Scott U. Adam; 1st Assistant Director: Michael Sturges; 2nd Assistant Director: John J. Eyler; Sound Effects Editor: Tom McMullen; Music Editor: Mark Green; Costume Designer: Darryl Martell; Costume Supervisor: Don Snyder; Produced In Association With: Glen A. Larson Productions And Universal Television; Exclusive Distributor: MCA Television Limited.

MR. INSIDE/MR. OUTSIDE (NBC WEDNESDAY MYSTERY MOVIE)

NBC Television Network, March 14, 1973; 1 episode in color on film; 90 minutes.

A drama about New York City police detectives Massi and Isaacs who were attacked when they answered a call at a foreign embassy. As a result, Massi's arm was later amputated. Although the two cops were forbidden to pursue the case because of diplomatic immunity, a bitter Massi persuaded his partner to help him find his assailant. An unsold pilot film.

Cast: Detective Massi (Tony Lo Bianco), Detective Isaacs (Hal Linden), Fred Wakeman (Ed Van Nuys), Capt. Valentine (Paul Benjamin), Vice Consul Luber (Stefan Schnabel), Renee Isaacs (Marcia Jean Kurtz).

Credits: Written by: Jerry Coopersmith; Based on a Story by: Sonny Grosso; Editorial Supervision: Richard Belding; Music Supervision: Hal Mooney; Color by: Technicolor; Titles & Optical Effects: Universal Title; Produced by: Universal Television; Exclusive Distributor: MCA Television Limited.

MR. TERRIFIC

CBS Television Network, January 4, 1967-August 28, 1967; 10 episodes in color on film; 30 minutes.

A situation comedy about a gas station attendant who became a super-hero when he took a "power pill" developed by the U.S. government.

Cast: Stanley Beamish/Mr. Terrific (Stephen Strimpell), Barton J. Reed (John McGiver), Hal Walters (Dick Gautier), Harley Trent (Paul Smith).

Credits: Music by: Gerald Fried; Produced by: Universal Television; In Association With: CBS-TV; Exclusive Distributor: MCA Television Limited.

MRS. COLUMBO (KATE COLUMBO, KATE THE DETECTIVE, KATE LOVES A MYSTERY)

NBC Television Network, February 26, 1979-March 29, 1979; 13 episodes in color on film; 120 minutes and 60 minutes.

A drama about Kate Columbo, wife of Lt. Detective Columbo. Kate was a mother, a homemaker and reporter for her neighborhood newspaper. She also had a knack for investigation and found herself caught up in murder cases. Based on the often-mentioned but never seen character from the series Columbo (which see).

Cast: Kate Columbo (Kate Mulgrew), Jenny (Lily Haydn), Alden (Henry Jones), Sgt. Mike Varrick (Don Stroud).

Credits: Executive Producer: Richard Alan Simmons; Supervising Producer: James McAdams; Produced by: David Levinson; Developed by: Richard Alan Simmons; Directors: Boris Sagal, others; Writers: Richard Alan Simmons, Lane Slate, others; Executive Story Consultant: Howard Berk; Associate Producer: Stuart Cohen; Music: John Cacavas; Director of Photography: Thomas Del Ruth; Art Director: Seymour Klate; Set Decorations: Richard B. Goddard; Casting by: Bob Manahan; Film Editors: Howard S. Deane, Larry Lester; Sound: Chuck Haggin; Color by: Technicolor; Titles & Optical Effects: Universal Title; Unit Production Manager: Dan Franklin; 1st Assistant Director: Phil Bowles; 2nd Assistant Director: Robert Villar; Sound Effects Editor: Jack C. May; Music Editor: Robert Mayer; Costume Designer: Brienne Von Glyttov; Produced In Association With: Gambit Productions, Inc. And Universal Television; Exclusive Distributor: MCA Television Limited.

MOBILE ONE

ABC Television Network, September 12, 1975-December 29, 1975; 13 episodes in color on film; 60 minutes.

A drama about KONE-TV news reporter Peter Campbell who covered the Los Angeles area with a mobile video unit. Based on the telefeature Mobile Two (which see).

Cast: Peter Campbell (Jackie Cooper), Maggie Spencer (Julie Gregg), Doug McKnight (Mark Wheeler).

Credits: Executive Producer: Jack Webb; Produced by: William Bowers; Directors: Joseph Pevney, Don Taylor, others; Music by: Nelson Riddle; Color by: Technicolor; Titles & Optical Effects: Universal Title; Produced by: Mark VII Limited; In Association With: Universal Television; Exclusive Distributor: MCA Television Limited.

MOMENT OF FEAR

NBC Television Network, May 1964-August 1965; in black & white on film; 30 minutes.

A suspense anthology which, in its first summer replacement season, rebroadcast episodes originally aired on General Electric Theatre, Heinz Studio 57, Lux Playhouse and Schlitz Playhouse of Stars (all produced by Revue Productions). In its second semester, the series added reruns from Pepsi-Cola Playhouse (which see) to those listed above. (An earlier version of this series [1960] which broadcast live productions was not produced by Revue.)

Moment of Fear / 73

Credits: Produced by: Revue Productions, Inc.; Exclusive Distributor: MCA Television Limited.

THE MUNSTERS

CBS Television Network, September 24, 1964-September 1, 1966; 70 episodes in black & white on film; 30 minutes.

A situation comedy about the inhabitants of 1313 Mockingbird Lane: the Munster clan. They were Herman, who bore an amazing resemblance to the Frankenstein monster; his wife Lily, a woman who was concerned with the little problems of everyday living: standing over a hot cauldron all day, dusting nine rooms and a dungeon and saving enough out of the household budget for her weekly beauty treatment at the mortician's; his father-in-law, Grandpa, an over-the-hill Dracula, whose age was somewhere between 62 and 479; his 10-year-old son Eddie who resembled a werewolf; and his beautiful niece Marilyn, the "ugly duckling" of the family. A theatrical film based on the series entitled Munster Go Home was produced by Universal Pictures in 1966.

Cast: Herman Munster (Fred Gwynne), Lily Munster (Yvonne DeCarlo), Grandpa Munster (Al Lewis), Edward Wolfgang Munster (Butch Patrick), Marilyn Munster (Beverly Owen, Pat Priest).

Credits: Producers: Joe Connelly, Bob Mosher; Directors: Lawrence Dobkin, Ezra Stone; Writers: Joe Connelly, Bob Mosher; Directors of Photography: Lionel Lindon, Monroe Askins; Music: Jack Marshall; Film Editor: Bud Isaacs; Music Supervision: Stanley Wilson; Produced by: Kayro-Vue Productions, Inc., Universal Television; Exclusive Distributor: MCA Television Limited.

THE NAME OF THE GAME

NBC Television Network, September 20, 1968-September 10, 1971; 76 episodes in color on film; 90 minutes.

A drama about the "behind-the-scenes" operations of Howard Publications as seen from the viewpoint of its owner, Glenn Howard, Crime magazine editor Dan Farrell, People magazine editor Jeff Dillon, and editorial assistant Peggy Maxwell. Based on the telefeature Fame Is the Name of the Game (which see).

Cast: Glenn Howard (Gene Barry), Dan Farrell (Robert Stack), Jeff Dillon (Tony Franciosa), Peggy Maxwell (Susan Saint James), Joe Sample (Ben Murphy), Andy Hill (Cliff Potter), Ross Craig (Mark Miller).

Credits: Executive Producer: Richard Irving; Producer for Gene Barry: Dean Hargrove; Producers for Robert Stack: George Eckstein, David Victor; Producers for Tony Franciosa: Norman Lloyd,

Leslie Stevens; Directors: Lamont Johnson, Harvey Hart, John Llewellyn Moxey, James Nielson, Bill Graham, Steven Spielberg, others; Writers: Richard Nelson, Robert Thompson, Richard Levinson, William Link, Robert White, Phyllis White, Henry Slesar, Mark Rodgers, Leslie Stevens, Robert Collins, Philip Wylie, others; Associate Producer for Gene Barry: William Koenig; Associate Producer for Robert Stack: Robert F. O'Neill; Associate Producer for Tony Franciosa: Frederick Shorr; Directors of Photography: E. Charles Straumer, Jack Marta, Benjamin H. Kline, A.S.C., Pietro Portalupi, Earl Rath, Ralph Woolsey; Art Directors: Russell C. Forrest, Robert Mackichan, Franco Sumagalli; Theme Music by: Dave Grusin; Music Score: Billy Goldenberg; Film Editors: Richard M. Sprague, Robert Watts, A.C.E., Richard G. Wray, A.C.E., Budd Small, Carl Pingitore; Set Decorations: John McCarthy, James S. Redd, Joseph Stone, Jerry Miggins, Charles Thompson; Sound: Roger H. Heman, Jr., William A. Russell, Earl Crain, Jr., Luciano Sacripanti, David H. Moriarty; Music Supervision: Stanley Wilson, Dominic Frontiere; Costumes: Grady Hunt, Burton Miller; Makeup: Bud Westmore; Hair Styles: Larry Germain; Color by: Technicolor; Titles & Optical Effects: Universal Title; Produced by: Universal Television; In Association With: NBC-TV; Exclusive Distributor: MCA Television Limited.

THE NANCY DREW MYSTERIES

ABC Television Network, February 6, 1977-January 1, 1978; 10 episodes in color on film; 60 minutes.

A mystery about the adventures of Nancy Drew, all-American girl detective and one of the first "liberated" young women of American literature. This series rotated with The Hardy Boys Mysteries (which see). In addition to the episodes listed above, there were 8 episodes of the combined The Hardy Boys/Nancy Drew Mysteries.

Cast: Nancy Drew (Pamela Sue Martin), Carson Drew (William Schallert), Ned Nickerson (George O'Hanlon, Jr.), George Fayne (Jean Rasey, Susan Buckner), Bess (Ruth Cox).

Credits: Executive Producer: Glen A. Larson; Supervising Producer: B. W. Sandefur; Producers: Arlene Sidaris, Joyce Brotman; Based on the Nancy Drew Books by: Carolyn Keene; Directors: E. W. Swackhamer, Andy Sidaris, others; Writers: Glen A. Larson, Lou Shaw, others; Music Score: Stu Phillips; Theme Music: Glen A. Larson; Director of Photography: Ben Colman; Art Director: William Campbell; Film Editor: Fred Baratta; Produced In Association With: Glen A. Larson Productions And Universal Television; Exclusive Distributor: MCA Television Limited.

NBC SUNDAY MYSTERY MOVIE

NBC Television Network, September 15, 1971-September 4, 1977; in color on film; 120 minutes and 90 minutes.

NBC Sunday Mystery Movie / 75

The umbrella title for nine rotating series. See Amy Prentiss, Columbo, Hec Ramsey, Lanigan's Rabbi, McCloud, McCoy, McMillan, McMillan and Wife and Quincy, M. E. for details.

NBC TUESDAY MYSTERY MOVIE

NBC Television Network, January 15, 1974-September 4, 1974; in color on film; 90 minutes.

The umbrella title for four rotating series. See Faraday and Company, Madigan, The Snoop Sisters and Tenafly for details.

NBC WEDNESDAY MYSTERY MOVIE

NBC Television Network, September 13, 1972-January 9, 1974; in color on film; 90 minutes.

The umbrella title for six rotating series. See Banacek, Cool Million, Faraday and Company, Madigan, The Snoop Sisters and Tenafly for details.

NBC'S BEST SELLERS

NBC Television Network, September 30, 1976-May 15, 1978; 8 mini-series in color on film.

Novels for television. See Aspen, Captains and the Kings, Loose Change, Once An Eagle, The Rhinemann Exchange, Seventh Avenue, 79 Park Avenue and Wheels for details.

THE NIGHT STALKER (KOLCHAK: THE NIGHT STALKER)

ABC Television Network, September 13, 1974-August 30, 1975; 20 episodes in color on film; 60 minutes.

A suspense-drama about Carl Kolchak, a dynamic wire service reporter based in Chicago who pursued stories appearing to be bizarre and unworldly--yet incredibly true. Kolchak battled not only the dark forces of evil but the suppression of his stories by his boss and authorities who believed it was in the public's interest for them not to know the facts as presented by the reporter. Based on the telefeatures The Night Stalker and The Night Strangler produced by ABC Circle Films.

Cast: Carl Kolchak (Darren McGavin), Tony Vincenzo (Simon Oakland), Updike (Jack Grinnage), Emily (Ruth McDevitt).

Credits: Executive Producer: Cy Chermak; Produced by: Paul Playdon; Created by: Jeff Rice; Directors: Allen Baron, Don Weis,

76 / Series

Alex Grasshoff, Gordon Hessler, Michael Caffey, Don McDougall, Bruce Kessler, Seymour Robbie, others; Writers: Rudolph Borchert, David Chase, Bill S. Ballinger, Stephen Lord, Michael Kozoll, L. Ford Neale, others; Story Consultant: David Chase; Music: Gil Melle; Director of Photography: Donald Peterman; Art Director: Raymond Beal; Film Editor: Robert Leeds; Sound: John Kean; Color by: Technicolor; Titles & Optical Effects: Universal Title; Assistant Director: John Gaudioso; Editorial Supervision: Richard Belding; Music Supervision: Hal Mooney; Main Title Design by: Jack Cole; Produced by: Francy Productions, Universal Television; Exclusive Distributor: MCA Television Limited.

90 BRISTOL COURT

NBC Television Network, October 5, 1964-January 4, 1965; 13 episodes in black & white on film; 90 minutes.

The umbrella title for three situation comedies. See Harris Against the World, Karen and Tom, Dick and Mary for details. The setting for all three shows was 90 Bristol Court, a balconied modern multi-unit apartment motel with eight bungalows and a swimming pool, located on the Los Angeles-Beverly Hills line.

NOBODY'S PERFECT

ABC Television Network, June 26, 1980-August 28, 1980; 8 episodes in color on film; 30 minutes.

A situation comedy about Inspector Roger Hart of Scotland Yard who was loaned out to the San Francisco Police Department. During production, this program was known as Hart in San Francisco.

Cast: Inspector Roger Hart (Ron Moody), Dempsey (Cassie Yates), DeGennaro (Michael Durrell), Jacobi (Victor Brandt), Ramsey (Renny Roker), Grauer (Tom Williams), Dreyfus (Greg Monaghan), Careful Eddie (Danny Wells).

Credits: Color by: Technicolor; Titles & Optical Effects: Universal Title; Produced by: Universal Television; Exclusive Distributor: MCA Television Limited.

O'HARA, U.S. TREASURY

CBS Television Network, September 17, 1971-September 8, 1972; 22 episodes in color on film; 60 minutes.

A drama about special agent Jim O'Hara of the United States Treasury who came to grips with violators of federal law as an operative with one of five separate enforcement agencies of the Department--Bureau of Customs, Secret Service, Internal Revenue Service

Intelligence Division, Internal Revenue Service Inspection Division and Internal Revenue Service Alcohol, Tobacco and Firearms Division. The program was produced with the approval and cooperation of every division of the Department of the Treasury. Based on the telefeature O'Hara, United States Treasury (which see).

Cast: Jim O'Hara (David Janssen).

Credits: Executive Producer: Jack Webb; Produced by: Leonard B. Kaufman; Created by: Jack Webb, James E. Moser; Directors: Gerald Mayer, others; Writers: Gilbert A. Ralston, others; Associate Producer: William Stark; Story Consultant: Norman Jolley; Director of Photography: Fred Mandl; Music by: Ray Heindorf; Film Editor: Bob Kagey; Art Director: Stan Jolley; Color by: Technicolor; Titles & Optical Effects: Universal Title; Produced by: Mark VII Limited, Universal Television; Exclusive Distributor: MCA Television Limited.

ONCE AN EAGLE (NBC'S BEST SELLERS)

NBC Television Network, December 2, 1976-January 13, 1977; 7 episodes in color on film; 60 minutes and 120 minutes (total: 9 hours).

The story of two American soldiers from 1918 through World War II: the idealistic Sgt. Sam Damon and the ruthless Lt. Courtney Massengale.

Cast: Sgt. Sam Damon (Sam Elliott), Lt. Courtney Massengale (Cliff Potts), Jack Devlin (Gary Grimes), Major Caldwell (Glenn Ford), Emily Pawlfrey (Amy Irving), Reb Rayburne (Andrew Robinson), Krazewski (Dennis Burkley), Michele (Patty D'Arbanville), Tommy Caldwell (Darleen Carr), Captain Townshend (John Saxon), Colonel Avery (Forrest Tucker), Marge (Lynda Day George), Ben (Robert Hogan), Colonel Terwilliger (David Wayne), Earl Preis (David Huddleston), Joe Brand (Kario Salem), Captain Lasovitch (Jim Antonio), Sergeant Ives (Jordan Rhodes), Donny (Andrew Stevens), Lt. Merrick (Clu Gulager), Lin Tso-Han (James Shigeta), Jinny (Melanie Griffith), Bert McConnadin (Albert Salmi), Joyce (Juliet Mills), Dave Shifkin (Anthony Zerbe), Ryetower (Kip Niven), General Pulleyne (William Windom).

Credits: Executive In Charge of Production: Charles Engel; Executive Producer: William Sackheim; Produced by: Peter S. Fischer; Directors: E. W. Swackhamer, Richard Michaels; Written by: Peter S. Fischer; Based on the Novel by: Anton Myrer; Director of Photography: J. J. Jones; Music by: Dana Kaproff; NBC's Best Sellers Theme by: Elmer Bernstein; Art Director: William Campbell; Film Editors: Chuck McClelland, Howard S. Deane, John Elias; Color by: Technicolor; Titles & Optical Effects: Universal Title; Produced by: Universal Television; Exclusive Distributor: MCA Television Limited.

OPERATION PETTICOAT

ABC Television Network, September 17, 1977-October 19, 1978; 24 episodes in color on film; 30 minutes.

A situation comedy about the crew of the shocking pink submarine U. S. S. Sea Tiger, which blundered its way toward the Pacific War Zone. In addition to the crew there was a bevy of beautiful nurses, and together they turned military protocol inside-out in a series of incredible misadventures on the high seas. Based on the 1959 film and the telefeature Operation Petticoat (which see).

Cast: Lt. Comdr. Matthew Sherman (John Astin), Lt. Nick Holden (John Gilliland), Major Edna Howard (Yvonne Wilder), Lt. Barbara Duran (Jamie Lee Curtis), Lt. Dolores Crandall (Melinda Naud), Lt. Ruth Colfax (Dorrie Thomson), Lt. Claire Reid (Bond Gideon), Ensign Stovall (Christopher J. Brown), Seaman Dooley (Kraig Cassity), Ramon Gallardo (Jesse Dizon), Pharmacist's Mate Williams (Richard Marion), Chief of Boat Herbert Molumphrey (Wayne Long), Radioman Gossett (Michael Mazes), Seaman Horwich (Peter Schuck), Chief Machinist's Mate Tostin (Jack Murdock), Lt. Watson (Raymond Singer), Lt. Mike Bender (Randolph Mantooth), Seaman Broom (Jim Varney), Lt. Betty Wheeler (Hilary Thompson), Lt. Comdr. Haller (Robert Hogan), Lt. Katherine O'Hara (JoAnn Pflug), Seaman Horner (Don Sparks), Seaman Dixon (Scott McGinnis), Chief Engineer Dobritch (Warren Berlinger), Doplos (Fred Kareman).

Credits: Executive Producer: Leonard B. Stern; Producers: David J. O'Connell, Si Rose; Music by: Artie Butler; Color by: Technicolor; Titles & Optical Effects: Universal Title; Produced by: Heyday Productions, Universal Television; Exclusive Distributor: MCA Television Limited.

THE OREGON TRAIL

NBC Television Network, September 21, 1977-October 26, 1977; 13 episodes in color on film; 60 minutes.

A Western about pioneer Evan Thorpe and the adventures of his fiercely courageous frontier family as they pulled up stakes and headed west in a wagon train. While crossing the treacherous, unknown wilderness, they encountered innumerable hardships, from Indian attacks to dread diseases. Based on the telefeature The Oregon Trail (which see).

Cast: Evan Thorpe (Rod Taylor), Andrew Thorpe (Andrew Stevens), Rachel Thorpe (Gina Marie Smika), William Thorpe (Tony Becker), Margaret Devlin (Darleen Carr), Luther Sprague (Charles Napier).

Credits: Executive Producer: Michael Gleason; Supervising Producer: Richard Collins; Produced by: Carl Vitale; Associate Producer: Terry Wilson; Music by: Dick De Benedictis; Theme Song

Sung by: Danny Darst; Color by: Technicolor; Titles & Optical Effects: Universal Title; Produced by: Universal Television; Exclusive Distributor: MCA Television Limited.

THE OUTSIDER

NBC Television Network, September 18, 1968-September 3, 1969; 26 episodes in color on film; 60 minutes.

A mystery-suspense program about the adventures of David Ross, a rugged, non-conforming private investigator who had a police record but had been pardoned after serving time. Set in Los Angeles. Based on the telefeature The Outsider (which see).

Cast: David Ross (Darren McGavin).

Credits: Executive Producer and Creator: Roy Huggins; Produced by: Gene Levitt; Directors: Alexander Singer, others; Writers: Edward J. Lasko, others; Associate Producer: Paul Freeman; Music by: Pete Rugolo; Music Supervision: Stanley Wilson; Produced by: Roy Huggins-Public Arts Productions; In Association With: Universal Television And NBC-TV; Exclusive Distributor: MCA Television Limited.

THE OVERLAND TRAIL

NBC Television Network, February 7, 1960-September 11, 1960; 17 episodes in black & white on film; 60 minutes.

A Western about Frederick Thomas Kelly, superintendent of a newly formed stagecoach line, operating between Independence, Missouri and California, and his best friend, Flip, who rode shotgun for the line.

Cast: Frederick Thomas Kelly (William Bendix), Frank "Flip" Flippen (Doug McClure).

Credits: Executive Producer: Nat Holt; Produced by: Samuel A. Peeples; Directors: Virgil W. Vogel, others; Writers: Samuel A. Peeples, others; Produced by: Stage Coach Productions, Revue Productions, Inc.; Exclusive Distributor: MCA Television Limited.

OWEN MARSHALL, COUNSELOR AT LAW

ABC Television Network, September 16, 1971-August 24, 1974; 69 episodes in color on film; 60 minutes. Major Sponsors and Agencies: Bristol-Myers through Boclaro; Colgate-Palmolive Co. through Ted Bates & Co., Inc.; Procter & Gamble Co., Inc. through Compton Advertising, Inc.; Sterling Drug, Inc. through Dancer-Fitzgerald-Sample, Inc.; General Foods Corporation through

Benton & Bowles, Inc.; The Clorox Co. through Ketchum, MacLeod & Groves, Inc.; S. C. Johnson & Son, Inc. through Benton & Bowles, Inc.

A drama about attorney Owen Marshall and his young associates, Jess Brandon and Danny Paterno, who pursued the general practice of law in Santa Barbara, California. Based on the telefeature Owen Marshall, Counselor at Law (which see).

Cast: Owen Marshall (Arthur Hill), Jess Brandon (Lee Majors), Danny Paterno (Reni Santoni), Melissa Marshall (Christine Matchett), Frieda Krause (Joan Darling), Ted Warrick (David Soul).

Credits: Executive Producer: David Victor; Producers: Jon Epstein, Douglas Benton; Created by: David Victor, John McNeely; Directors: David Lowell Rich, Lou Antonio, Walter Doniger, Harry Falk, Buzz Kulik, Allen Reisner, James Sheldon, Leo Penn, others; Writers: Michael Gleason, Jerry McNeely, Pat Fielder, Frank Granville, Edward DeBlasio, David Victor, Frank Telford, Margaret Schneider, Paul Schneider, others; Executive Story Consultant: Jerry McNeely; Directors of Photography: Harkness Smith, A.S.C., Walter Strenge; Music by: Elmer Bernstein, Richard Clements; Film Editors: Milton Shifman, A.C.E., Tony Martinelli, A.C.E., Robert F. Shugrue; Art Directors: Russell C. Forrest, Howard E. Johnson, John J. Lloyd; Sound: John Kean, Terry Kellum, Frank H. Wilkinson, David H. Moriarty; Color by: Technicolor; Titles & Optical Effects: Universal Title; Produced by: Groverton Productions, Ltd.; In Association With: Universal Television; Exclusive Distributor: MCA Television Limited.

PARIS 7000

ABC Television Network, January 22, 1970-June 4, 1970; 10 episodes in color on film; 60 minutes.

An adventure program about Jack Brennan, a compassionate troubleshooter for the consulate of the American Embassy in Paris, whose function was to help visiting Americans who found themselves in trouble in the City of Light. Their way of getting in touch with Brennan was the telephone number PAris 7000.

Cast: Jack Brennan (George Hamilton), Robert Stevens (Gene Raymond), Jules Maurois (Jacques Aubuchon).

Credits: Executive Producer: Richard Caffey; Producers: John Wilder, Michael Gleason; Directors: Marc Daniels, others; Writers: Gene L. Coon, John Wilder, others; Director of Photography: William Margulies, A.S.C.; Art Director: Howard E. Johnson; Theme Music by: Michael Colombier; Set Decorations: Joe Stone; Film Editor: Tony Martinelli; Assistant Directors: George Bisk, Kenny Williams; Music Supervision: Stanley Wilson; Sound: Lyle Cain; Hair Stylist: Shirley Althouse; Makeup: Jack Freeman; Unit

Manager: Bud Brill; Produced by: Universal Television; Exclusive Distributor: MCA Television Limited.

THE PARTNERS

NBC Television Network, September 18, 1971-September 8, 1972; 20 episodes in color on film; 30 minutes.

A situation comedy about two plainclothes policemen--Lennie Crooke and George Robinson--who had an incredible knack for being in the right place at the wrong time, in the wrong place at the right time and in big trouble with their precinct captain most of the time.

Cast: Det. Lennie Crooke (Don Adams), Det. George Robinson (Rupert Crosse), Capt. Andrews (John Doucette), Sgt. Higgenbottom (Dick Van Patten).

Credits: Executive In Charge of Production: Charles Engel; Executive Producer: Arne Sultan; Producers: Earl Barret, Lee Wolfberg; Created by: Don Adams; Directors: Gary Nelson, others; Writers: Don Adams, Earl Barret, Arne Sultan, others; Director of Photography: William Cronjager; Music by: Lalo Schifrin; Color by: Technicolor; Titles & Optical Effects: Universal Title; Produced by: Donlee Productions, Universal Television; Exclusive Distributor: MCA Television Limited.

PEPSI-COLA PLAYHOUSE

ABC Television Network, October 2, 1953-June 26, 1955; in black & white on film; 30 minutes.

A dramatic anthology which presented about 80 episodes, some of which were rebroadcast on Moment of Fear (which see).

Credits: Produced by: Revue Productions, Inc.; Exclusive Distributor: MCA Television Limited.

PISTOLS 'N' PETTICOATS

CBS Television Network, September 17, 1966-August 19, 1967; 26 episodes in color on film; 30 minutes.

A situation comedy about the three generations of the Hanks family, whose home was on the outskirts of Wretched, Colorado in the 1870s.

Cast: Henrietta Hanks (Ann Sheridan), Grandma Hanks (Ruth McDevitt), Grandpa Hanks (Douglas Fowley), Lucy Hanks (Carole Wells), Sheriff Harold Sikes (Gary Vinson).

Credits: Executive Producer: Joe Connelly; Produced by: Irving Paley; Directors: Joe Connelly, others; Music by: Jack Elliott; Music Supervision: Stanley Wilson; Produced by: Kayro Enterprises, Inc., Universal Television; Exclusive Distributor: MCA Television Limited.

PORTRAIT (DuPONT CAVALCADE OF TELEVISION)

ABC Television Network, December 17, 1972-March 11, 1974; 4 episodes in color on film; 60 minutes. Sponsored by DuPont.

The umbrella title for a series of four dramatic specials. See THE SPECIALS: Legend in Granite, The Man from Independence, A Man Whose Name Was John and The Woman I Love for details.

PRIDE OF THE FAMILY (THE PAUL HARTMAN SHOW)

ABC Television Network, October 2, 1953-September 24, 1954; 40 episodes in black & white on film; 30 minutes.

A situation comedy about Albie Morrison, an advertising department executive at a small town newspaper, his wife Catherine and his children, Ann and Albie, Jr.

Cast: Albie Morrison (Paul Hartman), Catherine Morrison (Fay Wray), Ann Morrison (Natalie Wood), Albie Morrison, Jr. (Junior) (Bobby Hyatt).

Credits: Produced by: Revue Productions, Inc.; Exclusive Distributor: MCA Television Limited.

THE PROTECTORS (THE BOLD ONES)

NBC Television Network, September 28, 1969-September 6, 1970; 6 episodes in color on film; 60 minutes.

A police drama about the cases of public protectors Sam Danforth and William Washburn. Based on the telefeature Deadlock! (which see).

Cast: Deputy Chief of Police Sam Danforth (Leslie Nielsen), District Attorney William Washburn (Hari Rhodes).

Credits: Executive Producer: Jack Laird; Produced by: Jerrold Freedman; Created by: Roland Wolpert, William Sackheim; Directors: Robert Day, Daryl Duke, others; Writers: L. T. Brentwood, Betty Deveraux, Adrian Spies, others; Director of Photography: Vilmos Zsigmond; Sound: Lyle Cain; Music Supervision: Stanley Wilson; Color by: Technicolor; Titles & Optical Effects: Universal Title; Produced by: Roy Huggins-Public Arts Productions, Universal Television; In Association With: NBC-TV; Exclusive Distributor: MCA Television Limited.

THE PSYCHIATRIST (FOUR-IN-ONE)

NBC Television Network, February 3, 1971-September 1, 1971; 6 episodes in color on film; 60 minutes.

A drama about the work of a young psychiatrist who utilized all of the effective techniques of modern psychiatry. Based on the telefeature The Psychiatrist: God Bless the Children (which see).

Cast: Dr. James Whitman (Roy Thinnes), Dr. Bernard Altman (Luther Adler).

Credits: Executive Producer: Norman Felton; Produced by: Jerrold Freedman; Based on Characters Created by: Richard Levinson, William Link; Directors: Jerrold Freedman, Steven Spielberg, Douglas Stewart, others; Writers: Jerrold Freedman, Charles Israel, Thomas Y. Drake, Herb Berman, others; Associate Producer: Bo May; Music by: Gil Melle; Directors of Photography: Lloyd Ahern, A. S. C. , Richard A. Kelley; Art Director: Joseph Alves, Jr.; Set Decorations: Charles S. Thompson; Unit Manager: James M. Walters, Jr.; Assistant Director: Ralph Sariego; Film Editor: John Kaufman, Jr.; Sound: David H. Moriarty; Special Consultant: J. Thomas Ungerleider, M. D.; Main Title Design: Brice Wood; Color by: Technicolor; Titles & Optical Effects: Universal Title; Editorial Supervision: Richard Belding; Music Supervision: Hal Mooney; Costumes by: Richard Hopper; Makeup: Bud Westmore; Hair Stylist: Larry Germain; Produced by: Arena Productions, Inc.; And Universal Television; Exclusive Distributor: MCA Television Limited.

QUINCY, M. E. (NBC SUNDAY MYSTERY MOVIE)

As an element of NBC Sunday Mystery Movie: NBC Television Network, October 3, 1976-January 2, 1977; 3 episodes in color on film; 90 minutes. As a regular series: NBC Television Network, February 4, 1977- ; 81 episodes in color on film; 60 minutes.

A drama about Medical Examiner Quincy who was employed by the Coroner's Department of Los Angeles County. A socially conscious program, Quincy, M. E. dealt effectively with such subjects as rape, drug abuse, alcoholism, child abuse and hazardous waste disposal.

Cast: Quincy (Jack Klugman), Lt. Frank Monahan (Gary Walberg), Dr. Robert Astin (John S. Ragin), Danny (Val Bisoglio), Sam Fujiyama (Robert Ito), Sgt. Brill (Joseph Roman), Lee (Lynette Mettey).

Credits: Executive Producers: Glen A. Larson, Peter J. Thompson, R. A. Cinader, Jud Kinberg; Producers: William Cairncross,

Lester William Berke, Lou Shaw, Christopher Morgan; Created by: Glen A. Larson, Lou Shaw; Directors: Rod Holcomb, Jackie Cooper, Corey Allen, Paul Krasny, David Moessinger, E. W. Swackhamer, Alvin Ganzer, Stephen Stern, others; Writers: Allan Cole, Chris Bunch, Wallace Ware, Mann Rubin, David Moessinger, others; Executive Story Consultants: Robert Crais, Sam Egan, David Shaw; Associate Producers: William Cairncross, Charles E. Dismukes, Maurice Klugman, Richard E. Rabjohn; Music Score: Bruce Broughton, Stu Phillips; Theme Music: Glen A. Larson, Stu Phillips; Directors of Photography: Fred Jackman, Alric Edens, A. S. C.; Art Director: Ira Diamond; Set Decorations: Claire P. Brown; Casting by: William J. Kenney, Joe Reich; Film Editors: Neil MacDonald, Jeanene Ambler; Sound: James F. Rogers, John R. McDonald; Color by: Technicolor; Titles & Optical Effects: Universal Title; Unit Production Manager: Bud Brill; 1st Assistant Directors: Gary Grillo, Paul Samuelson; 2nd Assistant Directors: Dick Erickson, Robert Villar; Mr. Klugman's Wardrobe Furnished by: Botany 500, McGregor Sportswear; Technical Advisors: Victor J. Rosen, M. D. , Marc Scott Taylor; Sound Effects Editors: Clive Smith, Ken Sweet; Music Editor: Gene L. Gillette; Costume Designer: Yvonne Wood; Produced In Association With: Glen A. Larson Productions And Universal Television; Exclusive Distributor: MCA Television Limited.

THE RAY MILLAND SHOW

CBS Television Network, September 16, 1954-September 30, 1955; 37 episodes in black & white on film; 30 minutes.

A situation comedy about Prof. Ray McNulty, the drama teacher at a Los Angeles university. This program was a continuation of Meet Mr. McNutley (which see) in which the professor was the head of the English Department at an elite women's college and had the last name of McNutley.

Cast: Prof. Ray McNulty (Ray Milland), Peggy McNulty (Phyllis Avery), Dean Dodsworth (Lloyd Corrigan).

Credits: Produced by: Revue Productions, Inc.; Exclusive Distributor: MCA Television Limited.

THE REBELS

Distributed by MCA Television Limited for Operation Prime Time, May 1979; 2 episodes in color on film; 120 minutes (total: 4 hours).

An historical drama about Philip Kent, the illegitimate son of an English nobleman and a French actress who joined the ranks of the Colonial revolutionaries and their budding democracy. His compatriots included Judson Fletcher, the libertine son of a wealthy plantation owner; and Eph Tait, a raucous backwoodsman. A sequel to The Bastard (which see). Followed by the sequel The Seekers (which see).

Cast: Philip Kent (Andrew Stevens), Judson Fletcher (Don Johnson), Eph Tait (Doug McClure), Henry Knox (John Chappell), Mrs. Brumple (Joan Blondell), Peggy McLean (Gwen Humble), Seth McLean (Robert Vaughn), Rachel (Tanya Tucker), Charlotte Waverly (Pamela Hensley), George Washington (Peter Graves), Benjamin Franklin (Tom Bosley), John Adams (William Daniels), Thomas Jefferson (Kevin Tighe), Anne Kent (Kim Cattrall), John Waverly (William Smith), Ambrose Waverly (Warren Stevens), Dr. Church (Macdonald Carey), Angus Fletcher (Forrest Tucker), Duke of Kentland (Richard Basehart), Von Steuben (Nehemiah Persoff), Lafayette (Marc Vahanian), General Howe (Wilfrid Hyde-White), Mrs. Harris (Anne Francis), Sam Gill (Bobby Troup), Breen (Rory Calhoun), John Hancock (Jim Backus), Rothman (David Matthau), Molly (Debi Richter), Donnigan (Ben Davidson), Smith (Duncan Gamble), Lt. Rorke (Gordon Steel), 2nd Congressman (Timothy O'Hagen), 1st Congressman (John Rayner), Doctor (Tom Williams), Alice (Jennifer Holmes), Masters (James L. Brown), Trumbold (Ross McGuin), Stable Boy (Kelly Flynn), Narrated by (William Conrad).

Credits: Executive Producer: R. A. Cinader; Producers: Gian R. Grimaldi, Hannah L. Shearer; Directed by: Russ Mayberry; Written by: Sean Bain; Based on the Novel by: John Jakes; Associate Producer: Bernadette Joyce; Director of Photography: Frank Thackery; Music by: Gerald Fried; Art Director: William Campbell; Film Editors: Skip Lusk, John Kaufman, Jr., Leon Garbers; Set Decorations: Lowell Chambers; Sound: Norman Webster; Titles & Optical Effects: Universal Title; Unit Production Manager: Brad H. Aronson; 1st Assistant Director: Dean Marks; 2nd Assistant Ditors: Armande Huerta, Stan Zabka; The American Bicentennial Series of Novels is Based Upon a Concept by: Lyle Engels; Casting by: Robert O. Edmiston; Costume Designer: Jean-Pierre Dorleac; Costume Supervisors: Wayne Reed, Opal Vils; Promotional Consideration Furnished by: Harcourt Brace Jovanovich; Sound Effects Editor: Wes Wolfe; Music Editor: Fred Prior; Color by: Technicolor; Produced by: Universal Television; Exclusive Distributor: MCA Television Limited.

THE RESTLESS GUN

NBC Television Network, September 23, 1957-September 14, 1959; 77 episodes in black & white on film; 30 minutes. Sponsors: Warner-Lambert Pharmaceutical Company, Inc.; Bell & Howell; Sterling Drug; Carter Products; Procter & Gamble.

A Western about Vint Bonner, who was feared and famed as the fastest man with a six-shooter the post-Civil War era had ever known. The word of his speed with a Colt .45 preceded him everywhere, involving Vint continually in blazing adventures. The pilot for this series was telecast on Schlitz Playhouse of Stars on March 29, 1957.

Cast: Vint Bonner (John Payne).

Credits: Executive Producer: John Payne; Produced by: David Dortort; Writers: David Dortort, others; Music Supervision: Stanley Wilson; Produced by: Window Productions, Revue Productions, Inc.; Exclusive Distributor: MCA Television Limited.

REVLON MIRROR THEATRE

CBS Television Network, September 19, 1953-December 12, 1953; 13 episodes in black & white on film; 30 minutes. Sponsored by Revlon Cosmetics.

A dramatic anthology. (An earlier version of this series was broadcast live by the NBC Television Network, June 23, 1953-September 12, 1953. It was not produced by Revue.)

Cast: Hostess/Spokeswoman for Revlon, Robin Chandler.

Credits: Executive in Charge of Production: Jennings Lang; Produced by: Revue Productions, Inc.; Exclusive Distributor: MCA Television Limited.

THE RHINEMANN EXCHANGE (NBC'S BEST SELLERS)

NBC Television Network, March 10, 1977-March 24, 1977; 3 episodes in color on film; 60 minutes and 120 minutes (total: 5 hours).

A tale about espionage and profiteering during World War II in which U.S. intelligence agent David Spaulding was sent to Argentina to arrange for an exchange of industrial diamonds for German gyroscope plans. Filmed in Mexico City and Cuernavaca.

Cast: David Spaulding (Stephen Collins), Leslie Hawkewood (Lauren Hutton), Colonel Pace (Larry Hagman), Kendall (Claude Akins), General Swanson (Vince Edwards), Altmuller (Werner Klemperer), Geoffrey Moore (Jeremy Kemp), Ambassador Granville (John Huston), Bobby Ballard (Roddy McDowall), Dietricht (John van Dreelen), Erich Rhinemann (José Ferrer), Stoltz (Bo Brundin), Mrs. Cameron (Kate Woodville), Uribe (Zitto Kazann), Dr. Lyons (Rene Auberjonois), Asher Feld (Len Berman).

With: Ben Wright, William Prince, Victoria Racimo, Claudio Brook, Roberto Dumont, Tricia Noble, Pedro Galvon, Bruno Schwebel, Thayer David, John Chappell, Edgar Winston, Lance Hoole, Anthony Charnota, Ramon Bieri, Pedro Armendariz, Jr., Vincent Bagetta, John Hoyt, Gene Evans, Isela Vega, John Astin, Bob Neill.

Credits: Executive In Charge of Production: Charles Engel; Executive Producer: George Eckstein; Produced by: Richard Collins;

Directed by: Burt Kennedy; Written by: Richard Collins; Based on the Novel by: Robert Ludlum; Director of Photography: Alex Phillips, Jr.; Music by: Michel Columbier; NBC's Best Sellers Theme by: Elmer Bernstein; Art Director: William H. Tuntke; Film Editors: Anthony Redman, Rod Stevens; Color by: Technicolor; Titles & Optical Effects: Universal Title; Produced by: Universal Television; Exclusive Distributor: MCA Television Limited.

RICH MAN, POOR MAN

ABC Television Network, February 1, 1976-March 15, 1976; 8 episodes in color on film; 120 minutes and 60 minutes (total: 12 hours).

A drama about 20 years in the divergent lives of two brothers. Beginning in 1945, the program followed 17-year-old Rudy Jordache, a conscientious youth who hoped to win a college scholarship, and his wild and irresponsible brother Tom through a series of adventures that ended with Rudy entering a political career and Tom running a yachting venture off the French coast. Followed by the series Rich Man, Poor Man--Book II (which see).

Cast: Rudy Jordache (Peter Strauss), Tom Jordache (Nick Nolte), Julie Prescott (Susan Blakely), Bayard Nichols (Steve Allen), Axel Jordache (Edward Asner), Willie Abbott (Bill Bixby), Al Fanducci (Dick Butkus), Virginia Calderwood (Kim Darby), Col. Deiner (Andrew Duggan), Smitty (Norman Fell), Clothilde (Fionnuala Flanagan), Linda Quales (Lynda Day George), Sue Prescott (Gloria Graham), Sid Gossett (Murray Hamilton), Marsh Goodwin (Van Johnson), Kate (Kay Lenz), Joey Quales (George Maharis), Irene Goodwin (Dorothy Malone), Mary Jordache (Dorothy McGuire), Brad Knight (Tim McIntire), Duncan Calderwood (Ray Milland), Teddy Boylan (Robert Reed), Teresa Santoro (Talia Shire), Asher Berg (Craig Stevens), Arnold Simms (Michael Evans), Claude Tinker (Dennis Dugan), Mr. Tinker (Frank Aletter), Dr. Tinker (John Furlong), Buddy (Mike Baird), Miss Lenaut (Josette Banzet), Martin (Martin Ash), Bill Denton (Lawrence Pressman), Harold Jordache (Bo Brundin), Theatre Manager (William Bronder), Augie (Julius Harris), Gloria Bartley (Jo Ann Harris), Jay Ledbetter (Ben Archibek), Lou Martin (Anthony Carbone), Roy Dwyer (Herbert Jefferson, Jr.), Pinky (Harvey Jason), Pete Tierney (Roy Jenson), Falconetti (William Smith), Papadakis (Ed Barth), Billy (Leigh J. McCloskey), Martha (Helen Craig), Wesley (Michael Morgan), Phil McGee (Gavan O'Herlihy), Barone (John Larroquette), O'Hara (Terrence Locke).

Credits: Executive Producer: Harve Bennett; Produced by: Jon Epstein; Directors: Boris Sagal, David Greene; Written by: Dean Riesner; Based on the Novel by: Irwin Shaw; Director of Photography: Howard R. Schwartz; Music by: Alex North; Art Director: John E. Chilberg II; Film Editors: Richard Bracken, Douglas Stewart; Set Decorations: Joseph J. Stone; Costumes by: Charles

Waldo; Color by: Technicolor; Titles & Optical Effects: Universal Title; Produced by: Universal Television; Exclusive Distributor: MCA Television Limited.

RICH MAN, POOR MAN--BOOK II

ABC Television Network, September 21, 1976-March 8, 1977; 21 episodes in color on film; 60 minutes.

A drama about the lives of Rudy Jordache, his stepson Billy Abbott, and his nephew Wes Jordache, the only child of Rudy's slain brother Tom, from 1965 to 1975. A sequel to Rich Man, Poor Man (which see).

Cast: Rudy Jordache (Peter Strauss), Billy Abbott (James Carroll Jordan), Wesley Jordache (Gregg Henry), Falconetti (William Smith), Roy Dwyer (Herbert Jefferson, Jr.), Maggie Porter (Susan Sullivan), Marie Falconetti (Dimitra Arliss), Ramona Scott (Penny Peyser), Charles Estep (Peter Haskell), Scotty (John Anderson), Diane Porter (Kimberly Beck), Phil Greenberg (Sorrell Booke), Arthur Raymond (Peter Donat), Annie Adams (Cassie Yates), Senator Paxton (Barry Sullivan), John Franklin (Philip Abbott), Claire Estep (Laraine Stephens), Kate Jordache (Kay Lenz), Max Vincent (George Gaynes), Senator Dillon (G. D. Spradlin), Al Barber (Ken Swofford).

Credits: Executive Producer: Michael Gleason; Produced by: Jon Epstein; Directors: Paul Stanley, Bill Bixby, Alex Segal, others; Music by: Alex North; Music Supervision: Stanley Wilson; Color by: Technicolor; Titles & Optical Effects: Universal Title; Produced by: Universal Television; Exclusive Distributor: MCA Television Limited.

RICHIE BROCKELMAN, PRIVATE EYE

NBC Television Network, March 17, 1978-August 24, 1978; 5 episodes in color on film; 60 minutes.

A detective program about Richie Brockelman, a young, inexperienced, college-educated private eye who undertook each case with an overwhelming amount of enthusiasm. As a 23-year-old independent businessman, his credit was bad, his insurance rates were high and his rent was overdue. Set in Los Angeles. Based on the telefeature Richie Brockelman, Private Eye (which see), the character was originally introduced in an episode of The Rockford Files (which see).

Cast: Richie Brockelman (Dennis Dugan), Sgt. Coopersmith (Robert Hogan), Sharon (Barbara Bosson).

Credits: Executive Producers: Stephen J. Cannell, Steven Bochco; Supervising Producer: Alex Beaton; Produced by: Peter S. Fischer; Directors: Arnold Laven, others; Writers: Stephen J. Cannell, Steven Bochco, Michael Kozoll; Color by: Technicolor; Titles & Optical Effects: Universal Title; Produced by: Universal Television; Exclusive Distributor: MCA Television Limited.

RIVERBOAT

NBC Television Network, September 13, 1959-January 16, 1961; 44 episodes in black & white on film; 60 minutes.

A drama about Grey Holden, operator of the riverboat Enterprise on the Mississippi in the 1840s, and his friend, Ben Frazer, a plainspoken, rough young riverman whom he appointed as pilot of the Enterprise. Their adventures took them up and down stream from New Orleans to St. Louis and as far north as the fur-trapping regions of Minnesota.

Cast: Grey Holden (Darren McGavin), Ben Frazer (Burt Reynolds), Travis (William D. Gordon), Joshua (Jack Lambert), Carney (Richard Wessel), Chip (Mike McGreevey), Terry Blake (Bart Patten), Bill Blake (Noah Beery, Jr.), Pickalong (Jack Mitchum).

Credits: Produced, Directed and Written by: Richard H. Bartlett, Norman Jolley; Music by: Elmer Bernstein, Richard Sendry; Produced by: Meladre Company, Revue Productions, Inc.; Exclusive Distributor: MCA Television Limited.

THE ROAD WEST

NBC Television Network, September 12, 1966-August 28, 1967; 26 episodes in black & white on film; 60 minutes. Sponsor and Agency: Kraft Foods through J. Walter Thompson Company.

A Western about Benjamin Pride, a widower farmer from Springfield, Ohio who moved his family out to the wild, lawless Territory of Kansas during the post-Civil War years. A theatrical motion picture entitled This Savage Land, edited from episodes of this series, was released by Universal Pictures in 1969.

Cast: Benjamin Pride (Barry Sullivan), Timothy Pride (Andrew Prine), Midge Pride (Brenda Scott), Kip Pride (Kelly Corcoran), Grandpa Pride (Charles Seel), Chance Reynolds (Glenn Corbett), Elizabeth Reynolds (Kathryn Hays).

Credits: Executive Producer: Norman Macdonnell; Produced by: James McAdams; Directors: Vincent McEveety, others; Associate Producer: Mort Zarcoff; Music Supervision: Stanley Wilson; Theme Music by: Leonard Rosenman; Produced by: Universal Television; In Association With: NBC-TV; Exclusive Distributor: MCA Television Limited.

90 / Series

THE ROCKFORD FILES

NBC Television Network, September 13, 1974- ; 113 episodes in color on film; 60 minutes.

A detective drama about private investigator Jim Rockford who operated out of a ramshackle trailer home in Paradise Cove, California and only handled cases which the police had closed. Based on the telefeature The Rockford Files (which see). The character Richie Brockelman was introduced on this series (see the telefeature Richie Brockelman, Private Eye and the series of the same title for details). For a time, while new episodes were still running on the network, old segments of The Rockford Files were syndicated under the title Jim Rockford, Private Investigator.

Cast: Jim Rockford (James Garner), Joseph "Rocky" Rockford (Noah Beery, Jr.), Beth Davenport (Gretchen Corbett), Det. Dennis Becker (Joe Santos), Lt. Deel (Tom Atkins), Angel Martin (Stuart Margolin), John Cooper (Bo Hopkins).

Credits: Executive Producer: Meta Rosenberg; Supervising Producer: Stephen J. Cannell; Producers: Stephen J. Cannell, David Chase, Chas. Floyd Johnson; Created by: Roy Huggins, Stephen J. Cannell; Directors: Russ Mayberry, William Wiard, Hy Averback, others; Executive Story Consultant and Story Editor: Juanita Bartlett; Associate Producers: David Chase, Chas. Floyd Johnson, J. Rickley Dumm; Music by: Mike Post, Pete Carpenter; Directors of Photography: Lamar Boren, A.S.C., Andrew Jackson, A.S.C.; Art Direction: Robert Crawley, Sr.; Set Decorations: Gary Moreno, Robert L. Zilliox; Casting by: Dodie McLean; Film Editors: Buford F. Hayes, I. Robert Levy, Diane Adler; Sound: John Carter; Color by: Technicolor; Titles & Optical Effects: Universal Title; Editorial Supervision: Richard Belding; Music Supervision: Hal Mooney; Unit Production Managers: Les Berke, Zane Radney; 1st Assistant Directors: Robert Jones, David Menteer; 2nd Assistant Director: Leonard R. Garner; Sound Effects Editor: Walt Jenevein; Music Editor: Morrie McNaughton; Costume Designers: Charles Waldo, Kent Warner; Main Title Design: Jack Cole; Produced by: Roy Huggins-Public Arts Productions; In Association With: Cherokee Productions And Universal Television; Exclusive Distributor: MCA Television Limited.

ROD SERLING'S NIGHT GALLERY (FOUR-IN-ONE)

As an element of Four-in-One: NBC Television Network, December 16, 1970-January 20, 1971; 6 episodes in color on film; 60 minutes. As a regular series: NBC Television Network, September 15, 1971 -May 27, 1973; 22 episodes in color on film; 60 minutes and 14 episodes in color on film; 30 minutes.

A horror anthology hosted by Rod Serling which presented stories in the genre of the occult, the weird and the fantastic. Based on the telefeature Night Gallery (which see).

Cast: Host/Narrator, Rod Serling.

Credits: Produced by: Jack Laird; Created by: Rod Serling; Directors: Douglas Heyes, John Meredyth Lucas, others; Writers: Rod Serling, Douglas Heyes, Matthew Howard, Gene R. Kearney, Jerrold Freedman, others; Music Score: Robert Prince; Theme Music by: Gil Melle; Directors of Photography: William Margulies, A.S.C., Gerald Perry Finnerman, A.S.C., Lionel Lindon; Art Director: Joseph Alves, Jr.; Set Decorations: Bert F. Allen; Unit Manager: Burt Astor; Assistant Directors: Jack Doran, Ralph Sariego; Film Editor: James Leicester; Sound: David H. Moriarty; Gallery Paintings by: Tom Wright; Main Title Design: Visual Computing Corp.; Color by: Technicolor; Titles & Optical Effects: Universal Title; Editorial Supervision: Richard Belding; Costumes by: Grady Hunt; Makeup: Bud Westmore; Hair Stylist: Larry Germain; Production Executive: Paul Freeman; Executive in Charge of Production: Norman Glenn; Produced by: Universal Television; In Association with: NBC-TV; Exclusive Distributor: MCA Television Limited.

THE ROSEMARY CLOONEY SHOW

Distributed by MCA Television Limited, 1956-1957; 39 episodes in black & white on film; 30 minutes.

A musical/variety program hosted by Rosemary Clooney.

Cast: Rosemary Clooney, Nelson Riddle Orchestra, the Hi-Los.

Credits: Music by: Nelson Riddle; Produced by: The Maysville Corporation And Revue Productions, Inc.; Exclusive Distributor: MCA Television Limited.

ROSETTI AND RYAN

NBC Television Network, September 22, 1977-November 10, 1977; 13 episodes in color on film; 60 minutes.

A courtroom drama about Rosetti and Ryan, two stylish defense attorneys who won not only every case but the heart of every female client. Based on the telefeature Rosetti and Ryan: Men Who Love Women (which see).

Cast: Joseph Rosetti (Tony Roberts), Frank Ryan (Squire Fridell), Jessica Hornesby (Jane Elliott), Judge Hardcastle (Dick O'Neill), Judge Black (William Marshall).

Credits: Executive Producer: Leonard B. Stern; Supervising Producers: Don Mankiewicz, Gordon Cotler; Produced by: Jerry Davis; Directors: Alex March, others; Writers: Richard Bluel, Pat Fielder, others; Music by: Peter Matz, Gordon Jenkins; Color

92 / Series

by: Technicolor; Titles & Optical Effects: Universal Title; Produced by: Heyday Productions; In Association With: Universal Television; Exclusive Distributor: MCA Television Limited.

RUN FOR YOUR LIFE

NBC Television Network, September 13, 1965-September 11, 1968; 85 episodes in color on film; 60 minutes. Major Sponsor and Agency: Brown & Williamson Tobacco Corporation through Post-Keyes-Gardner, Inc.

An adventure-drama about Paul Bryan, a successful young lawyer, who was told by his doctors that he had only two years to live. Trying to crowd a lifetime of living into the time left, Paul set out on an intensive global search for adventure. The pilot film for this series was the Kraft Suspense Theatre (which see) episode "Rapture at Two-Forty" (April 15, 1965).

Cast: Paul Bryan (Ben Gazzara).

Credits: Executive Producer: Roy Huggins; Producers: Jo Swerling, Jr., Robert Hamner, Gordon Hessler; Created by: Roy Huggins; Directors: George McGowan, John Llewellyn Moxey, others; Writers: Robert E. Thompson, John D. MacDonald, Howard Browne, John Thomas James, others; Associate Producer: Paul Freeman; Assistant to the Executive Producer: Robert Foster; Assistant to the Producer: Steve Heilpern; Music by: Pete Rugolo; Film Editors: Robert Watts, Carl Pingitore; Music Supervision: Stanley Wilson; Color by: Technicolor; Titles & Optical Effects: Universal Title; Produced by: Roncom Films-Roy Huggins Productions; In Association With: Universal Television And NBC-TV; Exclusive Distributor: MCA Television Limited.

SAN FRANCISCO INTERNATIONAL AIRPORT (FOUR-IN-ONE)

NBC Television Network, October 28, 1970-August 25, 1971; 6 episodes in color on film; 60 minutes.

A drama about the people who operated and used the San Francisco International Airport. Based on the telefeature San Francisco International Airport (which see).

Cast: Jim Conrad (Lloyd Bridges), Bob Hatten (Clu Gulager), June (Barbara Werle).

Credits: Executive Producer: Richard Irving; Produced by: Paul Mason; Created by: William Read Woodfield, Allan Balter; Directors: Richard Benedict, others; Writers: John Furia, Jr., Lionel E. Siegel, Paul Mason, others; Story Editor: Richard Landau; Associate Producer: Don Gold; Music by: George del Barrio; Director of Photography: Alric Edens; Art Director: Alexander A.

Mayer; Set Decorations: Joseph Stone; Unit Manager: Don Gold; Technical Advisor: Robert J. Serling; Film Editor: George Ohanian; Sound: Lyle Cain; Assistant Director: George Fenady; Editorial Supervision: Richard Belding; Costumes by: Burton Miller; Makeup: Bud Westmore; Hair Stylist: Larry Germain; Produced by: Universal Television; In Association With: NBC-TV; Exclusive Distributor: MCA Television Limited.

SARA

CBS Television Network, February 13, 1976-July 30, 1976; 13 episodes in color on film; 60 minutes.

A Western about Sara Yarnell, a school teacher from the East who set out to make a life for herself in a small town in Colorado in the 1870s.

Cast: Sara Yarnell (Brenda Vaccaro), Martha Higgins (Louise Latham), Emmet Ferguson (Bert Kramer), Martin Pope (Albert Stratton), Julia Bailey (Mariclare Costello), Claude Barstow (William Phipps), George Bailey (William Wintersole), Georgie Bailey (Kraig Metzinger), Emma Higgins (Hallie Morgan), Debbie Higgins (Debbie Lytton).

Credits: Executive Producer: George Eckstein; Produced and Created by: Richard Collins; Directors: William Wiard, Alf Kjellin, Stuart Margolin, Jud Taylor, others; Music by: Lee Holdridge; Music Supervision: Hal Mooney; Color by: Technicolor; Titles & Optical Effects: Universal Title; Produced by: Universal Television; Exclusive Distributor: MCA Television Limited.

SARGE

NBC Television Network, September 21, 1971-January 11, 1972; 13 episodes in color on film; 60 minutes.

A drama about Father Samuel Cavanaugh, better known as "Sarge," a compassionate man who entered the priesthood after a bombing attempt on his life resulted in the death of his young wife. Formerly a detective sergeant in the homicide division of the San Diego Police Department, he was assigned to a parish in the heart of his old precinct. A man of the cloth, Sarge was still drawn to police work and criminal investigation. Based on the telefeatures Sarge: The Badge or the Cross (which see) and The Priest Killer (which see) in which Raymond Burr played Chief Robert T. Ironside.

Cast: Father Samuel Cavanaugh (George Kennedy), Valerie (Sallie Shockley), Barney Verick (Ramon Bieri), Kenji Takichi (Harold Sakata).

Credits: Executive Producer: David Levy; Produced by: David Levinson; Created by: David Levy; Directors: John Badham,

94 / Series

others; Writers: Joel Oliansky, others; Associate Producer: Rita Dillon; Editorial Supervision: Richard Belding; Music Supervision: Hal Mooney; Color by: Technicolor; Titles & Optical Effects: Universal Title; Produced by: Universal Television; Exclusive Distributor: MCA Television Limited.

SCHLITZ PLAYHOUSE OF STARS

CBS Television Network, November 1956-March 27, 1959; 91 episodes in black & white on film; 30 minutes. Sponsored by the Schlitz Brewing Company.

A dramatic anthology which was seen weekly 1956-58 and then rotated with Lux Playhouse (which see) during the 1958-59 season. The pilot films for the series Tales of Wells Fargo (which see) and The Restless Gun (which see) were telecast on this program on December 14, 1956 and March 29, 1957, respectively. (An earlier version of Schlitz Playhouse of Stars which presented a combination of live shows and filmed episodes produced by Meridian Productions, Inc. was broadcast by the CBS Television Network, October 5, 1951-October 1956. Revue Productions was not involved in this earlier program.) Certain episodes of Schlitz Playhouse of Stars were rebroadcast on Moment of Fear (which see).

Credits: Executive Producer: Edward Lewis; Produced by: Lewman, Inc., Revue Productions, Inc.; Exclusive Distributor: MCA Television Limited.

THE SEEKERS

Distributed by MCA Television Limited for Operation Prime Time, November 1979; 2 episodes in color on film; 120 minutes (total: 4 hours).

An historical drama about the sons of American revolutionary Philip Kent: Abraham, who tried various occupations, and Gilbert, who was content to run his father's publishing business. A sequel to The Bastard (which see) and The Rebels (which see).

Cast: Abraham Kent (Randolph Mantooth), Elizabeth (Delta Burke), Gilbert Kent (George Deloy), Lt. Stovall (George Hamilton), Harriet (Harriet Karr), Elijah Weatherby (Brian Keith), Pleasant (Ross Martin), Philip Kent (Martin Milner), Clapper (Robert Reed), Peggy Kent (Barbara Rush).

With: Edie Adams, Neville Brand, John Carradine, Julie Gregg, Rosey Grier, Alex Hyde-White, Donald Mantooth, Gary Merrill, Vic Morrow, Timothy P. Murphy, Hugh O'Brian, Allan Rich, Sarah Rush, Stuart Whitman, Ed Harris, Michael Sullivan, Marty Gold, Skip Riley.

Credits: Executive Producer: R. A. Cinader; Produced by: Gian R. Grimaldi, Hannah L. Shearer; Directed by: Sidney Hayers; Written by: Steve Hayes; Based on the Novel by: John Jakes; Associate Producer: Bernadette Joyce; Director of Photography: Vincent A. Martinelli; Music by: Gerald Fried; Art Director: John E. Chilberg II; Film Editor: John Elias; Set Decorations: Morrie Hoffman; Sound: John R. Carter; Unit Production Manager: Burt Bluestein; Color by: Technicolor; Titles & Optical Effects: Universal Title; Produced by: Universal Television; Exclusive Distributor: MCA Television Limited.

THE SENATOR (THE BOLD ONES)

NBC Television Network, September 13, 1970-August 22, 1971; 8 episodes in color on film; 60 minutes.

A drama about Hays Stowe, a U.S. senator who was deeply concerned with the state of the nation. The series delved into the immediate problems of mankind and how they affected a man of high office. Based on the telefeature A Clear and Present Danger (which see).

Cast: Sen. Hays Stowe (Hal Holbrook), Jordan Boyle (Michael Tolan), Erin Stowe (Sharon Acker), Norma Stowe (Cindy Eilbacher).

Credits: Produced by: David Levinson; Directors: Daryl Duke, John Badham, others; Writers: Joel Oliansky, David W. Rintels, Preston Wood, others; Associate Producer: John Badham; Executive Consultant: William Sackheim; Executive Story Consultant and Story Editor: Fred Freiberger; Director of Photography: Jacques Marquette; Art Director: John J. Lloyd; Film Editors: Michael Economou, Douglas Stewart; Set Decorations: Jerry Miggins; Assistant Director: Dale Coleman; Unit Manager: Jimmy Walters; Editorial Supervision: Richard Belding; Camera Operator: Roger Sherman, Jr.; Sound: Lyle Cain; Makeup: Mike Germain; Technical Advisor: John Fuller; Color by: Technicolor; Titles & Optical Effects: Universal Title; Executive In Charge of Production: Stuart Erwin, Jr.; Produced by: Universal Television; In Association with: NBC-TV; Exclusive Distributor: MCA Television Limited.

SEVENTH AVENUE (NBC'S BEST SELLERS)

NBC Television Network, February 10, 1977-February 24, 1977; 3 episodes in color on film; 120 minutes (total: 6 hours).

The story of Jay Blackman's rags-to-riches climb in New York's garment industry in 1938. Filmed on location.

Cast: Jay Blackman (Steven Keats), Rhoda Gold (Dori Brenner), Al Blackman (Kristoffer Tabori), Gus Farber (Eli Wallach), Joe Vitelli (Herschel Bernardi), Myrna Gold (Anne Archer), Morris

Blackman (Mike Kellin), Eva Myers (Jane Seymour), Marty Cass (John Pleshette), Harry Lee (Alan King), Mr. Finkelstein (Jack Gilford), Frank Topo (Richard Dimitri), Celia Blackman (Anna Berger), Mr. Gold (Robert Symonds), Mrs. Gold (Leora Dana), Fredericks (Ray Milland), John Meyers (William Windom).

Credits: Executive In Charge of Production: Charles Engel; Executive Producer: Franklin Barton; Produced by: Richard Irving; Directed by: Richard Irving, Russ Mayberry; Written by: Laurence Heath; Based on the Novel by: Norman Bogner; Director of Photography: Jack Priestley; Music by: Nelson Riddle; NBC's Best Sellers Theme by: Elmer Bernstein; Production Designer: Philip Rosenberg; Art Director: Loyd S. Papez; Film Editor: Robert F. Shugrue; Color by: Technicolor; Titles & Optical Effects: Universal Title; Produced by: Universal Television; Exclusive Distributor: MCA Television Limited.

79 PARK AVENUE (NBC'S BEST SELLERS)

NBC Television Network, October 16, 1977-October 18, 1977; 3 episodes in color on film; 120 minutes (total: 6 hours).

The life story of Marja Fludjicki who escaped New York's ghetto, changed her identity, and both attracted and rejected lovers during a notorious career as a prostitute.

Marja Fludjicki/Marianne (Lesley Ann Warren), Ross Savitch (Marc Singer), Mike Koshko (David Dukes), Kaati Fludjicki (Barbara Barrie), Vera Keppler (Polly Bergen), Armand Perfido (Raymond Burr), Ben Savitch (Michael Constantine), John Stevens (Lloyd Haynes), Paulie Fludjicki (Scott Jacoby), Brian Whitfield (Peter Marshall), Frank Millerson (Alex Rocco), Peter Markevich (Albert Salmi), Harry Vito (John Saxon), John Hackson DeWitt (Robert Webber), Joker Martin (Jack Weston).

Credits: Executive Producer: George Eckstein; Produced by: Paul Wendkos; Directed by: Paul Wendkos; Written by: Richard DeRoy, Jack Guss, Lionel Siegel; Developed for Television by: Richard DeRoy; Based on the Novel by: Harold Robbins; Director of Photography: Enzo A. Martinelli; Music by: Nelson Riddle; Art Director: Loyd S. Papez; Film Editors: Robert F. Shugrue, Rod Stephens; Color by: Technicolor; Titles & Optical Effects: Universal Title; Produced by: Universal Television; Exclusive Distributor: MCA Television Limited.

SHIRLEY

NBC Television Network, October 26, 1979-January 25, 1980; 13 episodes in color on film; 60 minutes.

A comedy-drama about single parent Shirley Miller and her three children who moved from New York to Lake Tahoe in search of a better life.

Cast: Shirley Miller (Shirley Jones), Bill Miller (Peter Barton), Hemm Miller (Brett Shryer), Michelle Miller (Tracey Gold), Dutch (John McIntire), Charlotte (Ann Doran), Debra (Rosanna Arquette), Lew (Patrick Wayne), Tracey (Cynthia Eilbacher).

Credits: Color by: Technicolor; Titles & Optical Effects: Universal Title; Produced by: Procter & Gamble Productions; In Association with: Universal Television And NBC-TV; Exclusive Distributor: MCA Television Limited.

SHOTGUN SLADE

Distributed by MCA Television Limited, 1959-1961; 78 episodes in black & white on film; 30 minutes. Sponsored by Ballantine Beer through William Esty Co.

A Western about Shotgun Slade, a detective who pursued the lawless of the frontier.

Cast: Shotgun Slade (Scott Brady), Monica (Monica Lewis).

Credits: Executive Producer: Nat Holt; Produced by: Frank Gruber; Directors: Frank Gruber, others; Produced by: The Shotgun Production Company, Revue Productions, Inc.; Exclusive Distributor: MCA Television Limited.

SIERRA

NBC Television Network, September 12, 1974-December 12, 1974; 13 episodes in color on film; 60 minutes.

An adventure program about the forest rangers at Yosemite National Park in California. "Cruncher," the tourist-terrorizing bear, played himself. Based on the telefeature The Rangers (which see).

Cast: Ranger Tim Cassidy (James G. Richardson), Ranger Matt Harper (Ernest Thompson), Chief Ranger Jack Moore (Jack Hogan), Ranger Julie Beck (Susan Foster), Ranger P. J. Lewis (Mike Warren).

Credits: Executive Producer: Robert A. Cinader; Produced by: Bruce Johnson; Directors: Bruce Bilson, others; Writers: Preston Wood, others; Music by: Lee Holdridge; Color by: Technicolor; Titles & Optical Effects: Universal Title; Produced by: Mark VII Limited; In Association With: Universal Television; Exclusive Distributor: MCA Television Limited.

98 / Series

SING ALONG WITH MITCH

NBC Television Network, January 27, 1961-September 21, 1964; 42 episodes in black & white on tape; 60 minutes.

A musical/variety program hosted by Mitch Miller.

Cast: Mitch Miller, Leslie Uggams, Gloria Lambert, Diana Trask, Louise O'Brien, Sandy Stewart.

Credits: Music Director: Jimmy Carroll; Theme Song "Sing Along" by: Robert Allen; Produced by: All America Features; In Association With: MCA Television Limited; Distributed by: William Morris Agency.

THE SIX MILLION DOLLAR MAN

ABC Television Network, January 18, 1974-March 6, 1978; 126 episodes in color on film; 60 minutes. Major Sponsors and Agencies: American Home Products Corporation through John F. Murray Advertising, Inc.; Bristol-Myers Co. through Boclaro, Inc.; Colgate-Palmolive Co. through William Esty Co., Inc.; General Foods Corporation through Benton & Bowles, Inc.

An action-adventure program about Steve Austin, a former astronaut and NASA pilot who, after a devastating crash, was reconstructed by a team of aero-space physicians. The use of multimillion dollar bionic limbs gave him super-physical capabilities and he was employed by the Office of Scientific Information to combat super-villains. Based on the telefeature The Six Million Dollar Man (which see), the series also featured guest appearances by the Bionic Boy and the Bionic Dog. See the spin-off The Bionic Woman.

Cast: Col. Steve Austin (Lee Majors), Oscar Goldman (Richard Anderson), Dr. Rudy Wells (Alan Oppenheimer, Martin E. Brooks).

Credits: Executive Producers: Harve Bennett, Lionel E. Siegel; Supervising Producers: Lionel E. Siegel, Allan Balter; Producers: Kenneth Johnson, Fred Freiberger, Richard Landau, Michael Gleason, Sam Strangis, Don Boyle, Joe L. Cramer; Directors: Cliff Bole, Russ Mayberry, Jerry London, Alan Levi, Jeannot Szwarc, Lawrence Doheny, Jerry Johnson, Phil Bondelli, Barry Crane, Alan Crosland, Jr., Richard Moder, others; Writers: Arthur Weingarten, Elroy Schwartz, William Driskill, Larry Alexander, Richard Carr, Gustave Field, D. C. Fontana, Lionel E. Siegel, Tom Greene, Wilton Schiller, Margaret Schneider, Paul Schneider, Kenneth Johnson, others; Executive Script Consultant: Hilton Schiller; Executive Story Consultants: Lionel E. Siegel, Peter Allan Fields; Associate Producers: Rod Holcomb, Arthur E. McLaird, Arnold F. Turner; Story Editor: Richard Carr; Music Score: J. J. Johnson, Oliver Nelson, Richard Clements, Stu Phillips, Gil Melle;

Theme Music: Oliver Nelson; Directors of Photography: Allen M. Davey, Kenneth J. Williams, Tom Connors III, Enzo A. Martinelli, A.S.C., Alric Edens; Art Directors: Norman R. Newberry, Alfeo Bocchicchio, Frank Grieco, William Campbell; Set Decorations: Lowell Chambers, Jerry Adams; Assistant Director: Tom Connors III; Unit Manager: Ted Schilz; Film Editors: Jack W. Schoengarth, William Stark, Jamie Caylor, Howard Epstein; Casting by: Charles King; Color by: Technicolor; Titles & Optical Effects: Universal Title; Main Title Design: Jack Cole; Editorial Supervision: Richard Belding; Music Supervision: Hal Mooney; Costumes by: Burton Miller; Special Effects: Dale Johnston, Joe Goss; Sound: Charles King; Based on the Novel "Cyborg" by: Martin Caidin; Produced In Association With: Silverton Productions, Inc., Harve Bennett Productions And Universal Television; Exclusive Distributor: MCA Television Limited.

THE SIXTH SENSE

ABC Television Network, January 15, 1972-December 30, 1972; 25 episodes in color on film; 60 minutes. Major Sponsors and Agencies: S. C. Johnson & Son, Inc. through Foote, Cone & Belding; General Foods Corporation through Benton & Bowles, Inc.

A drama about psychic investigator Michael Rhodes, Ph.D. and his explorations of extrasensory perception (ESP).

Cast: Dr. Michael Rhodes (Gary Collins), Nancy Murphy (Catherine Ferrar).

Credits: Produced and Developed by: Stan Shpetner; Created by: Anthony Lawrence; Directors: Sutton Roley, Alf Kjellin, John Newland, others; Writers: Leonard Kantor, Don Ingalls, Anthony Lawrence, Merwin Gerard, others; Executive Story Consultant: Anthony Lawrence; Associate Producer: Robert F. O'Neill; Story Editors: Harlan Ellison, Ed Waters; Director of Photography: Enzo A. Martinelli, A.S.C.; Theme Music by: Lalo Schifrin; Music Score: Billy Goldenberg; Unit Manager: Frank Losee; Assistant Director: Bill Hole; Art Directors: William Tuntke, Arch Bacon; Film Editors: John Elias, Bud Hoffman; Set Decorations: Leonard Mazzola; Color by: Technicolor; Titles & Optical Effects: Universal Title; Executive In Charge of Production: Frank Price; Produced by: Universal Television; Exclusive Distributor: MCA Television Limited.

THE SNOOP SISTERS (NBC TUESDAY MYSTERY MOVIE, NBC WEDNESDAY MYSTERY MOVIE)

NBC Television Network, December 19, 1973-August 20, 1974; 4 episodes in color on film; 90 minutes.

A mystery-drama about Ernesta and Gwen Snoop, an eccentric whodone-it writing team whose insatiable curiosity all too often involved them in real-life murders. Based on the telefeature The Snoop Sisters (which see).

Cast: Ernesta Snoop (Helen Hayes), Gwen Snoop (Mildred Natwick), Barney (Lou Antonio), Lt. Steven Ostrowski (Bert Convy).

Credits: Executive Producer: Leonard B. Stern; Produced by: Tony Barrett; Created by: Alan Shayne; Editorial Supervision: Richard Belding; Music Supervision: Hal Mooney; Color by: Technicolor; Titles & Optical Effects: Universal Title; Produced by: Talent Associates-Norton Simon, Inc.; In Association With: Universal Television And NBC-TV; Exclusive Distributor: MCA Television Limited.

SOLDIERS OF FORTUNE

Distributed by MCA Television Limited, 1955-1956; 52 episodes in black & white on film; 30 minutes.

An adventure program about Tim Kelley and Toubo Smith, two soldiers of fortune who went from the Arabian Desert to the Pacific for a price.

Cast: Tim Kelly (John Russell), Toubo Smith (Chick Chandler).

Credits: Produced by: Revue Productions, Inc.; Exclusive Distributor: MCA Television Limited.

SONS AND DAUGHTERS

CBS Television Network, September 11, 1974-November 6, 1974; 13 episodes in color on film; 60 minutes. Major Sponsors and Agencies: Lever Brothers Co. through Sullivan, Stauffer, Colwell & Bayles, Inc.; Lehn & Fink through Sullivan, Stauffer, Colwell & Bayles, Inc.; Chevrolet through Campbell-Ewald Co.

A drama about Jeff Reed and Anita Cramer, sweethearts who attended the Southwest High School in Stockton, California in the 1950s. Based on the telefeature Senior Year (which see).

Cast: Jeff Reed (Gary Frank), Anita Cramer (Glynnis O'Connor), Stash Melnyck (Scott Colomby), Moose Kerner (Barry Livingston), Charlie Riddel (Lionel Johnston), Evie Karasek (Debralee Scott), Lucille Reed (Jay W. MacIntosh), Walter Cramer (John S. Ragin), Ruth Cramer (Jan Shutan), Cody (Christopher Stafford Nelson).

Credits: Executive Producer: David Levinson; Producers: Michael Gleason, Barney Rosenzweig; Created by: M. Charles Cohen; Directors: Charles Dubin, others; Writers: David Levinson, Joseph Calvelli, others; Executive Story Consultant: Richard De Roy; Script Editor: Joseph Calvelli; Associate Producer: Stu Cohen; Director of Photography: Gayne Rescher; Music Score and Theme Music by: James Di Pasquale; Art Director: John E. Chilberg II; Set Decorations: Don Webb; Unit Manager: Jack Stubbs; Color by: Technicolor; Titles & Optical Effects: Universal Title; Produced by: Universal Television; Exclusive Distributor: MCA Television Limited.

SPECIAL AGENT 7

Distributed by MCA Television Limited, 1958-1959; 26 episodes in black & white on film; 30 minutes.

A drama about Special Agent 7, Conroy of the Intelligence Bureau of the Department of Internal Revenue, who tracked down tax dodgers. This series was also known as SA 7 and Secret Agent 7.

Cast: Treasury Agent Conroy (Lloyd Nolan).

Credits: Produced by: Revue Productions, Inc.; Exclusive Distributor: MCA Television Limited.

STAR STAGE

NBC Television Network, September 9, 1955-September 7, 1956; 8 episodes in black & white on film; 30 minutes.

A dramatic anthology which presented a number of live broadcasts (produced by NBC-TV) and 8 episodes on film (produced by Revue).

Cast: Host, Jeffrey Lynn.

Credits: Produced by: Revue Productions, Inc.; Exclusive Distributor: MCA Television Limited.

STARTIME (FORD STARTIME, LINCOLN-MERCURY STARTIME)

NBC Television Network, October 6, 1959-May 31, 1960; 39 episodes in color on film and tape; 60 minutes. Sponsors and Agencies: The Ford Motor Company through J. Walter Thompson Company; Lincoln-Mercury Division of the Ford Motor Company through J. Walter Thompson Company.

A dramatic, musical, variety and comedy anthology. Guest stars included James Stewart, George Gobel, Tony Curtis, Vera Miles, Paul Hartman and George Peppard. Alfred Hitchcock directed one episode.

Credits: Executive Producer: Hubbell Robinson; Producers: William Frye, Alfred Hitchcock, Joan Harrison; Directors: Gower Champion, Bretaigne Windust, Ted Post, Alfred Hitchcock, others;

Writers: Jameson Brewer, Joseph Stefano, Charlotte Armstrong, others; Directors of Photography: John F. Warren, John L. Russell; Music by: Conrad Salinger; Art Directors: John Meehan, John J. Lloyd; Editorial Supervisor: Richard G. Wray; Film Editors: Edward Haire, Duncan Mansfield, Edward W. Williams; Music Supervision: Stanley Wilson, Frederick Herbert; Sound: Earl Cain, Sr., Frank Sarv, William Russell; Assistant Directors: James H. Brown, Hilton A. Green; Set Decorators: James S. Redd, Rudy Butler, George Mile; Costume Supervisor: Vincent Dee; Makeup: Jack Barron; Hair Stylist: Florence Bush; Produced by: Hubbell Robinson Productions, Shamley Productions, Inc.; Filmed by: Revue Productions, Inc.

STATE TROOPER

Distributed by MCA Television Limited, 1957-1959; 104 episodes in black & white on film; 30 minutes.

A drama about Rod Blake of the Nevada State Police force. Based on actual cases. The pilot for this series was the "Killer on Horseback" episode of NBC's Star Stage, telecast February 3, 1956.

Cast: Rod Blake (Rod Cameron).

Credits: Music by: Maury Leaf; Music Supervision: Stanley Wilson; Produced by: Revue Productions, Inc.; Exclusive Distributor: MCA Television Limited.

STRIPE PLAYHOUSE

Distributed by MCA Television Limited, 1959; 2 episodes in black & white on film; 30 minutes.

A dramatic anthology.

Credits: Produced by: Revue Productions, Inc.; Exclusive Distributor: MCA Television Limited.

SUNSHINE

NBC Television Network, March 6, 1975-June 19, 1975; 13 episodes in color on film; 30 minutes.

A situation comedy about a widowed musician who tried to make a life for himself and his daughter. Based on the telefeature Sunshine (which see). Followed by the telefeature Sunshine Christmas (which see).

Cast: Sam Hayden (Cliff De Young), Jill Hayden (Elizabeth Cheshire), Weaver (Bill Mumy), Nora (Meg Foster), Corey Givits (Corey Fischer).

Sunshine / 103

Credits: Produced by: George Eckstein; Music Supervision: Hal Mooney; Color by: Technicolor; Titles & Optical Effects: Universal Title; Produced by: Universal Television; Exclusive Distributor: MCA Television Limited.

SUSPICION

NBC Television Network, September 30, 1957-September 6, 1959; 21 episodes in black & white on film; 60 minutes and 10 episodes live in black & white; 60 minutes.

A mystery/suspense anthology. Guest stars included Bette Davis, Greer Garson, Ray Milland, Joan Fontaine, James Mason, Ronald Colman, Joseph Cotten and Robert Cummings. Alfred Hitchcock's Shamley Productions produced ten episodes on film and Revue Productions produced eleven episodes on film. Ten additional segments were telecast live. Hitchcock directed one episode of the series.

Cast: Hosts, Dennis O'Keefe, Walter Abel.

Credits: Executive Producer: S. Mark Smith; Producers: Alfred Hitchcock, Richard Lewis, Mort Abrams, William Frye; Directors: Alfred Hitchcock, others; Based on Stories by: Daphne Du Maurier, John Steinbeck, Cornell Woolrich, others; Produced by: Shamley Productions, Inc., Revue Productions, Inc.; Exclusive Distributor: MCA Television Limited.

SWITCH

CBS Television Network, September 9, 1975-September 3, 1978; 66 episodes in color on film; 60 minutes.

A detective drama about Pete Ryan, a sophisticated con man gone straight, and Frank MacBride, a retired ex-cop, who became private investigators and joined forces to "con" the con men. Based on the telefeature Switch (which see).

Cast: Pete Ryan (Robert Wagner), Frank MacBride (Eddie Albert), Malcolm Argos (Charlie Callas), Maggie (Sharon Gless), Lt. Griffin (Ken Swofford), Revel (Mindi Miller), Lt. Modeer (Richard X. Slattery), Wang (James Hong).

Credits: Executive Producers: Jon Epstein, Glen A. Larson, Matthew Rapf; Supervising Producer: James McAdams; Producers: Paul Playdon, Leigh Vance, Jack Laird, John Peyser; Created by: Glen A. Larson; Directors: Reza S. Badiyi, E. W. Swackhamer, Sigmund Neufeld, Jr., Walter Doniger, Leo Penn, others; Writers: Stephen Kandel, Dick Powell, David Chase, Paul Playdon, others; Associate Producers: Stuart Cohen, Cynthia Cherbak, Mort Zarcoff; Executive Story Consultant: Larry Forrester; Executive Story Editor:

Robert Earll; Story Consultant and Story Editor: David Chase; Story Editor: Steve Kandel; Music Score: Stu Phillips; Theme Music: Glen A. Larson; Directors of Photography: Ben Colman, Frank P. Beaschoechea, Charles Correll; Art Directors: Ira Diamond, John Leimanis; Set Decorations: Mary Swanson; Assistant Director: Thomas Blank; Unit Manager: Russell Vreeland; Film Editors: Alan Marks, Edward W. Williams, A.C.E.; Sound: Jean Valentino; Color by: Technicolor; Titles & Optical Effects: Universal Title; Editorial Supervision: Richard Belding; Music Supervision: Hal Mooney; Costumes by: George R. Whittaker; Main Title Design: Wayne Fitzgerald; Produced In Association With: Glen A. Larson Productions And Universal Television; Exclusive Distributor: MCA Television Limited.

SWORD OF JUSTICE

NBC Television Network, September 10, 1978-October 28, 1978; 13 episodes in color on film; 60 minutes.

A drama about Jack Cole, a wealthy playboy who was framed on tax evasion charges and sent to prison, where he planned a unique form of justice. After his release, he struck out to seek revenge against the corporate businessmen who were responsible for his incarceration.

Cast: Jack Cole (Dack Rambo), Hector Ramirez (Bert Rosario), Arthur Woods (Alex Courtney).

Credits: Executive Producer: Glen A. Larson; Supervising Producer: Michael Sloan; Producers: Joe Boston, Herman Groves; Music by: John Andrew Tartaglia; Color by: Technicolor; Titles & Optical Effects: Universal Title; Produced In Association With: Glen A. Larson Productions And Universal Television; Exclusive Distributor: MCA Television Limited.

TALES OF WELLS FARGO

NBC Television Network, March 18, 1957-September 8, 1962; 167 episodes in black & white on film; 30 minutes and 34 episodes in color on film; 60 minutes. Sponsor and Agency: The American Tobacco Co. through Sullivan, Stauffer, Colwell & Bayles, Inc.

A Western based on stories of the famed Wells Fargo Express Company, which played a major role in the West's expansion. The pilot for this series ("A Tale of Wells Fargo") was telecast on Schlitz Playhouse of Stars (which see).

Cast: Wells Fargo Agent Jim Hardie (Dale Robertson), Beau McCloud (Jack Ging), Jeb Gaine (William Demarest), Ovie (Virginia Christine), Mary Gee (Mary Jayne Saunders), Tina (Lory Patrick).

Credits: Produced by: Earle Lyon; Created by: Frank Gruber; Directors: Jerry Hopper, R. G. Springsteen, others; Writers: Milton S. Gelman, Anthony Lawrence, Jack Turley, others; Executive Story Consultant: Milton S. Gelman; Theme Music: Harry Warren; Music Score: Johnny Williams, Morton Stevens, Melvyn Lenard; Director of Photography: Bud Thackery, A. S. C.; Art Directors: Alexander A. Mayer, Loyd S. Papez; Sound: Earl Crain, Jr., Lyle Cain; Musical Supervision: Stanley Wilson; Film Editors: Jean Berthelot, Edward A. Biery, Irving Schoenberg, Richard G. Wray; Makeup: Jack Barron; Hair Stylist: Florence Bush; Assistant Directors: Donald Baer, George Bisk; Set Decorations: John McCarthy, Ralph Sylos, James Walters; Costume Supervisor: Vincent Dee; Produced by: Overland Productions, Juggernaut, Inc., Revue Productions, Inc.; Exclusive Distributor: MCA Television Limited.

THE TALL MAN

NBC Television Network, September 10, 1960-September 1, 1962; 75 episodes in black & white on film; 30 minutes. Sponsors and Agencies: R. J. Reynolds Tobacco Company through William Esty Company, Inc.; American Motors through Geyer, Morey, Madden & Ballard, Inc.; Norwich Pharmaceutical Co., Inc. through Benton & Bowles, Inc.; Beech-Nut Life Savers, Inc. through Young & Rubicam, Inc.

A Western about the adventures of two real-life characters: Deputy Sheriff Pat F. Garrett and William H. Bonney, better known as Billy the Kid. Though close friends, each sensed that eventually he would face the other in a showdown. Meanwhile, they were friendly rivals, struggling to avoid the inevitable day of reckoning between them. Set in New Mexico in the 1870s.

Cast: Deputy Sheriff Pat F. Garrett (Barry Sullivan), Billy the Kid (Clu Gulager).

Credits: Executive Producers: Nat Holt, Edward J. Montagne; Producers: Samuel A. Peeples, Frank Price; Created by: Samuel A. Peeples; Directors: Herschel Daugherty, Les Selander, others; Writers: Samuel A. Peeples, David Lang, others; Associate Producer: Frank Price; Director of Photography: Lionel Lindon; Art Director: John J. Lloyd; Music by: Esquivel; Editorial Supervision: Richard G. Wray, A. C. E., David J. O'Connell; Makeup: Jack Barron; Hair Stylist: Florence Bush; Costume Supervisor: Vincent Dee; Produced by: Lincoln County Production Company, Revue Productions, Inc.; Exclusive Distributor: MCA Television Limited.

TAMMY

ABC Television Network, September 17, 1965-July 15, 1966; 26 episodes in black & white on film; 30 minutes. Major Sponsors and

Agencies: S. C. Johnson & Son, Inc. through Benton & Bowles, Inc.; The Procter & Gamble Company through Benton & Bowles, Inc.

A situation comedy about the adventures of Tammy Tarleton, a backwoods heroine of two worlds: the bayou houseboat where she and her family lived and the plantation of her wealthy employer, John Brent. Based on the film Tammy and the Bachelor (1957) and its sequels. A theatrical motion picture entitled Tammy and the Millionaire (1967) was edited from episodes of this series.

Cast: Tammy Tarleton (Debbie Watson), Grandpa Tarleton (Denver Pyle), Uncle Lucius (Frank McGrath), John Brent (Donald Woods), Lavinia Tate (Dorothy Green), Dwayne Whitt (George Furth), Peter Tate (David Macklin), Gloria Tate (Linda Marshall), Steven Brent (Jay Sheffield), Cousin Cletus Tarleton (Dennis Robertson).

Credits: Produced by: Dick Wesson; Based on the Novels "Tammy Out of Time" and "Tammy Tell Me True" by: Cid Ricketts Sumner; Directors: Sidney Miller, Leslie Goodwins, Ezra Stone, others; Writers: George Tibbles, others; Theme Music by: Herbert Spencer; Director of Photography: Robert Wycoff; Art Director: Henry Larrecq; Film Editor: Danford Greene; Music Supervision: Stanley Wilson; Produced by: Uni-Bet Productions, Universal Television; Exclusive Distributor: MCA Television Limited.

TENAFLY (NBC TUESDAY MYSTERY MOVIE, NBC WEDNESDAY MYSTERY MOVIE)

NBC Television Network, October 10, 1973-August 6, 1974; 6 episodes in color on film; 90 minutes.

A drama about Los Angeles private detective Harry Tenafly and his family. Based on the telefeature Tenafly (which see).

Cast: Harry Tenafly (James McEachin), Ruth Tenafly (Lillian Lehman), Herb Tenafly (Paul Jackson), Lorrie (Rosanna Huffman), Lt. Sam Church (David Huddleston).

Credits: Executive Producers and Creators: Richard Levinson, William Link; Directors: Robert Day, others; Writers: Booker Bradshaw, David P. Lewis, others; Music by: Gil Melle; Color by: Technicolor; Titles & Optical Effects: Universal Title; Produced by: Universal Television; Exclusive Distributor: MCA Television Limited.

TESTIMONY OF TWO MEN

Distributed by MCA Television Limited for Operation Prime Time, May 1977; 3 episodes in color on film; 120 minutes (total: 6 hours).

Testimony of Two Men / 107

A drama about Jonathan Ferrier, a crusading doctor, and his fight to introduce modern methods of medicine to inept doctors and his struggle to overcome a disastrous marriage, a murder accusation and the dramatic obstacles that prevented him from being united with the woman he loved.

Cast: Jonathan Ferrier (David Birney), Marjorie Ferrier/Hilda Eaton (Barbara Parkins), Martin Eaton (Steve Forrest), Dr. Jim Spaulding (Ralph Bellamy), Peter Heger (Theodore Bikel), Dr. Louis Hedler/Narrator (Tom Bosley), Howard Best (Barry Brown), Kenton Campion (J. D. Cannon), Father McGuire (Dan Dailey), David Paxton (Leonard Frey), Harald Ferrier (David Huffman), Father Frank McNulty (Randolph Mantooth), Jonas Witherby (Ray Milland), Jeremiah Hadley (Cameron Mitchell), Edna Beamish (Trisha Noble), Myrtle Heger (Kathleen Nolan), Flora Bumstead Eaton (Margaret O'Brien), Jenny Heger (Laurie Prange), Adrian Ferrier (William Shatner), Amelia Foster (Inga Swenson), Priscilla Madden Witherby (Devon Ericson), Jane Robson (Joan Van Ark), Francis Campion (Kario Salem), Mavis Eaton (Linda Purl), Elizabeth Best (Lynn Tufeld), Jerome Eaton (John DeLancie).

Credits: Produced by: Jack Laird; Directors: Leo Penn, Larry Yust; Written by: William Hanley, James M. Miller, Jennifer Miller; Based on the Novel by: Taylor Caldwell; Directors of Photography: Jim Dickson, Isidore Mankofsky; Music by: Gerald Fried, Michel Colombier; Art Directors: John E. Chilberg II, William H. Tuntke; Film Editors: Jim Benson, Robert F. Shugrue, John Elias; Costumes by: Bill Jobe; Color by: Technicolor; Titles & Optical Effects: Universal Title; Produced by: Universal Television; Exclusive Distributor: MCA Television Limited.

THRILLER

NBC Television Network, September 13, 1960-July 9, 1962; 67 episodes in black & white on film; 60 minutes. Sponsors and Agencies: American Tobacco Company through Sullivan, Stauffer, Colwell & Bayles, Inc.; Pillsbury through Campbell-Mithun, Inc.; Glenbrook Labs through Dancer-Fitzgerald-Sample, Inc.; Colgate-Palmolive through Ted Bates & Co., Inc.; Union Carbide through William Esty Co., Inc.; Max Factor through Kenyon & Eckhardt, Inc.; Corning Glass Works through N. W. Ayer & Son, Inc.; Block Drug Co. through Gray Advertising, Inc.; Latex; Allstate Insurance Co. through Leo Burnett Co., Inc.; E. I. du Pont de Nemours & Co., Inc. through Batten, Barton, Durstine & Osborn, Inc.

A mystery/suspense anthology hosted by Boris Karloff. Guest stars included Richard Chamberlain, Boris Karloff, William Shatner, Marlo Thomas, John Ireland, Brandon de Wilde, Ann Todd, Elizabeth Montgomery, John Carradine, Phyllis Thaxter, Ursula Andress, Mary Tyler Moore and Edward Andrews.

Cast: Host, Boris Karloff.

108 / Series

Credits: Executive Producer: Hubbell Robinson; Producers: William Frye, Fletcher Markle; Directors: Fletcher Markle, Maxwell Shane, John Brahm, Arthur Hiller, Douglas Heyes, Herschel Daugherty, Lazlo Benedek, Ida Lupino, Ted Post, Ray Milland, Paul Henreid, John Newland, William Claxton, others; Writers: Evelyn Beckman, Charlotte Armstrong, Dolores Hitchens, Robert Dozier, John D. MacDonald, Douglas Heyes, Robert Andrews, Robert Hardy, Alan Caillou, Barre Lyndon, Robert Bloch, Donald S. Sanford, Ida Lupino, Richard Matheson, Jay Simms, others; Music by: Jerry Goldsmith, Pete Rugolo; Director of Photography: Lionel Lindon; Produced by: Hubbell Robinson Productions, Inc., Revue Productions, Inc.; In Association With: NBC-TV; Exclusive Distributor: MCA Television Limited.

TOM, DICK AND MARY (90 BRISTOL COURT)

NBC Television Network, October 5, 1964-January 4, 1965; 12 episodes in black & white on film; 30 minutes.

A situation comedy about newlywed Dr. Tom Gentry and his wife Mary, and their best man and star boarder Dr. Dick Moran. Gentry and Moran were interns at Valley General Hospital and Mary was secretary to the chief of staff there. For financial reasons, the young trio shared a two bedroom apartment, a situation little to the liking of the newlyweds, except on pay day. The three lived at 90 Bristol Court, a balconied modern multi-unit apartment motel on the Los Angeles-Beverly Hills line. The other residents of the Court were featured in Harris Against the World (which see) and Karen (which see).

Cast: Dr. Tom Gentry (Don Galloway), Mary Gentry (Joyce Bulifant), Dr. Dick Moran (Steve Franken).

Credits: Executive Producer: Joe Connelly; Produced by: Revue Productions, Inc.; Exclusive Distributor: MCA Television Limited.

TOMA

ABC Television Network, October 4, 1973-September 6, 1974; 24 episodes in color on film; 60 minutes. Major Sponsors and Agencies: Warner-Lambert Company through J. Walter Thompson Company; Procter & Gamble through Benton & Bowles, Inc.; General Foods Corporation through Benton & Bowles, Inc.; J. C. Penney Co., Inc. through McCaffrey & McCall, Inc.

An action-adventure program about the life and career of police detective David Toma, whose unorthodox methods of investigation won him national fame. A master of disguise and a loner, Toma was dogged in pursuit of criminals but compassionate in his concept of law enforcement. Based on the telefeature Toma (which see). The program Baretta (which see) was based on this series.

Cast: Det. David Toma (Tony Musante), Inspector Spooner (Simon Oakland), Patty Toma (Susan Strasberg).

Credits: Executive Producer: Roy Huggins; Associate Executive Producer: Jo Swerling, Jr.; Produced by: Stephen J. Cannell; Created by: Edward Hume; Directors: Jeannot Szwarc, Richard Bennett, Joseph Hardy, others; Writers: Stephen J. Cannell, Zekial Marko, Don Carlos Dunaway, John Thomas James, Tony Musante, Jane Musante; Production Consultant: David Toma; Director of Photography: Vilis Lapenieks; Music by: Mike Post, Pete Carpenter; Art Director: Robert Luthardt; Film Editor: Gloryette Clark; Music Supervision: Hal Mooney; Color by: Technicolor; Titles & Optical Effects: Universal Title; Produced by: Roy Huggins-Public Arts Productions; In Association With: Universal Television; Exclusive Distributor: MCA Television Limited.

TURNABOUT

NBC Television Network, January 26, 1979-March 30, 1979; 13 episodes in color on film; 30 minutes.

A situation comedy about Sam and Penny Alston, a husband and wife whose casual wish to change places with each other became a reality.

Cast: Sam Alston (John Schuck), Penny Alston (Sharon Gless), Jack Overmeyer (Richard Stahl), Judy Overmeyer (Bobbi Jordan), Geoffrey St. James (James Sikking), Brennan (Bruce Kirby).

Credits: Based on the Story by: Thorne Smith; Color by: Technicolor; Titles & Optical Effects: Universal Title; Produced by: Universal Television; Exclusive Distributor: MCA Television Limited.

THE VIRGINIAN

NBC Television Network, September 19, 1962-September 9, 1970; 225 episodes in color on film; 90 minutes.

A Western set in the Wyoming Territory during the 1890s with stories that revolved around life and personalities at the Shiloh Ranch where the Virginian was foreman. Based on the novel by Owen Wister and the 1929 film. The series was continued as The Men from Shiloh (which see). The Virginian episode "We've Lost a Train" (April 21, 1965) was the pilot for the series Laredo (which see). An expanded version of it was released theatrically as Backtrack by Universal Pictures in 1969.

Cast: The Virginian (James Drury), Judge Henry Garth (Lee J. Cobb), Trampas (Doug McClure), Steve (Gary Clarke), Betsy (Roberta Shore), Molly Wood (Pippa Scott), Randy (Randy Boone),

110 / Series

Jennifer (Diane Roter), Emmett Ryker (Clu Gulager), Stacy Grainger (Don Quine), John Grainger (Charles Bickford), Clay Grainger (John McIntire), Elizabeth Grainger (Sara Lane), Holly Grainger (Jeannette Nolan), Jim Horn (Tim Matheson), David Sutton (David Hartman).

Credits: Executive Producers: Richard Irving, Norman Macdonnell; Producers: Charles Marquis Warren, James McAdams, Howard Christie, Paul Freeman, Cy Chermak, Roy Huggins, Winston Miller, Jules Schermer, Frank Price, Joel Rogosin, David Levinson; Based on the Novel by: Owen Wister; Directors: Charles S. Dubin, Don McDougall, Abner Biberman, Robert Gist, Joel Rogosin, Tony Leader, others; Writers: Richard Fielder, Richard Wendley, Sy Salkowitz, W. R. Burnett, Andy Lewis, Joy Dexter, Robert Van Scoyk, Gerry Day, Bethel Leslie, Reuben Bercovitch, Don Tait, Abe Polsky, Gil Lasky, others; Associate Producers: Robert Van Scoyk, John Choy; Director of Photography: Enzo A. Martinelli; Theme Music by: Percy Faith; Music Score: Max Steiner, Leonard Rosenman, Leo Shuken, Hans Salter; Color Consultant: Alex Quigora; Set Decorations: James M. Walters; Film Editors: Lee Huntington, Danny Landres; Unit Manager: Henry Kline; Costumes by: Vincent Dee; Makeup: Jack Barron, Bud Westmore; Hair Stylist: Larry Germain; Music Supervision: Stanley Wilson; Color by: Technicolor; Titles & Optical Effects: Universal Title; Produced by: Revue Productions, Inc., Universal Television; In Association With: NBC-TV; Exclusive Distributor: MCA Television Limited.

WAGON TRAIN

NBC Television Network, September 18, 1957-September 12, 1962; ABC Television Network, September 19, 1962-September 5, 1965; 252 episodes in black & white on film; 60 minutes and 32 episodes in black & white on film; 90 minutes (1963-64 season).

A Western about the experiences of wagonmasters Seth Adams and Chris Hale, their aides and the emigrants with their wagon train as they trekked Westward during the pioneer days. Syndicated as Major Adams and Major Adams, Trailmaster.

Cast: Major Seth Adams (Ward Bond), Flint McCullough (Robert Horton), Bill Hawks (Terry Wilson), Charlie Wooster (Frank McGrath), Chris Hale (John McIntire), Duke Shannon (Scott Miller), Cooper Smith (Robert Fuller), Barnaby West (Michael Burns).

Credits: Produced by: Howard Christie; Directors: John Ford, Virgil W. Vogel, others; Writers: Tony Paulson, Norman Jolley, others; Directors of Photography: Benjamin H. Kline, Walter Strenge; Music Score: Hans Salter, Melvyn Lenard, Richard Sendry; Theme Music by: Jerome Moross; Art Directors: Howard E. Johnson, Martin Obzina; Editorial Supervisor: David J. O'Connell; Film Editors: Marsten Fay, Gene Palmer; Set Decorator: Ralph

Sylos; Music Supervision: Stanley Wilson; Sound: David H. Moriarty; Costume Supervisor: Vincent Dee; Makeup: Jack Barron; Hair Stylist: Florence Bush; Produced by: Revue Productions, Inc., Universal Television; Exclusive Distributor: MCA Television Limited.

WAYNE AND SHUSTER TAKE AN AFFECTIONATE LOOK AT...

CBS Television Network, June 17, 1966-July 29, 1966; 13 episodes in black & white on film; 60 minutes.

A documentary about the greatest comedians of the 20th century. Among those featured in film clips were Laurel and Hardy, George Burns, the Marx Brothers, W. C. Fields and Bob Hope.

Cast: Hosts, Johnny Wayne, Frank Shuster.

Credits: Produced by: CBS-Toronto; In Association with: MCA Television Limited; Exclusive Distributor: MCA Television Limited.

WESTINGHOUSE PLAYHOUSE STARRING NANETTE FABRAY AND WENDELL COREY

NBC Television Network, January 6, 1961-July 7, 1961; 13 episodes in black & white on film; 30 minutes. Sponsor and Agency: Westinghouse Electric Corporation through McCann-Erickson, Inc.

A situation comedy about Nan and Dan McGovern, based on events in the real family life of series star Nanette Fabray and her husband, Ranald MacDougall, who wrote the initial episode.

Cast: Nan McGovern (Nanette Fabray), Dan McGovern (Wendell Corey), Buddy (Bobby Diamond), Mrs. Harper (Doris Kemper), Nancy (Jacklyn O'Donnell).

Credits: Produced by: Larry Berns; Directors: Herschel Daugherty, Jerry Hopper; Writers: Ranald MacDougall, others; Director of Photography: Ray Rennahan; Music by: Axel Stordahl; Art Director: John Meehan; Editorial Supervisor: David J. O'Connell; Film Editor: Edward Haire, A. C. E.; Musical Supervision: Stanley Wilson; Sound: William Lynch; Set Decorator: Oliver Emert; Costume Supervisor: Vincent Dee; Makeup: Jack Barron; Hair Stylist: Florence Bush; Produced by: Beejay Productions; Filmed by: Revue Productions, Inc.; Exclusive Distributor: MCA Television Limited.

WHAT REALLY HAPPENED TO THE CLASS OF '65?

NBC Television Network, December 8, 1977-July 27, 1978; 13 episodes in color on film; 60 minutes.

A dramatic anthology about the members of the class of '65 at Bret Harte High School. The series focused on America in the 1960s and offered some insights into a turbulent era and its effect on the lives, aspirations, careers and dreams of its youth.

Cast: Sam Ashley (Tony Bill).

Credits: Executive Producer: Richard Irving; Producers: Richard Irving, Jim Miller, Jack Laird, Rick Husky, George Eckstein; Based on the Book by: Michael Medved, David Wallechinsky; Color by: Technicolor; Titles & Optical Effects: Universal Title; Produced by: Universal Television; Exclusive Distributor: MCA Television Limited.

WHEELS (NBC'S BEST SELLERS)

NBC Television Network, May 7, 1978-May 15, 1978; 5 episodes in color on film; 120 minutes (total: 10 hours).

The story of Adam Trenton, the director of project development for Detroit's National Motors in the late 1960s.

Cast: Adam Trenton (Rock Hudson), Erica Trenton (Lee Remick), Wingate (Fred Williamson), Peter Flodenhale (John Beck), Baxter (Ralph Bellamy), Hub Hewitson (Tim O'Connor), Rusty (Gerald S. O'Loughlin), Ursula (Jessica Walter), Smokey (Tony Franciosa), Teresa (Adele Mara), Greg (Howard McGillin), Jody (Lisa Eilbacher), Kirk (James Carroll Jordan), Beecham (James Ray), Brett (Stewart Moss), Rollie Knight (Harold Sylvester), Barbara Lipton (Blair Brown), Merv Rucks (John Durren), Val (Debi Richter), Nessel (Bob Hastings), Parkland (John Crawford), Newkirk (Al White), Emerson Vale (Anthony Costello), Caroline Horton (Marj Dusay), Al Holleb (Ray Singer), Dr. Patterson (David Spielberg), Sir Phillip (James Booth).

Credits: Executive Producer: Roy Huggins; Produced by: Robert F. O'Neill; Directed by: Jerry London; Written by: Millard Lampell, Robert Hamilton, Hank Searls, Nancy Lynn Schwartz; Based on the Novel by: Arthur Hailey; Associate Producer: Gary B. Winter; Director of Photography: Jacques R. Marquette; Music by: Morton Stevens; Art Director: William H. Tuntke; Film Editors: Edwin F. England, James T. Heckart, Gene Ranney, Larry Lester, Jamie Caylor; Color by: Technicolor; Titles & Optical Effects: Universal Title; Produced by: Universal Television; Exclusive Distributor: MCA Television Limited.

WHEN THE WHISTLE BLOWS

ABC Television Network, March 14, 1980-April 25, 1980; 6 episodes in color on film; 60 minutes.

A comedy-drama about a gang of hard-living construction workers who enjoyed their afterhours as much as "hanging iron" during the day. When the whistle blew, it was quitting time.

Cast: Norm (Dolph Sweet), Buzz (Doug Barr), Randy (Philip Brown), Hunk (Tim Rossovich), Lucy (Susan Buckner), Darlene (Sue Anne Langdon), Hanrahan (Gary Allen), Bulldog (Noble Willingham).

Credits: Executive Producer: Leonard Goldberg; Color by: Techcolor; Titles & Optical Effects: Universal Title; Produced by: Daydreams Productions; In Association with: Universal Television; Exclusive Distributor: MCA Television Limited.

WHISPERING SMITH

NBC Television Network, May 15, 1961-September 18, 1961; 25 episodes in black & white on film; 30 minutes.

A Western police-mystery program set in Denver, Colorado, about a detective who, in the 1870s, became the first in the West to adopt methods of tracing and apprehending outlaws standard in modern criminology. Based on the 1948 film Whispering Smith.

Cast: Det. Tom "Whispering" Smith (Audie Murphy), Det. George Romack (Guy Mitchell), Chief John Richards (Sam Buffington).

Credits: Executive Producer: Richard Lewis; Producers: Herbert Coleman, Willard Willingham; Director of Photography: Bud Thackery; Music by: Richard Shores, Leo Shuken; Editorial Supervisor: Richard G. Wray; Story Consultant: Borden Chase; Musical Supervision: Stanley Wilson; Costume Supervisor: Vincent Dee; Makeup: Jack Barron; Hair Stylist: Florence Bush; Produced by: The Whispering Smith Company, Revue Productions, Inc.; Exclusive Distributor: MCA Television Limited.

THE WIDE COUNTRY

NBC Television Network, September 20, 1962-September 12, 1963; 28 episodes in black & white on film; 60 minutes.

A contemporary Western about Mitch Guthrie, rodeo rider par excellence, and his younger brother Andy, who was smitten with "rodeo fever" and was Mitch's number one fan. Together they criss-crossed the West--and the entire country--in their search for money and glory on the rodeo circuit.

Cast: Mitch Guthrie (Earl Holliman), Andy Guthrie (Andrew Prine).

Credits: Executive Producer: Ralph Edwards; Produced by: Frank Telford; Writers: Harold Swanton, others; Musical Supervision: Stanley Wilson; Produced by: Gemini Productions, Inc., Revue Productions, Inc.; Exclusive Distributor: MCA Television Limited.

WOMEN IN WHITE

NBC Television Network, February 8, 1979-February 22, 1979; 3 episodes in color on film; 120 minutes and 60 minutes (total: 4 hours).

A medical drama about the patients and staff of a Florida Hospital and their personal crises.

Cast: Dr. Jill Bates (Kathryn Harrold), Dr. Rebecca Dalton (Susan Flannery), Dr. Mike Rayburn (David Ackroyd), Cathy Payson (Patty Duke Astin), Dr. Evanhauer (Howard McGillin), Dr. Karen Fletcher (Laraine Stephens), Anthony Broadhurst (Robert Culp), Lisa Gordon (Sheree North), Kevin Haggarty (Scott Brady), Deena Tyndall (Dena Crowder), Dr. Ken Dalton (Stuart Whitman), Virginia Tyndall (Tracy Reed).

Credits: Executive Producer: David Victor; Based on the Novel by: Frank G. Slaughter; Color by: Technicolor; Titles & Optical Effects: Universal Title; Produced by: Groverton Productions, Ltd.; In Association with: Universal Television And NBC-TV; Exclusive Distributor: MCA Television Limited.

Alfred Hitchcock in THE ALFRED HITCHCOCK HOUR.

Alfred Hitchcock in ALFRED HITCHCOCK PRESENTS.

Lauren Bacall in APPLAUSE.

The cast of BAA BAA BLACK SHEEP. Back row: Robert Ginty and W. K. Stratton. Front row: Jeff MacKay, Robert Conrad, James Whitmore, Jr., Dirk Blocker, and John Larroquette.

George Peppard and Christine Belford in BANACEK.

Robert Blake in BARETTA.

The cast of THE BOLD ONES assembled on the lot of Universal Studios. Back row: Joseph Campanella, James Farentino, and David Hartman; middle row: John Saxon, Hari Rhodes, and E. G. Marshall; front row: Leslie Nielsen and Burl Ives.

Anthony George in CHECKMATE.

Peter Falk in COLUMBO.

Bradford Dillman and Peter Graves in COURT MARTIAL.

Jack Webb and Harry Morgan in DRAGNET 1967-1970.

Randolph Mantooth in EMERGENCY!

Martin Sheen in THE EXECUTION OF PRIVATE SLOVIK.

Elizabeth Cheshire, Julie Harris, Lance Kerwin, and Glenn Ford in THE FAMILY HOLVAK.

Jan-Michael Vincent and Lana Turner in HAROLD ROBBINS' "THE SURVIVORS."

Parker Stevenson, Lisa Eilbacher, and Shaun Cassidy in THE HARDY BOYS MYSTERIES.

Bill Bixby and Lou Ferrigno in THE INCREDIBLE HULK.

Guest star Desi Arnaz and Raymond Burr in IRONSIDE.

Fred Astaire and Robert Wagner in IT TAKES A THIEF.

Eddie "Rochester" Anderson and Jack Benny in THE JACK BENNY SHOW.

THE TELEFEATURES

Note

This book does not cover the following types of films: (a) productions like The Killers which were made for television but initially released to theatres (omitted because they were not originally broadcast on television); (b) movies like Code Name: Heraclitus and Nightmare in Chicago which were edited from two-part episodes of the TV programs Bob Hope Presents, the Chrysler Theatre, and Kraft Suspense Theatre respectively (omitted because they were originally produced as series episodes, not telefeatures); and (c) telefeatures like The Night Stalker (omitted because, although they were pilots for Universal Television series, they were produced by other studios).

See APPENDIX I for a list of theatrical films edited from series episodes and APPENDIX II for a list of theatrical films based on Universal Television series.

THE ADVENTURES OF NICK CARTER
(THE ABC SUNDAY NIGHT MOVIE)

ABC Television Network, February 20, 1972; 90 minutes in color on film.

A drama about Nick Carter, the famous, brash, and brawling private detective of the early 1900s in New York City who discovered that the death of a fellow private eye was tied to the mysterious disappearance of a wealthy playboy's wife. The pilot for an unsold series.

Cast: Nick Carter (Robert Conrad), Bess Tucker (Shelley Winters), Otis Duncan (Broderick Crawford), Capt. Dan Keller (Neville Brand), Neal Duncan (Pernell Roberts), Hallelujah Harry (Pat O'Brien), Lloyd Deems (Sean Garrison), Joyce Jordan (Laraine Stephens), Freddy Duncan (Dean Stockwell), Roxy O'Rourke (Brooke Bundy), Dr. Zimmerman (Sorrell Booke), Archer (Joseph R. Maross), Maxie (Ned Glass), O'Hara (Paul Mantee), Plush Horse Singer (Jaye P. Morgan), Flo (Arlene Martel), Sam Bates (Byron Morrow).

Credits: Executive Producer: Richard Irving; Produced by: Stanley Kallis; Directed by: Paul Krasny; Written by: Ken Pettus; Director of Photography: Alric Edens; Music by: John Andrew Tartaglia;

116 / Telefeatures

Art Director: Henry Bumstead; Set Decorations: James Payne; Film Editor: Robert F. Shugrue; Costumes by: Burton Miller; Produced by: Universal Television; Exclusive Distributor: MCA Television Limited.

ALIAS SMITH AND JONES
(ABC MOVIE OF THE WEEK)

ABC Television Network, January 5, 1971; 90 minutes in color on film.

A comedy-western about two notorious outlaws who suddenly decided to go straight. The pilot for the series Alias Smith and Jones (which see).

Cast: Hannibal Hayes, alias Joshua Smith (Peter Deuel), Jed "Kid" Curry, alias Thaddeus Jones (Ben Murphy), Miss Porter (Susan Saint James), Lom Trevors (James Drury), Wheat (Earl Holliman), Harker (Forrest Tucker), Miss Birdie (Jeanette Nolan), Kyle (Dennis Fimple), Lobo (Bill McKinney).

Credits: Executive Producer: Frank Price; Produced by: Glen A. Larson; Directed by: Gene Levitt; Written by: Glen A. Larson, Matthew Howard; Director of Photography: John M. Stephens; Music by: Billy Goldenberg; Film Editor: Bob Cagey; Art Director: George Webb; Produced by: Universal Television; Exclusive Distributor: MCA Television Limited.

ALL MY DARLING DAUGHTERS
(ABC WEDNESDAY MOVIE OF THE WEEK)

ABC Television Network, November 22, 1972; 90 minutes in color on film.

A comedy-drama about Charles Raleigh, a widower-father and respected judge, who was confronted with his most perplexing decision when all four of his daughters decided to get married on the same day. Filmed on location in Malibu and Beverly Hills, California. Followed by the sequel My Darling Daughters' Anniversary (which see).

Cast: Charles Raleigh (Robert Young), The Grandfather (Raymond Massey), The Wedding Counselor (Eve Arden), Susan Raleigh (Darleen Carr), Robin Raleigh (Judy Strangis), Jennifer Raleigh (Sharon Gless), Charlotte Raleigh (Fawne Harriman), Andy O'Brien (Darrell Larson), Jerry Grene (Jerry Fogel), Bradley Coombs (Colby Chester), Biff Brynner (Michael Richardson), Anthony Stephanelli (Bruce Kirby, Jr.), Prosecuting Attorney (John Lupton), Defense Attorney (Richard Roat).

Credits: Executive Producer: David Victor; Produced by: David J. O'Connell; Directed by: David Lowell Rich; Written by: John

Gay; Based on a Story by: Robert Presnell, Jr., Stan Dreben; Director of Photography: Walter Strenge; Music by: Billy Goldenberg; Art Director: Russell C. Forrest; Set Decorations: George Hopkins; Film Editor: Richard G. Wray; Costumes by: Charles Waldo; Produced by: Groverton Productions, Ltd.; In Association with: Universal Television; Exclusive Distributor: MCA Television Limited.

ALOHA MEANS GOODBYE
(CBS FRIDAY NIGHT AT THE MOVIES)

CBS Television Network, October 11, 1974; 120 minutes in color on film.

A drama about Sara Moore, teacher of the blind, who left Colorado for Hawaii when she contracted a rare blood disease which could be cured on the islands by a brilliant young surgeon, Dr. Lawrence Maddux. The surgeon's motive for accepting Moore for treatment: he needed a heart-transplant donor for the son of his wealthy employer.

Cast: Sara Moore (Sally Struthers), Lawrence Maddux (James Franciscus), Pamela Crane (Joanna Miles), David Kalani (Henry Darrow), Torger Nilsson (Larry Gates), Dr. Frank Franklin (Russell Johnson), Christian Nilsson (Colin Losby), Mrs. Kalani (Pat Li), Connie (Tracy Reed).

Credits: Executive Producer: David Lowell Rich; Produced by: Sam Strangis; Directed by: David Lowell Rich; Written by: Dean Riesner, Joseph Stefano; Based on the Novel by: Naomi A. Hintze; Director of Photography: J. J. Jones; Music by: Charles Fox; Art Director: William Campbell; Film Editor: Richard M. Sprague; Color by: Technicolor; Titles & Optical Effects: Universal Title; Produced by: Universal Television; Exclusive Distributor: MCA Television Limited.

THE ALPHA CAPER
(ABC SUSPENSE MOVIE)

ABC Television Network, October 6, 1973; 90 minutes in color on film.

A drama about a scheme to rob six armored cars of $30,000,000 in gold.

Cast: Mark Forbes (Henry Fonda), Mitch (Leonard Nimoy), Scat (James McEachin), Tudor (Larry Hagman), Lee Saunders (John Marley), Hilda (Elena Verdugo), Harry Balsam (Noah Beery, Jr.), Harlan Moss (Tom Troupe), Minister (Woodrow Parfrey), Policeman (Vic Tayback), Police Captain (Kenneth Tobey), John Woodbury (Paul Kent), Henry Kellner (James B. Sikking), Tow Truck Driver (Paul Sorensen), Sergeant (Wally Taylor).

118 / Telefeatures

Credits: Executive Producer: Harve Bennett; Produced by: Aubrey Schenck; Directed by: Robert Michael Lewis; Written by: Elroy Schwartz; Associate Producer: Arnold Turner; Director of Photography: Enzo A. Martinelli; Music by: Oliver Nelson; Art Director: John J. Lloyd; Film Editors: Les Green, Albert J. Zuniga; Color by: Technicolor; Titles & Optical Effects: Universal Title; Produced by: Silverton Productions, Inc.; In Association with: Universal Television; Exclusive Distributor: MCA Television Limited.

AMATEUR NIGHT AT THE DIXIE BAR AND GRILL

ABC Television Network, January 8, 1979; 120 minutes in color on film.

A drama about the behind-the-scenes activities during a talent contest at the Dixie Bar and Grill.

Cast: Mac (Victor French), Sharee (Candy Clark), Fanny (Louise Latham), Cowboy (Don Johnson), Snuffy McCann (Jamie Farr), Lettie Norman (Sheree North), Sharon Singleton (Tanya Tucker), Marvin Laurie (Jeff Altman), Vera Elvira (Pat Ast), Moss Tillis (Ed Begley, Jr.), Roy (Gary Bisig), Marcy (Joan Goodfellow), Milt Cavanaugh (Henry Gibson), Harry (Rick Hurst), Duke (Howard Itzkowitz), with: Roz Kelly, Melinda Naud, Kyle Richards, Timothy Scott, Dennis Quaid.

Credits: Executive Producer: Rob Cohen; Produced by: Lauren Shuler; Directed by: Joel Schumacher; Written by: Joel Schumacher; Director of Photography: Ric Waite; Music by: Bradford Craig; Art Directors: Ray Brandt, Henry Berman; Film Editor: Anthony Redmond; Color by: Technicolor; Titles & Optical Effects: Universal Title; Produced by: Motown Corporation; In Association with: Universal Television; Exclusive Distributor: MCA Television Limited.

AMELIA EARHART
(WORLD PREMIERE)

NBC Television Network, October 25, 1976; 3 hours in color on film.

A drama about "the first lady of the skies," from her first flight in 1921 to her mysterious disappearance in 1937.

Cast: Amelia Earhart (Susan Clark), George Putnam (John Forsythe), Paul Mantz (Stephen Macht), Snooky (Susan Oliver), Pidge (Catherine Burns), Amy (Jane Wyatt), Sid Isaacs (Ed Barth), Mr. Earhart (Charles Aidman), Radio Operator (David Huffman), Bill Stultz (Jack Colvin), Fred Noonan (Bill Vint), Alan Bradford (Kip Niven), Billy Putnam (Lance Kerwin), Broadcaster (Lowell Thomas), Young Amelia (Kim Diamond), Miss Perkins (Florida Froebus), Dr. Paterson (John Archer).

Credits: Produced by: George Eckstein; Directed by: George Schaefer; Written by: Carol Sobieski; Director of Photography: Ted Voigtlander; Music by: David Shire; Art Director: William H. Tuntke; Set Decorations: Richard Freedman; Film Editor: Jim Benson; Sound: Jim Alexander; Aerial Sequences Staged by: Frank Tallman; Color by: Technicolor; Titles & Optical Effects: Universal Title; Produced by: Universal Television; In Association with: NBC-TV; Exclusive Distributor: MCA Television Limited.

ANY SECOND NOW
(WORLD PREMIERE/NBC TUESDAY NIGHT AT THE MOVIES)

NBC Television Network, February 11, 1969; 120 minutes in color on film.

A suspense drama about Paul Dennison, a philandering photographer whose wealthy wife was divorcing him. Dennison plotted her murder only to have his first attempt foiled, so a second attempt became imperative.

Cast: Paul Dennison (Stewart Granger), Nancy Dennison (Lois Nettleton), Dr. Raul Valdez (Joseph Campanella), Jane Peterson (Dana Wynter), Señora Vorhis (Katy Jurado), Howard Lenihan (Tom Tully), Mrs. Hoyt (Marion Ross), American Girl (Eileen Wesson).

Credits: Executive Producer: Roy Huggins; Produced and Directed by: Gene Levitt; Written by: Gene Levitt; Story by: Gene Levitt, Robert Mitchell, Harold Jack Bloom; Director of Photography: Jack Marta; Music by: Leonard Rosenman; Art Director: Howard E. Johnson; Set Decorations: John McCarthy, James M. Walters, Sr.; Film Editor: David Eric Rawlins; Costumes by: Grady Hunt; Make-up: Bud Westmore; Hair Stylist: Larry Germain; Color by: Technicolor; Titles & Optical Effects: Universal Title; Produced by: Universal Television; In Association with: NBC-TV; Exclusive Distributor: MCA Television Limited.

THE AQUARIANS
(WORLD PREMIERE/NBC SATURDAY NIGHT AT THE MOVIES)

NBC Television Network, October 24, 1970; 120 minutes in color on film.

A drama about a team of scientists that manned a nuclear-powered deep sea laboratory and their investigation of a mysterious pollution of the ocean that threatened to kill off marine life.

Cast: Luis Delgado (Ricardo Montalban), Alfred Vreeland (José Ferrer), Official (Leslie Nielsen), Barbara Brand (Kate Woodville), Bob Exeter (Lawrence Casey), Jerry Hollis (Tom Simcox), Ledring (Chris Robinson), Ehrlich (Curt Lowens), Jean Hollis (Elisa Ingram), Norma (Joan Murphy), Bogan (Austin Stoker), Aganda Official (Napoleon Reed), Bellboy (Henry Mortimer), 1st Technician (Phil Philbin), Sonar Man (Dan Chandler), Aide (Ted Swanson), Jim Morgan (William Evenson), 2nd Technician (Ken Harris), 3rd Technician (Roger Phillips), 1st Reporter (Myron Natwick), 2nd Reporter (Harlan Warde).

Credits: Produced by: Ivan Tors, Charles F. Engel; Directed by: Don McDougall; Written by: Leslie Stevens, Winston Miller; Story by: Ivan Tors, Alan Caillou; Director of Photography: Clifford Poland; Music by: Lalo Schifrin; Art Director: Gene Harris; Film Editor: Erwin Dumbrille; Underwater Sequences Directed by: Ricou Browning; Underwater Sequences Photographed by: Jordan Klein; Color by: Technicolor; Titles & Optical Effects: Universal Title; Produced by: Ivan Tors Productions; In Association with: Universal Television; Exclusive Distributor: MCA Television Limited.

THE ART OF CRIME
(WORLD PREMIERE/NBC WEDNESDAY NIGHT AT THE MOVIES)

NBC Television Network, December 3, 1975; 90 minutes in color on film.

A drama about murder in New York City's Gypsy subculture. Filmed on location in Manhattan, Staten Island, Long Island. The pilot for an unsold series called Roman Grey.

Cast: Roman Grey (Ron Leibman), Beckwith Sloan (José Ferrer), Parker Sharon (David Hedison), Dany (Jill Clayburgh), Sgt. Harry Isadore (Eugene Roche), Hillary Sloan (Diane Kagan), Nanoosh Pulneshti (Cliff Osmond), Madame Vera (Dimitra Arliss), Kore (Mike Kellin), Dodo (Louis Guss), Gypsy Queen (Tally Brown).

Credits: Executive Producer: Richard Irving; Produced by: Jules Irving; Directed by: Richard Irving; Written by: Martin Smith, Bill Davidson; Based on the Novel "Gypsy in Amber" by: Martin Smith; Directors of Photography: Jack Priestley, Bernie Abrahmson; Music by: Gil Melle; Art Directors: William Campbell, May Callas; Film Editor: Frederic Baratta; Color by: Technicolor; Titles & Optical Effects: Universal Title; Produced by: Universal Television; In Association with: NBC-TV; Exclusive Distributor: MCA Television Limited.

THE ASTRONAUT
(ABC MOVIE OF THE WEEKEND)

ABC Television Network, January 8, 1972; 90 minutes in color on film.

A drama about a young woman who fell in love with her astronaut-husband all over again when he returned from America's first mission to Mars, only to learn that he was not really her husband.

The Astronaut / 121

Cast: Kurt Anderson (Jackie Cooper), Col. Brice Randolph/Eddie Reese (Monte Markham), John Phillips (Robert Lansing), Gail Randolph (Susan Clark), Dr. Wylie (Richard Anderson), Don Masters (John Lupton), Tom Everett (Walter Brooke), Astronaut Higgins (James Sikking), Carl Samuels (Paul Kent), Toni Scott (Lorette Leversee).

Credits: Produced by: Harve Bennett; Directed by: Robert Michael Lewis; Written by: Gerald DiPego, Charles R. Kuenstle, Robert S. Biheller; Story by: Charles R. Kuenstle, Robert S. Biheller; Director of Photography: Alric Edens; Art Director: George Webb; Set Decorator: Joseph Reith; Film Editors: Les Green, John Kaufman, Jr.; Color by: Technicolor; Titles & Optical Effects: Universal Title; Produced by: Universal Television; Exclusive Distributor: MCA Television Limited.

BANACEK
(WORLD PREMIERE)

NBC Television Network, March 20, 1972; 120 minutes in color on film.

A drama about insurance investigator Thomas Banacek and his attempts to locate an armored truck which seemingly vanished into thin air in Texas with $1.6 million in gold. The pilot for the series Banacek (which see).

Cast: Thomas Banacek (George Peppard), Carlie Kirkland (Christine Belford), Sheriff Jessup (Don Dubbins), Felix Mulholland (Murray Matheson), Earl (Russell Wiggins), McKinney (Charles Knox Robinson), Jay (Ralph Manza), Cavanaugh (George Murdock), Geoff Holden (Ed Nelson), Mackey (Bill Vint), Indian Joe (Vic Mohica).

Credits: Produced by: George Eckstein; Directed by: Jack Smight; Written by: Anthony Wilson; Director of Photography: Sam Leavitt; Music by: Billy Goldenberg; Art Director: George Webb; Film Editor: Robert Watts; Costumes by: Grady Hunt; Color by: Technicolor; Titles & Optical Effects: Universal Title; Produced by: Universal Television; In Association with: NBC-TV; Exclusive Distributor: MCA Television Limited.

BEG, BORROW ... OR STEAL
(ABC TUESDAY MOVIE OF THE WEEK)

ABC Television Network, March 20, 1973; 90 minutes in color on film.

A drama about three handicapped men who tested their courage and abilities by plotting and executing a daring heist.

Cast: Victor Cummings (Mike Connors), Cliff Norris (Michael Cole),

Lester Yates (Kent McCord), Alex Langley (Russell Johnson), Hal Cooper (Henry Beckman), Kevin Turner (Joel Fabiani), Walter Beal (Logan Ramsey), Ray Buren (Ron Glass).

Credits: Produced by: Stanley Kallis; Directed by: David Lowell Rich; Written by: Paul Playdon; Director of Photography: Harkness Smith; Music by: Richard Markowitz; Art Director: George Webb; Film Editor: Robert F. Shugrue; Technical Advisor: Gene Gerwig; Color by: Technicolor; Titles & Optical Effects: Universal Title; Produced by: Universal Television; Exclusive Distributor: MCA Television Limited.

BENNY AND BARNEY: LAS VEGAS UNDERCOVER
(NBC MOVIE OF THE WEEK)

NBC Television Network, January 19, 1977; 90 minutes in color on film.

A comedy-drama about two policemen who moonlighted as nightclub singers. They were enlisted to solve the kidnapping of a big-name entertainer.

Cast: Benny Kowalski (Terry Kiser), Barney Tuscom (Timothy Thomerson), Davis (Hugh O'Brian), Margie (Jane Seymour), Lt. Callan (Jack Colvin), Rosen (Jack Cassidy), Manager (Rodney Dangerfield), Jake (Ted Cassidy), Higgie (Marty Allen), Will Dawson (Dick Gautier), Drunk (George Gobel), Joey Gallion (Pat Harrington).

Credits: Produced by: Glen A. Larson; Directed by: Ron Satlof; Written by: Glen A. Larson; Director of Photography: Ronald W. Browne; Music by: Stu Phillips; Art Director: Alexander A. Mayer; Film Editor: Ronald J. Fagan; Color by: Technicolor; Titles & Optical Effects: Universal Title; Produced by: Glen A. Larson Productions; In Association with: Universal Television; Exclusive Distributor: MCA Television Limited.

BERLIN AFFAIR

NBC Television Network, November 2, 1970; 120 minutes in color on film.

A drama about a private spy assigned to hunt down his close friend and former co-worker. Filmed on location in Berlin.

Cast: Killian (Darren McGavin), Mallicent (Fritz Weaver), Strand (Brian Kelly), Languin (Claude Dauphin), Wendi (Pascale Petit), Albert (Christian Roberts), Galt (Derren Nesbitt), Andrea (Kathie Browne), Juliet (Marian Collier), Klaus (Reinhard Kolldehoff), Mildred (Heidren Hankammer), Copy Girl (Gitta Schubert), Vendor (Manfred Meurer), Blonde (Isabelle Ervens).

Credits: Producers: E. Jack Neuman, Paul Donnelly; Directed by: David Lowell Rich; Written by: Richard Alan Simmons; Story by: Elliot West; Director of Photography: Michael Marszalek; Music by: Francis Lai; Art Director: Hans Jurgen Kiebach; Film Editor: Edward M. Abroms; Color by: Technicolor; Titles & Optical Effects: Universal Title; Produced by: Universal Television; In Association with: NBC-TV; Exclusive Distributor: MCA Television Limited.

THE BIG RIPOFF
(WORLD PREMIERE/NBC TUESDAY NIGHT AT THE MOVIES)

NBC Television Network, March 11, 1975; 90 minutes in color on film.

A drama about an in-debt gambler who developed a scheme to make enough money to pay off his mobster creditors. The pilot for the series McCoy (which see).

Cast: McCoy (Tony Curtis), Brenda (Brenda Vaccaro), Darnell (Larry Hagman), Bishop (John Dehner), Grace Bishop (Lynn Borden), Kelso (Morgan Woodward), Silky (Roscoe Lee Browne), Lt. Claypool (Jay Varela), Ship Captain (Vito Scotti), Lucy Meredith (Priscilla Pointer), Notch (Fuddle Bagley), Peabody (Woodrow Parfrey), Art (Nate Esformes), Phil (Len Lesser), Security Chief (Ed Peck), Hersh (Alan Fudge), with: Robert Symonds, Charles Macaulay, Lucille Meredith, Jack Krupnick, Linda Gray, Jefferson Kibbee, Barry Cahill, Robert Ball, John Lawrence Shaw, Owen Hithe Pace, Phil Diskin, Howard Storm, Manuel DePina, Jerry Mann, Lincoln Evans, Mario Gallo, William Benedict, Don Fenwick, Nancy Belle Fuller, Larry Burrell, James V. Christy, Wayne Bartlett, Tyree Glenn, Jr., Tobar Mayo, Tom McFadden, Brian O'Mullin, Carol Ann Susi, John Francis, Robert Gibbons, Ben Gage.

Credits: Producers: Roland Kibbee, Dean Hargrove; Directed by: Dean Hargrove; Written by: Dean Hargrove, Roland Kibbee; Director of Photography: Bill Butler; Music by: Dick De Benedictis; Art Director: Loyd S. Papez; Film Editor: Robert L. Kimble; Sound: Harold Lewis; Color by: Technicolor; Titles & Optical Effects: Universal Title; Produced by: Universal Television; In Association with: NBC-TV; Exclusive Distributor: MCA Television Limited.

THE BIRDMEN
(ABC MOVIE OF THE WEEKEND)

ABC Television Network, September 18, 1971; 90 minutes in color on film. Major Sponsors and Agencies: The Gillette Company through Moorgate Advertising; Warner-Lambert Pharmaceutical Company through J. Walter Thompson Company.

A World War II adventure, based on fact, about a daring escape attempt by Allied POWs held by the Germans in an impregnable medi-

124 / Telefeatures

eval castle. The men planned to build a glider and soar from the castle below the Alps to freedom in Switzerland, some 10 miles away. This was the premiere installment of The ABC Movie of the Weekend.

Cast: Maj. Harry Cook (Doug McClure), Col. Morgan Crawford (Chuck Connors), Schiller (Richard Basehart), Halden Brevik (Rene Auberjonois), Tanker (Max Baer, Jr.), Focus Flaherty (Don Knight), Fitz (Tom Skerritt), Sparrow (Greg Mullavey), Davies (Paul Koslo), Donnely (Barry Brown).

Credits: Produced by: Harve Bennett; Directed by: Philip Leacock; Written by: David Kidd; Director of Photography: Jack Marta; Music by: David Rose; Production Supervisor: Paul Freeman; Art Director: Henry Bumstead; Film Editor: Robert F. Shugrue; Color by: Technicolor; Titles & Optical Effects: Universal Title; Produced by: Universal Television; Exclusive Distributor: MCA Television Limited.

BJ AND THE BEAR
(WORLD PREMIERE)

NBC Television Network, October 4, 1978; 120 minutes in color on film.

A comedy-drama about independent trucker BJ McKay who took on unusual cargo: 11 women fleeing white slavery. The pilot for the series BJ and the Bear (which see).

Cast: BJ McKay (Greg Evigan), Stilts (Penny Peyser), Sheriff Lobo (Claude Akins), Perkins (Mills Watson), Store Proprietor (Woodrow Parfrey), Marcia (Kristine DeBell), Willie (Antoinette Stella), Col. Whitmore (Julius Harris), Julie (Elena Eileen Frank).

Credits: Executive Producer: Glen A. Larson; Producers: Christopher Crowe, John Peyser; Directed by: Bruce Bilson; Written by: Glen A. Larson, Christopher Crowe; Director of Photography: Sy Hoffberg; Aerial Photography: Frank Holgate; Music by: Glen A. Larson; Art Director: Vince Cresciman; Film Editor: Michael S. Murphy; Color by: Technicolor; Titles & Optical Effects: Universal Title; Produced in Association with: Glen A. Larson Productions And Universal Television; Exclusive Distributor: MCA Television Limited.

THE BOOK OF MURDER
(ABC WIDE WORLD OF ENTERTAINMENT/WIDE WORLD MYSTERY)

ABC Television Network, March 19, 1974; 90 minutes in color on tape.

A mystery about three ex-wives suspected of murdering their former husband.

Cast: Henry (Fritz Weaver), Mary (Pamela Bellwood), Anne (Louise Latham), Catherine (Nan Martin), with: Joyce Van Patten, Barry Primus.

Credits: Produced by: Barbara Schultz; Directed by: Lloyd Richards; Written by: Ron Owen; Produced by: Universal Television; Exclusive Distributor: MCA Television Limited.

THE BORGIA STICK
(WORLD PREMIERE/NBC SATURDAY NIGHT AT THE MOVIES)

NBC Television Network, February 25, 1967; 120 minutes in color on film.

A drama about big crime's scheme to invade big business. Filmed on location in New York City.

Cast: Tom Harrison (Don Murray), Eve Harrison (Inger Stevens), Hal Carter (Barry Nelson), Anderson (Sorrell Booke) Davenport (Marc Donnelly), Ruth (Kathleen Maguire), Craigmeyer (Dana Elcar), Dr. Helm (Barnard Hughes), Wilma (Sudi Bond), Rigley (Frederick Rolf), Willoughby (Hugh Franklin), Man from Toledo (Ralph Waite), Louise (Valeria Allen).

Credits: Produced by: Richard Lewis; Directed by: David Lowell Rich; Written by: A. J. Russell; Director of Photography: Morris Hartzband, A. S. C.; Music by: Kenyon Hopkins; Art Director: Robert Gundlach; Set Decorations: Robert Drumheller; Film Editor: Sidney Katz; Sound: Newton Avrutis; Costumes by: Mary Merrill; Makeup: Robert Phillipee; Hair Stylist: Philip Nasox; Produced by: Universal Television; Exclusive Distributor: MCA Television Limited.

BRAVE NEW WORLD
(NBC FRIDAY NIGHT AT THE MOVIES)

NBC Television Network, March 7, 1980; 3 hours in color on film.

A drama about a frightening futuristic society where people are mass-produced, sex is compulsory and love is against the law. The focus is on three people: Thomas Grahmbell, director of the hatcheries; Linda Lysenko, his girlfriend and a social outcast (a mother); and John Savage, a man who refused to adapt to the world of automatons.

Cast: John Savage (Kristoffer Tabori), Bernard Marx (Bud Cort), Lenina Disney (Marcia Strassman), Mustapha Mond (Ron O'Neal), Helmholtz Watson (Dick Anthony Williams), Thomas Grahmbell (Keir Dullea), Linda Lysenko (Julie Cobb), Maoina Krupps (Trish O'Neil), Stalina Shell (Valerie Curtin).

Credits: Directed by: Burt Brinckerhoff; Written by: Robert E. Thompson; Based on the Novel by: Aldous Huxley; Color by: Technicolor; Titles & Optical Effects: Universal Title; Produced by: Universal Television; Exclusive Distributor: MCA Television Limited.

THE BRAVOS
(THE ABC SUNDAY NIGHT MOVIE)

ABC Television Network, January 9, 1972; 120 minutes in color on film.

A Western about the commander of a beleaguered cavalry post whose precarious friendship with Indians was destroyed, resulting in the abduction of his son.

Cast: Maj. John Harkness (George Peppard), Jackson Buckley (Pernell Roberts), Heller Chase (Belinda J. Montgomery), Ben Lawler (L. Q. Jones), Capt. Macdowell (George Murdock), Garratt (Barry Brown), Peter Harkness (Vincent Van Patten), Capt. Detroville (Dana Elcar), Sgt. Marcy (John Kellog), Raeder (Bo Svenson), Satanta (Joaquin Martinez), Lt. Lewis (Randolph Mantooth), Corp. Love (Clint Ritchie), Sgt. Boyd (Michael Bow).

Credits: Executive Producer: David Victor; Produced by: Norman Lloyd; Directed by: Ted Post; Written by: Christopher Knopf; Director of Photography: Enzo A. Martinelli; Music by: Leonard Rosenman; Film Editors: Robert L. Kimble, Michael R. McAdam; Sound: James R. Alexander; Color by: Technicolor; Titles & Optical Effects: Universal Title; Produced by: Universal Television; Exclusive Distributor: MCA Television Limited.

BREAKOUT
(WORLD PREMIERE/NBC TUESDAY NIGHT AT THE MOVIES)

NBC Television Network, December 8, 1970; 120 minutes in color on film.

A drama about a man who planned to escape from a maximum security state prison to be reunited with his wife and the $50,000 stolen in a bank robbery.

Cast: Joe Baker (James Drury), Pipes (Red Buttons), Ann Baker (Kathryn Hays), Skip Manion (Woody Strode), Frank McCready (Sean Garrison), Fletcher (Bert Freed), Middleton (Mort Mills), Banks (William Mims), Phil Caprio (Harold J. Stone), Mackey (Don Wilbanks), Ranger (Kenneth Tobey), Bianchi (Ric Roman), Marian (Victoria Meyerink), Cook (Charles Lampkin), Donnie (Teddy Quinn), Hunter (Kent McCord), Hogan (Buck Kartalian).

Credits: Produced and Directed by: Richard Irving; Written by:

Sy Gomberg; Director of Photography: Ray Flin; Music by: Shorty Rogers; Art Director: Henry Larrecq; Film Editor: Milton Shifman; Color by: Technicolor; Titles & Optical Effects: Universal Title; Produced by: Universal Television; In Association with: NBC-TV; Exclusive Distributor: MCA Television Limited.

BRIDGER
(THE ABC FRIDAY NIGHT MOVIE)

ABC Television Network, September 10, 1976; 120 minutes in color on film.

A Western about Jim Bridger, a mountain man who blazed a trail through the Rocky Mountains to California in the 1830s. The pilot for an unsold series.

Cast: Jim Bridger (James Wainwright), Kit Carson (Ben Murphy), Jennifer Melford (Sally Field), Joe Meek (Dirk Blocker), Senator Webster (William Windom), President Jackson (John Anderson).

Credits: Produced and Directed by: David Lowell Rich; Written by: Merwin Gerard; Director of Photography: Bud Thackery; Music by: Elliot Kaplan; Art Director: Loyd S. Papez; Set Decorations: Joseph J. Stone; Film Editor: Boyd Clark; Color by: Technicolor; Titles & Optical Effects: Universal Title; Produced by: Universal Television; Exclusive Distributor: MCA Television Limited.

BROCK'S LAST CASE
(WORLD PREMIERE/NBC MONDAY NIGHT AT THE MOVIES)

NBC Television Network, March 5, 1973; 120 minutes in color on film.

A mystery drama about a police lieutenant who quit the New York Police Department to raise oranges out West but was forced into local crime-solving. The pilot for an unsold series.

Cast: Lt. Max Brock (Richard Widmark), Arthur Goldencorn (Henry Darrow), Ellen Ashley (Beth Brickell), Smiley Crenshaw (Will Geer), Joe Cuspie (John Anderson), Stretch Willis (Michael Burns), Jack Dawson (David Huddleston), Jake Hinkley (Henry Beckman).

Credits: Executive Producer: Leonard B. Stern; Produced by: Roland Kibbee; Directed by: David Lowell Rich; Written by: Martin Donaldson, Alex Gordon; Director of Photography: Russell L. Metty, A.S.C.; Music by: Charles Gross; Art Director: John E. Chilberg II; Set Decorations: Robert C. Bradfield; Film Editor: Frank Morriss; Unit Manager: Don Gold; Sound: Victor H. Carpenter; Color by: Technicolor; Titles & Optical Effects: Universal Title; Editorial Supervision: Richard Belding; Music Supervision: Hal Mooney; Costumes by: Charles Waldo; Produced by: Talent

Associates/Norton Simon, Inc., Oden Productions, Inc. And Universal Television; In Association with: NBC-TV; Exclusive Distributor: MCA Television Limited.

THE CALIFORNIA KID
(ABC MOVIE OF THE WEEK)

ABC Television Network, September 25, 1974; 90 minutes in color on film.

A drama about Michael McCord who set out to turn the tables on evil Sheriff Roy, a man who punished speeders by running them off hairpin mountain curves. This telefeature was the 200th ABC Movie of the Week.

Cast: Michael McCord (Martin Sheen), Sheriff Roy (Vic Morrow), Maggie (Michelle Phillips), Deputy (Stuart Margolin), Buzz Stafford (Nick Nolte), Sissy (Janit Baldwin), Lyle (Gary Morgan), Don McCord (Joe Estevez), Tom (Gavan O'Herlihy).

Credits: Executive Producer: Paul Mason; Produced by: Howie Horwitz; Directed by: Richard T. Heffron; Written by: Richard Compton; Director of Photography: Terry K. Meade; Music by: Lucio DeJesus; Art Director: Raymond Beal; Film Editor: Robert F. Shugrue; Color by: Technicolor; Titles & Optical Effects: Universal Title; Produced by: Universal Television; Exclusive Distributor: MCA Television Limited.

CAPTAIN AMERICA
(CBS SPECIAL MOVIE PRESENTATION)

CBS Television Network, January 19, 1979; 120 minutes in color on film.

A drama about Steve Rogers, an athletic ex-Marine, who became crime-fighter Captain America--as his father had years earlier--and, augmented by a secret super-steroid, pursued an arch-criminal who planned to decimate Phoenix, Arizona with a neutron bomb. Based on the Marvel Comics Group character. The pilot for an unsold series.

Cast: Steve Rogers (Reb Brown), Dr. Simon Mills (Len Birman), Dr. Wendy Day (Heather Menzies), Harley (Lance LeGault), Charles Barber (Frank Marth), Tina Hayden (Robin Mattson), Rudy Sandrini (Joseph Ruskin), Lou Brackett (Steve Forrest), Throckmorton (Nocona Aranda), Ortho (Michael McManus), Jerry (Chip Johnson), Jeff Hayden (Dan Barton), Lester Wiant (James Ingersoll), FBI Assistant (Jim Smith), 1st Doctor (Ken Chandler), 2nd Doctor (Jason Wingreen), 3rd Doctor (Buster Jones), Secretary (June Dayton), Nurse (Diana Webster).

Credits: Executive Producer: Allan Balter; Produced by: Martin Goldstein; Directed by: Rod Holcomb; Written by: Don Ingalls; Story by: Don Ingalls, Chester Krumholz; Director of Photography: Ronald W. Browne; Art Director: Lou Montejano; Film Editor: Miki Murphy; Sound: Bill Griffith; Color by: Technicolor; Titles & Optical Effects: Universal Title; Produced by: Universal Television; Exclusive Distributor: MCA Television Limited.

A CASE OF RAPE
(WORLD PREMIERE/NBC WEDNESDAY NIGHT AT THE MOVIES)

NBC Television Network, February 20, 1974; 120 minutes in color on film.

A drama about the humiliation a housewife was put through in court when she sought redress for being raped. Based on true incidents from the District Attorney's files.

Cast: Ellen (Elizabeth Montgomery), David (Ronny Cox), Leonard Alexander (William Daniels), Larry (Cliff Potts), Defense Attorney (Rosemary Murphy), Marge Bracken (Patricia Smith), Det. Riley (Ken Swofford), Det. Parker (Jonathan Lippe), Judge (Robert Karnes), Dr. Marsden (Charles Macauley), Dr. Goldstone (Alex Henteloff).

Credits: Executive Producer: David Levinson; Produced by: Louis Randolph; Directed by: Boris Sagal; Written by: Robert E. Thompson; Story by: Louis Randolph; Director of Photography: Terry K. Meade; Music by: Hal Mooney; Art Director: George Webb; Film Editor: Richard Bracken; Color by: Technicolor; Titles & Optical Effects: Universal Title; Produced by: Universal Television; In Association with: NBC-TV; Exclusive Distributor: MCA Television Limited.

THE CHADWICK FAMILY
(ABC WEDNESDAY MOVIE OF THE WEEK)

ABC Television Network, April 17, 1974; 90 minutes in color on film.

A drama about the hectic lives of the Chadwick family. Filmed on location on Coronado Peninsula, San Diego, California. The pilot for an unsold series.

Cast: Ned Chadwick (Fred MacMurray), Valeria Chadwick (Kathleen Maguire), Joan Chadwick McTaggert (Darleen Carr), Tim Chadwick (Stephen Nathan), Duffy McTaggert (Barry Bostwick), Lisa Chadwick (Jane Actman), Alex Hawthorne (Alan Fudge), Lee Wu-Tsaung (Frank Michael Liu), Eileen Chadwick Hawthorne (Lara Parker), Cindy Hawthorne (Carlena Gower), Sari Hawthorne (Kim Durso), Jimmy Hawthorne (Eben George), Danny (Bruce Boxleitner).

130 / Telefeatures

Credits: Executive Producer: David Victor; Produced by: David J. O'Connell; Directed by: David Lowell Rich; Written by: David Victor; Story by: David Victor, John Gay; Director of Photography: Walter Strenge; Music by: Hal Mooney; Art Director: Howard E. Johnson; Film Editor: Richard G. Wray; Color by: Technicolor; Titles & Optical Effects: Universal Title; Produced by: Groverton Productions, Ltd.; In Association with: Universal Television; Exclusive Distributor: MCA Television Limited.

THE CHALLENGERS
(CBS FRIDAY NIGHT MOVIE)

CBS Television Network, February 20, 1970; 120 minutes in color on film.

A drama about race-car drivers who competed for the Grand Prix. The challengers were Cody Scanlon, Paco Ortega and Jim McBade. Filmed in 1969, this was CBS's first made-for-TV movie.

Cast: Jim McCabe (Darren McGavin), Cody Scanlon (Sean Garrison), Paco (Nico Minardos), Stephanie (Anne Baxter), Ritchie (Richard Conte), Mary McCabe (Juliet Mills), Nealy (Farley Granger), Catherine Burroughs (Susan Clark), "Angel" de Angelo (Sal Mineo), Brad York (William Sylvester), Ambrose (John Holland).

Credits: Produced by: Roy Huggins; Directed by: Leslie H. Martinson; Written by: Dick Nelson; Story by: Robert Hamner, John Thomas James; Director of Photography: Jack Marta; Music by: Pete Rugolo; Art Director: John T. McCormack; Film Editors: Edward A. Biery, Nick Archer; Color by: Technicolor; Titles & Optical Effects: Universal Title; Produced by: Roy Huggins-Public Arts Productions; In Association with: Universal Television; Exclusive Distributor: MCA Television Limited.

CHARLIE CHAN
(HAPPINESS IS A WARM CLUE)
(CBS LATE MOVIE)

CBS Television Network, July 17, 1979; 120 minutes in color on film.

A crime drama about the famed fictional sleuth, a former member of the Honolulu Police Department, who was lured out of self-imposed retirement to solve a series of murders aboard a yacht. As a private investigator, Chan's modern approach to detective work retained the wisdom and insight of his cultural heritage. Filmed in 1971, this telefeature was not broadcast on American television until 1979. Filmed on location in Vancouver, British Columbia, Canada.

Cast: Charlie Chan (Ross Martin), Andrew Kidder (Richard Haydn), Ariane Hadrachi (Louise Sorel), Paul Hadrachi (Joseph Hindy), Irene

Hadrachi (Kathleen Widdoes), Lambert (Don Gordon), Noel Adamson (Peter Donat), Alexander Hadrachi (Leslie Nielsen), Peter Chan (Rocky Gunn), Doreen Chan (Virginia Lee), Stephen Chan (Soon Taik-Oh), Oliver Chan (Ernest Harada), Fielding (William Nunn), Sylvia Grombach (Pat Gage), Dr. Howard Jamison (Ted Greenhalgh), Inspector McKenzie (Graham Campbell), Richard Lovell (Neil Dainard), Anton Grombach (Otto Lowy), Giancarlo Tui (John Guiliani), Mai-Ling Chan (Adele Yoshioda), Jan Chan (Pearl Hong).

Credits: Executive Producer: John J. Cole; Produced by: Jack Laird; Directed by: Daryl Duke; Written by: Gene Kearney; Story by: Simon Last, Gene Kearney; Director of Photography: Richard C. Glouner; Music by: Robert Prince; Art Director: Frank Arrigo; Film Editor: Frank Morriss; Color by: Technicolor; Titles & Optical Effects: Universal Title; Produced by: Sandler, Burns & Marmer; In Association with: Universal Television And NBC-TV; Exclusive Distributor: MCA Television Limited.

CHARLIE COBB: NICE NIGHT FOR A HANGING
(WORLD PREMIERE/NBC THURSDAY NIGHT AT THE MOVIES)

NBC Television Network, June 9, 1977; 120 minutes in color on film.

A Western set in 1877 about a private investigator who was hired by a wealthy Texas rancher to return his daughter to him. The detective's mission was imperilled by would-be kidnappers who were after the girl. The pilot for an unsold series.

Cast: Charlie Cobb (Clu Gulager), Charity (Blair Brown), McVea (Ralph Bellamy), Martha McVea (Stella Stevens), Angelica Adams (Tricia O'Neil), Sheriff Yates (Pernell Roberts), Conroy (George Furth), Waco (Christopher Connelly), Miss Cumberland (Carmen Matthews), Vurg (Josh Taylor), Potter (Ted Chapman).

Credits: Executive Producers: Richard Levinson, William Link; Produced by: Peter S. Fischer; Directed by: Richard Michaels; Written by: Peter S. Fischer; Director of Photography: Andrew Jackson, A.S.C.; Music by: Mike Post, Pete Carpenter; Art Director: John E. Chilberg II; Film Editor: Howard S. Deane; Color by: Technicolor; Titles & Optical Effects: Universal Title; Produced by: Fairmount/Foxcroft Productions; In Association with: Universal Television And NBC-TV; Exclusive Distributor: MCA Television Limited.

CHASE
(WORLD PREMIERE/NBC DOUBLE FEATURE NIGHT AT THE MOVIES)

NBC Television Network, March 24, 1973; 90 minutes in color on film.

132 / Telefeatures

A drama about four Los Angeles police officers who formed a specialized quasi-official unit which was assigned major criminal cases. The team was headed by Chase Reddick. The pilot for the series Chase (which see).

Cast: Chase Reddick (Mitchell Ryan), Norm Hamilton (Reid Smith), Steve Baker (Michael Richardson), Fred Sing (Brian Fong), Nora Devlon (Brenda Scott), Frank Dawson (Albert Reed), Tom Traynor (John Chandler), Lt. Joe Salizar (Valentin DeVargas), Judge Mary Foreman (Virginia Gregg), May Munro (Ann Morgan Guilbert).

Credits: Produced and Directed by: Jack Webb; Written by: Stephen J. Cannell; Director of Photography: Jack Marta; Music by: Oliver Nelson; Art Director: John J. Lloyd; Film Editor: Warren H. Adams; Assistant Director: Phil Bowles; Color by: Technicolor; Titles & Optical Effects: Universal Title; Produced by: Mark VII Limited; In Association with: Universal Television And NBC-TV; Exclusive Distributor: MCA Television Limited.

THE CITY
(ABC MONDAY NIGHT MOVIE)

ABC Television Network, May 17, 1971; 120 minutes in color on film.

A drama about Thomas Jefferson Alcala, a man whose combination of brilliant politics and unorthodox life style had given him three terms as mayor of his city. But pollution, campus unrest, spiraling costs, a tough opponent and a would-be assassin threatened to end Alcala's long and colorful career. The pilot for the series The Man and the City (which see). Filmed on location in Albuquerque, New Mexico.

Cast: Mayor Thomas Jefferson Alcala (Anthony Quinn), Sheridan Hugotor (E. G. Marshall), Sealy Graham (Robert Reed), Sabina Menard (Skye Aubrey), Ira Groom (Pat Hingle), Unknown Man (Kaz Garas), Mrs. Lockney (Peggy McKay), Holland Yermo (John Larch), Victoria Ulysses (Lorraine Gray), Det. Loop (Manny Smith), Bishop Bremend (W. R. Stevens), Nutwood (Jose Rey Toledo), Det. Kosse (Paul Lees), Mrs. Laboe (Felicita Jojola).

Credits: Produced by: Frank Price; Directed by: Daniel Petrie; Written by: Howard Rodman; Director of Photography: Jack Marta; Music by: Billy Goldenberg; Song "Satisfied with You" by: Billy Goldenberg, Bobby Russell; Sung by: Bobby Russell; Art Director: Howard E. Johnson; Film Editors: Robert Watts, Larry Lester; Color by: Technicolor; Titles & Optical Effects: Universal Title; Produced by: Universal Television; Exclusive Distributor: MCA Television Limited.

A CLEAR AND PRESENT DANGER
(WORLD PREMIERE/NBC SATURDAY NIGHT AT THE MOVIES)

NBC Television Network, March 21, 1970; 120 minutes in color on film.

A drama about Deputy U. S. Attorney General Hays Stowe, a candidate for the U. S. Senate, who defied his father, a veteran Senator and all his advisors, in his determination to do something about air pollution and its threat to human lives, even if it meant not being senator. The pilot for The Senator (which see) segment of the series The Bold Ones (which see).

Cast: Hays Stowe (Hal Holbrook), Senator Stowe (E. G. Marshall), Jordan Boyle (Joseph Campanella), Dr. Chanute (Jack Albertson), Salem Chase (Pat Hingle), Erin Stowe (Sharon Acker), Howard Eager (James Douglas), Professor Duke (Mike Kellin), Beiseker (Jeff Corey), House (Bernie Hamilton), Elliot Morse (Michael Bell), Norma Stowe (Cindy Eilbacher), Amanda Shamokin (Adrienne Marden), Health Commissioner (Harry Basch), Preston Gardiner (Robert Heinz), Nurse (Marian Collier).

Credits: Produced by: William Sackheim; Directed by: James Goldstone; Written by: A. J. Russell, Henri Simoun; Story by: S. S. Schweitzer, A. J. Russell; Associate Producer: John Badham; Director of Photography: Bill Butler; Music by: Billy Goldenberg; Art Director: John J. Lloyd; Film Editors: Edward A. Biery, A. C. E., Richard M. Sprague; Assistant Director: Donald Roberts; Unit Manager: Arthur Newman; Sound: James A. Alexander; Costumes by: Vincent Dee; Makeup: Bud Westmore; Hair Stylist: Larry Germain; Color by: Technicolor; Titles & Optical Effects: Universal Title; Produced by: Universal Television; In Association with: NBC-TV; Exclusive Distributor: MCA Television Limited.

COMPANIONS IN NIGHTMARE
(WORLD PREMIER/NBC SATURDAY NIGHT AT THE MOVIES)

NBC Television Network, November 23, 1968; 120 minutes in color on film.

A drama about Dr. Strelson, a famous psychiatrist who had to identify a psychotic killer in the midst of patients engaged in a group therapy project.

Cast: Eric Nicholson (Gig Young), Carlotta Mauridge (Anne Baxter), Jeremy Siddack (Patrick O'Neal), Julie Klanton (Dana Wynter), Dr. Neesden (Leslie Nielsen), Dr. Strelson (Melvyn Douglas), Richard Lyle (William Redfield), Sara Nicholson (Bettye Ackerman), Adam McKay (Lou Gossett, Jr.), Det. Cort (Tom Bellin), Young Man in Funeral Parlor (Gregory Mullavy), Phillip Rootes (Stacy Harris), Cab Driver (Syl Lamont), Waitress (Connie Hunter).

Credits: Produced and Directed by: Norman Lloyd; Written by: Robert L. Joseph; Director of Photography: William Margulies, A. S. C.; Music by: Bernard Herrmann; Art Director: Alexander A. Mayer; Film Editor: Douglas Stewart; Costumes by: Burton Miller; Makeup: Bud Westmore; Hair Stylist: Larry Germain; Color by: Technicolor; Titles & Optical Effects: Universal Title; Produced by: Universal Television; Exclusive Distributor: MCA Television Limited.

COOL MILLION
(WORLD PREMIERE)

NBC Television Network, October 16, 1972; 120 minutes in color on film.

A mystery drama about Jefferson Keyes, a private investigator whose fee was one million dollars, and his search for the daughter of one of the world's richest men. Filmed on location in Greece and Italy. The pilot for the series Cool Million (which see).

Cast: Jefferson Keyes (James Farentino), Inspector Duprez (John Vernon), Carla Miles (Barbara Bouchet), Merrill H. Cossack (Jackie Coogan), Adrienne (Christine Belford), Mme. Martine (Lila Kedrova), Dr. Emile Snow (Patrick O'Neal), Tomlin (Guido Alberti), Werner (John Karlsen), Frederick (Michael Hargitay).

Credits: Executive Producer: George Eckstein; Produced by: David J. O'Connell; Directed by: Gene Levitt; Written by: Larry Cohen; Director of Photography: Gabor Pogany; Music by: Robert Prince; Art Director: Aurelio Crugnola; Film Editor: Michael Economou; Color by: Technicolor; Titles & Optical Effects: Universal Title; Produced by: Universal Television; In Association with: NBC-TV; Exclusive Distributor: MCA Television Limited.

THE COUPLE TAKES A WIFE
(ABC TUESDAY MOVIE OF THE WEEK)

ABC Television Network, December 5, 1972; 90 minutes in color on film.

A comedy-drama about an attractive young woman hired by a working couple to take care of the domestic chores. She turned the household upside down by taking a very personal interest in her job.

Cast: Jeff Hamilton (Bill Bixby), Barbara Hamilton (Paula Prentiss), Jennifer Allen (Valerie Perrine), Marion Randolph (Nanette Fabray), Randy Perkins (Robert Goulet), Mother (Myrna Loy), David Stevens (Larry Storch), Maria (Carmen Zapata), Christy Hamilton (Mia Bendixson), Mindy Hamilton (Dana Laurita), Mrs. Flannigan (Ruth McDevitt), Miss Robbins (Helen Kleeb), Clerk (Shirley Mitchell), Paula (Penny Marshall), Mr. Kaplan (Bert Holland), Singer (Dwan Smith).

Credits: Produced by: George Eckstein; Directed by: Jerry Paris; Written by: Susan Silver; Director of Photography: F. Bud Mautino; Music by: Dick De Benedictis; Art Director: Lester L. Green; Set Decorations: John Sturtevant; Film Editors: Aaron Stell, Bill Brame; Color by: Technicolor; Titles & Optical Effects: Universal Title; Produced by: Universal Television; Exclusive Distributor: MCA Television Limited.

CRIME CLUB
(CBS THURSDAY NIGHT AT THE MOVIES)

CBS Television Network, April 3, 1975; 90 minutes in color on film.

A drama about a group of detectives, writers and lawyers who formed a society to prevent and solve crimes. Their latest case involved a series of ice-pick murders to which a publicity hound convincingly confessed. The pilot for an unsold series.

Cast: John Keesey (Scott Thomas), Daniel Lawrence (Eugene Roche), Alex Norton (Robert Lansing), Frank Swoboda (Michael Christofer), Peter Karpf (David Clennon), Angela Swoboda (Barbara Rhoades), Pam Agostino (Kathy Beller), Jorge Gamos (Carl Gottlieb), Schroeder (Martine Beswick), Lt. Jack Doyle (M. Emmett Walsh), Mary Jo (Jennifer Shaw), Jack Dowd (Regis J. Cordic), Byron Craine (Biff McGuire).

Credits: Executive Producer: Matthew Rapf; Produced by: James McAdams; Directed by: Jeannot Szwarc; Written by: Gene R. Kearney; Director of Photography: Gayne Rescher; Art Director: Peter M. Wooley; Film Editors: Sigmund Neufeld, Jr., Jim Benson; Color by: Technicolor; Titles & Optical Effects: Universal Title; Produced by: Universal Television; Exclusive Distributor: MCA Television Limited.

A CRY FOR HELP
(ABC WEDNESDAY MOVIE OF THE WEEK)

ABC Television Network, February 12, 1975; 90 minutes in color on film.

A drama about an acid-tongued radio talk show host who rebuffed a listener threatening suicide, and then came to suspect that his caller may have been sincere.

Cast: Harry (Robert Culp), Ingrid (Elayne Heilveil), Paul (Ken Swofford), Buddy (Chuck McCann), George Rigney (Julius Harris), Irene Schullman (Jean Allison), Arthur Schullman (Donald Mantooth), Eddie (Joseph George), Richie Danko (Bruce Boxleitner), Philip Conover (Michael Lerner), Sgt. Lou Shirley (Lee DeBroux), Brother Stephen Tyler (Granville Van Dusen).

136 / Telefeatures

Credits: Executive Producers: Richard Levinson, William Link; Produced by: Howie Horwitz; Directed by: Daryl Duke; Written by: Peter S. Fischer; Director of Photography: Richard C. Glouner; Music by: Gil Melle; Art Director: Jack T. Collis; Film Editors: Frank Morriss, Douglas Stewart; Color by: Technicolor; Titles & Optical Effects: Universal Title; Produced by: Universal Television; Exclusive Distributor: MCA Television Limited.

A CRY IN THE WILDERNESS
(ABC TUESDAY MOVIE OF THE WEEK)

ABC Television Network, March 26, 1974; 90 minutes in color on film.

A drama about a farmer who was bitten by a rabid skunk. To protect his family from his future madness, he chained himself inside his barn, only to discover that a flood was coming. His wife set out for help, but was delayed by car trouble, a rape attempt and near-electrocution in the oncoming storm.

Cast: Sam (George Kennedy), Delda (Joanna Pettet), Gus (Lee H. Montgomery), Rex Millard (Roy Poole), Bess Millard (Collin Wilcox-Horne), Hainie (Liam Dunn), Griffey (Bing Russell), Old Woman (Irene Tedrow), Doctor (Robert Brubaker).

Credits: Produced by: Lou Morheim; Directed by: Gordon Hessler; Written by: Stephen Karpf, Elinor Karpf; Story by: Gilbert Wright; Director of Photography: J. J. Jones; Music by: Robert Prince; Film Editor: Bud Hoffman; Color by: Technicolor; Titles & Optical Effects: Universal Title; Produced by: Universal Television; Exclusive Distributor: MCA Television Limited.

CUTTER
(NBC MYSTERY MOVIE)

NBC Television Network, January 26, 1972; 90 minutes in color on film.

A drama about a black detective who searched Chicago's ghetto and affluent Lake Shore Drive area for his missing friend, a professional football quarterback. Filmed on location.

Cast: Cutter (Peter DeAnda), Riggs (Cameron Mitchell), Linda (Barbara Rush), Leone (Gabriel Dell), Meredith (Robert Webber), Susan Macklin (Marlene Warfield), Ray Brown (Archie Moore), Macklin (Herbert Jefferson, Jr.), Miss Aguilera (Anna Navarro), Shineman (Stepin Fetchit), Janice (Karen Carlson), Billy (John Alexander, Jr.), Arlene French (Arlene Banas), Benedict (Thomas Erhart).

Credits: Executive Producer: Richard Irving; Produced by: Dean Hargrove; Directed by: Richard Irving; Written by: Dean Hargrove;

Director of Photography: Jack Priestley; Color by: Technicolor; Titles & Optical Effects: Universal Title; Produced by: Universal Television; Exclusive Distributor: MCA Television Limited.

THE D. A.: CONSPIRACY TO KILL
(WORLD PREMIERE)

NBC Television Network, January 11, 1971; 120 minutes in color on film.

A crime drama about Deputy District Attorney Paul Ryan who had second thoughts about his key witness, after winning a manslaughter conviction. This was the second pilot for the series The D. A. (which see). The first was The D. A.: Murder One (which see).

Cast: Paul Ryan (Robert Conrad), Vincent Kovac (William Conrad), Thomas Bertrand (Don Stroud), James Fletcher (Steve Ihnat), Luanne Gibson (Belinda J. Montgomery), Bob Ramires (Armando Silvestre), Rochelle De Haven (Linda Marsh), Stevens (Roger Perry), Ramona Bertrand (Leslie Parrish), Arthur De Haven (Michael Strong), Sgt. Webster (Morgan Sterne), Judge Adamson (Virginia Gregg), Pullman (Lew Brown), Eddie Jewell (James McEachin), Doctor Leonard (Stacy Harris), Judge Bellamy (William Wintersole), Martha Grimes (Ann Morgan Guilbert), Pinkney (Ray Ballard), Shadlock (Tom Geas), Ben Chambers (Joe E. Tate), Grace (Sonja Dunson), Dr. Samuels (Olan Soule), Lambert (Arthur Balinger), Eve (Arleen Starr), Gibson (Thomas J. Huff), Willis (Ron Cavallo), Foreman (Dick Cangey), Bailiff (Dallas Mitchell), Deputy Sheriff (David Tyrone), Jimmy (Andrew Mac Heath), Time Keeper (Larry Levine), Corcoran (Don Edwards), Trainer (Ralph Gambina), Himself (Cisco Andrade).

Credits: Produced by: Robert H. Forward; Directed by: Paul Krasny; Written by: Stanford Whitmore; Director of Photography: Alric Edens; Music by: Frank Comstock; Art Director: Arch Bacon; Set Decorations: Mickey S. Michaels; Film Editors: Robert F. Shugrue, Richard M. Sprague; Unit Manager: Mel A. Bishop; Assistant Director: Jack Terry; Sound: Melvin M. Metcalfe, Sr.; Editorial Supervision: Richard Belding; Costume Supervision: Vincent Dee; Makeup: Bud Westmore; Hair Stylist: Larry Germain; Technical Advice: The Office of Joseph P. Busch, Jr., District Attorney, Los Angeles County; Color by: Technicolor; Titles & Optical Effects: Universal Title; Produced by: Mark VII Limited; In Association with: Universal Television And NBC-TV; Exclusive Distributor: MCA Television Limited.

THE D. A.: MURDER ONE
(WORLD PREMIERE)

NBC Television Network, December 8, 1969; 120 minutes in color on film.

138 / Telefeatures

A drama about Deputy District Attorney Paul Ryan's attempt to prove that a pretty nurse killed her husbands and relatives by injecting them with insulin. This was the first pilot for the series The D. A. (which see). The second was The D. A.: Conspiracy to Kill (which see). The D. A.: Murder One was selected as the winner of the annual Gavel Award for Outstanding Public Service by the American Bar Association.

Cast: Paul Ryan (Robert Conrad), District Attorney Lynn Compton (Howard Duff), Mary Brokaw (Diane Baker), Nicholas Devany (J. D. Cannon), Andrushian (Gerald S. O'Loughlin), Dr. Grainger (David Opatoshu), Dr. Stuart (Alfred Ryder), Cherniss (Scott Brady), Dr. Enright (Dana Elcar), Ramirez (Carlos Romero), Charles Lloyd (Patrick Knowles), Dr. Ellis Anders (Ford Rainey).

Credits: Executive Producer: Robert H. Forward; Produced by: Harold Jack Bloom; Directed by: Boris Sagal; Written by: Harold Jack Bloom; Associate Producer: Edward K. Dodds; Director of Photography: Alric Edens; Music by: Frank Comstock; Art Director: George Webb; Film Editor: Tony Martinelli; Sound: Stanley Cooley; Assistant Director: Ralph Ferrin; Color by: Technicolor; Titles & Optical Effects: Universal Title; Produced by: Mark VII Limited; In Association with: Universal Television And NBC-TV; Exclusive Distributor: MCA Television Limited.

THE DARK SECRET OF HARVEST HOME
(NBC NOVEL FOR TELEVISION/THE BIG EVENT)

NBC Television Network, January 23 and 24, 1978; 5 hours in color on film.

A drama about a New York family that moved to a secluded New England village where strange, supernatural goings-on belied its placid rural charm.

Cast: Widow Fortune (Bette Davis), Nick Constantine (David Ackroyd), Beth Constantine (Joanna Miles), Kate Constantine (Rosanna Arquette), Justin Hooke (John Calvin), Sophie Hooke (Laurie Prange), Tamar Penrose (Lina Raymond), Worthy Pettinger (Michael O'Keefe), Amys Penrose (Norman Lloyd), Jack Stump (Rene Auberjonois), Robert Dodd (Stephen Joyce), Maggie Dodd (Linda Marsh), Richard (Richard Venture), Missy Penrose (Tracy Gold), Ty Harth (Michael Durrell), Jimmy Minerva (Stephen Gustafson), Roy Soakes (Dick Durock).

Credits: Produced by: Jack Laird; Directed by: Leo Penn; Written by: Charles E. Israel, Jack Guss; Adapted by: James Miller, Jennifer Miller; Based on the Novel "Harvest Home" by: Thomas Tryon; Directors of Photography: Ken Dickson, Frank V. Phillips, Charles Correll; Music by: Paul Chihara; Art Director: Philip Barber; Film Editors: Robert F. Shugrue, Robert Watts; Costumes by: Bill Jobe; Color by: Technicolor; Titles & Optical Effects:

The Dark Secret of Harvest Home / 139

Universal Title; Produced by: Universal Television; In Association with: NBC-TV; Exclusive Distributor: MCA Television Limited.

DARK VICTORY
(WORLD PREMIERE)

NBC Television Network, February 5, 1976; 3 hours in color on film.

A drama about a successful television producer who had a brain tumor and fell in love with her doctor. Based on the play, the 1939 film and the 1963 remake, Stolen Hours.

Cast: Katherine Merrill (Elizabeth Montgomery), Dr. Michael Grant (Anthony Hopkins), Dolores Marsh (Michele Lee), Jeremy (John Elerick), Dr. Kassiter (Herbert Berghof), Eileen (Janet MacLachlan), Manny (Michael Lerner), Archie (Vic Tayback), Sandy (Mario Roccuzzo), Veronica (Julie Rogers).

Credits: Executive Producer: Richard Irving; Produced by: Jules Irving; Directed by: Robert Butler; Written by: M. Charles Cohen; Based on the Stage Play by: George Emerson Brewer, Jr., Bertram Bloch; Director of Photography: Michael Margulies; Music by: Billy Goldenberg; Art Director: William H. Tuntke; Film Editor: John Dumas; Color by: Technicolor; Titles & Optical Effects: Universal Title; Produced by: Universal Television; Exclusive Distributor: MCA Television Limited.

DEADLOCK!
(WORLD PREMIERE/NBC SATURDAY NIGHT AT THE MOVIES)

NBC Television Network, February 22, 1969; 120 minutes in color on film.

A drama about a black district attorney and a white police lieutenant who tried to find the killer of a newspaperman in a racially troubled city. The pilot for The Protectors (which see) element of The Bold Ones (which see).

Cast: Lt. Sam Danforth (Leslie Nielsen), Leslie Washburn (Hari Rhodes), Coley Walker (Max Julien), Melissa (Beverly Todd), George Stack (Dana Elcar), Lucinda (Ruby Dee), Logan (Aldo Ray), Gamel (Melvin Stuart), Ski (Roger Bowen), with: James McEachin.

Credits: Produced by: William Sackheim; Directed by: Lamont Johnson; Written by: William Sackheim, Chester Krumholz, Robert E. Thompson; Story by: Roland Wolpert, William Sackheim; Director of Photography: Vilis Lapenieks; Music by: Stanley Wilson; Song "Even When You Cry" Sung by: The Blossoms; Art Director: John T. McCormack; Film Editor: Edward M. Abroms; Sound: James T. Porter; Color by: Technicolor; Titles & Optical Effects:

140 / Telefeatures

Universal Title; Produced by: Universal Television; In Association with: NBC-TV; Exclusive Distributor: MCA Television Limited.

THE DEADLY DREAM
(ABC MOVIE OF THE WEEKEND)

ABC Television Network, September 25, 1971; 90 minutes in color on film. Major Sponsor and Agency: Warner-Lambert Pharmaceutical Company through J. Walter Thompson Company.

A suspense drama about a man who had a recurring and continuing dream in which he was marked for death by a mysterious tribunal. The man became terrified when he was unable to separate his dreams from reality--and vice versa. This was the first ABC Movie of the Weekend presentation.

Cast: Jim Hanley (Lloyd Bridges), Laurel Hanley (Janet Leigh), Dr. Harold Malcolm (Leif Erickson), Dr. Howard Geary (Carl Betz), Kagen (Don Stroud), Delgreve (Richard Jaeckel), Dr. Farrow (Phillip Pine), Dr. Goodman (Herbert Nelson).

Credits: Produced by: Stan Shpetner; Directed by: Alf Kjellin; Written by: Barry Oringer; Director of Photography: Jack Marta; Music by: Dave Grusin; Art Director: Loyd S. Papez; Film Editor: Robert L. Kimble; Produced by: Universal Television; Exclusive Distributor: MCA Television Limited.

DEATH IS A BAD TRIP
(ABC WIDE WORLD OF ENTERTAINMENT/WIDE WORLD MYSTERY)

ABC Television Network, July 23, 1974; 90 minutes in color on tape.

A suspense drama about an eyewitness to a syndicate murder. Even though she refused to cooperate with the police, the mob pegged her to die.

Cast: Kimberly (Tisha Sterling), Jerry Gerard (Peter Coffield), Corrigan (Tim O'Connor), Charlie (Charles Dierkop), Randy (Tom Heaton), Male Poet (Kendrew Lascelles), Pub Manager (Geoffrey Scott).

Credits: Produced by: Barbara Schultz; Produced by: Universal Television; Exclusive Distributor: MCA Television Limited.

DEATH RACE
(ABC SUSPENSE MOVIE)

ABC Television Network, November 10, 1973; 90 minutes in color on film.

An action/suspense yarn about the battle between a Nazi tank and a disabled American airplane in the North African desert during World War II.

Cast: General Beimier (Lloyd Bridges), Culpepper (Doug McClure), McMillan (Roy Thinnes), Stoeffer (Eric Braeden), Voelke (Dennis Rucker), Huffman (Brendon Boone), Becker (Dennis Dugan).

Credits: Executive Producer: Harve Bennett; Produced by: Terry K. Meade; Directed by: David Lowell Rich; Written by: Charles Kuenstle; Director of Photography: Terry K. Meade; Music by: Milton Rosen; Film Editors: Carl Pingitore, Les Green; Sound: James E. Alexander; Color by: Technicolor; Titles & Optical Effects: Universal Title; Produced by: Universal Television; Exclusive Distributor: MCA Television Limited.

DEATH TAKES A HOLIDAY
(ABC MOVIE OF THE WEEKEND)

ABC Television Network, October 23, 1971; 90 minutes in color on film.

A drama about Death, in human form, who came to earth to find out why people hang onto life so tenaciously. He unexpectedly fell in love with a beautiful young woman. Based on the stage play and the 1934 film.

Cast: Judge Earl Chapman (Melvyn Douglas), Peggy Chapman (Yvette Mimieux), David Smith (Monte Markham), Selena Chapman (Myrna Loy), John Cummings (Bert Convy), Earl Chapman, Jr. (Kerwin Mathews), Marion Chapman (Priscilla Pointer), Martin Herndon (Austin Willis), Tony Chapman (Colby Chester), Ellen Chapman (Maureen Reagan), TV Announcer (Regis Cordic), TV Announcer (Mario Machado).

Credits: Produced by: George Eckstein; Directed by: Robert Butler; Written by: Rita Lakin; Based on a Play by: Alberto Casella; Adapted by: Walter Ferris; Director of Photography: Michael Margulies; Music by: Laurindo Almeida; Art Director: Eugene Lourie; Set Decorations: Robert C. Bradfield; Film Editor: Michael Economou; Color by: Technicolor; Titles & Optical Effects: Universal Title; Produced by: Universal Television; Exclusive Distributor: MCA Television Limited.

THE DESPERATE MILES
(ABC WEDNESDAY MOVIE OF THE WEEK)

ABC Television Network, March 5, 1975; 90 minutes in color on film.

A drama about one-legged Vietnam Veteran Joe Larkin and his journey in a wheelchair from Los Angeles to San Diego, California. Based on the real-life adventures of Jim Mayo.

Cast: Joe Larkin (Tony Musante), Ruth Merrick (Joanna Pettet), Ruiz (Pepe Serna), Al (Richard Reicheg), Lou (Shelly Novack), Ted (Michael Richardson), Mrs. Larkin (Jeanette Nolan), Jill (Lynn Loring), Dr. Bryson (John Larch), Rhodes (Stacy Keach, Sr.), Jason (Purvis Atkins), Spaulding (Marcus Smith).

Credits: Executive Producer: Joel Rogosin; Producers: Frank von Zerneck, Robert Greenwald; Directed by: Daniel Haller; Written by: Joel Rogosin, Arthur Ross; Story by: Arthur Ross; Director of Photography: Jack Woolf; Music by: Robert Prince; Song "Many Miles to Morning" Music by: Robert Prince; Lyrics by: Bill Dyer; Sung by: Denny Brooks; Film Editors: J. Howard Terrill, Chuck McClelland; Color by: Technicolor; Titles & Optical Effects: Universal Title; Produced by: Universal Television; Exclusive Director: MCA Television Limited.

DESTINY OF A SPY
(WORLD PREMIERE/NBC MONDAY NIGHT AT THE MOVIES)

NBC Television Network, October 27, 1969; 120 minutes in color on film.

A spy drama about veteran Russian secret agent Peter Vanin, who was sent to discover why a mysterious letter caused a top British scientist to suffer a heart attack. In London, he was aided by Megan Thomas--a double agent actually working for the British, who was eager to find out what made Vanin accept the assignment after being in retirement for eight years. Megan fell in love with Vanin and had difficulty carrying out her orders. Filmed on location in London.

Cast: Peter Vanin (Lorne Greene), Megan Thomas (Rachel Roberts), Col. Malendin (Anthony Quayle), Sir Martin Rolfe (James Donald), Gen. Kirk (Harry Andrews), John Flack (Patrick Magee), Julius Bates (Patrick Newell), Superintendent Pode (Raymond Huntley), Igor Trubenoff (Olaf Beaumont), Karl Kronig (Victor Beaumont), Elena Vanin (Janina Faye), Elizaveta (Josephine Stuart), Colonel (Richard Vernon), Peace Girl (Angels Pleasance), Lady Rolfe (Mary Kerridge).

Credits: Produced by: Jack Laird; Directed by: Boris Sagal; Written by: Stanford Whitmore; Based on a Novel by: John Blackburn; Director of Photography: Arthur Grant; Music by: Ron Grainger; Production Designer: Bernard Robinson; Film Editor: Archie Ludski, G. B. F. E.; Sound Editor: Roy Baker, G. B. F. E.; Production Manager: Don Toms; Wardrobe: Rosemary Burrows; Makeup: George Blackler; Hair Stylist: Joan White; Color by: Technicolor; Titles & Optical Effects: Universal Title; Produced by: Universal Television; In Association with: NBC-TV; Exclusive Distributor: MCA Television Limited.

THE DEVIL AND MISS SARAH
(ABC MOVIE OF THE WEEKEND)

ABC Television Network, December 4, 1971; 90 minutes in color on film. Major Sponsor and Agency: Warner-Lambert Pharmaceutical Company through J. Walter Thompson Company.

A drama about a legendary outlaw with the powers of Satan who was being escorted to justice by a homesteading couple. The outlaw used hypnosis to possess the woman's soul, making her betray her husband and help him escape. Filmed on location in southern Utah.

Cast: Rankin (Gene Barry), Gil Turner (James Drury), Sarah Turner (Janice Rule), Marshall Duncan (Charles McGraw), Stoney (Slim Pickens), Appleton (Donald Moffat), Holmes (Logan Ramsey).

Credits: Produced by: Stan Shpetner; Directed by: Michael Caffey; Written by: Calvin Clements; Director of Photography: Harry Wolf; Music by: David Rose; Art Director: Arch Bacon; Set Decorations: Chester R. Bayhi; Film Editor: Budd Small; Color by: Technicolor; Titles & Optical Effects: Universal Title; Produced by: Universal Television; Exclusive Distributor: MCA Television Limited.

DIAL: HOT LINE
(THE ABC SUNDAY NIGHT MOVIE)

ABC Television Network, March 8, 1970; 120 minutes in color on film.

A drama about David Leopold, a hip psychiatric social worker and his desperate attempt to prevent the collapse of his unique telephone counseling service. Filmed on location in San Diego, California. The pilot for the series Matt Lincoln (which see) in which the central character's name was changed.

Cast: David Leopold (Vince Edwards), Tag (Chelsea Brown), Mrs. Carruthers (Kim Hunter), Pam Carruthers (Lane Bradbury), Ann (June Harding), Kevin (Michael Larraine), Jimmy (Felton Perry), Earl (Robert Pratt), Stevie (Vinnie [Vincent] Van Patten), Joe (Elliott Street), Peter (Michael McGreevey), Dr. Stone (G. D. Spradlin), Hippie (Kevin Burchett), Gail (Leslie Freeman).

Credits: Produced by: William Sackheim; Directed by: Jerry Thorpe; Written by: Carol Sobieski; Associate Producer: John Badham; Director of Photography: Jack Marta; Music by: Oliver Nelson; Art Director: George Webb; Film Editor: Edward M. Abroms; Assistant Director: Harker Wade; Sound: David H. Moriarty; Costumes by: Leah Rhodes; Color by: Technicolor; Titles & Optical Effects: Universal Title; Produced by: Universal Television; Exclusive Distributor: MCA Television Limited.

144 / Telefeatures

DO YOU TAKE THIS STRANGER
(WORLD PREMIERE)

NBC Television Network, January 18, 1971; 120 minutes in color on film.

A drama about a man who schemed to come into a million-dollar inheritance by switching identities with another man who had a limited time to live.

Cast: Murray Jarvis (Gene Barry), Steven Breck (Lloyd Bridges), Rachel Jarvis (Diane Baker), Dr. Carson (Joseph Cotten), G. R. Jarvis (Sidney Blackmer), Mildred Crandall (Susan Oliver), Dr. Bamber (Ivor Barry), Night Man (Arthur Mallet), Karen (Cara Burgess), Taxi Driver (Byron Webster), Lawyer (Bart Burns), Airport Officer (Marc Seaton), Judy (Linda Marie).

Credits: Executive Producer: Roy Huggins; Produced by: Jo Swerling, Jr.; Directed by: Richard Heffron; Written by: Matthew Howard; Associate Producer: Steve Heilpern; Director of Photography: Lionel Lindon; Music by: Pete Rugolo; Art Director: John J. Lloyd; Film Editor: John Dumas; Assistant Director: Kenny Williams; Sound: Melvin M. Metcalfe, Sr.; Color by: Technicolor; Titles & Optical Effects: Universal Title; Produced by: Roy Huggins-Public Arts Productions; In Association with: Universal Television And NBC-TV; Exclusive Distributor: MCA Television Limited.

DR. SCORPION
(THE ABC FRIDAY NIGHT MOVIE)

ABC Television Network, February 24, 1978; 120 minutes in color on film.

An action drama about a deadly and power-mad genius who threatened world peace with an astonishing scheme involving the theft of atomic missiles from the United States. Only one man stood in his way.

Cast: John Shackelford (Nick Mancuso), Tania Reston (Christine Lahti), Bill Worthington (Richard T. Herd), Sandra Shackelford (Sandra Kerns), Dr. Cresus (Roscoe Lee Browne), The Dane (Denny Miller), Terry Batliner (Granville Van Dusen), Admiral Gunwilder (Philip Sterling), Eddie (Lincoln Kilpatrick), Lt. Reed (Joseph Ruskin), Whitey Ullman (Bill Lucking).

Credits: Executive Producer: Stephen J. Cannell; Produced by: Alex Beaton; Directed by: Richard Lang; Written by: Stephen J. Cannell; Director of Photography: Charles Correll; Music by: Mike Post, Pete Carpenter; Film Editors: Diane Adler, George R. Rohrs; Color by: Technicolor; Titles & Optical Effects: Universal Title; Produced by: Stephen J. Cannell Productions; In Association with: Universal Television; Exclusive Distributor: MCA Television Limited.

Dr. Strange / 145

DR. STRANGE

CBS Television Network, September 6, 1978; 120 minutes in color on film.

A drama about a sorcerer who enlisted the aid of a psychiatrist in defeating a satanic goddess who threatened to unlease her evil powers on the world. The pilot for an unsold series.

Cast: Dr. Stephen Strange (Peter Hooten), Wong (Clyde Kusatsu), Morgan Le Fay (Jessica Walter), Clea (Eddie Benton), Lindmer (John Mills), Dr. Frank Taylor (Philip Sterling), Sarah (June Barrett), Nurse (Sarah Rush), The Nameless One (David Hooks), Head Nurse (Diana Webster), Department Chief (Blake Marion), Intern (Bob Delegall), Orderly (Frank Catalano), Magician (Larry Anderson), Agnes Carson (Inez Pedroza), Mrs. Sullivan (Lady Rowlands).

Credits: Executive Producer: Philip DeGuere; Produced by: Alex Beaton; Directed by: Philip DeGuere; Written by: Philip DeGuere; Based on the Marvel Comics Group Characters Created by: Stan Lee; Director of Photography: Enzo A. Martinelli; Music by: Paul Chihara; Art Director: William H. Tuntke; Film Editor: Christopher Nelson; Color by: Technicolor; Titles & Optical Effects: Universal Title; Produced by: Universal Television; Exclusive Distributor: MCA Television Limited.

DON'T PUSH, I'LL CHARGE WHEN I'M READY

NBC Television Network, December 18, 1977; 120 minutes in color on film.

A comedy about the World War II adventures of an Italian Prisoner of War who was conscripted into the U.S. Army. Produced in 1969, this telefeature was not broadcast until 1977.

Cast: Wendy Sutherland (Sue Lyon), Sgt. Ed Hutchins (Dwayne Hickman), Angelo Rossini (Enzo Cerusico), Maj. Ralph Watson (Edward Andrews), Teodoro Bruzizi (Cesar Romero), Santola (Soupy Sales), Tony Esposito (Gino Conforti), Phil Parsons (Parley Baer), Oliver (Kenneth Tobey), Himself (Jerry Colonna), Fabrizio (Mikel Angel), Lauren (Victoria Meyerink), Announcer (Avery Schreiber).

Credits: Produced and Directed by: Nathaniel Lande; Written by: Al Ramus, John Shaner; Associate Producer: Lloyd Richards; Director of Photography: Lionel Lindon; Music by: Lyn Murray; "Don't Push, I'll Charge When I'm Ready" Sung by: Rita Gardner; Art Director: Henry Bumstead; Film Editor: Robert L. Kimble; Color by: Technicolor; Titles & Optical Effects: Universal Title; Produced by: Universal Television; Exclusive Distributor: MCA Television Limited.

146 / Telefeatures

THE DOOMSDAY FLIGHT
(WORLD PREMIERE)

NBC Television Network, December 13, 1966; 120 minutes in color on film.

A suspense drama about a hidden bomb aboard a New York-bound jet liner. The bomb was set to go off at a certain altitude, which the man who planted it refused to reveal until he was payed a ransom of $100,000.

Cast: Special Agent Frank Thompson (Jack Lord), The Man (Edmond O'Brien), Captain Anderson (Van Johnson), Jean (Katherine Crawford), George Ducette (John Saxon), Chief Pilot Shea (Richard Carlson), Engineer "Chips" (Tom Simcox), Army Corporal (Michael Sarrazin), Feldman (Edward Asner), Bartender (Malachi Throne), Willoughby (Robert Pickering), Mrs. Thompson (Jan Shepard), FBI Agent Balaban (Gregg Morris), Mr. Rierdon (David Lewis), L. A. Dispatcher (Howard Caine), Seaton (John Kellogg), Virginia (Bernadette Hale), Elderly Woman (Celia Lovsky), Speedijet Messenger (Dee Pollock), Co-pilot Reilly (Edward Faulkner), Bomb Disposal Man (Don Wilbanks), Charlie (Don Stewart).

Credits: Produced by: Frank Price; Directed by: William Graham; Written by: Rod Serling; Director of Photography: William Margulies, A. S. C.; Music by: Lalo Schifrin; Art Director: Frank Arrigo; Film Editor: Robert F. Shugrue; Sound: Thom Piper; Costume Supervision: Vincent Dee; Makeup: Bud Westmore; Hair Stylist: Larry Germain; Produced by: Universal Television; Exclusive Distributor: MCA Television Limited.

DOUBLE INDEMNITY

ABC Television Network, October 13, 1973; 90 minutes in color on film.

A suspense drama about a woman and an insurance man who plotted to kill her husband and collect on his policy. Based on the 1944 film and the novel Three of a Kind by James M. Cain.

Cast: Walter Neff (Richard Crenna), Barton Keyes (Lee J. Cobb), Phyllis Dietrichson (Samantha Eggar), Lola Dietrichson (Kathleen Cody), Dietrichson (Arch Johnson), Jackson (John Fiedler), Edward Norton (Robert Webber), Sam Bonaventura (Gene Dynarski), Donald Franklin (John Elerick), Neff's Secretary (Joan Pringle).

Credits: Executive Producer: David Victor; Produced by: Robert F. O'Neill; Directed by: Jack Smight; Written by: Steve Bochco; Based on the Screenplay by: Raymond Chandler, Billy Wilder; Based on the Novel "Three of a Kind" by: James M. Cain; Director of Photography: Haskell Boggs; Music by: Billy Goldenberg; Art Director: Joseph Alves, Jr.; Film Editor: Edward A. Biery; Color by: Technicolor; Titles & Optical Effects: Universal Title; Produced by: Universal Television; Exclusive Distributor: MCA Television Limited.

DRAGNET 1966
(WORLD PREMIERE/NBC MONDAY NIGHT AT THE MOVIES)

NBC Television Network, January 27, 1969; 120 minutes in color on film.

A drama about Sgt. Joe Friday and Officer Bill Gannon's dogged search for an elusive murderer who preyed on photographic models. The pilot for the series Dragnet 1967-1970 (which see), this film was produced in 1966 as the second World Premiere attraction, but was not telecast until 1969.

Cast: Sgt. Joe Friday (Jack Webb), Officer Bill Gannon (Harry Morgan), Don Negler (Vic Perrin), Mrs. Kruger (Virginia Gregg), Capt. Hugh Brown (Gene Evans), Sgt. Dave Bradford (John Roseboro), George Freeman (Bobby Troup), Melvin Gannon (Tom Williams), Carl Rockwell (Jack Ragotzy), William Smith (Roger Till), Claude La Borg (Gerald Michenaud), Freddie (Bruce Watson), Ricky Markell (Herb Ellis), Max Shelton (Eddie Firestone), Eve Sorenson (Elizabeth Rogers).

Credits: Produced and Directed by: Jack Webb; Written by: Richard L. Breen; Associate Producer: Burt Nodella; Director of Photography: Walter Strenge, A.S.C.; Music by: Lyn Murray; Art Director: Russell Kimball; Film Editor: Richard Belding; Costume Supervisor: Vincent Dee; Makeup: Bud Westmore; Hair Stylist: Larry Germain; Technical Advisor: Lt. Pierce Brooks, Homicide Division, Los Angeles Police Department; Produced by: Mark VII Limited; In Association with: Universal Television And NBC-TV; Exclusive Distributor: MCA Television Limited.

DRIVE HARD, DRIVE FAST
(WORLD PREMIERE)

NBC Television Network, September 11, 1973; 120 minutes in color on film.

A drama about a race car driver who agreed to drive a wealthy woman from Mexico City to New Orleans and became the target of a murderer. Produced in 1969, this film was not telecast until 1973.

Cast: Mark Driscoll (Brian Kelly), Carole Bradley (Joan Collins), Richard LaCosta (Henry Silva), Eric Bradley (Joseph Campanella), Ellen (Karen Huston), William Fielder (Todd Martin), Blond Man (Charles H. Gray), Cartier (Patrick Whyte), Gerald Ives (John Trayne), Mechanic (Jacques Denbeaux).

148 / Telefeatures

Credits: Executive Producer: Roy Huggins; Produced by: Jo Swerling, Jr.; Directed by: Douglas Heyes; Written by: Matthew Howard; Story by: John Thomas James; Associate Producers: Steve Heilpern, Carl Pingitore; Director of Photography: Gene Polito; Music by: Pete Rugolo; Art Director: Robert Luthardt; Film Editor: John Dumas; Assistant Director: James A. Westman; Sound: Lyle Cain; Color by: Technicolor; Titles & Optical Effects: Universal Title; Produced by: Universal Television; In Association with: NBC-TV; Exclusive Distributor: MCA Television Limited.

DUEL
(ABC MOVIE OF THE WEEKEND)

ABC Television Network, November 13, 1971; 90 minutes in color on film. Major Sponsor and Agency: Warner-Lambert Pharmaceutical Company through J. Walter Thompson Company.

A suspense drama about a motorist on a lonely highway who became engaged in a deadly cat and mouse game with a vengeful truck driver who was determined to force him off the road regardless of the consequences. Filmed on location in the Mint Canyon-Soledad Canyon area of Saugus, California.

Cast: David Mann (Dennis Weaver), Mrs. Mann (Jacqueline Scott), Cafe Owner (Eddie Firestone), Bus Driver (Lou Frizzell), Man in Cafe (Gene Dynarski), Lady at Snakerama (Lucille Benson), Gas Station Attendant (Tim Herbert), Old Man (Charles Seel), Waitress (Shirley O'Hara), Old Man in Car (Alexander Lockwood), Old Woman in Car (Amy Douglass), Radio Interviewer (Dick Whittington), The Truck Driver (Cary Loftin), Car Driver (Dale Van Sickle).

Credits: Produced by: George Eckstein; Directed by: Steven Spielberg; Written by: Richard Matheson; Based on the "Playboy" Story by: Richard Matheson; Director of Photography: Jack A. Marta; Music by: Billy Goldenberg; Art Director: Robert E. Smith; Set Decorations: S. Blydenburgh; Film Editor: Frank Morriss; Sound: Edwin S. Hall; Color by: Technicolor; Titles & Optical Effects: Universal Title; Produced by: Universal Television; Exclusive Distributor: MCA Television Limited.

THE ELEVATOR
(ABC SUSPENSE MOVIE)

ABC Television Network, February 9, 1974; 90 minutes in color on film.

A suspense drama about a claustrophobic armed robber who found himself trapped in an elevator with a diverse group of people while fleeing from his latest "job."

Cast: Eddie Holcomb (James Farentino), Mrs. Kenyon (Myrna Loy),

Marvin Ellis (Roddy McDowall), Dr. Reynolds (Craig Stevens), Pete Howarth (Don Stroud), Irene Turner (Carol Lynley), Robert Peters (Barry Livingston), Wendy Thompson (Arlene Golonka), Mrs. Reynolds (Theresa Wright), Mrs. Peters (Jean Allyson).

Credits: Produced by: William Frye; Directed by: Jerry Jameson; Written by: Bruce Shelley, David Ketchum, Rhoda Blecker; Director of Photography: Matthew F. Leonetti; Music by: John Cacavas; Art Director: Leroy G. Deane; Film Editors: J. Jerry Williams, Philip Haberman; Color by: Technicolor; Titles & Optical Effects: Universal Title; Produced by: Universal Television; Exclusive Distributor: MCA Television Limited.

ELLERY QUEEN
(NBC SUNDAY MYSTERY MOVIE)

NBC Television Network, March 23, 1975; 120 minutes in color on film.

A detective drama about the 1940s criminologist-author's investigation into the killing of a well-known fashion designer. The pilot for the series Ellery Queen (which see). An earlier pilot for a series which didn't sell was 1971's Ellery Queen: Don't Look Behind You (which see) starring Peter Lawford.

Cast: Ellery Queen (Jim Hutton), Inspector Richard Queen (David Wayne), Carson McKell (Ray Milland), Tom McKell (Monte Markham), Simon Brimmer (John Hillerman), Gail Stevens (Gail Strickland), Marion McKell (Kim Hunter), Sgt. Velie (Tom Reese), Ben Waterson (Tim O'Connor), District Attorney (John Larch), Eddie Carter (Warren Berlinger), Announcer (Harry Von Zell), Maid (Dwan Smith).

Credits: Producers: Richard Levinson, William Link; Directed by: David Greene; Written by: Richard Levinson, William Link; Based on the Novel "The Fourth Side of the Triangle" by: Ellery Queen; Director of Photography: Howard R. Schwartz; Music by: Elmer Bernstein; Art Director: George Webb; Film Editor: Douglas Stewart; Color by: Technicolor; Titles & Optical Effects: Universal Title; Produced by: Fairmount/Foxcroft Productions; In Association with: Universal Television And NBC-TV; Exclusive Distributor: MCA Television Limited.

ELLERY QUEEN: DON'T LOOK BEHIND YOU
(WORLD PREMIERE)

NBC Television Network, November 19, 1971; 120 minutes in color on film.

A detective drama about author-criminologist Ellery Queen's investigation of a strangler whose victims had numerically descending ages,

150 / Telefeatures

and were strangled with blue cords when they were male and pink ones when they were female. Queen was drawn into the case by his Uncle, Inspector Richard Queen of the New York City Police Department. This was the pilot for an unsold series, although a later version, Ellery Queen (which see), did become a series starring Jim Hutton.

Cast: Ellery Queen (Peter Lawford), Inspector Richard Queen (Harry Morgan), Dr. Cazalis (E. G. Marshall), Celeste (Stefanie Powers), Christy (Skye Aubrey), Mrs. Cazalis (Coleen Gray), Police Commissioner (Morgan Sterne), Sgt. Velie (Bill Zuckert), Hal Hunter (Bob Hastings), Registrar (Than Wyeen).

Credits: Executive Producer: Edward J. Montagne; Produced by: Leonard J. Ackerman; Directed by: Barry Shear; Written by: Ted Leighton; Based on the Novel "Cat of Many Tails" by: Ellery Queen; Director of Photography: William Margulies; Music by: Jerry Fielding; Art Director: Alexander A. Mayer; Film Editor: Sam E. Waxman, A. C. E.; Animation: Felix Zelenka Productions; Color by: Technicolor; Titles & Optical Effects: Universal Title; Produced by: Universal Television; In Association with: NBC-TV; Exclusive Distributor: MCA Television Limited.

EMERGENCY!
(WORLD PREMIERE)

NBC Television Network, January 15, 1972; 120 minutes in color on film.

A film comprised of a series of events dramatizing the vital need for paramedics. Among them: an automobile accident and a tunnel explosion. Martin Milner and Kent McCord appeared in their Adam-12 roles as police officers Malloy and Reed of the L. A. P. D. The pilot for the series Emergency! (which see) and the basis for the animated cartoon series Emergency Plus Four (which see).

Cast: Dr. Kelly Brackett (Robert Fuller), Nurse Dixie McCall (Julie London), Dr. Joe Early (Bobby Troup), John Gage (Randolph Mantooth), Roy DeSoto (Kevin Tighe), Mike Wolski (Jack Kruschen), Officer Pete Malloy (Martin Milner), Officer Jim Reed (Kent McCord), Tony (Colby Chester), Battalion Chief (Arthur Balinger), Second Chief (Arthur Gilmore), Woman (Ann Morgan Guilbert).

Credits: Executive Producer: Jack Webb; Produced by: R. A. Cinader; Created and Written by: Harold Jack Bloom, R. A. Cinader; Directed by: Jack Webb; Associate Producer: William Stark; Director of Photography: Jack Marta; Music by: Nelson Riddle; Art Director: John J. Lloyd; Film Editor: Warren H. Adams; Sound: Robert Bertrand; Color by: Technicolor; Titles & Optical Effects: Universal Title; Produced by: Mark VII Limited; In Association with: Universal Television And NBC-TV; Exclusive Distributor: MCA Television Limited.

ESCAPE FROM COLDITZ

NBC Television Network, August 25, 1977; 120 minutes in color on film.

A drama about three Allied POWs who broke out of World War II Germany's famed maximum-security prison. Filmed in 1972 but not aired until 1977, this film was edited from episodes of the series Colditz (which see) which was never broadcast on American television.

Cast: Robert Wagner, David McCallum, Jack Hedley, Edward Hardwicke, Christopher Neame, Bernard Hepton.

Credits: Produced by: Gerard Glaister; Directed by: Michael Ferguson; Written by: N. J. Crisp; Produced by: BBC-TV, Universal Television.

ESCAPE TO MINDANAO
(WORLD PREMIERE/NBC SATURDAY NIGHT AT THE MOVIES)

NBC Television Network, December 7, 1968; 120 minutes in color on film.

A drama about two American soldiers, among 5,000 imprisoned by the Japanese in a Luzon compound during World War II, who came into possession of a secret Japanese decoding device. The two escaped the compound, aided by the Filipino underground, in an attempt to deliver the device to Allied forces in Mindanao. On their journey they encountered a black marketeer and an opportunistic Merchant Marine captain and his daughter. Filmed on location on Luzon, Philippine Islands.

Cast: Joe Walden (George Maharis), Capt. Kramer (Nehemiah Persoff), Anne (Willi Koopman), Lt. Takahashi (James Shigeta), Lt. Parang (Ronald Remy), Sokuri (Vic Diaz), Capt. Aquino (Eddie Arenas), Zairin (Gil De Leon), Viray (Andres Centenera), Sgt. Major (Vic Uematsu).

Credits: Produced by: Jack Leewood; Directed by: Don McDougall; Written by: Harold Livingston; Story by: Orville H. Hampton; Director of Photography: Ray Flin; Music by: Lyn Murray; Art Director: Napoleon Enriquez; Film Editor: Richard G. Wray, A. C. E.; Costumes by: Grady Hunt; Wardrobe: Alice Garcia; Makeup: Pat De Lara; Color by: Technicolor; Titles & Optical Effects: Universal Title; Produced by: Universal Television; In Association with: NBC-TV; Exclusive Distributor: MCA Television Limited.

EVIL ROY SLADE
(WORLD PREMIERE)

NBC Television Network, February 18, 1972; 120 minutes in color on film.

A comedy-Western about Evil Roy Slade, the meanest outlaw in the West, whose friends and enemies were determined to reform him or kill him. The pilot for an unsold series.

Cast: Evil Roy Slade (John Astin), Nelson Stool (Mickey Rooney), Marshal Bing Bell (Dick Shawn), Clifford Stool (Henry Stool), Logan Delp (Dom DeLuise), Flossie (Edie Adams), Betsy (Pamela Austin), Harry Fern (Milton Berle), Lee (Arthur Batanides), Snake (Larry Hankin).

Credits: Executive Producer: Howie Horwitz; Produced and Written by: Jerry Belson, Garry Marshall; Directed by: Jerry Paris; Director of Photography: Sam Leavitt; Music by: Stuart Margolin, Murray MacLeod, Jerry Riopelle, James Prigmore; Art Director: Alexander A. Mayer; Film Editor: Richard M. Sprague; Color by: Technicolor; Titles & Optical Effects: Universal Title; Produced by: Universal Television; In Association with: NBC-TV; Exclusive Distributor: MCA Television Limited.

THE EXECUTION OF PRIVATE SLOVIK
(WORLD PREMIERE)

NBC Television Network, March 13, 1974; 150 minutes in color on film.

A drama about Private Eddie Slovik, a soldier in World War II, who was the only American to be executed for desertion since the Civil War. The telefeature followed Slovik's life from the time he was paroled from prison to his death by firing squad in 1945 in St. Marie Aux Mines, France. In between, the program explored his marriage, induction into the Army rifle corps, fear of combat, desertion and court martial. Based on the 1954 book by William Bradford Huie. Filmed in Montreal and Quebec.

Cast: Eddie Slovik (Martin Sheen), Antoinette Slovik (Mariclare Costello), Father Stafford (Ned Beatty), Jimmy Freedek (Gary Busey), Margaret (Kathryn Grody), Maj. Fellman (Warren Kemmerling), Dunn (Matt Clark), Lt. Col. Leacock (Ben Hamer), Joe Sirelli (Paul Lambert), Brockmeyer (Charles Haid), with: Jon Cedar, Joseph George, Laurence Haddon, James-Burr Johnson, Tom Ligon, Bill McKinney, Paul Shenar, George Sperdakos, William Traylor, Sandy Ward.

Credits: Executive Producers: Richard Levinson, William Link; Produced by: Richard Dubleman; Directed by: Lamont Johnson; Written by: Richard Levinson, William Link; Based on the Book by: William Bradford Huie; Director of Photography: Bill Butler; Music by: Hal Mooney; Art Director: Walter Tyler; Film Editor: Frank Morriss; Set Decorations: Richard Friedman; Color by: Technicolor; Titles & Optical Effects: Universal Title; Produced by: Universal Television; In Association with: NBC-TV; Exclusive Distributor: MCA Television Limited.

EXO-MAN
(WORLD PREMIERE/NBC SATURDAY NIGHT AT THE MOVIES)

NBC Television Network, June 18, 1977; 120 minutes in color on film.

An action-adventure film about a physics professor, paralyzed below the waist, who developed a device that revitalized his legs and endowed him with super-human abilities. The pilot for an unsold series.

Cast: Nick Conrad (David Ackroyd), Emily Frost (Anne Schedeen), Raphael (A Martinez), Kermit Haas (José Ferrer), Travis (Harry Morgan), Kamenski (Kevin McCarthy), Martin (Jack Colvin), Rubenstein (Jonathan Segal), Yamaguchi (Richard Narita), Dominic Leandro (John Moio), with: Eve McVeagh, W. T. Zacha, Martin Speer, Frances Osborne, Greg Barnett, Max Kleven, Terry Leonard, Alan Oliney, John Robotham, Wina Sturgeon, Allan Wyatt, Jr., Joe Brooks, Chuck Walsh, Wally Rose, Russ Saunders, Henri Kingi, Nick David, Randy Fausting, Fritz Ford, Bill Lane, Donald Moffat, Norma Storch.

Credits: Executive Producer: Richard Irving; Produced by: Lionel E. Siegel; Directed by: Richard Irving; Written by: Lionel E. Siegel, Martin Caidin, Howard Rodman; Story by: Martin Caidin, Henri Simoun; Director of Photography: Enzo A. Martinelli; Music by: Dana Kaproff; Art Director: John W. Corso; Film Editor: Howard Leeds; Color by: Technicolor; Titles & Optical Effects: Universal Title; Produced by: Universal Television; In Association with: NBC-TV; Exclusive Distributor: MCA Television Limited.

THE FAILING OF RAYMOND
(ABC MOVIE OF THE WEEKEND)

ABC Television Network, November 27, 1971; 90 minutes in color on film.

A suspense drama about a dedicated high school teacher who faced the greatest challenge of her career when one of her former pupils, a disturbed young man she flunked, threatened her life in a deserted classroom.

Cast: Mary Bloomquist (Jane Wyman), Raymond (Dean Stockwell), Allan McDonald (Dana Andrews), Dr. Abel (Paul Henreid), Sgt. Manzak (Murray Hamilton), Cliff Roeder (Tim O'Connor), History Teacher (Priscilla Pointer), Latin Teacher (Mary Jackson), Librarian (Adrienne Marden), Girl Patient (Catherine Louise Sagal), City Editor (Robert Karnes), Store Owner (Ray Ballard).

Credits: Produced by: George Eckstein; Directed by: Boris Sagal; Written by: Adrian Spies; Director of Photography: Ben Colman; Music by: Pat Williams; Art Director: Robert Clatworthy; Set Decorations: Charles S. Thompson; Film Editor: John Kaufman, Jr.; Color by: Technicolor; Titles & Optical Effects: Universal Title; Produced by: Universal Television; Exclusive Distributor: MCA Television Limited.

FAME IS THE NAME OF THE GAME
(WORLD PREMIERE)

NBC Television Network, November 26, 1966; 120 minutes in color on film.

A mystery drama about Fame magazine reporter Jeff Dillon who, while on assignment, accidentally discovered the body of a slain girl. Based on the novel One Woman by Tiffany Thayer and the 1949 film Chicago Deadline, this telefeature served as the pilot for the series The Name of the Game (which see). In the series, Fame was changed to People magazine and Gene Barry took over the role of publisher Glenn Howard. The telefeature was the first of the NBC-Universal World Premiere movies.

Cast: Jeff Dillon (Tony Franciosa), Leona (Jill St. John), Ben Welcome (Jack Klugman), Peggy Maxwell (Susan Saint James), Cruikshank (Lee Bowman), Glenn Howard (George Macready), Griffin (Jack Weston), Belle (Melodie Johnson), Eddie (Robert Duvall), Pat (Nanette Fabray), Dizzy (Jay C. Flippen).

Credits: Produced by: Ranald MacDougall; Directed by: Stuart Rosenberg; Written by: Ranald MacDougall; Based on the Novel "One Woman" by: Tiffany Thayer; Director of Photography: John F. Warren; Music by: Benny Carter; Art Director: John J. Lloyd; Film Editor: Edward W. Williams; Sound: Earl Craine, Jr.; Color by: Technicolor; Titles & Optical Effects: Universal Title; Produced by: Universal Television; In Association with: NBC-TV; Exclusive Distributor: MCA Television Limited.

FAMILY FLIGHT
(ABC WEDNESDAY MOVIE OF THE WEEK)

ABC Television Network, October 25, 1972; 90 minutes in color on film.

A drama about a flying vacation to Mexico for a disunited family that turned into a near-hopeless battle for survival after a crash-landing in an isolated section of Baja California. Filmed on location at Lucerne Valley, California. U.S. Navy sequences were filmed off the California coast at Monterey and San Diego.

Cast: Jason Carlyle (Rod Taylor), Florence Carlyle (Dina Merrill),

David Carlyle (Kristoffer Tabori), Carol Rutledge (Janet Margolin), Carrier Captain (Gene Nelson), Officer of the Deck (Richard Roat), 1st Controller (Paul Kent), 2nd Controller (James Sikking), Frank Gross (Bill Zuckert), Driver (Ed Begley, Jr.).

Credits: Produced by: Harve Bennett; Directed by: Marvin Chomsky; Written by: Guerdon Trueblood; Director of Photography: Emil Oster; Music by: Fred Steiner; Art Director: John J. Lloyd; Set Decorations; Ralph Hurst; Film Editor: Charles K. McClelland; Aerial Sequences by: Frank Tallman, Tallmantz Aviation; Color by: Technicolor; Titles & Optical Effects: Universal Title; Produced by: Universal Television; Exclusive Distributor: MCA Television Limited.

THE FAMILY NOBODY WANTED
(ABC WEDNESDAY MOVIE OF THE WEEK)

ABC Television Network, February 19, 1975; 90 minutes in color on film.

A drama about an impoverished minister and his wife who fought to find a home for their racially mixed, adopted children.

Cast: Helen Doss (Shirley Jones), Carl Doss (James Olson), Elmer Franklin (Woodrow Parfrey), Eunice Franklin (Claudia Bryar), Judge Goldman (Lindsay Workman), Rick (Ernest Esparza III), Donny (Willy Ames), James Collins (Beeson Carroll), Mrs. Bittner (Katherine Helmond), Mrs. Kimberly (Ann Doran), with: Dawn Biglay, Guillermo San Juan, Gina Tan, Tina Toyota, Haig Movsesian, Knar Keshishian, Charlene Wong, Tim Kim, Sherry Kupahu, Michael Stadnik, Robert Stadnik.

Credits: Executive Producer: David Victor; Produced by: William Kayden; Directed by: Ralph Senensky; Written by: Suzanne Clauser; Based on the Book by: Helen Doss; Director of Photography: Jack Woolf; Music by: George Romanis; Art Director: Ira Diamond; Film Editor: Chuck McClelland; Color by: Technicolor; Titles & Optical Effects: Universal Title; Produced by: Universal Television; Exclusive Distributor: MCA Television Limited.

FAREWELL TO MANZANAR
(NBC THURSDAY NIGHT AT THE MOVIES)

NBC Television Network, March 11, 1976; 120 minutes in color on film.

A drama about a Japanese-American family whose well-ordered lives were disrupted by the concern for national security that followed the attack on Pearl Harbor. The father, accused of supplying fuel to Japanese submarines, was imprisoned, while the rest of the family was sent to the internment camp of Manzanar in California's Mojave Desert.

156 / Telefeatures

Cast: Misa/Jeanne Wakatsuki (Nobu McCarthy), Ko Wakatsuki (Yuki Shimoda), Teddy Wakatsuki (Clyde Kusatu), Richard Wakatsuki (James Saito), Young Jeanne (Dori Takeshita), Koro (Akemi Kikumura), Fukimoto (Mako), Alice (Momo Yashima), Lois (Gretchen Corbett), Zenahiro (Pat Morita), Captain Curtis (Kip Niven), Himself (Lou Frizzell), Narrator (Greta Chi).

Credits: Executive Producer: George J. Santoro; Produced and Directed by: John Korty; Written by: Jeanne Wakatsuki Houston, John Korty, James D. Houston; Based on the Book by: Jeanne Wakatsuki Houston, James D. Houston; Director of Photography: Hiro Narita; Music by: Paul Chihara; Production Designer: Robert Konoshita; Film Editor: Eric Albertson; Color by: Technicolor; Titles & Optical Effects: Universal Title; Produced by: Korty Films, Inc.; In Association with: Universal Television; Exclusive Distributor: MCA Television Limited.

FEAR NO EVIL
(WORLD PREMIERE)

NBC Television Network, March 3, 1969; 120 minutes in color on film.

A drama about psychiatrist Paul Varney who bought a strange mirror for his apartment, despite his girlfriend's dislike for it. But she soon became entranced with it as well. When Varney died in an automobile accident, his grief-stricken girlfriend learned that the mirror could bring her lover back. Followed by the sequel Ritual of Evil (which see). The pilot for an unsold series.

Cast: David Sorell (Louis Jourdan), Paul Varney (Bradford Dillman), Barbara (Lynda Day), Mrs. Varney (Marsha Hunt), Myles Donovan (Carroll O'Connor), Harry Snowden (Wilfrid Hyde-White), Ingrid Dorne (Kate Woodville), Wyant (Harry Davis).

Credits: Produced by: Richard Alan Simmons; Directed by: Paul Wendkos; Written by: Richard Alan Simmons; Story by: Guy Endore; Associate Producer: David Levinson; Director of Photography: Andrew J. McIntyre; Music by: Billy Goldenberg; Art Director: Howard E. Johnson; Film Editor: Byron Chudnow; Assistant Director: Kenny Williams; Color by: Technicolor; Titles & Optical Effects: Universal Title; Produced by: Universal Television; In Association with: NBC-TV; Exclusive Distributor: MCA Television Limited.

FEMALE ARTILLERY
(ABC WEDNESDAY MOVIE OF THE WEEK)

ABC Television Network, January 17, 1973; 90 minutes in color on film.

Female Artillery / 157

A Western about a rugged outlaw and a wagon train of bawdy frontier women who became unlikely combatants when they were forced to take a stand together at an abandoned cavalry fort. Filmed on location in Antelope Valley, California.

Cast: Deke Chambers (Dennis Weaver), Martha Lindstrom (Ida Lupino), Sybil Townsend (Sally Ann Howes), Charlotte Paxton (Linda Evans), Brian Townsend (Lee H. Montgomery), Frank Taggart (Albert Salmi), Sarah De La O (Anna Navarro), Amelia Craig (Nina Foch), Sam (Charles Dierkop), Johnny (Nate Esformes), Squat (Lee de Broux), John Townsend (Bobby Eilbacher), Billy (Robby Weaver).

Credits: Produced by: Winston Miller; Directed by: Marvin Chomsky; Written by: Bud Freeman; Story by: Jack Sher, Bud Freeman; Director of Photography: Enzo A. Martinelli; Music by: Frank DeVol; Art Director: Sydney Z. Litwack; Film Editors: John Elias, John Kaufman, Jr., Albert J. Zuniga; Color by: Technicolor; Titles & Optical Effects: Universal Title; Produced by: Universal Television; Exclusive Distributor: MCA Television Limited.

FORCE FIVE
(CBS FRIDAY NIGHT MOVIE)

CBS Television Network, March 28, 1975; 90 minutes in color on film.

A drama about police Lt. Kessler who gathered together a group of ex-cons to solve the toughest, most baffling crimes in his district. The pilot for an unsold series.

Cast: Lt. Roy Kessler (Gerald Gordon), James T. O'Neil (Nick Pryor), Vic Bauer (William Lucking), Lester White (James Hampton), Arnier Kogan (Roy Jenson), Norman Ellsworth (David Spielberg), Cal Newkirk (Leif Erickson), Arthur Haberman (Normann Burton), Michael Dominick (Bradford Dillman), Frankie Hatcher (Victor Argo), Steve Ritchie (Lee Paul).

Credits: Producers: Michael Gleason, David Levinson; Directed by: Walter Grauman; Written by: Michael Gleason, David Levinson; Director of Photography: Jack Swain; Music by: James Di Pasquale; Art Director: John E. Chilberg II; Film Editor: Richard Bracken; Color by: Technicolor; Titles & Optical Effects: Universal Title; Produced by: Universal Television; Exclusive Distributor: MCA Television Limited.

FRANKENSTEIN: THE TRUE STORY

NBC Television Network, November 30, 1973 and December 1, 1973; 4 hours in color on film.

A remake of the 1931 film based on Mary Shelley's novel about the tragic results of Dr. Frankenstein's experiment of creating a living creature out of the body parts of dead men.

Cast: Dr. Polidori/Narrator (James Mason), Dr. Victor Frankenstein (Leonard Whiting), The Creature (Michael Sarrazin), Henri Clerval (David McCallum), Elizabeth Fanschawe (Nicola Paget), Agatha/Prima (Jane Seymour), Sir Richard Fanschawe (Michael Wilding), Mrs. Blair (Agnes Moorehead), Lady Fanschawe (Clarissa Kaye), Françoise DuVal (Margaret Leighton), Chief Constable (John Gielgud), Mr. Lacy (Ralph Richardson), Sea Captain (Tom Baker), Young Man (Julian Barnes), Felix (Dallas Adams).

Credits: Produced by: Hunt Stromberg, Jr.; Directed by: Jack Smight; Written by: Christopher Isherwood, Don Bachardy; Based on the Novel by: Mary Shelley; Director of Photography: Arthur Ibbetson; Music by: Gil Melle; Art Director: Wilfrid Shingleton; Film Editor: Richard Marden; Color by: Technicolor; Titles & Optical Effects: Universal Title; Produced by: Universal Television; Exclusive Distributor: MCA Television Limited.

GEMINI MAN
(WORLD PREMIERE)

NBC Television Network, May 10, 1976; 120 minutes in color on film.

A science fiction drama about INTERSECT (International Security Technics) agent Sam Casey who was made invisible by the radiation aftereffects of an underwater explosion. He set out to use his newfound powers to nail the saboteurs who planted the explosive device. This pilot for the series Gemini Man (which see) was inspired by the earlier telefeature The Invisible Man (which see) which was also turned into a series.

Cast: Sam Casey (Ben Murphy), Dr. Abby Lawrence (Katherine Crawford), Leonard Driscoll (Richard A. Dysart), Royce (Paul Shenar), Dr. Harold Schyler (Dana Elcar), Vince Rogers (Quinn Redeker), Capt. Taggart (Greg Walcott), Capt. Ballard (H. M. Wynant), Capt. Whelan (Len Wayland), Receptionist (Cheryl Miller).

Credits: Executive Producer: Harve Bennett; Produced by: Robert F. O'Neill; Directed by: Alan Levi; Written by: Leslie Stevens; Suggested by the Novel "The Invisible Man" by: H. G. Wells; Director of Photography: Enzo A. Martinelli; Music by: Billy Goldenberg; Art Director: David Marshall; Set Decorations: Lowell Chambers; Film Editor: Robert F. Shugrue; Color by: Technicolor; Titles & Optical Effects: Universal Title; Produced by: Harve Bennett Productions; In Association with: Universal Television; Exclusive Distributor: MCA Television Limited.

THE GREAT MAN'S WHISKERS
(WORLD PREMIERE/NBC TUESDAY NIGHT AT THE MOVIES)

NBC Television Network, February 13, 1973; 120 minutes in color on film.

A drama about a small-town school teacher who was suddenly thrust into the limelight when his 10-year-old daughter wrote a letter to the newly-elected President, Abraham Lincoln, urging him to grow a beard. Filmed in 1969, this telefeature was not broadcast until 1973.

Cast: Abraham Lincoln (Dennis Weaver), James Cooper (Dean Jones), Aunt Margaret (Ann Sothern), Andrew Hogan (John McGiver), Minstrel (Harve Presnell), Catherine (Beth Brickell), Elizabeth (Cindy Eilbacher), Somerby (Richard Erdman), Ella (Isabel Sanford), Mr. Philbrick (Charles Lane).

Credits: Produced by: Adrian Scott; Directed by: Philip Leacock; Written by: John Paxton; Based on the One Act Play by: Adrian Scott; Director of Photography: John F. Warren; Music by: Earl Robinson; Lyrics by: E. Y. Harburg; Art Director: George Webb; Film Editor: John Elias; Color by: Technicolor; Titles & Optical Effects: Universal Title; Produced by: Universal Television; Exclusive Distributor: MCA Television Limited.

THE GREATEST GIFT
(NBC MONDAY NIGHT AT THE MOVIES)

NBC Television Network, November 4, 1974; 120 minutes in color on film.

A drama about a 13-year-old boy's relationship with his preacher father. Set in the rural South in 1940. Filmed on location in Statesboro, Georgia, this telefeature was the pilot for the series The Family Holvak (which see). The working title was Holvak.

Cast: Reverend Holvak (Glenn Ford), Elizabeth Holvak (Julie Harris), Ramey Holvak (Lance Kerwin), Hog Yancey (Harris Yulin), Julie Mae Holvak (Cari Anne Warder), Amos Goodloe (Charles Tyner), Deacon Hurd (Dabbs Greer), Willis Graham (Furman Walters), Eli Wiggins (Albert Smith), Tincey Bell (Leslie Thorsen), Abraham Morrison (Ken Renard), Mrs. Goodloe (Elsie Travis), Jim Friedland (J. Don Ferguson), Narrated by Burt Douglas.

Credits: Produced by: Dean Hargrove; Directed by: Boris Sagal; Written by: Abby Mann; Based on the Novel "Ramey" by: Jack Farris; Director of Photography: Stevan Larner; Music by: Dick De Benedictis; Art Director: Dick T. Smith; Film Editors: Douglas Stewart, Howard Epstein; Color by: Technicolor; Titles & Optical Effects: Universal Title; Produced by: Universal Television; Exclusive Distributor: MCA Television Limited.

160 / Telefeatures

GUILTY OR INNOCENT: THE SAM SHEPPARD MURDER CASE
(WORLD PREMIERE/NBC MONDAY NIGHT AT THE MOVIES)

NBC Television Network, November 17, 1975; 3 hours in color on film.

A drama about Cleveland osteopathic surgeon Sam Sheppard who in 1954 was accused of the brutal slaying of his wife. Sent to prison for 10 years, Sheppard was finally re-tried and found not guilty, with the help of attorney F. Lee Bailey.

Cast: Dr. Sam Sheppard (George Peppard), Attorney Philip J. Madden (Barnard Hughes), F. Lee Bailey (Walter McGinn), Walt Adamson (William Windom), Ilse Brandt (Nina Van Pallandt), Prosecutor Simmons (George Murdock), Fred Stoner (John Crawford), Medical Examiner (John Harkins), Jack (John Carter), Dr. Richard Sheppard, Sr. (William Dozier), Marilyn Sheppard (Claudette Nevins), Supreme Court Justice (Paul Fix), Det. Moore (Jack Night), Jerry Wyman (James Whitmore III), Judge Edwards (Russell Thorsen).

Credits: Executive Producer: Harve Bennett; Produced by: Harold Gast; Directed by: Robert Michael Lewis; Written by: Harold Gast; Based on a Story by: Lou Randolph; Director of Photography: Stevan Larner; Music by: Lalo Schifrin; Art Director: William Campbell; Film Editor: Robert F. Shugrue; Color by: Technicolor; Titles & Optical Effects: Universal Title; Produced by: Silverton Productions; In Association with: Universal Television And NBC-TV; Exclusive Distributor: MCA Television Limited.

THE GUN
(ABC WEDNESDAY MOVIE OF THE WEEK)

ABC Television Network, November 13, 1974; 90 minutes in color on film.

A drama about the odyssey of a .38 police special that passed through the hands of a suicidal man, a middle-class suburbanite, a deranged youngster and a small-time hood, among others.

Cast: Art Hilliard (Stephen Elliott), Wayne (David Huffman), Natcho (Pepe Serna), Senor Peralta (Felipe Turich), Gloria (Edith Diaz), Fran (Jean LeBouvier), Howie (Wallace Rooney), Frank (Val DeVargas), Walt Kelsy (Ramon Bieri), Braverman (John Sylvester White), Wilke (Michael McGuire), Tom (Ron Thompson), Kenny (Randy Gray), Gil Strauss (Richard Bright), Beryl Strauss (Mariclare Costello).

Credits: Producers: Richard Levinson, William Link; Directed by: John Badham; Written by: Richard Levinson, William Link; Story by: Jay Benson, Richard Levinson, William Link; Director of Photography: Stevan Larner; Art Director: Walter M. Simonds; Film Editor: Frank Morriss; Color by: Technicolor; Titles & Optical Effects:

Universal Title; Produced by: Fairmount/Foxcroft Productions; In Association with: Universal Television; Exclusive Distributor: MCA Television Limited.

THE HANGED MAN
(PROJECT 120)

NBC Television Network, November 18, 1964; 120 minutes in color on film.

A drama about Harry Pace, a man who hunted for the slayer of his best friend during the Mardi Gras festivities in New Orleans. A remake of the 1947 film Ride the Pink Horse, this telefeature was the second of the NBC-Universal Project 120 movies.

Cast: Harry Pace (Robert Culp), Arnie Seeger (Edmond O'Brien), Lois Seeger (Vera Miles), Gaylor Greb (Norman Fell), Whitey Devlin (Gene Raymond), Celine (Brenda Scott), Uncle Picaud (J. Carroll Naish), Otis Honeywell (Pat Buttram), Hotel Clerk (Edgar Bergen), Xavier (Archie Moore), The Boy (Randy Boone), Al (Al Lettieri), TV Newsman (Scott Hale), Bellboy (Seymour Cassel).

Credits: Produced by: Ray Wagner; Directed by: Don Siegel; Written by: Jack Laird, Stanford Whitmore; Based on the Novel by: Dorothy B. Hughes; Director of Photography: Bud Thackery; Music by: Stanley Wilson; Art Director: John J. Lloyd; Film Editor: Richard Belding; Produced by: Universal Television; Exclusive Distributor: MCA Television Limited.

THE HARNESS
(WORLD PREMIERE)

NBC Television Network, November 12, 1971; 120 minutes in color on film.

A drama about a middle-aged rancher, whose life was regulated by his ailing wife, and the disturbance of their relationship by the appearance of a free-spirited young woman and her son passing through on their way to the Big Sur camping area.

Cast: Peter Randall (Lorne Greene), Jennifer Shagaris (Julie Sommars), Roy Kern (Murray Hamilton), Tor Shagaris (Lee Harcourt Montgomery), Emma Randall (Louise Latham), Doc Marn (Henry Beckman), Millie Chappel (Joan Tompkins), Edgar Chappel (Robert Karnes), Minister (John Lasell), Charles Pitts (William Lanteau).

Credits: Produced by: William Sackheim; Directed by: Boris Sagal; Written by: Leon Tokatyan, Edward Hume; Suggested by the Story by: John Steinbeck; Director of Photography: Russell Metty; Music by: Billy Goldenberg; Song "We Are What We See" Music by: Billy Goldenberg; Lyrics by: David Wilson; Art Director: Alexander

A. Mayer; Film Editor: Frank Morriss; Color by: Technicolor; Titles & Optical Effects: Universal Title; Produced by: Universal Television; In Association with: George Lefferts And NBC-TV; Exclusive Distributor: MCA Television Limited.

HAUSER'S MEMORY
(WORLD PREMIERE)

NBC Television Network, November 24, 1970; 120 minutes in color on film.

A drama about Nobel Prize-winning biochemist Ernst Kramer who had been working for 15 years on a simple memory transfer which had proved successful with animals. He was then ready to transfer the memory of a mortally ill German physicist named Hauser to another subject. Before a subject could be chosen, Kramer's young assistant Hillel Mondoro injected himself with the fluid from Hauser's brain. Mondoro's mind merged with Hauser's and he was drawn back to the time of Nazi Germany.

Cast: Hillel Mondoro (David McCallum), Karen Mondoro (Susan Strasberg), Kramer (Helmut Kautner), Slaughter (Leslie Nielsen), Dorsey (Robert Webber), Renner (Herbert Fleischmann), Anna (Lilli Palmer), Van Kungen (Hans Elwenspoek), Shepilov (Peter Capell), Kucera (Peter Ehrlich), Angelika (Barbara Lass), Koroviev (Guenther Meisner), Gessler (Otto Stern), Sorsen (Manfred Reddemann), Bak (Art Brauss), Dieter (Jochen Busse), Young Anna (Barbara Capell).

Credits: Produced by: Jack Laird; Directed by: Boris Sagal; Written by: Adrian Spies; Based on the Novel by: Curt Siodmack; Director of Photography: Petrus Schloemp; Music by: Billy Byers; Art Director: Ellen Schmidt; Film Editor: Frank Morriss; Color by: Technicolor; Titles & Optical Effects: Universal Title; Produced by: Universal Television; In Association with: NBC-TV; Exclusive Distributor: MCA Television Limited.

HEAT WAVE
(ABC SUSPENSE MOVIE)

ABC Television Network, January 26, 1974; 90 minutes in color on film.

A suspense drama about the struggle of a young man and his pregnant wife to endure a 17-day heat wave. Filmed on location in Long Beach and the Saugus-Newhall area of California.

Cast: Frank Taylor (Ben Murphy), Laura Taylor (Bonnie Bedelia), Dr. Grayson (Lew Ayres), Toler (John Anderson), Arnold Brady (David Huddleston), Harry (Robert Hogan), Prescott (Dana Elcar), Terry (Lionel Johnson), Susan (Janit Baldwin), with: Clete Roberts, Joe Perry, Naomi Stevens, Donald Mantooth, Robert DoQui, Richard Bull, Stuart Nisbet, Christine Bennet.

Credits: Executive Producer: Harve Bennett; Produced by: Herbert F. Solow; Directed by: Jerry Jameson; Written by: Peter Allen Fields, Mark Weingart; Story by: Herbert F. Solow; Director of Photography: Enzo A. Martinelli; Music by: Fred Steiner; Art Director: Robert Jillson; Film Editors: Doug Young, J. Jerry Williams; Color by: Technicolor; Titles & Optical Effects: Universal Title; Produced by: Harve Bennett Productions; In Association with: Universal Television; Exclusive Distributor: MCA Television Limited.

HITCHED
(NBC DOUBLE FEATURE NIGHT AT THE MOVIES)

NBC Television Network, March 31, 1973; 90 minutes in color on film.

A comedy-Western about young Clare Bridgeman who accepted a job with the railroad in another city but, after arguing with his bride, there was a mix-up at the train station and he inadvertently left without her. While trying to find each other, his wife encountered an unsavory gang of railroad workers, a wild-spirited wagon driver named Rainbow, and some unfriendly Indians. Clare ran into a pair of crooked horse traders and was mistaken for an outlaw and nearly hanged. A sequel to the telefeature Lock, Stock and Barrel (which see).

Cast: Roselle Bridgeman (Sally Field), Clare Bridgeman (Tim Matheson), Barnstable (Henry Jones), Banjo Riley (Neville Brand), Homer Cruett (John Anderson), The Dawson Brothers (Slim Pickens), Henry (John Fiedler), P. Hunter (John McLiam), Reese (Don Knight), Round Tree (Charles Lane), Rainbow McLeod (Kathleen Freeman), Jay Appleby (Bo Svenson).

Credits: Produced by: Richard Alan Simmons; Directed by: Boris Sagal; Written by: Richard Alan Simmons; Director of Photography: Gerald Perry Finnerman; Music by: Pat Williams; Film Editor: Frank Morriss; Color by: Technicolor; Titles & Optical Effects: Universal Title; Produced by: Universal Television; In Association with: NBC-TV; Exclusive Distributor: MCA Television Limited.

HITCHHIKE!

ABC Television Network, February 23, 1974; 90 minutes in color on film.

A suspense drama about a woman motorist who picked up a moody young hitchhiker, unaware that he had just killed his stepmother.

Cast: Claire Stevens (Cloris Leachman), Keith Miles (Michael Brandon), Mary Reardon (Clairborne Cary), Hadley (Cameron Mitchell), Sgt. Hanranty (John Elerick), Ken Reardon, Jr. (Linden

Chiles), Gardner (Henry Darrow), Tim Moore (Les Lannon), Matt Benton (Jack Manning), Agatha Carlyle (Elizabeth Kerr), Dr. Schlesinger (Nadyne Turney), Sheriff Bentley (James Griffith), Counterman (Eddie Quillan), Gas Station Attendant (Terry Wilson).

Credits: Produced by: Jay Benson; Directed by: Gordon Hessler; Written by: Yale M. Udoff; Story by: Yale M. Udoff; Director of Photography: Leonard J. South; Music by: Gil Melle; Art Director: Arch Bacon; Film Editor: John F. Schreyer; Color by: Technicolor; Titles & Optical Effects: Universal Title; Produced by: Universal Television; Exclusive Distributor: MCA Television Limited.

THE HOUND OF THE BASKERVILLES
(ABC MOVIE OF THE WEEKEND)

ABC Television Network, February 12, 1972; 90 minutes in color on film.

A suspense drama in which Sherlock Holmes investigated the baffling death of an heir to the Baskerville fortune on the English moors. Holmes had to discover a way to save another heir from the same fate. A re-make of the 1939 film.

Cast: Sherlock Holmes (Stewart Granger), Stapleton (William Shatner), Laura Frankland (Sally Ann Howes), Arthur Frankland (John Williams), Dr. Watson (Bernard Fox), Dr. Mortimer (Anthony Zerbe), Beryl Stapleton (Jane Merrow), Cartwright (Billy Bowles), Barrymore (Brendon Dillon), Mrs. Barrymore (Arline Anderson), Inspector Lestrade (Alan Callio), Seldon (Chuck Hicks), Mrs. Mortimer (Karen Kondon).

Credits: Executive Producer: Richard Irving; Produced by: Stanley Kallis; Directed by: Barry Crane; Written by: Robert E. Thompson; Based on the Novel by: Sir Arthur Conan Doyle; Director of Photography: Harry Wolf; Art Director: Howard E. Johnson; Set Decorations: Arthur Jeph Parker; Film Editor: Bill Mosher; Special Photographic Effects: Albert Whitlock; Costumes by: Richard Hopper; Color by: Technicolor; Titles & Optical Effects: Universal Title; Produced by: Universal Television; Exclusive Distributor: MCA Television Limited.

THE HOUSE OF EVIL
(ABC WIDE WORLD OF ENTERTAINMENT/WIDE WORLD MYSTERY)

ABC Television Network, May 31, 1974; 90 minutes in color on tape.

A mystery about a girl who reappeared after vanishing to claim that she was held prisoner by devil worshipers at "The House of Evil" in a small New England town.

Cast: Sheriff Moore (Andy Robinson), Kitty (Jamie Smith Jackson), Rachel (Salome Jens), Rose (Elayne Heilveil), Dr. Cates (Sarah Cunningham), Howard Dale (Dabney Coleman), Deputy (Lou Frizzell), Mary Hogan (Mary Carver).

Credits: Produced by: Barbara Schultz; Produced by: Universal Television; Exclusive Distributor: MCA Television Limited.

HOUSTON, WE'VE GOT A PROBLEM
(ABC SUSPENSE MOVIE)

ABC Television Network, March 2, 1974; 90 minutes in color on film.

A suspense drama about the ill-fated Apollo 13 moon mission of 1970 which was aborted when an explosion damaged the craft in flight. Filmed on location at NASA's Johnson Spaceflight Center in Houston, Texas.

Cast: Steve Bell (Robert Culp), Tim Cordell (Gary Collins), Angie Cordell (Sandra Dee), Lisa Bell (Sheila Sullivan), Lou Matthews (Clu Gulager), Gene Kranz (Ed Nelson), Shimon Levin (Steve Franken), Abraham Levin (Robert Corff), Kerwin (Jack Hogan), Lousma (Quinn Rederker), Donna (Barbara Baldwin), Mrs. Levin (Zolya Tolma), Mel Anderson (Geoffrey Scott), Mike Matthews (Eric Shea), Newsman (James N. Harrell).

Credits: Executive Producer: Harve Bennett; Produced by: Herman Saunders; Directed by: Lawrence Doheny; Written by: Rick Nelson; Director of Photography: J. J. Jones; Music by: Richard Clements; Art Director: Lester L. Green; Film Editor: Robert F. Shugrue; Color by: Technicolor; Titles & Optical Effects: Universal Title; Produced by: Harve Bennett Productions; In Association with: Universal Television; Exclusive Distributor: MCA Television Limited.

HOW I SPENT MY SUMMER VACATION
(WORLD PREMIERE/NBC SATURDAY NIGHT AT THE MOVIES)

NBC Television Network, January 7, 1967; 120 minutes in color on film.

A drama about Jack Washington, an idealistic U.S. college student who lived in Paris, and who was marked for death by two wealthy, powerful behind-the-scenes figures in the international scene when they discovered his notebook on their illegal dealings entitled "How I Spent My Summer Vacation."

Cast: Jack Washington (Robert Wagner), Ned Pine (Peter Lawford), Mrs. Pine (Lola Albright), Lewis Gannet (Walter Pidgeon), Nikki Fine (Jill St. John), Pucci (Michael Ansara), The Greek (Len Les-

166 / Telefeatures

ser), Jewelry Dealer (Alberto Morin), Mr. Amin (Ralph Smiley), Yoshiro (Tiger Joe Marsh), Miss Karali (Joni Webster), The Interviewer (Lyn Peters), Spanish Sailor (Asher Dann), Croupier (Peter Camlin), Croupier Assistant (Frank Delfino), 1st Spaniard (Francisco Ortega), 2nd Spaniard (Victor Dunlap), 1st Guard (Horst Ebersberg), Helicopter Pilot (Peter Pascal), Waiter (Rolf Sedan).

Credits: Produced by: Jack Laird; Directed by: William Hale; Written by: Gene Kearney; Director of Photography: Bud Thackery, A.S.C.; Music by: Lalo Schifrin; Art Director: Henry Larrecq; Film Editor: Douglas Stewart; Sound: Melvin M. Metcalfe, Sr.; Costumes by: Helen Colvig; Makeup: Bud Westmore; Hair Stylist: Larry Germain; Color by: Technicolor; Titles & Optical Effects: Universal Title; Produced by: Universal Television; In Association with: NBC-TV; Exclusive Distributor: MCA Television Limited.

HOW TO STEAL AN AIRPLANE
(WORLD PREMIERE)

NBC Television Network, December 10, 1971; 120 minutes in color on film.

A drama about Sam Rollins, an American, and Evan Brice, a Welshman, who posed as tourists in a Latin American country to repossess a jet from the dictator's irresponsible playboy son, Luis Ortega. Filmed on location at Lancaster, this telefeature was completed in 1969 but not telecast until 1971.

Cast: Sam Rollins (Peter Deuel), Evan Brice (Clinton Greyn), Michelle Chivot (Claudine Longet), Jan (Katherine Crawford), Dorothy (Julie Sommars), Luis Ortega (Sal Mineo).

Credits: Executive Producer: Roy Huggins; Produced by: Jo Swerling, Jr.; Directed by: Leslie H. Martinson; Written by: Robert Foster, Philip De Guere, Jr.; Associate Producers: Robert Foster, Philip De Guere, Jr., Carl Pingitore; Director of Photography: Jack Marta; Music by: Pete Rugolo; Song "The Sadness of a Happy Time" Music by: Pete Rugolo; Lyrics by: Norman Gimbel; Sung by: Claudine Longet; Art Director: Frank Arrigo; Film Editors: Budd Small, John Dumas; Color by: Technicolor; Titles & Optical Effects: Universal Title; Produced by: Roy Huggins-Public Arts Productions; In Association with: Universal Television And NBC-TV; Exclusive Distributor: MCA Television Limited.

A HOWLING IN THE WOODS
(WORLD PREMIERE)

NBC Television Network, November 5, 1971; 120 minutes in color on film.

A Howling in the Woods / 167

A mystery drama in which a husband and wife with marital problems returned to a small town where something seemed terribly wrong; the wife's stepmother was strangely cool, her father was absent, there was the constant howling of a dog, and the story of a small girl's death.

Cast: Liza Crocker (Barbara Eden), Eddie Crocker (Larry Hagman), Justin Conway (John Rubinstein), Rose (Vera Miles), Sally (Tyne Daly), Sharon (Ruta Lee), Mel (George Murdock), Henshaw (Ford Rainey), Lonnie Henshaw (Bill Vint), Apperson (Karl Swenson), Betsy Warren (Lisa Gerritsen).

Credits: Produced by: Douglas Benton; Directed by: Daniel Petrie; Written by: Richard DeRoy; Based on the Novel by: Velda Johnson; Director of Photography: Jack Marta; Music by: Dave Grusin; Art Director: Howard E. Johnson; Film Editor: Robert F. Shugrue; Color by: Technicolor; Titles & Optical Effects: Universal Title; Produced by: Universal Television; In Association with: NBC-TV; Exclusive Distributor: MCA Television Limited.

I LOVE A MYSTERY
(WORLD PREMIERE/NBC TUESDAY NIGHT AT THE MOVIES)

NBC Television Network, February 27, 1973; 120 minutes in color on film.

A mystery spoof about three airborne detectives who were hunting for a missing billionaire who was insured for $12 million. The pilot for an unsold series.

Cast: Randy Cheyne (Ida Lupino), Doc Long (David Hartman), Jack Packard (Les Crane), Job Cheyne (Jack Weston), Reggie York (Hagan Beggs), Gordon Elliott (Terry-Thomas), Alexander Archer (Don Knotts), Faith Cheyne (Karen Jensen), Charity Cheyne (Melodie Johnson), Hope Cheyne (Deanna Lund), Andre (Andre Philippe), Telegram Girl (Francine York).

Credits: Produced by: Frank Price; Directed by: Leslie Stevens; Written by: Leslie Stevens; Based on the Radio Series by: Carlton E. Morse; Director of Photography: Ray Rennahan; Music by: Oliver Nelson; Art Director: John J. Lloyd; Film Editor: Robert F. Shugrue; Color by: Technicolor; Titles & Optical Effects: Universal Title; Produced by: Universal Television; In Association with: NBC-TV; Exclusive Distributor: MCA Television Limited.

THE IMPATIENT HEART
(WORLD PREMIERE)

NBC Television Network, October 8, 1971; 120 minutes in color on film.

168 / Telefeatures

A drama about social worker Grace McCormack who cared so deeply about the various cases she handled for Winslow House, that she drove her boss, Murray Kane, to distraction. Her penchant for turning every human relationship into a case study prompted her to be a meddler in a potentially explosive situation between would-be suitor Frank Pescadero and his father.

Cast: Grace McCormack (Carrie Snodgress), Frank Pescadero (Michael Brandon), Murray Kane (Michael Constantine), Nellie Santschi (Marian Hailey), Mr. Hernandez (Hector Elizondo), Brewster Crowley (Brad David), Mr. Pescadero (Harry Davis), Dr. Felix Mandez (Victor Millan), Mrs. Hernandez (Anna Navarro), Mrs. Esposito (Penny Stanton).

Credits: Produced by: William Sackheim; Directed by: John Badham; Written by: Alvin Sargent, William Sackheim; Director of Photography: Jacques R. Marquette; Music by: David Shire; Art Director: Joseph Alves, Jr.; Film Editor: Edward M. Abroms; Color by: Technicolor; Titles & Optical Effects: Universal Title; Produced by: Universal Television; In Association with: NBC-TV; Exclusive Distributor: MCA Television Limited.

THE INCREDIBLE HULK
(THE CBS FRIDAY NIGHT MOVIE)

CBS Television Network, November 4, 1977; 120 minutes in color on film.

A drama about Dr. David Banner, a scientist who, experimenting on human strength under stress, overexposed himself to gamma rays. Whenever he found himself in a threatening situation he turned into a raging creature known as The Hulk. The pilot for the series The Incredible Hulk (which see).

Cast: Dr. David Banner (Bill Bixby), The Hulk (Lou Ferrigno), Elaina (Susan Sullivan), McGee (Jack Colvin), Ben (Charles Siebert), Mrs. Maier (Susan Batson), Bram (Mario Gallo), Policeman (Eric Server), B. J. Maier (Eric Devon), Jerry (Jake Mitchell), Laura Banner (Lara Parker), Minister (William Larsen), Girl at Lake (Olivia Barash), Man at Lake (George Brenlin), Mrs. Epstein (June Whitley Taylor), Young Man (Terence Locke).

Credits: Produced and Directed by: Kenneth Johnson; Written by: Kenneth Johnson; Based on: The Marvel Comics Group Character; Director of Photography: Howard R. Schwartz; Art Director: Charles R. Davis; Film Editors: Jack Schoengarth, Alan Marks; Color by: Technicolor; Titles & Optical Effects: Universal Title; Produced by: Universal Television; Exclusive Distributor: MCA Television Limited.

INDICT AND CONVICT
(THE ABC SUNDAY NIGHT MOVIE)

ABC Television Network, January 6, 1974; 120 minutes in color on film.

A drama based on the real-life Jack Kirschke murder case where a deputy district attorney was convicted of killing his wife and her lover even though the accused man was 150 miles away when the murders were committed.

Cast: Bob Mathews (George Grizzard), Mike Flores (Reni Santoni), Joanna Garrett (Susan Howard), Timothy Fitzgerald (Ed Flanders), DeWitt Foster (Eli Wallach), Sam Belden (William Shatner), Judge Taylor (Myrna Loy), Mel Thomas (Harry Guardino), Norman Hastings (Kip Niven), Phyllis Dorfman (Ruta Lee), Frank Rogers (Del Russel), Barbara Mathews (Marie Cheatham), Muriel Fitzgerald (Eunice Christopher), Pathologist (Alfred Ryder).

Credits: Executive Producer: David Victor; Produced by: Winston Miller; Directed by: Boris Sagal; Written by: Winston Miller; Based on the Book by: Bill Davidson; Director of Photography: Bill Butler; Music by: Jerry Goldsmith; Art Director: John T. McCormack; Film Editor: Robert F. Shugrue; Color by: Technicolor; Titles & Optical Effects: Universal Title; Produced by: Groverton Productions, Ltd.; In Association with: Universal Television; Exclusive Distributor: MCA Television Limited.

THE INTRUDERS
(WORLD PREMIERE)

NBC Television Network, November 10, 1970; 120 minutes in color on film.

A drama about fear among frontier townsmen in the path of a lawless gang. When the Jesse James-Cole Younger gang threatened to invade Medelia, Minnesota, the people turned to town pillar Col. Bodeen for help.

Cast: Sam Garrison (Don Murray), Col. Bodeen (Edmond O'Brien), Billy Pye (John Saxon), Leora Garrison (Anne Francis), Cole Younger (Gene Evans), Elton Dykstra (Edward Andrews), Whit Dykstra (Dean Stanton), Theron Pardo (Shelly Novack), Jesse James (Stuart Margolin), Harold Gilman (Phillip Alford), Appleton (John Hoyt), Carl (Harrison Ford), Bob Younger (Zalman King), Kate Guerrera (Marlene Tracy), Pomerantz (Ken Swofford), Roy Kirsh (Robert Donner), Bill Riley (Edward Falkner), Chaunce Dykstra (James Gammon), George Ganzer (Len Wayland).

Credits: Executive Producer: Bert Granet; Produced by: James Duff McAdams; Directed by: William Graham; Written by: Dean Riesner; Based on the Story by: William Lansford; Director of

Photography: Ray Flin; Music by: Dave Grusin; Art Director: Loyd S. Papez; Set Decorations: John McCarthy, James S. Redd; Film Editor: J. Howard Terrill; Sound: Frank H. Wilkinson; Color by: Technicolor; Titles & Optical Effects: Universal Title; Produced by: Universal Television; In Association with: NBC-TV; Exclusive Distributor: MCA Television Limited.

THE INVASION OF JOHNSON COUNTY
(NBC SATURDAY NIGHT AT THE MOVIES)

NBC Television Network, July 31, 1976; 120 minutes in color on film.

A Western about a group of Wyoming land barons who put together a private army of gunslingers to wipe out small-time ranchers and homesteaders. They were challenged by a wily Bostonian and a righteous cowboy who wanted to stop a range war.

Cast: Sam Lowell (Bill Bixby), George Dunning (Bo Hopkins), Maj. Wolcott (John Hillerman), Frank Canton (Billy Green Bush), Col. Van Horn (Stephen Elliott), Richard Allen (Lee de Broux), Irvine (M. Emmet Walsh), Sheriff Angus (Mills Watson), Teschmacher (Alan Fudge), Deputy Sheriff Brooks (Luke Askew), Maj. Edward Fershay (Edward Winter).

Credits: Executive Producer: Jo Swerling, Jr.; Produced by: Roy Huggins; Directed by: Jerry Jameson; Written by: Nicholas E. Baehr; Director of Photography: Rexford Metz; Music by: Mike Post, Pete Carpenter; Art Director: Alexander A. Mayer; Film Editors: Gloryette Clark, Chuck McClelland, Jim Benson; Color by: Technicolor; Titles & Optical Effects: Universal Title; Produced by: Roy Huggins-Public Arts Productions; In Association with: Universal Television; Exclusive Distributor: MCA Television Limited.

THE INVISIBLE MAN
(WORLD PREMIERE)

NBC Television Network, May 6, 1975; 90 minutes in color on film.

A drama about Daniel Weston, a noted scientist who discovered a way to make himself invisible. An updated version of the 1933 film based on H. G. Wells' classic novel The pilot for the series The Invisible Man (which see).

Cast: Daniel Weston (David McCallum), Kate Weston (Melinda Fee), Dr. Nick Maggio (Henry Darrow), Carlson (Jackie Cooper), Steiner (Alex Henteloff), Gen. Turner (Arch Johnson), Blind Man (John McLiam), Gate Guard (Ted Gehring), Security Chief (Paul Kent).

Credits: Executive Producer: Harve Bennett; Produced by: Steven Bochco; Directed by: Robert Michael Lewis; Written by: Steven

Bochco; Story by: Harve Bennett, Steven Bochco; Based on the Novel by: H. G. Wells; Director of Photography: Enzo A. Martinelli; Music by: Richard Clements; Art Director: Frank T. Smith; Film Editor: Robert F. Shugrue; Color by: Technicolor; Titles & Optical Effects: Universal Title; Produced by: Silverton Productions, Inc.; In Association with: Universal Television; Exclusive Distributor: MCA Television Limited.

IRONSIDE
(WORLD PREMIERE/NBC TUESDAY NIGHT AT THE MOVIES)

NBC Television Network, March 28, 1967; 120 minutes in color on film.

A detective drama about Robert T. Ironside, a veteran San Francisco police chief, who set out to find the gunman who made him a permanent wheelchair case. The pilot for the series Ironside (which see).

Cast: Robert T. Ironside (Raymond Burr), Honor Thompson (Geraldine Brooks), Comm. Dennis Randell (Gene Lyons), Det. Sgt. Brown (Don Galloway), Eve Whitfield (Barbara Anderson), Mark Sanger (Donald Mitchell), Scoutmaster (Wally Cox), Ellen Wells (Kim Darby), Doctor (David Sheiner), Sister Agatha (Lilia Skala).

Credits: Produced by: Collier Young; Directed by: James Goldstone; Written by: Don Mankiewicz; Story by: Collier Young; Director of Photography: John F. Warren, A.S.C.; Music by: Quincy Jones; Art Director: Loyd S. Papez; Film Editor: Edward W. Williams, A.C.E.; Sound: Lyle Cain; Costumes by: Grady Hunt; Color by: Technicolor; Titles & Optical Effects: Universal Title; Produced by: Universal Television; Exclusive Distributor: MCA Television Limited.

THE ISLANDER

CBS Television Network, September 16, 1978; 120 minutes in color on film.

A drama about a lawyer who moved to Hawaii and got caught up in a gangland murder.

Cast: Gable McQueen (Dennis Weaver), Shauna Cooke (Sharon Gless), Lt. Larkin (Peter Mark Richman), Trudy Engles (Bernadette Peters), Sen. Gerald Stratton (Robert Vaughn), Bishop Hatch (John S. Ragin), Al Kahala (Dick Jensen), Kimo (Ed Kaahea), Paul Lazarro (Sheldon Leonard), Simms (George Wyner).

Credits: Produced by: Glen A. Larson; Directed by: Paul Krasny; Written by: Glen A. Larson; Director of Photography: Ron Browne; Music by: Stu Phillips; Art Director: Ira Diamond; Film

Editor: Budd Small; Color by: Technicolor; Titles & Optical Effects: Universal Title; Produced in Association with: Glen A. Larson Productions And Universal Television; Exclusive Distributor: MCA Television Limited.

ISTANBUL EXPRESS
(WORLD PREMIERE/NBC TUESDAY NIGHT AT THE MOVIES)

NBC Television Network, October 22, 1968; 120 minutes in color on film.

A thriller about art dealer Michael London who was sent by the Western powers to compete with representatives of several countries at an auction of the research notes of a deceased scientist. Aboard the Trans-Europa Express between Paris and Istanbul were a number of spies--each determined to prevent London from reaching the auction. Filmed on location in the European cities of Paris, Milan, Venice, Belgrade and Istanbul.

Cast: Michael London (Gene Barry), Cheval (John Saxon), Mila Darvos (Senta Berger), Leland McCord (Tom Simcox), Peggy Coopersmith (Mary Ann Mobley), Doctor Lenz (Werner Peters), Shepherd (Donald Woods), Capt. Granicek (Jack Kruschen), Gustav (Moustache).

Credits: Produced and Directed by: Richard Irving; Written by: Richard Levinson, William Link; Associate Producer: Jerrold Freedman; Director of Photography: Benjamin H. Kline, A.S.C.; Music by: Oliver Nelson; Art Director: John J. Lloyd; Set Decorations: John McCarthy, Perry Murdock; Film Editor: Richard G. Wray, A.C.E.; 2nd Unit Director: Hal Polaire; Music Supervision: Stanley Wilson; Editorial Supervision: Richard Belding; Sound: Robert Bertrand; Costumes by: Grady Hunt; Makeup: Bud Westmore; Hair Stylist: Larry Germain; Color Coordinator: Robert Brower; Color by: Technicolor; Titles & Optical Effects: Universal Title; Produced by: Universal Television; In Association with: NBC-TV; Exclusive Distributor: MCA Television Limited.

IT HAPPENED ONE CHRISTMAS

ABC Television Network, December 11, 1977; 150 minutes in color on film.

A drama about a guardian angel who took a disenchanted woman on an imaginary tour of her home town to show her what it would have been like without her. A remake of the 1946 film It's a Wonderful Life.

Cast: Mary Hatch (Marlo Thomas), George Hatch (Wayne Rogers), Henry F. Potter (Orson Welles), Clara (Cloris Leachman), Uncle Willy (Barney Martin), Bailey (Richard Dysart), Mrs. Bailey (Doris

Roberts), Cousin Tillie (Ceil Cabot), Harry Bailey (Christopher Guest), Ernie (Archie Hahn), Bert (Morgan Upton), Violet (Karen Carlson), Gower (Dick O'Neill), Sam Wainwright (Jim Lovelett), Martini (Cliff Norton), Judge (Robert Emhardt), Doctor (Bryan O'Byrne), Sassini (Gino Conforti), Nick (Med Flory).

Credits: Producers: Marlo Thomas, Carole Hart; Directed by: Donald Wrye; Written by: Lionel Chetwynd; Based on the Story "The Greatest Gift" by: Philip Van Doren Stern; Director of Photography: Conrad Hall; Music by: Stephen Lawrence; Art Director: John J. Lloyd; Film Editors: Robbe Roberts, Bill Martin; Set Decorations: Hal Guasman; Color by: Technicolor; Titles & Optical Effects: Universal Title; Produced by: Daisy Productions; In Association with: Universal Television; Exclusive Distributor: MCA Television Limited.

IT TAKES A THIEF

ABC Television Network, January 9, 1968; 90 minutes in color on film.

An action-adventure film about Alexander Mundy, a swinging master thief with an eye for the ladies as well as the loot, who was paroled from prison to exercise his light-fingered talents exclusively for the SIA, a U.S. intelligence agency. The pilot for the series It Takes a Thief (which see). Filmed on locations including Montreal's Expo '67.

Cast: Alexander Mundy (Robert Wagner), Noah Bain (Malachi Throne), Claire Vickers (Senta Berger), Dead Man (John Saxon), SIA Bureau Chief (Raymond Burr), Tourist (Wally Cox), Mr. Clifton (James Drury), Nightclub Manager (Kurt Kasznar), Prizefighter (Joe Louis), Mr. Sanders (Doug McClure), Control Officer (Leslie Nielsen), Anne Edwards (Susan Saint James), Courier (Michael Forest), Hilary Dickensen (Anita Eubank), Jessica Teague (Willi Koopman), Prison Chaplain (Stuart Margolin), Airline Captain (Donald Barry), with: Eddie "Rochester" Anderson.

Credits: Produced by: Frank Price; Directed by: Leslie Stevens; Written by: Roland Kibbee, Leslie Stevens; Director of Photography: Ralph Woolsey; Music by: Ernie Freeman; Film Editor: Tony Martinelli; Sound: Ed Sommers; Color by: Technicolor; Titles & Optical Effects: Universal Title; Produced by: Universal Television; Exclusive Distribution: MCA Television Limited.

JIGSAW
(THE ABC SUNDAY NIGHT MOVIE)

ABC Television Network, March 26, 1972; 120 minutes in color on film.

174 / Telefeatures

A mystery drama in which a framed police lieutenant was caught in a web of deception when he couldn't produce the body of a suspect he said he shot or the female witness he claimed was there. The pilot for the series Jigsaw (which see).

Cast: Frank Dain (James Wainwright), Lilah Beth (Vera Miles), Dan Bellington (Richard Kiley), Harrison Delando (Andrew Duggan), Ed Burtelson (Edmond O'Brien), Dr. Gehlen (Marsha Hunt), Mrs. Cummings (Irene Dailey), Eric (Gene Andrusco), The Hood (Mills Watson), Police Psychologist (Milton Selzer), Adelle Collier (Pamela Rodgers), Motel Clerk (Elliott Street), Deputy Sheriff Coley (Ted Gehring), Mr. Cummings (Ken Lynch).

Credits: Produced by: Stanley Kallis; Directed by: William Graham; Written by: Robert E. Thompson; Director of Photography: Mike Margulies; Music by: Robert Drasnin; Art Director: Bill Kenny; Film Editor: Jim Benson; Color by: Technicolor; Titles & Optical Effects: Universal Title; Produced by: Universal Television; Exclusive Distributor: MCA Television Limited.

THE JORDAN CHANCE
(CBS TUESDAY NIGHT MOVIES)

CBS Television Network, December 12, 1978; 120 minutes in color on film.

A drama about Frank Jordan, head of the Jordan Foundation, an organization which came to the aid of those who were sent to jail on trumped up charges, as Jordan himself was. The pilot for an unsold series.

Cast: Frank Jordan (Raymond Burr), Brian Klosky (Ted Shackelford), Jimmy Foster (James Canning), Karen Wagner (Jeannie Fitzsimmons), Virna Stewart (Stella Stevens), Sheriff DeVega (George DiCenzo), Jasper Colton (John McIntire), Lee Southerland (Peter Haskell), Elena Delgado (Maria-Elena Cordero), Sid Burton (Gerald McRaney), Lew Mayfield (John Dennis), Mike Anderson (Grant Owen), Judge Miller (Michael Don Wagner).

Credits: Executive Producer: Roy Huggins; Produced by: Jo Swerling, Jr.; Directed by: Jules Irving; Written by: Stephen J. Cannell; Story by: John Thomas James, Stephen J. Cannell; Director of Photography: Enzo A. Martinelli; Music by: Pete Rugolo; Art Director: John J. Jeffries; Film Editor: Larry Lester; Color by: Technicolor; Titles & Optical Effects: Universal Title; Produced by: Roy Huggins-Public Arts Productions; In Association with: R. B. Productions And Universal Television; Exclusive Distributor: MCA Television Limited.

THE JUDGE AND JAKE WYLER
(WORLD PREMIERE)

NBC Television Network, December 2, 1972; 120 minutes in color on film.

A drama about a retired judge who opened a detective agency and, assisted by an ex-convict on probation to her, investigated a girl's claim that her father's death was murder, not suicide. The pilot for an unsold series.

Cast: Judge Meredith (Bette Davis), Jake Wyler (Doug McClure), Anton Granicek (Eric Braeden), Alicia Dodd (Joan Van Ark), Frank Morrison (Gary Conway), Lt. Wolfson (Lou Jacobi), Quint (James McEachin), Caroline Dodd (Lisabeth Hush), Robert Dodd (Kent Smith), Chloe Jones (Barbara Rhoades).

Credits: Producers: Richard Levinson, Willian Link; Directed by: David Lowell Rich; Written by: David Shaw, Richard Levinson, William Link; Associate Producer: Jay Benson; Director of Photography: William Margulies; Music by: Gil Melle; Art Director: Alexander A. Mayer; Film Editor: Budd Small; Color by: Technicolor; Titles & Optical Effects: Universal Title; Produced by: Universal Television; In Association with: NBC-TV; Exclusive Distributor: MCA Television Limited.

JUST A LITTLE INCONVENIENCE
(THE BIG EVENT)

NBC Television Network, October 2, 1977; 120 minutes in color on film.

A drama about the physical and emotional rehabilitation of an embittered amputee who lost an arm and a leg in the Vietnam war.

Cast: Frank Logan (Lee Majors), Kenny Briggs (James Stacy), Nikki Klausing (Barbara Hershey), Maj. Bloom (Charles Cioffi), Dave Erickson (Jim Davis), Bartender (John Furey), B-Girl (Lane Bradbury), Harry (Bob Hastings).

Credits: Executive Producer: Lee Majors; Produced by: Allan Balter; Directed by: Theodore J. Flicker; Written by: Theodore J. Flicker, Allan Balter; Director of Photography: Duke Callaghan; Theme Music by: Jim Weatherly; Music Score: Jim Haskell; Art Director: David Marshall; Film Editor: Bernard J. Small; Color by: Technicolor; Titles & Optical Effects: Universal Title; Produced by: Fawcett-Majors Productions; In Association with: Universal Television And NBC-TV; Exclusive Distributor: MCA Television Limited.

THE KEEGANS

CBS Television Network, May 3, 1976; 90 minutes in color on film.

176 / Telefeatures

A drama about investigative reporter Larry Keegan who set out to prove that his brother Pat Keegan, a professional football player, was innocent of the murder of his sister's attacker.

Cast: Larry Keegan (Adam Roarke), Pat Keegan (Spencer Milligan), Brandy Keegan (Heather Menzies), Tim Keegan (Tom Clancy), Mary Keegan (Joan Leslie), Helen Hunter McVey (Priscilla Pointer), Lt. Marco Giardi (Judd Hirsch), Rudi Portinari (Paul Shenar), Tracy McVey (Janit Baldwin), Penny Voorhees Keegan (Penelope Windust), Vinnie Cavell (Robert Yuro), Martha Carechal (Anna Navarro), Angie Carechal (Smith Evans), Bill Richardson (Michael McGuire), Don Guido Carechal (George Skaff), Slim Montana (James Louis Watkins).

Credits: Produced by: George Eckstein; Directed by: John Badham; Written by: Dean Riesner; Director of Photography: Stevan Larner; Music by: Paul Chihara; Art Director: Ira Diamond; Film Editor: Jamie Caylor; Color by: Technicolor; Titles & Optical Effects: Universal Title; Produced by: Universal Television; Exclusive Distributor: MCA Television Limited.

KILLDOZER

ABC Television Network, February 2, 1974; 90 minutes in color on film.

A suspense drama about a group of construction workers who were terrorized by a bulldozer operated by an alien being.

Cast: Lloyd Kelly (Clint Walker), Dennis Holvig (Carl Betz), Dutch Krasner (James Wainwright), Chub Foster (Neville Brand), Beltran (James Watson, Jr.), Mack McCarthy (Robert Urich).

Credits: Produced by: Herbert F. Solow; Directed by: Jerry London; Written by: Theodore Sturgeon, Ed MacKillop; Based on the Novella by: Theodore Sturgeon; Director of Photography: Terry K. Meade; Music by: Gil Melle; Art Director: James Martin Buchanan; Film Editor: Fabien Tordjmann; Stunt Coordinator: Carey Loftin; Special Effects: Albert Whitlock; Color by: Technicolor; Titles & Optical Effects: Universal Title; Produced by: Universal Television; Exclusive Distributor: MCA Television Limited.

KILLING STONE

NBC Television Network, May 2, 1978; 120 minutes in color on film.

A drama about a writer who returned from serving a lengthy term in prison and attempted to discover who was really responsible for the murder for which he was framed.

Cast: Gil Stone (Gil Gerard), Sheriff Harky (J. D. Cannon), Sen. Barry Tyler (Jim Davis), Christopher Stone (Matthew Laborteaux),

Ellen Rizzi (Corinne Michaels), Harold Rizzi (Joshua Bryant), Earl Stone (Nehemiah Persoff), Daniel Tyler (Dick DeCoit), Cindy (Valentina Quinn), Barney Dawes (Ken Johnson), Bobby Joe (Dan McBride).

Credits: Produced and Directed by: Michael Landon; Written by: Michael Landon; Director of Photography: Ted Voigtlander; Music by: David Rose; Art Director: Walter M. Jeffries; Film Editor: Jerry Taylor; Color by: Technicolor; Titles & Optical Effects: Universal Title; Produced by: Universal Television; Exclusive Distributor: MCA Television Limited.

KINGSTON: THE POWER PLAY
(NBC WEDNESDAY NIGHT AT THE MOVIES)

NBC Television Network, September 15, 1976; 120 minutes in color on film.

A drama about free-lance journalist R. B. Kingston who was hired by the head of a newspaper chain to investigate why one of their award-winning editors suddenly changed his editorial policy. When his investigation proved successful, Kingston was hired on as one of the paper's top reporters. The pilot for the series Kingston: Confidential (which see).

Cast: R. B. Kingston (Raymond Burr), Tony Kolsky (James Canning), Avery Stanton (Bradford Dillman), Beth Kelly (Pamela Hensley), Pat Martinson (Biff McGuire), Helen Martinson (Dina Merrill), Laura Frazier (Lenka Peterson), Lt. Vokeman (Milt Kogan), Sam Trowbridge (Robert Sampson), Dr. Eberly (Stacy Keach, Sr.), Father Riordan (R. G. Armstrong), Deeley (Martin Kove), Senator Hobath (Robert Mandan), Ethelmae Turner (Claire Brennan).

Credits: Executive Producer: David Victor; Produced by: David J. O'Connell; Directed by: Robert Day; Written by: Dick Nelson; Story by: David Victor, Dick Nelson; Director of Photography: Sy Hoffberg; Music by: Leonard Rosenman; Art Director: Howard E. Johnson; Film Editor: Richard G. Wray; Sound: Harold Lewis; Color by: Technicolor; Titles & Optical Effects: Universal Title; Produced by: Groverton Productions, Ltd.; In Association with: R. B. Productions And Universal Television; Exclusive Distributor: MCA Television Limited.

LANIGAN'S RABBI
(NBC THURSDAY NIGHT AT THE MOVIES)

NBC Television Network, June 17, 1976; 120 minutes in color on film.

A comedy-drama about a police chief who was aided in his investigation of a murder by a rabbi who was adept at digging up leads and clues. The pilot for the series Lanigan's Rabbi (which see) in which Bruce Solomon took over the role of Rabbi Small from Stuart Margolin.

Cast: Police Chief Paul Lanigan (Art Carney), Rabbi David Small (Stuart Margolin), Kate Lanigan (Janis Paige), Miriam Small (Janet Margolin), Myra Galen (Lorraine Gary), Galen (Robert Reed), Blake (Jim Antonio), Becker (David Sheiner), Norman (Andy Robinson), Bobbi (Barbara Carney), Osgood (Robert Doyle), Basserman (Stefan Zacharias), Stanley (William Wheatley), Mrs. Blake (Barbara Flicker).

Credits: Executive Producer: Leonard B. Stern; Produced by: Robert C. Thompson, Rod Paul; Directed by: Lou Antonio; Written by: Don M. Mankiewicz, Gordon Cotler; Based on the Novel "Friday the Rabbi Slept Late" by: Harry Kemelman; Director of Photography: Andrew Jackson; Music by: Leonard Rosenman; Art Director: Norman R. Newberry; Film Editor: Volney Howard III; Color by: Technicolor; Titles & Optical Effects: Universal Title; Produced by: Heyday Productions; In Association with: Universal Television; Exclusive Distributor: MCA Television Limited.

THE LAW
(WORLD PREMIERE)

NBC Television Network, October 22, 1974; 150 minutes in color on film.

A drama about a youth who was arrested on a drug violation and was subsequently charged with murder, and a public defender's efforts to clear him. The pilot for the series The Law (which see).

Cast: Murray Stone (Judd Hirsch), Gene Carey (John Beck), William Bright (Gary Busey), Judge Fornier (Barbara Baxley), Bobbie Stone (Bonnie Franklin), Jules Benson (Sam Wanamaker), Thomas Q. Rachel (John Hillerman), Leonard Caproni (Allan Arbus), Judge Arnold Lerner (Gerald Hiken), Cliff Wilson (Michael Bell), Maxwell Fall (Herb Jefferson, Jr.), Arthur Winchell (Frank Marth), Judge Philip Shields (John Sylvester White), Speaker at Bar Dinner (Robert Q. Lewis), with: Logan Ramsey, Sandy Ward, George Wyner, Ernie Anderson, Reb Brown, Dennis Burkley, Don Calfa, Helen Page Camp, Alex Colon, Regis J. Cordic, Corey Fisher, Ted Gehring, Pamela Hensley, Milt Kogan, Luis Moreno, Joel Oliansky, Eugene Peterson, Anne Ramsey, Brad Sullivan, Keith Walker, Charles White, Alex Wilson.

Credits: Produced by: William Sackheim; Directed by: John Badham; Written by: William Sackheim, Joel Oliansky; Director of Photography: Michael Margulies; Art Director: Raymond Beal; Film Editor: Frank Morriss; Color by: Technicolor; Titles & Optical Effects: Universal Title; Produced by: Universal Television; In Association with: NBC-TV; Exclusive Distributor: MCA Television Limited.

LET'S SWITCH
(ABC TUESDAY MOVIE OF THE WEEK)

ABC Television Network, January 7, 1975; 90 minutes in color on film.

A comedy about what happened when the editor of a women's magazine switched roles with her best friend, a housewife.

Cast: Kate Fleming (Barbara Feldon), Lucy Colbert (Barbara Eden), Ross Daniels (Richard Schaal), Alice Wright (Penny Marshall), Linette Robbin (Joyce Van Patten), Sidney King (George Furth), Randy Colbert (Pat Harrington), Morgan Ames (Barra Grant), Inez Dulin (Bella Bruck), Flo Moore (Kaye Stevens), LaRue Williams (Ron Glass), Greta Bennett (Barbara Cason), with: Bill Balance, Tanya Matarazzo, Jerry Bishop, Paul Hansen, Roger Til, Gene Krischer, Reb Brown, Oaky Miller, Mary Ann Kosica, Barbara Baldavin, Donald Mantooth.

Credits: Produced by: Bruce Johnson; Directed by: Alan Rafkin; Written by: Peter Lefcourt, Ruth Brooks Flippen, Sid Arthur, Andy Chubby Williams; Story by: Peter Lefcourt; Director of Photography: Stevan Larner; Music by: Harry Geller; Film Editor: Albert J. Zuniga; Color by: Technicolor; Titles & Optical Effects: Universal Title; Produced by: Universal Television; Exclusive Distributor: MCA Television Limited.

LIEUTENANT SCHUSTER'S WIFE
(ABC WEDNESDAY MOVIE OF THE WEEK)

ABC Television Network, October 11, 1972; 90 minutes in color on film.

A drama about a woman who became determined to clear the name of her late policeman-husband, accused of being on the take after he was shot in ambush, even if it cost her own life. Filmed on location in New York City.

Cast: Ellie Schuster (Lee Grant), Capt. Patrick Lonergan (Jack Warden), Danny Reilly (Don Galloway), Lt. Lou Schuster (Paul Burke), Joe Carroll (Nehemiah Persoff), Lady (Eartha Kitt), Mr. Abbott (Murray Matheson), Butrick (George Brenlin), Det. McCann (Robert DoQui), Guide (Lew Palter), The Junkie (John Herzfeld).

Credits: Produced by: Steven Bochco; Directed by: David Lowell Rich; Written by: Bernie Kukoff, Steven Bochco; Director of Photography: Bud Thackery; Music by: Gil Melle; Art Director: Loyd S. Papez; Set Decorations: Ira Bates; Film Editor: John M. Woodcock; Costumes by: Burton Miller; Color by: Technicolor; Titles & Optical Effects: Universal Title; Produced by: Universal Television; Exclusive Distributor: MCA Television Limited.

180 / Telefeatures

LINDA
(ABC SUSPENSE MOVIE)

ABC Television Network, November 3, 1973; 90 minutes in color on film.

A suspense film about a woman who murdered her lover's wife, then set up her own husband to be suspected as the killer.

Cast: Linda Reston (Stella Stevens), Paul Reston (Ed Nelson), Jeff Braden (John Saxon), Marshall Journeyman (John McIntire), Chief Vernon (Ford Rainey), Ann Braden (Mary Robin-Redd), Brownell (John Fink), Officer Carr (Alan Fudge), Louella (Joyce Cunning), Young Man (Gary Morgan), Officer Ramsey (Ross Elliott).

Credits: Produced by: William Frye; Directed by: Jack Smight; Written by: Merwin Gerard; Director of Photography: Leonard J. South; Music by: John Cacavas; Art Director: George Webb; Film Editor: Edward A. Biery; Color by: Technicolor; Titles & Optical Effects: Universal Title; Produced by: Universal Television; Exclusive Distributor: MCA Television Limited.

A LITTLE BIT LIKE MURDER
(ABC WIDE WORLD OF ENTERTAINMENT/WIDE WORLD MYSTERY)

ABC Television Network, March 29, 1973; 90 minutes in color on tape.

A suspense drama about an evil house which exerted a malevolent force on its occupants.

Cast: Camilla (Elizabeth Hartman), Jeff (Roger Davis), Linda (Sharon Farrell), Nellie (Nina Foch), with: Sharon Gless.

Credits: Produced by: Barbara Schultz; Directed by: Nick Havinga; Written by: Sandra Scoppettone; Taped at: KTLA-TV; Produced by: Universal Television; Exclusive Distributor: MCA Television Limited.

A LITTLE GAME
(ABC MOVIE OF THE WEEKEND)

ABC Television Network, October 30, 1971; 90 minutes in color on film. Major Sponsor and Agency: Warner-Lambert Pharmaceutical Company through J. Walter Thompson Company.

A thriller about a 13-year-old boy who would stop at nothing to break up the marriage of his mother and stepfather. At the same time, the stepfather became convinced the boy was capable of murder. Filmed on location in Thousand Oaks, California.

Cast: Paul Hamilton (Ed Nelson), Elaine Hamilton (Diane Baker), Dunlap (Howard Duff), Laura (Katy Jurado), Robert Mueller (Mark Gruner), Stuart Parker (Christopher Shea), Secretary (Helen Kleeb).

Credits: Produced by: George Eckstein; Directed by: Paul Wendkos; Written by: Carol Sobieski; Based on the Novel by: Fielden Farrington; Director of Photography: Henry Wolf; Music by: Robert Prince; Art Director: Frank Arrigo; Set Decorations: James M. Walters; Film Editor: Michael Economou; Color by: Technicolor; Titles & Optical Effects: Universal Title; Produced by: Universal Television; Exclusive Distributor: MCA Television Limited.

LITTLE WOMEN

NBC Television Network, October 2, 1978 and October 3, 1978; 4 hours in color on film.

A drama about the lives of the March sisters: their conflicts, joys and heartbreaks. Based on Louisa May Alcott's novel of 19th-century manners and mores. The pilot for the series Little Women (which see) in which Mildred Natwick assumed the role of Aunt March.

Cast: Meg March (Meredith Baxter-Birney), Jo March (Susan Dey), Amy March (Ann Dusenberry), Beth March (Eve Plumb), Marmee (Dorothy McGuire), Grandpa Lawrence (Robert Young), Aunt March (Greer Garson), Laurie (Richard Gilliland), John Brooke (Cliff Potts), Professor Bhaer (William Shatner), Reverend March (William Schallert), Hannah (Virginia Gregg), Mrs. Kirke (Joyce Bulifant), Frank Vaughn (John DeLancie), Sally Gardiner (Carlene Watkins), J. T. Dashwood (Logan Ramsey), Mrs. Hummel (Carol Baxter).

Credits: Produced by: David Victor; Directed by: David Lowell Rich; Written by: Suzanne Clauser; Based on the Novel by: Louisa May Alcott; Director of Photography: Joseph Biroc; Music by: Elmer Bernstein; Art Director: Howard E. Johnson; Film Editors: James Benson, Donald Douglas; Set Decorations: Richard B. Goddard; Costumes by: Edith Head; Color by: Technicolor; Titles & Optical Effects: Universal Title; Produced by: Groverton Productions, Ltd.; In Association with: Universal Television And NBC-TV; Exclusive Distributor: MCA Television Limited.

LIVE AGAIN, DIE AGAIN

ABC Television Network, February 16, 1974; 90 minutes in color on film.

A suspense drama about a woman who returned to her family after being frozen for 34 years. But the joy of her reunion was squelched when she learned that somebody was trying to kill her.

182 / Telefeatures

Cast: Caroline Carmichael (Donna Mills), Sissie O'Neil (Geraldine Page), Thomas Carmichael (Walter Pidgeon), Joe Dolan (Cliff Potts), Marcia Carmichael (Vera Miles), James Carmichael (Mike Farrell), Betty Simpson (Lurene Tuttle), Wilson (Stewart Moss), Nurse (Irene Tedrow), Dr. Fellman (Peter Bromilow), Larry Brice (Walker Edmiston).

Credits: Executive Producer: David Victor; Produced by: Robert F. O'Neill; Directed by: Richard A. Colla; Written by: Joseph Stefano; Based on the Novel "Come to Mother" by: David Sale; Director of Photography: Michael Margulies; Music by: George Romanis; Art Director: George Webb; Film Editors: Jamie Caylor, David Newhouse; Color by: Technicolor; Titles & Optical Effects: Universal Title; Produced by: Groverton Productions, Ltd.; In Association with: Universal Television; Exclusive Distributor: MCA Television Limited.

LOCK, STOCK AND BARREL
(WORLD PREMIERE)

NBC Television Network, September 24, 1971; 120 minutes in color on film.

A comedy-Western about Clare and Roselle Bridgeman who eloped. They were pursued by Roselle's displeased father as they made their way to Oregon. During the journey, their lives were further complicated as they met a purported murderer, a con man who sold them property and a group of rough soldiers. Followed by the sequel Hitched (which see).

Cast: Clare Bridgeman (Tim Matheson), Roselle Bridgeman (Belinda J. Montgomery), Punch Logan (Claude Akins), Mr. Brucker (Jack Albertson), Sgt. Markey (Neville Brand), Rev. Willie Pursle (Burgess Meredith), Beth Lambert (Felicia Farr), Hartwig (Robert Emhardt), Micah (John Beck), Cpl. Fowler (Charles Dierkop).

Credits: Produced by: Richard Alan Simmons; Directed by: Jerry Thorpe; Written by: Richard Alan Simmons; Directors of Photography: Russell Metty, Harry J. May; Music by: Pat Williams; Art Director: William D. DeCinces; Film Editor: Edward M. Abroms; Color by: Technicolor; Titles & Optical Effects: Universal Title; Produced by: Universal Television; In Association with: NBC-TV; Exclusive Distributor: MCA Television Limited.

THE LOG OF THE BLACK PEARL
(WORLD PREMIERE)

NBC Television Network, January 4, 1975; 120 minutes in color on film.

A drama about a young stockbroker who inherited his grandfather's ship, the Black Pearl, hired a captain and continued his grandfather's quest for a sunken treasure. The pilot for an unsold series. Filmed on location in Mazatlan, Mexico.

Cast: Christopher Sand (Kiel Martin), Capt. Fitz (Ralph Bellamy), Lila Bristol (Anne Archer), Jock Roper (Jack Kruschen), Devlin (Glenn Corbett), Kort (John Anderson), Fenner (Edward Faulkner), Alexander Sand (Henry Wilcoxin), Eric Kort (John Alderson), Archie Hector (Pedro Armendariz, Jr.), Velasquez (Jose Angel Espinosa), Stockbroker (Dale Johnson).

Credits: Executive Producer: Jack Webb; Produced by: William Stark; Directed by: Andrew McLaglen; Written by: Harold Jack Bloom; Story by: Harold Jack Bloom, Eric Bercovici, Jerry Ludwig; Director of Photography: Gabriel Torres; Music by: Laurence Rosenthal; Art Director: James Martin Buchanan; Film Editor: John Kaufman; Jr.; Color by: Technicolor; Titles & Optical Effects: Universal Title, Produced by: Mark VII Limited; In Association with: Universal Television And NBC-TV; Exclusive Distributor: MCA Television Limited.

THE LONELY PROFESSION
(WORLD PREMIERE/NBC TUESDAY NIGHT AT THE MOVIES)

NBC Television Network, October 21, 1969; 120 minutes in color on film.

A mystery drama about a private investigator who attempted to solve the murder of a client after he became a suspect.

Cast: Lee Gordon (Harry Guardino), Charles Van Cleve (Dean Jagger), Donna Travers (Barbara McNair), Martin Bannister (Joseph Cotten), Karen Menardos (Ina Balin), Beatrice Savorona (Dina Merrill), Freddie Farber (Jack Carter), Julian Thatcher (Troy Donahue), Lt. Joseph Webber (Stephen McNally), Dominic Savarona (Fernando Lamas).

Credits: Produced by: Jo Swerling, Jr.; Directed by: Douglas Heyes; Written by: Douglas Heyes; Director of Photography: Ralph Woolsey; Music by: Pete Rugolo; Art Director: Robert Luthardt; Set Decorations: John McCarthy, James M. Walters, Sr.; Film Editor: Robert Watts; Costumes by: Charles Waldo; Makeup: Bud Westmore; Hair Stylist: Larry Germain; Color by: Technicolor; Titles & Optical Effects: Universal Title; Produced by: Universal Television; In Association with: NBC-TV; Exclusive Distributor: MCA Television Limited.

THE LONGEST HUNDRED MILES
(WORLD PREMIERE/NBC SATURDAY NIGHT AT THE MOVIES)

NBC Television Network, January 21, 1967; 120 minutes in color on film.

184 / Telefeatures

A World War II adventure about a GI and a nurse in the Philippines, where they persuaded a priest and seven orphans to attempt escape with them from Japanese soldiers. Filmed on location in the Philippines.

Cast: Corporal Steve Bennett (Doug McClure), Father Sanchez (Ricardo Montalban), Lt. Laura Huntington (Katharine Ross), Miguel (Ronald Remy), Lupe (Helen Thompson), Pedro (Berting Labra), Paz (Loaki Bay), Maria (Vilma Santos), Vincente (Danilo Jurado), Teresa (Debra Gaza), Jose (Juan Marcelo), Chico (Danny Tariuam), Coro (Tommy Bismark), Hiko (captured Japanese) (Victor Uematsu).

Credits: Produced by: Jack Leewood; Directed by: Don Weis; Written by: Winston Miller; Adapted by: Paul Mason; Story by: Hennie Leon; Director of Photography: Ray Flin; Music by: Franz Waxman; Art Director: Russ Lecap; Film Editor: Richard G. Wray, A.C.E.; Sound: Joe Keener; Color by: Technicolor; Titles & Optical Effects: Universal Title; Men's Wardrobe: Isaias Betsayda; Women's Wardrobe: Rosa France; Makeup: Pat De Lara; Produced by: Universal Television; Exclusive Distributor: MCA Television Limited.

THE LONGEST NIGHT
(ABC TUESDAY MOVIE OF THE WEEK)

ABC Television Network, September 12, 1972; 90 minutes in color on film.

A thriller, based on an actual incident, about a girl who was kidnapped and buried alive in a coffin with a life-support system limited to 83 hours. With time running out, her father and federal authorities engaged in a desperate search to find her before she died. Filmed on location in Thousand Oaks, California.

Cast: Alan Chambers (David Janssen), John Danbry (James Farentino), Norma Chambers (Phyllis Thaxter), Ellen Gunther (Skye Aubrey), Agent Wills (Mike Farrell), Karen Chambers (Sallie Shockley), Agent Barris (Joel Fabiani), Harvey Eaton (Richard Anderson), Father Chase (Charles McGraw), Agent Jones (John Kerr), Frank Cavanaugh (Robert Cornthwaite), Dr. Steven Clay (Ross Elliott).

Credits: Produced by: William Frye; Directed by: Jack Smight; Written by: Merwin Gerard; Director of Photography: Sam Leavitt; Music by: Hal Mooney; Art Director: John J. Lloyd; Film Editor: Robert F. Shugrue; Color by: Technicolor; Titles & Optical Effects: Universal Title; Produced by: Universal Television; Exclusive Distributor: MCA Television Limited.

LOVE IS NOT ENOUGH

NBC Television Network, June 12, 1978; 120 minutes in color on film.

A situation comedy about the Harrises, a black family that left Los Angeles for Detroit in hopes of finding a better life. The pilot for the series Harris and Company (which see).

Cast: Mike Harris (Bernie Casey), David Harris (Stuart K. Robinson), Angie Adams (Carol Tillery Banks), Liz Morris (Renne Brown), Richard Allen (Dain Turner), Tommy (Eddie Singleton), J. P. (Lia Jackson), Cousin Charley Adams (Stu Gilliam).

Credits: Produced by: Stanley L. Robinson; Directed by: Ivan Dixon; Written by: Arthur Ross; Director of Photography: Lamar Boren; Music by: Coleridge-Taylor Perkinson; Art Director: Sherman Loudermilk; Film Editor: Larry Strong; Color by: Technicolor; Titles & Optical Effects: Universal Title; Produced by: Universal Television; Exclusive Distributor: MCA Television Limited.

LUCAS TANNER
(NBC DOUBLE FEATURE NIGHT AT THE MOVIES)

NBC Television Network, May 8, 1974; 90 minutes in color on film.

A drama about schoolteacher Lucas Tanner whose career was jeopardized after a student's death. Rumor had it that it was his negligence which caused the accident that killed the boy. The pilot for the series Lucas Tanner (which see). Filmed on location in Los Angeles and St. Louis, Missouri.

Cast: Lucas Tanner (David Hartman), Joyce Howell (Kathleen Quinlan), Margaret Blumenthal (Rosemary Murphy), Craig Willemon (Ramon Bieri), Jaytee (Alan Abelew), Glendon (Robbie Rist), Himself (Joe Garagiola), Nancy Howell (Nancy Malone), Mr. Howell (Michael Baseleon).

Credits: Executive Producer: David Victor; Produced by: Jerry McNeely; Directed by: Richard Donner; Written by: Jerry McNeely; Director of Photography: Harry L. Wolf; Music by: David Shire; Art Director: Sydney Z. Litwack; Film Editor: Richard Bracken; Color by: Technicolor; Titles & Optical Effects: Universal Title; Produced by: Groverton Productions, Ltd.; In Association with: Universal Television; Exclusive Distributor: MCA Television Limited.

MAGIC CARPET
(WORLD PREMIERE)

NBC Television Network, November 6, 1972; 120 minutes in color on film.

A comedy-mystery about Timothea Bentley, a language and art major working her way through college in Rome. Ranato Caruso, office manager of Magic Carpet Tours, asked her to take over a tour when one of his regular girls became ill. She met the group in Florence and soon discovered that it included a mysterious freeloader, Josh Tracy. Though she was suspicious of him (as were the police), she was attracted to him. Filmed on location.

Cast: Timothea (Susan Saint James), Josh Tracy (Robert Pratt), Roger Warden (Cliff Potts), Renato Caruso (Enzo Cerusico), Mr. Benson (Jim Backus), Mrs. Benson (Henny Backus), Mr. Kane (Wally Cox), Mrs. Kane (Abby Dalton), Mrs. Vogel (Selma Diamond), Virginia Wolfe (Nanette Fabray), Mr. Tracy (John Larch).

Credits: Produced by: Ranald MacDougall; Directed by: William Graham; Written by: Ranald MacDougall; Director of Photography: Pietro Portalupi; Music by: Lyn Murray; Art Director: Franco Fumagelli; Film Editor: Richard G. Wray; Color by: Technicolor; Titles & Optical Effects: Universal Title; Produced by: Westward Productions; In Association with: Universal Television; And NBC-TV; Exclusive Distributor: MCA Television Limited.

MALLORY: CIRCUMSTANTIAL EVIDENCE
(WORLD PREMIERE/NBC SUNDAY MYSTERY MOVIE)

NBC Television Network, February 8, 1976; 120 minutes in color on film.

A drama about Arthur Mallory, a once-successful lawyer who had been accused of causing a witness to perjure himself. Though the bar association cleared him, many people still considered him guilty. Mallory's latest client was Joe Celli, a man accused first of grand theft, auto and then of slaying a fellow prisoner. The pilot for an unsold series.

Cast: Arthur Mallory (Raymond Burr), Joe Celli (Mark Hamill), Angelo Rondello (Robert Loggia), Roberto Ruiz (A Martinez), Tony Garcia (Vic Mohica), Cole (Stanley Kamel), Georgie (Bill Lucking), Hanigan (Walter Lott), Martinez (Armando Federico), Clifford Wilson (Roger Robinson), Bob Latimer (Eugene Roche), John Shields (Peter Mark Richman), Judge Paul Pieter (Allan Rich), Richmond (Peter Stirling), Sandra Wiley (Joyce Easton), Ron Wymer (Cliff Emmich), George (Bill Lucking), with: Alexander Courtney, Mark Travis, John Finnegan, Jay Varela, Karen Somerville, Sandy Ward, Wil Albert, J. Jay Saunders, Don Barrows, Richard Eastham, Harry Hickox, Bert Holland.

Credits: Produced by: William Sackheim; Directed by: Boris Sagal; Written by: Joel Oliansky, Joseph Polizzi; Based on a Story by: Tom Greene; Director of Photography: Russell Metty; Music by: James Di Pasquale; Art Director: John Corso; Film Editor: Robert F. Shugrue; Music Supervision: Hal Mooney; Color by: Technicolor; Titles & Optical Effects: Universal Title; Produced by: Crescendo Productions; In Association with: R. B. Productions; And

Universal Television; Exclusive Distributor: MCA Television Limited.

MAN ON THE OUTSIDE
(THE ABC SUNDAY NIGHT MOVIE)

ABC Television Network, June 29, 1975; 120 minutes in color on film.

A drama about former police lieutenant Wade Griffin who came out of retirement after his private investigator son was killed and his grandson kidnapped by the syndicate. This pilot for the series Griff (which see) was produced in 1973 but not telecast until 1975.

Cast: Wade Griffin (Lorne Greene), Nora (Lorraine Gary), Mark (Lee H. Montgomery), Ellen (Jean Allison), Gerald (James Olson), Ames (William C. Watson), Sandra Ames (Brooke Bundy), Lt. Matthews (Ken Swofford), Detective (Alan Fudge), Scully (Bruce Kirby), Arnold (Charles Knox Robinson), Benny (Gary Walberg), Stella (Ruth McDevitt), Ruben (Scat Man Crothers).

Credits: Executive Producer: David Victor; Produced by: George Eckstein; Directed by: Boris Sagal; Written by: Larry Cohen; Director of Photography: Mario Tosi; Music by: Elliot Kaplan; Art Director: Walter M. Simonds; Film Editors: Douglas Stewart, Bud Hoffman; Color by: Technicolor; Titles & Optical Effects: Universal Title; Produced by: Groverton Productions, Ltd.; In Association with: Universal Television; Exclusive Distributor: MCA Television Limited.

THE MAN WITH THE POWER

NBC Television Network, May 24, 1977; 120 minutes in color on film.

An action-adventure film about Eric Smith, a man who inherited strange powers from his father, a being from another planet. His psychokinetic abilities were enlisted by the government to ensure the safety of a visiting princess.

Cast: Eric Smith (Bob Neill), Princess Siri (Persis Khambatta), Agent Bloom (Tim O'Connor), Paul (Vic Morrow), Farnsworth (Roger Perry), Maj. Sajid (Rene Assa), Shanda (Noel de Souza), Driver (James Ingersoll), Dilling (Bill Fletcher).

Credits: Produced by: Allan Balter; Directed by: Nicholas Sgarro; Written by: Allan Balter; Director of Photography: J. J. Jones; Music by: Pat Williams; Art Director: George Reune; Film Editors: Jerrold Ludwig, Chuck McClelland; Color by: Technicolor: Titles & Optical Effects: Universal Title; Produced by: Universal Television; In Association with: NBC-TV; Exclusive Distributor: MCA Television Limited.

188 / Telefeatures

MANDRAKE

NBC Television Network, January 24, 1979; 120 minutes in color on film.

A drama about Mandrake the Magician, who set out to foil a crazed criminal who was trying to extort $10,000,000 from the head of a large corporation while planning multiple murders. The pilot for an unsold series.

Cast: Mandrake (Anthony Herrera), Stacy (Simone Griffeth), Lothar (Ji-Tu Cumbuka), Alec Gordon (Hank Brandt), Jennifer Lindsay (Gretchen Corbett), Dr. Malcolm Lindsay (David Hooks), William Romero (Peter Haskell), Arkadian (Robert Reed).

Credits: Produced by: Rick Husky; Directed by: Harry Falk; Written by: Rick Husky; Director of Photography: Vincent A. Martinelli; Music by: Morton Stevens; Art Director: John T. Bruce; Film Editors: Fredric Knudsten, Edward W. Williams; Color by: Technicolor; Titles & Optical Effects: Universal Title; Produced by: Universal Television; Exclusive Distributor: MCA Television Limited.

MANEATER
(ABC SUSPENSE MOVIE)

ABC Television Network, December 8, 1973; 90 minutes in color on film.

A suspense drama about a crazed animal trainer who unleashed two hungry Bengal tigers on a group of tourists.

Cast: Carl Brenner (Richard Basehart), Nick Baron (Ben Gazzara), Gloria Baron (Sheree North), Shep Sanders (Kip Niven), Polly (Laurette Spang), Paula Brenner (Claire Brennen), Louis (Stewart Raffill), 1st Ranger (Lou Ferragher), 2nd Ranger (Jerry Fitzpatrick).

Credits: Produced by: Robert F. O'Neill; Directed by: Vince Edwards; Written by: Vince Edwards, Marcus Demian, Jimmy Sangster; Story by: Vince Edwards; Director of Photography: Haskell Boggs; Music by: George Romanis; Art Director: William Newberry; Film Editor: John F. Schreyer; Color by: Technicolor; Titles & Optical Effects: Universal Title; Produced by: Universal Television; Exclusive Distributor: MCA Television Limited.

THE MANHUNTER
(NBC SATURDAY NIGHT AT THE MOVIES)

NBC Television Network, April 3, 1976; 120 minutes in color on film.

A suspense drama about a bank-robbery suspect hiding in the Louisiana swamp country and the big-game hunter who was hired to flush him out.

Cast: David Farrow (Roy Thinnes), Mara Bocock (Sandra Dee), Rafe Augustine (Albert Salmi), Carl Auscher (Sorrell Booke), Clel Bocock (William Smith), Walter Sinclair (David Brian), Pa Bocock (Royal Dano), Ma Bocock (Madeleine Sherwood), Teresa Taylor (Madlyn Rhue), Prof. Mike Mellick (Pitt Herbert), Himself (Al Hirt), Police Sergeant (Lew Brown), Stephen Sinclair (Richard Van Fleet), Fronie (Eric Laneuville), with: Foster Brooks.

Credits: Produced by: Ron Roth; Directed by: Don Taylor; Written by: Meyer Dolinsky; Based on the Novel by: Wade Miller; Director of Photography: Benjamin H. Kline; Music by: Benny Carter; Art Director: Henry Larrecq; Film Editor: Howard G. Epstein; Color by: Technicolor; Titles & Optical Effects: Universal Title; Produced by: Universal Television; Exclusive Distributor: MCA Television Limited.

THE MARCUS-NELSON MURDERS
(THE CBS THURSDAY NIGHT MOVIES)

CBS Television Network, March 8, 1973; 3 hours in color on film.

A crime drama about Det. Lt. Theo Kojak and his mammoth investigation into the murder of two young women named Marcus and Nelson in their Manhattan apartment. A black youth, Lewis Humes, was arrested on very flimsy evidence for attempted rape and subsequently confessed to the two murders. He claimed his confession was the result of being beaten by the police. When Kojak discovered discrepancies between the facts in the case and Humes' confession, he tried to help the youth but was thwarted at every turn by fellow law-enforcement officials who seemed to be interested only in a quick conviction. The pilot for the series Kojak (which see), this telefeature was based on the real-life Wylie-Hoffert murder case detailed in Selwyn Raab's book Justice in the Back Room.

Cast: Det. Lt. Theo Kojak (Telly Savalas), Teddy Hopper (Marjoe Gortner), Jake Weinhaus (José Ferrer), Det. Dan Corrigan (Ned Beatty), Mario Portello (Allen Garfield), Ruthie (Lorraine Gary), Bobby Martin (Roger Robinson), Ginny (Harriet Karr), Lewis Humes (Gene Woodbury), Det. Matt Black (William Watson), Det. Jacarrio (Val Bisoglio), Rita Alvarez (Antonia Rey), Josie Hopper (Chita Rivera), Sgt. McCartney (Bruce Kirby), Mr. Fisher (Robert Walden), Asst. D.A. Goodman (Robert Fields), Inspector MacNeill (Lloyd Gough), Arless Humes (Lynn Hamilton), Cabot (Lawrence Pressman), Inspector Hoffstetter (John Sylvester White), Melissa Karr (Carolyn Nelson), Al Stabile (Paul Jenkins), Mrs. Hopper (Helen Page Camp), Lynn Peyser (Ellen Moss), Jack Deems (George Savalas), Sgt. Roberts (Alan Manson), Sgt. Topf (Fred Holliday), Abe Humes (Henry Brown, Jr.), Mr. Sack (Joshua Shelley), Marge Corrigan (Patricia

O'Connel), Roberto Timoteo (Alex Colon), Judge DeKana (Ben Hammer), Justice Redding (Tol Avery), Judge Mathews (Bill Zuckert), Jo-Ann Marcus (Elizabeth Berger), Kathy Nelson (Lora Kaye), Irwin David (Steven Gravers).

Credits: Executive Producer: Abby Mann; Produced by: Matthew Rapf; Directed by: Joseph Sargent; Written by: Abby Mann; Suggested by the Book "Justice in the Back Room" by: Selwyn Raab; Director of Photography: Mario Tosi; Music by: Billy Goldenberg; Art Director: John J. Lloyd; Film Editors: Carl Pingitore, Richard M. Sprague; Color by: Technicolor; Titles & Optical Effects: Universal Title; Produced by: Universal Television; Exclusive Distributor: MCA Television Limited.

MARCUS WELBY, M. D.
(ABC WEDNESDAY NIGHT MOVIE)

ABC Television Network, March 26, 1969; 120 minutes in color on film.

A medical drama about the very human, very real experiences of general practitioner Marcus Welby. Welby was representative of a vanishing breed of doctor, the kind of man who was more committed to people than to symptoms and who knew that illness could best be treated when medicine was tempered with both knowledge of --and compassion for--the patient. The pilot for the series Marcus Welby, M. D. (which see).

Cast: Marcus Welby (Robert Young), Steve Kiley (James Brolin), Myra Sherwood (Anne Baxter), Tina Sawyer (Susan Strasberg), Lew Sawyer (Peter Deuel), Andrew Swanson (Lew Ayres), Sandy Welby (Sheila Larken), Ray Wells (Mercer Harris), Kenji Yamashita (Richard Loo), Tiny Baker (Tom Bosley), Consuelo (Penny Santon), with: Ben Wright.

Credits: Executive Producer: David Victor; Produced by: David J. O'Connell; Directed by: David Lowell Rich; Written by: Don Mankiewicz; Story by: David Victor; Director of Photography: Russell Metty; Music by: Leonard Rosenman; Art Director: George Patrick; Film Editor: Gene Palmer; Color by: Technicolor; Titles & Optical Effects: Universal Title; Produced by: Groverton Productions, Ltd.; In Association with: Universal Television; Exclusive Distributor: MCA Television Limited.

MARRIAGE: YEAR ONE
(WORLD PREMIERE)

NBC Television Network, October 15, 1971; 120 minutes in color on film.

A drama about a struggling young medical student and a girl from a wealthy family who attempt to adjust to their first year of marriage.

Cast: Jane Duden (Sally Field), L. T. Millens (Robert Pratt), Duden (William Windom), Grandma Duden (Agnes Moorehead), Golonkas (Neville Brand), Bernie (Bob Balaban), Phil (Lonny Chapman), Lemberg (Michael Lerner), Luke (Robert Lipton), Shirley Lemberg (Susan Silo), Emma Teasley (Cicely Tyson).

Credits: Executive Producer: Norman Felton; Produced by: Stephen Karpf; Directed by: William Graham; Written by: Stephen Karpf, Elinor Karpf; Director of Photography: William Margulies, A. S. C.; Art Director: William D. DeCinces; Set Decorations: F. Keogh Gleason, Film Editor: Douglas Stewart; Color by: Technicolor; Titles & Optical Effects: Universal Title; Produced by: Arena Productions, Inc.; In Association with: Universal Television And NBC-TV; Exclusive Distributor: MCA Television Limited.

McCLOUD: WHO KILLED MISS U. S. A. ?
(WORLD PREMIERE/NBC TUESDAY NIGHT AT THE MOVIES)

NBC Television Network, February 17, 1970; 120 minutes in color on film.

A police drama about U. S. Deputy Marshal Sam McCloud who was dispatched from Taos, New Mexico to New York City to deliver a prisoner wanted as a witness in the murder trial of a Puerto Rican busboy. Upon arrival in New York, the prisoner was kidnapped. McCloud set out to find the prisoner and prove that he was an expert marshal even if he wasn't familiar with city ways. Along the way, he got entangled with a lady novelist, a Wall Street lawyer and a dead beauty queen. The pilot for the series McCloud (which see).

Cast: Deputy Marshal Sam McCloud (Dennis Weaver), Whitman (Craig Stevens), Peter B. Clifford (Mark Richman), Chris Coughlin (Diana Muldaur), Sgt. Joe Broadhurst (Terry Carter), Peralta (Mario Alcalde), Father Nieves (Raul Julia), James Waldron (Shelly Novack), Adrienne Redman (Julie Newmar), Billy (Michael Bow), Ramos (Nefti Millet), Merri Ann Coleman (Kathy Stritch), Guard (Albert Popwell), 2nd Reporter (Ira Cook), 1st Deputy (Gregory Sierra), 2nd Deputy (Tony Dante), Black Reporter (Victor Bozeman), 1st Reporter (Bill Baldwin), Vejar (Ron Henriquez), Receptionist (Lee Pulford), Chico (Roberto Vargas).

Credits: Produced by: Leslie Stevens; Directed by: Richard A. Colla; Written by: Stanford Whitmore, Richard Levinson, William Link; Director of Photography: Ben Colman; Music by: David Shire; Art Director: Henry Bumstead; Film Editors: Robert L. Kimble, Bob Kagey, Edwin H. Bryant, A. C. E.; Assistant Directors: Edward K. Dodds, Steve Marshall; Unit Manager: Joseph E. Kenny; Music Supervision: Stanley Wilson; Sound: Stanley Cooley; Costumes by: Bill Hargate; Makeup: Bud Westmore; Hair Stylist:

Larry Germain; Color by: Technicolor; Titles & Optical Effects: Universal Title; Produced by: Universal Television; In Association with: NBC-TV; Exclusive Distributor: MCA Television Limited.

McNAUGHTON'S DAUGHTER
(NBC THURSDAY NIGHT AT THE MOVIES)

NBC Television Network, March 4, 1976; 120 minutes in color on film.

A drama about Laurel McNaughton, daughter of a great defense lawyer, who, as a deputy D.A., prosecuted a well-known missionary accused of murder. The pilot for the series McNaughton's Daughter (which see).

Cast: Laurel McNaughton (Susan Clark), Grace Coventry (Vera Miles), Quintero (Ricardo Montalban), Moses Bellman (Ralph Bellamy), Ed Hughes (John Elerick), Lew Farragut (James Callahan), Aprili (Tina Andrews), Jardine (Ramon Bieri), Zareb (Roger Aaron Brown), Dick Vanderback (Quinn Redeker), Cassie Garnet (Louise Latham), Pierce (Mike Farrell).

Credits: Executive Producer: David Victor; Produced by: David J. O'Connell; Directed by: Jerry London; Written by: Ken Trevey; Story by: David Victor, Ken Trevey; Director of Photography: Sy Hoffberg; Music by: David Shire; Art Director: Howard E. Johnson; Film Editors: John Elias, Richard Watts; Color by: Technicolor; Titles & Optical Effects: Universal Title; Produced by: Groverton Productions, Ltd., In Association with: Universal Television; Exclusive Distributor: MCA Television Limited.

MOBILE TWO
(ABC SPECIAL MOVIE)

ABC Television Network, September 2, 1975; 90 minutes in color on film.

A drama about Peter Campbell, an experienced broadcast journalist whose past drinking problems made it hard for him to find a job. His luck changed when a TV producer signed him on to the station's mobile reporting unit. His stories included investigations into an arsonist and the search for an ill youngster's missing father. The pilot for the series Mobile One (which see).

Cast: Peter Campbell (Jackie Cooper), Maggie Spencer (Julie Gregg), Doug McKnight (Mark Wheeler), Robert Brice (Edd Byrnes), Bill Hopkins (Jack Hogan), Father John Lucas (Joe E. Tata), Phillip Ganzer (Harry Bartell), Lt. Don Carter (Bill Boyett), Wally (Burt Mustin), Surgeon (Barney Phillips).

Credits: Executive Producer: Jack Webb; Produced by: William

Bowers; Directed by: David Moessinger; Written by: David Moessinger, James M. Miller; Director of Photography: Enzo A. Martinelli; Music by: Nelson Riddle; Film Editor: Robert Leeds; Color by: Technicolor; Titles & Optical Effects: Universal Title; Produced by: Mark VII Limited; In Association with: Universal Television; Exclusive Distributor: MCA Television Limited.

MONEY TO BURN
(ABC SUSPENSE MOVIE)

ABC Television Network, October 27, 1973; 90 minutes in color on film.

A suspense drama about Jed Finnegan, a clever prison trustee who taught art and ran the prison printshop. He managed to manufacture $1,000,000 in counterfeit bills and planned to exchange them for real money scheduled to be burned in a treasury building.

Cast: Jed Finnegan (E. G. Marshall), Emily Finnegan (Mildred Natwick), Caesar Rodriguez (Alejandro Ray), Calvin Baker (Cleavon Little), Warden Caulfield (David Doyle), Neil Davis (Charles McGraw), Big Maury (Ronald Feinberg), Guard Sergeant (Lou Frizzell), Team Leader (Robert Karnes), Guard (Lew Brown), Parking Lot Attendant (Paul Sorenson).

Credits: Produced by: Harve Bennett; Directed by: Robert Michael Lewis; Written by: Elroy Schwartz; Director of Photography: Enzo A. Martinelli; Music by: Oliver Nelson; Art Director: Joseph Alves, Jr.; Film Editor: Les Green; Color by: Technicolor; Titles & Optical Effects: Universal Title; Produced by: Silverton Productions, Inc.; In Association with: Universal Television; Exclusive Distributor: MCA Television Limited.

MOUSEY
(ABC SUSPENSE MOVIE)

ABC Television Network, March 9, 1974; 90 minutes in color on film.

A suspense drama about a milquetoast biology teacher who was determined to get revenge on his ex-wife. Filmed on location in Montreal and London.

Cast: George Anderson (Kirk Douglas), Laura Anderson (Jean Seberg), David Richardson (John Vernon), Mrs. Richardson (Bessie Love), Sandra (Beth Porter), Inspector (Sam Wanamaker), Private Detective (James Bradford), Nancy (Suzanne Lloyd), Simon (Stuart Chandler), Miss Wainwright (Valerie Colgan), Martha (Mavis Villiers), Harry (Elliott Sullivan), Barman (Bob Sherman), Headmaster (James Berwick), Miss Carter (Margo Alexis).

Credits: Executive Producer: Beryl Vertue; Produced by: Aida Young; Directed by: Daniel Petrie; Written by: John Peacock; Director of Photography: Jack Hildyard; Music by: Ron Grainger; Art Director: Roy Stannard; Film Editor: John Trumper; Color by: Technicolor; Titles & Optical Effects: Universal Title; Produced by: Associated British Films; In Association with: Universal Television; Exclusive Distributor: MCA Television Limited.

THE MOVIE MURDERER
(WORLD PREMIERE/NBC MONDAY NIGHT AT THE MOVIES)

NBC Television Network, February 2, 1970; 120 minutes in color on film.

A drama about two insurance investigators who tracked down an arsonist who set fire to buildings that stored motion picture films.

Cast: Angus MacGregor (Arthur Kennedy), Alfred Fisher (Warren Oates), Mike Beaudine (Tom Selleck), Collier Landis (Jeff Corey), Ellen Farrington (Norma Crane), Karel Kessler (Robert Webber), Cliff Thomas (Russell Johnson), Lois Warwick (Nita Talbot), Jimmy Apache (Severn Darden), Willie Peanuts (Elisha Cook, Jr.), J. M. Cole (David Astor), Martin Moss (Henry Jones), King Kong (Steve Sandor), Hotel Clerk (Ned Glass), Linderman (Woodrow Parfrey), Beaver (Sally Ann Richards), Arson Lieutenant (Frank Campanella), Pete Holland (Mark Allen), Jacob Silas (Milton Frome).

Credits: Produced by: Jack Laird; Directed by: Boris Sagal; Written by: Stanford Whitmore; Story by: Bernard Taper, Stanford Whitmore; Director of Photography: Lionel Lindon; Music Supervision: Stanley Wilson; Art Director: Henry Bumstead; Film Editor: Frank E. Morriss; Assistant Director: Carl Beringer; Unit Manager: Burt Astor; Sound: Earl Schwarz; Costumes by: Bill Hargate; Makeup: Bud Westmore; Hair Stylist: Larry Germain; Color by: Technicolor; Titles & Optical Effects: Universal Title; Produced by: Universal Television; In Association with: NBC-TV; Exclusive Distributor: MCA Television Limited.

MURDER BY PROXY
(ABC WIDE WORLD OF ENTERTAINMENT/WIDE WORLD MYSTERY)

ABC Television Network, April 23, 1974; 90 minutes in color on tape.

A mystery about the president of an electronics firm who promised all of his potential successors that they would join him in the grave.

Cast: Dan Keeley (Lawrence Pressman), MacShane (John Randolph), Mason (Edward Andrews), Jenny (Amanda McBroom), Alex Baron (Ramon Bieri), Jace Gilbert (Tom Troupe), Ada Walden (Zina Jasper), Sgt. Wilson (Don Dubbins), Miss Todd (Dana Hansen).

Credits: Produced by: Universal Television; Exclusive Distributor: MCA Television Limited.

MURDER WORKS OVERTIME
(ABC WIDE WORLD OF ENTERTAINMENT/WIDE WORLD MYSTERY)

ABC Television Network, August 27, 1974; 90 minutes in color on tape.

A mystery about an executive secretary who was robbed and strangled while working late at night. Her assailant apparently knew that she was carrying a large sum of money.

Cast: Donna Ederle (Lee Purcell), Jack Goss (Joseph Hindy), Andy (James G. Richardson), Canavan (Alan Oppenheimer), Pacciardi (George DiCenzo), with: Juno Dawson, George Tyne, Jason Wingreen, Connie Milton, Ray Ballard, Paula Victor, Larry Simpasa, Joe Cortese, Anna Karen.

Credits: Executive Producer: Barbara Schultz; Produced by: Matthew N. Herman; Directed by: Nick Havinga; Written by: Philip Reisman, Jr.; Produced by: Universal Television; Exclusive Distributor: MCA Television Limited.

MY DARLING DAUGHTERS' ANNIVERSARY
(ABC WEDNESDAY MOVIE OF THE WEEK)

ABC Television Network, November 7, 1973; 90 minutes in color on film.

A drama about Judge Charles Raleigh, a widower who wanted to remarry on the anniversary of his daughters' quadruple wedding ceremony. A sequel to the telefeature All My Darling Daughters (which see).

Cast: Judge Charles Raleigh (Robert Young), Maggie Cartwright (Ruth Hussey), Matthew Cunningham (Raymond Massey), Susan (Darleen Carr), Andy (Darrell Lawson), Robin (Judy Strangis), Jerry (Jerry Fogel), Jennifer (Sharon Gless), Brad (Colby Chester), Charlotte (Lara Parker), Biff (Alan Vint), Carter (Ben Wright), Judge Harline (Anna Lee).

Credits: Executive Producer: David Victor; Produced by: David J. O'Connell; Directed by: Joseph Pevney; Written by: John Gay; Director of Photography: Walter Strenge; Music by: Hal Mooney; Art Director: Howard E. Johnson; Film Editor: Sam E. Waxman; Color by: Technicolor; Titles & Optical Effects: Universal Title; Produced by: Groverton Productions, Ltd.; In Association with: Universal Television; Exclusive Distributor: MCA Television Limited.

196 / Telefeatures

MY SWEET CHARLIE
(WORLD PREMIERE/NBC TUESDAY NIGHT AT THE MOVIES)

NBC Television Network, January 20, 1970; 120 minutes in color on film.

A drama about a Southern white girl and a Northern black man who overcame their objections to each other in order to stay alive. Marlene Chambers, who was expecting a baby, was ordered to leave her father's home and traveled to a small Texas town where she hid in a vacant house. After she had been there for some time, Charlie Roberts, a black man, arrived and decided to hide in the house too. Marlene considered Charlie inferior and despised him. Charlie, a New York lawyer, was running away from law enforcement officers who wanted him in connection with an incident resulting from his traveling to the South. This telefeature was the recipient of the Golden Gate Award for "outstanding film contribution to the field of television entertainment" at the San Francisco International Film Festival. It was later put into theatrical distribution.

Cast: Marlene Chambers (Patty Duke), Charles Roberts (Al Freeman, Jr.), Treadwell (Ford Rainey), Mr. Larrabee (William Hardy), Mrs. Larrabee (Chris Wilson), Grady (Noble Willingham), Sheriff (Dave Ward).

Credits: Produced by: Richard Levinson, William Link; Directed by: Lamont Johnson; Written by: Richard Levinson, William Link; Based on the Novel by: David Westheimer; Director of Photography: Gene Polito; Music by: Gil Melle; Art Director: Robert Luthardt; Film Editor: Edward M. Abroms; Assistant Director: Ralph Ferrin; Unit Manager: Kenneth L. Grossman; Sound: Melvin M. Metcalfe, Sr.; Costumes by: Charles Waldo; Makeup: Bud Westmore; Hair Stylist: Larry Germain; Color by: Technicolor; Titles & Optical Effects: Universal Title; Produced by: Universal Television; In Association with: NBC-TV; Exclusive Distributor: MCA Television Limited.

THE NEON CEILING
(WORLD PREMIERE)

NBC Television Network, February 8, 1971; 120 minutes in color on film.

A drama about an unhappily married woman and her daughter who ran away from home and became stranded in the desert at a roadside cafe and gas station run by a gruff loner.

Cast: Jones (Gig Young), Carrie (Lee Grant), Paula (Denise Nickerson), Harry (Herb Edelman), Miller (William Smithers), Carnival Boy (Robert Pratt), Highway Patrolman (James McEachin).

Credits: Produced by: William Sackheim; Directed by: Frank A.

Pierson; Written by: Carol Sobieski, Henri Simoun; Story by: Carol Sobieski; Director of Photography: Edward Rosson; Music by: Billy Goldenberg; Art Director: Alexander A. Mayer; Film Editor: Robert F. Shugrue; Color by: Technicolor; Titles & Optical Effects: Universal Title; Produced by: Universal Television; In Association with: NBC-TV; Exclusive Distributor: MCA Television Limited.

NIGHT GALLERY
(WORLD PREMIERE/NBC SATURDAY NIGHT AT THE MOVIES)

NBC Television Network, November 8, 1969; 120 minutes in color on film.

A three-part drama about ironic human relationships. The first story involved a man haunted by his participation in Nazi war crimes. The second involved a wealthy woman who was blind and wanted an eye transplant to regain her sight; and the third concerned a young man who was anxious to inherit his dying uncle's wealth.

Cast: Miss Menlo (Joan Crawford), Portifoy (Ossie Davis), Strobe (Richard Kiley), Jeremy (Roddy McDowall), Dr. Heatherton (Barry Sullivan), Resnick (Tom Bosley), Hendrickes (George Macready), Bleum (Sam Jaffee), Gretchen (Norman Crane), Carson (Barry Atwater), 1st Agent (George Murdock), Gibson (Tom Basham), Packer (Byron Morrow), Louis (Garry Goodrow), 1st Nurse (Shannon Farnon), Doctor (Richard Hale).

Credits: Produced by: William Sackheim; Directed by: Boris Sagal; Written by: Rod Serling; Directors of Photography: Richard Batcheller, William Margulies, A.S.C.; Music by: Billy Goldenberg; Art Director: Howard E. Johnson; Set Decorations: John McCarthy, Joseph Stone, Perry Murdock; Film Editor: Edward M. Abroms; Sound: James Porter, Elbert Franklin; Costumes by: Burton Miller; Makeup: Bud Westmore; Hair Stylist: Larry Germain; Color by: Technicolor: Titles & Optical Effects: Universal Title; Produced by: Universal Television; In Association with: NBC-TV; Exclusive Distributor: MCA Television Limited.

NIGHT LIFE
(ABC WIDE WORLD OF ENTERTAINMENT/WIDE WORLD MYSTERY)

ABC Television Network, March 28, 1973; 90 minutes in color on tape.

A suspense drama about a restaurant owner who rented his entire club to a couple only to find out too late that they were his mistress and her vengeful husband.

Cast: Midge Ross (Anne Francis), Paul Ross (Charles Aidman), Tommy Martino (Tim Matheson), Pete Martino (Joel Fabiani), Lila Street (Heather MacRae), Giorgio (Jay Novello), Eddie (Henry Shed).

Credits: Produced by: Barbara Schultz; Directed by: Burt Brinckerhoff; Written by: Robert Van Scoyk; Technical Director: Mike Maloof; Music by: Michael Lang; Production Designer: Ralph Holmes; Audio: Dick Sartor; Video: Dean Terrell; Taped at: KTLA-TV; Produced by: Universal Television; Exclusive Distributor: MCA Television Limited.

THE NIGHT RIDER

ABC Television Network, May 11, 1979; 90 minutes in color on film.

A drama about a dashing Southerner who transformed himself into a swashbuckling crusader for justice. The pilot for an unsold series.

Cast: Lord Thomas Earl (David Selby), Robert (Percy Rodrigues), Regina Kenton (Kim Cattrall), Dan Kenton (George Grizzard), Tru Sheridan (Anthony Herrera), Lady Earl (Anna Lee), Alex Sheridan (Pernell Roberts), Chock Hollister (Young Thomas) (Michael Sharrett), Billy "Bowlegs" Baines (Harris Yulin), Marie Hollister (Hildy Brooks), Hans Klaus (Curt Lowens), Jim Hollister (Van Williams).

Credits: Executive Producers: Stephen J. Cannell, Alex Beaton; Supervising Producer: Bill Phillips; Produced by: J. Rickley Dumm; Directed by: Hy Averback; Written by: Stephen J. Cannell; Director of Photography: Steve Poster; Music by: Mike Post, Pete Carpenter; Art Director: John J. Jeffries; Film Editor: Christopher Nelson; Color by: Technicolor; Titles & Optical Effects: Universal Title; Produced by: Stephen J. Cannell Productions; In Association with: Universal Television; Exclusive Distributor: MCA Television Limited.

THE NIGHTMARE STEP
(ABC WIDE WORLD OF ENTERTAINMENT/WIDE WORLD MYSTERY)

ABC Television Network, March 27, 1973; 90 minutes in color on tape.

A suspense drama about a young woman who hired a professional killer to murder her husband and then found herself caught in her own deadly trap.

Cast: Rafe (Don Stroud), Allen (John Vernon), Claire (Louise Sorel), Steven (Mike Farrell), Francine (Lillian Lehman), Carol (Sue Ane Langdon).

Credits: Produced by: Barbara Schultz; Directed by: Burt Brinckerhoff; Written by: George Bellak; Technical Director: Roy White; Music by: Michael Lang; Production Designer: Ralph Holmes; Audio: Jerry Pattison; Video: Dick Browning; Taped at: KTLA-TV; Produced by: Universal Television; Exclusive Distributor: MCA Television Limited.

NOW YOU SEE IT, NOW YOU DON'T
(WORLD PREMIERE/NBC MONDAY NIGHT AT THE MOVIES)

NBC Television Network, November 11, 1968; 120 minutes in color on film.

A drama about an art expert, hired by an insurance company to protect a priceless Rembrandt, who devised a scheme to trap an unscrupulous art collector.

Cast: Jerry Klay (Jonathan Winters), Gabrielle (Luciana Paluzzi), Herschel (Steve Allen), Ida (Jayne Meadows), Prince Haroun (Jack Weston), Herman (Lewis Charles), M. Moulle (Marcel Hillaire), Haggerty (Richard X. Slattery), Capt. Boyle (James Westerfield), Dr. Von Gansa (Than Wyenn), Inspector Delon (Michael Fox), Dalrymple (George Neise), Nori (Richard Kiel), Miss Ross (Lucille Meredith), Taxi Driver (Joseph Corey), Mr. Stockman (Roy Roberts), Achmed (John Aniston), Hamid (Michael Forest).

Credits: Produced by: Roland Kibbee; Directed by: Don Weis; Written by: Roland Kibbee; Director of Photography: John L. Russell, A.S.C.; Music by: Lyn Murray; Art Director: Loyd S. Papez; Set Decorations: John McCarthy, James S. Redd; Film Editor: Edward W. Williams, A.C.E.; Sound: Lyle Cain; Color Coordinator: Robert Brower; Color by: Technicolor; Titles & Optical Effects: Universal Title; Editorial Supervision: Richard Belding; Music Supervision: Stanley Wilson; Costumes by: Vincent Dee; Makeup: Bud Westmore; Hair Stylist: Larry Germain; Produced by: Universal Television; In Association with: NBC-TV; Exclusive Distributor: MCA Television Limited.

O'HARA, UNITED STATES TREASURY
(THE CBS FRIDAY NIGHT MOVIES)

CBS Television Network, April 2, 1971; 120 minutes in color on film.

A drama about James O'Hara, a small-town sheriff, who after passing the examination for Secret Service agent was instead asked to become a U.S. Customs inspector to help track down smugglers who were bringing in hashish from Mexico. He was led to the smuggler's number-one man who was about to distribute $9 million worth of hashish smuggled in as dinner plates. The pilot for the series O'Hara, U.S. Treasury (which see).

Cast: James O'Hara (David Janssen), Harry Fish (Gary Crosby), Fran Harper (Lana Wood), Joe Flagg (Charles McGraw), Marty Baron (Jerome Thor), Agent Garrick (Jack Ging), Agent Ben Hazzard (Stacy Harris), Keegan (William Conrad).

Credits: Executive Producers: Jack Webb, James B. Moser; Produced by: Leonard B. Kaufman; Directed by: Jack Webb; Written by: James E. Moser; Director of Photography: Alric Edens; Music by: Ray Heindorf, William Lava; Art Director: William D. DeCinces; Film Editor: Warren H. Adams; Color by: Technicolor; Titles & Optical Effects: Universal Title; Produced by: Mark VII Limited; In Association with: Universal Television; Exclusive Distributor: MCA Television Limited.

ONCE UPON A DEAD MAN
(WORLD PREMIERE)

NBC Television Network, September 17, 1971; 120 minutes in color on film.

A comedy-drama about Police Commissioner Stewart McMillan who became more involved than he'd planned to in his wife Sally's charity auction when a rare Egyptian sarcophagus disappeared. He and Sally investigate two art dealers, and the case soon became complicated by murder. The pilot for the series McMillan and Wife (which see).

Cast: Commissioner Stewart McMillan (Rock Hudson), Sally McMillan (Susan Saint James), Chief Andrew Yeakel (Jack Albertson), Andre Stryker (Rene Auberjonois), Edmond Corday (Kurt Kasznar), Mr. Wortzel (Jonathan Harris), Gregory Constantine (Herb Edelman), Sgt. Enright (John Schuck), John Patterson (James Wainwright), Madame Jarnac (Lilyan Chauvin), Dewhawk (Frank Orsatti), Dr. Hinton (Stacy Keach, Sr.), Emily Hull (Linda Watkins), Etienne Jacoby (Gerald Hiken).

Credits: Executive Producer: Leonard B. Stern; Produced by: Paul Mason; Directed by: Leonard B. Stern; Written by: Chester Krumholz, Leonard B. Stern; Director of Photography: Stanley M. Lazan; Music by: Jerry Fielding; Art Director: John J. Lloyd; Film Editor: Michael Economou; Color by: Technicolor; Titles & Optical Effects: Universal Title; Produced by: Talent Associates-Norton Simon, Inc.; In Association with: Universal Television And NBC-TV; Exclusive Distributor: MCA Television Limited.

ONE OF OUR OWN
(NBC MONDAY NIGHT AT THE MOVIES)

NBC Television Network, May 5, 1975; 120 minutes in color on film.

A medical drama about Dr. Jake Goodwin, the head of neurosurgery at Lowell Memorial Hospital. He found himself involved with a hypocritical cardiologist, a failing surgeon and a paralyzed boy. The pilot for the series Doctors' Hospital (which see).

Cast: Dr. Jake Goodwin (George Peppard), Dr. Norah Purcell (Zohra Lampert), Dr. Moresby (William Daniels), Carole Simon (Louise Sorel), LeRoy Atkins (Strother Martin), Dr. Ortega (Victor

Campos), Sanantonio (Giorgio Tozzi), Dr. Janos Varga (Albert Paulsen), Dr. Madison (Peter Hooten), Frances Hollander (Jacqueline Brooks), Dr. Helmut Von Schulthers (Oscar Homolka), Felix Needham (Ben Masters), Scotty (Maxine Stuart), Grance Chang (Mary Von Toy), Sabina (Trish Noble), Rose Sanantonio (Rose Gregorio), Mavis Porter (Eleonor Zee), Bill Hinshaw (William Traylor), Adrian Hollander (Scott McKay), Debbie Hinshaw (Wendy Phillips), Dr. Korngold (Milt Kogan), Myrna (Karen Knotts), Muriel Emhardt (Frances Osborne), Glick (Larry Gelman).

Credits: Executive Producer: Matthew Rapf; Produced by: Jack Laird; Directed by: Richard Sarafian; Written by: Jack Laird; Director of Photography: Howard R. Schwartz; Music by: Hal Mooney; Art Director: Jack T. Collis; Film Editor: Douglas Stewart; Color by: Technicolor; Titles & Optical Effects: Universal Title; Produced by: Universal Television; In Association with: NBC-TV; Exclusive Distributor: MCA Television Limited.

OPERATION: PETTICOAT
(THE ABC SUNDAY NIGHT MOVIE)

ABC Television Network, September 4, 1977; 120 minutes in color on film.

A situation comedy about the World War II adventures of the men of the U.S.S. Sea Tiger, a shocking pink submarine, and the bevy of beautiful nurses they rescued from a Pacific Island. Based on the 1959 film, this telefeature was the pilot for the series Operation: Petticoat (which see).

Cast: Lt. Cmdr. Matthew Sherman (John Astin), Lt. Nick Holden (Richard Gilliland), Ensign Stovall (Christopher J. Brown), Yeoman Hunkle (Richard Brestoff), The Admiral (Jackie Cooper), Maj. Edna Hayward (Yvonne Wilder), Chief Molumphrey (Wayne Long), Seaman Dooley (Kraig Cassity), Williams (Richard Marion), Seaman Gossett (Michael Mazes), Chief Tostin (Jack Murdock), Lt. Watson (Raymond Singer), Seaman Horwich (Peter Schuck), Seaman Broom (Jim Varney), Admiral Hatfield (George O. Petrie), Lt. Barbara Duran (Jamie Lee Curtis), Lt. Dolores Crandell (Melinda Naud), Lt. Ruth Colfax (Dorrie Thomson), Lt. Claire Reid (Bond Gideon).

Credits: Executive Producer: Leonard B. Stern; Produced by: David J. O'Connell; Directed by: John Astin; Written by: Leonard B. Stern; Story by: Paul King, Joe Stone; Director of Photography: Frank Thackery; Music by: Artie Butler; Art Director: John J. Jeffries; Film Editor: Clay Bartels; Color by: Technicolor; Titles & Optical Effects: Universal Title; Produced by: Heyday Productions; In Association with: Universal Television; Exclusive Distributor: MCA Television Limited.

THE OREGON TRAIL
(NBC SATURDAY NIGHT AT THE MOVIES)

NBC Television Network, January 10, 1976; 120 minutes in color on film.

A western about a pioneer family that encountered Indian attacks, disease and the harshness of the elements on a wagon-train trek. The pilot for the series The Oregon Trail (which see).

Cast: Evan Thorpe (Rod Taylor), Andrew Thorpe (Andrew Stevens), Jessica Thorpe (Blair Brown), Eli Thorpe (Douglas V. Fowley), Painted Face Kelly (David Huddleston), Thomas Hearn (G. D. Spradlin), Rachel Thorpe (Gina Marie Smika), William Thorpe (Tony Becker), Deborah Randal (Linda Purl), Trenchard (George Jeymas).

Credits: Produced by: Michael Gleason; Directed by: Boris Sagal; Written by: Michael Gleason; Director of Photography: Jack Woolf; Music by: David Shire; Art Director: A. C. Montenaro; Film Editor: Jamie Caylor; Color by: Technicolor; Titles & Optical Effects: Universal Title; Produced by: Universal Television; In Association with: NBC-TV; Exclusive Distributor: MCA Television Limited.

THE OTHER MAN
(WORLD PREMIERE/NBC MONDAY NIGHT AT THE MOVIES)

NBC Television Network, October 19, 1970; 120 minutes in color on film.

A thriller about a lawyer and wife who suspected each other in a playboy's death. Filmed on location at Big Sur, California.

Cast: Johnny Brant (Roy Thinnes), Kathy (Joan Hackett), Paul (Arthur Hill), Denise (Tammy Grimes), George Dunning (James Gavin), Lt. Lorca (Rodolfo Hoyos), Maria Soledad (Zolya Talma), Brant's Wife (Linda Burton), Mrs. Turley (Anne Collings), Dr. Brookner (Bruce Kirby), Mrs. Baird (Virginia Gregg), Miss Miller (Julie Foley).

Credits: Produced by: William Frye; Directed by: Richard A. Colla; Written by: Michael Blankfort, Eric Bercovici; Based on a Novel by: Margaret Lynn; Director of Photography: E. Charles Straumer; Music by: Stanley Wilson; Art Director: John J. Lloyd; Set Decorations: John McCarthy, Joseph Reith; Film Editor: Robert L. Kimble; Sound: Melvin M. Metcalfe, Sr.; Assistant Director: Marty Hornstein; Color by: Technicolor; Titles & Optical Effects: Universal Title; Produced by: Universal Television; In Association with: NBC-TV; Exclusive Distributor: MCA Television Limited.

THE OUTSIDER
(WORLD PREMIERE/NBC TUESDAY NIGHT AT THE MOVIES)

NBC Television Network, November 21, 1967; 120 minutes in color on film.

A drama about private investigator David Ross, a man with a prison-scarred past who checked out suspected embezzlement charges against a beautiful woman only to become a suspect in her murder. The pilot for the series The Outsider (which see).

Cast: David Ross (Darren McGavin), Collin Kenniston III (Sean Garrison), Peggy Leydon (Shirley Knight), Honora Dundas (Nancy Malone), Marvin Bishop (Edmond O'Brien), Mrs. Kozzek (Ann Sothern), Ernest Grimes (Joseph Wiseman), Lt. Wagner (Ossie Davis), Mrs. Bishop (Audrey Totter), Sgt. Delgado (Mario Alcalde), Carol Dorfman (Anna Hagan), Della (Madame Spivy), Officer Dutton (Kent McCord).

Credits: Produced by: Roy Huggins; Directed by: Michael Ritchie; Written by: Roy Huggins; Director of Photography: Bud Thackery, A. S. C.; Music by: Pete Rugolo; Art Director: Frank Arrigo; Film Editors: Carl Pingitore, David Rawlins; Set Decorations: John McCarthy, Claude Carpenter; Music Supervision: Stanley Wilson; Costumes by: Grady Hunt; Makeup: Bud Westmore; Hair Stylist: Larry Germain; Sound: Frank H. Wilkinson; Color Coordinator: Robert Brower; Color by: Technicolor; Titles & Optical Effects: Universal Title; Produced by: Roy Huggins-Public Arts Productions; In Association with: Universal Television And NBC-TV; Exclusive Distributor: MCA Television Limited.

OWEN MARSHALL, COUNSELOR AT LAW
(THE ABC SUNDAY NIGHT MOVIE)

ABC Television Network, September 12, 1971; 120 minutes in color on film. Major Sponsors and Agencies: The Procter & Gamble Company through Grey Advertising, Inc.; Sterling Drug through Dancer-Fitzgerald-Sample, Inc.

A drama about Owen Marshall, who while defending a hippie charged with the murder of a Santa Barbara matron made some startling revelations about the lady's private life. The pilot for the series Owen Marshall, Counselor at Law (which see). Filmed on location in Santa Barbara, California.

Cast: Owen Marshall (Arthur Hill), Joan Baldwin (Vera Miles), Dr. Eric Gibson (Joseph Campanella), Dave Blankenship (William Shatner), Jim McGuire (Tim Matheson), Dr. Thomas Hershey (Ramon Bieri), Murray Gale (Sorrell Booke), Raymond "Cowboy" Leatherberry (Bruce Davison), Judge Lynn Oliver (Dana Wynter), Frieda Krause (Joan Darling), Melissa Marshall (Christine Matchett), Ray Baldwin (Walter Brooke), Gloria (Kathy Lloyd), Baird Marshall (Rick Lenz).

Credits: Executive Producer: David Victor; Produced by: Douglas Benton; Directed by: Buzz Kulik; Written by: Jerry McNeely; Story by: David Victor, Jerry McNeely; Director of Photography: Walter Strenge; Music by: Elmer Bernstein; Art Director: George Patrick; Film Editor: Robert F. Shugrue; Sound: David H. Moriarty; Color by: Technicolor; Titles & Optical Effects: Universal Title; Produced by: Groverton Productions, Ltd.; In Association with: Universal Television; Exclusive Distributor: MCA Television Limited.

PARTNERS IN CRIME
(WORLD PREMIERE/NBC DOUBLE FEATURE NIGHT AT THE MOVIES)

NBC Television Network, March 24, 1973; 90 minutes in color on film.

A drama about a retired judge turned private eye who helped an ex-convict with amnesia discover where he hid $750,000 in bank robbery loot. The pilot for an unsold series. Filmed on locations in and around Los Angeles.

Cast: Judge Meredith Leland (Lee Grant), Sam Hatch (Lou Antonio), Frank Jordan (Richard Jaeckel), Walt Connors (Harry Guardino), Lt. Fred Harnett (Charles Drake), Charles Leland (John Randolph), Mrs. Margery Jordan (Lorraine Gary), Ralph Elsworth (Bob Cummings), Trooper (Gary Crosby), Mrs. Harris (Maxine Stuart), with: Vic Tayback.

Credits: Executive Producers: Richard Levinson, William Link; Produced by: Jon Epstein; Directed by: Jack Smight; Written by: David Shaw; Director of Photography: Jack Marta; Music by: Gil Melle; Art Director: Raymond Beal; Film Editor: Robert F. Shugrue; Color by: Technicolor; Titles & Optical Effects: Universal Title; Produced by: Universal Television; In Association with: NBC-TV; Exclusive Distributor: MCA Television Limited.

PERILOUS VOYAGE

NBC Television Network, July 29, 1976; 120 minutes in color on film.

A drama about a Latin American revolutionary who hijacked a ship in hopes of becoming his country's dictator. Produced in 1968, this telefeature was not broadcast until 1976.

Cast: Antonio De Leon (Michael Parks), Virginia Monroe (Lee Grant), Steve Monroe (William Shatner), General Salazar (Frank Silvera), Dr. Henry Merrill (Victor Jory), Capt. Humphreys (Charles McGraw), Alicia Salazar (Louise Sorel), Maggie Merrill (Barbara Werle), Reynaldo Solis (Michael Tolan), Rico (Stuart Margolin).

Perilous Voyage / 205

Credits: Produced by: Jack Laird; Directed by: William A. Graham; Written by: Robert Weverka, Sidney Stebel, Oscar Millard; Associate Producer: Jerrold Freedman; Director of Photography: Bud Thackery; Music by: Gil Melle; Art Director: George Patrick; Film Editor: Carl Pingitore; Color by: Technicolor; Titles & Optical Effects: Universal Title; Produced by: Universal Television; In Association with: NBC-TV; Exclusive Distributor: MCA Television Limited.

PINE CANYON IS BURNING
(NBC DOUBLE FEATURE NIGHT AT THE MOVIES)

NBC Television Network, May 18, 1977; 90 minutes in color on film.

A drama about Capt. William Stone, a widower with two children who operated a one-man fire station in California. The pilot for an unsold series.

Cast: Capt. William Stone (Kent McCord), Michael Stone (Shane Sinutko), Margaret Stone (Megan McCord), Sandra (Diana Muldaur), Capt. Ed Wilson (Andrew Duggan), Charlie Edison (Dick Bakalyan), Anne Walker (Brit Lind), Whitney Olson (Curtis Credel).

Credits: Executive Producer: R. A. Cinader; Producers: Gino Grimaldi, Hannah Shearer; Directed by: Chris Nyby III; Written by: R. A. Cinader; Director of Photography: Frank Thackery; Music by: Lee Holdridge; Art Director: George Renne; Film Editor: Albert Zuniga; Color by: Technicolor; Titles & Optical Effects: Universal Title; Produced by: Universal Television; In Association with: NBC-TV; Exclusive Distributor: MCA Television Limited.

PRESCRIPTION: MURDER
(WORLD PREMIERE/NBC TUESDAY NIGHT AT THE MOVIES)

NBC Television Network, February 20, 1968; 120 minutes in color on film.

A suspense drama about stubborn police detective Lt. Columbo who doggedly pursued a suave psychiatrist who he was convinced had murdered his wife in a "perfect crime." This telefeature was the first pilot for the series Columbo (which see). The second was Ransom for a Dead Man (which see).

Cast: Lt. Columbo (Peter Falk), Dr. Ray Flemming (Gene Barry), Joan Hudson (Katherine Justice), Carol Flemming (Nina Foch), Burt Gordon, (William Windom), Cynthia Gordon (Andrea King), Miss Petrie (Virginia Gregg), Paul (Brian Avery), Blonde (Suzanne Benton), Young Man (Jim Creech), Tommy (Anthony James), Stewardess (Sherry Boucher), Airline Clerk (Tom Williams), Doctor (Clark Howat), Delivery Boy (John Maurer), Nurse (Ena Hartman), Old Codger (Grandon Rhodes), Policeman (Don Stewart).

Credits: Produced and Directed by: Richard Irving; Written by: Richard Levinson, William Link; Director of Photography: Ray Rennahan, A. S. C.; Music by: Dave Grusin; Art Director: Russell Kimball; Set Decorations: John McCarthy, James S. Redd; Film Editor: Richard G. Wray, A. C. E.; Costumes by: Burton Miller; Makeup: Bud Westmore; Hair Stylist: Larry Germain; Color Coordinator: Robert Brower; Color by: Technicolor; Titles & Optical Effects: Universal Title; Produced by: Universal Television; In Association with: NBC-TV; Exclusive Distributor: MCA Television Limited.

THE PRIEST KILLER
(WORLD PREMIERE)

NBC Television Network, September 14, 1971; 120 minutes in color on film.

A drama about Chief Ironside and Sarge, a policeman-turned-priest, who made a joint effort to track down a psychopathic killer who had murdered three priests. This telefeature, which featured the stars of Ironside (which see) and Sarge (which see) was the second pilot for the latter series. Filmed on location in San Francisco.

Cast: Chief Robert T. Ironside (Raymond Burr), Sarge (George Kennedy), Sgt. Ed Brown (Don Galloway), Mark Sanger (Don Mitchell), Marla Gordon (Louise Latham), Vincent Wiertel (Anthony Zerbe), Father Miles (Peter Brocco), Father McMurtry (Robert Sampson), Father Wendell (Robert Shayne), Publisher (Kermit Murdock), Author (Fred Slyter), Patrolman (Max Gail).

Credits: Executive Producer: Richard A. Colla; Produced by: David Levinson; Directed by: Richard A. Colla; Written by: Robert Van Scoyk, Joel Oliansky; Director of Photography: Jacques R. Marquette; Music by: David Shire; Art Director: Joseph Alves, Jr.; Film Editor: Robert L. Kimble; Color by: Technicolor; Titles & Optical Effects: Universal Title; Produced by: Harbour Productions; In Association with: Universal Television; Exclusive Distributor: MCA Television Limited.

A PROWLER IN THE HEART
(ABC WIDE WORLD OF ENTERTAINMENT/WIDE WORLD MYSTERY)

ABC Television Network, March 26, 1973; 90 minutes in color on tape.

A mystery drama about a wealthy writer of popular mystery novels who married a much younger man and was forced to concoct an alibi for him in order to shield him from a murder charge.

Cast: Margery Landing (Colleen Dewhurst), Tony Parrish (Martin Sheen), Doreen (Ruth McDevitt), Liz Elliott (Lorraine Gary), Luigi (Lee Bergere), Harry (Ted Gehring).

Credits: Produced by: Barbara Schultz; Directed by: Glenn Jordan; Written by: Sherman Yellen; Technical Director: Roy White; Music by: Michael Lang; Production Designer: Ralph Holmes; Audio: Jerry Pattison; Video: Dick Browning; Taped at: KTLA-TV; Produced by: Universal Television; Exclusive Distributor: MCA Television Limited.

THE PSYCHIATRIST: GOD BLESS THE CHILDREN
(WORLD PREMIERE/NBC MONDAY NIGHT AT THE MOVIES)

NBC Television Network, December 14, 1970; 120 minutes in color on film.

A drama about a psychiatrist who enlisted the aid of his patient, an ex-addict, in dealing with a small community's drug epidemic. The pilot for the series The Psychiatrist (which see).

Cast: Dr. James Whitman (Roy Thinnes), Casey Poe (Pete Deuel), Dr. Bernard Altman (Luther Adler), Teddy (John Rubinstein), Kendell (Joy Bang), Sheriff Glenn (Norman Alden), Fritz (Barry Brown), Persephone (Katherine Justice), Mrs. Pilgrim (Marion Ross), Dr. Lewis (Gilbert Green), Ellen (Shannon Farnon), Weasel (David Alan Bailey), Pusher (Michael C. Gwynne), Maxwell (John Lasell), Danny (Danny Smaller), Michael (Michael Laird), Themselves (The Staple Singers).

Therapy Group: Beatrice (Lynn Hamilton), Jane (Jackie Burroughs), Cathy (Gloria Manon), Don (Phillip E. Pine), Mary (Virginia Vincent), Art (George Sperdakos), Steve (Jere Brian).

Credits: Executive Producer: Norman Felton; Produced by: Edgar Small; Directed by: Daryl Duke; Written by: Jerrold Freedman; Story by: Richard Levinson, William Link; Director of Photography: Richard C. Glouner; Music by: Roger Kellaway; Art Director: William D. DeCinces; Film Editor: Robert F. Shugrue; Assistant Director: Phil Bowles; Color by: Technicolor; Titles & Optical Effects: Universal Title; Produced by: Arena Productions, Inc.; In Association with: Universal Television; Exclusive Distributor: MCA Television Limited.

THE QUESTOR TAPES
(NBC WEDNESDAY NIGHT AT THE MOVIES)

NBC Television Network, January 23, 1974; 120 minutes in color on film.

A science fiction film about Questor, a robot in human form developed by a Nobel Prize-winning scientist. When the scientist disappeared, Questor set out in search of his creator. The pilot for an unsold series.

Cast: Questor (Robert Foxworth), Jerry Robinson (Mike Farrell),

Lady Trimbal (Dana Wynter), Darrow (John Vernon), Allison Sample (Ellen Weston), Dr. Chen (James Shigeta), Dr. Michaels (Robert Douglas), Vaslovik (Lew Ayres), Dr. Bradley (Majel Barrett), Dr. Gorlov (Reuben Singer), Administrative Assistant (Walter Koenig), Dr. Audret (Fred Sadoff), Randolph (Gerald Sanderson), Immigration Officer (Alan Caillou), Stewardess (Eydse Girard), Col. Henderson (Lal Baum), Secretary (Patti Cibbison).

Credits: Executive Producer: Gene Roddenberry; Produced by: Howie Horwitz; Directed by: Richard A. Colla; Written by: Gene Roddenberry, Gene L. Coon; Story by: Gene Roddenberry; Director of Photography: Michael Margulies; Music by: Gil Melle; Art Director: Phil Barber; Film Editors: Robert L. Kimble, Jerry Williams; Special Effects: Albert Whitlock; Color by: Technicolor; Titles & Optical Effects: Universal Title; Editorial Supervision: Richard Belding; Produced by: Universal Television; In Association with: NBC-TV; Exclusive Distributor: MCA Television Limited.

THE RANGERS
(WORLD PREMIERE)

NBC Television Network, December 24, 1974; 90 minutes in color on film.

A drama about the adventures of park rangers. The pilot for the series Sierra (which see) in which Ernest Thompson took over the part of Ranger Matt Harper, and Jack Hogan assumed the role of Chief Ranger Jack Moore.

Cast: Ranger Tim Cassidy (James G. Richardson), Ranger Matt Harper (Colby Chester), Chief Ranger Jack Moore (Jim B. Smith), Edie (Laraine Stephens), Bob (Laurence Delaney), Frank (Michael Conrad), Sam (Roger Bowen), with: Roger Breedlove, Dave Birkoff.

Credits: Executive Producer: Jack Webb; Produced by: Edwin Self; Directed by: Chris Nyby III; Written by: Robert A. Cinader, Michael Donovan, Preston Wood; Director of Photography: Robert H. Wyckoff; Music by: Lee Holdridge; Art Director: James Martin Buchanan; Film Editors: Bill Parker, John Kaufman, Jr.; Color by: Technicolor; Titles & Optical Effects: Universal Title; Produced by: Mark VII Limited; In Association with: Universal Television And NBC-TV; Exclusive Distributor: MCA Television Limited.

RANSOM FOR A DEAD MAN
(WORLD PREMIERE)

NBC Television Network, March 1, 1971; 120 minutes in color on film.

A drama about a woman lawyer who killed her husband and tried to outsmart the law. Lt. Columbo was convinced that she was guilty and pursued his own hunches. This telefeature was the second pilot for the series Columbo (which see). The first was Prescription: Murder (which see).

Cast: Lt. Columbo (Peter Falk), Leslie Williams (Lee Grant), Michael Clarke (John Fink), Carlson (Harold Gould), Margaret (Patricia Mattick), Hammond (Paul Carr), Phil (Jed Allan), Richard (Charles Macaulay), Attorney (Henry Brandt), Pat (Jeane Byron), Perkins (Richard Roat), Celia (Norma Connolly), Paul Williams (Harlan Warde), Crowell (Bill Walker), Bert (Timothy Carey), Judge (Judson Morgan), Priest (Richard O'Brien), Gloria (Celeste Yarnall), Nancy (Lisa Moore), Waitress (Lois Battle), Mechanic (Reginald Fenderson).

Credits: Executive Producer: Richard Irving; Produced by: Dean Hargrove; Directed by: Richard Irving; Written by: Dean Hargrove; Story by: Richard Levinson, William Link; Director of Photography: Lionel Lindon; Music by: Billy Goldenberg; Art Director: John J. Lloyd; Film Editor: Edward M. Abroms; Assistant Director: George Bisk; Color by: Technicolor; Titles & Optical Effects: Universal Title; Produced by: Universal Television; In Association with: NBC-TV; Exclusive Distributor: MCA Television Limited.

THE RETURN OF THE WORLD'S GREATEST DETECTIVE

NBC Television Network, June 16, 1976; 90 minutes in color on film.

A comedy-drama about a wacky Los Angeles cop who came to think he was Sherlock Holmes. With the help of Dr. Watson, a psychiatric social worker, he set out to solve the murder of an embezzler.

Cast: Sherman Holmes (Larry Hagman), Dr. Watson (Jenny O'Hara), Lt. Tinker (Nicholas Colasanto), Himmel (Woodrow Parfrey), Landlady (Helen Verbit), Spiner (Ivor Francis), Judge Harley (Charles Macaulay), Dr. Collins (Ron Silver), Vince Cooley (Sid Haig), Psychiatrist (Booth Colman), Mrs. Slater (Lieux Dressler), Detective (Fuddle Bagley), Klinger (Benny Rubin).

Credits: Producers: Roland Kibbee, Dean Hargrove; Directed by: Dean Hargrove; Written by: Roland Kibbee, Dean Hargrove; Director of Photography: William Mendenhall; Music by: Dick DeBenedictis; Art Director: William Campbell; Film Editor: John Kaufman, Jr.; Color by: Technicolor; Titles & Optical Effects: Universal Title; Produced by: Universal Television; In Association with: NBC-TV; Exclusive Distributor: MCA Television Limited.

RICHIE BROCKELMAN, PRIVATE EYE
(RICHIE BROCKELMAN: THE MISSING 24 HOURS)
(NBC MOVIE OF THE WEEK)

NBC Television Network, October 27, 1976; 90 minutes in color on film.

A detective drama about Richie Brockelman, a young gumshoe who was hired by an amnesiac who believed that she was involved in a murder. The pilot for the series Richie Brockelman, Private Eye (which see). The Brockelman character was introduced in an episode of The Rockford Files (which see).

Cast: Richie Brockelman (Dennis Dugan), Elizabeth Morton (Suzanne Pleshette), Sharon Deterson (Barbara Bosson), Darcy Davenport (Sharon Gless), Davenport (Lloyd Bochner), Mrs. Brockelman (Helen Page Camp), Brockelman (Norman Fell), Arnold Springfield (William Windom), McNeil (Ned Wilson), Mitch (Harold Sylvester), Marine (Hunter Von Leer), Hooker (Gloria LeRoy).

Credits: Executive Producers: Stephen J. Cannell, Steven Bochco; Produced by: William F. Phillips; Directed by: Hy Averback; Written by: Stephen J. Cannell, Steven Bochco; Director of Photography: William Mendenhall; Music by: Mike Post, Pete Carpenter; Art Director: Lester L. Green; Film Editor: John Elias; Color by: Technicolor; Titles & Optical Effects: Universal Title; Produced by: Universal Television; In Association with: NBC-TV; Exclusive Distributor: MCA Television Limited.

RITUAL OF EVIL
(WORLD PREMIERE/NBC MONDAY NIGHT AT THE MOVIES)

NBC Television Network, February 23, 1970; 120 minutes in color on film.

A suspense drama about psychiatrist David Sorrell who found one of his patients dead, an apparent suicide, and set out to find the reason. Through investigation, he found that the girl, a beautiful heiress with everything to live for, belonged to a supernatural cult which practiced ritualistic murder. A sequel to Fear No Evil (which see).

Cast: David Sorrell (Louis Jourdan), Jolene Wiley (Anne Baxter), Leila Barton (Diana Hyland), Edward Bolander (John McMartin), Harry Snowden (Wilfrid Hyde-White), Loey Wiley (Belinda J. Montgomery), Aline Wiley (Carla Borelli), Larry Richmond (Georg Stanford Brown), Sheriff (Rege Cordic), Mora (Dehl Berti), Hippie (Richard Alan Knox), Newscaster (Johnny Williams), 1st Reporter (Jimmy Joyce), 2nd Reporter (James LaSane).

Credits: Produced by: David Levinson; Directed by: Robert Day; Written by: Robert Presnell, Jr.; Director of Photography: Lionel Lindon, A.S.C.; Music by: Billy Goldenberg; Art Director: William D. DeCinces; Film Editor: Douglas Stewart; Sound: Stanley Cooley; Assistant Director: Carl Beringer; Unit Manager: George Lollier; Costumes by: Helen Colvig; Makeup: Bud Westmore; Hair Stylist: Larry Germain; Color by: Technicolor; Titles & Optical Effects:

Universal Title; Produced by: Universal Television; In Association with: NBC-TV; Exclusive Distributor: MCA Television Limited.

RIVER OF MYSTERY
(WORLD PREMIERE)

NBC Television Network, October 1, 1971; 120 minutes in color on film.

A drama about a pair of adventurers searching for diamonds in Brazil's interior. Their quest was interrupted by guerilla fighters and government mercenaries. Filmed on location in Brazil in 1969, this telefeature was not broadcast until 1971.

Cast: Phil Munger (Vic Morrow), Ernie Dorate (Claude Akins), R. J. Twitchell (Edmond O'Brien), Drum (Niall MacGinnis), Elena (Louise Sorel), El Alacron (Nico Minardos), Torres (Cicero Shadler), Cleo (Dilma Loes), Pablo (Waldir Maia), Gold (Earl Parker).

Credits: Produced by: Steve Shagan; Directed by: Paul Stanley; Written by: Albert Ruben; Director of Photography: Gabriel Torres Garces; Music by: Luis Bonfa; Art Director: Robert Machado; Film Editor: Richard G. Wray; Color by: Technicolor; Titles & Optical Effects: Universal Title; Produced by: Universal Television; In Association with: NBC-TV; Exclusive Distributor: MCA Television Limited.

THE ROCKFORD FILES
(NBC WEDNESDAY NIGHT AT THE MOVIES)

NBC Television Network, March 27, 1974; 90 minutes in color on film.

A detective drama about private investigator Jim Rockford who only handled cases that the police considered closed. In this one, a young woman asked him to find out whether her father's death was suicide or murder. The pilot for the series The Rockford Files (which see) in which Noah Beery, Jr. assumed the role of Joseph Rockford.

Cast: Jim Rockford (James Garner), Sara Butler (Lindsay Wagner), Jerry Grimes (William Smith), Mildred Elias (Nita Talbot), Joseph Rockford (Robert Donley), Det. Becker (Joe Santos), Morrie Talbot (Pat Renella), Angel (Stuart Margolin), Nick Butler (Bill Mumy), Danford Baker (Mike Steele).

Credits: Executive Producer: Jo Swerling, Jr.; Produced by: Stephen J. Cannell; Directed by: Richard T. Heffron; Written by: Stephen J. Cannell; Story by: John Thomas James; Director of Photography: Lamar Boren; Music by: Mike Post, Pete Carpenter; Art Director: Robert Luthardt; Film Editor: John Dumas; Color by:

Technicolor; Titles & Optical Effects: Universal Title; Produced by: Roy Huggins-Public Arts Productions And Cherokee Productions; In Association with: Universal Television; Exclusive Distributor: MCA Television Limited.

ROSETTI AND RYAN: MEN WHO LOVE WOMEN
(WORLD PREMIERE)

NBC Television Network, May 23, 1977; 120 minutes in color on film.

A drama about lawyers Rosetti and Ryan who were hired by a wealthy woman accused of murdering her husband. The pilot for the series Rosetti and Ryan (which see).

Cast: Joseph Rosetti (Tony Roberts), Frank Ryan (Squire Fridell), Jessica Hornesby (Jane Elliot), Sylvia Crawford (Patty Duke Astin), Sgt. Pete Agopian (Bill Dana), Beverly Dresden (Susan Anspach), Judge Hardcastle (Dick O'Neill), Druscilla Gerard (Roberta Leighton), Benny (Al Molinaro), Judge Marcus Black (William Marshall), Sister Constanza (Andrea Howard), Medical Examiner (Richard Stahl), Ma Rosetti (Penny Stanton), Greta Gerber (Barbara Alston).

Credits: Executive Producer: Leonard B. Stern; Produced by: Jerry Davis; Directed by: John Astin; Written by: Don M. Mankiewicz, Gordon Dotler, Sam Rolfe; Director of Photography: William Mendenhall; Music by: Peter Matz; Art Director: George Reune; Film Editor: James T. Hackert; Color by: Technicolor; Titles & Optical Effects: Universal Title; Produced by: Heyday Productions; In Association with: Universal Television And NBC-TV; Exclusive Distributor: MCA Television Limited.

RUN A CROOKED MILE
(WORLD PREMIERE/NBC TUESDAY NIGHT AT THE MOVIES)

NBC Television Network, November 18, 1969; 120 minutes in color on film.

A drama about a swinging young math teacher at a London private school who became the victim of a secret organization plotting the financial collapse of Europe through gold manipulation. Filmed on location in London and Geneva.

Cast: Richard Stuart (Louis Jourdan), Elizabeth Sutton (Mary Tyler Moore), Dr. Ralph Sawyer (Wilfrid Hyde-White), Caretaker (Stanley Holloway), Sir Howard Nettleton (Alexander Knox), Peter Martin (Terence Alexander), Inspector Huntington (Ronald Howard), Lord Dunnfield (Laurence Naismith), Sgt. Hooper (Norman Bird), Chairman (Ernest Clark), Business Spokesman (Bernard Archard).

Credits: Produced by: Charles F. Engel; Directed by: Gene

Levitt; Written by: Trevor Wallace, Richard Levinson, William Link, Gene Levitt; Director of Photography: Arthur Grant, B.S.C.; Music by: Mike Leander; Art Director: Bernard Robinson; Film Editor: Bert Rule, G.B.F.E.; Sound Editor: William Trent; Assistant Director: Bert Batt; Production Manager: Don Toms; Casting by: Weston Drury, Jr.; Costumes by: Rosemary Burrows; Makeup: George Blackler; Hair Stylist: Betty Glasow; Color by: Technicolor; Titles & Optical Effects: Universal Title; Produced by: Universal Television; In Association with: NBC-TV; Exclusive Distributor: MCA Television Limited.

RUNAWAY!
(ABC SUSPENSE MOVIE)

ABC Television Network, September 29, 1973; 90 minutes in color on film.

A suspense drama about the lives of 200 people hanging in the balance during a battle between man and machine, as railroad officials and courageous passengers struggled to stop a runaway ski train hurtling down a mountain towards impending disaster. This telefeature was the first produced for the ABC Suspense Movie. Filmed on location in Denver, Colorado.

Cast: Holly Gibson (Ben Johnson), Les Reaver (Ben Murphy), Nick Staffo (Ed Nelson), Carol Lerner (Darleen Carr), Mark (Lee H. Montgomery), John Shedd (Martin Milner), Ellen Staffo (Vera Miles), Professor Dunn (Ray Danton), Dispatcher (Frank Marth), Conductor (John McLiam), Brakeman (Lou Frizzell), Chief Dispatcher (Frank Maxwell), Fireman (Bing Russell), College Man (Kip Niven), Coed (Laurette Spang), Dr. Phillips (Ross Elliott), Screaming Girl (Kelley Miles), Bill Travers (Judson Pratt), Man in Shock (Than Wyenn).

Credits: Executive Producer: Harve Bennett; Produced and Directed by: David Lowell Rich; Written by: Gerald DiPego; Director of Photography: Bud Thackery; Music by: Hal Mooney; Art Director: Loyd S. Papez; Film Editor: Douglas Stewart; Color by: Technicolor; Titles & Optical Effects: Universal Title; Produced by: Universal Television; Exclusive Distributor: MCA Television Limited.

SAM HILL: WHO KILLED THE MYSTERIOUS MR. FOSTER?
(WORLD PREMIERE)

NBC Television Network, February 1, 1971; 120 minutes in color on film.

A Western about Sam Hill, a lovable drifter who found himself challenged to run for sheriff and solve the mysterious murder of a preacher. The pilot for an unsold series.

Cast: Sam Hill (Ernest Borgnine), Jethro (Stephen Hudis), Jody

214 / Telefeatures

Kenyon (Judy Geeson), Simon Anderson (Will Geer), Mal Yeager (J. D. Cannon), Doyle Pickett (Bruce Dern), Toby (Sam Jaffe), Abigail Booth (Carmen Mathews), Judge Hathaway (John McGiver), Kilpatrick (Slim Pickens), Sheriff (Jay C. Flippen), Doc Waters (Woodrow Parfrey), Fletcher (George Furth), George Millbrook (Milton Selzer), Reed (Dub Taylor), Rev. Foster (G. D. Spradlin), Lucas (Ted Gehring), Hotel Clerk (Dennis Fimple), Telegraph Operator (Robert Gooden).

Credits: Executive Producer: Roy Huggins; Produced by: Jo Swerling, Jr.; Directed by: Fielder Cook; Written by: Richard Levinson, William Link; Director of Photography: Gene Polito; Music by: Pete Rugolo; Art Director: Robert E. Smith; Film Editors: John Dumas, Gloryette Clark; Color by: Technicolor; Titles & Optical Effects: Universal Title; Produced by: Roy Huggins-Public Arts Productions; In Association with: Universal Television And NBC-TV; Exclusive Distributor: MCA Television Limited.

SAN FRANCISCO INTERNATIONAL AIRPORT
(WORLD PREMIERE/NBC TUESDAY NIGHT AT THE MOVIES)

NBC Television Network, September 29, 1970; 120 minutes in color on film.

A drama about the behind-the-scenes operation of a major international airport. Among the goings-on were the kidnapping of a pilot's wife, the disintegration of a marriage, and a $3,000,000 robbery. The pilot for the series San Francisco International Airport (which see) in which Lloyd Bridges assumed the role of Jim Conrad.

Cast: Jim Conrad (Pernell Roberts), Bob Hatten (Clu Gulager), Katie Barrett (Beth Brickell), Lester Scott (Van Johnson), Tina Scott (Nancy Malone), Ross Edwards (David Hartman), Davey Scott (Teddy Eccles), Clifford Foster Evans (Walter Brooke), William Sturtevant (Cliff Potts), Joan Edwards (Jill Donohue), Frank Davis (Chuck Daniel), George Woodruff (Dana Elcar), Stayczek (Tab Hunter), Dan (Robert Sorrells), Senator (Jason Wingreen), Amato (Jim B. Smith), Sgt. Dobkin (Marc Hannibal), Congressman (Frank Gerstle).

Credits: Executive Producer: Frank Price; Producers: William Read Woodfield, Allan B. Balter; Directed by: John Llewellyn Moxey; Written by: William Read Woodfield, Allan B. Balter; Associate Producer: John Orland; Director of Photography: Andrew Jackson; Music by: Pat Williams; Art Director: Henry Larrecq; Film Editors: Budd Small, John Elias; Color by: Technicolor; Titles & Optical Effects: Universal Title; Produced by: Universal Television; In Association with: NBC-TV; Exclusive Distributor: MCA Television Limited.

SARAH T.--PORTRAIT OF A TEENAGE ALCOHOLIC
(WORLD PREMIERE)

NBC Television Network, February 11, 1975; 120 minutes in color on film.

A drama about the ruinous effects of alcohol on the school and personal life of an emotionally disturbed teenager.

Cast   Sarah Travis (Linda Blair), Jean Hodges (Verna Bloom), Ken Newkirk (Mark Hamill), Matt Hodges (William Daniels), Jerry Travis (Larry Hagman), Dr. Kittredge (Michael Lerner), Margaret (Hilda Haynes), Mr. Peterson (M. Emmet Walsh), Nancy (Laurette Spang), Marsha Cooper (Karen Purcil), with: Eric Olson, Steve Benedict, Richard Roat, Marian Collier, Jessica Rains, Sheila Larken, Heather Totten, Dean Franklin.

Credits: Produced by: David Levinson; Directed by: Richard Donner; Written by: Richard Shapiro, Esther Shapiro; Director of Photography: Gayne Rescher; Music by: Jim DiPasquale; Art Director: John E. Chilberg II; Film Editor: Richard Bracken; Color by: Technicolor; Titles & Optical Effects: Universal Title; Produced by: Universal Television; In Association with: NBC-TV; Exclusive Distributor: MCA Television Limited.

SARGE: THE BADGE OR THE CROSS
(WORLD PREMIERE)

NBC Television Network, February 22, 1971; 120 minutes in color on film.

A drama about Sarge, a police detective who reevaluated his life when his wife was killed, and decided to enter the priesthood as fellow officers proceeded with the investigation. The first pilot for the series Sarge (which see). The second was The Priest Killer (which see). Filmed on location in San Diego, California.

Cast   Sarge (George Kennedy), Matteo (Ricardo Montalban), Carol (Diane Baker), Nico (Nico Minardos), Father Terence (Stewart Moss), Valerie (Sallie Shockley), Kenji Takichi (Harold Sakata), Mama Bain (Naomi Stevens), Bigelow (Larry Gates), Chief Dewey (Ramon Bieri), Rector (Walter Brooke), Bishop Andrade (Henry Wilcoxon), Chaplain Dinsmore (Dana Elcar), Charlie (Stanley Livingston).

Credits: Executive Producer: Richard A. Colla; Produced by: David Levy; Directed by: Richard A. Colla; Written by: Don M. Mankiewicz; Director of Photography: Jacques Marquette; Music by: Dave Grusin; Art Directors: Joseph Alves, Jr., Sydney Litwack; Set Decorations: Charles S. Thompson; Film Editor: Robert L. Kimble; Sound: David H. Moriarty; Assistant Director: George Fenady; Color by: Technicolor; Titles & Optical Effects: Universal

216 / Telefeatures

Title; Produced by: Universal Television; In Association with: NBC-TV; Exclusive Distributor: MCA Television Limited.

SAVAGE
(WORLD PREMIERE/NBC DOUBLE FEATURE NIGHT AT THE MOVIES)

NBC Television Network, March 31, 1973; 90 minutes in color on film.

A drama about a TV news commentary team which investigated the moral fitness of a Supreme Court nominee. The pilot for an unsold series. Filmed on location in the Los Angeles area.

Cast: Paul Savage (Martin Landau), Gail Abbott (Barbara Bain), Joel Ryker (Will Geer), Judge Stern (Barry Sullivan), Marion Stern (Louise Latham), Russell (Pat Harrington), Lee Reynolds (Susan Howard), Ted Seligson (Dabney Coleman), Phillip Brooks (Paul Richards), Allison Baker (Michele Carey).

Credits: Executive Producers: Richard Levinson, William Link; Produced by: Paul Mason; Directed by: Steven Spielberg; Written by: Mark Rodgers, Richard Levinson, William Link; Story by: Mark Rodgers; Director of Photography: Bill Butler; Music by: Gil Melle; Film Editor: Edward M. Abroms; Color by: Technicolor; Titles & Optical Effects: Universal Title; Produced by: Universal Television; In Association with: NBC-TV; Exclusive Distributor: MCA Television Limited.

SCOTT FREE
(NBC MOVIE OF THE WEEK)

NBC Television Network, September 13, 1976; 90 minutes in color on film.

A drama about a smooth-talking, two-fisted hustler who was approached by Federal agents with a dangerous proposition: he would get a break on his troubles with the Internal Revenue Service if he helped to expose a syndicate front. The pilot for an unsold series.

Cast: Tony Scott (Michael Brandon), Holly (Susan Saint James), Ed McGraw (Ken Swofford), Tom Little Lion (Cal Bellini), Donaldson (Robert Loggia), Santini (Michael Lerner), George Running Bear (Dehl Berti), Kevin Southerland (Stephen Nathan), Al (Paul Koslo), Rosa (Peter Brocco), Max (Allan Rich), Lillie Lion (Cal Bellini).

Credits: Executive Producers: Meta Rosenberg, Stephen J. Cannell; Produced by: Alex Beaton; Directed by: William Wiard; Written by: Stephen J. Cannell; Director of Photography: Jacques R. Marquette; Music by: Mike Post, Pete Carpenter; Art Director:

Seymour Klate; Film Editor: Howard S. Deane; Color by: Technicolor; Titles & Optical Effects: Universal Title; Produced by: Cherokee Productions; In Association with: Universal Television And NBC-TV; Exclusive Distributor: MCA Television Limited.

SCREAM, PRETTY PEGGY
(ABC SUSPENSE MOVIE)

ABC Television Network, November 24, 1973; 90 minutes in color on film.

A suspense drama about a mother and son who rented a room above their garage to a mysterious young woman.

Cast: Mrs. Elliot (Bette Davis), Jeffrey Elliot (Ted Bessell), Peggy Johns (Sian Barbara Allen), George Thornton (Charles Drake), Dr. Saks (Allen Arbus), Agnes Thornton (Tovah Feldshuh), Jennifer Elliot (Christiane Schmidtner), Student (Johnie Collins III), Office Girl (Jessica Rains).

Credits: Produced by: Lou Morheim; Directed by: Gordon Hessler; Written by: Jimmy Sangster, Arthur Hoffe; Director of Photography: Leonard J. South; Music by: Robert Prince; Art Director: Joseph Alves, Jr.; Film Editor: Larry Strong; Color by: Technicolor; Titles & Optical Effects: Universal Title; Produced by: Universal Television; Exclusive Distributor: MCA Television Limited.

THE SCREAMING WOMAN
(ABC MOVIE OF THE WEEKEND)

ABC Television Network, January 29, 1972; 90 minutes in color on film.

A drama about a wealthy dowager--and former mental patient--who claimed to have found a woman buried alive on the grounds of her estate. When no evidence of a burial was found, her family feared for the woman's sanity.

Cast: Laura Wynant (Olivia de Havilland), George Tresvant (Joseph Cotten), Dr. Amos Larkin (Walter Pidgeon), Carl Nesbitt (Ed Nelson), Caroline Wynant (Laraine Stephens), Howard Wynant (Charles Robinson), Evie Carson (Alexandra Hay), Ken Bronson (Charles Drake), Bernice Wilson (Joyce Cunning), Ted Wilson (Ray Montgomery), David (Gene Andrusco), Martin (Jan Arvan), Harry Sands (Russell C. Wiggins), Slater (John Alderman).

Credits: Produced by: William Frye; Directed by: Jack Smight; Written by: Merwin Gerard; Based on a Short Story by: Ray Bradbury; Director of Photography: Sam Leavitt; Music by: John Williams; Art Director: John E. Chilberg II; Set Decorations: Don

Sullivan; Film Editor: Robert F. Shugrue; Costumes by: Technicolor; Titles & Optical Effects: Universal Title; Produced by: Universal Television; Exclusive Distributor: MCA Television Limited.

SEE HOW THEY RUN
(PROJECT 120)

NBC Television Network, October 7, 1964; 120 minutes in color on film.

A drama about the father of three gifted children who was murdered after he collected evidence in Europe that could have exposed a crooked international cartel. But he had concealed the evidence in a copy of the book Alice in Wonderland which the children unwittingly took to America when they went to visit an aunt. Filmed on location in New York City, this telefeature was the first of the NBC-Universal Project 120 films, and the first TV movie to be telecast. The first TV movie to be produced, Universal's The Killers, for Project 120, was considered to be too violent for television, and was released theatrically.

Cast: Martin Young (John Forsythe), Orlando Miller (Senta Berger), Augusta Flanders (Jane Wyatt), Tirza Green (Pamela Franklin), Baron Frood (Franchot Tone), Elliott Green (Leslie Nielsen), Rudy (George Kennedy), Maggie Green (Jami Fields), Jamesy Green (Jackie Jones), Manley (Harlan Warde).

Credits: Produced by: Jack Laird; Directed by: David Lowell Rich; Written by: Michael Blankfort; Based on the Novel "The Widow-Makers" by: Michael Blankfort; Director of Photography: Lionel Lindon; Music by: Lalo Schifrin; Film Editor: George Jay Nicholson; Produced by: Universal Television; In Association with: NBC-TV; Exclusive Distributor: MCA Television Limited.

SEE THE MAN RUN
(ABC MOVIE OF THE WEEKEND)

ABC Television Network, December 11, 1971; 90 minutes in color on film.

A drama about a struggling actor who was faced with a dangerous decision when tempted by an enormous sum of money. He decided to cast himself as the middleman in a kidnap plot.

Cast: Ben Taylor (Robert Culp), Joanne Taylor (Angie Dickinson), Dr. Spencer (June Allyson), Capt. Dan Dorsey (Charles Cioffi), Peggy Larson (Antoinette Bower), Ralph Larson (Ross Elliott), Water and Power Man (John Goddard), Mike (Michael Bell), Dex (Robert Lipton).

Credits: Produced by: Stan Shpetner; Directed by: Corey Allen;

Written by: Mann Rubin; Director of Photography: Gerald Perry Finnerman; Music by: David Shire; Art Director: Joseph Alves, Jr.; Set Decorations: Robert C. Bradfield; Film Editor: Lovel Ellis; Costumes by: Grady Hunt; Color by: Technicolor; Titles & Optical Effects: Universal Title; Produced by: Universal Television; Exclusive Distributor: MCA Television Limited.

SENIOR YEAR
(CBS FRIDAY NIGHT AT THE MOVIES)

CBS Television Network, March 22, 1974; 90 minutes in color on film.

A drama about the adventures of five students at Southwest High School in Stockton, California during the 1950s. The pilot for the series Sons and Daughters (which see).

Cast: Jeff Reed (Gary Frank), Anita Cramer (Glynnis O'Connor), Stash (Scott Colomby), Moose Kerner (Barry Livingston), Paul Reed (Dana Elcar), Lucille Reed (Jay W. McIntosh), Charlie (Lionel Johnson), Evie Mortenson (Debralee Scott), Danny Reed (Michael Morgan), Walter Cramer (John S. Ragin), Ruth Cramer (Jan Shutan), Cody (Christopher Stafford Nelson), with: Maida Severn, Al Dunlap, Chris Norris, Randi Kallan, Teresa Medaris, Cheryl Linde, Bonnie Van Dyke, Wallace Rooney, Ted Gehring.

Credits: Produced by: David Levinson; Directed by: Richard Donner; Written by: M. Charles Cohen; Director of Photography: Jack Woolf; Music by: James DiPasquale; Art Director: Walter M. Simonds; Film Editor: Richard Bracken; Color by: Technicolor; Titles & Optical Effects: Universal Title; Produced by: Universal Television; Exclusive Distributor: MCA Television Limited.

SET THIS TOWN ON FIRE
(WORLD PREMIERE)

NBC Television Network, January 8, 1973; 120 minutes in color on film.

A drama about a newspaper publisher who developed doubts about his own courtroom testimony which sent a politician to jail for manslaughter. Filmed in 1969, this telefeature was not broadcast until 1973.

Cast: Buddy Bates (Chuck Connors), Andy Wells (Carl Betz), Molly Thornburgh (Lynda Day), Brad Wells (Charles Robinson), Henry Kealey (John Anderson), Walter Stafford (Jeff Corey), Carl Rickter (James Westerfield), Sen. Porter (Paul Fix), Shirley Hammond (Nancy Malone), Stabler (Vaughn Taylor).

Credits: Executive Producer: Roy Huggins; Produced and Directed by: David Lowell Rich; Written by: John Thomas James; Director of Photography: Gene Polito; Music by: Pete Rugolo; Art Director: Robert Luthardt; Film Editor: John Dumas; Color by: Technicolor; Titles & Optical Effects: Universal Title; Produced by: Roy Huggins-Public Arts Productions; In Association with: Universal Television And NBC-TV; Exclusive Distributor: MCA Television Limited.

SEX AND THE MARRIED WOMAN
(NBC MOVIE OF THE WEEK)

NBC Television Network, September 13, 1977; 120 minutes in color on film.

A comedy-drama about a housewife who wrote a book on her neighbors' sex lives only to win overnight success and have her marriage disintegrate because of a jealous husband.

Cast: Leslie Fitch (Joanna Pettet), Alan Fitch (Barry Newman), Uncle June (Keenan Wynn), Duke Skaggs (F. Murray Abraham), Louie Grosscup (Dick Gautier), Peter Nebben (Angus Duncan), Virginia Ladysmith (Fannie Flagg), Irma Caddish (Jayne Meadows), Alan "Arnie" Fish (Larry Hovis), Carolyn Fish (Jeanne M. Lange), Jim Cutler (Chuck McCann), Stan Oberfield (John Lawrence), Heidi Lomax (Nita Talbot), with: Marco Battaglia, Robin Cohen, Liz Ingleson, Jessica Rains, Bryan O'Bryne, Gregg Forrest, Andy Stone, Rori King, Lance Gordon, Bert Holland, Roy Stuart, Jordan Rhodes, Jack Stryker, Lin Shaye, Jackie Joseph, Tamar Cooper, Dennis McCarthy, Maureen Reagan, Hugh Benson, Bill Dyer, Pamela Davenport, Laura Gile, Judith Woodbury, June Fenley, Kathy Longinaker, Sharri Zak, Dave Armstrong.

Credits: Executive Producer: George J. Santoro; Produced and Directed by: Jack Arnold; Written by: Michael Norell; Director of Photography: Ben Colman; Music by: Gerald Fried; Art Director: Jack DeGovia; Film Editors: Jamie Caylor, Robert Watts; Color by: Technicolor; Titles & Optical Effects: Universal Title; Produced by: Universal Television; Exclusive Distributor: MCA Television Limited.

SHADOW OVER ELVERON
(WORLD PREMIERE/NBC TUESDAY NIGHT AT THE MOVIES)

NBC Television Network, March 5, 1968; 120 minutes in color on film.

A drama about a young doctor who found a small town medical practice distasteful when citizens preferred to ignore corruption after a teen-age boy was unjustly accused of murder by an ambitious sheriff who held the town in his grip.

Cast: Dr. Matthew Tregaskis (James Franciscus), Sheriff Verne

Drover (Leslie Nielsen), Joanne Tregaskis (Shirley Knight), Barney Conners (Franchot Tone), Luke Travers (James Dunn), Justin Pettit (Don Ameche), Tino Silvera (Vic Dana), Arturo Silvera (Thomas Gomez), Emily Maslan (Josephine Hutchinson), Dr. Parker (Wright King), Merle Hotchkiss (Stuart Erwin), Jessie Drover (Jill Banner), Gordon Yaeger (Clinton Sundberg), Deputy Kelly (Robert Osterloh), Teddy (Kent McCord).

Credits: Produced by: Jack Laird; Directed by: James Goldstone; Written by: Chester Krumholz; Based on a Novel by: Michael Kingsley; Director of Photography: William Margulies, A.S.C.; Music by: Leonard Rosenman; Art Director: Alexander A. Mayer; Film Editor: Edward A. Biery; Costumes by: Burton Miller; Makeup: Bud Westmore; Hair Stylist: Larry Germain; Color by: Technicolor; Titles & Optical Effects: Universal Title; Produced by: Universal Television; In Association with: NBC-TV; Exclusive Distributor: MCA Television Limited.

SHORT WALK TO DAYLIGHT
(ABC TUESDAY MOVIE OF THE WEEK)

ABC Television Network, October 24, 1972; 90 minutes in color on film.

A drama about eight terrified people who were trapped in a subway tunnel when a devastating earthquake leveled New York City. Portions of this telefeature were filmed on location.

Cast: Tom Phelan (James Brolin), Alvin (Don Mitchell), Ed (James McEachin), Dorella (Abbey Lincoln), Joanne (Brooke Bundy), Jax (Lazaro Perez), Sylvia (Suzanne Charny), Sandy (Laurette Spang), Conductor (Franklin Cover).

Credits: Produced by: Edward J. Montagne; Directed by: Barry Shear; Written by: Philip H. Reisman, Jr., Gerald DiPego; Story by: Edward J. Montagne; Directors of Photography: Terry K. Meade, Ed Brown; Music by: Pat Williams; Art Director: John J. Lloyd; Film Editor: Sam E. Waxman; Special Photographic Effects: Albert Whitlock; Color by: Technicolor; Titles & Optical Effects: Universal Title; Produced by: Universal Television; Exclusive Distributor: MCA Television Limited.

SILENT NIGHT, LONELY NIGHT
(WORLD PREMIERE/NBC TUESDAY NIGHT AT THE MOVIES)

NBC Television Network, December 16, 1969; 120 minutes in color on film.

A drama about a man and a woman who had a brief New England romance while each was enduring marital difficulties. Based on the 1959 Broadway play by Robert Anderson.

Cast: John (Lloyd Bridges), Katherine (Shirley Jones), Jennifer (Lynn Carlin), Janet (Carrie Snodgress), Ginny (Cloris Leachman), Philip (Robert Lipton), Paul (Richard Eastham), Jerry (Stefan Arngrim), Mae (Nydia Westman), Physician (Woodrow Parfrey), Mac (Edward R. Leadbetter), Desk Clerk (Walter Boughton), Saleswoman (Amzie Strickland), Young Ginny (Marjorie Anne Short), Young John (Jeffrey Bridges).

Credits: Produced by: Jack Farren; Directed by: Daniel Petrie; Written by: John Vlahos; Based on a Play by: Robert Anderson; Director of Photography: Jack Marta; Music by: Billy Goldenberg; Art Director: William D. DeCinces; Set Decorations: John McCarthy, James S. Redd; Film Editor: Budd Small; Sound: David H. Moriarty; Assistant Director: Harker Wade; Unit Manager: Burt Astor; Costumes by: Charles Waldo; Makeup: Bud Westmore; Hair Stylist: Larry Germain; Color by: Technicolor; Titles & Optical Effects: Universal Title; Produced by: Universal Television; In Association with: NBC-TV; Exclusive Distributor: MCA Television Limited.

THE SIX MILLION DOLLAR MAN
(ABC WEDNESDAY MOVIE OF THE WEEK)

ABC Television Network, March 7, 1973; 90 minutes in color on film.

A drama about Steve Austin, a test pilot all but killed in a plane crash, who was "remade" through the science of bionics into a superman superior to the flesh-and-blood man he had been. His new assignment: working for the United States on secret missions. The pilot for the series The Six Million Dollar Man (which see) in which Alan Oppenheimer, and later Martin E. Brooks, assumed the role of Dr. Rudy Wells. The character known as Oliver Spencer in the telefeature was changed to Oscar Goldman in the series, with Richard Anderson taking over the role. The telefeature was filmed on location at Yuma, Ariz. and Edwards Air Force Base, California.

Cast: Steve Austin (Lee Majors), Oliver Spencer (Darren McGavin), Dr. Rudy Wells (Martin Balsam), Jean Manners (Barbara Anderson), Prisoner (Charles Knox Robinson), Geraldton (Ivory Barry), Mrs. McKay (Dorothy Green), Young Woman (Anne Whitfield), General (George Wallace), Dr. Ashburn (Robert Cornthwaite), Saltillo (Olan Soule), Nudaylah (Maurice Sherbanee), Woman (Norma Storch), Aide (John Mark Robinson).

Credits: Produced and Directed by: Richard Irving; Written by: Henri Simoun; Based on the Novel "Cyborg" by: Martin Caidin; Director of Photography: Emil Oster; Music by: Gil Melle; Art Director: Raymond Beal; Set Decorations: Jerry Adams; Film Editors: Budd Small, Richard M. Sprague; Color by: Technicolor; Titles & Opitcal Effects: Universal Title; Produced by: Universal Television; Exclusive Distributor: MCA Television Limited.

SKYWAY TO DEATH
(ABC SUSPENSE MOVIE)

ABC Television Network, January 19, 1974; 90 minutes in color on film.

A suspense drama about a group of people trapped thousands of feet above the ground in a tramway car sabotaged by a former mechanic. Filmed on location near Palm Springs, California.

Cast: Barney Taylor (Bobby Sherman), Bob Parsons (Joseph Campanella), Martin Leonard (Ross Martin), Nancy Sorenson (Stefanie Powers), Louise (Ruth McDevitt), Andrew Tustin (John Astin), Steve Kramer (Severn Darden), Sam Nichols (Tige Andrews), Ann Leonard (Nancy Malone), Bill Carter (David Sheiner), Walter Benson (Billy Green Bush), Kathy Reed (Lissa Morrow).

Credits: Produced by: Lou Morheim; Directed by: Gordon Hessler; Written by: David Spector; Director of Photography: J. J. Jones; Music by: Lee Holdridge; Art Director: William Campbell; Film Editor: Bud Hoffman; Color by: Technicolor; Titles & Optical Effects: Universal Title; Produced by: Universal Television; Exclusive Distributor: MCA Television Limited.

THE SMUGGLERS
(WORLD PREMIERE/NBC TUESDAY NIGHT AT THE MOVIES)

NBC Television Network, December 24, 1968; 120 minutes in color on film.

A drama about an American woman's innocent involvement in a European smuggling plot.

Cast: Mrs. Hudson (Shirley Booth), Jo Hudson (Carol Lynley), Adriana (Gayle Hunnicutt), Piero (Michael J. Pollard), Herr Willi Raben (Kurt Kasznar), Alfredo Faggio (David Opatoshu), M. Antoine Cirret (Donnelly Rhodes), Inspector Cesare Brunelli (Emilio Fernandez), Harry Miller (Charles Drake), Anton (Albert Szabo), Battisto (Ralph Manza), Sgt. Rossi (Rico Cattani), Customs Official (George Tyne), Italian Hotel Clerk (Edward Colmans), Freight Agent (John Indrisano), Waiter (Gino Gottarelli).

Credits: Produced and Directed by: Norman Lloyd; Written by: Alfred Hayes; Based on the Novel by: Elizabeth Hely; Director of Photography: John F. Warren, A.S.C.; Music by: Lyn Murray; Art Director: Loyd S. Papez; Set Decorations: John McCarthy, George Milo; Film Editor: Douglas Stewart; Costumes by: Grady Hunt; Makeup: Bud Westmore; Hair Stylist: Larry Germain; Color by: Technicolor; Titles & Optical Effects: Universal Title; Produced by: Universal Television; In Association with: NBC-TV; Exclusive Distributor: MCA Television Limited.

224 / Telefeatures

THE SNOOP SISTERS
(WORLD PREMIERE)

NBC Television Network, December 18, 1972; 120 minutes in color on film.

A mystery drama about Ernestine and Gwendolyn Snoop, quaint sisters who write murder mysteries and become personally involved in the murder of a glamorous retired movie star. The pilot for the series The Snoop Sisters (which see), in which Lou Antonio assumed the role of Barney, and Bert Convy took over the part of Lt. Ostrowski.

Cast: Ernestine Snoop (Helen Hayes), Gwendolyn "G." Snoop Ostrowski (Mildred Natwick), Norma Treat (Paulette Goddard), Barney (Art Carney), Lt. Ostrowski (Lawrence Pressman), Charlie (Charlie Callas), Mary Nero (Jill Clayburgh), Melvin Kaplan (Bill Dana), Milo Perkins (Ed Flanders), Alexander Scalanandre (Kurt Kasznar), Julius Nero (Ed Platt), Warren Packer (Kent Smith), Charles Corman (Craig Stevens), Anton De Touralay (Fritz Weaver).

Credits: Executive Producer: Leonard B. Stern; Produced by: Douglas Benton; Directed by: Leonard B. Stern; Written by: Leonard B. Stern, Hugh Wheeler; Story by: Leonard B. Stern; Based on Characters Created by: Alan Shayne; Director of Photography: Harry L. Wolf; Music by: Jerry Fielding; Art Director: Kenneth A. Reid; Film Editor: Edward W. Williams; Color by: Technicolor; Titles & Optical Effects: Universal Title; Produced by: Talent Associates-Norton Simon, Inc.; In Association with: Universal Television And NBC-TV; Exclusive Distributor: MCA Television Limited.

SOMETHING FOR A LONELY MAN
(WORLD PREMIERE/NBC TUESDAY NIGHT AT THE MOVIES)

NBC Television Network, November 26, 1968; 120 minutes in color on film.

A Western about a man's struggle to regain his reputation by proving to a spiteful town that he could provide it with a means of livelihood. Filmed on location in Sonora, Calif., Columbia, Calif., and the Ward Ranch in San Fernando Valley, California.

Cast: John Killibrew (Dan Blocker), Mary Duren (Susan Clark), Sam Batt (John Dehner), Angus Duren (Warren Oates), Pete Duren (Paul Peterson), Eben Duren (Don Stroud), R. J. Hoferkamp (Henry Jones), Bleeck (Sandy Kenyon), Old Man Wolenski (Edgar Buchanan), Rafe Runkel (Tommy Nolan), Joe Gillespie (Conlon Carter), Sheriff (Dub Taylor), Male Secretary (Grady Sutton), Hooker (Joan Shawlee), Preacher (Ralph Neff).

Credits: Produced by: Richard E. Lyons; Directed by: Don Taylor;

Written by: John Fante, Frank Fenton; Director of Photography: Benjamin H. Kline, A.S.C.; Music by: Jack Marshall; Art Director: Henry Larrecq; Film Editor: Robert F. Shugrue; Costumes by: Vincent Dee; Makeup: Bud Westmore; Hair Stylist: Larry Germain; Color by: Technicolor; Titles & Optical Effects: Universal Title; Produced by: Universal Television; In Association with: NBC-TV; Exclusive Distributor: MCA Television Limited.

THE SOUND OF ANGER
(WORLD PREMIERE/NBC TUESDAY NIGHT AT THE MOVIES)

NBC Television Network, December 10, 1968; 120 minutes in color on film.

A drama about a pair of lawyer brothers and a shrewd older lawyer from San Francisco who defended a pair of teenagers on a charge of murdering the girl's wealthy father in a small California town. This telefeature was the first pilot for the series The Lawyers (which see). The second was The Whole World Is Watching (which see).

Cast: Walter Nichols (Burl Ives), Brad Darrell (Guy Stockwell), Neil Darrell (James Farentino), Marge Carruthers (Dorothy Provine), Gerald Thompson (Charles Aidman), Judge Prentiss (Jay C. Flippen), Barbara Keeley (Lynda Day), Barry Kochek (David Macklin), Andrew Pearce (Dana Elcar), Ann Kochek (Collin Wilcox), Sheriff Turner (John Milford), Dorothy Daley (Sannon Farnon), Judy Schaffer (Nina Roman), Grebe (George Murdock), Lt. Morrisy (Gene Dyanarski), 2nd Sheriff (Arch Whiting).

Credits: Produced by: Roy Huggins; Directed by: Michael Ritchie; Written by: Dick Nelson; Story by: Roy Huggins; Director of Photography: Eugene Polito; Music by: Pete Rugolo; Art Director: Alexander A. Mayer; Film Editor: Carl Pingitore; Costumes by: Burton Miller; Makeup: Bud Westmore; Hair Stylist: Larry Germain; Color by: Technicolor; Titles & Optical Effects: Universal Title; Produced by: Roy Huggins-Public Arts Productions; In Association with: Universal Television And NBC-TV; Exclusive Distributor: MCA Television Limited.

THE SPECIALISTS
(NBC DOUBLE FEATURE NIGHT AT THE MOVIE)

NBC Television Network, January 6, 1975; 90 minutes in color on film.

A drama about the medical team at the Epidemic Intelligence Service who investigated, among other things, a rare strain of venereal disease and cases of typhoid contracted by American tourists in Europe. Filmed on location at the Center for Disease Control in Atlanta, Georgia. This telefeature was originally titled Vector while in production. The pilot for an unsold series.

Cast: Dr. William Nugent (Robert York [Robert Urich]), Dr. Christine Scholfield (Maureen Reagan), Dr. Edward Grey (Jack Hogan), Dick Rowdon (Jed Allan), Dr. Al Masdan (Alfred Ryder), Dr. Burkhart (Harry Townes), Eileen (Anne Whitefield), Ruth Conoyer (Corinne Camacho), Resident Doctor (Lillian Lehman).

Credits: Executive Producer: R. A. Cinader; Directed by: Richard Quine; Written by: Preston Wood, R. A. Cinader; Director of Photography: F. Bud Mautino; Music by: Billy May; Film Editor: Chuck McClelland; Color by: Technicolor; Titles & Optical Effects: Universal Title; Produced by: Mark VII Limited; In Association with: Universal Television And NBC-TV; Exclusive Distributor: MCA Television Limited.

STONESTREET: WHO KILLED THE CENTERFOLD MODEL? (WORLD PREMIERE)

NBC Television Network, January 16, 1977; 90 minutes in color on film.

A mystery drama about a widowed cop-turned-private eye who went undercover in the pornographic movie theatres on Santa Monica Boulevard in Los Angeles to locate the missing son of a client. The pilot for an unsold series.

Cast: Liz Stonestreet (Barbara Eden), Max Pierce (Joseph Mascolo), Elliot Osborn (Richard Basehart), Jessica Hilliard (Joan Hackett), Eddie Shroeder (James Ingersoll), Arlene (Elaine Giftos), Mrs. Shroeder (Louise Latham), Chuck Voit (Val Avery), Della (Sally Kirkland), Davis (Gino Conforti), Dale Anderson (Robert Burton), Erna (LaWanda Page), Amory Osborn (Ann Dusenberry), Watch Commander (Ryan MacDonald).

Credits: Executive Producer: David J. O'Connell; Produced by: Leslie Stevens; Directed by: Russ Mayberry; Written by: Leslie Stevens; Director of Photography: Terry K. Meade; Music by: Pat Williams; Art Director: John E. Chilberg II; Film Editor: Robert F. Shugrue; Color by: Technicolor; Titles & Optical Effects: Universal Title; Produced by: Universal Television; In Association with: NBC-TV; Exclusive Distributor: MCA Television.

THE STORY OF PRETTY BOY FLOYD (ABC TUESDAY MOVIE OF THE WEEK)

ABC Television Network, May 7, 1974; 90 minutes in color on film.

A drama about Charles Arthur Floyd, a sodbuster who turned to a life of crime. As the infamous "Pretty Boy," Floyd was into bootlegging, robbery and murder. He was finally gunned down by Melvin Purvis' men when he would not surrender in 1934. Filmed on location in southern California.

The Story of Pretty Boy Floyd / 227

Cast: Charles Arthur Floyd (Martin Sheen), Ruby Hardgrave (Kim Darby), Bradley Floyd (Michael Parks), Ma Floyd (Ellen Corby), E. W. Floyd (Joseph Estevez), Mary Floyd (Kitty Carl), Melvin Purvis (Geoffrey Binney), Bill Miller (Bill Vint), Shine Rush (Mills Watson), Dominic Mirell (Abe Vigoda), Eddie Ferchetti (Steven Keats), George Burtwell (Rod McCarey), Suggs (Ford Rainey), Secretary (Ann Doran), Juanita (Arlene Faber), Phil Donnati (Frank Cristi), Decker (Ted Gehring), Deputy (Ron Applegate).

Credits: Executive Producer: Roy Huggins; Produced by: Jo Swerling, Jr.; Directed by: Clyde Ware; Written by: Clyde Ware; Director of Photography: J. J. Jones; Music by: Pete Rugolo; Art Director: Alfeo Bocchicchio; Film Editors: Chuck McClelland, Gloryette Clark; Color by: Technicolor; Titles & Optical Effects: Universal Title; Produced by: Roy Huggins-Public Arts Productions; In Association with: Universal Television; Exclusive Distributor: MCA Television Limited.

THE STORYTELLER
(NBC MONDAY NIGHT AT THE MOVIES)

NBC Television Network, December 5, 1977; 120 minutes in color on film.

A drama about a television writer who set out to find if he was in some way guilty of a 12-year-old boy's death. The youngster was a viewer of the writer's TV movie about an arsonist, and later set his school on fire only to die of smoke inhalation. The writer wanted to learn whether the child was emotionally disturbed or whether his script really did motivate the tragedy.

Cast: Ira Davidson (Martin Balsam), Marion Davidson (Doris Roberts), Sue Davidson (Patty Duke Astin), Mrs. Eberhardt (Rose Gregorio), Arthur Huston (James Daly), Donaldson (David Spielberg), Eberthardt (Tom Aldredge), Lee Gardner (Peter Masterson), Reporter (James Staley), Curry (Milt Kogan), Chrissie (Shelby Balik), Whitman (Ivan Bonar).

Credits: Producers: Richard Levinson, William Link; Directed by: Robert Markowitz; Written by: Richard Levinson, William Link; Director of Photography: Terry K. Meade; Music by: David Shire; Additional Music by: Hal Mooney; Art Director: Lawrence G. Paull; Film Editor: Bud S. Isaacs; Color by: Technicolor; Titles & Optical Effects: Universal Title; Produced by: Fairmont/Foxcroft Productions; In Association with: Universal Television; Exclusive Distributor: MCA Television Limited.

STRANGER ON THE RUN
(WORLD PREMIERE/NBC TUESDAY NIGHT AT THE MOVIES)

NBC Television Network, October 31, 1967; 120 minutes in color on film.

228 / Telefeatures

A drama about an itinerant alcoholic who ran for his life from a posse when he was accused of murdering a girl in a bleak New Mexico railroad town.

Cast: Ben Chamberlain (Henry Fonda), Valverda Johnson (Anne Baxter), Vince McKay (Michael Parks), O. E. Hotchkiss (Dan Duryea), George Blaylock (Sal Mineo), Mr. Gorman (Lloyd Bochner), Matt Johnson (Michael Burns), Leo Weed (Tom Reese), Dickory (Bernie Hamilton), Larkin (Zalman King), Alma Britton (Madlyn Rhue), Berk (Walter Burke), Mercurio (Rodolfo Acosta), Pilney (George Dunn), Manolo (Pepe Hern).

Credits: Produced by: Richard E. Lyons; Directed by: Donald Siegel; Written by: Dean Riesner; Based on a Story by: Reginald Rose; Director of Photography: Bud Thackery, A. S. C.; Music by: Leonard Rosenman; Theme Song "Stranger on the Run" Written by: Kay Scott; Sung by: Bill Anderson; Art Director: William D. DeCinces; Set Decorations: John McCarthy, Audrey Blasdel; Film Editor: Richard G. Wray, A. C. E.; Sound: David H. Moriarty; Music Supervision: Stanley Wilson; Costumes by: Vincent Dee; Makeup: Bud Westmore; Hair Stylist: Larry Germain; Color Coordinator: Robert Brower; Color by: Technicolor; Titles & Optical Effects: Universal Title; Produced by: Universal Television; In Association with: NBC-TV; Exclusive Distributor: MCA Television Limited.

THE SUICIDE CLUB
(ABC WIDE WORLD OF ENTERTAINMENT/WIDE WORLD MYSTERY)

ABC Television Network, February 13, 1973; 90 minutes in color on tape.

A suspense drama about a bored gambler whose search took him to a unique card club where the stakes were life and death.

Cast: Tommy Kennicot (Peter Haskell), Gerry Totten (Margot Kidder), Silverado (Joseph Wiseman), Mr. Mullery (George Coulouris), Mr. Palmieri (Logan Ramsey), Mrs. Higbee (Maxine Stuart), Charlie Summerhayes (Ron Rifkin), Leslie Woodruff (Ellen Weston).

Credits: Produced by: Barbara Schultz; Directed by: Bill Glenn; Written by: Philip Reisman, Jr.; Based on a Story by: Robert Louis Stevenson; Technical Director: Roy White; Music by: Michael Lang; Production Designer: Ralph Holmes; Audio: Jerry Pattison; Video: Dick Browning; Taped at: KTLA-TV; Produced by: Universal Television; Exclusive Distributor: MCA Television Limited.

SUNSHINE
(CBS SPECIAL MOVIE PRESENTATION)

CBS Television Network, November 9, 1973; 150 minutes in color on film.

A drama suggested by the journals of a young wife and mother who lost a courageous battle against cancer but left a unique legacy of love to her husband and two-year-old daughter. Followed by the sequel Sunshine Christmas (which see). The pilot for the series Sunshine (which see). Filmed on location in British Columbia.

Cast: Dr. Carol Gillman (Brenda Vaccaro), Kate Hayden (Cristina Raines), Sam Hayden (Cliff DeYoung), Nora (Meg Foster), Weaver (Bill Mumy), Jill Hayden (Lindsay Green Bush), David (Alan Fudge), Givits (Corey Fischer), Jill at $2\frac{1}{2}$ years (Robin Bush), Jill at 6 months (Sarah Valentini), Dr. Wilde (James Hong), Bartender (Noble Willingham), Nurse (Adrian Ricard), Interviewer (Bill Stout).

Credits: Produced by: George Eckstein; Directed by: Joseph Sargent; Written by: Carol Sobieski; Based on the Journals of: Jacquelyn Helton; Director of Photography: Bill Butler; Music by: Lee Holdridge; Songs by: John Denver; Art Director: George Webb; Film Editors: Budd Small, Richard M. Sprague; Color by: Technicolor; Titles & Optical Effects: Universal Title; Produced by: Universal Television; Exclusive Distributor: MCA Television Limited.

SUNSHINE CHRISTMAS
(NBC MONDAY NIGHT AT THE MOVIES)

NBC Television Network, December 12, 1977; 120 minutes in color on film.

A drama about widower Sam Hayden and his young daughter who left British Columbia to return to Hayden's home town of Claude, Texas to visit his parents and celebrate Christmas. A sequel to the telefeature Sunshine (which see) on which the series of the same title was based. Filmed on location, in Claude, Texas and southern California.

Cast: Sam Hayden (Cliff DeYoung), Jill (Elizabeth Cheshire), Weaver (Bill Mumy), Corey Givits (Corey Fischer), Nora (Meg Foster), Bertha Hayden (Eileen Heckart), Joe Hayden (Pat Hingle), Cody (Barbara Hershey), Hugh Bob (James Keane), Stanley (Douglas V. Fowley), Ray Griff (Michael Alldredge).

Credits: Produced by: George Eckstein; Directed by: Glenn Jordan; Written by: Carol Sobieski; Director of Photography: Edward Rosson; Music by: Tony Berg; Art Director: William H. Tuntke; Film Editor: Gordon Scott; Costumes by: Edith Head; Color by: Technicolor; Titles & Optical Effects: Universal Title; Produced by: Universal Television; Exclusive Distributor: MCA Television Limited.

THE SUNSHINE PATRIOT
(WORLD PREMIERE/NBC MONDAY NIGHT AT THE MOVIES)

NBC Television Network, December 16, 1968; 120 minutes in color on film.

A drama about master spy Christopher Ross, who accepted one last assignment from his superior--to go behind the Iron Curtain to retrieve microfilm of vital interest to the Western powers. He switched identities with a traveling American businessman to insure the success of his mission.

Cast: Christopher Ross/Arthur Selby (Cliff Robertson), Brancie Hagen (Dina Merrill), Imre Hyneck (Luther Adler), Morris Vanders (Wilfrid Hyde-White), Dr. Novack (Lilia Skala), Iris (Antoinette Bower), Benedeck (Donald Sutherland), Janosi (Sandor Szabo), Scopes (Clarke Gordon), Beamis (Woodrow Parfrey), Tibor (Victor Brandt), Guard (Danny Klega), Reisling (Charles H. Radilac), Vander's Secretary (Jill Curzon), Tageris (George Sawaya), Janosi's Secretary (Hanna Landy).

Credits: Produced by: Joel Rogosin; Directed by: Joseph Sargent; Written by: Gustave Field, Joel Rogosin, John Kneubuhl; Story by: Gustave Field; Director of Photography: Jerry Finnerman (Gerald Perry Finnerman); Music by: Stanley Wilson; Art Director: Howard E. Johnson; Set Decorations: John McCarthy, Ralph Sylos; Film Editor: Budd Small; Sound: Earl Crain, Jr.; Costumes by: Burton Miller; Makeup: Bud Westmore; Hair Stylist: Larry Germain; Color by: Technicolor; Titles & Optical Effects: Universal Title; Produced by: Universal Television; In Association with: NBC-TV; Exclusive Distributor: MCA Television Limited.

SWITCH
(CBS FRIDAY NIGHT AT THE MOVIES)

CBS Television Network, March 21, 1975; 90 minutes in color on film.

A drama about former cop Frank MacBride and onetime felon Pete Ryan, who teamed up to form a private investigation firm. Their first case was to prove that a cop, rather than an ex-con, was responsible for a jewel robbery. The pilot for the series Switch (which see).

Cast: Pete Ryan (Robert Wagner), Frank MacBride (Eddie Albert), Phil Beckman (Charles Durning), Capt. Griffin (Ken Swofford), Murray Franklin (Alan Manson), Maggie (Sharon Gless), Chuck Powell (Greg Mullavey), Malcolm (Charlie Callas), Franks (Marc Lawrence), Alice (Jaclyn Smith), Lisa (Ann Schedeen).

Credits: Produced by: Glen A. Larson; Directed by: Robert Day; Written by: Glen A. Larson; Directors of Photography: John Morley Stephens, Ben Colman; Music by: Stu Phillips; Art Director: George Renne; Film Editors: Budd Small, Frank Morriss; Color by: Technicolor; Titles & Optical Effects: Universal Title; Produced by: Glen A. Larson Productions; In Association with: Universal Television; Exclusive Distributor: MCA Television Limited.

TAIL GUNNER JOE
(WORLD PREMIERE/THE BIG EVENT)

NBC Television Network, February 6, 1977; 3 hours in color on film.

A drama about the rise and fall of anti-Communist crusader Sen. Joseph McCarthy, who caused a reign of terror in the 1950s.

Cast: Sen. Joseph McCarthy (Peter Boyle), Paul Cunningham (John Forsythe), Joseph Welch (Burgess Meredith), Logan (Heather Menzies), Sen. Margaret Chase Smith (Patricia Neal), Jean Kerr (Karen Carlson), President Eisenhower (Andrew Duggan), Roy Cohn (George Wyner), Sylvester (Ned Beatty), Mrs. DeCamp (Jean Stapleton), Drew Pearson (Robert F. Simon), President Truman (Robert Symonds), Sen. Symington (Lin McCarthy), Sen. Lucas (Philip Abbott), Middleton (Wesley Addy), Gen. Lamkin (John Randolph), Armitage (Henry Jones), Wisconsin Farmer (John Carradine), Logan's Boss (Charles Cioffi), Sarah (Diana Douglas), Farmer (Andrew Prine), Publisher (Murray Matheson), Gen Zwicker (William Schallert), Gen. Marshall (John Anderson), Dean Acheson (Alan Hewitt), Richard M. Nixon (Richard M. Dixon), Robert F. Kennedy (Sam Chew, Jr.), Sen. Bolland (Herb Voland).

Credits: Produced by: George Eckstein; Directed by: Jud Taylor; Written by: Lane Slate; Director of Photography: Ric Waite; Music by: Billy May; Art Director: Lawrence G. Paull; Film Editor: Bernard J. Small; Sound: Don Parker; Color by: Technicolor; Titles & Optical Effects: Universal Title; Produced by: Universal Television; Exclusive Distributor: MCA Television Limited.

TARGET RISK
(NBC DOUBLE FEATURE NIGHT AT THE MOVIES)

NBC Television Network, January 6, 1975; 90 minutes in color on film.

A drama about a bonded courier whose girlfriend was kidnapped and held for a ransom of $2,000,000 in diamonds. The pilot for an unsold series.

Cast: Lee Driscoll (Bo Svenson), Linda Frayly (Meredith Baxter), Ralph Sloan (John P. Ryan), Julian Ulrich (Robert Coote), Simon Cusack (Keenan Wynn), Marty (Philip Burns), Harry (Lee Paul), Bill Terek (Charles Shull).

Credits: Executive Producer: Jo Swerling, Jr.; Produced by: Robert F. O'Neill; Directed by: Robert Scheerer; Written by: Don Carlos Dunaway; Director of Photography: Bill Butler; Music by: Eumir Deodato; Film Editor: John A. Martinelli; Color by: Technicolor; Titles & Optical Effects: Universal Title; Produced by: Roy Huggins-Public Arts Productions; In Association with: Universal Television And NBC-TV; Exclusive Distributor: MCA Television Limited.

TENAFLY
(WORLD PREMIERE/NBC MONDAY NIGHT AT THE MOVIES)

NBC Television Network, February 12, 1973; 90 minutes in color on film.

A drama about Harry Tenafly, a private eye with a wife and two youngsters trying to manage a typical middle-class life. He also tried to do his job, which involved finding out who murdered the wife of a caustic radio talk show host. The pilot for the series Tenafly (which see).

Cast: Harry Tenafly (James McEachin), Ted Harris (Ed Nelson), Charles Rush (Mel Ferrer), Uncle Walter (Bill Walter), Ken Shepherd (Jon Ericson), Lorrie (Rosanna Huffman), Ruth Tenafly (Lillian Lehman), Herb Tenafly (Paul M. Jackson, Jr.), Lt. Church (David Huddleston), Aunt Gertrude (Lillian Randolph).

Credits: Executive Producers: Richard Levinson, William Link; Produced by: Jon Epstein; Directed by: Richard A. Colla; Written by: Richard Levinson, William Link; Director of Photography: Emil Oster; Music by: Gil Melle; Art Director: George Webb; Film Editor: Robert L. Kimble; Color by: Technicolor; Titles & Optical Effects: Universal Title; Produced by: Universal Television; In Association with: NBC-TV; Exclusive Distributor: MCA Television Limited.

THAT CERTAIN SUMMER
(ABC MOVIE OF THE WEEK)

ABC Television Network, November 1, 1972; 90 minutes in color on film.

A drama about a 14-year-old boy who went to San Francisco to visit his divorced father, as he had for the past three years. His world was shattered when he accidentally discovered that his father was a homosexual.

Cast: Doug Salter (Hal Holbrook), Janet Salter (Hope Lange), Gary McClain (Martin Sheen), Phil Bonner (Joe Don Baker), Nick Salter (Scott Jacoby), Lauren Hyatt (Marlyn Mason), Conductor (James McEachin), Artist (Clarke Gordon), Jody Bonner (Jan Shepard), Mrs. Michele (Carolyn Bueno).

Credits: Produced by: Richard Levinson, William Link; Directed by: Lamont Johnson; Written by: Richard Levinson, William Link; Director of Photography: Vilis Lapenieks; Music by: Gil Melle; Art Director: John T. McCormack; Set Decorations: Ralph Hurst;

That Certain Summer / 233

Film Editor: Edward M. Abroms; Sound: Melvin Metcalfe; Color by: Technicolor; Titles & Optical Effects: Universal Title; Produced by: Universal Television; Exclusive Distributor: MCA Television Limited.

THIS IS THE WEST THAT WAS
(WORLD PREMIERE)

NBC Television Network, December 17, 1974; 90 minutes in color on film.

A whimsical Western about the adventures of Wild Bill Hickok, an innocent bystander who came to be feared as a deadly gunslinger. The pilot for an unsold series.

Cast: Wild Bill Hickok (Ben Murphy), Calamity Jane (Kim Darby), Buffalo Bill Cody (Matt Clark), Sarah Shaw (Jane Alexander), J. W. McCanles (Tony Franciosa), Blind Pete (Stuart Margolin), Oscar Wellman (Bill McKinney), Carmedly (Stefan Gierasch), Hearts (W. L. LeGault), Narrated by (Roger Davis).

Credits: Executive Producer: Roy Huggins; Produced by: Jo Swerling, Jr.; Directed by: Fielder Cook; Written by: Sam H. Rolfe; Director of Photography: Earl Rath; Music by: Dick DeBenedictis; Art Director: Walter M. Simonds; Film Editors: Gloryette Clark, Fred Knudtson; Color by: Technicolor; Titles & Optical Effects: Universal Title; Produced by: Roy Huggins-Public Arts Productions; In Association with: Universal Television And NBC-TV; Exclusive Distributor: MCA Television Limited.

THE 3,000 MILE CHASE
(NBC MOVIE OF THE WEEK)

NBC Television Network, June 16, 1977; 120 minutes in color on film.

A drama about Matthew Considine, a bonded courier who was paid $25,000 to deliver key witness Paul Dvorak to a murder trial safely. Filmed on location in Antelope Valley, California.

Cast: Matthew Considine/Marty Scanlon (Cliff DeYoung), Paul Dvorak/Leonard Staveck (Glenn Ford), Rachel Kane (Blair Brown), Frank Oberon (David Spielberg), Emma Dvorak (Priscilla Pointer), Ambrose Finn (Brendan Dillon), Livingston (Lane Allan), Inspector (John Zenda), Santeen (Carmen Argenziano), Richette (Tom Bower), Prosecutor (Rogar Aaron Brown), Vince Leone (Titos Vandis), Richards (Marc Alaimo), with: Michael Mancini, Don Maxwell, Jerry Hardin, Richard LePore, Hugh Gillin, June Whitley Taylor, George Fisher, Abraham Alvarez, Tanya Swerling, Michael Dan Wagner, Stephen Colt, Michael J. London.

234 / Telefeatures

Credits: Executive Producer: Roy Huggins; Produced by: Jo Swerling, Jr.; Directed by: Russ Mayberry; Written by: Philip DeGuere, Jr.; Story by: Roy Huggins; Director of Photography: Charles G. Arnold; Music by: Elmer Bernstein; Art Director: Mark Hassbinder; Film Editors: Larry Lester, Lawrence J. Vallario; Color by: Technicolor; Titles & Optical Effects: Universal Title; Produced by: Roy Huggins-Public Arts Productions; In Association with: Universal Television And NBC-TV; Exclusive Distributor: MCA Television Limited.

TOM SAWYER

CBS Television Network, March 23, 1973; 90 minutes in color on film. Sponsor and Agency: Dr. Pepper through Young & Rubicam, Inc.

A new adaptation about the adventures of Tom Sawyer and Huckleberry Finn in Hannibal, Missouri. Filmed on location in Ontario, Canada on the banks of the St. Lawrence. Based on the 1938 film The Adventures of Tom Sawyer and Mark Twain's novel of the same title.

Cast: Tom Sawyer (Josh Albee), Huckleberry Finn (Jeff Tyler), Aunt Polly (Jane Wyatt), Muff Potter (Buddy Ebsen), Injun Joe (Vic Morrow), Judge Thatcher (John McGiver), Becky Thatcher (Karen Pearson), Mary Sawyer (Sue Petrie), Sid Sawyer (Scott Fisher), with: Dawn Greenlogh, Leonard Bernardo, Gwen Thomas, Bob Goodier, David Yorstan, Kay Hawtrey, Al Bernardo, Colin Fox, Scott Carlson, Ricky O'Neill, Chris Pellett, Susan Stacey, Alysia Pascaris, Leo Leyden, Peter Mews.

Credits: Executive Producer: Earl A. Glick; Produced by: Trevor Wallace; Directed by: James Neilson; Written by: Jean Holloway; Based on "The Adventures of Tom Sawyer" by: Mark Twain; Director of Photography: Fred Mandl; Music by: Hal Mooney; Art Director: Chris Adney; Film Editor: John McSweeney; Color by: Technicolor; Titles & Optical Effects: Universal Title; Produced by: Hal Roach Productions; In Association with: Universal Television And CBS-TV; Exclusive Distributor: MCA Television Limited.

TOMA
(ABC WEDNESDAY MOVIE OF THE WEEK)

ABC Television Network, March 21, 1973; 90 minutes in color on film.

A drama about New Jersey police detective David Toma, whose mastery of disguises allowed him to infiltrate and singlehandedly destroy a syndicate gambling operation. The pilot for the series Toma (which see), this telefeature was also the basis for the series Baretta (which see).

Cast: David Toma (Tony Musante), Lt. Spooner (Simon Oakland), Patty Toma (Susan Strasberg), Prolaci (Nicholas Colasanto), Frank Barber (Robert Yuro), Vinnie Cecca (David Toma), Sam Hooper (Philip Thomas), Bags Roland (David Mauro), Andretti (Robert Phillips), Donzer (Abe Vigoda), Dox (Ron Soble), Jim Toma (Sean Manning), Donna Toma (Michelle Livingston), Mark (Eugene Mazzola).

Credits: Executive Producer: Roy Huggins; Produced by: Jo Swerling, Jr.; Directed by: Richard T. Heffron; Written by: Edward Hume; Director of Photography: Vilis Lapenieks; Music by: Pete Rugolo; Film Editors: John Dumas, Gloryette Clark; Technical Advisor: Det. David Toma; Color by: Technicolor; Titles & Optical Effects: Universal Title; Produced by: Roy Huggins-Public Arts Productions; In Association with: Universal Television; Exclusive Distributor: MCA Television Limited.

TRAPPED
(ABC WEDNESDAY MOVIE OF THE WEEK)

ABC Television Network, November 14, 1973; 90 minutes in color on film.

A suspense drama about a man who was locked in a department store with six ferocious guard dogs.

Cast: Chuck Brenner (James Brolin), Elaine Moore (Susan Clark), David Moore (Earl Holliman), Carrie (Tammy Harrington), Sgt. Connaught (Robert Hooks), Salesgirl (Ivy Jones), Bartender (Bob Hastings), First Boy (Gerald Brutsche), Steward (Marco Lopez), Mr. Higgins (Elliott Lindsey), Waitress (Mary Robinson), Stewardess (Erica Hagen).

Credits: Executive Producer: Richard Irving; Produced by: Gary L. Messenger; Directed by: Frank DeFelitta; Written by: Frank DeFelitta; Director of Photography: Fred Mandl; Music by: Gil Melle; Art Director: George Webb; Film Editors: John F. Schreyer, Larry Lester; Color by: Technicolor; Titles & Optical Effects: Universal Title; Produced by: Universal Television; Exclusive Distributor: MCA Television Limited.

TRIAL RUN
(WORLD PREMIERE/NBC SATURDAY NIGHT AT THE MOVIES)

NBC Television Network, January 18, 1969; 120 minutes in color on film.

A drama about how a young criminal lawyer's ambition and his senior attorney's anguish over his wife's behavior affected their defense of a man charged with murder.

Cast: Louis Coleman (James Franciscus), Lucille Harkness (Janice Rule), Jason Harkness (Leslie Nielsen), Carol Trenet (Diane Baker), Leo D'Agosta (John Vernon), Noel Ferguson (David Sheiner), Charles Andrews (Fred Beir), Tyler Peters (Paul Carr), Mrs. Menderes (Lili Valenty), Henry Wycoff (Jack Collins), Karlson (William Bramley), Larkin (Bartlett Robinson), Jeanne (Vicki Medlin).

Credits: Produced by: Jack Laird; Directed by: William Graham; Written by: Chester Krumholz; Story by: Richard Levinson, William Link; Associate Producer: Jerrold Freedman; Director of Photography: Alric Edens; Music by: Stanley Wilson; Art Director: Robert MacKichan; Film Editor: Douglas Stewart; Sound: James T. Porter; Editorial Supervision: Richard Belding; Costumes by: Burton Miller; Makeup: Bud Westmore; Hair Stylist: Larry Germain; Color Coordinator: Robert Brower; Color by: Technicolor; Titles & Optical Effects: Universal Title; Produced by: Universal Television; In Association with: NBC-TV; Exclusive Distributor: MCA Television Limited.

THE TRIBE
(ABC WEDNESDAY MOVIE OF THE WEEK)

ABC Television Network, December 11, 1974; 90 minutes in color on film.

A drama about the simple and often brutal lives of Cro-Magnons, mankind's nomadic forefathers. Filmed in Beaumont, California.

Cast: Mathis (Victor French), Gorin (Warren Vanders), Perron (Mark Gruner), Gato (Stewart Moss), Cana (Henry Wilcoxon), Rouse (Sam Gilman), Jen (Adriana Shaw), Hertha (Meg Wylie), Ardis (Nancy Elliott), Orda (Jeannine Brown), Kiska (Dominique Pinassi), The Neanderthal (Jack Scalici), Narrated by (Paul Richards).

Credits: Produced by: George Eckstein; Directed by: Richard A. Colla; Written by: Lane Slate; Director of Photography: Rexford Metz; Music by: Hal Mooney; Art Director: William Newberry; Film Editor: Robert F. Shugrue; Color by: Technicolor; Titles & Optical Effects: Universal Title; Produced by: Universal Television; Exclusive Distributor: MCA Television Limited.

TWO ON A BENCH
(ABC MOVIE OF THE WEEK)

ABC Television Network, November 2, 1971; 90 minutes in color on film.

A comedy about a hip girl and a square stockbroker who were suspected of being international spies. Filmed on location in Boston, Massachusetts.

Two on a Bench / 237

Cast: Macy Kramer (Patty Duke), Preston Albright (Ted Bessell), Brubaker (Andrew Duggan), Dr. Remmington (John Astin), Mrs. Kramer (Alice Ghostley), Kingston (Terry Carter), Lukens (Dick Balduzzi), Hayes (Robert Cornthwaite), Harriet (Jeannie Berlin), Ralph (Gary Waynesmith), Agent (Ken Sansom).

Credits: Produced by: Richard Levinson, William Link; Directed by: Jerry Paris; Written by: Richard Levinson, William Link; Directors of Photography: Harry Wolf, Howard Block; Music by: Mike Post, Pete Carpenter; Art Director: Walter M. Simonds; Film Editor: Stefan Arnsten; Color by: Technicolor; Titles & Optical Effects: Universal Title; Produced by: Universal Television; Exclusive Distributor: MCA Television Limited.

THE UFO INCIDENT
(NBC MONDAY NIGHT AT THE MOVIES)

NBC Television Network, September 20, 1975; 120 minutes in color on film.

A drama about Barney and Betty Hill, an interracially married couple who claimed that they were taken into an alien spaceship for physical examinations in New Hampshire in 1961.

Cast: Betty Hill (Estelle Parsons), Barney Hill (James Earl Jones), Dr. Benjamin Simon (Barnard Hughes), MacRainey (Beeson Carroll), Gen. Davidson (Dick O'Neill), Lisa MacRainey (Terrence O'Connor), Examiner (Jeanne Joe), Leader (Lou Wagner), Henderson (Joe Stefano), Gill (Tony Swartz), with: Eric Murphy, Eric Server.

Credits: Produced by: Richard A. Colla, Joe L. Cramer; Directed by: Richard A. Colla; Written by: S. Lee Pogostin, Hesper Anderson; Based on the Book "The Interrupted Journey" by: John G. Fuller; Director of Photography: Rexford Metz; Music by: Billy Goldenberg; Art Director: Peter M. Wooley; Film Editor: Richard Bracken; Color by: Technicolor; Titles & Optical Effects: Universal Title; Produced by: Universal Television; In Association with: NBC-TV; Exclusive Distributor: MCA Television Limited.

VANISHED
(WORLD PREMIERE)

NBC Television Network, March 8, 1971 and March 9, 1971; 4 hours in color on film.

A drama about the disappearance at a period set in the future of the top advisor to the President of the United States, and its national and international repercussions. This telefeature was the first two-parter to be produced, paving the way for the expanded TV movie and the mini-series.

Cast: President Paul Roudebush (Richard Widmark), Jill Nichols

(Skye Aubrey), Johnny Cavanaugh (Tom Bosley), Gene Culligan (James Farentino), Jerry Freytag (Larry Hagman), Nick McCann (Murray Hamilton), Arnold Greer (Arthur Hill), Larry Storm (Robert Hooks), Arthur Ingram (E. G. Marshall), Sue Greer (Eleanor Parker), Dave Paulick (William Shatner), Sen. Earl Gannon (Robert Young), Newscaster (Chet Huntley), TV Hostess (Betty White), Gen. Palfrey (Stephen McNally), Beverly West (Sheree North), Mike Loomis (Robert Lipton), Capt. Cooledge (Jim Davis), Pete Descowicz (Michael Strong), Gretchen Greer (Christine Belford), Grace Lally (Catherine McLeod), Big Bubba Toubo (Denny Miller), Mercurio (Don Pedro Colley), Clyde Morehouse (Russell Johnson), Butter Nygaard (Susan Kussman), Merrihew (Neil Hamilton), Phyllis (Judy Jordan), Dr. Winthrop (Richard Dix), Miss Rogers (Nancy Lee Dix), Kate McGuiness (Athena Lorde), Gov. Wolcott (Stacy Keach, Sr.), Matthew Silkworth (Kevin Hagen), Joe Hotchkiss (Herb Vigran), Hester Portinari (Ilka Windish), Ensign (Randolph Mantooth), Admiral Fairclough (Russ Conway), Commander Fyfield (Clark Howat), Whitelaw (Gil Stuart), Admiral Houton (Art Balinger), Dr. Geoffrey Page (Barry Atwater), Ned Lee (James Hong), Admiral Claypool (Earl Ebi), Walters (Lawrence Linville), Capt. Fonseca (Leo G. Morrell), Baldomero (Pery Ribeiro), Capt. Meadowcroft (Stacy Harris), Maj. Spear (Vince Howard), Rupe (Stephen Coit), Loren Kupperman (Frances DeSales), Officer of the Deck (Fred Holliday), Commander Prescott (William Boyett), Leonard Carey (Carleton Young), Mrs. Erdlatz (Helen Kleeb), Reporters (Herbert Kaplow, Martin Agronsky, Dick Kleiner, Vernon Scott, Joseph Finnigan).

Credits: Executive Producer: David Victor; Produced by: David J. O'Connell; Directed by: Buzz Kulik; Written by: Dean Riesner; Based on the Novel by: Fletcher Knebel; Associate Producer: Joseph Cavalier; Director of Photography: Lionel Lindon, A.S.C.; Music by: Leonard Rosenman; Art Director: John J. Lloyd; Set Decorations: Ruby R. Levitt; Film Editor: Robert Watts, A.C.E.; Sound: James Z. Flaster; Unit Manager: Joseph Cavalier; Assistant Director: Jim Fargo; Special Photographic Effects: Albert J. Whitlock; Color by: Technicolor; Titles & Optical Effects: Universal Title; Editorial Supervision: Richard Belding; Costumes by: Charles Waldo; Makeup: Bud Westmore; Hair Stylist: Larry Germain; Produced by: Universal Television; In Association with: NBC-TV; Exclusive Distributor: MCA Television Limited.

A VERY MISSING PERSON
(ABC MOVIE OF THE WEEKEND)

ABC Television Network, March 4, 1972; 90 minutes in color on film.

A detective drama about Hildegarde Withers, a flamboyant ex-school-teacher-turned-private eye, who investigated the disappearance of a young woman and soon found herself trying to solve a murder case. Based on the novel by Stuart Palmer and Fletcher

A Very Missing Person / 239

Flora and the Hildegarde Withers films of the 1930s, this pilot for an unsold series was filmed on location in New York City.

Cast: Hildegarde Withers (Eve Arden), Aletha (Julie Newmar), Oscar Piper (James Gregory), Lenore Gregory/Isobel (Skye Aubrey), Capt. Westering (Ray Denton), Onofree (Robert Easton), Al Fister (Dennis Rucker), Eberhardt (Woodrow Parfrey), Malloy (Bob Hastings), Bernadine Toller (Linda Gillin), Delmar Faulkenstein (Pat Morita), Ora (Dwan Smith), Dr. Singer (Peter Morrison Jacobs), Mrs. Singer (Savannah Bentley), Mariette (Udana Power).

Credits: Produced by: Edward J. Montagne; Directed by: Russ Mayberry; Written by: Philip H. Reisman, Jr.; Based on the Novel "Hildegarde Withers Makes the Scene" by: Stuart Palmer, Fletcher Flora; Director of Photography: William Margulies; Music by: Vic Mizzy; Art Director: William H. Tuntke; Set Decorations: Perry Murdock; Film Editor: Richard M. Sprague; Costumes by: Grady Hunt; Color by: Technicolor; Titles & Optical Effects: Universal Title; Produced by: Universal Television; Exclusive Distributor: MCA Television Limited.

THE VICTIM

ABC Television Network, November 14, 1972; 90 minutes in color on film.

A chiller about a young woman who was trapped in a storm while searching for her missing sister. The woman was unaware that she was the next target of an unknown killer. Filmed on location in Monterey, California.

Cast: Katherine Wainwright (Elizabeth Montgomery), Ben Chappel (George Maharis), Mrs. Hawks (Eileen Heckart), Edith Jordan (Sue Ane Langdon), Susan (Jess Walton), Highway Patrolman (Richard Derr), 1st Policeman (Ross Elliott), 2nd Policeman (John Furlong).

Credits: Produced by: William Frye; Directed by: Herschel Daugherty; Written by: Merwin Gerard; Based on a Short Story by: McKnight Malmar; Director of Photography: Michael Joyce; Music by: Gil Melle; Art Director: Henry Bumstead; Set Decorations: James Payne; Film Editors: Douglas Stewart, John Kaufman, Jr.; Color by: Technicolor; Titles & Optical Effects: Universal Title; Produced by: Universal Television; Exclusive Distributor: MCA Television Limited.

WHAT'S A NICE GIRL LIKE YOU...?
(ABC MOVIE OF THE WEEKEND)

ABC Television Network, December 18, 1971; 90 minutes in color on film.

240 / Telefeatures

A comedy-drama about a poor girl from the Bronx who was drawn into an elaborate extortion plot by impersonating a rich socialite after being kidnapped by a gang of sophisticated con men.

Cast: Shirley Campbel (Brenda Vaccaro), Mr. Stillman (Edmond O'Brien), Spevin (Vincent Price), Lt. Burton (Jack Warden), Soames (Roddy McDowall). Cynthia (Jo Anne Worley), Flint (Arthur Batanides), Adam Newman (Morgan Sterne), Fats Detroit (Michael Lerner), Francis Malone (Robert Doyle), Seltzer (Gino Conforti), Mr. Foley (Curt Conway).

Credits: Produced by: Norman Lloyd; Directed by: Jerry Paris; Written by: Howard Fast; Based on the Novel "Shirley" by: E. V. Cunningham (Howard Fast); Director of Photography: Harry Wolf; Music by: Bob Prince; Art Director: Alexander A. Mayer; Set Decorations: Robert C. Bradfield; Film Editor: Richard M. Sprague; Costumes by: Grady Hunt; Color by: Technicolor; Titles & Optical Effects: Universal Title; Produced by: Universal Television; Exclusive Distributor: MCA Television Limited.

THE WHOLE WORLD IS WATCHING
(WORLD PREMIERE)

NBC Television Network, March 11, 1969; 120 minutes in color on film.

A drama about the legal team of Nichols, Darrell & Darrell, who were hired to defend a student leader accused of killing a campus policeman during a student revolt. This telefeature was the second pilot for the series The Lawyers (which see). The first was The Sound of Anger (which see).

Cast: Walter Nichols (Burl Ives), Brian Darrell (Joseph Campanella), Neil Darrell (James Farentino), Chancellor Graham (Hal Holbrook), Officer Platt (Steve Ihnat), The Governor (Stephen McNally), Gil Bennett (Rick Ely), Ed Shepp (Dennis Olivieri), Jim Church (Roy Poole), Huston (Dana Elcar), Megan Baker (Carrie Snodgress), Debbie (Eileen Wesson), 2nd Judge (Kermit Murdock), Mrs. Harbeson (Juanita Moore), Student Witness (Charles Brewer), Arresting Officer (John S. Ragin), Dr. Sloan (Bennes Mardenn), Jail Guard (Stuart Nisbet).

Credits: Executive Producer: Roy Huggins; Produced by: Jo Swerling, Jr.; Directed by: Richard A. Colla; Written by: Richard Levinson, William Link; Associate Producers: Steve Heilpern, Carl Pingitore; Director of Photography: E. Charles Straumer; Music by: Pete Rugolo; Art Director: Robert Luthardt; Film Editor: Robert L. Kimble; Sound: Melvin M. Metcalfe, Sr.; Assistant Director: Marty Hornstein; Color by: Technicolor; Titles & Optical Effects: Universal Title; Produced by: Roy Huggins-Public Arts Productions; In Association with: Universal Television And NBC-TV; Exclusive Distributor: MCA Television Limited.

WINCHESTER 73
(WORLD PREMIERE/NBC TUESDAY NIGHT AT THE MOVIES)

NBC Television Network, March 14, 1967; 120 minutes in color on film.

A Western about gunsmith Bart McAdam who donated his "one in a thousand" Winchester rifle as a prize to the best marksman at a frontier town celebration. His nephew Lin, who was the sheriff, won the contest, but the gunsmith's son Dakin, an ex-convict, got the gun--by theft and murder. He quickly lost it in a poker game to "High Spade" Johnny Dean, who sold guns to the Indians. Lin, tracking cousin Dakin, caught up with him at a saloon run by Larouge. Dakin and henchman Preacher then cooked up a scheme to get rid of the sheriff. This telefeature was a remake of the 1950 film of the same title.

Cast: Lin McAdam (Tom Tryon), Dakin McAdam (John Saxon), Bart McAdam (Dan Duryea), The Preacher (John Drew Barrymore), Larouge (Joan Blondell), High Spade Johnny Dean (John Dehner), Jake Starret (John Doucette), Dan McAdam (David Pritchard), Ben McAdam (Paul Fix), Scots (Jack Lambert), Sun Rider (John Hoyt), Meriden (Barbara Luna), Santiago Ortega (Jan Arvan), Doc Beneke (Robert Bice), Young Bull (Ned Romero), Breed (George Keymas), Christmas Jones (Doodles Weaver), Col. Septimus Vane (Terry Wilson), Fat Sally (Jenie Jackson).

Credits: Produced by: Richard E. Lyons; Directed by: Herschel Daugherty; Written by: Stephen Kandel, Richard L. Adams; Based on a Screenplay by: Robert L. Richards, Borden Chase; Director of Photography: Bud Thackery, A.S.C.; Music by: Sol Kaplan; Art Director: Frank Arrigo; Set Decorations: John McCarthy, James Walters; Film Editor: Richard G. Wray, A.C.E.; Sound: Lyle Cain; Costumes by: Helen Colvig; Makeup: Bud Westmore; Color Coordinator: Robert Brower; Color by: Technicolor; Titles & Optical Effects: Universal Title; Produced by: Universal Television; In Association with: NBC-TV; Exclusive Distributor: MCA Television Limited.

WINGS OF FIRE
(WORLD PREMIERE/NBC TUESDAY NIGHT AT THE MOVIES)

NBC Television Network, February 14, 1967; 120 minutes in color on film.

The love of Kitty Sanborn for Taff Malloy was interrupted when he was called to Vietnam. Shaken, Kitty tried to find substitutes among other men. Meanwhile, financial troubles beset the small air freight service she ran with her father and his associate. Only her victory in an air race could provide the needed money. Before the race, Taff returned from Vietnam with a bride. On race day, Kitty winged into the clouds, but Taff wasn't sure whether she wanted to win or die.

242 / Telefeatures

Cast: Kitty Sanborn (Suzanne Pleshette), Taff Malloy (James Farentino), Max Clarity (Lloyd Nolan), Lisa (Juliet Mills), Hal Random (Jeremey Slate), Doug Sanborn (Ralph Bellamy), Scott (Gary Crosby), Luis Passos (Jaime Sanchez), Hotel Manager (John Hubbard), Naval Officer (William Boyett), Doctor (Than Wyenn), 1st Reporter (Frank Roach), 2nd Reporter (Bill Baldwin), 3rd Reporter (Clyde Howdy).

Credits: Produced and Directed by: David Lowell Rich; Written by: Stirling Silliphant; Director of Photography: Bud Thackery, A.S.C.; Music by: Samuel Matlovsky; Art Director: Frank Arrigo; Film Editor: Tony Martinelli, A.C.E.; Sound: James T. Porter; Aerial Photography by: Ray Fernstrom, A.S.C.; Costumes by: Burton Miller; Makeup: Bud Westmore; Color Coordinator: Robert Brower; Color by: Technicolor; Titles & Optical Effects: Universal Title; Produced by: Universal Television; In Association with: NBC-TV; Exclusive Distributor: MCA Television Limited.

YOU LIE SO DEEP, MY LOVE
(ABC TUESDAY MOVIE OF THE WEEK)

ABC Television Network, February 25, 1975; 90 minutes in color on film.

A suspense drama about a man who killed his mistress when he mistook her for his wife in a dark house. He buried the body in a pavilion under construction on his front lawn.

Cast: Neal Collins (Don Galloway), Susan Collins (Barbara Anderson), Jennifer Pierce (Angel Tompkins), Uncle Joe Padway (Walter Pidgeon), Ellen (Anne Schedeen), The Foreman (Russell Johnson), The Maid (Virginia Gregg), Tom File (Robert Rothwell), Phyllis (Bobbi Jordan), Jordan (Pitt Herbert).

Credits: Produced and Directed by: David Lowell Rich; Written by: John Neufeld, Robert Hamner; Story by: William L. Stuart, Robert Hamner; Director of Photography: Leonard J. South; Music by: Elliot Kaplan; Art Director: Ira Diamond; Film Editor: Asa Clark; Color by: Technicolor; Titles & Optical Effects: Universal Title; Produced by: Universal Television; Exclusive Distributor: MCA Television Limited.

YOU'LL NEVER SEE ME AGAIN
(ABC WEDNESDAY MOVIE OF THE WEEK)

ABC Television Network, February 28, 1973; 90 minutes in color on film.

A drama about a young wife who mysteriously disappeared after a quarrel with her husband. His frantic search uncovered evidence which implicated him as her murderer.

Cast: Ned Bliss (David Hartman), Lt. Stillman (Joseph Campanella), Mary Alden (Jane Wyatt), Will Alden (Ralph Meeker), Vicki Bliss (Jess Walton), Sam (Bo Svenson), Bob (Colby Chester), Desk Sergeant (George Murdock).

Credits: Executive Producer: Harve Bennett; Produced by: David J. O'Connell; Directed by: Jeannot Szwarc; Written by: William Wood, Gerald DiPego; Based on a Short Story by: Cornell Woolrich; Director of Photography: Walter Strenge; Music by: Richard Clements; Art Director: Sydney Z. Litwack; Film Editor: Richard G. Wray; Color by: Technicolor; Titles & Optical Effects: Universal Title; Produced by: Silverton Productions, Inc.; In Association with: Universal Television; Exclusive Distributor: MCA Television Limited.

THE YOUNG COUNTRY
(ABC MOVIE OF THE WEEK)

ABC Television Network, March 17, 1970; 90 minutes in color on film.

A rollicking Western about a young gambler and his search for the rightful heir to a mysterious fortune of $38,000.

Cast: Sheriff Fenley (Walter Brennan), Clementine Hale (Joan Hackett), Aron Grimes (Wally Cox), Honest John Smith (Pete Deuel), Stephen Foster Moody (Roger Davis), Parker (Steve Sandor), Harvey "Fat" Chance (Robert Driscoll), Randy Wills (Richard Van Fleet).

Credits: Produced and Directed by: Roy Huggins; Written by: Roy Huggins; Associate Producers: Carl Pingitore, Steve Heilpern; Director of Photography: Vilis Lapenieks; Music by: Pete Rugolo; Art Director: Joseph Alves, Jr.; Film Editor: Robert Watts; Unit Manager: Marty Hornstein; Assistant Director: Richard Bennett; Color by: Technicolor; Titles & Optical Effects: Universal Title; Produced by: Roy Huggins-Public Arts Productions; In Association with: Universal Television; Exclusive Distributor: MCA Television Limited.

THE PILOTS

Note

This section covers only 30-minute and 60-minute pilots. Most Universal Television pilots were produced as 90-minute and 120-minute TV-movies. They are listed in the TELEFEATURES section.

THE BAY CITY AMUSEMENT COMPANY

NBC Television Network, July 28, 1977; 30 minutes in color on film.

A situation comedy set at a zany TV station in San Francisco.

Cast: Alan (Dennis Howard), Ann (Barrie Youngfellow), Clifford (Terry Kiser), Howie (Pat McCormick), Gail (June Gable), Bradshaw (Ted Gehring), Warren (Jim Scott).

Credits: Executive Producer: Norman Steinberg; Produced by: Bo Kaprall; Directors: Norman Steinberg, Gary Shimokawa; Writers: Ken Levine, David Isaacs; Color by: Technicolor; Titles & Optical Effects: Universal Title; Produced by: Universal Television; Exclusive Distributor: MCA Television Limited.

BOBBY PARKER AND COMPANY

NBC Television Network, April 22, 1974; 30 minutes in color on film.

A situation comedy about a man whose hangups followed him around in imagined human form. Produced in 1970.

Cast: Bobby Parker (Ted Bessell).

Credits: Color by: Technicolor; Titles & Optical Effects: Universal Title; Produced by: Universal Television; Exclusive Distributor: MCA Television Limited.

246 / Pilots

BOSTON AND KILBRIDE

CBS Television Network, March 3, 1979; 60 minutes in color on film.

A pair of freewheeling private detectives and a girl pilot took on a wacky but perilous mission in Central America involving a stolen jetliner, a multi-million dollar swindler who was a fugitive from U.S. law, and a blueprint for a revolutionary but bogus Chinese typewriter. This was the second pilot to feature the team of James Whitmore, Jr. and Tom Selleck. The first was The Gypsy Warriors (which see).

Cast: Tom Boston (Tom Selleck), Jim Kilbride (James Whitmore, Jr.), Jill Miller (Jamie Lyn Bauer), Devlin (William Daniels), Beller (Don Ameche), Louise (Lane Bradbury), Toby Nash (Kathryn Leigh Scott), Turgeyev (David Palmer), Markov (George Fisher), Manolito (Walt Davis), Dianne (Elizabeth Halliday), Vince (Michael Brick), Mrs. Beller (June Whitley Taylor), Marie Sangria (Marlena Amey).

Credits: Executive Producers: Stephen J. Cannell, Alex Beaton; Directed by: Lou Antonio; Written by: Stephen J. Cannell; Color by: Technicolor; Titles & Optical Effects: Universal Title; Produced by: Stephen J. Cannell Productions, Universal Television; Exclusive Distributor: MCA Television Limited.

CAR WASH

NBC Television Network, May 24, 1979; 30 minutes in color on film.

A situation comedy about the zany goings on at an "auto laundry." Based on the 1976 film of the same title.

Cast: Danny Aiello, Hilary Beane, Stuart Pankin, Sheryl Lee Ralph, Matt Landers, and John Anthony Bailey.

Credits: Executive Producers: Leonard B. Stern, Arne Sultan; Color by: Technicolor; Titles & Optical Effects: Universal Title; Produced by: Heyday Productions; In Association with: Universal Television; Exclusive Distributor: MCA Television Limited.

THE DETECTIVE: BULL IN A CHINA SHOP

NBC Television Network, October 12, 1975; 30 minutes in color on film.

A comedy-drama about Det. Dennis O'Finn, who became involved in a murder case with four old women.

Cast: Det. Dennis O'Finn (Larry Hagman), Miss Hildy-Lou (Helen Kleeb), Miss Bessie (Hope Summers), Miss Amantha (Helen Craig), Miss Birdie (Shirley O'Hara).

Credits: Produced by: Jules Irving; Directed by: Jules Irving; Written by: Sarett Rudley; Color by: Technicolor; Titles & Optical Effects: Universal Title; Produced by: Universal Television; Exclusive Distributor: MCA Television Limited.

DOCTOR DAN

NBC Television Network, April 22, 1974; 30 minutes in color on film.

A situation comedy about a child guidance psychologist whose problems included a distrustful patient and a rebellious teenage daughter. Produced in 1970.

Cast: The Psychologist (Jackie Cooper), His Wife (Barbara Stuart).

Credits: Color by: Technicolor; Titles & Optical Effects: Universal Title; Produced by: Cooper-Finkel Co.; In Association with: Universal Television; Exclusive Distributor: MCA Television Limited.

·DUFFY

CBS Television Network, May 6, 1977; 30 minutes in color on film.

A situation comedy about a canine with lots of personality who became the mascot of a small-town high school.

Cast: Cliff Sellers (Fred Grandy), Marty Carter (Lane Binkley), Thomas N. Tibbles (Roger Bowen), Happy Jack (George Wyner), Mrs. Dreifuss (Jane Lambert), Postman (Dick Yarmy), Nick (John Sheldon), Danny (Jarrod Johnson), Craig (John Herbsleb), Friendly Bum (Robert E. Ball), Neighbor (Jane Dulo), Duffy (Himself).

Credits: Produced by: George Eckstein; Directed by: Bruce Bilson; Written by: Richard DeRoy; Titles & Optical Effects: Universal Title; Color by: Technicolor; Produced by: Universal Television; Exclusive Distributor: MCA Television Limited.

THE GYPSY WARRIORS

CBS Television Network, May 12, 1978; 60 minutes in color on film.

An action program about the World War II adventures of Capt. Shelly Alhern and Capt. Ted Brinkerhoff. This was the first pilot to feature the team of James Whitmore, Jr. and Tom Selleck. The second was Boston and Kilbride (which see).

Cast: Capt. Shelly Alhern (James Whitmore, Jr.), Capt. Ted Brinkerhoff (Tom Selleck), Ganault (Joseph Ruskin), Lela (Lina Raymond), Androck (Michael Lane), Bruno Schlagel (Albert Paulsen), Schulman (Kenneth L. Tigar), Ramon Pierre Cammus (William Wheatley), Henry Deseau (Hubert Noel), Lady Britt Austin-Forbes (Kathryn Leigh Scott), Communications Officer (Chris Anders).

Credits: Executive Producer: Stephen J. Cannell; Produced by: Alex Beaton; Directed by: Lou Antonio; Written by: Stephen J. Cannell, Philip DeGuere; Director of Photography: Enzo A. Martinelli, A.S.C.; Art Director: John D. Jefferies; Film Editors: George R. Potter, Christopher Nelson; Set Decorations: Robert Freer; Color by: Technicolor; Titles & Optical Effects: Universal Title; Produced by: Stephen J. Cannell Productions, Universal Television; Exclusive Distributor: MCA Television Limited.

HAZARD'S PEOPLE

CBS Television Network, April 9, 1976; 60 minutes in color on film.

A drama about defense attorney John Hazard and his client, a renowned doctor who was accused of slaying his girlfriend. Telecast on The CBS Friday Night Movies.

Cast: John Hazard (John Houseman), Michael Crowder (John Elerick), Trish Corelli (Jesse Welles), Ernest Clay (Roger Hill), Dr. Carl DeLacy (Michael Tolan), Mrs. DeLacy (Hope Lange), D.A. Robert Powell (Stefan Gierasch), Sylvia Freed (Doreen Lang), with: Cliff Emmich, Richard Herd, E. A. Sirianni, Eric Server, James Whitmore, Jr., Don Maxwell, Joseph Burke, Rod Colbin.

Credits: Executive Producer: Jo Swerling, Jr.; Produced by: Roy Huggins; Directed by: Jeannot Szwarc; Written by: Heywood Gould; Director of Photography: Charles Correll; Music by: John Cacavas; Film Editors: Tony Redman, Robert Leeds; Color by: Technicolor; Titles & Optical Effects: Universal Title; Produced by: Roy Huggins-Public Arts Productions; In Association with: Universal Television And NBC-TV; Exclusive Distributor: MCA Television Limited.

IF I HAD A MILLION

NBC Television Network, December 31, 1973; 60 minutes in color on film.

This pilot probed the effects of a million tax-free dollars on several people, including a syndicate chauffeur afraid to tell his sinister employees about the money; an old, unwanted lady with a selfish family; and a man torn between his wife and his mistress. Telecast on the NBC Monday Movie.

"The Good Boy"
Cast: John Schuck, Louis Zorich, Val Bisoglio, Doolie Brown.

"The Searchers"
Cast: Joseph Wiseman, Ruth McDevitt, Gerald Hiken, Rae Allen.

"Three"
Cast: Kenneth Mars, Elayne Heilveil, Melendy Britt.

"First the Tube, and Now You, Darling"
Cast: Brett Somers, Ted Gehring.

Credits: Executive Producer: David Levinson; Produced by: James McAdams; Directed by: Daryl Duke; Director of Photography: Sam Leavitt; Film Editors: Richard Bracken, Sigmund Neufeld, Jr.; Sound: David H. Moriarty; "The Good Boy" Written by: Lionel E. Siegel, Herbert Wright, From a Story by: Lionel E. Siegel; "The Searchers" Written by: Robert Van Scoyk; "Three" Written by: M. Charles Cohen; "First the Tube, and Now You, Darling" Written by: Oliver Hailey; Color by: Technicolor; Titles & Optical Effects: Universal Title; Produced by: Universal Television; In Association with: NBC-TV; Exclusive Distributor: MCA Television Limited.

JAMISON'S KIDS

ABC Television Network, 1971; 30 minutes in color on film.

A comedy drama about a dedicated worker in a rural adoption and foster care agency.

Cast: Jamison (Gary Collins).

Credits: Color by: Technicolor; Titles & Optical Effects: Universal Title; Produced by: Universal Television; Exclusive Distributor: MCA Television Limited.

KOSKA AND HIS FAMILY

NBC Television Network, December 31, 1973; 60 minutes in color on film.

A situation comedy about an unemployed aerospace technician who was too qualified for the few jobs he might have found. But his irrepressible optimism and slightly crazy family pulled him through. Telecast on the NBC Monday Movie.

Cast: Koska (Herb Edelman), Isabel (Barbara Barrie), Grandpa (Liam Dunn), Jimmy (Jack David Walker), Gina (Ellen Sherman), Al (Albert Henderson), Eugene (Jack Sollins), Wilhelmina (Nora Marlowe).

Credits: Executive Producer: Leonard B. Stern; Produced by: Ted Rich; Directed by: Dan Dailey; Writers: Roger Price, Leonard B. Stern; Director of Photography: Lloyd Ahern; Film Editor: Ted Rich; Color by: Technicolor; Titles & Optical Effects: Universal Title; Produced by: Universal Television; Exclusive Distributor: MCA Television Limited.

LADY LUCK

NBC Television Network, February 12, 1973; 30 minutes in color on film.

A situation comedy about a mysterious woman who popped into people's lives when they needed a little luck. Telecast on the NBC World Premiere movie.

Cast: Lady Luck (Laura) (Valerie Perrine), Roger (Paul Sand), Clay (Bert Convy), Penny (Sallie Shockley), Walter (J.D. Cannon).

Credits: Color by: Technicolor; Titles & Optical Effects: Universal Title; Produced by: Universal Television; Exclusive Distributor: MCA Television Limited.

OFF THE WALL

NBC Television Network, May 7, 1977; 30 minutes in color on film.

A situation comedy about the advisor in a western university's co-ed dorm.

Cast: Arthur (Frank O'Brien), Matthew Bozeman (Todd Susman), Flash (Harry Gold), Gordon (Sean Roche), Melvin (Sandy Helberg), Jeanie (Dana House), Mother (Hal Williams), Lenny (Barbara Deutsch).

Credits: Executive Producer: Franklin Barton; Producers: George Tricker, Neil Rosen; Directed by: Bob LaHendro; Writers: George Tricker, Neil Rosen; Music by: Mike Post, Pete Carpenter; Lyrics by: Harry Gold; Color by: Technicolor; Titles & Optical Effects: Universal Title; Produced by: Franklin Barton Productions, Universal Television; In Association with: NBC-TV; Exclusive Distributor: MCA Television Limited.

PETE 'N' TILLIE

CBS Television Network, March 28, 1974; 30 minutes in color on film.

A situation comedy about a newly-married social worker who drove her husband crazy by bringing her work home from the office.

Cast: Tillie (Cloris Leachman), Pete (Carmine Caridi), Norma Jean (Mabel Albertson).

Credits: Color by: Technicolor; Titles & Optical Effects: Universal Title; Produced by: Universal Television; Exclusive Distributor: MCA Television Limited.

ROOSEVELT AND TRUMAN

CBS Television Network, May 25, 1977; 30 minutes in color on film.

A situation comedy about Roosevelt and Truman, two crazies who ran a combination security-guard and bail-bond agency. Their motto: "We Nail 'Em, We Bail 'Em."

Cast: Roosevelt (Art Evans), Truman (Philip Thomas), Juanita (Ika Payan), Richie (Richard Karron), Reverend Davis (Hank Rolike), Rodriguez (Danny Mora), Mrs. Tilson (Minnie S. Lindsey), Garcia (Bert Rosario), Savoyan (Bob Manuel), Crawford (Tim Pelt), Quinn (Michael Keaton).

Credits: Executive Producer: Norman Steinberg; Produced by: Richard Dmitri; Created by: Norman Steinberg, Robert Dmitri; Directed by: James Burrows; Writers: Norman Steinberg, Richard Dmitri; Color by: Technicolor; Titles & Optical Effects: Universal Title; Produced by: Universal Television; Exclusive Distributor: MCA Television Limited.

SNAFU

NBC Television Network, August 23, 1976; 30 minutes in color on film.

A situation comedy about a World War II combat unit in Europe.

Cast: Sgt. Mike Conroy (Tony Roberts), Cpl. Billy Kaminski (James Cromwell), Lt. Hemsley Hauser (Kip Niven), Wiggins (Fred Fate), Crosetti (Joey Aresco), Hinkley (Wally Dalton), Capt. Robinson (Phillip R. Allen), Lockwood (Terry Hinz), Braverman (Jay Leno), Fowler (Rick Podell).

Credits: Executive Producer: Leonard B. Stern; Produced by: Arnie Rosen; Directed by: Jackie Cooper; Written by: Arnie Rosen, Leonard B. Stern; Color by: Technicolor; Titles & Optical Effects: Universal Title; Produced by: Heyday Productions; In Association with: Universal Television And NBC-TV; Exclusive Distributor: MCA Television Limited.

252 / Pilots

STRANDED

CBS Television Network, May 26, 1976; 60 minutes in color on film.

An action-adventure drama about the survivors of an Australia-bound airliner which crashed on an isolated South Pacific island.

Cast: Sgt. Rafe Harder (Kevin Dobson), Crystal Norton (Lara Parker), Rose Orselli (Marie Windsor), Julie Blake (Devon Ericson), Tim Blake (Jimmy McNichol), John Rados (Rex Everhart), Ali Baba (Erin Blunt), Burt Hansen (Lal Baum), Jerry Holmes (James Cromwell), Charley Lee (John Fujioka).

Credits: Executive Producer: David Victor; Produced by: Howie Horwitz; Directed by: Earl Bellamy; Written by: Anthony Lawrence; Based on a Story by: Anthony Lawrence, David Victor; Director of Photography: Allen M. Davey; Music by: Gordon Jenkins; Film Editor: Robert F. Shugrue; Art Director: David Marshall; Set Decorations: Anthony Montenaro; Color by: Technicolor; Titles & Optical Effects: Universal Title; Produced by: Groverton Productions, Ltd. And Universal Television; Exclusive Distributor: MCA Television Limited.

THE SWEET LIFE

NBC Television Network, March 7, 1966; 60 minutes in color on film.

The pilot for an unsold series to star Bobby Darin, telecast as "Who's Watching the Fleshpot?," an episode of Run for Your Life.

Cast: Bobby Darin, Eve Arden, Jeff Corey, Davey Davison.

Credits: Executive Producer: Roy Huggins; Produced by: Jo Swerling, Jr.; Written by: John Thomas James; Color by: Technicolor; Titles & Optical Effects: Universal Title; Produced by: Roy Huggins-Public Arts Productions; In Association with: Universal Television And NBC-TV; Exclusive Distributor: MCA Television Limited.

THREE TIMES DALEY

CBS Television Network, August 3, 1976; 30 minutes in color on film.

A situation comedy about a divorced newspaper columnist.

Cast: Bob Daley (Don Adams), Alex Daley (Liam Dunn), Wes Daley (Jerry Houser), Stacy (Bibi Besch), Jenny (Ayn Ruyman).

Credits: Executive Producer: Leonard B. Stern; Produced and Created by: John Rappaport; Directed by: Jay Sandrich; Written by: John Rappaport; Musical Director: Don Costa; Color by: Technicolor; Titles & Optical Effects: Universal Title; Produced by: Heyday Productions; In Association with: Universal Television; Exclusive Distributor: MCA Television Limited.

THE TWO-FIVE

ABC Television Network, January 7, 1979; 60 minutes in color on film.

A comedy-drama about two bungling undercover detectives (Charlie Morgan and Frank Sarno) who stumbled onto a mob accountant and his computer printout for the entire illegal operation and competed with hitmen, FBI agents and special police as they tried to get official credit for the bust.

Cast: Charlie Morgan (Don Johnson), Frank Sarno (Joe Bennett), Capt. Paul Carter (John Crawford), Commander Malloy (George Murdock), Vinnie Lombardo (Michael Durrell), J. Edward Ward (Shelley Berman).

Credits: Executive Producer: R. A. Cinader; Producers: Gino Grimaldi, Hannah Shearer; Directed by: Jules Irving; Written by: R. A. Cinader; Story by: R. A. Cinader, Joseph Pelizzi; Director of Photography: Frank Thackery; Film Editor: John Kaufman; Art Director: Richard Lewis; Produced by: Universal Television; Exclusive Distributor: MCA Television Limited.

THE SPECIALS

THE ADVENTURES OF DON QUIXOTE

CBS Television Network, April 23, 1973; 120 minutes in color on film. Sponsored by IBM.

A drama about the funny, sad, romantic adventures of the man of La Mancha. Based on the 17th-century classic by Cervantes. Filmed on location on the Spanish plains of La Mancha.

Cast: Don Quixote (Rex Harrison), Sancho Panza (Frank Finlay), Dulcinea (Rosemary Leach), The Priest (Bernard Hepton), The Duke (Robert Eddison), Traveling Barber (Murray Melvin), The Monk (Roger Delgado).

Credits: Produced by: Gerald Savory; Directed by: Alvin Rakoff; Written by: Hugh Whitmore; Based on the Novel by: Cervantes; Director of Photography: Peter Bartlett; Music by: Michel Legrand; Produced by: Universal Television, BBC-TV.

ALONE WITH TERROR
(ABC MATINEE TODAY)

ABC Television Network, December 5, 1973; 90 minutes in color on tape.

Susan Maroni put her life in jeopardy to set a trap for the killer of her policeman husband.

Cast: Susan Maroni (Juliet Mills), Leonard Walters (Colby Chester), Joe Maroni (Paul Shenar), Marian (Virginia Vincent), Ryan (Charles Shull), Sam (Joe Bernard), Betty (Lilliam Lehman), Roperman (Nancy Stephens), Mr. Stone (Patrick O'Moore), Frank Loomis (Vince Howard), Anthony (Allen Price), Helen (Shelly Hines).

Credits: Executive Producer: Barbara Schultz; Directed by: Mike Onofrio; Written by: Art Wallace; Produced by: Universal Television.

APPLAUSE

CBS Television Network, March 15, 1973; 120 minutes in color on tape. Sponsored by Connecticut General Life Insurance Co. and Volkswagen.

A special performance of the 1970 Tony award winner (Best Musical; Best Actress in a Musical, Lauren Bacall) taped in London. Based on the 1950 film All About Eve. The songs included "Who's That Girl?," "The Best Night of My Life," "But Alive," "Fasten Your Seat Belts," "One of a Kind," "Something Greater," "Welcome to the Theatre," and "Applause."

Cast: Margo Channing (Lauren Bacall), Eve Harrington (Penny Fuller), Bill Sampson (Larry Hagman), Howard Benedict (Robert Mandan), Duane Fox (Harvey Evans), Buzz Richards (Rod McLennan), Karen Richards (Sarah Marshall), Bert (Bob Sherman), Peter (David Knight), Stan (James Berwick), Bonnie (Debbie Bowen).

Credits: Produced by: Richard Rosenbloom, Lawrence Kasha, Joseph Kipness; Directed by: Ron Field, Bill Foster; Written by: Betty Comden, Adolph Green; Music and Lyrics by: Charles Strouse, Lee Adams; Choreography by: Ron Field; Produced by: Universal Pictures Television, Ltd.

THE CAY
(BELL SYSTEM FAMILY THEATRE)

NBC Television Network, October 21, 1974; 60 minutes in color on film. Sponsor and Agency: The American Telephone and Telegraph Company through N. W. Ayer & Son, Inc.

Timothy was an aging West Indian crew member of a tramp steamer in the Caribbean Sea during World War II. He rescued Phillip, an 11-year-old American boy, when their ship was torpedoed by a Nazi submarine. Together they reached a tiny island where Timothy taught Phillip the art of survival. Filmed on location at Grand Caye Isle and Belize City, Belize (British Honduras).

Cast: Timothy (James Earl Jones), Phillip (Alfred Lutter III), Phillip's Mother (Gretchen Corbett).

Credits: Executive Producer: Frank O'Connor; Produced by: Russell Thacher, Walter Seltzer; Directed by: Patrick Garland; Written by: Russell Thacher; Based on the Novel by: Theodore Taylor; Directors of Photography: Rosalio Solano, Alric Edens; Music by: Carl Davis; Film Editor: Douglas Stewart; Produced by: Russell Thacher-Walter Seltzer Productions; In Association with: Universal Television.

FUNNY BUSINESS

CBS Television Network, July 26, 1978; 120 minutes in color on film.

A retrospective which spotlighted the greatest comedies of the 1930s and 1940s, with more than 100 film clips including Laurel and Hardy, the Marx Brothers in Duck Soup, Abbott and Costello in One Night in the Tropics, Hope and Crosby in the Road pictures, Mae West in She Done Him Wrong, W. C. Fields in The Old Fashioned Way, and Fields and West in My Little Chickadee.

Cast: Host, Walter Matthau.

Credits: Executive Producer: Leonard B. Stern; Produced, Written and Directed by: Richard Schickel; Associate Producer: Volney Howard; Produced by: Heyday Productions; In Association with: Universal Television; Exclusive Distributor: MCA Television Limited.

HAMLET
(HALLMARK HALL OF FAME)

NBC Television Network, November 17, 1970; 120 minutes in color on tape. Sponsor and Agency: Hallmark Cards, Inc. through Foote, Cone & Belding, Inc.

A new production of Shakespeare's classic set in the early 1800s. Produced on location at historic Raby Castle in the north of England, and in London.

Cast: Hamlet (Richard Chamberlain), Polonius (Sir Michael Redgrave), Gertrude (Margaret Leighton), Claudius (Richard Johnson), The Ghost (Sir John Gielgud), Ophelia (Ciaran Madden), Laertes (Nicholas Jones), Horatio (Martin Shaw), Rosencrantz (James Laurenson), Guildenstern (Desmond McNamara), Osric (Alan Bennett), Gravedigger (Norman Rossington), First Player (Nigel Stock), Marcellus (Godfrey James), Barnardo (Philip Brack), Francisco (Robert Oates), Fortinbras (Robert Coleby), Priest (Donald Layne-Smith), Captain (Roger Green), Players (David Belcher, Helen Bourne, Alan Adams, Stephen Williams, Donald Barclay).

Credits: Executive Producer: Cecil Clarke; Produced by: George LeMaire; Directed by: Peter Wood; Adapted for Television by: John Barton; Based on the Play by: William Shakespeare; Music Composed and Conducted by: John Addison; Duel Staged by: John Barton; Pantomime Staged by: Claude Chagrin; Choral Singing by: The Wandsworth Boys' School Choir; Scenery Designer: Peter Roden; Senior Cameraman: Bill Brown; Audio: Henry Bird; Senior Video Engineer: Jim Reeves; Video Tape Editor: Ray Knipe; Film Editor: George Clark; Graphic Design: George Wallder; Stage Manager: Sheila Atha; Assistant Producer: Lorna Mason; Lighting

258 / Specials

Director: John Rook; Costume Supervisor: Martin Baugh; Makeup Supervisor: Marie Roche; Assistant to the Director: David Walker; Produced by: Chamberlain-LeMaire Productions; In Association with: ATV Network Limited And Universal Television.

THE JACK BENNY SPECIAL

NBC Television Network, March 20, 1968; 60 minutes in color on tape. Sponsored by Celanese Fortrel.

A "carnival of comedy" which featured Johnny Carson as a carnival barker who did a take-off on Benny; Lucille Ball as a stripper who did impersonations of Cleopatra and Helen of Troy; vaudevillian Ben Blue, who performed pantomime; rock 'n' roll artists Paul Revere and the Raiders, who did "Too Much Talk" and "What's It Gonna Be, Him or Me?"--aided by Mr. Benny on the violin.

Cast: Jack Benny, Lucille Ball, Johnny Carson, Ben Blue, Paul Revere and the Raiders, Bob Hope, Danny Thomas, George Burns, Dean Martin, Tom Smothers, Dick Smothers, Don Drysdale.

Credits: Choreography by: Jack Regas; Music by: Earl Brown, Jack Elliot; Music Conducted by: Jack Elliot; Choral Director: Earl Brown; Produced by: J.B. Productions, Universal Television; Exclusive Distributor: MCA Television Limited.

LEGEND IN GRANITE
(PORTRAIT/DuPONT CAVALCADE OF TELEVISION)

ABC Television Network, December 14, 1973; 60 minutes in color on film. Sponsor and Agency: DuPont through Batten, Barton, Durstine & Osborn, Inc.

A drama about professional football player Vince Lombardi in his last two years, during which he led the last-place Green Bay Packers to an NFL playoff spot.

Cast: Vince Lombardi (Ernest Borgnine), Marie Lombardi (Colleen Dewhurst), Max McGee (James Olson), Paul Hornung (John Calvin), Dom Olejniczak (John McLiam), Tony Canadeo (Alex Rocco).

Credits: Executive Producer: David Victor; Color by: Technicolor; Titles & Optical Effects: Universal Title; Produced by: Groverton Productions, Ltd.; In Association with: Universal Television; Exclusive Distributor: MCA Television Limited.

THE MAN FROM INDEPENDENCE
(PORTRAIT/DuPONT CAVALCADE OF TELEVISION)

ABC Television Network, March 11, 1974; 60 minutes in color on

The Man from Independence / 259

film. Sponsor and Agency: DuPont through Batten, Barton, Durstine & Osborn, Inc.

A drama about an eventful year in the life of Harry S Truman. In 1929, his judgeship in Independence, Missouri put him in conflict with political boss Tom Pendergast and various contractors.

Cast: Harry S Truman (Robert Vaughn), Tom Pendergast (Arthur Kennedy), Mamma Truman (Martha Scott), Bess Truman (June Dayton), Linaver (Russell Johnson), Constance (Ronne Troup), Mooney (Alan Fudge), Margaret Truman (age 6) (Tasha Lee), Stranger (James Luisi), Quilling (Lou Frizzell), Werner (Leonard Stone), Dayton (Michael Vandever), Teacher (Alice Backes), Pete (Jay Virela).

Credits: Executive Producer: David Victor; Produced by: Jon Epstein; Directed by: Jack Smight; Written by: Edward DeBlasio; Director of Photography: Leonard J. South; Music by: Elmer Bernstein; Art Director: George C. Webb; Film Editor: J. Jerry Williams; Makeup: John Chambers; Color by: Technicolor; Titles & Optical Effects: Universal Title; Produced by: Groverton Productions, Ltd.; In Association with: Universal Television; Exclusive Distributor: MCA Television Limited.

THE MAN WHO CAME TO DINNER
(HALLMARK HALL OF FAME)

NBC Television Network, November 29, 1972; 90 minutes in color on tape. Sponsor and Agency: Hallmark Cards, Inc. through Foote, Cone & Belding, Inc.

A comedy about Sheridan Whiteside, a noted personality who liked to have his own way. He injured his hip and was forced to stay in the home of a family in a small Ohio town. He immediately took over and held court for friends as he tried to run the lives of those around him.

Cast: Sheridan Whiteside (Orson Welles), Maggie Cutler (Lee Remick), Lorraine Sheldon (Joan Collins), Bert Jefferson (Peter Haskell), Mr. Stanley (Edward Andrews), Miss Preen (Mary Wickes), Banjo (Marty Feldman), Dr. Bradley (Don Knotts), Mrs. Stanley (Marcella Markham), Harriet Stanley (Anita Sharp Bolster), Beverly Carlton (Michael Gough), Professor Metz (George Pravda), June Stanley (Kim Braden), John (Frank Singuinea), Sarah (Elisabeth Welch), Zoltan (Tutte Lemkow), Mrs. McCutcheon (Betty McDowall), Westcott (Al Mancini), Delivery Express Man (Hal Calili).

Credits: Executive Producer for Foote, Cone & Belding Productions: Duane C. Bogie; Executive Producer for Universal Television: Frank O'Connor; Producers: Bill Persky, Sem Denoff; Directed by: Buzz Kulik; Adapted for Television by: Bill Persky, Sam Denoff; Based on the Play by: George S. Kaufman, Moss Hart;

Set Decorator: John Dilly; Costume Supervisor: Beatrice Dawson; Floor Manager: Peter Lover; Music by: Roy Budd; Casting by: Maude Spector; Taped at: Independent Television Corporation Studios, Southampton, England; Produced by: Foote, Cone & Belding Productions; In Association with: Universal Television.

A MAN WHOSE NAME WAS JOHN
(PORTRAIT/DuPONT CAVALCADE OF TELEVISION)

ABC Television Network, April 22, 1973; 60 minutes in color on film. Sponsor and Agency: DuPont through Batten, Barton, Durstine & Osborn, Inc.

A drama about Archbishop Angelo Roncalli, the man who became Pope John XXIII. Apostolic delegate to Turkey during World War II, Roncalli had to stop a ship carrying Jewish children from going to Nazi Germany.

Cast: Archbishop Angelo Roncalli (Pope John XXIII) (Raymond Burr), Monsignor Thomas Ryan (Don Galloway), Rabbi Isaac Herzog (David Opatoshu), Under-Secretary Numan Menemengioglu (John Colicos), Minister Calheiros De Menezes (Henry Darrow), Col. Gunter Kroll (Eric Braeden), Capt. Melech Ben Zvi (Scott Hylands), Rachael Friedman (Alizia Gur), Joseph Kahn (Gil Anov), Maria Roncalli (Penny Santon), Ambassador Franz Von Papen (Peter Von Zerneck), Clete Roberts (Himself), Marta (Diana Ferziger).

Credits: Executive Producer: David Victor; Produced by: David J. O'Connell; Directed by: Buzz Kulik; Written by: John Mc-Greevey; Color by: Technicolor; Titles & Optical Effects: Universal Title; Makeup: Nick Marcellino, James Lee McCoy; Produced by: Groverton Productions, Ltd.; In Association with: Universal Television; Exclusive Distributor: MCA Television Limited.

THE MASK OF LOVE
(ABC MATINEE TODAY)

ABC Television Network, December 7, 1973; 90 minutes in color on tape.

John Connors, a writer working on a biography of the famous author Jeffrey Aspern, desperately needed the author's valuable unpublished papers to compete his work. He duped Tina Bordereau, the niece of the author's mistress, into participating in a scheme of trickery and deceit to obtain the papers.

Cast: Tina Bordereau (Barbara Barrie), John Connors (Harris Yulin), Juliana Bordereau (Cathleen Nesbitt), Maria (Geraldine Brooks).

Credits: Executive Producer: Barbara Schultz; Directed by: Burt

Brinckerhoff; Written by: Sherman Yellen; Produced by: Universal Television.

MOTHER OF THE BRIDE
(ABC AFTERNOON PLAYBREAK)

ABC Television Network, January 9, 1974; 90 minutes in color on tape.

A comedy-drama about Mrs. Owens, a woman who had six days to arrange an all-stops-out wedding for her daughter. There was just one problem: the daughter wanted a simple ceremony with her own vows and health food at the reception.

Cast: Mrs. Owens (Eve Arden), Jody Owens (Jennifer Salt), Steve Whitman (Kip Niven), George Owens (Don Porter), Harry Prosnick (Philip Sterling), Mrs. Whitman (Elizabeth Allen), Mr. Whitman (Elliott Reid), with: Regis J. Cordic.

Credits: Produced by: Jay Benson; Directed by: Burt Brinckerhoff; Written by: Lila Garrett, Sandy Krinski; Produced by: Universal Television; Exclusive Distributor: MCA Television Limited.

MY SECRET MOTHER
(ABC MATINEE TODAY)

ABC Television Network, December 6, 1973; 90 minutes in color on tape.

A drama about Nora Sells, an 18-year-old adopted child who set out in search of her real mother.

Cast: Nora Sells (Sandra Locke), Mrs. Sells (Marge Redmond), Mary (Lola Albright), Carol (Rue McClanahan), Ellen (Maxine Stuart).

Credits: Executive Producer: Barbara Schultz; Directed by: Lela Swift; Written by: Roger Hirson; Produced by: Universal Television; Exclusive Distributor: MCA Television Limited.

THE RED PONY
(BELL SYSTEM FAMILY THEATRE)

NBC Television Network, March 18, 1973; 120 minutes in color on film. Sponsor and Agency: American Telephone and Telegraph Company through N. W. Ayer & Son, Inc.

The story of a poor farm family in turn-of-the-century California. Based on the 1949 film. Filmed on location in Sonora, Calif. and at the Samuel Goldwyn Studios in Hollywood.

262 / Specials

Cast: Carl Tiflin (Henry Fonda), Ruth Tiflin (Maureen O'Hara), Jess Taylor (Ben Johnson), The Grandfather (Jack Elam), Ditano (Julian Rivero), Jody Tiflin (Clint Howard), James Creighton (Richard Jaeckel), Sheriff Bill Smith (Rance Howard), Dearie (Lieux Dressler), Barton (Warren Douglas), Mr. Sing/Mr. Green (Victor Sen Yung), Orville Frye (Woodrow Chambliss), Toby (Roy Jenson).

Credits: Executive In Charge of Production: Fred Hamilton; Produced by: Frederick Brogger; Directed by: Robert Totten; Written by: Robert Totten, Ron Bishop; Based on the Novel by: John Steinbeck; Associate Producer: Ray Kellogg; Music Composed & Conducted by: Jerry Goldsmith; Director of Photography: Andrew Jackson, A.S.C.; Art Directors: Robert Boyle, James Hulsey; Set Decorations: John Kuri; Film Editor: Marsh Hendry; Production Supervisor: Clarence Eurist; Additional Photography: Frank Phillips, A.S.C., Lloyd Ahern, A.S.C.; Makeup: Allan Snyder, Richard Cobos; Hair Stylist: Bette Iverson; Wardrobe: Frank Balchus, Yvonne Wood; Technical Advisor: E. W. "Bud" Johnston; Produced by: Omnibus Productions And Universal Television; In Association with: Robert Aller And NBC-TV.

SHORT STORIES OF LOVE

NBC Television Network, May 1, 1974; 120 minutes in color on film.

Three romantic stories by famous authors: "The Epicac," about a computer which fell in love with its programmer; "Kiss Me Again, Stranger," about a World War II veteran's romance with a murderess; and "The Fortunate Painter," about a man's scheme to help his daughter marry a penniless artist.

Cast: Host: Rex Harrison

"Epicac"
Cast: Julie Sommars, Bill Bixby, Roscoe Lee Browne.

"Kiss Me Again, Stranger"
Cast: Leonard Nimoy, Juliet Mills.

"The Fortunate Painter"
Cast: Lorne Greene, Agnes Moorehead, Jess Walton, Lawrence Casey, Claude Woolman, Fred Holliday, Robert Emhardt, Alan Hale, Jr.

Credits:
"Epicac"
Directed by: John Badham; Written by: Liam O'Brien; Based on the Story by: Kurt Vonnegut, Jr.

"Kiss Me Again, Stranger"
Directed by: Arnold Laven; Written by: Arthur Dales; Based on the Story by: Daphne du Maurier.

"The Fortunate Painter"
Based on the Story by: Somerset Maugham; Color by: Technicolor; Titles & Optical Effects: Universal Title; Produced by: Universal Television; Exclusive Distributor: MCA Television Limited.

THE SLOWEST GUN IN THE WEST
(THE PHIL SILVERS SPECIAL)

CBS Television Network, May 7, 1960; 60 minutes in black & white on film. Sponsor and Agencies: Carling Brewing Co. through Benton & Bowles, Inc. and Lang, Fisher & Stashower, Inc.

A Western spoof about Fletcher Bissell III, alias the Silver Dollar Kid, a violence-shunning Bostonian who used his lack of courage to tame the most turbulent hamlet in the history of the frontier.

Cast: The Silver Dollar Kid/Fletcher Bissell III (Phil Silvers), Chicken Finsterwald (Jack Benny), Nick Nolan (Bruce Cabot), Black Bart (Ted De Corsia), Ike Dalton (Jack Elam), Jack Dalton (Karl Lukas), Butcher Blake (Robert J. Wilke), Wild Bill (John Dierkes), Sam Bass (Lee Van Cleef), Kathy McQueen (Jean Willes), Collingwood (Parley Baer), Jebb Slocum (Tom Fadden), Elsie May (Marion Ross), Lulu Belle (Kathie Browne), Col. Dexter (Jack Albertson), Bartender (Edward Brophy), Jud McCoy (George Keymas), Mrs. Hotchkiss (Hallene Hill), Indian Woman (Bella Bruck), Mr. Simpson (George Chandler), Clerk (Byron Foulger), Man (Alan Dester), Boy (Billy Booth), Girl (Gina Gillespie), Wife (Jeanne Bates).

Credits: Executive Producer: William Frye; Produced and Written by: Nat Hiken; Directed by: Herschel Daugherty; Assistant Director: James H. Brown; Set Decorator: Rudy Butler; Costume Supervisor: Vincent Dee; Makeup: Jack Barron; Hair Stylist: Florence Bush; Produced by: Tra-Nan Productions, Revue Productions, Inc.; Exclusive Distributor: MCA Television Limited.

THE SNOW GOOSE
(HALLMARK HALL OF FAME)

NBC Television Network, November 15, 1971; 60 minutes in color on film. Sponsor and Agency: Hallmark Cards, Inc. through Foote, Cone & Belding, Inc.

Caring for a wounded snow goose in England during the late 1930s changed the lives of an embittered, lonely artist and a shy orphan girl. The drama reached a climax as the artist took part in rescue operations during the Battle of Dunkirk. Filmed on location on the east coast of England at Landermere, Essex.

Cast: Philip Rhayader (Richard Harris), Fritha (Jenny Agutter), Recruiting Officer (Graham Crowden), Postmistress (Freda Bamford), Naval Captain (Noel Johnson), Soldier (William Marlowe), Jane (Ludmila Nova).

Credits: Executive Producer for Foote, Cone & Belding Productions: Duane C. Bogie; Executive Producer for BBC-TV: Innes Lloyd; Produced by: Frank O'Connor; Directed by: Patrick Garland; Written for Television by: Paul Gallico; Based on the Story by: Paul Gallico; Director of Photography: Ray Henman; Music by: Carl Davis; 2nd Unit Photography by: Patrick Carey; Set Designer: Stanley Morris; Film Editor: Ken Pearce; Snow Goose Trainer: Ray Berwick; Paintings: Peter Scott (Severn Wildfowl Trust); Sound: Colin March; Special Effects: Jim Ward; Makeup: Anna Chesterman, Bill Lodge; Wardrobe: Ken Morey; Produced by: BBC-TV; In Association with: Universal Television.

A SPECIAL ACT OF LOVE
(ABC AFTERNOON PLAYBREAK)

ABC Television Network, November 14, 1973; 90 minutes in color on tape. Major Sponsors and Agency: Clairol, Inc., The Drackett Company and Bristol-Myers Products through Boclaro.

A drama about nurse Anne Ricciardi, a nun in a Catholic nursing order who married Dr. Howard Wellman only to discover that he was dying of Hodgkin's disease.

Cast: Anne Ricciardi (Diana Muldaur), Dr. Howard Wellman (Laurence Luckinbill), Mother Superior Elizabeth Vanier (Barbara Baxley), Dr. Jack Easton (Martin Brooks), Dr. Lesser (Norman Foster), Maureen Easton (Pat Hindy), Mark Berdon (Taldo Kenyon), Lydia Berdon (Ellen Moss), The Priest (Jason Johnson), Dr. Doland (Robert Burr), The Uncle (Peter Eastman), The Aunt (Barbara Smith).

Credits: Produced by: John Choy; Directed by: Burt Brinkerhoff; Written by: D. C. Fontana; Associate Producer: Matt Harmon; Assistant Director: Zane Radney; Production Designer: Ralph Holmes; Set Designer: Rick Goddard; Audio: Phil Dager; Video: Dean Terrell; Unit Manager: Russell Llewellyn; Executive In Charge of Production: Michael Scheff; Produced by: Universal Television; Exclusive Distributor: MCA Television Limited.

THE WOMAN I LOVE
(PORTRAIT /DuPONT CAVALCADE OF TELEVISION)

ABC Television Network, December 17, 1972; 60 minutes in color on film. Sponsor and Agency: DuPont through Batten, Barton, Durstine & Osborn, Inc.

A drama about the first meeting between twice-divorced American socialite Wallis Warfield Simpson and the dashing Prince of Wales, their courtship, his endeavors to marry the lady of his choice after becoming Edward VIII, King of England and, finally, his irrevocable decision to abdicate.

Cast: King Edward VIII (Richard Chamberlain), Mrs. Wallis Warfield Simpson (Faye Dunaway), Lord Brownlow (Patrick Macnee), Queen Mary (Eileen Herlie), Winston Churchill (Henry Oliver), Prime Minister Stanley Baldwin (Robert Douglas), Walter Monckton (Murray Matheson).

Credits: Executive Producer: David Victor; Produced by: David J. O'Connell; Directed by: Paul Wendkos; Written by: John McGreevey; Miss Dunaway's Costumes by: Theadora van Runkle; Mr. Chamberlain's Costumes by: Berman's of London; Color by: Technicolor; Titles & Optical Effects: Universal Title; Produced by: Groverton Productions, Ltd.; In Association with: Universal Television; Exclusive Distributor: MCA Television Limited.

THE EMMY AWARDS

NOMINEES AND WINNERS

*Denotes Winner

1955

BEST ACTION OR ADVENTURE SERIES
Alfred Hitchcock Presents (CBS)

BEST M.C. OR PROGRAM HOST--MALE OR FEMALE
Alfred Hitchcock (CBS)

BEST DIRECTOR--FILM SERIES
Alfred Hitchcock, Alfred Hitchcock Presents ("The Case of Mr. Pelham") (CBS)

BEST EDITING OF A TELEVISION FILM
*Edward W. Williams, Alfred Hitchcock Presents ("Breakdown") (CBS)

1956

BEST SERIES--HALF HOUR OR LESS
Alfred Hitchcock Presents (CBS)

BEST MALE PERSONALITY--CONTINUING PERFORMANCE
Alfred Hitchcock (CBS)

BEST FEMALE PERSONALITY--CONTINUING PERFORMANCE
Rosemary Clooney (Syndicated)

BEST DIRECTION--HALF HOUR OR LESS
Herschel Daugherty, General Electric Theatre ("The Road That Led Afar") (CBS)

BEST ART DIRECTION--HALF HOUR OR LESS
Martin Obzina, John Robert Lloyd, John J. Lloyd, John Meehan and George Patrick, General Electric Theatre (CBS)

BEST CINEMATOGRAPHY FOR TELEVISION
 Robert W. Pittack, General Electric Theatre ("The Glorious Gift of Molly Malloy") (CBS)
 John L. Russell, General Electric Theatre ("The Night Goes On") (CBS)

BEST MUSICAL CONTRIBUTION FOR TELEVISION
 Nelson Riddle, Arrangement of Musical Score, The Rosemary Clooney Show (Syndicated)

1957

BEST NEW PROGRAM SERIES OF THE YEAR
 Leave It to Beaver (CBS)
 Wagon Train (NBC)

BEST DRAMATIC ANTHOLOGY SERIES
 Alfred Hitchcock Presents (CBS)

BEST DRAMATIC SERIES WITH CONTINUING CHARACTERS
 Wagon Train (NBC)

ACTOR--BEST SINGLE PERFORMANCE--LEAD OR SUPPORT
 David Wayne as Menick, Suspicion ("Heartbeat")

BEST TELEPLAY WRITING--HALF HOUR OR LESS
 Joe Connelly and Bob Mosher, Leave It to Beaver ("Beaver Gets Spelled") (CBS)

BEST DIRECTION--HALF HOUR OR LESS
 *Robert Stevens, Alfred Hitchcock Presents ("The Glass Eye") (CBS)

BEST ART DIRECTION
 Howard E. Johnson, Wagon Train (NBC)

BEST EDITING OF A FILM FOR TELEVISION
 Michael R. McAdam, General Electric Theatre ("Trail to Christmas") (CBS)

1958-59

BEST DRAMATIC SERIES--LESS THAN ONE HOUR
 Alfred Hitchcock Presents (CBS)
 General Electric Theatre (CBS)

BEST WESTERN SERIES
 Wagon Train (NBC)

BEST DIRECTION OF A SINGLE PROGRAM OF A DRAMATIC
SERIES--LESS THAN ONE HOUR
  Herschel Daugherty, General Electric Theatre ("One is a Wanderer") (CBS)
  Alfred Hitchcock, Alfred Hitchcock Presents ("Lamb to the Slaughter") (CBS)
  James Neilsen, General Electric Theatre ("Kid at the Stick") (CBS)

BEST WRITING OF A SINGLE PROGRAM OF A DRAMATIC SERIES,
LESS THAN ONE HOUR
  Roald Dahl, Alfred Hitchcock Presents ("Lamb to the Slaughter") CBS
  Samuel Taylor, General Electric Theatre ("One is a Wanderer") (From a story by James Thurber) (CBS)

1959-60

OUTSTANDING ACHIEVEMENT IN ART DIRECTION AND SCENIC DESIGN
  John J. Lloyd, Alfred Hitchcock Presents (CBS)

OUTSTANDING ACHIEVEMENT IN FILM EDITING FOR TELEVISION
  Dan Landres, General Electric Theatre ("The Patsy") (CBS)
  Edward Williams, Alfred Hitchcock Presents ("Man from the South") (CBS)

1960-61

OUTSTANDING PERFORMANCE IN A SUPPORTING ROLE BY AN ACTOR OR ACTRESS IN A SINGLE PROGRAM
  Charles Bronson, General Electric Theatre ("Memory in White") (CBS)

OUTSTANDING ACHIEVEMENT IN THE FIELD OF MUSIC FOR TELEVISION
  Pete Rugolo and Jerry Goldsmith, Thriller (NBC)

OUTSTANDING ACHIEVEMENT IN ART DIRECTION AND SCENIC DESIGN
  *John J. Lloyd, Checkmate (CBS)

OUTSTANDING ACHIEVEMENT IN CINEMATOGRAPHY FOR TELEVISION
  Walter Strenge, Wagon Train ("The Sam Elder Story") (NBC)

OUTSTANDING ACHIEVEMENT IN FILM EDITING FOR TELEVISION
  Edward W. Williams, Alfred Hitchcock Presents ("Incident in a Small Jail") (CBS)

1961-62

OUTSTANDING ACHIEVEMENT IN ORIGINAL MUSIC COMPOSED FOR TELEVISION
John Williams, Alcoa Premiere (ABC)

OUTSTANDING WRITING ACHIEVEMENT IN DRAMA
Henry F. Greenberg, Alcoa Premiere ("People Need People") (ABC)

OUTSTANDING DIRECTORIAL ACHIEVEMENT IN DRAMA
Alex Segal, Alcoa Premiere ("People Need People") (ABC)

OUTSTANDING ACHIEVEMENT IN CINEMATOGRAPHY FOR TELEVISION
Walter Strenge, Wagon Train (NBC)

OUTSTANDING ACHIEVEMENT IN FILM EDITING FOR TELEVISION
Marston Fay and Gene Palmer, Wagon Train (NBC)

1962-63

OUTSTANDING PROGRAM ACHIEVEMENT IN THE FIELD OF HUMOR
McHale's Navy (ABC)

OUTSTANDING PROGRAM ACHIEVEMENT IN THE FIELD OF DRAMA
Alcoa Premiere/Premiere (ABC)

OUTSTANDING SINGLE PERFORMANCE BY AN ACTOR IN A LEADING ROLE
Bradford Dillman as Charlie Pont, Premiere ("The Voice of Charlie Pont") (ABC)

OUTSTANDING SINGLE PERFORMANCE BY AN ACTRESS IN A LEADING ROLE
Diana Hyland as Liza Laurents, Premiere ("The Voice of Charlie Pont") (ABC)

OUTSTANDING CONTINUED PERFORMANCE BY AN ACTOR IN A SERIES (LEAD)
Ernest Borgnine as Lt. Cmdr. Quinton McHale, McHale's Navy (ABC)

OUTSTANDING PERFORMANCE IN A SUPPORTING ROLE BY AN ACTOR
Tim Conway as Ensign Charles Parker, McHale's Navy (ABC)
Robert Redford as George Laurents, Premiere ("The Voice of Charlie Pont") (ABC)

OUTSTANDING ACHIEVEMENT IN COMPOSING ORIGINAL MUSIC
FOR TELEVISION
Johnny Williams, Alcoa Premiere/Premiere (ABC)

OUTSTANDING WRITING ACHIEVEMENT IN DRAMA
Halsted Welles, Premiere ("The Voice of Charlie Pont") (ABC)

OUTSTANDING DIRECTORIAL ACHIEVEMENT IN DRAMA
Robert Ellis Miller, Premiere ("The Voice of Charlie Pont") (ABC)

OUTSTANDING ACHIEVEMENT IN FILM EDITING FOR TELEVISION
Howard Epstein, Richard Belding and Tony Martinelli, Alcoa Premiere/Premiere (ABC)

1963-64

OUTSTANDING PROGRAM ACHIEVEMENT IN THE FIELD OF COMEDY
McHale's Navy (ABC)

OUTSTANDING PROGRAM ACHIEVEMENT IN THE FIELD OF DRAMA
Bob Hope Presents the Chrysler Theatre (NBC)

OUTSTANDING PERFORMANCE BY AN ACTOR IN A LEADING ROLE
Roddy McDowall as Paul LeDoux, Arrest and Trial ("Journey into Darkness") (ABC)
Rod Steiger as Mike Kirsch, Bob Hope Presents the Chrysler Theatre ("A Slow Fade to Black") (NBC)

OUTSTANDING PERFORMANCE BY AN ACTRESS IN A LEADING ROLE
*Shelley Winters as Jenny Dworak, Bob Hope Presents the Chrysler Theatre ("Two Is the Number") (NBC)

OUTSTANDING PERFORMANCE IN A SUPPORTING ROLE BY AN ACTOR
*Albert Paulsen as Lt. Volkovoi, Bob Hope Presents the Chrysler Theatre ("One Day in the Life of Ivan Denisovich") (NBC)

OUTSTANDING PERFORMANCE IN A SUPPORTING ROLE BY AN ACTRESS
Martine Bartlett as Miranda, Arrest and Trial ("Journey into Darkness") (ABC)
Anjanette Comer as Annabelle, Arrest and Trial ("Journey into Darkness") (ABC)

OUTSTANDING WRITING ACHIEVEMENT IN DRAMA--ORIGINAL

David Rayfiel, Bob Hope Presents the Chrysler Theatre ("Something About Lee Wiley") (NBC)

OUTSTANDING WRITING ACHIEVEMENT IN DRAMA--ADAPTATION
*Rod Serling, Bob Hope Presents the Chrysler Theatre ("It's Mental Work") (From the story by John O'Hara) (NBC)
James Bridges, The Alfred Hitchcock Hour ("The Jar") (From a short story by Ray Bradbury) (CBS)

OUTSTANDING DIRECTORIAL ACHIEVEMENT IN DRAMA
Sydney Pollack, Bob Hope Presents the Chrysler Theatre ("Something About Lee Wiley") (NBC)

OUTSTANDING DIRECTORIAL ACHIEVEMENT IN COMEDY
Sidney Lanfield, McHale's Navy (ABC)

OUTSTANDING ACHIEVEMENT IN CINEMATOGRAPHY FOR TELEVISION
Ellis F. Thackery, Kraft Suspense Theatre ("Once Upon a Savage Night") (NBC)

OUTSTANDING ACHIEVEMENT IN FILM EDITING FOR TELEVISION
Danny Landres, Milton Shifman and Richard G. Wray, Arrest and Trial (ABC)

1964-65

OUTSTANDING PROGRAM ACHIEVEMENTS IN ENTERTAINMENT
Bob Hope Presents the Chrysler Theatre (NBC) Dick Berg, Executive Producer

1965-66

OUTSTANDING SINGLE PERFORMANCE BY AN ACTOR IN A LEADING ROLE IN A DRAMA
*Cliff Robertson as Quincey Parker, Bob Hope Presents the Chrysler Theatre ("The Game") (NBC)

OUTSTANDING SINGLE PERFORMANCE BY AN ACTRESS IN A LEADING ROLE IN A DRAMA
*Simone Signoret as Sara Lescaut, Bob Hope Presents the Chrysler Theatre ("A Small Rebellion") (NBC)
Shelley Winters as Edith, Bob Hope Presents the Chrysler Theatre ("Back to Back") (NBC)

OUTSTANDING WRITING ACHIEVEMENT IN DRAMA
S. Lee Pogostin, Bob Hope Presents the Chrysler Theatre ("The Game") (NBC)

OUTSTANDING DIRECTORIAL ACHIEVEMENT IN DRAMA
  *Sidney Pollack, Bob Hope Presents the Chrysler Theatre ("The Game") (NBC)

INDIVIDUAL ACHIEVEMENTS IN MUSIC
  Pete Rugolo, Run for Your Life (NBC)

1966-67

OUTSTANDING DRAMATIC SERIES
  Run for Your Life (NBC) Jo Swerling, Jr., Producer

OUTSTANDING CONTINUED PERFORMANCE BY AN ACTOR IN A LEADING ROLE IN A DRAMATIC SERIES
  Ben Gazzara as Paul Bryan, Run for Your Life (NBC)

INDIVIDUAL ACHIEVEMENTS IN MUSIC
  Pete Rugolo, Run for Your Life (NBC)

1967-68

OUTSTANDING DRAMATIC SERIES
  Run for Your Life (NBC) Roy Huggins, Executive Producer

OUTSTANDING SINGLE PERFORMANCE BY AN ACTOR IN A LEADING ROLE IN A DRAMA
  Raymond Burr as Chief Ironside, World Premiere ("Ironside") (NBC)

OUTSTANDING CONTINUED PERFORMANCE BY AN ACTOR IN A LEADING ROLE IN A DRAMATIC SERIES
  Raymond Burr as Chief Ironside, Ironside (NBC)
  Ben Gazzara as Paul Bryan, Run for Your Life (NBC)

OUTSTANDING PERFORMANCE BY AN ACTRESS IN A SUPPORTING ROLE IN A DRAMA
  *Barbara Anderson as Officer Eve Whitfield, Ironside (NBC)

OUTSTANDING WRITING ACHIEVEMENT IN DRAMA
  Don M. Mankiewicz, World Premiere ("Ironside") (NBC)

OUTSTANDING ACHIEVEMENT IN MUSICAL COMPOSITION
  Pete Rugolo, Run for Your Life ("Cry Hard, Cry Fast") (NBC)

OUTSTANDING ACHIEVEMENT IN CINEMATOGRAPHY
  *Ralph Woolsey, It Takes a Thief ("A Thief Is a Thief Is a Thief") (ABC)

1968-69

OUTSTANDING DRAMATIC SERIES
Ironside (NBC) Cy Chermak, Executive Producer
The Name of the Game (NBC) Richard Irving, Leslie Stevens and David Victor, Producers

OUTSTANDING SINGLE PERFORMANCE BY AN ACTRESS IN A LEADING ROLE
Anne Baxter, The Name of the Game ("The Bobbie Currier Story") (NBC)

OUTSTANDING CONTINUED PERFORMANCE BY AN ACTOR IN A LEADING ROLE IN A DRAMATIC SERIES
Raymond Burr, Ironside (NBC)

OUTSTANDING SINGLE PERFORMANCE BY AN ACTOR IN A SUPPORTING ROLE
Hal Holbrook, World Premiere ("The Whole World Is Watching") (NBC)

OUTSTANDING CONTINUED PERFORMANCE BY AN ACTRESS IN A SUPPORTING ROLE IN A SERIES
*Susan Saint James, The Name of the Game (NBC)
Barbara Anderson, Ironside (NBC)

1969-70

OUTSTANDING DRAMATIC SERIES
*Marcus Welby, M.D. (ABC) David Victor, Executive Producer; David J. O'Connell, Producer
Ironside (NBC) Cy Chermak, Executive Producer; Douglas Benton, Winston Miller, Joel Rogosin and Albert Aley, Producers
The Name of the Game (NBC) Richard Irving, Executive Producer; George Eckstein, Dean Hargrove, Norman Lloyd and Boris Sagal, Producers

OUTSTANDING DRAMATIC PROGRAM
Marcus Welby, M.D. ("Hello, Goodbye, Hello") (ABC) David Victor, Executive Producer; David J. O'Connell, Producer
World Premiere ("My Sweet Charlie") (NBC) Bob Banner, Executive Producer; Richard Levinson and William Link, Producers

OUTSTANDING SINGLE PERFORMANCE BY AN ACTOR IN A LEADING ROLE
Al Freeman, Jr., World Premiere ("My Sweet Charlie") (NBC)

OUTSTANDING SINGLE PERFORMANCE BY AN ACTRESS IN A

LEADING ROLE
*Patty Duke, World Premiere ("My Sweet Charlie") (NBC)
Shirley Jones, World Premiere ("Silent Night, Lonely Night") (NBC)

OUTSTANDING CONTINUED PERFORMANCE BY AN ACTOR IN A LEADING ROLE IN A DRAMATIC SERIES
*Robert Young, Marcus Welby, M.D. (ABC)
Raymond Burr, Ironside (NBC)
Robert Wagner, It Takes a Thief (ABC)

OUTSTANDING PERFORMANCE BY AN ACTOR IN A SUPPORTING ROLE IN A DRAMA
*James Brolin, Marcus Welby, M.D. (ABC)

OUTSTANDING PERFORMANCE BY AN ACTRESS IN A SUPPORTING ROLE IN A DRAMA
Barbara Anderson, Ironside (NBC)
Susan Saint James, The Name of the Game (NBC)

OUTSTANDING WRITING ACHIEVEMENT IN DRAMA
*Richard Levinson and William Link, World Premiere ("My Sweet Charlie") (NBC)
Don M. Mankiewicz, The ABC Wednesday Night Movie ("Marcus Welby, M.D.") (ABC)

OUTSTANDING DIRECTORIAL ACHIEVEMENT IN DRAMA
Lamont Johnson, World Premiere ("My Sweet Charlie") (NBC)

OUTSTANDING ACHIEVEMENT IN MUSIC COMPOSITION--FOR A SPECIAL PROGRAM
*Pete Rugolo, CBS Friday Night Movie ("The Challengers") (CBS)

OUTSTANDING ACHIEVEMENT IN CINEMATOGRAPHY FOR ENTERTAINMENT PROGRAMMING--FOR A SINGLE PROGRAM OF A SERIES
*Walter Strenge, Marcus Welby, M.D. ("Hello, Goodbye, Hello") (ABC)

OUTSTANDING ACHIEVEMENT IN CINEMATOGRAPHY FOR ENTERTAINMENT PROGRAMMING--FOR A SPECIAL PROGRAM
*Lionel Lindon, NBC Monday Night at the Movies ("Ritual of Evil") (NBC)
Gene Polito, World Premiere ("My Sweet Charlie") (NBC)

OUTSTANDING ACHIEVEMENT IN FILM EDITING FOR ENTERTAINMENT PROGRAMMING--FOR A SPECIAL PROGRAM
*Edward M. Abroms, World Premiere ("My Sweet Charlie") (NBC)
Gene Palmer, ABC Wednesday Night Movie ("Marcus Welby, M.D.") (ABC)

OUTSTANDING ACHIEVEMENT IN FILM SOUND MIXING
Melvin M. Metcalfe, Sr., John A. Stransky, Jr., Clarence Self and Roger Heman, World Premiere ("My Sweet Charlie") (NBC)

1970-71

OUTSTANDING SERIES--DRAMA
*The Bold Ones ("The Senator") (NBC) David Levinson, Producer
Ironside (NBC) Cy Chermak, Executive Producer; Douglas Benton, Winston Miller, Joel Rogosin and Albert Aley, Producers
Marcus Welby, M.D. (ABC) David Victor, Executive Producer; David J. O'Connell, Producer

OUTSTANDING SINGLE PROGRAM--DRAMA OR COMEDY
World Premiere/NBC Monday and Tuesday Night at the Movies ("Vanished") (NBC) David Victor, Executive Producer; David J. O'Connell, Producer

OUTSTANDING NEW SERIES
The Bold Ones ("The Senator") David Levinson, Producer

OUTSTANDING SINGLE PERFORMANCE BY AN ACTOR IN A LEADING ROLE
Hal Holbrook, World Premiere/NBC Saturday Night at the Movies ("A Clear and Present Danger") (NBC)
Richard Widmark, World Premiere/NBC Monday and Tuesday Night at the Movies ("Vanished") (NBC)
Gig Young, World Premiere/NBC Monday Night at the Movies ("The Neon Ceiling") (NBC)

OUTSTANDING SINGLE PERFORMANCE BY AN ACTRESS IN A LEADING ROLE
*Lee Grant, World Premiere/NBC Monday Night at the Movies ("The Neon Ceiling") (NBC)
Lee Grant, World Premiere/NBC Monday Night at the Movies ("Ransom for a Dead Man") (NBC)

OUTSTANDING CONTINUED PERFORMANCE BY AN ACTOR IN A LEADING ROLE IN A DRAMATIC SERIES
*Hal Holbrook, The Bold Ones ("The Senator") (NBC)
Raymond Burr, Ironside (NBC)
Robert Young, Marcus Welby, M.D. (ABC)

OUTSTANDING PERFORMANCE BY AN ACTOR IN A SUPPORTING ROLE IN DRAMA
James Brolin, Marcus Welby, M.D. (ABC)
Robert Young, World Premiere/NBC Monday and Tuesday Night at the Movies ("Vanished") (NBC)

Emmy Awards / 277

OUTSTANDING PERFORMANCE BY AN ACTRESS IN A SUPPORTING ROLE IN DRAMA
*Margaret Leighton, Hallmark Hall of Fame ("Hamlet") (NBC)
Susan Saint James, The Name of the Game (NBC)
Elena Verdugo, Marcus Welby, M.D. (ABC)

OUTSTANDING DIRECTORIAL ACHIEVEMENT IN DRAMA--SERIES EPISODE
*Daryl Duke, The Bold Ones ("The Senator": "The Day the Lion Died") (NBC)
John M. Badham, The Bold Ones ("The Senator": "A Single Blow of a Sword") (NBC)

OUTSTANDING DIRECTORIAL ACHIEVEMENT IN DRAMA--SINGLE PROGRAM
Peter Wood, Hallmark Hall of Fame ("Hamlet") (NBC)
James Goldstone, World Premiere/NBC Saturday Night at the Movies ("A Clear and Present Danger") (NBC)

OUTSTANDING ACHIEVEMENT IN CHOREOGRAPHY
Claude Chagrin, Hallmark Hall of Fame ("Hamlet") (NBC)

OUTSTANDING WRITING ACHIEVEMENT IN DRAMA--SERIES EPISODE
*Joel Oliansky, The Bold Ones ("The Senator": "To Taste of Death But Once") (NBC)
David W. Rintels, The Bold Ones ("The Senator": "A Continual Roar of Musketry, Parts I and II") (NBC)
Jerrold Freedman, Four-in-One ("The Psychiatrist": "In Death's Other Kingdom") (NBC)

OUTSTANDING WRITING ACHIEVEMENT IN DRAMA--SINGLE PROGRAM--ORIGINAL
William Read Woodfield and Allan Balter, World Premiere/ NBC Tuesday Night at the Movies ("San Francisco International Airport") (NBC)

OUTSTANDING WRITING ACHIEVEMENT IN DRAMA--SINGLE PROGRAM--ADAPTATION
John Barton, Hallmark Hall of Fame ("Hamlet") (NBC)
Dean Riesner, World Premiere/NBC Monday and Tuesday Night at the Movies ("Vanished") (NBC)

OUTSTANDING ACHIEVEMENT IN MUSIC COMPOSITION--SERIES EPISODE
Robert Prince and Billy Goldenberg, The Name of the Game ("LA 2017") (NBC)
Frank Comstock, Adam-12 ("Elegy for a Pig") (NBC)

OUTSTANDING ACHIEVEMENT IN MUSIC COMPOSITION--SPECIAL PROGRAM
John Addison, Hallmark Hall of Fame ("Hamlet") (NBC)
Pete Rugolo, World Premiere/NBC Monday Night at the Movies ("Do You Take This Stranger") (NBC)

OUTSTANDING ACHIEVEMENT IN MUSIC DIRECTION OF A VARIETY, MUSICAL OR DRAMATIC PROGRAM
John Addison, Hallmark Hall of Fame ("Hamlet") (NBC)

OUTSTANDING ACHIEVEMENT IN MUSIC, LYRICS AND SPECIAL MATERIAL
Billy Goldenberg and David Wilson, The Name of the Game ("All the Old Familiar Faces") (NBC)

OUTSTANDING ACHIEVEMENT IN CINEMATOGRAPHY FOR ENTERTAINMENT PROGRAMMING--SERIES EPISODE
*Jack Marta, The Name of the Game ("Cynthia Is Alive and Living in Avalon") (NBC)
Walter Strenge, A.S.C., Marcus Welby, M.D. ("A Spanish Saying I Made Up") (ABC)

OUTSTANDING ACHIEVEMENT IN CINEMATOGRAPHY FOR ENTERTAINMENT PROGRAMMING—FEATURE LENGTH PROGRAM
*Lionel Lindon, A.S.C., World Premiere/NBC Monday and Tuesday Night at the Movies ("Vanished") (NBC)
Edward Rosson, World Premiere/NBC Monday Night at the Movies ("The Neon Ceiling") (NBC)

OUTSTANDING ACHIEVEMENT IN ART DIRECTION AND SCENIC DESIGN
*Peter Roden, Hallmark Hall of Fame ("Hamlet") (NBC)
John J. Lloyd (Art Director) and Ruby R. Levitt (Set Decorator), World Premiere/NBC Monday and Tuesday Night at the Movies ("Vanished") (NBC)

OUTSTANDING ACHIEVEMENT IN COSTUME DESIGN
*Martin Baugh and David Walker, Hallmark Hall of Fame ("Hamlet") (NBC)

OUTSTANDING ACHIEVEMENT IN MAKE-UP
Marie Roche, Hallmark Hall of Fame ("Hamlet") (NBC)

OUTSTANDING ACHIEVEMENT IN FILM EDITING FOR ENTERTAINMENT PROGRAMMING--SERIES EPISODE
*Michael Economou, The Bold Ones ("The Senator": "A Continual Roar of Musketry, Parts I and II") (NBC)
Douglas Stewart, The Bold Ones ("The Senator": "To Taste of Death But Once") (NBC)

OUTSTANDING ACHIEVEMENT IN FILM EDITING FOR ENTERTAINMENT PROGRAMMING--FEATURE LENGTH PROGRAM
Robert F. Shugrue, World Premiere/NBC Monday Night at the Movies ("The Neon Ceiling") (NBC)
Robert Watts, World Premiere/NBC Monday and Tuesday Night at the Movies ("Vanished") (NBC)

OUTSTANDING ACHIEVEMENT IN FILM SOUND MIXING
Ronald K. Pierce and James Z. Flaster, World Premiere/NBC

Monday and Tuesday Night at the Movies ("Vanished") (NBC)
Roger Parish and Robert L. Hoyt, World Premiere/NBC Tuesday Night at the Movies ("San Francisco International Airport") (NBC)

OUTSTANDING ACHIEVEMENT IN LIGHTING DIRECTION
*John Rook, Hallmark Hall of Fame ("Hamlet") (NBC)

OUTSTANDING ACHIEVEMENT IN VIDEO TAPE EDITING
Ray Knipe, Hallmark Hall of Fame ("Hamlet") (NBC)

1971-72

OUTSTANDING SERIES--DRAMA
NBC Mystery Movie ("Columbo") (NBC) Richard Levinson and William Link, Executive Producers; Everett Chambers, Producer

OUTSTANDING SINGLE PROGRAM--DRAMA OR COMEDY
Hallmark Hall of Fame ("The Snow Goose") (NBC) Frank O'Connor, Producer

OUTSTANDING NEW SERIES
NBC Mystery Movie ("Columbo") (NBC) Richard Levinson and William Link, Executive Producers; Everett Chambers, Producer

OUTSTANDING SINGLE PERFORMANCE BY AN ACTOR IN A LEADING ROLE
Richard Harris, Hallmark Hall of Fame ("The Snow Goose") (NBC)

OUTSTANDING CONTINUED PERFORMANCE BY AN ACTOR IN A LEADING ROLE IN A DRAMATIC SERIES
*Peter Falk, NBC Mystery Movie ("Columbo") (NBC)
Robert Young, Marcus Welby, M.D. (ABC)

OUTSTANDING CONTINUED PERFORMANCE BY AN ACTRESS IN A LEADING ROLE IN A DRAMATIC SERIES
Susan Saint James, NBC Mystery Movie ("McMillan and Wife") (NBC)

OUTSTANDING PERFORMANCE BY AN ACTOR IN A SUPPORTING ROLE IN A DRAMA
James Brolin, Marcus Welby, M.D. (ABC)

OUTSTANDING PERFORMANCE BY AN ACTRESS IN A SUPPORTING ROLE IN A DRAMA
*Jenny Agutter, Hallmark Hall of Fame ("The Snow Goose") (NBC)
Elena Verdugo, Marcus Welby, M.D. (ABC)

OUTSTANDING DIRECTORIAL ACHIEVEMENT IN DRAMA--SERIES EPISODE
   *Alexander Singer, The Bold Ones ("The Lawyers": "The Invasion of Kevin Ireland") (NBC)
   Edward M. Abroms, NBC Mystery Movie ("Columbo": "Short Fuse") (NBC)
   Daniel Petrie, The Man and the City ("Hands of Love") (ABC)

OUTSTANDING DIRECTORIAL ACHIEVEMENT IN DRAMA--SINGLE PROGRAM
   Patrick Garland, Hallmark Hall of Fame ("The Snow Goose") (NBC)

OUTSTANDING WRITING ACHIEVEMENT IN DRAMA--SERIES EPISODE
   *Richard Levinson and William Link, NBC Mystery Movie ("Columbo": "Death Lends a Hand") (NBC)
   Steven Bochco, NBC Mystery Movie ("Columbo": "Murder by the Book") (NBC)
   Jackson Gillis, NBC Mystery Movie ("Columbo": "Suitable for Framing") (NBC)

OUTSTANDING WRITING ACHIEVEMENT IN DRAMA--ADAPTATION
   Paul W. Gallico, Hallmark Hall of Fame ("The Snow Goose") (NBC)

OUTSTANDING ACHIEVEMENT IN MUSIC COMPOSITION
   *Pete Rugolo, The Bold Ones ("The Lawyers": "In Defense of Ellen McKay") (NBC)
   Billy Goldenberg, NBC Mystery Movie ("Columbo": "Lady in Waiting") (NBC)

OUTSTANDING ACHIEVEMENT IN ART DIRECTION OR SCENIC DESIGN
   Stanley Morris, Hallmark Hall of Fame ("The Snow Goose") (NBC)

OUTSTANDING ACHIEVEMENT IN CINEMATOGRAPHY FOR ENTERTAINMENT PROGRAMMING--SERIES EPISODE
   *Lloyd Ahern, A.S.C., NBC Mystery Movie ("Columbo": "Blue Print for Murder") (NBC)

OUTSTANDING ACHIEVEMENT IN CINEMATOGRAPHY FOR ENTERTAINMENT PROGRAMMING--FEATURE LENGTH PROGRAM
   Ray Henman, Hallmark Hall of Fame ("The Snow Goose") (NBC)
   Jack A. Marta, ABC Movie of the Weekend ("Duel") (ABC)

OUTSTANDING ACHIEVEMENT IN FILM EDITING FOR ENTERTAINMENT PROGRAMMING--SERIES EPISODE OR SERIES
   *Edward M. Abroms, NBC Mystery Movie ("Columbo": "Death Lends a Hand") (NBC)
   Richard Bracken, Gloryette Clark and Terry Williams, The Bold Ones ("The Lawyers") (NBC)

OUTSTANDING ACHIEVEMENT IN FILM EDITING FOR ENTERMENT PROGRAMMING--SPECIAL
Ken Pearce, Hallmark Hall of Fame ("The Snow Goose") (NBC)

OUTSTANDING ACHIEVEMENT IN FILM SOUND EDITING
*Jerry Christian, James Troutman, Ronald LaVine, Sidney Lubow, Richard Raderman, Dale Johnston, Sam Caylor, John Stacy and Jack Kirschner, ABC Movie of the Weekend ("Duel") (ABC)

1972-73

OUTSTANDING DRAMA SERIES--CONTINUING
NBC Sunday Mystery Movie ("Columbo") (NBC) Dean Hargrove, Producer

OUTSTANDING SINGLE PROGRAM--DRAMA OR COMEDY
The CBS Thursday Night Movies ("The Marcus-Nelson Murders") (CBS) Abby Mann, Executive Producer; Matthew Rapf, Producer
Bell System Family Theatre ("The Red Pony") (NBC) Frederick W. Brogger, Producer
ABC Wednesday Movie of the Week ("That Certain Summer") (ABC) Richard Levinson and William Link, Producers

OUTSTANDING SINGLE PROGRAM--VARIETY AND POPULAR MUSIC
Applause (CBS) Alexander Cohen, Executive Producer; Joseph Kipness, Lawrence Kasha and Dick Rosenbloom, Producers

OUTSTANDING SINGLE PERFORMANCE BY AN ACTOR IN A LEADING ROLE
Henry Fonda, Bell System Family Theatre ("The Red Pony") (NBC)
Hal Holbrook, ABC Wednesday Movie of the Week ("That Certain Summer") (ABC)
Telly Savalas, The CBS Thursday Night Movies ("The Marcus-Nelson Murders") (CBS)

OUTSTANDING SINGLE PERFORMANCE BY AN ACTRESS IN A LEADING ROLE
Lauren Bacall, Applause (CBS)
Hope Lange, ABC Wednesday Movie of the Week ("That Certain Summer") (ABC)

OUTSTANDING CONTINUED PERFORMANCE BY AN ACTOR IN A LEADING ROLE
Peter Falk, NBC Sunday Mystery Movie ("Columbo") (NBC)

OUTSTANDING CONTINUED PERFORMANCE BY AN ACTRESS IN A LEADING ROLE--DRAMA SERIES

Susan Saint James, NBC Sunday Mystery Movie ("McMillan and Wife") (NBC)

OUTSTANDING PERFORMANCE BY AN ACTOR IN A SUPPORTING ROLE IN DRAMA
*Scott Jacoby, ABC Wednesday Movie of the Week ("That Certain Summer") (ABC)
James Brolin, Marcus Welby, M.D. (ABC)

OUTSTANDING PERFORMANCE BY AN ACTRESS IN A SUPPORTING ROLE IN DRAMA
Nancy Walker, NBC Sunday Mystery Movie ("McMillan and Wife") (NBC)

OUTSTANDING DIRECTORIAL ACHIEVEMENT IN DRAMA--SERIES EPISODE
Edward M. Abroms, NBC Sunday Mystery Movie ("Columbo": "The Most Dangerous Match") (NBC)

OUTSTANDING DIRECTORIAL ACHIEVEMENT IN DRAMA--SINGLE PROGRAM
*Joseph Sargent, The CBS Thursday Night Movies ("The Marcus-Nelson Murders") (CBS)
Lamont Johnson, ABC Wednesday Movie of the Week ("That Certain Summer") (ABC)

OUTSTANDING WRITING ACHIEVEMENT IN DRAMA--SERIES EPISODE
Steven Bochco, NBC Sunday Mystery Movie ("Columbo": "Etude in Black") (NBC)

OUTSTANDING WRITING ACHIEVEMENT IN DRAMA--ORIGINAL TELEPLAY
*Abby Mann, The CBS Thursday Night Movies ("The Marcus-Nelson Murders") (CBS)
Richard Levinson and William Link, ABC Wednesday Movie of the Week ("That Certain Summer") (ABC)

OUTSTANDING WRITING ACHIEVEMENT IN DRAMA--ADAPTATION
Robert Totten and Ron Bishop, Bell System Family Theatre ("The Red Pony") (NBC)

OUTSTANDING ACHIEVEMENT IN MUSIC COMPOSITION--SPECIAL
*Jerry Goldsmith, Bell System Family Theatre ("The Red Pony") (NBC)

OUTSTANDING ACHIEVEMENT IN MUSIC, LYRICS AND SPECIAL MATERIAL
Billy Goldenberg and Bobby Russell, The CBS Thursday Night Movies ("The Marcus-Nelson Murders") (CBS)

OUTSTANDING ACHIEVEMENT IN ART DIRECTION OR SCENIC DESIGN

Robert Boyle and James Hulsey (Art Directors), John Kurl (Set
Decorator), Bell System Family Theatre ("The Red Pony")
(NBC)

OUTSTANDING ACHIEVEMENT IN MAKE-UP
Allan Snyder and Richard Cobos, Bell System Family Theatre
("The Red Pony") (NBC)

OUTSTANDING ACHIEVEMENT IN CINEMATOGRAPHY FOR ENTERTAINMENT PROGRAMMING--SERIES
Sam Leavitt, NBC Wednesday Mystery Movie ("Banacek") (NBC)

OUTSTANDING ACHIEVEMENT IN CINEMATOGRAPHY FOR ENTERTAINMENT PROGRAMMING--SPECIAL
Andrew Jackson, Bell System Family Theatre ("The Red Pony")
(NBC)

OUTSTANDING ACHIEVEMENT IN FILM SOUND EDITING
*Ross Taylor, Fred Brown and David Marshall, Bell System
Family Theatre ("The Red Pony") (NBC)
Peter Berkos, John Singleton, Brian Courcier, Gordon Ecker,
John Stacy, James Nownes, George Luckenbacher, Walter
Jenevein and Sidney Lubow, ABC Tuesday Movie of the Week
("Short Walk to Daylight") (ABC)

OUTSTANDING ACHIEVEMENT IN FILM SOUND MIXING
Melvin M. Metcalfe, Sr. and Thom Piper, ABC Wednesday
Movie of the Week ("That Certain Summer") (ABC)

1973-74

OUTSTANDING DRAMA SERIES
Kojak (CBS) Abby Mann and Matthew Rapf, Executive Producers;
James McAdams, Producer

OUTSTANDING LIMITED SERIES
*NBC Sunday Mystery Movie ("Columbo") (NBC) Dean Hargrove
and Roland Kibbee, Executive Producers; Douglas Benton,
Robert F. O'Neill and Edward K. Dodds, Producers
NBC Sunday Mystery Movie ("McCloud") (NBC) Glen A. Larson,
Executive Producer; Michael Gleason, Producer

OUTSTANDING SPECIAL--COMEDY OR DRAMA
NBC Wednesday Night at the Movies ("The Execution of Private
Slovik") (NBC) Richard Levinson and William Link, Executive Producers; Richard Dubelman, Producer

BEST LEAD ACTOR IN A DRAMA SERIES
*Telly Savalas, Kojak (CBS)

BEST LEAD ACTOR IN A LIMITED SERIES

Peter Falk, NBC Sunday Mystery Movie ("Columbo") (NBC)
Dennis Weaver, NBC Sunday Mystery Movie ("McCloud") (NBC)

BEST LEAD ACTOR IN A DRAMA
    Martin Sheen, NBC Wednesday Night at the Movies ("The Execution of Private Slovik") (NBC)

BEST LEAD ACTRESS IN A LIMITED SERIES
    *Mildred Natwick, NBC Tuesday Mystery Movie ("The Snoop Sisters") (NBC)
    Helen Hayes, NBC Tuesday Mystery Movie ("The Snoop Sisters") (NBC)

BEST LEAD ACTRESS IN A DRAMA
    Elizabeth Montgomery, NBC Wednesday Night at the Movies ("A Case of Rape") (NBC)

BEST SUPPORTING ACTRESS IN DRAMA
    Nancy Walker, NBC Sunday Mystery Movie ("McMillan and Wife") (NBC)

BEST DIRECTING IN DRAMA
    Boris Sagal, NBC Wednesday Night at the Movies ("A Case of Rape") (NBC)
    Lamont Johnson, NBC Wednesday Night at the Movies ("The Execution of Private Slovik") (NBC)

BEST WRITING IN DRAMA--SERIES EPISODE
    Gene R. Kearney, Kojak ("Death Is Not a Passing Grade") (CBS)

BEST WRITING IN DRAMA--ADAPTATION
    Richard Levinson and William Link, NBC Wednesday Night at the Movies ("The Execution of Private Slovik") (NBC)

BEST SONG OR THEME
    Billy Goldenberg, Kojak (CBS)

BEST ART DIRECTION OR SCENIC DESIGN--FEATURE LENGTH PROGRAM
    Walter H. Tyler (Art Director), Richard Friedman (Set Decorator), NBC Wednesday Night at the Movies ("The Execution of Private Slovik") (NBC)

OUTSTANDING ACHIEVEMENT IN COSTUME DESIGN
    Grady Hunt, NBC Tuesday Mystery Movie ("The Snoop Sisters": "The Devil Made Me Do It") (NBC)

OUTSTANDING ACHIEVEMENT IN MAKE-UP
    Nick Marcellino and James Lee McCoy, Portrait ("A Man Whose Name Was John") (ABC)

BEST CINEMATOGRAPHY FOR ENTERTAINMENT PROGRAMMING

--SERIES EPISODE OR SERIES
*Harry Wolf, A.S.C., NBC Sunday Mystery Movie ("Columbo": "Any Old Port in a Storm") (NBC)
Gerald Perry Finnerman, A.S.C., Kojak (CBS)

BEST CINEMATOGRAPHY FOR ENTERTAINMENT PROGRAMMING
--SPECIAL
Walter Strenge, A.S.C., Portrait ("A Man Whose Name Was John") (ABC)

BEST FILM EDITING FOR ENTERTAINMENT PROGRAMMING--
FEATURE LENGTH PROGRAM
*Frank Morriss, NBC Wednesday Night at the Movies ("The Execution of Private Slovik") (NBC)
Richard Bracken, NBC Wednesday Night at the Movies ("A Case of Rape") (NBC)

FILM EDITOR OF THE YEAR
*Frank Morriss, NBC Wednesday Night at the Movies ("The Execution of Private Slovik") (NBC)

OUTSTANDING ACHIEVEMENT IN FILM SOUND EDITING
Sid Lubow, Sam Caylor, Jack Kirschner, Richard Raderman, Stanley Frazen and John Singleton, Kojak ("Marker for a Dead Bookie") (CBS)

OUTSTANDING ACHIEVEMENT IN FILM OR TAPE SOUND MIXING
John K. Kean and Thom K. Piper, NBC Wednesday Night at the Movies ("The Execution of Private Slovik") (NBC)

OUTSTANDING DRAMA SPECIAL--DAYTIME
ABC Afternoon Playbreak ("A Special Act of Love") (ABC) John Choy, Producer

BEST ACTRESS IN DAYTIME DRAMA--SPECIAL
*Cathleen Nesbitt, ABC Matinee Today ("The Mask of Love") (ABC)

DAYTIME ACTRESS OF THE YEAR
*Cathleen Nesbitt, ABC Matinee Today ("The Mask of Love") (ABC)

BEST INDIVIDUAL DIRECTOR FOR A SPECIAL PROGRAM--
DAYTIME
Burt Brinckerhoff, ABC Matinee Today ("The Mask of Love") (ABC)

BEST WRITING FOR A SPECIAL PROGRAM--DAYTIME
*Lila Garrett and Sandy Krinski, ABC Afternoon Playbreak ("Mother of the Bride") (ABC)

1974-75

OUTSTANDING DRAMA SERIES
Kojak (CBS) Matthew Rapf, Executive Producer; Jack Laird and James McAdams, Producers

OUTSTANDING LIMITED SERIES
NBC Sunday Mystery Movie ("McCloud") (NBC) Glen A. Larson, Executive Producer; Michael Gleason and Ronald Satlof, Producers
NBC Sunday Mystery Movie ("Columbo") (NBC) Roland Kibbee and Dean Hargrove, Executive Producers; Everett Chambers and Edward K. Dodds, Producers

OUTSTANDING SPECIAL--DRAMA OR COMEDY
*World Premiere ("The Law") (NBC) William Sackheim, Producer

OUTSTANDING LEAD ACTOR IN A DRAMA SERIES
*Robert Blake, Baretta (ABC)
Telly Savalas, Kojak (CBS)

OUTSTANDING LEAD ACTOR IN A LIMITED SERIES
*Peter Falk, NBC Sunday Mystery Movie ("Columbo") (NBC)
Dennis Weaver, NBC Sunday Mystery Movie ("McCloud") (NBC)

OUTSTANDING LEAD ACTRESS IN A LIMITED SERIES
*Jessica Walter, NBC Sunday Mystery Movie ("Amy Prentiss") (NBC)
Susan Saint James, NBC Sunday Mystery Movie ("McMillan and Wife") (NBC)

OUTSTANDING CONTINUED PERFORMANCE BY A SUPPORTING ACTOR IN A DRAMA SERIES
J. D. Cannon, NBC Sunday Mystery Movie ("McCloud") (NBC)

OUTSTANDING SINGLE PERFORMANCE BY A SUPPORTING ACTOR IN A COMEDY OR DRAMA SERIES
*Patrick McGoohan, NBC Sunday Mystery Movie ("Columbo": "By Dawn's Early Light") (NBC)

OUTSTANDING CONTINUED PERFORMANCE BY A SUPPORTING ACTRESS IN A DRAMA SERIES
Nancy Walker, NBC Sunday Mystery Movie ("McMillan and Wife") (NBC)

OUTSTANDING DIRECTING IN A DRAMA SERIES
David Friedkin, Kojak ("Cross Your Heart and Hope to Die") (CBS)
Telly Savalas, Kojak ("I Want to Report a Dream...") (CBS)

OUTSTANDING DIRECTING IN A SPECIAL PROGRAM--DRAMA OR

COMEDY
John Badham, World Premiere ("The Law") (NBC)

OUTSTANDING WRITING IN A SPECIAL PROGRAM--DRAMA OR COMEDY--ORIGINAL TELEPLAY
Joel Oliansky (Story by William Sackheim and Joel Oliansky), World Premiere ("The Law") (NBC)

OUTSTANDING ACHIEVEMENT IN ART DIRECTION OR SCENIC DESIGN
Michael Baugh (Art Director), Jerry Adams (Set Decorator), NBC Sunday Mystery Movie ("Columbo": "Playback") (NBC)

OUTSTANDING ACHIEVEMENT IN CINEMATOGRAPHY FOR ENTERTAINMENT PROGRAMMING--SERIES
*Richard C. Glouner, A.S.C., NBC Sunday Mystery Movie ("Columbo": "Playback") (NBC)
Vilis Lapenieks, A.S.C. and Sol Negrin, A.S.C., Kojak ("Wall Street Gunslinger") (CBS)

1975-76

OUTSTANDING DRAMA SERIES
Baretta (ABC) Bernard L. Kowalski, Executive Producer; Jo Swerling, Jr., Robert Harris, Howie Horwitz and Robert Lewin, Producers

OUTSTANDING LIMITED SERIES
Rich Man, Poor Man (ABC) Harve Bennett, Executive Producer; Jon Epstein, Producer

OUTSTANDING LEAD ACTOR IN A DRAMA SERIES
*Peter Falk, NBC Sunday Mystery Movie ("Columbo") (NBC)
James Garner, The Rockford Files (NBC)

OUTSTANDING LEAD ACTOR IN A LIMITED SERIES
Nick Nolte, Rich Man, Poor Man (ABC)
Peter Strauss, Rich Man, Poor Man (ABC)

OUTSTANDING LEAD ACTOR FOR A SINGLE APPEARANCE IN A DRAMA OR COMEDY SERIES
*Edward Asner, Rich Man, Poor Man (ABC)

OUTSTANDING LEAD ACTRESS IN A COMEDY SERIES
Lee Grant, Fay (NBC)

OUTSTANDING LEAD ACTRESS IN A DRAMA SERIES
Brenda Vaccaro, Sara (CBS)

OUTSTANDING LEAD ACTRESS IN A LIMITED SERIES
Susan Blakely, Rich Man, Poor Man (ABC)

OUTSTANDING LEAD ACTRESS FOR A SINGLE APPEARANCE IN
A DRAMA OR COMEDY SERIES
  Sheree North, Marcus Welby, M.D. ("How Do You Know What
    Hurts Me?") (ABC)
  Martha Raye, NBC Sunday Mystery Movie ("McMillan and Wife":
    "Greed") (NBC)

OUTSTANDING CONTINUING PERFORMANCE BY A SUPPORTING
ACTOR IN A DRAMA SERIES
  Ray Milland, Rich Man, Poor Man (ABC)
  Robert Reed, Rich Man, Poor Man (ABC)

OUTSTANDING SINGLE PERFORMANCE BY A SUPPORTING ACTOR
IN A COMEDY OR DRAMA SERIES
  Bill Bixby, Rich Man, Poor Man (ABC)
  Norman Fell, Rich Man, Poor Man (ABC)
  Van Johnson, Rich Man, Poor Man (ABC)

OUTSTANDING SINGLE PERFORMANCE BY A SUPPORTING AC-
TRESS IN A COMEDY OR DRAMA SERIES
  *Fionnuala Flanagan, Rich Man, Poor Man (ABC)
  Kim Darby, Rich Man, Poor Man (ABC)
  Kay Lenz, Rich Man, Poor Man (ABC)

OUTSTANDING DIRECTING IN A DRAMA SERIES
  *David Greene, Rich Man, Poor Man (Episode 8) (ABC)

OUTSTANDING WRITING IN A DRAMA SERIES
  Dean Riesner, Rich Man, Poor Man (ABC)

OUTSTANDING WRITING IN A SPECIAL PROGRAM--DRAMA OR
COMEDY--ADAPTATION
  Jeanne Wakatsuki Houston, James D. Houston and John Korty,
    World Premiere ("Farewell to Manzanar") (NBC)

OUTSTANDING ACHIEVEMENT IN MUSIC COMPOSITION FOR A
SERIES
  *Alex North, Rich Man, Poor Man (ABC)
  John Cacavas, Kojak ("A Question of Answers") (CBS)

OUTSTANDING ACHIEVEMENT IN MUSIC COMPOSITION FOR A
SPECIAL
  Billy Goldenberg, Dark Victory (NBC)

OUTSTANDING ACHIEVEMENT IN ART DIRECTION OR SCENIC
DESIGN--SERIES EPISODE
  William Hiney (Art Director), Joseph J. Stone (Set Decorator),
    Rich Man, Poor Man (ABC)

OUTSTANDING ACHIEVEMENT IN COSTUME DESIGN FOR A
DRAMA OR COMEDY SERIES
  Charles Waldo, Rich Man, Poor Man (ABC)

OUTSTANDING ACHIEVEMENT IN CINEMATOGRAPHY FOR ENTERTAINMENT PROGRAMMING--SERIES
*Harry L. Wolf, A.S.C., Baretta ("Keep Your Eye on the Sparrow") (ABC)
Howard Schwartz, Rich Man, Poor Man (ABC)
Sol Negrin, A.S.C., Kojak ("A Question of Answers") (CBS)

OUTSTANDING ACHIEVEMENT IN CINEMATOGRAPHY FOR ENTERTAINMENT PROGRAMMING--SPECIAL
Hiro Narita, World Premiere ("Farewell to Manzanar") (NBC)

OUTSTANDING FILM EDITING FOR ENTERTAINMENT PROGRAMMING--SERIES
Douglas Stewart, Rich Man, Poor Man (ABC)
Richard Bracken, Rich Man, Poor Man (ABC)

OUTSTANDING ACHIEVEMENT IN FILM SOUND EDITING--SERIES EPISODE
Jerry Christian, Ken Sweet, Thomas M. Patchett, Jack Jackson, David A. Schonleber, John W. Singleton, Dale Johnston, George E. Luckenbacher, Walter Jenevein and Dennis Diltz, The Six Million Dollar Man ("The Secret of Bigfoot Part I and II") (ABC)

1976-77

OUTSTANDING DRAMA SERIES
Baretta (ABC) Anthony Spinner, Bernard Kowalski and Leigh Vance, Executive Producers; Charles E. Dismukes, Producer
NBC Sunday Mystery Movie ("Columbo") (NBC) Everett Chambers, Producer

OUTSTANDING LIMITED SERIES
NBC's Best Sellers ("Captains and the Kings") (NBC) Roy Huggins, Executive Producer; Jo Swerling, Jr., Producer

OUTSTANDING LEAD ACTOR IN A DRAMA SERIES
*James Garner, The Rockford Files (NBC)
Robert Blake, Baretta (ABC)
Peter Falk, NBC Sunday Mystery Movie ("Columbo") (NBC)
Jack Klugman, Quincy, M.E. (NBC)

OUTSTANDING LEAD ACTOR IN A LIMITED SERIES
Richard Jordan, NBC's Best Sellers ("Captains and the Kings") (NBC)
Steven Keats, NBC's Best Sellers ("Seventh Avenue") (NBC)

OUTSTANDING LEAD ACTOR IN A DRAMA OR COMEDY SPECIAL
Peter Boyle, World Premiere/The Big Event ("Tail Gunner Joe") (NBC)

OUTSTANDING LEAD ACTRESS IN A LIMITED SERIES
    *Patty Duke Astin, NBC's Best Sellers ("Captains and the
        Kings") (NBC)
    Dori Brenner, NBC's Best Sellers ("Seventh Avenue") (NBC)
    Jane Seymour, NBC's Best Sellers ("Captains and the Kings")
        (NBC)

OUTSTANDING LEAD ACTRESS IN A DRAMA OR COMEDY SPECIAL
    Susan Clark, NBC Monday Night at the Movies ("Amelia Earhart") (NBC)

OUTSTANDING LEAD ACTRESS FOR A SINGLE APPEARANCE IN A DRAMA OR COMEDY SERIES
    Susan Blakely, Rich Man, Poor Man (ABC)

OUTSTANDING CONTINUING PERFORMANCE BY A SUPPORTING ACTOR IN A DRAMA SERIES
    Noah Beery, Jr., The Rockford Files (NBC)
    Tom Ewell, Baretta (ABC)

OUTSTANDING PERFORMANCE BY A SUPPORTING ACTOR IN A COMEDY OR DRAMA SPECIAL
    *Burgess Meredith, World Premiere/The Big Event ("Tail
        Gunner Joe") (NBC)

OUTSTANDING SINGLE PERFORMANCE BY A SUPPORTING ACTOR IN A COMEDY OR DRAMA SERIES
    Charles Durning, NBC's Best Sellers ("Captains and the Kings"
        Chapter 2) (NBC)

OUTSTANDING PERFORMANCE BY A SUPPORTING ACTRESS IN A COMEDY OR DRAMA SPECIAL
    Patricia Neal, World Premiere/The Big Event ("Tail Gunner
        Joe") (NBC)
    Susan Oliver, NBC Monday Night at the Movies ("Amelia Earhart") (NBC)

OUTSTANDING WRITING IN A SPECIAL PROGRAM--DRAMA OR COMEDY--ORIGINAL TELEPLAY
    *Lane Slate, World Premiere/The Big Event ("Tail Gunner
        Joe") (NBC)

OUTSTANDING DIRECTING IN A SPECIAL PROGRAM--DRAMA OR COMEDY
    Jud Taylor, World Premiere/The Big Event ("Tail Gunner Joe")
        (NBC)

OUTSTANDING ACHIEVEMENT IN MUSIC COMPOSITION FOR A SERIES
    Elmer Bernstein, NBC's Best Sellers ("Captains and the Kings"
        Chapter 8) (NBC)

OUTSTANDING CINEMATOGRAPHY IN ENTERTAINMENT PROGRAM-

MING--SERIES
    *Ric Waite, NBC's Best Sellers ("Captains and the Kings" Chapter 1) (NBC)
    John J. Jones, NBC's Best Sellers ("Once an Eagle" Part 1) (NBC)
    Sherman Kunkel, Baretta ("Soldier in the Jungle") (ABC)
    Sol Negrin, A.S.C., Kojak ("A Shield for Murder" Part 2) (CBS)

OUTSTANDING CINEMATOGRAPHY IN ENTERTAINMENT PROGRAMMING--SPECIAL
    Ric Waite, World Premiere/The Big Event ("Tail Gunner Joe") (NBC)

OUTSTANDING FILM EDITING IN A DRAMA SERIES
    Jerrold Ludwig, Rich Man, Poor Man--Book II (ABC)

OUTSTANDING ACHIEVEMENT IN FILM SOUND EDITING--SERIES
    Dale Johnston, James A. Bean, Carl J. Brandon, Joe Divitale, Don Tomlinson, Don Weinman and Gene Craig, The Six Million Dollar Man ("The Return of Bigfoot" Part 1) (ABC)

OUTSTANDING ART DIRECTION OR SCENIC DESIGN FOR A DRAMATIC SERIES
    John Corso (Art Director), Jerry Adams (Set Decorator), NBC's Best Sellers ("Captains and the Kings" Chapter 2) (NBC)

OUTSTANDING ART DIRECTION OR SCENIC DESIGN FOR A DRAMATIC SPECIAL
    William H. Tuntke (Art Director), Richard Friedman (Set Decorator), NBC Monday Night at the Movies ("Amelia Earhart") (NBC)

1977-78

OUTSTANDING DRAMA SERIES
    *The Rockford Files (NBC) Meta Rosenberg, Executive Producer; David Chase and Chas. Floyd Johnson, Producers
    Quincy, M.E. (NBC) Glen A. Larson, Executive Producer; Lou Shaw, Producer

OUTSTANDING LEAD ACTOR IN A DRAMA SERIES
    Peter Falk, NBC Sunday Mystery Movie ("Columbo") (NBC)
    James Garner, The Rockford Files (NBC)
    Jack Klugman, Quincy, M.E. (NBC)

OUTSTANDING LEAD ACTOR IN A DRAMA OR COMEDY SPECIAL
    James Stacy, Just a Little Inconvenience (NBC)

OUTSTANDING LEAD ACTRESS IN A LIMITED SERIES
    Lee Remick, NBC's Best Sellers ("Wheels") (NBC)

OUTSTANDING LEAD ACTRESS FOR A SINGLE APPEARANCE IN A DRAMA OR COMEDY SERIES
*Rita Moreno, The Rockford Files ("The Paper Palace") (NBC)

OUTSTANDING WRITING IN A SPECIAL PROGRAM--DRAMA OR COMEDY--ORIGINAL TELEPLAY
Richard Levinson and William Link, The Storyteller (NBC)

OUTSTANDING ART DIRECTION FOR A DRAMATIC SPECIAL
John J. Lloyd (Art Director), Hal Guasman (Set Decorator), It Happened One Christmas (ABC)
Loyd S. Papez (Art Director), Richard Friedman (Set Decorator), The Bastard (Syndicated)

OUTSTANDING ACHIEVEMENT IN COSTUME DESIGN FOR A DRAMA OR COMEDY SERIES
Bill Jobe, Testimony of Two Men (Part 3) (Syndicated)

OUTSTANDING ACHIEVEMENT IN COSTUME DESIGN FOR A DRAMA SPECIAL
Jean-Pierre Dorleac, The Bastard (Syndicated)
Bill Jobe, The Dark Secret of Harvest Home (NBC)

OUTSTANDING FILM EDITING IN A DRAMA SERIES
Robert Watts, NBC Sunday Mystery Movie ("Columbo": "How to Dial a Murder") (NBC)

OUTSTANDING FILM EDITING FOR A SPECIAL
Bernard J. Small, Just a Little Inconvenience (NBC)

OUTSTANDING ACHIEVEMENT IN FILM EDITING FOR A SERIES
Larry Carow, David Pettijohn, Don Warner, Colin Mouat, Chuck Moran and Pieter Hubbard, Baa Baa Black Sheep/Black Sheep Squadron ("The Hawk Flied on Sunday") (NBC)

OUTSTANDING ACHIEVEMENT IN FILM SOUND EDITING FOR A SPECIAL
Bernard F. Pincus, Patrick R. Somerset, Jeffrey Bushelman, A. Jeremy Hoenack, John Bushelman, Edward L. Sandlin, Robert A. Biggart and Jerry Rosenthal, The Dark Secret of Harvest Home (NBC)

OUTSTANDING ACHIEVEMENT IN MUSIC COMPOSITION FOR A SERIES
Morton Stevens, NBC's Best Sellers ("Wheels") (NBC)
Patrick Williams, NBC Sunday Mystery Movie ("Columbo": "Try and Catch Me") (NBC)

1978-79

OUTSTANDING DRAMA SERIES

The Rockford Files (NBC) Meta Rosenberg, Executive Producer; David Chase and Chas. Floyd Johnson, Producers

OUTSTANDING SUPPORTING ACTOR IN A DRAMA SERIES
*Stuart Margolin, The Rockford Files (NBC)
Noah Beery, Jr., The Rockford Files (NBC)
Joe Santos, The Rockford Files (NBC)

OUTSTANDING LEAD ACTRESS IN A DRAMA SERIES
*Mariette Hartley, The Incredible Hulk ("Married") (CBS)
Rita Moreno, The Rockford Files ("Rosendahl and Gilda Stern Are Dead") (NBC)

OUTSTANDING LEAD ACTOR IN A DRAMA SERIES
James Garner, The Rockford Files (NBC)
Jack Klugman, Quincy, M.E. (NBC)

OUTSTANDING ART DIRECTION FOR A SERIES
*Howard E. Johnson (Art Director), Richard B. Goddard (Set Decorator), Little Women (Part 1) (NBC)
John E. Chilberg II (Art Director), Battlestar: Galactica ("Saga of a Star World") (ABC)

OUTSTANDING ART DIRECTION FOR A LIMITED SERIES OR A SPECIAL
Jack Senter (Production Designer), John W. Corso (Art Director), Sherman Loudermilk (Art Director), Joseph J. Stone (Set Decorator), John M. Dwyer (Set Decorator) and Robert G. Freer (Set Decorator), Centennial ("The Shepherds") (NBC)

OUTSTANDING COSTUME DESIGN FOR A SERIES
*Jean-Pierre Dorleac, Battlestar: Galactica ("Furlon")

OUTSTANDING FILM EDITING FOR A LIMITED SERIES OR SPECIAL
Robert Watts, Centennial ("Only the Rocks Live Forever") (NBC)

OUTSTANDING INDIVIDUAL ACHIEVEMENT--CREATIVE TECHNICAL CRAFTS
*John Dykstra (Special Effects Coordinator), Richard Edlund (Director of Miniature Photography) and Joseph Goss (Mechanical Special Effects), Battlestar: Galactica ("Saga of a Star World") (ABC)

1979-80

OUTSTANDING DRAMA SERIES
The Rockford Files (NBC) Meta Rosenberg, Executive Producer; Stephen J. Cannell, Supervising Producer; David Chase, Chas. Floyd Johnson and Juanita Bartlett, Producers

OUTSTANDING LEAD ACTOR IN A DRAMA SERIES
　　James Garner, The Rockford Files (NBC)
　　Jack Klugman, Quincy, M.E. (NBC)

OUTSTANDING LEAD ACTRESS IN A DRAMA SERIES
　　Lauren Bacall, The Rockford Files ("Lions, Tigers, Monkeys and Dogs") (NBC)
　　Mariette Hartley, The Rockford Files ("Paradise Cove") (NBC)

OUTSTANDING SUPPORTING ACTOR IN A DRAMA SERIES
　　*Stuart Margolin, The Rockford Files (NBC)
　　Noah Beery, Jr., The Rockford Files (NBC)

OUTSTANDING CINEMATOGRAPHY FOR A SERIES
　　Alric Edens, A.S.C., Quincy, M.E. ("Riot") (NBC)
　　John McPherson, A.S.C., The Incredible Hulk ("Broken Image") (NBC)

OUTSTANDING CINEMATOGRAPHY FOR A LIMITED SERIES OR A SPECIAL
　　Harry L. Wolf, A.S.C., Brave New World (NBC)

OUTSTANDING ART DIRECTION FOR A SERIES
　　Hub Braden and Fred Luff (Art Directors) and Frank Lombardo (Set Decorator), Buck Rogers in the 25th Century ("Ardala Returns") (NBC)

OUTSTANDING ART DIRECTION FOR A LIMITED SERIES OR A SPECIAL
　　Tom H. John (Art Director) and Mary Ann Biddle (Set Decorator), Brave New World (NBC)

OUTSTANDING COSTUME DESIGN FOR A SERIES
　　Jean-Pierre Dorleac, Galactica 1980 ("Starbuck's Last Journey") (ABC)
　　Alfred E. Lehman, Buck Rogers in the 25th Century ("Flight of the War Witch" Part II) (NBC)

Telly Savalas in KOJAK.

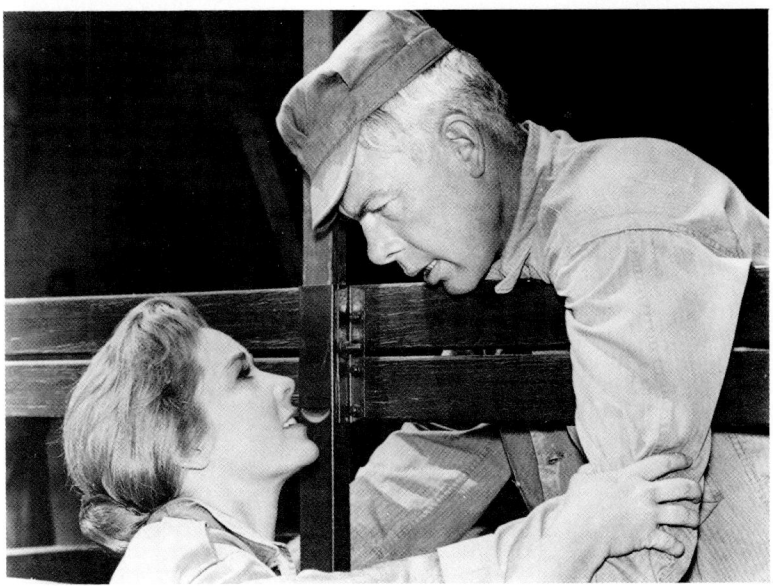

Vera Miles and Lee Marvin in the KRAFT SUSPENSE THEATRE episode "The Case Against Paul Ryker."

The cast of LEAVE IT TO BEAVER in 1957 (clockwise from top left): Barbara Billingsley, Hugh Beaumont, Tony Dow, and Jerry Mathers.

Lee Marvin and friend in M SQUAD.

Raymond Burr, Robert Loggia, and Mark Hamill in MALLORY: CIRCUMSTANTIAL EVIDENCE.

Guest star John Denver and Dennis Weaver in McCLOUD.

The cast of McHALE'S NAVY, c. 1962. Top row: Edson Stroll, Gavin MacLeod, Ernest Borgnine, Billy Sands, and Yoshio Yoda. Bottom row: John Wright, Gary Vinson, Tim Conway, and Carl Ballantine.

Susan Saint James and Rock Hudson in McMILLAN AND WIFE.

Ray Milland and Phyllis Avery in MEET MR. McNUTLEY.

Guest ghoul Teddie Blue and Darren McGavin in THE NIGHT STALKER.

Robert Stack, Tony Franciosa, and Gene Barry, the stars of separate segments of THE NAME OF THE GAME.

Andrew Stevens in THE OREGON TRAIL.

John Payne (right) and unidentified actor in THE RESTLESS GUN.

Peter Strauss, Susan Blakely, and Nick Nolte in RICH MAN, POOR MAN.

Darren McGavin (second from right) and Burt Reynolds (center) in RIVERBOAT.

Noah Berry, Jr. and James Garner in THE ROCKFORD FILES.

Mildred Natwick and Helen Hayes in THE SNOOP SISTERS.

Dale Robertson in TALES OF WELLS FARGO.

Boris Karloff of THRILLER in a publicity photograph taken in Universal's mask-making department.

Tim Matheson in THE VIRGINIAN.

APPENDIX I:

THEATRICAL FILMS EDITED FROM SERIES EPISODES

The following is a list of films released to motion picture theatres which were "made" by splicing together episodes of Universal Television series. The majority of these shows were released theatrically three or four years after being broadcast on television --by which time, it was assumed, the public had forgotten that they had already seen them on the home screen.

BACKTRACK

Released by Universal Pictures, June 1969; 95 minutes in color.

A Western, with comic overtones, about Trampas, cowhand at the Shiloh Ranch in the Wyoming Territory in the 1890s, who was sent to Texas by his boss, The Virginian, to secure a prize bull. While in the Lone Star State, Trampas met up with three Texas Rangers and their captain. This film was actually The Virginian episode "We've Lost a Train" (telecast on NBC, April 21, 1965), with some additional footage tacked on. The episode served as the pilot for the Laredo series which starred Brand, Brown, Smith, and Carey. The Virginian regulars were Drury, McClure, Clarke and Boone, and the guest stars, in addition to the Laredo people, were Lamas, Fleming, Lupino and Dano. Another theatrical release which featured the cast of Laredo was Three Guns for Texas (which see).

Cast: The Virginian (James Drury), Reese Bennett (Neville Brand), Trampas (Doug McClure), Chad Cooper (Peter Brown), Joe Riley (William Smith), Capt. Edward Parmalee (Philip Carey), Capt. Estrada (Fernando Lamas), Carmelita (Rhonda Fleming), Dolores (Ida Lupino), Faraway (Royal Dano), Steve (Gary Clarke), Randy (Randy Boone).

Credits: Produced by: David J. O'Connell; Directed by: Earl Bellamy; Written by: Borden Chase; Music by: Jack Marshall.

BATTLESTAR: GALACTICA

Released by Universal Pictures, May 1979; 148 minutes in color.

296 / Appendix I

This film was actually an edited version of the pilot episode for the series of the same title, enhanced with the rumbling effects of Sensurround, an audio process. It was released just weeks after the series was canceled and was a substantial success.

Cast: Captain Apollo (Richard Hatch), Lt. Starbuck (Dirk Benedict), Commander Adama (Lorne Greene), Lt. Boomer (Herbert Jefferson, Jr.), Count Baltar (John Colicos), Athena (Maren Jensen), Boxey (Noah Hathaway), Cassiopea (Laurette Spang), Col. Tigh (Terry Carter), Flight Sgt. Jolly (Tony Swartz), Uri (Ray Milland), Adar (Lew Ayres), Anton (Wilfrid Hyde-White), Serina (Jane Seymour), Dr. Paye (John Fink), Zac (Rick Springfield).

Credits: Executive Producer: Glen A. Larson; Producers: John Dykstra, Leslie Stevens; Directed by: Richard A. Colla; Written by: Glen A. Larson; Music by: Stu Phillips; Music Performed by: The Los Angeles Philharmonic Orchestra; Color by: Technicolor; Titles & Optical Effects: Universal Title; Produced by: Glen A. Larson Productions.

BUCK ROGERS IN THE 25th CENTURY

Released by Universal Pictures, Spring 1979; 89 minutes in color.

This film was actually the pilot for the series of the same title, released theatrically about four months before the TV program premiered. It cannot really be classified as a telefeature because it was first screened in theatres.

Cast: Buck Rogers (Gil Gerard), Princess Ardala (Pamela Hensley), Col. Wilma Deering (Erin Gray), Kane (Henry Silva), The Voice of Twiki (Mel Blanc).

Credits: Executive Producer: Glen A. Larson; Produced by: Richard Caffey, Leslie Stevens; Directed by: Daniel Haller; Written by: Glen A. Larson, Leslie Stevens; Color by: Technicolor; Titles & Optical Effects: Universal Title; Produced by: Glen A. Larson Productions.

SERGEANT RYKER

Released by Universal Pictures, February 1968; 85 minutes in color.

This film was actually an edited version of the Kraft Suspense Theatre episode "The Case Against Paul Ryker" (telecast on NBC, October 10 and 17, 1963) which was the basis for the series Court Martial in which Dillman and Graves continued their roles. Sergeant Ryker was about a U.S. Army non-com who was convicted of being a Red spy and was sentenced to die.

Cast: Sgt. Paul Ryker (Lee Marvin), Capt. David Young (Bradford

Appendix I / 297

Dillman), Ann Ryker (Vera Miles), Maj. Frank Whitaker (Peter Graves), Gen. Amos Bailey (Lloyd Nolan), Capt. Appleton (Murray Hamilton), Sgt. Max Winkler (Norman Fell), Col. Arthur Merriam (Walter Brooke), Pres. of Court Martial (Francis DeSales), Corp. Jenks (Don Marshall).

Credits: Produced by: Frank Telford; Directed by: Buzz Kulik; Written by: Seeleg Lester, William D. Gordon; Story by: Seeleg Lester; Director of Photography: Walter Strenge, A.S.C.; Music by: Johnny Williams; Art Director: John J. Lloyd; Film Editor: Robert B. Warwick; Set Decorators: John McCarthy, Robert C. Bradfield; Assistant Director: John Clarke Bowman; Sound: William Lynch; Costume Supervisor: Vincent Dee; Makeup: Jack Barron; Hair Stylist: Florence Bush; Music Supervision: Stanley Wilson.

STRATEGY OF TERROR

Released by Universal Pictures, January 1969; 90 minutes in color.

This film was actually an edited version of the Kraft Suspense Theatre episode "In Darkness Waiting" (telecast on NBC, January 14 and 21, 1965). It was about a terrorist group that set out to assasinate three important members of the United Nations and the female journalist and Manhattan cop who tried to stop it.

Cast: Matt (Hugh O'Brian), Karen (Barbara Rush), Mr. Harkin (Neil Hamilton), Jacques (Frederick O'Neal), Wally (Will Corry), Bit (Mort Mills).

Credits: Executive Producer: Frank P. Rosenberg; Produced by: Arthur H. Nadel; Directed by: Jack Smight; Written by: Robert L. Joseph; Music by: Lyn Murray.

TAMMY AND THE MILLIONAIRE

Released by Universal Pictures, May 1967; 87 minutes in color.

This film was edited from four episodes of the series Tammy. It was a comedy about a millionaire who employed a pretty backwoods girl to be his secretary and was released a year after the series went off the air.

Cast: Tammy Tarleton (Debbie Watson), John Brent (Donald Woods), Lavinia Tate (Dorothy Green), Steven Brent (Jay Sheffield), Dwayne Witt (George Furth), Uncle Lucius (Frank McGrath), Grandpa Tarleton (Denver Pyle), Peter Tate (David Macklin), Gloria Tate (Linda Marshall), Gov. Alden (Roy Roberts).

Credits: Produced by: Dick Wesson; Directed by: Ezra Stone, Sidney Miller, Leslie Goodwins; Written by: George Tibbles;

298 / Appendix I

Based on the Novels "Tammy Tell Me True" and "Tammy Out of Time" by: Cid Ricketts Summer.

THIS SAVAGE LAND

Released by Universal Pictures, August 1969; 98 minutes in color.

This film was actually an edited version of the The Road West episode of the same title (telecast on NBC, September 12 and 19, 1966). It was about an Ohio widower who moved his family out West where they were victimized by a vigilante gang.

Cast: Benjamin Pride (Barry Sullivan), Timothy Pride (Andrew Prine), Midge Pride (Brenda Scott), Kip Pride (Kelly Corcoran), Grandpa Pride (Charles Seel), Chance Reynolds (Glenn Corbett), Elizabeth Reynolds (Kathryn Hays), Grandma Pride (Katherine Squire), Elizabeth's Father (Roy Roberts), Stacey (John Drew Barrymore), with: George C. Scott.

Credits: Executive Producer: Norman Macdonnell; Produced by: James McAdams; Directed by: Vincent McEveety; Music Supervision: Stanley Wilson.

THREE GUNS FOR TEXAS

Released by Universal Pictures, May 1968; 99 minutes in color.

This Western with comic overtones was about three Texas Rangers and their captain, who helped a young Indian girl in her search for a husband. It was edited from the Laredo episodes "Yahoo," "Jinx" and "No Bugles, One Drum," all of which featured guest star Shelley Morrison, telecast on NBC September 30, 1965, December 2, 1965 and February 24, 1966, respectively. Another theatrical release which featured the cast of Laredo was Backtrack (which see).

Cast: Reese Bennett (Neville Brand), Chad Cooper (Peter Brown), Joe Riley (William Smith), Capt. Edward Parmalee (Philip Carey), MacMillan (Martin Milner), Indian Girl (Shelley Morrison), with: Michael Conrad, Ralph Manza, Albert Salmi and Dub Taylor.

Credits: Produced by: Richard Irving; Directors: Earl Bellamy, David Lowell Rich, Paul Stanley; Written by: John D. F. Black; Music by: Russ Garcia.

APPENDIX II:

THEATRICAL FILMS BASED ON SERIES

The following is a list of films, created especially for release to motion picture theatres, which were based on Universal Television series. They are not to be confused with the type of films listed in APPENDIX I, which were "made" by splicing together existing episodes of series.

McHALE'S NAVY

Released by Universal Pictures, June 1964; 93 minutes in color.

A comedy about the crew of PT 73, stationed on the South Pacific island of Taratupa during World War II, who rigged a horse race to get themselves out of debt. Based on the TV series of the same title. Followed by the sequel listed below.

Cast: Lt. Commander McHale (Ernest Borgnine), Capt. Binghamton (Joe Flynn), Ensign Charles Parker (Tim Conway), Lester Gruber (Carl Ballantine), "Happy" Hanes (Gavin MacLeod), "Christy" Christopher (Gary Vinson), "Tinker" Bell (Billy Sands), Willy Moss (John Wright), Virgil Farrell (Edson Stroll), Fuji (Yoshio Yoda), Lt. Carpenter (Bob Hastings), Andrea (Claudine Longet), Margot (Jean Willes), Henri Le Clerc (George Kennedy), Chief of Police (Marcel Hillaire).

Credits: Produced and Directed by: Edward J. Montagne; Writers: Frank Gill, Jr., G. Carleton Brown; Story by: Si Rose; Associate Producer: Si Rose; Director of Photography: William Margulies, A.S.C.; Music by: Jerry Fielding; Art Directors: Alexander Golitzen, Russell Kimball; Film Editor: Sam E. Waxman, A.C.E.; Set Decorations: John McCarthy, James S. Redd; Sound: Waldon O. Watson, Earl Crain, Sr.; Unit Production Manager: Wallace Worsley; Costumes: Helen Colvig; Makeup: Bud Westmore; Hair Stylist: Larry Germain; Assistant Director: Phil Bowles.

McHALE'S NAVY JOINS THE AIR FORCE

Released by Universal Pictures, June 1965; 90 minutes in color.

A comedy about the crew of PT 73 in the South Pacific during World War II and their involvement with Russian agents, a hard-nosed Army general, and some nubile WACs. Ernest Borgnine was conspicuous for his absence from this sequel to the theatrical film McHale's Navy (which see).

Cast: Capt. Wallace Burton Binghamton (Joe Flynn), Ensign Charles Parker (Tim Conway), Lt. Elroy Carpenter (Bob Hastings), Quartermaster George "Christy" Christopher (Gary Vinson), Machnist "Tinker" Bell (Billy Sands), Gunner's Mate Virgil Edwards (Edson Stroll), Radioman Will Moss (John Wright), Seaman Joseph "Happy" Haines (Gavin MacLeod), Takeo "Fuji" Fujiwara (Yoshio Yoda), General Harkness (Tom Tully), Smitty (Susan Silo), Col. Platt (Henry Beckman), Madge (Jean Hale), Dimitri (Jacques Aubuchon).

Credits: Produced and Directed by: Edward J. Montagne; Written by: John Fenton Murray; Story by: William J. Lederer; Associate Producer: Si Rose; Director of Photography: Lionel Lindon, A.S.C.; Music by: Jerry Fielding; Art Directors: Alexander Golitzen, Russell Kimball; Film Editor: Sam E. Waxman; Set Decorations: John McCarthy, James S. Redd; Sound: Waldon O. Watson, Earl Crain, Sr.; Unit Production Manager: Wes Thompson; Assistant Director: George Bisk; Makeup: Bud Westmore; Hair Stylist: Larry Germain.

MUNSTER, GO HOME

Released by Universal Pictures, June 1966; 96 minutes in color.

A comedy about the ghoulish Munster clan who inherited a castle and journeyed to England to claim it. This film was made after the TV series The Munsters had ceased production and, as Pat Priest, who played the role of Marilyn Munster, had become involved in other projects, her role was taken over by Debbie Watson. The stars of the series were Gwynne, De Carlo, Lewis and Patrick.

Cast: Herman Munster (Fred Gwynne), Lily Munster (Yvonne De Carlo), Grandpa Munster (Al Lewis), Eddie Munster (Butch Patrick), Marilyn Munster (Debbie Watson), Lady Effigie Munster (Hermione Gingold), Freddie Munster (Terry-Thomas), Grace Munster (Jeanne Arnold), Roger Morseby (Robert Pine), Cruckshank (John Carradine), Shipmate (Jack Dodson), Squire Moresby (Bernard Fox), Joey (Richard Dawson), Millie (Marie Lennard), Herbert (Cliff Norton), Mrs. Moresby (Diana Chesney), Hennesy (Ben Wright), Alfie (Arthur Malet).

Credits: Producers: Joe Connelly, Bob Mosher; Directed by: Earl Bellamy; Written by: George Tibbles, Joe Connelly, Bob Mosher; Color by: Technicolor.

INDEX

The names listed below can be found by their cited show titles, which are listed alphabetically within each of the main sections: Series, Telefeatures, Pilots, and Specials.

ATV NETWORK LIMITED (production company)
   Special
      Hamlet
ABBOTT, NORMAN (director)
   Series
      Leave It to Beaver
ABEL, WALTER (host)
   Series
      Suspicion
ABRAHMSON, BERNIE (director of photography)
   Telefeature
      The Art of Crime
ABRAMS, MORT (producer)
   Series
      Suspicion
ABRAMS, ROBERT (director)
   Series
      Doctors' Hospital
ABROMS, EDWARD M. (film editor)
   Series
      Columbo (and director)
      Doctors' Hospital (director only)
   Telefeatures
      Berlin Affair
      Deadlock!
      Dial: Hot Line
      The Impatient Heart
      Lock, Stock and Barrel
      My Sweet Charlie
      Night Gallery
      Ransom for a Dead Man
      Savage
      That Certain Summer
ACKER, SHARON (actress)
   Series
      The Senator
ACKERMAN, HARRY (producer)
   Series
      Bachelor Father
      Leave It to Beaver (executive producer)
ACKERMAN, LEONARD J. (producer)
   Telefeature
      Ellery Queen: Don't Look Behind You
ACKROYD, DAVID (actor)
   Telefeatures
      The Dark Secret of Harvest Home
      Exo-Man
ADAM, SCOTT U. (unit production manager)
   Series
      The Misadventures of Sheriff Lobo
ADAM-12 PRODUCTIONS (production company)
   Series
      Adam-12
ADAMS, DON (actor)
   Series
      Don Adams' Screen Test (and executive producer/creator)
      The Partners (and creator/writer)
   Pilot
      Three Times Daley
ADAMS, EDIE (actress)
   Series
      The Seekers
   Telefeature
      Evil Roy Slade
ADAMS, JEB (actor)
   Series
      Black Sheep Squadron
ADAMS, JERRY (set decorator)
   Series
      Aspen
      Banacek

Captains and the Kings
The Six Million Dollar Man
Telefeature
The Six Million Dollar Man
ADAMS, LEE (composer/lyricist)
Special
Applause
ADAMS, RICHARD L. (writer)
Telefeature
Winchester 73
ADAMS, WARREN H., A.C.E.
 (film editor)
Series
Emergency!
Telefeatures
Chase
Emergency!
O'Hara, United States Treasury
ADDISON, JOHN (composer)
Series
The Bastard
Black Beauty
Centennial
The Eddie Capra Mysteries
 (theme only)
Special
Hamlet
ADLER, DIANE (film editor)
Series
The Rockford Files
Telefeature
Dr. Scorpion
ADLER, LUTHER (actor)
Series
The Psychiatrist
Telefeatures
The Psychiatrist: God Bless
 the Children
The Sunshine Patriot
ADNEY, CHRIS (art director)
Telefeature
Tom Sawyer
AGUTTER, JENNY (actress)
Special
The Snow Goose
AHERN, LLOYD, A.S.C. (director
 of photography)
Series
Columbo
The Psychiatrist
Pilot
Koska and His Family
Special
The Red Pony
AIDMAN, CHARLES (actor)
Telefeatures
Amelia Earhart
Night Life

The Sound of Anger
AKINS, CLAUDE (actor)
Series
The Misadventures of Sheriff
 Lobo
The Rhinemann Exchange
Telefeatures
BJ and the Bear
Lock, Stock and Barrel
River of Mystery
ALBERT, EDDIE (actor)
Series
Evening in Byzantium
Switch
Telefeature
Switch
ALBERT, EDWARD (actor)
Series
Black Beauty
The Last Convertible
ALBERTSON, ERIC (film editor)
Telefeature
Farewell to Manzanar
ALBERTSON, JACK (actor)
Telefeatures
A Clear and Present Danger
Lock, Stock and Barrel
Special
The Slowest Gun in the West
ALETTER, FRANK (actor)
Series
Bringing Up Buddy
ALEX WINITSKY-ARLENE SELL-
 ERS PRODUCTIONS (produc-
 tion company)
Series
House Calls
ALEXANDER, DAVID (director)
Series
Marcus Welby, M.D.
ALEXANDER, JAMES A. (sound
 mixer)
Telefeature
A Clear and Present Danger
ALEXANDER, JAMES E. (sound
 mixer)
Telefeature
Death Race
ALEXANDER, JAMES R. (sound
 mixer)
Telefeature
The Bravos
ALEXANDER, JEFF (composer)
Series
Columbo
Frontier Circus
ALEXANDER, JIM (sound mixer)
Telefeature

Amelia Earhart
ALEXANDER, LARRY (writer)
  Series
  Kingston: Confidential
  The Six Million Dollar Man
ALEY, ALBERT (producer/story editor)
  Series
  Ironside
ALL AMERICA FEATURES (production company)
  Series
  Sing Along with Mitch
ALLARDICE, JAMES (writer)
  Series
  General Electric Theatre
  It's a Man's World
ALLEN, BERT F. (set decorator)
  Series
  Alias Smith and Jones
  Rod Serling's Night Gallery
ALLEN, COREY (director)
  Series
  The Family Holvak
  Quincy, M.E.
  Telefeature
  See the Man Run
ALLEN, LEWIS (director)
  Series
  Harold Robbins' "The Survivors"
ALLEN, MARTY (actor)
  Telefeature
  Benny and Barney: Las Vegas Undercover
ALLEN, ROBERT (theme composer)
  Series
  Sing Along with Mitch
ALLEN, SIAN BARBARA (actress)
  Telefeature
  Scream, Pretty Peggy
ALLEN, STEVE (actor)
  Series
  Rich Man, Poor Man
  Telefeature
  Now You See It, Now You Don't
ALLER, ROBERT (producer)
  Special
  The Red Pony
ALLISON, JEAN (actress)
  Telefeature
  Man on the Outside
ALLYSON, JUNE (actress)
  Telefeatures
  The Elevator
  See the Man Run
ALMEIDA, LAURINDO (composer)
  Telefeature
  Death Takes a Holiday
ALSTON, Howard (producer)
  Series
  Centennial
ALTHOUSE, SHIRLEY (hair stylist)
  Series
  PAris 7000
ALTMAN, ROBERT (producer/director/writer)
  Series
  Kraft Suspense Theatre
ALVES, JOSEPH, JR. (art director)
  Series
  Escape
  The Psychiatrist
  Rod Serling's Night Gallery
  Telefeatures
  Double Indemnity
  The Impatient Heart
  Money to Burn
  The Priest Killer
  Sarge: The Badge or the Cross
  Scream, Pretty Peggy
  See the Man Run
  The Young Country
AMBLER, ERIC (producer)
  Series
  Alcoa Premiere/Premiere
  Checkmate (creator only)
AMBLER, JEANENE (film editor)
  Series
  Quincy, M.E.
AMECHE, DON (actor)
  Telefeature
  Shadow Over Elveron
  Pilot
  Boston and Kilbride
AMES, MORGAN (theme lyricist)
  Series
  Baretta
AMES, WILLY (actor)
  Telefeature
  The Family Nobody Wanted
ANDERSON, BARBARA (actress)
  Series
  Ironside
  Telefeatures
  Ironside
  The Six Million Dollar Man
  You Lie So Deep, My Love
ANDERSON, BILL (theme vocalist)
  Telefeature
  Stranger on the Run
ANDERSON, EDDIE "ROCHESTER" (actor)
  Series
  The Jack Benny Show

Telefeature
It Takes a Thief
ANDERSON, HESPER (writer)
  Series
  Marcus Welby, M.D.
  Telefeature
  The UFO Incident
ANDERSON, JOHN (actor)
  Telefeatures
  Heat Wave
  Hitched
  The Log of the Black Pearl
ANDERSON, RICHARD (actor)
  Series
  The Bionic Woman
  Condominium
  The Immigrants
  The Six Million Dollar Man
  Telefeatures
  The Astronaut
  The Longest Night
ANDREWS, DANA (actor)
  Telefeature
  The Failing of Raymond
ANDREWS, EDWARD (actor)
  Series
  Broadside
  Telefeatures
  Don't Push, I'll Charge When I'm Ready
  The Intruders
  Murder by Proxy
  Special
  The Man Who Came to Dinner
ANDREWS, ROBERT HARDY (writer)
  Series
  Going My Way
  Thriller
ANDREWS, TIGE (actor)
  Telefeature
  Skyway to Death
ANHALT, EDWARD (writer)
  Series
  Bob Hope Presents the Chrysler Theatre
ANSARA, MICHAEL (actor)
  Telefeature
  How I Spent My Summer Vacation
ANTON, SUSAN (actress)
  Series
  Cliffhangers
ANTONIO, LOU(IS) (director)
  Series
  Griff
  McMillan and Wife
  Owen Marshall, Counselor at Law
  Telefeatures
  Lanigan's Rabbi
  Pilots
  Boston and Kilbride
  The Gypsy Warriors
ARCHER, NICK (film editor)
  Telefeature
  The Challengers
ARDEN, EVE (actress)
  Telefeatures
  All My Darling Daughters
  A Very Missing Person
  Special
  Mother of the Bride
ARENA PRODUCTIONS, INC.
  (Norman Felton's production company)
  Series
  The Psychiatrist
  Telefeatures
  Marriage: Year One
  The Psychiatrist: God Bless the Children
ARESCO, JOEY (actor)
  Pilot
  Snafu
ARKIN, ALAN (director)
  Series
  Fay
ARLISS, DIMITRA (actress)
  Series
  Rich Man, Poor Man--Book II
  Telefeature
  The Art of Crime
ARMSTRONG, CHARLOTTE (writer)
  Series
  Startime
  Thriller
ARMUS, BURTON (writer)
  Series
  Delvecchio
  Kojak (technical advisor only)
ARNOLD, CHARLES G. (director of photography)
  Telefeature
  The 3,000 Mile Chase
ARNOLD, JACK (director)
  Series
  Alias Smith and Jones
  Ellery Queen
  Holmes and Yoyo
  It Takes a Thief (and executive producer)
  McNaughton's Daughter
  Telefeature
  Sex and the Married Woman

(and producer)
ARNSTEN, STEFAN (film editor)
  Telefeature
  Two on a Bench
ARONSON, BRAD H. (unit production manager)
  Series
  The Eddie Capra Mysteries
  The Rebels
ARRIGO, FRANK (art director)
  Series
  Going My Way
  The Jack Benny Show
  Telefeatures
  Charlie Chan
  The Doomsday Flight
  How to Steal an Airplane
  A Little Game
  The Outsider
  Winchester 73
  Wings of Fire
ARTHUR, JEAN (actress)
  Series
  The Jean Arthur Show
ARTHUR, SID (writer)
  Telefeature
  Let's Switch
ASKINS, MONROE (director of photography)
  Series
  The Munsters
ASNER, EDWARD (actor)
  Series
  Rich Man, Poor Man
  Telefeature
  The Doomsday Flight
ASSOCIATED BRITISH FILMS (production company)
  Telefeature
  Mousey
ASTAIRE, FRED (actor)
  Series
  Alcoa Premiere/Premiere (host only)
  It Takes a Thief
ASTIN, JOHN (actor)
  Series
  Holmes and Yoyo (director only)
  Operation Petticoat
  Telefeatures
  Evil Roy Slade
  Operation Petticoat (and director)
  Rosetti and Ryan: Men Who Love Women (director only)
  Skyway to Death
  Two on a Bench

ASTIN, PATTY DUKE (actress)
  Series
  Captains and the Kings
  Women in White
  Telefeatures
  My Sweet Charlie
  Rosetti and Ryan: Men Who Love Women
  The Storyteller
  Two on a Bench
ASTOR, BURT (unit manager)
  Series
  Rod Serling's Night Gallery
  Telefeatures
  The Movie Murderer
  Silent Night, Lonely Night
ASTORI, GABRIO (film editor)
  Series
  It Takes a Thief
ATHA, SHEILA (stage manager)
  Special
  Hamlet
ATHERTON, WILLIAM (actor)
  Series
  Centennial
ATKINS, TOM (actor)
  Series
  The Rockford Files
ATWATER, BARRY (actor)
  Telefeatures
  Night Gallery
  Vanished
AUBERJONOIS, RENE (actor)
  Series
  The Rhinemann Exchange
  Telefeatures
  The Birdmen
  The Dark Secret of Harvest Home
  Once Upon a Dead Man
AUBREY, SKYE (actress)
  Telefeatures
  Vanished
  A Very Missing Person
AUMONT, JEAN-PIERRE (actor)
  Series
  Beggarman, Thief
AUSTIN, RAY (director)
  Series
  House Calls
AVASTA PRODUCTIONS (production company)
  Series
  Alcoa Premiere/Premiere
AVERBACK, HY (director)
  Series
  McCloud
  The Rockford Files

306 / Index

Telefeatures
The Night Rider
Richie Brockelman, Private Eye
AVERY, PHYLLIS (actress)
Series
Meet Mr. McNulty
The Ray Milland Show
AVRUTIS, NEWTON (sound mixer)
Telefeature
The Borgia Stick
AYER, SIMON (casting director)
Series
Buck Rogers in the 25th Century
AYRES, LEW
Telefeatures
Heat Wave
Marcus Welby, M.D.
The Questor Tapes

BBC-TV see BRITISH BROADCASTING COMPANY
BACALL, LAUREN (actress)
Special
Applause
BACHARDY, DON (writer)
Telefeature
Frankenstein: The True Story
BACHELOR PRODUCTIONS (production company)
Series
Bachelor Father
BACKUS, JIM (actor)
Series
The Rebels
Telefeature
Magic Carpet
BACON, ARCH (art director)
Series
Columbo
The Sixth Sense
Telefeatures
The D.A.: Conspiracy to Kill
The Devil and Miss Sarah
Hitchhike!
BADHAM, JOHN (director)
Series
Sarge
The Senator (associate producer only)
Telefeatures
A Clear and Present Danger (associate producer only)
Dial: Hot Line (associate producer only)

The Gun
The Impatient Heart
The Keegans
The Law
Special
Short Stories of Love
BADIYI, REZA S. (director)
Series
Holmes and Yoyo
Switch
BAEHR, NICHOLAS E. (associate producer)
Series
Alias Smith and Jones
Telefeature
The Invasion of Johnson County (writer only)
BAEHR, NICK see BAEHR, NICHOLAS E.
BAER, DONALD (assistant director)
Series
Tales of Wells Fargo
BAER, ED (set decorator)
Series
Baretta
The Hardy Boys Mysteries
BAER, MAX, JR. (actor)
Telefeature
The Birdmen
BAGGETTA, VINCENT (actor)
Series
The Eddie Capra Mysteries
BAILEY, DOROTHY J. (associate producer)
Series
Aspen
BAIN, BARBARA (actress)
Telefeature
Savage
BAIN, SEAN (writer)
Series
The Rebels
BAKER, DIANE (actress)
Telefeature
Do You Take This Stranger
BAKER, JOE DON (actor)
Telefeature
That Certain Summer
BAKER, ROY, G.B.F.E. (sound editor)
Telefeature
Destiny of a Spy
BALCHUS, FRANK (costume designer)
Special
The Red Pony
BALL, LUCILLE (actress)
Special

The Jack Benny Special
BALLAS, JAMES D. (film editor)
Series
The Deputy
BALLINGER, BILL S. (writer)
Series
The Night Stalker
BALSAM, MARTIN (actor)
Telefeatures
The Six Million Dollar Man
The Storyteller
BALTER, ALLAN B. (producer)
Series
San Francisco International
 Airport (creator only)
The Six Million Dollar Man
 (supervising producer only)
Telefeatures
Captain America (executive
 producer only)
Just a Little Inconvenience
 (and writer)
The Man with the Power (and
 writer)
San Francisco International
 Airport (and writer)
BALZER, GEORGE (writer)
Series
The Jack Benny Show
BARATTA, FRED(ERIC) (film
 editor)
Series
The Nancy Drew Mysteries
Telefeature
The Art of Crime
BARBER, PHIL(IP) (art director)
Telefeatures
The Dark Secret of Harvest
 Home
The Questor Tapes
BARNETT, STEVE (assistant director)
Series
Kojak
BARON, ALLEN (director)
Series
The Night Stalker
BARRETT, EARL (producer/
 writer)
Series
The Partners
BARRETT, TONY (producer)
Series
Faraday and Company
The Snoop Sisters
BARRIE, BARBARA (actress)
Series
79 Park Avenue

Pilot
Koska and His Family
Special
The Mask of Love
BARRON, JACK (makeup artist)
Series
The Deputy
87th Precinct
Laramie
Leave It to Beaver
Startime
Tales of Wells Fargo
The Tall Man
The Virginian
Wagon Train
Westinghouse Playhouse Starring
 Nanette Fabray and Wendell
 Corey
Whispering Smith
Special
The Slowest Gun in the West
BARROWS, ROBERT GUY (writer)
Series
Destry
BARRY, GENE (actor)
Series
Aspen
The Name of the Game
Telefeatures
The Devil and Miss Sarah
Do You Take This Stranger
Istanbul Express
Prescription: Murder
BARRYMORE, JOHN DREW (actor)
Telefeature
Winchester 73
BARTELS, CLAY (film editor)
Telefeature
Operation Petticoat
BARTLETT, JUANITA (executive
 story consultant/story editor)
Series
The Rockford Files
BARTLETT, PETER (director of
 photography)
Special
The Adventures of Don Quixote
BARTLETT, RICHARD H. (producer)
Series
Cimarron City
Riverboat (and director/writer)
BARTON, FRANKLIN (executive
 producer)
Series
Seventh Avenue
Pilot
Off the wall

BARTON, JOHN (director/writer)
  Special
  Hamlet
BARTON, PETER (actor)
  Series
  Shirley
BASEHART, RICHARD (actor)
  Series
  The Rebels
  Telefeatures
  The Birdmen
  Maneater
  Stonestreet: Who Killed the Centerfold Model?
BASIE, COUNT (theme composer)
  Series
  M Squad
BASS, SAUL (main title designer)
  Series
  Alcoa Premiere/Premiere
BATANIDES, ARTHUR (actor)
  Series
  Johnny Midnight
BATCHELLER, RICHARD (director of photography)
  Telefeature
  Night Gallery
BATES, IRA (set decorator)
  Series
  Escape
  Telefeature
  Lieutenant Schuster's Wife
BATT, BERT (assistant director)
  Telefeature
  Run a Crooked Mile
BAUGH, MARTIN (costume designer)
  Special
  Hamlet
BAUR, ELIZABETH (actress)
  Series
  Ironside
BAUR, FRANK (associate producer)
  Series
  Alcoa Premiere/Premiere
BAXLEY, BARBARA (actress)
  Telefeature
  The Law
  Special
  A Special Act of Love
BAXTER, ANNE (actress)
  Series
  Marcus Welby, M.D.
  Telefeatures
  The Challengers
  Companions in Nightmare
  Marcus Welby, M.D.
  Ritual of Evil
  Stranger on the Run
BAXTER, MEREDITH see BAXTER-BIRNEY, MEREDITH
BAXTER-BIRNEY, MEREDITH (actress)
  Telefeatures
  Little Women
  Target Risk
BAYHI, CHESTER R. (set decorator)
  Telefeature
  The Devil and Miss Sarah
BEAL, RAYMOND (art director)
  Series
  Destry
  It's a Man's World
  The Night Stalker
  Telefeatures
  The California Kid
  The Law
  Partners in Crime
  The Six Million Dollar Man
BEASCOECHEA, FRANK P. (director of photography)
  Series
  BJ and the Bear
  Galactica 1980
  Switch
BEATON, ALEX (producer)
  Series
  Black Sheep Squadron
  Centennial
  The Duke
  Richie Brockelman, Private Eye (supervising producer only)
  Telefeatures
  Dr. Scorpion
  The Night Rider (executive producer only)
  Scott Free
  Pilots
  Boston and Kilbride (executive producer only)
  The Gypsy Warriors
BEATTY, NED (actor)
  Telefeatures
  The Execution of Private Slovik
  The Marcus-Nelson Murders
  Tail Gunner Joe
BEAUMONT, DAN (writer)
  Series
  Bachelor Father
BEAUMONT, HUGH (actor/director)
  Series
  Leave It to Beaver

BECKMAN, EVELYN (writer)
  Series
    Thriller
BECKNER, NEIL (director of
    photography)
  Series
    The Bob Cummings Show
BEDELIA, BONNIE (actress)
  Telefeature
    Heat Wave
BEEJAY PRODUCTIONS (production company)
  Series
    Westinghouse Playhouse Starring Nanette Fabray and Wendell Corey
BEERY, NOAH, JR. (actor)
  Series
    The Bastard
    Riverboat
    The Rockford Files
  Telefeature
    The Alpha Caper
BEGLEY, ED, JR. (actor)
  Telefeatures
    Amateur Night at the Dixie Bar and Grill
    Family Flight
BELDING, RICHARD (editorial supervisor)
  Series
    Adam-12
    Alcoa Premiere/Premiere (film editor only)
    Alias Smith and Jones
    Banacek
    Checkmate (film editor only)
    Columbo
    Cool Million
    The Doctors
    Emergency!
    Escape
    Hec Ramsey
    Hernandez: Houston P.D.
    It Takes a Thief
    Lanigan's Rabbi
    The Lawyers
    Leave It to Beaver (film editor only)
    Madigan
    The Man and the City
    Marcus Welby, M.D.
    Matt Lincoln
    McCloud
    McCoy
    McMillan
    McMillan and Wife
    McNaughton's Daughter
    Mr. Inside/Mr. Outside
    The Night Stalker
    The Psychiatrist
    The Rockford Files
    Rod Serling's Night Gallery
    San Francisco International Airport
    Sarge
    The Senator
    The Six Million Dollar Man
    The Snoop Sisters
    Switch
  Telefeatures
    Brock's Last Case
    The D.A.: Conspiracy to Kill
    Dragnet 1966 (film editor only)
    Istanbul Express
    Now You See It, Now You Don't
    The Questor Tapes
    Trial Run
    Vanished
BELFORD, CHRISTINE (actress)
  Series
    Banacek
  Telefeatures
    Banacek
    Cool Million
BELLAK, GEORGE (writer)
  Telefeature
    The Nightmare Step
BELLAMY, EARL (director)
  Series
    Bachelor Father
    Laredo
    McHale's Navy
    Pilot
    Stranded
BELLAMY, RALPH (actor)
  Series
    Condominium
    Harold Robbins' "The Survivors"
    Testimony of Two Men
    Wheels
  Telefeatures
    Charlie Cobb: Nice Night for a Hanging
    The Log of the Black Pearl
    McNaughton's Daughter
    Wings of Fire
BELLISARIO, DONALD (supervising producer)
  Series
    Battlestar: Galactica
    Black Sheep Squadron (and writer)
BELOUS, PAUL M. (story editor)
  Series
    The Misadventures of Sheriff

310 / Index

Lobo
BELSON, JERRY (producer/ writer)
Telefeature
Evil Roy Slade
BENDIX, WILLIAM (actor)
Series
The Overland Trail
BENEDICT, DIRK (actor)
Series
Battlestar: Galactica
BENEDICT, RICHARD (director)
Series
San Francisco International Airport
BENEVEDS, ROBERT (production executive)
Series
Ironside
BENJAMIN, PHIL (casting director)
Series
The Incredible Hulk
BENNETT, HARVE (executive producer and head of Harve Bennett Productions and Silverton Productions, Inc.)
Series
The Bionic Woman (and writer)
Gemini Man
The Invisible Man
Rich Man, Poor Man
The Six Million Dollar Man
Telefeatures
The Alpha Caper
The Astronaut (producer only)
The Birdmen (producer only)
Death Race
Family Flight (producer only)
Gemini Man
Guilty or Innocent: The Sam Sheppard Murder Case
Heat Wave
Houston, We've Got a Problem
The Invisible Man (and writer)
Money to Burn (producer only)
Runaway!
You'll Never See Me Again
BENNETT, PHIL (art director)
Series
Alias Smith and Jones
BENNETT, RICHARD (director)
Series
Toma
Telefeature
The Young Country (assistant director only)
BENNY, JACK (actor and head
of J & M Productions and J. B. Productions)
Series
The Jack Benny Show
Specials
The Jack Benny Special
The Slowest Gun in the West
BENSON, JAMES see BENSON, JIM
BENSON, JAY (producer)
Series
The Doctors (associate producer only)
Lucas Tanner
Telefeatures
The Gun (writer only)
Hitchhike!
The Judge and Jake Wyler (associate producer only)
Special
Mother of the Bride
BENSON, JIM (film editor)
Series
Testimony of Two Men
Telefeatures
Amelia Earhart
Crime Club
The Invasion of Johnson County
Jigsaw
Little Women
BENTON, DOUGLAS (producer)
Series
Hec Ramsey (and director/ writer)
Ironside
Owen Marshall, Counselor at Law
Telefeatures
A Howling in the Woods
Owen Marshall, Counselor at Law
The Snoop Sisters
BERCOVICI, ERIC (writer)
Telefeatures
The Log of the Black Pearl
The Other Man
BERCOVITCH, REUBEN (writer)
Series
The Doctors
The Virginian
BERG, DICK see BERG, RICHARD
BERG, RICHARD (producer)
Series
Alcoa Premiere/Premiere
Bob Hope Presents the Chrysler Theater (and executive producer)

Checkmate
  Johnny Staccato (writer only)
BERG, TONY (composer)
  Telefeature
  Sunshine Christmas
BERGEN, POLLY (actress)
  Series
  79 Park Avenue
BERGER, SENTA (actress)
  Telefeatures
  Istanbul Express
  It Takes a Thief
  See How They Run
BERGMAN, ALAN (director)
  Series
  House Calls
BERINGER, CARL (assistant director)
  Telefeatures
  The Movie Murderer
  Ritual of Evil
BERK, HOWARD (executive story consultant)
  Series
  Mrs. Columbo
BERKE, LES(TER WILLIAM) (unit production manager)
  Series
  Baretta
  BJ and the Bear (producer only)
  Centennial
  The Hardy Boys Mysteries
  Quincy, M.E. (producer only)
  The Rockford Files
BERLIN, ABBY (director)
  Series
  Bachelor Father
BERMAN, HENRY (art director)
  Telefeature
  Amateur Night at the Dixie Bar and Grill
BERMAN, HERB (writer)
  Series
  The Psychiatrist
BERNARDI, HERSCHEL (actor)
  Series
  Seventh Avenue
BERNS, LARRY (producer)
  Series
  Westinghouse Playhouse Starring Nanette Fabray and Wendell Corey
BERNSTEIN, ELMER (composer)
  Series
  Captains and the Kings
  Ellery Queen
  General Electric Theatre
  Johnny Staccato
  NBC's Best Sellers (theme only)
  Owen Marshall, Counselor at Law
  Riverboat
  Telefeatures
  Ellery Queen
  Little Women
  Owen Marshall, Counselor at Law
  The 3,000 Mile Chase
  Special
  The Man from Independence
BERTHELOT, JEAN (film editor)
  Series
  Tales of Wells Fargo
BERTRAND, ROBERT (sound mixer)
  Telefeatures
  Emergency!
  Istanbul Express
BESSELL, TED (actor)
  Series
  It's a Man's World
  Telefeatures
  Scream, Pretty Peggy
  Two on a Bench
  Pilot
  Bobby Parker and Company
BETFORD PRODUCTIONS (production company)
  Series
  Buckskin
  Channing
BETSAYDA, ISAIAS (costume designer)
  Telefeature
  The Longest Hundred Miles
BETTMAN, GILBERT, JR. (associate producer)
  Series
  BJ and the Bear
BETZ, CARL (actor)
  Telefeatures
  The Deadly Dream
  Killdozer
  Set This Town on Fire
BIBERMAN, ABNER (director)
  Series
  Ironside
  The Virginian
BICKFORD, CHARLES (actor)
  Series
  The Man Behind the Badge (and narrator)
  The Virginian
BIERY, EDWARD A., A.C.E. (film editor)

Series
Hec Ramsey
Marcus Welby, M.D.
Tales of Wells Fargo
Telefeatures
The Challengers
A Clear and Present Danger
Double Indemnity
Linda
Shadow Over Elveron
BIHELLER, ROBERT S. (writer)
Telefeature
The Astronaut
BIKEL, THEODORE (actor)
Series
Loose Change
Testimony of Two Men
BILL, TONY (actor)
Series
What Really Happened to the Class of '65?
BILLINGSLEY, BARBARA (actress)
Series
Leave It to Beaver
BILSON, BRUCE (director)
Series
BJ and the Bear
Sierra
Telefeature
BJ and the Bear
BINNS, EDWARD (actor)
Series
It Takes a Thief
BIRD, HENRY (sound mixer)
Special
Hamlet
BIRNEY, DAVID (actor)
Series
Testimony of Two Men
BIRNKRANT, DON H. (director of photography)
Series
The Hardy Boys Mysteries
BIROC, JOSEPH (director of photography)
Telefeature
Little Women
BISHOP, BEN (producer)
Series
Alias Smith and Jones (unit manager only)
Black Beauty
BISHOP, MEL A. (unit manager)
Series
Adam-12
Kojak
Telefeature
The D.A.: Conspiracy to Kill

BISHOP, RON (writer)
Special
The Red Pony
BISK, GEORGE (assistant director)
Series
McMillan and Wife
PAris 7000
Tales of Wells Fargo
Telefeature
Ransom for a Dead Man
BISOGLIO, VAL (actor)
Series
Quincy, M.E.
Telefeature
The Marcus-Nelson Murders
Pilot
If I Had a Million
BIXBY, BILL (actor)
Series
The Incredible Hulk
Rich Man, Poor Man
Rich Man, Poor Man--Book II (director only)
Telefeatures
The Couple Takes a Wife
The Incredible Hulk
The Invasion of Johnson County
Special
Short Stories of Love
BLACK, JOHN D.F. (writer)
Series
Kraft Suspense Theatre
Laredo
BLACKLER, GEORGE (makeup artist)
Telefeatures
Destiny of a Spy
Run a Crooked Mile
BLACKMER, SIDNEY (actor)
Telefeature
Do You Take This Stranger
BLAIR, LINDA (actress)
Telefeature
Sarah T.--Portrait of a Teenage Alcoholic
BLAKE, ROBERT (actor)
Series
Baretta
BLAKELY, SUSAN (actress)
Series
Rich Man, Poor Man
BLANC, MEL (actor)
Series
Buck Rogers in the 25th Century
BLANK, THOMAS (assistant director)
Series

Switch
BLANKFORT, MICHEAL (writer)
  Telefeatures
  The Other Man
  See How They Run
BLASDELL, AUDREY (set decorator)
  Series
  The John Forsythe Show
  Telefeature
  Stranger on the Run
BLAU, RAPHAEL DAVID (writer)
  Series
  Bob Hope Presents the Chrysler Theatre
  Leave It to Beaver
BLECKER, RHODA (writer)
  Telefeature
  The Elevator
BLEES, ROBERT (producer)
  Series
  Kraft Suspense Theatre
BLITZER, BARRY (writer)
  Series
  Broadside
BLOCH, ROBERT (writer)
  Series
  The Alfred Hitchcock Hour
  Thriller
BLOCK, HOWARD (director of photography)
  Telefeature
  Two on a Bench
BLOCKER, DAN (actor)
  Series
  Cimarron City
  Telefeature
  Something for a Lonely Man
BLOCKER, DIRK (actor)
  Series
  Baa Baa Black Sheep
  Black Sheep Squadron
  Telefeature
  Bridger
BLONDELL, GLORIA (actress)
  Series
  Calvin and the Colonel
BLONDELL, JOAN (actress)
  Series
  The Rebels
  Telefeature
  Winchester 73
BLOOM, HAROLD JACK (writer)
  Series
  Emergency! (creator only)
  Hec Ramsey (and producer)
  Telefeatures
  Any Second Now

  The D.A.: Murder One (and producer)
  Emergency! (and creator)
  The Log of the Black Pearl
BLOSSOMS, THE (vocalists)
  Telefeature
  Deadlock!
BLUE, BEN (actor)
  Special
  The Jack Benny Special
BLUEL, RICHARD (writer)
  Series
  The Hardy Boys Mysteries
  Rosetti and Ryan
BLUESTEIN, BURT (unit production manager)
  Series
  The Seekers
BLYDENBURGH, S. (set decorator)
  Telefeature
  Duel
BOCCHICCHIO, ALFEO (art director)
  Series
  The Six Million Dollar Man
  Telefeature
  The Story of Pretty Boy Floyd
BOCHCO, STEVEN (producer)
  Series
  Delvecchio
  Griff
  The Invisible Man
  Richie Brockelman, Private Eye (executive producer/writer)
  Telefeatures
  Double Indemnity (writer only)
  The Invisible Man (and writer)
  Lieutenant Schuster's Wife (and writer)
  Richie Brockelman, Private Eye (executive producer/writer)
BOCHNER, LLOYD (actor)
  Series
  The Immigrants
  Telefeatures
  Richie Brockelman, Private Eye
  Stranger on the Run
BOGGS, HASKELL (director of photography)
  Telefeatures
  Double Indemnity
  Maneater
BOGIE, DUANE C. (executive producer for Foote, Cone & Belding Productions)
  Specials
  The Man Who Came to Dinner
  The Snow Goose

BOLE, CLIFF (director)
  Series
    The Six Million Dollar Man
BOND, WARD (actor)
  Series
    Wagon Train
BONDELLI, PHIL (director)
  Series
    The Six Million Dollar Man
BONERZ, PETER (actor)
  Series
    The Bastard
BONFA, LUIS (composer)
  Telefeature
    River of Mystery
BOOKE, SORRELL (actor)
  Series
    Rich Man, Poor Man--Book II
  Telefeatures
    The Adventures of Nick Carter
    The Borgia Stick
    The Manhunter
    Owen Marshall, Counselor at Law
BOOTH, EARL (executive story editor)
  Series
    Marcus Welby, M.D.
BOOTH, SHIRLEY (actress)
  Telefeature
    The Smugglers
BOONE, RANDY (actor)
  Series
    It's a Man's World
BOONE, RICHARD (actor)
  Series
    Hec Ramsey
BORCHERT, RUDOLPH (writer)
  Series
    Get Christie Love!
    The Night Stalker
BORCHERT, RUDY see BORCHERT, RUDOLPH
BOREN, LAMAR, A.S.C. (director of photography)
  Series
    The Rockford Files
  Telefeatures
    Love Is Not Enough
    The Rockford Files
BORGNINE, ERNEST (actor)
  Series
    McHale's Navy
  Telefeature
    Sam Hill: Who Killed the Mysterious Mr. Foster?
  Special
    Legend in Granite

BOSLEY, TOM (actor)
  Series
    The Bastard
    The Rebels
    Testimony of Two Men (and narrator)
  Telefeatures
    Marcus Welby, M.D.
    Night Gallery
    Vanished
BOSTON, JOE (producer)
  Series
    BJ and the Bear
    The Hardy Boys Mysteries
    Sword of Justice
BOSTWICK, BARRY (actor)
  Telefeature
    The Chadwick Family
BOUCHET, BARBARA (actress)
  Telefeature
    Cool Million
BOWERS, WILLIAM (producer)
  Series
    Mobile One
  Telefeature
    Mobile Two
BOWLES, PHIL (1st assistant director)
  Series
    Mrs. Columbo
  Telefeatures
    Chase
    The Psychiatrist: God Bless the Children
BOWMAN, CHUCK (producer)
  Series
    Black Sheep Squadron (associate producer only)
    The Incredible Hulk (and supervising producer)
BOXLEITNER, BRUCE (actor)
  Series
    The Last Convertible
  Telefeatures
    The Chadwick Family
    A Cry for Help
BOYLE, BESS (writer)
  Series
    The Man and the City
BOYLE, DON (producer)
  Series
    The Six Million Dollar Man
BOYLE, PETER (actor)
  Telefeature
    Tail Gunner Joe
BOYLE, ROBERT (art director)
  Special
    The Red Pony

BRACKEN, RICHARD (film editor)
  Series
    Alias Smith and Jones
    Rich Man, Poor Man
  Telefeatures
    A Case of Rape
    Force Five
    Lucas Tanner
    Sarah T. --Portrait of a Teenage Alcoholic
    Senior Year
    The UFO Incident
  Pilot
    If I Had a Million
BRADBURY, RAY (writer)
  Series
    Alcoa Premiere/Premiere
    Alfred Hitchcock Presents
BRADFIELD, MARTIN C. (set decorator)
  Series
    Alcoa Premiere/Premiere
BRADFIELD, ROBERT C. (set decorator)
  Telefeatures
    Brock's Last Case
    Death Takes a Holiday
    See the Man Run
    What's a Nice Girl Like You...?
BRADSHAW, BOOKER (writer)
  Series
    Tenafly
BRADY, SCOTT (actor)
  Series
    Shotgun Slade
BRAHM, JOHN (director)
  Series
    Alfred Hitchcock Presents
    Arrest and Trial
    Thriller
BRAIN, STEPHEN L. (associate producer)
  Series
    The Misadventures of Sheriff Lobo
BRALVER, JOE (2nd unit director)
  Series
    Galactica 1980
BRAM, LEN (1st assistant director)
  Series
    BJ and the Bear
BRAME, BILL, A.C.E. (film editor)
  Series
    Banacek

  Telefeature
    The Couple Takes a Wife
BRAND, NEVILLE (actor)
  Series
    Captains and the Kings
    Laredo
    The Seekers
  Telefeatures
    The Adventures of Nick Carter
    Hitched
    Killdozer
    Lock, Stock and Barrel
    Marriage: Year One
BRANDON, MICHAEL (actor)
  Telefeatures
    Hitchhike!
    The Impatient Heart
    Scott Free
BRANDT, RAY (art director)
  Telefeature
    Amateur Night at the Dixie Bar and Grill
BRAZZI, ROSSANO (actor)
  Series
    Harold Robbins' "The Survivors"
BRECK, PETER (actor)
  Series
    Black Beauty
BREEN, RICHARD L. (writer)
  Series
    Dragnet 1967-1970
  Telefeature
    Dragnet 1966
BRENNAN, EILEEN (actress)
  Series
    Black Beauty
BRENNAN, WALTER (actor)
  Telefeature
    The Young Country
BRENNER, DORI (actress)
  Series
    Seventh Avenue
BRENNER, RAY (writer)
  Series
    Broadside
BRENTWOOD, L.T. (writer)
  Series
    The Protectors
BREWER, JAMESON (writer)
  Series
    Alcoa Premiere/Premiere
    Startime
BRICKEN, JULES (director)
  Series
    Cimarron City
BRIDGES, JAMES (writer)
  Series
    The Alfred Hitchcock Hour

BRIDGES, JEFF (actor)
  Telefeature
  Silent Night, Lonely Night
BRIDGES, LLOYD (actor)
  Series
  San Francisco International
    Airport
  Telefeatures
  The Deadly Dream
  Death Race
  Do You Take This Stranger
  Silent Night, Lonely Night
BRILL, BUD (unit production
    manager)
  Series
  Alias Smith and Jones
  PAris 7000
  Quincy, M. E.
BRINCKERHOFF, BURT (director)
  Telefeatures
  Brave New World
  Night Life
  The Nightmare Step
  Specials
  The Mask of Love
  Mother of the Bride
  A Special Act of Love
BRITISH BROADCASTING COR-
    PORATION (production com-
    pany)
  Series
  Colditz
  Telefeature
  Escape from Colditz
  Special
  The Snow Goose
BROGGER, FREDERICK (pro-
    ducer)
  Special
  The Red Pony
BROLIN, JAMES (actor)
  Series
  Marcus Welby, M. D.
  Telefeatures
  Marcus Welby, M. D.
  Short Walk to Daylight
  Trapped
BROOKS, DENNY (theme vocalist)
  Series
  The Family Holvak
  Telefeature
  The Desperate Miles
BROOKS, GERALDINE (actress)
  Series
  Faraday and Company
  Telefeature
  Ironside
BROOKS, MARTIN E. (actor)

  Series
  The Bionic Woman
  The Six Million Dollar Man
  Special
  A Special Act of Love
BROPHY, SALLY (actress)
  Series
  Buckskin
BROTMAN, JOYCE (producer)
  Series
  The Hardy Boys Mysteries (and
    co-producer)
  The Nancy Drew Mysteries
BROUGHTON, BRUCE (composer)
  Series
  Quincy, M. E.
BROUGHTON, WILLIAM (composer)
  Series
  BJ and the Bear
BROWER, ROBERT (color coor-
    dinator)
  Series
  The Doctors
  Telefeatures
  Istanbul Express
  Now You See It, Now You Don't
  The Outsider
  Prescription: Murder
  Stranger on the Run
  Trial Run
  Winchester 73
  Wings of Fire
BROWN, BARRY (actor)
  Series
  Testimony of Two Men
  Telefeatures
  The Birdmen
  The Bravos
BROWN, BILL (senior cameraman)
  Special
  Hamlet
BROWN, BLAIR (actress)
  Series
  Captains and the Kings
  Wheels
  Telefeatures
  Charlie Cobb: Nice Night for a
    Hanging
  The Oregon Trail
  The 3,000 Mile Chase
BROWN, CHELSEA (actress)
  Series
  Matt Lincoln
  Telefeature
  Dial: Hot Line
BROWN, CLAIRE P. (set decorator)
  Series
  McCloud

Quincy, M. E.
BROWN, EARL (composer/choral director)
Special
The Jack Benny Special
BROWN, ED (director of photography)
Telefeature
Short Walk to Daylight
BROWN, G. CHARLETON (writer)
Series
Broadside
McHale's Navy
BROWN, JAMES H. (assistant director)
Series
Startime
Special
The Slowest Gun in the West
BROWN, REB (actor)
Series
Centennial
Telefeatures
Captain America
Let's Switch
BROWNE, HOWARD (producer)
Series
Destry
Run for Your Life (writer only)
BROWNE, RON(ALD W.) (director of photography)
Series
Centennial
McCloud
Telefeatures
Benny and Barney: Las Vegas Undercover
Captain America
The Islander
BROWNE, ROSCOE LEE (actor)
Series
McCoy
Telefeatures
The Big Ripoff
Dr. Scorpion
Special
Short Stories of Love
BROWNING, DICK (video engineer)
Telefeatures
The Nightmare Step
A Prowler in the Heart
The Suicide Club
BROWNING, RICOU (director)
Telefeature
The Aquarians
BRUCE, JOHN P. (art director)
Series

Baretta
Centennial
Telefeature
Mandrake
BRUCE LANSBURY PRODUCTIONS, LTD. (production company)
Series
Buck Rogers in the 25th Century
BRUNDIN, BO (actor)
Series
Centennial
The Rhinemann Exchange
Rich Man, Poor Man
BRYANT, EDWIN H., A.C.E. (film editor)
Series
McHale's Navy
Telefeature
McCloud: Who Killed Miss U.S.A.?
BUCHANAN, JAMES MARTIN (art director)
Telefeatures
Killdozer
The Log of the Black Pearl
The Rangers
BUDD, ROY (composer)
Special
The Man Who Came to Dinner
BULIFANT, JOYCE (actress)
Series
Tom, Dick and Mary
Telefeature
Little Women
BUMSTEAD, HENRY (art director)
Telefeatures
The Adventures of Nick Carter
The Birdmen
Don't Push, I'll Charge When I'm Ready
McCloud: Who Killed Miss U.S.A.?
The Movie Murderer
BUNCH, CHRIS (writer)
Series
Quincy, M. E.
BURBRUDGE, EDWARD (art director)
Series
Kojak
BURLEY, MARK A. (unit production manager)
Series
The Incredible Hulk
BURNETT, W. R. (writer)
Series

The Virginian
BURNS, GEORGE (actor)
  Special
  The Jack Benny Special
BURNS, JUDY (writer)
  Series
  Marcus Welby, M.D.
BURNS, MICHAEL (actor)
  Series
  It's a Man's World
  Wagon Train
  Telefeatures
  Brock's Last Case
  Stranger on the Run
BURNS, SEYMOUR (producer)
  Series
  The Jack Benny Show
BURR, RAYMOND (actor and head of R.B. Productions)
  Series
  The Bastard (narrator only)
  Centennial
  Ironside
  Kingston: Confidential
  79 Park Avenue
  Telefeatures
  Ironside
  It Takes a Thief
  The Jordan Chance
  Kingston: The Power Play
  Mallory: Circumstantial Evidence
  The Priest Killer
  Special
  A Man Whose Name Was John
BURROWS, JAMES (director)
  Series
  Fay
  Pilot
  Roosevelt and Truman
BURROWS, ROSEMARY (costume designer)
  Telefeatures
  Destiny of a Spy
  Run a Crooked Mile
BUSEY, GARY (actor)
  Telefeatures
  The Execution of Private Slovik
  The Law
BUSH, FLORENCE (hair stylist)
  Series
  Alfred Hitchcock Presents
  The Deputy
  87th Precinct
  Laramie
  Leave It to Beaver
  McHale's Navy
  Startime
  Tales of Wells Fargo
  The Tall Man
  Wagon Train
  Westinghouse Playhouse Starring Nanette Fabray and Wendell Corey
  Whispering Smith
  Special
  The Slowest Gun in the West
BUSHKIN, JOE (composer)
  Series
  Johnny Midnight
BUTKUS, DICK (actor)
  Series
  Rich Man, Poor Man
BUTLER, ARTIE (composer)
  Series
  Operation Petticoat
  Telefeature
  Operation Petticoat
BUTLER, BILL (director of photography)
  Series
  Hernandez: Houston P.D.
  Telefeatures
  The Big Ripoff
  A Clear and Present Danger
  The Execution of Private Slovik
  Indict and Convict
  Savage
  Sunshine
  Target Risk
BUTLER, MICHAEL PHILIP (writer)
  Series
  Ironside
BUTLER, ROBERT (director)
  Telefeatures
  Dark Victory
  Death Takes a Holiday
BUTLER, RUDY (set decorator)
  Series
  Startime
  Special
  The Slowest Gun in the West
BUTTOLPH, DAVID (composer)
  Series
  Frontier Circus
BUTTONS, RED (actor)
  Telefeature
  Breakout
BYERS, BILLY (composer)
  Telefeature
  Hauser's Memory
BYINGTON, SPRING (actress)
  Series
  Laramie

BYRNE, JOE (producer)
Series
The Bastard
BYRNES, EDD (actor)
Telefeature
Mobile Two

CABOT, BRUCE (actor)
Special
The Slowest Gun in the West
CABOT, SEBASTIAN (actor)
Series
Checkmate
CACAVAS, JOHN (composer)
Series
The Eddie Capra Mysteries
Kojak
Mrs. Columbo
Telefeatures
The Elevator
Linda
Pilot
Hazard's People
CAFFEY, MICHAEL (director)
Series
Gemini Man
The Hardy Boys Mysteries
Harold Robbins' "The Survivors"
Ironside
Kingston: Confidential
The Night Stalker
Telefeature
The Devil and Miss Sarah
CAFFEY, RICHARD (producer)
Series
Centennial (supervising producer only)
Harold Robbins' "The Survivors" (and writer)
PAris 7000 (executive producer only)
CAFFREY, MICHAEL (executive producer)
Series
Emergency Plus Four
CAGEY, BOB (film editor)
Telefeature
Alias Smith and Jones
CAHN, DANN, A.C.E. (film editor)
Series
Going My Way
CAIDIN, MARTIN (writer)
Telefeature
Exo-Man
CAILLOU, ALAN (writer)
Series

It Takes a Thief
Thriller
Telefeature
The Aquarians
CAIN, EARL, SR. (sound mixer)
Series
Startime
CAIN, LYLE (sound mixer)
Series
The Doctors
PAris 7000
The Protectors
San Francisco International Airport
The Senator
Tales of Wells Fargo
Telefeatures
Drive Hard, Drive Fast
Ironside
Now You See It, Now You Don't
Winchester 73
CAINE, HOWARD (actor)
Telefeature
The Doomsday Flight
CAIRNCROSS, WILLIAM (producer/associate producer)
Series
Quincy, M.E.
CALDWELL, STEPHEN P. (associate producer)
Series
The Incredible Hulk
CALHOUN, RORY (actor)
Series
The Rebels
CALLAGHAN, DUKE (director of photography)
Series
Centennial
Telefeature
Just a Little Inconvenience
CALLAS, CHARLIE (actor)
Series
Switch
Telefeatures
The Snoop Sisters
Switch
CALLAS, MAY (art director)
Telefeature
The Art of Crime
CALLIOPE PRODUCTIONS, INC. (production company)
Series
Frontier Circus
CALVELLI, JOSEPH MICHAEL (writer)
Series
Adam-12

Sons and Daughters (and script editor)
CALVERT, FRED (executive producer/producer/director)
Series
Emergency Plus Four
CAMDEN, BILL (art director)
Series
Buck Rogers in the 25th Century
CAMERON, ROD (actor)
Series
City Detective
Coronado 9
State Trooper
CAMPANELLA, JOSEPH (actor)
Series
The Lawyers
Telefeatures
Any Second Now
A Clear and Present Danger
Drive Hard, Drive Fast
Owen Marshall, Counselor at Law
Skyway to Death
The Whole World Is Watching
You'll Never See Me Again
CAMPBELL, NORMAN (director)
Series
General Electric Theatre
CAMPBELL, WILLIAM (art director)
Series
Ellery Queen
Loose Change
The Nancy Drew Mysteries
Once an Eagle
The Rebels
The Six Million Dollar Man
Telefeatures
Aloha Means Goodbye
The Art of Crime
Guilty or Innocent: The Sam Sheppard Murder Case
The Return of the World's Greatest Detective
Skyway to Death
CANNELL, STEPHEN J. (executive producer and head of Stephen J. Cannell Productions)
Series
Adam-12 (story editor only)
Baa Baa Black Sheep (and creator/writer)
Baretta (creator only)
Black Sheep Squadron (and creator/writer)

Chase (writer only)
City of Angels (creator/writer only)
The D. A. (writer only)
The Duke (and writer)
Escape (writer only)
Richie Brockelman, Private Eye (and writer)
The Rockford Files (supervising producer/producer/creator only)
Toma (producer/writer only)
Telefeatures
Chase (writer only)
Dr. Scorpion (and writer)
The Jordan Chance (writer only)
The Night Rider (and writer)
Richie Brockelman, Private Eye (and writer)
The Rockford Files (producer/writer only)
Scott Free (and writer)
Pilots
Boston and Kilbride (and writer)
The Gypsy Warriors (and writer)
CANNON, J. D. (actor)
Series
McCloud
Testimony of Two Men
Telefeatures
The D. A.: Murder One
Killing Stone
Sam Hill: Who Killed the Mysterious Mr. Foster?
Pilot
Lady Luck
CAREY, PATRICK (director of photography)
Special
The Snow Goose
CARLIN, LYNN (actress)
Telefeature
Silent Night, Lonely Night
CARLSON, RICHARD (actor)
Telefeature
The Doomsday Flight
CARMICHAEL, HOAGY (actor)
Series
Laramie
CARNEY, ART (actor)
Series
Lanigan's Rabbi
Telefeatures
Lanigan's Rabbi
The Snoop Sisters
CAROTHERS, A. J. (story editor)
Series
General Electric Theatre

CARPENTER, CLAUDE (set decorator)
  Telefeature
  The Outsider
CARPENTER, PETE (composer with partner Mike Post)
  Series
  Baa Baa Black Sheep
  Black Sheep Squadron
  Griff
  The Rockford Files
  Toma
  Telefeatures
  Charlie Cobb: Nice Night for a Hanging
  Dr. Scorpion
  The Invasion of Johnson County
  The Night Rider
  Richie Brockelman, Private Eye
  The Rockford Files
  Scott Free
  Two on a Bench
  Pilot
  Off the Wall
CARPENTER, VICTOR H. (sound mixer)
  Telefeature
  Brock's Last Case
CARR, DARLEEN (actress)
  Series
  The John Forsythe Show
  Once an Eagle
  The Oregon Trail
  Telefeatures
  All My Darling Daughters
  The Chadwick Family
  My Darling Daughters' Anniversary
  Runaway!
CARR, JACKIE J. (set decorator)
  Series
  The Eddie Capra Mysteries
CARR, RICHARD (writer/story editor)
  Series
  The Six Million Dollar Man
CARRADINE, JOHN (actor)
  Series
  Captains and the Kings
  The Seekers
  Telefeature
  Tail Gunner Joe
CARRERA, BARBARA (actress)
  Series
  Centennial
CARROLL, BEESON (actor)
  Telefeatures
  The Family Nobody Wanted
  The UFO Incident
CARROLL, FRANCINE (writer)
  Series
  Ironside
CARROLL, JIMMY (conductor)
  Series
  Sing Along with Mitch
CARROLL, LEO G. (actor)
  Series
  Going My Way
CARROLL, SIDNEY (writer)
  Series
  General Electric Theatre
CARSON, JOHNNY (actor)
  Special
  The Jack Benny Special
CARTER, BENNY (composer)
  Telefeatures
  Fame Is the Name of the Game
  The Maneater
CARTER, JACK (actor)
  Telefeature
  The Lonely Profession
CARTER, JOHN R. (sound mixer)
  Series
  Banacek
  McMillan and Wife
  The Rockford Files
  The Seekers
CARTER, TERRY (actor)
  Series
  Battlestar: Galactica
  McCloud
  Telefeatures
  McCloud: Who Killed Miss U.S.A.?
  Two on a Bench
CARUSO, DEE (writer)
  Series
  Don Adams' Screen Test
CASEY, BERNIE (actor)
  Series
  Harris and Company
  Telefeature
  Love Is Not Enough
CASSAVETES, JOHN (actor)
  Series
  Johnny Staccato
CASSIDY, ALAN (composer)
  Series
  The Incredible Hulk
CASSIDY, JACK (actor)
  Telefeature
  Benny and Barney: Las Vegas Undercover
CASSIDY, SHAUN (actor)
  Series

The Hardy Boys Mysteries
CASSIDY, TED (actor)
  Telefeature
    Benny and Barney: Las Vegas Undercover
CATTRALL, KIM (actress)
  Series
    The Bastard
    The Rebels
  Telefeature
    The Night Rider
CAVALIER, JOSEPH (associate producer)
  Series
    The Man and the City
  Telefeature
    Vanished (and unit manager)
CAYLOR, JAMIE (film editor)
  Series
    The Six Million Dollar Man
    Wheels
  Telefeatures
    The Keegans
    Live Again, Die Again
    The Oregon Trail
    Sex and the Married Woman
CAYLOR, SAMUEL (sound effects editor)
  Series
    Leave It to Beaver
CECIL, HENRY (writer)
  Series
    Alcoa Premiere/Premiere
CHAGRIN, CLAUDE (director)
  Special
    Hamlet
CHAMBERLAIN, RICHARD (actor)
  Series
    Centennial
  Specials
    Hamlet
    The Woman I Love
CHAMBERLAIN-LeMAIRE PRODUCTIONS (production company)
  Special
    Hamlet
CHAMBERS, EVERETT (producer)
  Series
    Columbo
    Johnny Staccato
CHAMBERS, JOHN (makeup artist)
  Special
    The Man from Independence
CHAMBERS, LOWELL (set decorator)
  Series
    Battlestar: Galactica
    The Rebels
    The Six Million Dollar Man
  Telefeature
    Gemini Man
CHAMPION, GOWER (director)
  Series
    Startime
CHAMPION, JOHN (producer)
  Series
    Laramie
CHANDLER, CHICK (actor)
  Series
    Soldiers of Fortune
CHANDLER, GEORGE (actor)
  Series
    Ichabod and Me
CHAPMAN, LONNY (actor)
  Series
    Black Beauty
CHASE, BORDEN (story consultant)
  Series
    Whispering Smith
CHASE, DAVID (writer/story consultant)
  Series
    The Night Stalker
    The Rockford Files (producer/associate producer only)
    Switch
CHASE, STANLEY (producer)
  Series
    Bob Hope Presents the Chrysler Theatre
CHERBACK, CYNTHIA (associate producer)
  Series
    Switch
CHERMAK, CY (producer)
  Series
    Amy Prentiss
    Convoy
    The Doctors (executive producer/writer only)
    Ironside (executive producer/writer only)
    The Night Stalker (executive producer only)
    The Virginian
CHEROKEE PRODUCTIONS (James Garner's production company)
  Series
    The Rockford Files
  Telefeature
    Scott Free
CHERRY, STANLEY Z. (director)
  Series
    Bachelor Father

CHERTOK, JACK (producer and head of Jack Chertok TV, Inc.)
Series
Johnny Midnight
CHESHIRE, ELIZABETH (actress)
Series
Sunshine
CHESTERMAN, ANNA (makeup artist)
Special
The Snow Goose
CHETWYND, LIONEL (writer)
Telefeature
It Happened One Christmas
CHIHARA, PAUL (composer)
Telefeatures
The Dark Secret of Harvest Home
Dr. Strange
Farewell to Manzanar
The Keegans
CHILBERG, JOHN E., II (art director)
Series
Delvecchio
The Doctors
Hernandez: Houston P.D.
Rich Man, Poor Man
The Seekers
Sons and Daughters
Testimony of Two Men
Telefeatures
Brock's Last Case
Charlie Cobb: Nice Night for a Hanging
Force Five
Sarah T.--Portrait of a Teen-age Alcoholic
The Screaming Woman
Stonestreet: Who Killed the Centerfold Model?
CHILES, LINDEN (actor)
Series
Convoy
Telefeature
Hitchhike!
CHOMSKY, MARVIN (director)
Telefeatures
Family Flight
Female Artillery
CHOY, JOHN (associate producer)
Series
Escape
The Virginian
Special
A Special Act of Love (pro-ducer only)

CHRISTIE, HOWARD (producer and vice-president of Revue Productions and Universal Television in the 1960s)
Series
Laredo (executive producer only)
The Virginian
Wagon Train
CHUDNOW, BYRON (film editor)
Telefeature
Fear No Evil
CHULAY, JOHN C. (unit production manager)
Series
Galactica 1980
CINADER, R.A. see CINADER, ROBERT A.
CINADER, ROBERT A. (executive producer originally with Jack Webb's Mark VII Limited production company)
Series
Adam-12 (producer and creator only)
Chase
The D.A. (executive story consultant only)
Dragnet 1967-1970 (associate producer only)
Emergency! (and producer/creator)
Escape
The Immigrants
Quincy, M.E.
The Rebels (and writer)
The Seekers
Sierra
Telefeatures
Emergency! (producer/creator/writer only)
Pine Canyon Is Burning (and writer)
The Rangers (writer only)
The Specialists (and writer)
Pilot
The Two-Five (and writer)
CIOFFI, CHARLES (actor)
Series
Get Christie Love!
Telefeatures
Just a Little Inconvenience
See the Man Run
Tail Gunner Joe
CLARK, ASA (film editor)
Telefeature
You Lie So Deep, My Love
CLARK, BOYD (film editor)
Telefeature

Bridger
CLARK, CANDY (actress)
  Telefeature
   Amateur Night at the Dixie Bar and Grill
CLARK, CECIL (executive producer)
  Special
   Hamlet
CLARK, GEORGE (film editor)
  Special
   Hamlet
CLARK, GLORYETTE (film editor)
  Series
   Baretta
   Toma
  Telefeatures
   The Invasion of Johnson County
   Sam Hill: Who Killed the Mysterious Mr. Foster?
   The Story of Pretty Boy Floyd
   This Is the West That Was
   Toma
CLARK, SUSAN (actress)
  Series
   McNaughton's Daughter
  Telefeatures
   Amelia Earhart
   McNaughton's Daughter
CLATWORTHY, ROBERT (art director)
  Telefeature
   The Failing of Raymond
CLAUSER, SUZANNE (writer)
  Telefeatures
   The Family Nobody Wanted
   Little Women
CLAYBURGH, JILL (actress)
  Telefeatures
   The Art of Crime
   The Snoop Sisters
CLEMENTS, CALVIN J. (writer)
  Series
   Convoy
   Get Christie Love!
   Jigsaw
  Telefeature
   The Devil and Miss Sarah
CLEMENTS, RICHARD (composer)
  Series
   Delta House
   Delvecchio
   The Doctors
   Owen Marshall, Counselor at Law
   The Six Million Dollar Man
  Telefeatures

   Houston, We've Got a Problem
   The Invisible Man
   You'll Never See Me Again
CLAXTON, WILLIAM (director)
  Series
   Thriller
CLOONEY, ROSEMARY (actress/vocalist)
  Series
   The Rosemary Clooney Show
CLOTHIER, WILLIAM H. (director of photography)
  Series
   Alcoa Premiere/Premiere
COBB, JULIE (actress)
  Series
   The D. A.
  Telefeature
   Brave New World
COBB, LEE J. (actor)
  Series
   The Virginian
  Telefeature
   Double Indemnity
COBOS, RICHARD (makeup artist)
  Special
   The Red Pony
COHEN, JERRY (music editor)
  Series
   BJ and the Bear
COHEN, LARRY (writer)
  Series
   Columbo
   Griff (creator only)
  Telefeatures
   Cool Million
   Man on the Outside
COHEN, M. CHARLES (writer)
  Series
   Sons and Daughters (creator only)
  Telefeatures
   Dark Victory
   Senior Year
  Pilot
   If I Had a Million
COHEN, ROB (executive producer)
  Telefeature
   Amateur Night at the Dixie Bar and Grill
COHEN, STU(ART) (associate producer)
  Series
   The Eddie Capra Mysteries
   Mrs. Columbo
   Sons and Daughters
   Switch
COLASANTO, NICHOLAS (director)

Series
McCloud
COLE, ALLAN (writer)
Series
Quincy, M. E.
COLE, JACK (main title designer)
Series
The Night Stalker
The Rockford Files
The Six Million Dollar Man
COLE, JOHN J. (executive producer)
Telefeature
Charlie Chan
COLE, MICHAEL (actor)
Series
Evening in Byzantium
Telefeature
Beg, Borrow ... or Steal
COLEMAN, DALE (assistant director)
Series
The Senator
COLEMAN, HERB(ERT) (producer)
Series
Checkmate
Whispering Smith
COLLA, RICHARD A. (director)
Series
Battlestar: Galactica
Ironside
Telefeatures
Live Again, Die Again
McCloud: Who Killed Miss U. S. A. ?
The Other Man
The Priest Killer (and executive producer)
The Questor Tapes
Sarge: The Badge or the Cross (and executive producer)
Tenafly
The Tribe
The UFO Incident (and producer)
The Whole World Is Watching
COLLINS, GARY (actor)
Series
The Sixth Sense
Telefeature
Houston, We've Got a Problem
Pilot
Jamison's Kids
COLLINS, RICHARD (producer)
Series
The Family Holvak
The Immigrants (writer only)

The Oregon Trail (supervising producer only)
The Rhinemann Exchange (and writer)
Sara (and creator)
COLLINS, ROBERT (writer)
Series
The Name of the Game
COLLINS, STEPHEN (actor)
Series
The Rhinemann Exchange
COLLIS, JACK T. (art director)
Telefeatures
A Cry for Help
One of Our Own
COLMAN, BEN, A. S. C. (director of photography)
Series
Buck Rogers in the 25th Century
McCloud
The Nancy Drew Mysteries
Switch
Telefeatures
The Failing of Raymond
McCloud: Who Killed Miss U. S. A. ?
Sex and the Married Woman
Switch
COLOMBIER, MICHAEL (composer)
Series
PAris 7000 (theme only)
The Rhinemann Exchange
Testimony of Two Men
COLOMBY, SCOTT (actor)
Series
Sons and Daughters
Telefeature
Senior Year
COLVIG, HELEN (costume designer)
Series
Centennial
Telefeatures
How I Spent My Summer Vacation
Ritual of Evil
Winchester 73
COMDEN, BETTY (writer)
Special
Applause
COMPTON, RICHARD (writer)
Telefeature
The California Kid
COMSTOCK, FRANK (composer)
Series
Adam-12
The D. A.
Dragnet 1967-1970

Telefeatures
The D.A.: Conspiracy to Kill
The D.A.: Murder One
CONNELLY, CHRISTOPHER
  (actor)
  Telefeature
  Charlie Cobb: Nice Night for
    a Hanging
CONNELLY, JOE (producer and,
  with partner Bob Mosher,
  head of Kayro Productions
  and Kayro-Vue Productions)
  Series
  Bringing Up Buddy (and creator)
  Calvin and the Colonel
  Going My Way (and writer)
  Harris Against the World
    (executive producer only)
  Ichabod and Me (executive
    producer/writer only)
  Karen (executive producer
    only)
  Leave It to Beaver (and
    creator/writer)
  The Munsters (and writer)
  Pistols 'n' Petticoats (execu-
    tive producer/director
    only)
  Tom, Dick and Mary (execu-
    tive producer only)
CONNORS, CHUCK (actor)
  Series
  Arrest and Trial
  Telefeatures
  The Birdmen
  Set This Town on Fire
CONNORS, MIKE (actor)
  Telefeature
  Beg, Borrow ... or Steal
CONNORS, TOM, III (assistant
  director/2nd unit photog-
  rapher)
  Series
  The Six Million Dollar Man
CONRAD, NANCY (actress)
  Series
  Black Sheep Squadron
CONRAD, ROBERT (actor)
  Series
  Baa Baa Black Sheep
  Black Sheep Squadron (and
    director)
  Centennial
  The D.A.
  The Duke (and director)
  Telefeatures
  The Adventures of Nick
    Carter

The D.A.: Conspiracy to Kill
The D.A.: Murder One
CONRAD, WILLIAM (actor)
  Series
  The Rebels (narrator only)
  Telefeatures
  The D.A.: Conspiracy to Kill
  O'Hara, United States Treasury
CONSTANTINE, MICHAEL (actor)
  Series
  79 Park Avenue
  Telefeature
  The Impatient Heart
CONTE, RICHARD (actor)
  Telefeature
  The Challengers
CONVY, BERT (actor)
  Series
  The Snoop Sisters
  Telefeature
  Death Takes a Holiday
  Pilot
  Lady Luck
CONWAY, TIM (actor)
  Series
  McHale's Navy
COOK, ELISHA, JR. (actor)
  Telefeature
  The Movie Murderer
COOK, FIELDER (director)
  Series
  McCloud
  Telefeatures
  Sam Hill: Who Killed the
    Mysterious Mr. Foster?
  This Is the West That Was
COOLEY, STANLEY (sound mixer)
  Telefeatures
  The D.A.: Murder One
  McCloud: Who Killed Miss
    U.S.A.?
  Ritual of Evil
COON, GENE L. (writer)
  Series
  Cimarron City
  It Takes a Thief (producer
    only)
  McHale's Navy
  PAris 7000
  Telefeature
  The Questor Tapes
COOPER, JACKIE (actor)
  Series
  Baa Baa Black Sheep (director
    only)
  McMillan (director only)
  Mobile One
  Quincy, M.E. (director only)

Telefeatures
The Astronaut
Mobile Two
Operation Petticoat
Pilots
Doctor Dan
Snafu (director only)
COOPER-FINKEL CO. (Jackie Cooper's production company)
Pilot
Doctor Dan
COOPERSMITH, JERRY (writer)
Series
Mr. Inside/Mr. Outside
CORBETT, GLENN (actor)
Series
It's a Man's World
The Road West
Telefeature
The Log of the Black Pearl
CORBETT, GRETCHEN (actress)
Series
The Rockford Files
Telefeature
Mandrake
Special
The Cay
CORCORAN, KELLY (actor)
Series
The Road West
CORCORAN, NOREEN (actress)
Series
Bachelor Father
COREA, NICHOLAS (producer/writer)
Series
The Incredible Hulk
COREY, JEFF (actor)
Telefeatures
A Clear and Present Danger
The Movie Murderer
Set This Town on Fire
COREY, WENDELL (actor)
Series
Westinghouse Playhouse Starring Nanette Fabray and Wendell Corey
CORRELL, CHARLES (actor/creator with partner Freeman Gosden)
Series
Calvin and the Colonel
CORRELL, CHARLES (director of photography)
Series
Kojak
Switch
Telefeatures
The Dark Secret of Harvest Home
Dr. Scorpion
Pilot
Hazard's People
CORSARO, FRANK (director)
Series
Bob Hope Presents the Chrysler Theatre
CORSO, JOHN W. (art director)
Series
Aspen
Captains and the Kings
Centennial
Columbo
Telefeature
Mallory: Circumstantial Evidence
CORT, BUD (actor)
Telefeature
Brave New World
CORY, RAY, A.S.C. (director of photography)
Series
General Electric Theatre
COSTA, DON (composer)
Series
Lanigan's Rabbi
Loose Change
Pilot
Three Times Daley (musical director only)
COSTELLO, MARICLARE (actress)
Telefeatures
The Execution of Private Slovik
The Gun
COTLER, GORDON (producer)
Series
Lanigan's Rabbi
Rosetti and Ryan (supervising producer only)
Telefeature
Lanigan's Rabbi (writer only)
COTTEN, JOSEPH (actor)
Series
Aspen
Telefeatures
Do You Take This Stranger
The Lonely Profession
The Screaming Woman
COULOURIS, GEORGE (actor)
Telefeature
The Suicide Club
COURCIER, BRIAN (sound effects editor)
Series
Centennial
COX, RONNY (actor)
Telefeature

A Case of Rape
COX, WALLY (actor)
  Telefeatures
  Ironside
  It Takes a Thief
  Magic Carpet
  The Young Country
COX, WILLIAM R. (writer)
  Series
  General Electric Theatre
  Hec Ramsey
CRAIG, BRADFORD (composer)
  Telefeature
  Amateur Night at the Dixie Bar and Grill
CRAIN, EARL N., Jr. (sound mixer)
  Series
  Alias Smith and Jones
  Buck Rogers in the 25th Century
  Laramie
  McHale's Navy
  The Name of the Game
  Tales of Wells Fargo
  Telefeatures
  Fame Is the Name of the Game
  The Sunshine Patriot
CRAIS, ROBERT (executive story consultant)
  Series
  Quincy, M.E.
CRAMER, JOE L. (producer)
  Series
  Kingston: Confidential
  The Six Million Dollar Man
  Telefeature
  The UFO Incident
CRANE, BARRY (director)
  Series
  The Bionic Woman
  The Six Million Dollar Man
  Telefeature
  The Hound of the Baskervilles
CRAWFORD, BRODERICK (actor)
  Telefeature
  The Adventures of Nick Carter
CRAWFORD, CHARLES D. (film editor)
  Series
  The Misadventures of Sheriff Lobo
CRAWFORD, FRANK (1st assistant director)
  Series
  Buck Rogers in the 25th Century
CRAWFORD, JOAN (actress)
  Telefeature
  Night Gallery
CRAWFORD, KATHERINE (actress)
  Telefeatures
  The Doomsday Flight
  Gemini Man
  How to Steal an Airplane
CRAWFORD, OLIVER (story consultant)
  Series
  Madigan
CRAWLEY, ROBERT, SR. (art director)
  Series
  The Rockford Files
CRENNA, RICHARD (actor)
  Series
  Centennial
  Telefeature
  Double Indemnity
CRESCENDO PRODUCTIONS, INC. (production company)
  Series
  Delvecchio
  Telefeature
  Mallory: Circumstantial Evidence
CRESCIMAN, VINCE (art director)
  Telefeature
  BJ and the Bear
CRESTON PRODUCTIONS (production company of Freeman Gosden and Charles Correll)
  Series
  Calvin and the Colonel
CRISP, N.J. (writer)
  Series
  Colditz
  Telefeature
  Escape from Colditz
CRONJAGER, WILLIAM, A.S.C. (director of photography)
  Series
  Alias Smith and Jones
  BJ and the Bear
  Columbo
  The Partners
CROSBY, GARY (actor)
  Series
  Adam-12
  Chase
  Telefeatures
  O'Hara, United States Treasury
  Partners in Crime
  Wings of Fire
CROSBY, GEORGE E. (producer/

associate producer)
Series
Centennial
CROSLAND, ALAN, JR. (director)
Series
Adam-12
Alcoa Premiere/Premiere
Alfred Hitchcock Presents
The Bionic Woman
Chase
The D.A.
The Six Million Dollar Man
CROSLAND, STAN (director)
Series
Adam-12
CROSSE, RUPERT (actor)
Series
The Partners
CROTHERS, SCATMAN (actor)
Telefeature
Man on the Outside
CROWE, CHRISTOPHER (writer)
Series
BJ and the Bear (and creator)
The Hardy Boys Mysteries (and producer/story editor)
Telefeature
BJ and the Bear (and producer)
CRUGNOLA, AURELIO (art director)
Series
It Takes a Thief
Madigan
Telefeature
Cool Million
CUESTA, ALBERT D. (sound mixer)
Series
The Hardy Boys Mysteries
CULP, ROBERT (actor)
Series
Women in White
Telefeatures
A Cry for Help
Houston, We've Got a Problem
See the Man Run
CUMMINGS, BOB (actor)
Series
The Bob Cummings Show
Telefeature
Partners in Crime
CURTIS, JAMIE LEE (actress)
Series
Operation Petticoat
CURTIS, KEN (actor)
Series
Black Beauty

CURTIS, TONY (actor)
Series
McCoy
Telefeature
The Big Ripoff

DAGER, PHIL (sound mixer)
Special
A Special Act of Love
D'AGOSTA, JOSEPH (associate producer)
Series
Baretta
DAILEY, DAN (actor)
Series
Faraday and Company
Testimony of Two Men
Pilot
Koska and His Family
DAISY PRODUCTIONS (production company)
Telefeature
It Happened One Christmas
DALES, ARTHUR (writer)
Special
Short Stories of Love
DANA, BILL (actor)
Telefeatures
Rosetti and Ryan: Men Who Love Women
The Snoop Sisters
D'ANGELO, WILLIAM P. (executive producer)
Series
The Misadventures of Sheriff Lobo
DANGERFIELD, RODNEY (actor)
Telefeature
Benny and Barney: Las Vegas Undercover
DANIELS, MARC (director)
Series
Harold Robbins' "The Survivors"
PAris 7000
Marcus Welby, M.D.
DANIELS, WILLIAM (actor)
Series
The Bastard
The Rebels
Telefeatures
A Case of Rape
One of Our Own
Sarah T.--Portrait of a Teenage Alcoholic
Pilot
Boston and Kilbride
DANNY THOMAS PRODUCTIONS

(production company)
Series
Fay
DARBY, KIM (actress)
Series
The Last Convertible
Rich Man, Poor Man
Telefeatures
Ironside
The Story of Pretty Boy Floyd
This Is the West That Was
DARIN, BOBBY (actor)
Pilot
The Sweet Life
DARLING, JOAN (actress)
Series
Owen Marshall, Counselor at Law
Telefeature
Owen Marshall, Counselor at Law
DARROW, HENRY (actor)
Series
Hernandez: Houston P.D.
Telefeatures
Aloha Means Goodbye
Brock's Last Case
Hitchhike!
The Invisible Man
Special
A Man Whose Name Was John
DARST, DANNY (theme vocalist)
Series
The Oregon Trail
DAUGHERTY, HERSCHEL (director)
Series
Alfred Hitchcock Presents
General Electric Theatre
The Tall Man
Thriller
Westinghouse Playhouse Starring Nanette Fabray and Wendell Corey
Telefeatures
The Victim
Winchester 73
Special
The Slowest Gun in the West
DAUPHIN, CLAUDE (actor)
Telefeature
Berlin Affair
DAVEY, ALLEN M. (director of photography)
Series
The Six Million Dollar Man
Pilot
Stranded

DAVIDSON, BILL (writer)
Telefeature
The Art of Crime
DAVIS, ANN B. (actress)
Series
The John Forsythe Show
DAVIS, BETTE (actress)
Telefeatures
The Dark Secret of Harvest Home
The Judge and Jake Wyler
Scream, Pretty Peggy
DAVIS, CARL (composer)
Specials
The Cay
The Snow Goose
DAVIS, CHARLES R. (art director)
Series
The Incredible Hulk
Telefeature
The Incredible Hulk
DAVIS, CHUCK see DAVIS, CHARLES R.
DAVIS, JEROME see DAVIS, JERRY
DAVIS, JERRY (producer)
Series
House Calls (executive producer only)
Rosetti and Ryan
Telefeature
Rosetti and Ryan: Men Who Love Women
DAVIS, OSSIE (actor)
Telefeatures
Night Gallery
The Outsider
DAVIS, ROGER (actor)
Series
Alias Smith and Jones
DAVIS, SAMMY, JR. (theme vocalist)
Series
Baretta
DAVISON, BRUCE (actor)
Telefeature
Owen Marshall, Counselor at Law
DAWN, ROBERT (makeup artist)
Series
Leave It to Beaver
DAWSON, BEATRICE (costume designer)
Special
The Man Who Came to Dinner
DAY, DENNIS (actor/vocalist)
Series
The Jack Benny Show

DAY, GERRY (writer)
Series
The Virginian
DAY, LYNDA see GEORGE, LYNDA DAY
DAY, ROBERT (director)
Series
The Protectors
Tenafly
Telefeatures
Kingston: The Power Play
Ritual of Evil
Switch
DAYDREAMS PRODUCTIONS (production company)
Series
When the Whistle Blows
DEACON, RICHARD (actor)
Series
Leave It to Beaver
DEANE, HOWARD S. (film editor)
Series
Centennial
Delvecchio
Mrs. Columbo
Once an Eagle
Telefeatures
Charlie Cobb: Nice Night for a Hanging
Scott Free
DEANE, LEROY G. (art director)
Telefeature
The Elevator
DE BENEDICTIS, DICK (composer)
Series
Columbo
The Family Holvak
McCoy
The Oregon Trail
Telefeatures
The Big Ripoff
The Couple Takes a Wife
The Greatest Gift
The Return of the World's Greatest Detective
This Is the West That Was
DeBLASIO, EDWARD (writer)
Series
Owen Marshall, Counselor at Law
Marcus Welby, M.D.
Special
The Man from Independence
DE BONO, JERRY (writer)
Series
Marcus Welby, M.D.
DeCARLO, YVONNE (actress)
Series
The Munsters
DeCINCES, WILLIAM D. (art director)
Telefeatures
Lock, Stock and Barrel
Marriage: Year One
O'Hara, United States Treasury
The Psychiatrist: God Bless the Children
Ritual of Evil
Silent Night, Lonely Night
Stranger on the Run
DE CORDOVA, FRED (producer/director)
Series
The Jack Benny Show
DEE, RUBY (actress)
Telefeature
Deadlock!
DEE, SANDRA (actress)
Telefeatures
Houston, We've Got a Problem
The Manhunter
DEE, VINCENT (costume designer)
Series
Adam-12
Alfred Hitchcock Presents
Alias Smith and Jones
Convoy
The Deputy
Dragnet 1967-1970
87th Precinct
The John Forsythe Show
Laramie
Leave It to Beaver
McHale's Navy
The Men from Shiloh
Startime
Tales of Wells Fargo
The Tall Man
The Virginian
Wagon Train
Westinghouse Playhouse Starring Nanette Fabray and Wendell Corey
Whispering Smith
Telefeatures
A Clear and Present Danger
The Doomsday Flight
Dragnet 1966
Now You See It, Now You Don't
Something for a Lonely Man
Stranger on the Run
Special
The Slowest Gun in the West
DeFELITTA, FRANK (director/writer)

Telefeature
Trapped
DE FORE, DON (actor)
Series
Black Beauty
DeGOVIA, JACK (art director)
Telefeature
Sex and the Married Woman
DeGUERE, PHILIP, JR. (writer)
Series
Baa Baa Black Sheep (and producer)
Black Sheep Squadron (supervising producer only)
Telefeatures
Dr. Strange (and executive producer/director)
How to Steal an Airplane (and associate producer)
The 3,000 Mile Chase
Pilot
The Gypsy Warriors
DE HAVEN, CARTER, III (associate producer)
Series
Destry
DeHAVEN, GLORIA (actress)
Series
Evening in Byzantium
DE HAVILLAND, OLIVIA (actress)
Telefeature
The Screaming Woman
DEHNER, JOHN (actor)
Telefeatures
The Big Ripoff
Something for a Lonely Man
Winchester 73
DEIN, EDWARD (director)
Series
Baa Baa Black Sheep
DE JESUS, LUCHI (composer)
Series
Get Christie Love!
Telefeature
The California Kid
DE JESUS, LUCIO see DE JESUS, LUCHI
DE LADO, ATTILA (main title designer)
Series
The Man and the City
DE LARA, PAT (makeup artist)
Telefeatures
Escape to Mindanao
The Longest Hundred Miles
DEL BARRIO, GEORGE (composer)
Series

San Francisco International Airport
DELL, GABRIEL (actor)
Telefeature
Cutter
DEL RUTH, THOMAS (director of photography)
Series
Mrs. Columbo
DeLUISE, DOM (actor)
Telefeature
Evil Roy Slade
DEMAREST, WILLIAM (actor)
Series
Tales of Wells Fargo
DeMARTINI, ALDO (sound mixer)
Series
Madigan
DE MAUPASSANT, GUY (writer)
Series
General Electric Theatre
DEMIAN, MARCUS (writer)
Telefeature
Maneater
DEMOSTHENES see SAVALAS, GEORGE
DENNING, RICHARD (actor)
Series
Karen
DENNIS, ROBERT C. (writer)
Series
The D. A.
Escape
DENOFF, SAM (producer/writer with partner Bill Persky)
Special
The Man Who Came to Dinner
DENVER, JOHN (composer/lyricist)
Telefeature
Sunshine
DEODATO, EUMIR (composer)
Telefeature
Target Risk
DEREK, JOHN (actor)
Series
Frontier Circus
DERN, BRUCE (actor)
Telefeature
Sam Hill: Who Killed the Mysterious Mr. Foster?
DeROY, RICHARD (writer)
Series
79 Park Avenue (and developer for television)
Sons and Daughters (executive story consultant only)
Telefeature

A Howling in the Woods
DEUEL, PETE(R) (actor)
  Series
    Alias Smith and Jones
  Telefeatures
    Alias Smith and Jones
    How to Steal an Airplane
    Marcus Welby, M.D.
    The Psychiatrist: God Bless the Children
    The Young Country
DE VALLY, RAY C., SR. (film editor)
  Series
    Laramie
DEVANE, WILLIAM (actor)
  Series
    Black Beauty
DEVERAUX, BETTY (writer)
  Series
    The Protectors
DEVERMAN, DALE (director of photography)
  Series
    Checkmate
DEVLIN, DON (associate producer)
  Series
    Convoy
DeVOL, FRANK (composer)
  Telefeature
    Female Artillery
DEWHURST, COLLEEN (actress)
  Telefeature
    A Prowler in the Heart
  Special
    Legend in Granite
DEXTER, JOY (writer)
  Series
    The Virginian
DEY, SUSAN (actress)
  Telefeature
    Little Women
DeYOUNG, CLIFF (actor)
  Series
    Captains and the Kings
    Centennial
    Sunshine
  Telefeatures
    Sunshine
    Sunshine Christmas
    The 3,000 Mile Chase
DIAMOND, DON (actor)
  Series
    The Adventures of Kit Carson
DIAMOND, IRA (art director)
  Series
    Quincy, M.E.
    Switch
  Telefeatures
    The Family Nobody Wanted
    The Islander
    The Keegans
    You Lie So Deep, My Love
DIAMOND, MEL (story consultant/writer)
  Series
    The Bob Cummings Show
DiCENZO, GEORGE (actor)
  Series
    Aspen
  Telefeature
    Murder Works Overtime
DICKINSON, ANGIE (actress)
  Telefeature
    See the Man Run
DICKSON, JIM (director of photography)
  Series
    Testimony of Two Men
DICKSON, KEN (director of photography)
  Telefeature
    The Dark Secret of Harvest Home
DIERKOP, CHARLES (actor)
  Telefeatures
    Death Is a Bad Trip
    Female Artillery
    Lock, Stock and Barrel
DIGNAN, JOHN C. (sound mixer)
  Series
    Battlestar: Galactica
    Delta House
    The Misadventures of Sheriff Lobo
DiLEO, MARIO (director of photography)
  Series
    The Eddie Capra Mysteries
DILLMAN, BRADFORD (actor)
  Series
    Court Martial
  Telefeatures
    Fear No Evil
    Force Five
    Kingston: The Power Play
DILLON, RITA (associate producer)
  Series
    Sarge
DILLY, JOHN (set decorator)
  Special
    The Man Who Came to Dinner
DINALLO, GREGORY S. (writer)
  Series

The Hardy Boys Mysteries
DI PASQUALE, JAMES (composer)
Series
Sons and Daughters
Telefeatures
Force Five
Mallory: Circumstantial Evidence
Sarah T.--Portrait of a Teenage Alcoholic
Senior Year
DiPEGO, GERALD (writer)
Telefeatures
The Astronaut
Runaway!
Short Walk to Daylight
You'll Never See Me Again
DISMUKES, CHARLES E. (producer)
Series
Baretta (and unit manager)
Quincy, M.E. (associate producer only)
DIVITALE, JOSEPH B. (sound effects editor)
Series
BJ and the Bear
DIXON, IVAN (director)
Series
Baa Baa Black Sheep
The Hardy Boys Mysteries
Telefeature
Love Is Not Enough
DMITRI, RICHARD (producer/creator/writer)
Pilot
Roosevelt and Truman
DOBKIN, LAWRENCE (director)
Series
Alcoa Premiere/Premiere
Emergency!
The Munsters
DOBSON, KEVIN (actor)
Series
The Immigrants
Kojak
Pilot
Stranded
DODDS, EDWARD K. (associate producer)
Series
Columbo (and producer)
Dragnet 1967-1970 (unit manager only)
The Family Holvak
Madigan
McCoy
Telefeatures

The D.A.: Murder One
McCloud: Who Killed Miss U.S.A.? (assistant director only)
DODSON, MARY WEAVER (art director)
Series
Battlestar: Galactica
Delta House
DOHANOS, PETER (art director)
Series
Kojak
DOHENY, LARRY (director)
Series
Baa Baa Black Sheep
Black Sheep Squadron
The Duke
The Six Million Dollar Man
Telefeature
Houston, We've Got a Problem
DOHENY, LAWRENCE see DOHENY, LARRY
DOHERTY, JAMES (writer)
Series
Adam-12 (and producer/director)
Ironside
DOLINSKY, MEYER (writer)
Telefeature
The Manhunter
DONAHUE, TROY (actor)
Telefeature
The Lonely Profession
DONALDSON, MARTIN (writer)
Telefeature
Brock's Last Case
DONIGER, WALTER (director)
Series
Delvecchio
The Doctors
Griff
Harold Robbins' "The Survivors" (and executive producer/writer)
Jigsaw
Owen Marshall, Counselor at Law
Switch
DONLEE PRODUCTIONS (Don Adams' production company)
Series
The Partners
DONNELLY, DENNIS (director)
Series
Adam-12
Emergency! (and assistant director)
The Hardy Boys Mysteries
DONNELLY, KEVIN (assistant di-

Index / 335

rector)
Series
Columbo
DONNELLY, PAUL (producer)
Telefeature
Berlin Affair
DONNER, RICHARD (director)
Series
Hernandez: Houston P.D.
Kojak
Telefeatures
Lucas Tanner
Sarah T.--Portrait of a Teenage Alcoholic
Senior Year
DONOVAN, MICHAEL (writer)
Series
Adam-12
Chase
Dragnet 1967-1970
Telefeature
The Rangers
DoQUI, ROBERT (actor)
Series
Centennial
Telefeatures
Heat Wave
Lieutenant Schuster's Wife
DORAN, JACK (assistant director)
Series
Alias Smith and Jones
Rod Serling's Night Gallery
DORLEAC, JEAN-PIERRE (costume designer)
Series
Battlestar: Galactica
The Rebels
DORTORT, DAVID (producer/writer)
Series
The Restless Gun
DORWARD, KENNETH (writer)
Series
Emergency!
DOTLER, GORDON (writer)
Telefeature
Rosetti and Ryan: Men Who Love Women
DOUGLAS, DONALD (film editor)
Series
The Eddie Capra Mysteries
Telefeature
Little Women
DOUGLAS, KIRK (actor)
Telefeature
Mousey
DOUGLAS, MELVYN (actor)
Telefeatures

Companions in Nightmare
Death Takes a Holiday
DOUGLAS, ROBERT (director)
Series
Adam-12
Baretta
City of Angels
Columbo
DOW, TONY (actor)
Series
Leave It to Beaver
DOWELL, DAVID M. (assistant director)
Series
Columbo
DOWNEY, MARVIN (animal supervisor)
Series
BJ and the Bear
DOWNING, BARRY (costume designer)
Series
Buck Rogers in the 25th Century
DOZIER, ROBERT (writer)
Series
General Electric Theatre
Thriller
DRAGNET PRODUCTIONS (production company)
Series
Dragnet 1967-1970
DRAKE, THOMAS Y. (writer)
Series
The Psychiatrist
DRASNIN, ROBERT (composer)
Series
Jigsaw
Telefeature
Jigsaw
DREBEN, STAN (writer)
Telefeature
All My Darling Daughters
DRISKILL, WILLIAM (writer)
Series
Griff
The Six Million Dollar Man
DRUMHELLER, ROBERT (set decorator)
Telefeature
The Borgia Stick
DRURY, JAMES (actor)
Series
The Men from Shiloh
The Virginian
Telefeatures
Alias Smith and Jones
Breakout
The Devil and Miss Sarah

It Takes a Thief
DRURY, WESTON, JR. (casting director)
Telefeature
Run a Crooked Mile
DuBARRY, DENISE (actress)
Series
Black Sheep Squadron
DUBIN, CHARLES S. (director)
Series
Ellery Queen
Lucas Tanner
Kojak
Sons and Daughters
The Virginian
DUBLEMAN, RICHARD (producer)
Telefeature
The Execution of Private Slovik
DUFF, HOWARD (actor)
Telefeatures
The D.A.: Murder One
A Little Game
DUFF, WARREN (producer)
Series
Markham
DUFFY, PAT (1st assistant director)
Series
Galactica 1980
DUGAN, DENNIS (actor)
Series
Rich Man, Poor Man
Richie Brockelman, Private Eye
Telefeatures
Death Race
Richie Brockelman, Private Eye
DUGAN, JOHN T. (executive story consultant)
Series
Adam-12
Court Martial (writer only)
DUGGAN, ANDREW (actor)
Series
Rich Man, Poor Man
Telefeatures
Jigsaw
Pine Canyon Is Burning
Tail Gunner Joe
Two on a Bench
DUKE, DARYL (director)
Series
Banacek
The Protectors
The Senator
Telefeatures

Charlie Chan
A Cry for Help
The Psychiatrist: God Bless the Children
Pilot
If I Had a Million
DUKE, PATTY see ASTIN, PATTY DUKE
DUKES, DAVID (actor)
Series
79 Park Avenue
DULLEA, KEIR (actor)
Telefeature
Brave New World
DUMAS, JOHN (film editor)
Series
Alias Smith and Jones
The Hardy Boys Mysteries
Telefeatures
Dark Victory
Do You Take This Stranger
Drive Hard, Drive Fast
How to Steal an Airplane
The Rockford Files
Sam Hill: Who Killed the Mysterious Mr. Foster?
Set This Town on Fire
Toma
DUMBRILLE, ERWIN (film editor)
Telefeature
The Aquarians
DUMM, J. RICKLEY (producer)
Series
The Rockford Files (associate producer only)
Telefeature
The Night Rider
DUNAWAY, DON CARLOS (writer)
Series
The Duke (producer only)
Toma
Telefeature
Target Risk
DUNAWAY, FAYE (actress)
Special
The Woman I Love
DURNING, CHARLES (actor)
Series
Captains and the Kings
Telefeature
Switch
DURYEA, DAN (actor)
Telefeatures
Stranger on the Run
Winchester 73
DUSENBERRY, ANN (actress)
Series
Captains and the Kings

Little Women
  Telefeatures
  Little Women
  Stonestreet: Who Killed the
    Centerfold Model?
DUVALL, ROBERT (actor)
  Telefeature
  Fame Is the Name of the Game
DWYER, JOHN (set decorator)
  Series
  Kojak
DYER, BILL (lyricist)
  Telefeature
  The Desperate Miles
DYKSTRA, JOHN (producer/
    photographic effects creator)
  Series
  Battlestar: Galactica
DYSART, RICHARD (actor)
  Telefeature
  It Happened One Christmas

EARLL, ROBERT (executive
    story editor)
  Series
  Switch
EARNSHAW, FENTON (writer)
  Series
  Cimarron City
EBSEN, BUDDY (actor)
  Series
  The Bastard
  Telefeature
  Tom Sawyer
ECKSTEIN, GEORGE (producer)
  Series
  Banacek (executive producer
    only)
  The Name of the Game
  The Rhinemann Exchange
    (executive producer only)
  Sara (executive producer only)
  79 Park Avenue (executive pro-
    ducer only)
  Sunshine
  What Really Happened to the
    Class of '65?
  Telefeatures
  Amelia Earhart
  Banacek
  Cool Million (executive pro-
    ducer only)
  The Couple Takes a Wife
  Death Takes a Holiday
  Duel
  The Failing of Raymond
  The Keegans

  A Little Game
  Man on the Outside
  Sunshine
  Sunshine Christmas
  Tail Gunner Joe
  The Tribe
ECONOMOU, MICHAEL (film
    editor)
  Telefeatures
  Cool Million
  Death Takes a Holiday
  A Little Game
  Once Upon a Dead Man
EDELMAN, HERB (actor)
  Telefeatures
  The Neon Ceiling
  Once Upon a Dead Man
  Pilot
  Koska and His Family
EDEN, BARBARA (actress)
  Series
  Condominium
  Telefeatures
  A Howling in the Woods
  Let's Switch
  Stonestreet: Who Killed the
    Centerfold Model?
EDENS, ALRIC, A.S.C. (director
    of photography)
  Series
  Quincy, M.E.
  San Francisco International Air-
    port
  The Six Million Dollar Man
  Telefeatures
  The Adventures of Nick Carter
  The Astronaut
  The D.A.: Conspiracy to Kill
  The D.A.: Murder One
  O'Hara, United States Treasury
  Trial Run
  Special
  The Cay
EDMISTON, ROBERT O. (casting
    director)
  Series
  The Rebels
EDWARDS, RALPH (executive
    producer)
  Series
  The Wide Country
EDWARDS, VINCE(NT) (actor)
  Series
  Evening in Byzantium
  The Hardy Boys Mysteries (di-
    rector only)
  Matt Lincoln
  The Rhinemann Exchange

338 / Index

Telefeatures
Dial: Hot Line
Maneater (director/writer only)
EGAN, SAM (executive story consultant)
Series
Quincy, M. E.
EGGAR, SAMANTHA (actress)
Telefeature
Double Indemnity
EHRLICH, MAX (writer)
Series
General Electric Theatre
EISENMANN, IKE (actor)
Series
Black Beauty
EISENSON, ART (writer)
Series
Beggarman, Thief
ELAM, JACK (actor)
Series
Black Beauty
Specials
The Red Pony
The Slowest Gun in the West
ELCAR, DANA (actor)
Series
Baa Baa Black Sheep
Baretta
Black Sheep Squadron
Telefeatures
The Borgia Stick
The Bravos
The D.A.: Murder One
Deadlock!
Gemini Man
Heat Wave
San Francisco International Airport
Sarge: The Badge or the Cross
Senior Year
The Sound of Anger
The Whole World Is Watching
ELDER, LONNIE (writer)
Series
McCloud
ELIAS, JOHN (film editor)
Series
Centennial
Loose Change
Once an Eagle
The Seekers
The Sixth Sense
Telefeatures
Female Artillery
The Great Man's Whiskers
McNaughton's Daughter

Richie Brockelman, Private Eye
San Francisco International Airport
ELLIOT, JACK (composer, often with partner Allyn Ferguson)
Series
Banacek
Get Christie Love!
Pistols 'n' Petticoats
Special
The Jack Benny Special (and conductor)
ELLIOTT, ROSS (actor)
Telefeatures
Linda
The Longest Night
Runaway!
See the Man Run
The Victim
ELLIOTT, SAM (actor)
Series
Aspen
Once an Eagle
ELLIOTT, STEPHEN (actor)
Telefeatures
The Gun
The Invasion of Johnson County
ELLIOTT, WALTER ULRIC (music editor)
Series
Aspen
The Incredible Hulk
ELLIS, LOVEL (film editor)
Telefeature
See the Man Run
ELLIS, SIDNEY (executive story consultant)
Series
Baretta
BJ and the Bear
ELLISON, HARLAN (story editor)
Series
The Sixth Sense
ELLSWORTH, ROBERT (costume designer)
Series
Centennial
ELMAN, IRVING (producer)
Series
Matt Lincoln
ELSENBACH, JOHN (director of photography)
Series
Loose Change
EMERT, OLIVER (set decorator)
Series
Westinghouse Playhouse Starring

Nanette Fabray and Wendell Corey
EMHARDT, ROBERT (actor)
Special
Short Stories of Love
ENDORE, GUY (writer)
Telefeature
Fear No Evil
ENGEL, CHARLES F. (executive in charge of production)
Series
Captains and the Kings
Once an Eagle
The Partners
The Rhinemann Exchange
Seventh Avenue
Telefeatures
The Aquarians (producer only)
Run a Crooked Mile (producer only)
ENGLAND, EDWIN F. (film editor)
Series
Aspen
Captains and the Kings
Wheels
ENRIQUEZ, NAPOLEON (art director)
Telefeature
Escape to Mindanao
EPSTEIN, HOWARD G. (film editor)
Series
Alcoa Premiere/Premiere
Emergency!
Jigsaw
The Six Million Dollar Man
Telefeatures
The Greatest Gift
The Manhunter
EPSTEIN, JON (producer)
Series
McMillan
McMillan and Wife
Owen Marshall, Counselor at Law
Rich Man, Poor Man
Rich Man, Poor Man--Book II
Switch (executive producer only)
Telefeatures
Partners in Crime
Tenafly
Special
The Man from Independence
EPSTEIN, JULIUS J. (creator)
Series

House Calls
ERICKSON, DICK (2nd assistant director)
Series
Quincy, M. E.
ERICKSON, LEIF (actor)
Telefeatures
The Deadly Dream
Force Five
ERWIN, STUART (actor)
Telefeature
Shadow Over Elveron
ERWIN, STUART, JR. (executive in charge of production)
Series
The Doctors
The Senator
ESQUIVEL, JUAN (composer)
Series
The Bob Cummings Show
The Tall Man
EURIST, CLARENCE (production supervisor)
Special
The Red Pony
EVANS, LINDA (actress)
Telefeature
Female Artillery
EVERETT, CHAD (actor)
Series
Centennial
EVERS, JASON (actor)
Series
Channing
EVIGAN, GREG (actor)
Series
BJ and the Bear (and theme vocalist)
Telefeature
BJ and the Bear
EWELL, TOM (actor)
Series
Baretta
EYLER, JOHN J. (2nd assistant director)
Series
The Misadventures of Sheriff Lobo

FABRAY, NANETTE (actress)
Series
Westinghouse Playhouse Starring Nanette Fabray and Wendell Corey
Telefeatures
The Couple Takes a Wife
Fame Is the Name of the Game

Magic Carpet
FAGAN, RONALD J. (film editor)
Telefeature
Benny and Barney: Las Vegas Undercover
FAIRMOUNT/FOXCROFT PRODUCTIONS (production company of Richard Levinson and William Link)
Series
Ellery Queen
Telefeatures
Charlie Cobb: Nice Night for a Hanging
Ellery Queen
The Storyteller
FAIRWAY PRODUCTIONS (production company)
Series
Challenge Golf
FAITH, PERCY (theme composer)
Series
The Virginian
FALK, HARRY (director)
Series
Centennial
Marcus Welby, M.D.
McCloud
McMillan and Wife
Owen Marshall, Counselor at Law
Telefeature
Mandrake
FALK, PETER (actor)
Series
Columbo
Telefeatures
Prescription: Murder
Ransom for a Dead Man
FANTE, JOHN (writer)
Telefeature
Something for a Lonely Man
FARENTINO, JAMES (actor)
Series
Cool Million
The Lawyers
Telefeatures
Cool Million
The Elevator
The Longest Night
The Sound of Anger
Vanished
The Whole World Is Watching
Wings of Fire
FARGO, JIM (assistant director)
Telefeature
Vanished
FARLOW, WAYNE (assistant director)
Series
Aspen
FARR, JAMIE (actor)
Telefeature
Amateur Night at the Dixie Bar and Grill
FARRELL, MIKE (actor)
Series
The Man and the City
Telefeatures
Live Again, Die Again
The Longest Night
McNaughton's Daughter
The Nightmare Step
The Questor Tapes
FARRELL, SHARON (actress)
Telefeature
A Little Bit Like Murder
FARREN, JACK (producer)
Telefeature
Silent Night, Lonely Night
FAST, HOWARD (writer)
Telefeature
What's a Nice Girl Like You...?
FAULKNER, WILLIAM (writer)
Series
General Electric Theatre
FAWCETT-MAJORS PRODUCTIONS (production company of Lee Majors and Farrah Fawcett-Majors)
Telefeature
Just a Little Inconvenience
FAY, MARSTEN (film editor)
Series
Wagon Train
FAY, WILLIAM (writer)
Series
Going My Way
FEIN, IRVING A. (executive producer)
Series
The Jack Benny Show
FELDMAN, MARTY (actor)
Special
The Man Who Came to Dinner
FELDMAN, RICHARD (set decorator)
Series
The Bastard
FELDON, BARBARA (actress)
Telefeature
Let's Switch
FELDSHUH, TOVAH (actress)
Series
Beggarman, Thief

Telefeature
Scream, Pretty Peggy
FELIX ZELENKA PRODUCTIONS
   (animators)
   Telefeature
   Ellery Queen: Don't Look
      Behind You
FELL, NORMAN (actor)
   Series
   87th Precinct
   Rich Man, Poor Man
   Telefeature
   Richie Brockelman, Private
      Eye
FELTON, NORMAN (executive
      producer and head of Arena
      Productions, Inc.)
   Series
   General Electric Theatre
   The Psychiatrist
   Telefeatures
   Marriage: Year One
   The Psychiatrist: God Bless
      the Children
FENADY, GEORGE (director)
   Series
   Emergency!
   Harold Robbins' "The Sur-
      vivors"
   San Francisco International
      Airport (assistant director
      only)
   Telefeature
   Sarge: The Badge or the
      Cross
FENTON, FRANK (writer)
   Telefeature
   Something for a Lonely Man
FERBER, MEL (director)
   Series
   Alias Smith and Jones
FERGUSON, ALLYN (composer
      with partner Jack Elliot)
   Series
   Banacek
   Get Christie Love!
FERGUSON, MICHAEL (director)
   Series
   Colditz
   Telefeature
   Escape from Colditz
FERNSTROM, RAY, A.S.C.
      (aerial photographer)
   Telefeature
   Wings of Fire
FERRARO, RALPH (composer)
   Series
   It Takes a Thief

FERRER, JOSE (actor)
   Series
   The Rhinemann Exchange
   Telefeatures
   The Aquarians
   The Art of Crime
   Exo-Man
   The Marcus-Nelson Murders
FERRER, MEL (actor)
   Series
   Black Beauty
   Telefeature
   Tenafly
FERRIGNO, LOU (actor)
   Series
   The Incredible Hulk
   Telefeature
   The Incredible Hulk
FERRIN, RALPH (assistant direc-
      tor)
   Series
   McCloud
   Telefeatures
   The D.A.: Murder One
   My Sweet Charlie
FETCHIT, STEPIN (actor)
   Telefeature
   Cutter
FIEDLER, JOHN (actor)
   Telefeatures
   Double Indemnity
   Hitched
FIELD, GUSTAVE (writer)
   Series
   The Doctors
   The Six Million Dollar Man
   Telefeature
   The Sunshine Patriot
FIELD, RON (director/choreograph-
      er)
   Special
   Applause
FIELD, SALLY (actress)
   Series
   Alias Smith and Jones
   Telefeatures
   Bridger
   Hitched
   Marriage: Year One
FIELDER, PAT (writer)
   Series
   Owen Marshall, Counselor at
      Law
   Rosetti and Ryan
FIELDER, RICHARD (writer)
   Series
   Checkmate
   Marcus Welby, M.D.

McCloud (director only)
Kingston: Confidential
The Virginian
FIELDING, JERRY (composer)
Series
Broadside
Faraday and Company
McMillan
McMillan and Wife
Telefeatures
Ellery Queen: Don't Look Behind You
Once Upon a Dead Man
The Snoop Sisters
FIELDS, PETER ALLAN (executive story consultant)
Series
The Eddie Capra Mysteries
The Six Million Dollar Man
Telefeature
Heat Wave (writer only)
FINK, MARK (story editor)
Series
The Misadventures of Sheriff Lobo
FINKEL, ROBERT (producer)
Series
The Bob Cummings Show
FINLAY, FRANK (actor)
Special
The Adventures of Don Quixote
FINN, RAY (director of photography)
Series
McHale's Navy
FINNEGAN, WILLIAM (producer)
Series
Hec Ramsey
FINNERMAN, GERALD PERRY, A.S.C. (director of photography)
Series
The Doctors
Kojak
Rod Serling's Night Gallery
Telefeatures
Hitched
See the Man Run
The Sunshine Patriot
FINNERMAN, JERRY see FINNERMAN, GERALD PERRY
FISCHER, PETER S. (writer)
Series
Black Beauty (and executive producer)
Columbo (and executive story consultant)
The Eddie Capra Mysteries (and executive producer/creator)
Ellery Queen (and producer)
Griff
Once an Eagle (and producer)
Richie Brockelman, Private Eye (producer only)
Telefeatures
Charlie Cobb: Nice Night for a Hanging (and producer)
A Cry for Help
FITZGERALD, WAYNE (main title designer)
Series
NBC Sunday Mystery Movie
NBC Tuesday/Wednesday Mystery Movie
Switch
FIX, PAUL (actor)
Telefeatures
Guilty or Innocent: The Sam Sheppard Murder Case
Set This Town on Fire
Winchester 73
FLAGG, FANNIE (actress)
Telefeature
Sex and the Married Woman
FLANDERS, ED (actor)
Telefeatures
Indict and Convict
The Snoop Sisters
FLANNERY, SUSAN (actress)
Series
Women in White
FLASTER, JAMES Z. (sound mixer)
Telefeature
Vanished
FLICKER, THEODORE J. (director/writer)
Telefeature
Just a Little Inconvenience
FLIN, RAY (director of photography)
Series
It's a Man's World
Telefeatures
Breakout
Escape to Mindanao
The Intruders
The Longest Hundred Miles
FLIPPEN, JAY C. (actor)
Telefeatures
Fame Is the Name of the Game
Sam Hill: Who Killed the Mysterious Mr. Foster?
The Sound of Anger
FLIPPEN, RUTH BROOKS (writer)

Telefeature
   Let's Switch
FLOREY, ROBERT (director)
  Series
   Alcoa Premiere/Premiere
FLOYD, JOHN (art director)
  Series
   Ellery Queen
FLYNN, JOE (actor)
  Series
   McHale's Navy
FOCH, NINA (actress)
  Telefeatures
   Female Artillery
   A Little Bit Like Murder
   Prescription: Murder
FONDA, HENRY (actor)
  Series
   Captains and the Kings
   The Deputy
  Telefeatures
   The Alpha Caper
   Stranger on the Run
  Special
   The Red Pony
FONTANA, D.C. (writer)
  Series
   The Six Million Dollar Man
  Special
   A Special Act of Love
FOOTE, CONE & BELDING PRODUCTIONS (production company of the advertising agency Foote, Cone & Belding)
  Special
   The Man Who Came to Dinner
FORD, GLENN (actor)
  Series
   Beggarman, Thief
   Evening in Byzantium
   The Family Holvak
   Once an Eagle
  Telefeatures
   The Greatest Gift
   The 3,000 Mile Chase
FORD, HARRISON (actor)
  Telefeature
   The Intruders
FORD, JOHN (director)
  Series
   Alcoa Premiere/Premiere
   Wagon Train
FORD, OLGA (writer)
  Series
   Get Christie Love!
FORREST, RICHARD J. (2nd assistant director)

Series
  The Incredible Hulk
FORREST, RUSSELL C. (art director)
  Series
   Marcus Welby, M.D.
   The Name of the Game
   Owen Marshall, Counselor at Law
  Telefeature
   All My Darling Daughters
FORREST, STEVE (actor)
  Series
   Condominium
   Testimony of Two Men
  Telefeature
   Captain America
FORRESTER, LARRY (executive story consultant)
  Series
   Switch
FORSYTHE, JOHN (actor)
  Series
   Bachelor Father
   The John Forsythe Show
  Telefeatures
   Amelia Earhart
   See How They Run
   Tail Gunner Joe
FORSYTHE PRODUCTIONS (John Forsythe's production company)
  Series
   The John Forsythe Show
FORWARD, ROBERT H. (producer with Mark VII Limited)
  Series
   The D.A.
  Telefeatures
   The D.A.: Conspiracy to Kill
   The D.A.: Murder One (executive producer only)
FOSTER, BILL (director)
  Special
   Applause
FOSTER, GENE (director)
  Series
   Loose Change
FOSTER, MEG (actress)
  Series
   Sunshine
  Telefeatures
   Sunshine
   Sunshine Christmas
FOSTER, ROBERT (writer/associate producer)
  Series
   Run for Your Life (assistant to

the executive producer only)
Telefeature
How to Steal an Airplane
FOX, BERNARD (actor)
Telefeature
The Hound of the Baskervilles
FOX, CHARLES (composer)
Telefeature
Aloha Means Goodbye
FOX, MICHAEL (actor)
Telefeature
Now You See It, Now You Don't
FOX, NORMAN (associate producer)
Series
Black Beauty
FOXWORTH, ROBERT (actor)
Telefeature
The Questor Tapes
FRANCE, ROSA (costume designer)
Telefeature
The Longest Hundred Miles
FRANCIOSA, TONY (actor)
Series
Aspen
The Name of the Game
Wheels
Telefeatures
Fame Is the Name of the Game
This Is the West That Was
FRANCIS, ANNE (actress)
Series
Beggarman, Thief
The Rebels
Telefeatures
The Intruders
Night Life
FRANCISCUS, JAMES (actor)
Series
The Investigators
Telefeatures
Aloha Means Goodbye
Shadow Over Elveron
Trial Run
FRANCY PRODUCTIONS (production company)
Series
The Night Stalker
FRANK, GARY (actor)
Series
Sons and Daughters
Telefeature
Senior Year
FRANKEN, STEVE (actor)

Series
Tom, Dick and Mary
FRANKLIN, BONNIE (actress)
Telefeature
The Law
FRANKLIN, DON (unit production manager)
Series
Mrs. Columbo
FRANKLIN, ELBERT (sound mixer)
Telefeature
Night Gallery
FRANKLIN BARTON PRODUCTIONS (production company)
Pilot
Off the Wall
FRANKOVICH, MIKE, JR. (unit production manager)
Series
BJ and the Bear
FRAZER, DAN (actor)
Series
Kojak
FRED CALVERT PRODUCTIONS (production company)
Series
Emergency Plus Four
FREDERICKS, ELLSWORTH (director of photography)
Series
The Deputy
FREEDLE, SAM (unit production manager)
Series
Delta House
FREEDMAN, JERROLD (associate producer)
Series
The Protectors (producer only)
The Psychiatrist (producer/director/writer only)
Rod Serling's Night Gallery (writer only)
Telefeatures
Istanbul Express
Perilous Voyage
The Psychiatrist: God Bless the Children (writer only)
Trial Run
FREEDMAN, RICHARD (set decorator)
Telefeature
Amelia Earhart
FREEMAN, BUD (writer)
Telefeature
Female Artillery
FREEMAN, ERNEST (composer)

Series
It Takes a Thief
Telefeature
It Takes a Thief
FREEMAN, ERNIE see FREE-
   MAN, ERNEST
FREEMAN, EVERETT (producer)
Series
Alcoa Premiere/Premiere
Bachelor Father
FREEMAN, JACK (makeup artist)
Series
PAris 7000
FREEMAN, KATHLEEN (actress)
Telefeature
Hitched
FREEMAN, PAUL (associate pro-
   ducer)
Series
The Outsider
Rod Serling's Night Gallery
   (production executive only)
Run for Your Life
The Virginian (producer only)
Telefeature
The Birdmen (production super-
   visor only)
FREER, ROBERT (set decorator)
Pilot
The Gypsy Warriors
FREIBERGER, FRED (producer)
Series
The Senator (executive story
   consultant/story editor only)
The Six Million Dollar Man
FRENCH, VICTOR (actor)
Telefeatures
Amateur Night at the Dixie
   Bar and Grill
The Tribe
FRIDELL, SQUIRE (actor)
Series
Rosetti and Ryan
Telefeature
Rosetti and Ryan: Men Who
   Love Women
FRIED, GERALD (composer)
Series
The Immigrants
Mr. Terrific
The Rebels
The Seekers
Testimony of Two Men
Telefeature
Sex and the Married Woman
FRIEDKIN, DAVID (director)
Series
Chase

Jigsaw
Kojak
FRIEDMAN, RICHARD (set decor-
   ator)
Telefeature
The Execution of Private Slovik
FRONTIERE, DOMINIC (music
   supervisor)
Series
The Name of the Game
FRYE, WILLIAM (producer)
Series
The Bob Cummings Show
The Deputy (executive producer
   only)
Johnny Staccato (executive pro-
   ducer only)
Startime
Suspicion
Thriller
Telefeatures
The Elevator
Linda
The Longest Night
The Other Man
The Screaming Woman
The Victim
Special
The Slowest Gun in the West
   (executive producer only)
FULLER, ROBERT (actor)
Series
Emergency!
Laramie
Wagon Train
Telefeature
Emergency!
FUMAGELLI, FRANCO (art direc-
   tor)
Telefeature
Magic Carpet
FURIA, JOHN, JR. (writer)
Series
San Francisco International Air-
   port

GAFFEY, NICK (sound mixer)
Series
The Eddie Capra Mysteries
GALLICO, PAUL (writer)
Special
The Snow Goose
GALLO, FRED (assistant director)
Series
Madigan
GALLOWAY, DON (actor)
Series

Arrest and Trial
Ironside
Tom, Dick and Mary
Telefeatures
Ironside
Lieutenant Schuster's Wife
The Priest Killer
You Lie So Deep, My Love
Special
A Man Whose Name Was John
GAMBIT PRODUCTIONS, INC. (production company)
Series
Mrs. Columbo
GANTMAN, JOSEPH (associate producer)
Series
General Electric Theatre
GANZER, ALVIN (director)
Series
Quincy, M. E.
GARBER, DAVID W. (production and special effects consultant)
Series
Battlestar: Galactica
Buck Rogers in the 25th Century (miniature effects creator only)
GARBERS, LEON (film editor)
Series
The Rebels
GARCES, GABRIEL TORRES (director of photography)
Telefeature
River of Mystery
GARCIA, ALICE (costume designer)
Telefeature
Escape to Mindanao
GARCIA, RUSS (theme composer)
Series
Laredo
GARDNER, GERALD (writer)
Series
Don Adams' Screen Test
GARDNER, RITA (vocalist)
Telefeature
Don't Push, I'll Charge When I'm Ready
GARLAND, PATRICK (director)
Specials
The Cay
The Snow Goose
GARNER, JAMES (actor and head of Cherokee Productions)
Series

The Rockford Files
Telefeature
The Rockford Files
GARNER, LEONARD R. (2nd assistant director)
Series
The Rockford Files
GARRETT, LILA (writer)
Special
Mother of the Bride
GARSON, GREER (actress)
Telefeature
Little Women
GAST, HAROLD (producer)
Series
McNaughton's Daughter
Telefeature
Guilty or Innocent: The Sam Sheppard Murder Case
GAUDIOSO, JOHN (assistant director)
Series
The Night Stalker
GAUTIER, DICK (actor)
Telefeatures
Benny and Barney: Las Vegas Undercover
Sex and the Married Woman
GAVIN, JOHN (actor)
Series
Convoy
Destry
GAY, JOHN (writer)
Telefeatures
All My Darling Daughters
The Chadwick Family
My Darling Daughters' Anniversary
GAYNOR, JOHN (actor)
Series
Buck Rogers in the 25th Century
GAZZARA, BEN (actor)
Series
Arrest and Trial
Run for Your Life
Telefeature
Maneater
GEER, WILL (actor)
Telefeatures
Brock's Last Case
Sam Hill: Who Killed the Mysterious Mr. Foster?
Savage
GELLER, HARRY (composer)
Telefeature
Let's Switch
GELMAN, MILTON S. (writer)
Series

Tales of Wells Fargo
GEMINI PRODUCTIONS, INC.
    (production company)
  Series
  The Wide Country
GEORGE, ANTHONY (actor)
  Series
  Checkmate
GEORGE, CHIEF DAN (actor)
  Series
  Centennial
GEORGE, LYNDA DAY (actress)
  Series
  Once an Eagle
  Rich Man, Poor Man
  Telefeatures
  Fear No Evil
  Set This Town on Fire
  The Sound of Anger
GERARD, GIL (actor)
  Series
  Buck Rogers in the 25th
    Century
  Telefeature
  Killing Stone
GERARD, MERWIN (writer)
  Series
  The Sixth Sense
  Telefeatures
  Bridger
  Linda
  The Longest Night
  The Screaming Woman
  The Victim
GERMAIN, LARRY (hair stylist)
  Series
  Adam-12
  Dragnet 1967-1970
  The Lawyers
  McCloud
  The Men from Shiloh
  The Name of the Game
  The Psychiatrist
  San Francisco International
    Airport
  The Virginian
  Telefeatures
  Any Second Now
  A Clear and Present Danger
  Companions in Nightmare
  The D.A.: Conspiracy to
    Kill
  The Doomsday Flight
  Dragnet 1966
  How I Spent My Summer Vacation
  Istanbul Express
  The Lonely Profession

McCloud: Who Killed Miss
  U.S.A.?
The Movie Murderer
My Sweet Charlie
Night Gallery
Now You See It, Now You Don't
The Outsider
Prescription: Murder
Ritual of Evil
Shadow Over Elveron
Silent Night, Lonely Night
The Smugglers
Something for a Lonely Man
Stranger on the Run
The Sunshine Patriot
The Sound of Anger
Trial Run
Vanished
GERMAIN, MIKE (makeup artist)
  Series
  The Senator
GHOSTLEY, ALICE (actress)
  Telefeature
  Two on a Bench
GIBSON, HENRY (actor)
  Telefeature
  Amateur Night at the Dixie Bar
    and Grill
GIELGUD, JOHN (actor)
  Telefeature
  Frankenstein: The True Story
  Special
  Hamlet
GILBERT, KEN(NETH) (director)
  Series
  The Bionic Woman
  The Incredible Hulk
GILL, FRANK, JR. (writer)
  Series
  Broadside
  McHale's Navy
GILLETTE, GENE L. (music
    editor)
  Series
  Quincy, M.E.
GILLILAND, RICHARD (actor)
  Series
  Little Women
  McMillan
  Operation Petticoat
  Telefeatures
  Little Women
  Operation Petticoat
GILLIS, JACKSON (writer/executive story consultant)
  Series
  Columbo
GILMORE, ANDREW (sound mixer)

Series
Baretta
GILMORE, ROBERT W. (story editor)
Series
Buck Rogers in the 25th Century
GIMBEL, NORMAN (lyricist)
Telefeature
How to Steal an Airplane
GIRARD, BERNARD (director)
Series
Alcoa Premiere/Premiere
The Alfred Hitchcock Hour
GIST, ROBERT (director)
Series
The Virginian
GLAISTER, GERARD (producer)
Series
Colditz
Telefeature
Escape from Colditz
GLASOW, BETTY (hair stylist)
Telefeature
Run a Crooked Mile
GLAZER, HERMAN (production supervisor)
Series
The Jack Benny Show
GLEASON, F. KEOGH (set decorator)
Telefeature
Marriage: Year One
GLEASON, LAWRENCE J. (film editor)
Series
BJ and the Bear
GLEASON, MICHAEL (producer)
Series
Harold Robbins' "The Survivors" (and writer)
McCloud (and writer)
The Oregon Trail (executive producer only)
Owen Marshall, Counselor at Law (writer only)
PAris 7000
Rich Man, Poor Man (executive producer only)
The Six Million Dollar Man
Sons and Daughters
Telefeatures
Force Five (and writer)
The Oregon Trail (and writer)
GLEITSMAN, RICK (music editor)
Series
Delta House
GLEN A. LARSON PRODUCTIONS (production company)
Series
Battlestar: Galactica
BJ and the Bear
Buck Rogers in the 25th Century
Galactica 1980
The Hardy Boys Mysteries
McCloud
The Misadventures of Sheriff Lobo
The Nancy Drew Mysteries
Quincy, M. E.
Switch
Sword of Justice
Telefeatures
Benny and Barney: Las Vegas Undercover
BJ and the Bear
Switch
GLENN, BILL (director)
Telefeature
The Suicide Club
GLENN, NORMAN (executive in charge of production)
Series
Rod Serling's Night Gallery
GLESS, SHARON (actress)
Series
Centennial
Faraday and Company
The Immigrants
The Last Convertible
Marcus Welby, M. D.
Switch
Turnabout
Telefeatures
All My Darling Daughters
The Islander
A Little Bit Like Murder
My Darling Daughters' Anniversary
Richie Brockelman, Private Eye
Switch
GLICK, EARL A. (executive producer)
Telefeature
Tom Sawyer
GLOUNER, RICHARD C., A.S.C. (director of photography)
Series
Columbo
Telefeatures
Charlie Chan
A Cry for Help
The Psychiatrist: God Bless the Children
GOBEL, GEORGE (actor and partner in Gomalco Productions,

Inc. with David P. O'Malley)
Telefeature
Benny and Barney: Las Vegas Undercover
GODDARD, PAULETTE (actress)
Telefeature
The Snoop Sisters
GODDARD, RICHARD B. (set decorator)
Series
Kojak
Mrs. Columbo
Telefeature
Little Women
GODDARD, RICK (art director)
Special
A Special Act of Love
GODFREY, ALAN (producer)
Series
Baretta
GOLD, DONALD (unit manager)
Series
McMillan and Wife
San Francisco International Airport (and associate producer)
Telefeature
Brock's Last Case
GOLD, HARRY (lyricist)
Pilot
Off the Wall
GOLDBERG, LEONARD (executive producer)
Series
When the Whistle Blows
GOLDEN, DAVID (unit manager)
Series
Kojak
GOLDEN, MURRAY (director)
Series
The Men from Shiloh
GOLDENBERG, BILLY (composer)
Series
Alias Smith and Jones (theme only)
Banacek
Columbo
Delvecchio (theme only)
Kojak (theme only)
McCoy
The Name of the Game
The Sixth Sense
Telefeatures
Alias Smith and Jones
All My Darling Daughters
Banacek
The City

A Clear and Present Danger
Dark Victory
Double Indemnity
Duel
Fear No Evil
Gemini Man
The Harness
The Marcus-Nelson Murders
The Neon Ceiling
Night Gallery
Ransom for a Dead Man
Ritual of Evil
Silent Night, Lonely Night
The UFO Incident
GOLDMAN, HAL (writer)
Series
The Jack Benny Show
GOLDSMITH, GLORIA (writer)
Series
McMillan and Wife
GOLDSMITH, JERRY (composer)
Series
Bob Hope Presents the Chrysler Theatre
General Electric Theatre
Thriller
Telefeature
Indict and Convict
Special
The Red Pony
GOLDSTEIN, MARTIN (producer)
Telefeature
Captain America
GOLDSTONE, JAMES (director)
Series
Bob Hope Presents the Chrysler Theatre
Telefeatures
A Clear and Present Danger
Ironside
Shadow Over Elveron
GOLSON, BENNY (composer)
Series
It Takes a Thief
GOMALCO PRODUCTIONS, INC. (production company of George Gobel and his business partner David P. O'Malley [the name Gomalco was formed by using letters from the men's last names])
Series
Leave It to Beaver
GOMBERG, SY (writer)
Telefeature
Breakout
GOODWINS, LESLIE (director)
Series

Tammy
GORDON, AL (writer)
 Series
 The Jack Benny Show
GORDON, ALEX (writer)
 Telefeature
 Brock's Last Case
GORDON, WILLIAM (writer)
 Series
 Ironside
GORTNER, MARJOE (actor)
 Telefeature
 The Marcus-Nelson Murders
GOSDEN, FREEMAN (actor/creator and, with partner Charles Correll, head of Creston Productions)
 Series
 Calvin and the Colonel
GOSS, JOE (special effects creator)
 Series
 The Six Million Dollar Man
GOSSETT, LOU, JR. (actor)
 Telefeature
 Companions in Nightmare
GOULD, CHARLES S. (assistant director)
 Series
 The Jack Benny Show
GOULD, HAROLD (actor)
 Telefeature
 Ransom for a Dead Man
GOULD, HEYWOOD (writer)
 Pilot
 Hazard's People
GOULET, ROBERT (actor)
 Telefeature
 The Couple Takes a Wife
GRAHAM, BILL see GRAHAM, WILLIAM A.
GRAHAM, GLORIA (actress)
 Series
 Rich Man, Poor Man
GRAHAM, WILLIAM A. (director)
 Series
 The Name of the Game
 Telefeatures
 The Doomsday Flight
 The Intruders
 Jigsaw
 Magic Carpet
 Marriage: Year One
 Perilous Voyage
 Trial Run
GRAINGER, RON (composer)
 Telefeatures
 Destiny of a Spy

Mousey
GRANET, BERT (executive producer)
 Telefeature
 The Intruders
GRANGER, FARLEY (actor)
 Series
 Black Beauty
 Telefeature
 The Challengers
GRANGER, STEWART (actor)
 Series
 The Men from Shiloh
 Telefeatures
 Any Second Now
 The Hound of the Baskervilles
GRANT, ARTHUR, B.S.C. (director of photography)
 Telefeatures
 Destiny of a Spy
 Run a Crooked Mile
GRANT, LEE (actress)
 Series
 Fay
 Telefeatures
 Lieutenant Schuster's Wife
 The Neon Ceiling
 Partners in Crime
 Perilous Voyage
 Ransom for a Dead Man
GRANVILLE, FRANK (writer)
 Series
 Owen Marshall, Counselor at Law
GRASSHOFF, ALEX (director)
 Series
 The Night Stalker
GRAUMAN, WALTER (director)
 Telefeature
 Force Five
GRAVES, PETER (actor)
 Series
 Court Martial
 The Rebels
GRAVES, TERESA (actress)
 Series
 Get Christie Love!
GRAY, ERIN (actress)
 Series
 Buck Rogers in the 25th Century
GREEN, ADOLPH (writer)
 Special
 Applause
GREEN, CLARENCE (producer)
 Series
 Bob Hope Presents the Chrysler Theatre
GREEN, HILTON A. (assistant

director)
Series
Startime
GREEN, LES (film editor)
Series
McMillan and Wife
Telefeatures
The Alpha Caper
The Astronaut
Death Race
Money to Burn
GREEN, LESTER L. (art director)
Series
Adam-12
Telefeatures
The Couple Takes a Wife
Houston, We've Got a Problem
Richie Brockelman, Private Eye
GREEN, MARK (music editor)
Series
The Misadventures of Sheriff Lobo
GREEN, MORT (composer)
Series
Buckskin
GREENBERG, HENRY F. (writer)
Series
Alcoa Premiere/Premiere
GREENE, DANFORD (film editor)
Series
It's a Man's World
Tammy
GREENE, DAVID (director)
Series
Ellery Queen
General Electric Theatre
Rich Man, Poor Man
Telefeature
Ellery Queen
GREENE, LORNE (actor)
Series
The Bastard
Battlestar: Galactica
Galactica 1980
Griff
Telefeatures
Destiny of a Spy
The Harness
Man on the Outside
Special
Short Stories of Love
GREENE, TOM (writer)
Series
The Six Million Dollar Man
Telefeature

Mallory: Circumstantial Evidence
GREENWALD, ROBERT (producer)
Telefeature
The Desperate Miles
GREER, DABBS (actor)
Telefeature
The Greatest Gift
GREER, KATHY (supervising producer/writer)
Series
House Calls
GREGG, VIRGINIA (actress)
Series
Calvin and the Colonel (voice only)
Telefeatures
Chase
The D.A.: Conspiracy to Kill
Dragnet 1966
Little Women
The Other Man
Prescription: Murder
You Lie So Deep, My Love
GREGORY, ARTHUR U. (executive producer)
Series
House Calls
GREGORY, JAMES (actor)
Series
The Bastard
Telefeature
A Very Missing Person
GRIECO, FRANK (art director)
Series
The Six Million Dollar Man
GRIER, ROSEY (actor)
Series
The Seekers
GRIFFITH, ANDY (actor)
Series
Centennial
GRIFFITH, BILL (sound mixer)
Telefeature
Captain America
GRILLO, GARY (1st assistant director)
Series
Quincy, M.E.
GRIMALDI, GIAN R. (producer with partner Hannah L. Shearer)
Series
The Rebels
The Seekers
GRIMALDI, GINO (producer)
Series
Emergency! (associate producer

only)
The Immigrants
Telefeature
Pine Canyon Is Burning
Pilot
The Two-Five
GRIMES, GARY (actor)
Series
Once an Eagle
GRIMES, TAMMY (actress)
Telefeature
The Other Man
GRIZZARD, GEORGE (actor)
Telefeatures
Indict and Convict
The Night Rider
GROSS, CHARLES (composer)
Telefeature
Brock's Last Case
GROSS, SAM (set decorator)
Series
The Hardy Boys Mysteries
GROSSMAN, KENNETH L. (unit manager)
Telefeature
My Sweet Charlie
GROVERTON PRODUCTIONS, LTD. (David Victor's production company)
Series
Griff
Little Women
Lucas Tanner
The Man and the City
Marcus Welby, M.D.
McNaughton's Daughter
Owen Marshall, Counselor at Law
Women in White
Telefeatures
All My Darling Daughters
Indict and Convict
Kingston: The Power Play
Little Women
Live Again, Die Again
Lucas Tanner
Man on the Outside
Marcus Welby, M.D.
McNaughton's Daughter
My Darling Daughters' Anniversary
Owen Marshall, Counselor at Law
Pilot
Stranded
Specials
Legend in Granite
The Man from Independence

A Man Whose Name Was John
The Woman I Love
GROVES, HERMAN (supervising producer)
Series
The Hardy Boys Mysteries
Sword of Justice (producer only)
GROW, RON (1st assistant director)
Series
Centennial
GRUBB, JOHN C. (sound mixer)
Series
Alfred Hitchcock Presents
GRUBER, FRANK (producer/director)
Series
Shotgun Slade
Tales of Wells Fargo (creator only)
GRUSIN, DAVE (composer)
Series
Baretta (theme only)
It Takes a Thief (theme only)
The Name of the Game (theme only)
Telefeatures
The Deadly Dream
A Howling in the Woods
The Intruders
Prescription: Murder
Sarge: The Badge or the Cross
GUARDINO, HARRY (actor)
Series
Evening in Byzantium
Telefeatures
Indict and Convict
The Lonely Profession
Partners in Crime
GUASMAN, HAL (set decorator)
Telefeature
It Happened One Christmas
GUILBERT, ANN MORGAN (actress)
Telefeatures
Chase
The D.A.: Conspiracy to Kill
Emergency!
GULAGER, CLU (actor)
Series
Black Beauty
Once an Eagle
San Francisco International Airport
The Tall Man
The Virginian
Telefeatures
Charlie Cobb: Nice Night for a Hanging

Houston, We've Got a Problem
San Francisco International Airport
GUNDLACH, ROBERT (art director)
  Telefeature
  The Borgia Stick
GUNN, JAMES (writer)
  Series
  Alcoa Premiere/Premiere
GUSS, JACK (writer)
  Series
  Channing (producer only)
  79 Park Avenue
  Telefeature
  The Dark Secret of Harvest Home
GWYNNE, FRED (actor)
  Series
  The Munsters

HAAS, CHARLES (director)
  Series
  General Electric Theatre
HABERMAN, PHILIP (film editor)
  Telefeature
  The Elevator
HACKERT, JAMES T. (film editor)
  Telefeature
  Rosetti and Ryan: Men Who Love Women
HACKETT, JOAN (actress)
  Telefeatures
  The Other Man
  Stonestreet: Who Killed the Centerfold Model?
  The Young Country
HAGGARD, MERLE (actor)
  Series
  Centennial
HAGGERTY, DAN (actor)
  Series
  Condominium
HAGGIN, CHUCK (sound mixer)
  Series
  Aspen
  Mrs. Columbo
HAGMAN, LARRY (actor)
  Series
  The Rhinemann Exchange
  Telefeatures
  The Alpha Caper
  The Big Ripoff
  A Howling in the Woods
  The Return of the World's Greatest Detective
  Sarah T.--Portrait of a Teenage Alcoholic
  Vanished
  Pilot
  The Detective: Bull in a China Shop
  Special
  Applause
HAILEY, OLIVER (executive story consultant)
  Series
  McMillan and Wife
  Pilot
  If I Had a Million (writer only)
HAIRE, EDWARD, A.C.E. (film editor)
  Series
  Escape
  Leave It to Beaver
  Startime
  Westinghouse Playhouse Starring Nanette Fabray and Wendell Corey
HAL ROACH PRODUCTIONS (production company)
  Telefeature
  Tom Sawyer
HALE, ALAN, JR. (actor)
  Series
  Biff Baker, U.S.A.
  Special
  Short Stories of Love
HALE, WILLIAM (director)
  Telefeature
  How I Spent My Summer Vacation
HALL, CONRAD (director of photography)
  Telefeature
  It Happened One Christmas
HALL, EDWIN S. (sound mixer)
  Series
  Columbo
  McCloud
  Telefeature
  Duel
HALLER, DANIEL (director)
  Series
  Black Beauty
  Escape
  Ironside
  Kojak
  McNaughton's Daughter
  Telefeature
  The Desperate Miles
HALLICK, TOM (host)
  Series

American Flyer
HALLIGAN, DICK (composer)
Series
Holmes and Yoyo
HAMILL, MARK (actor)
Telefeatures
Mallory: Circumstantial Evidence
Sarah T. --Portrait of a Teenage Alcoholic
HAMILTON, FRED (executive in charge of production)
Special
The Red Pony
HAMILTON, GEORGE (actor)
Series
Harold Robbins' "The Survivors"
PAris 7000
The Seekers
HAMILTON, ROBERT (writer)
Series
Wheels
HAMNER, ROBERT (writer)
Series
Adam-12
Run for Your Life (producer only)
Telefeatures
The Challengers
You Lie So Deep, My Love
HAMPTON, ORVILLE H. (writer)
Telefeature
Escape to Mindanao
HANLEY, WILLIAM (writer)
Series
Testimony of Two Men
HARBOUR PRODUCTIONS UNLIMITED (production company)
Series
The Doctors
Ironside
Telefeature
The Priest Killer
HARBURG, E.Y. (lyricst)
Telefeature
The Great Man's Whiskers
HARDING, MALCOLM R. (producer)
Series
Centennial
HARDY, JOSEPH (director)
Series
Toma
HARDY, ROBERT (writer)
Series
Thriller

HARGATE, BILL (costume designer)
Telefeatures
McCloud: Who Killed Miss U.S.A.?
The Movie Murderer
HARGROVE, DEAN (producer)
Series
Columbo (and executive producer)
The Family Holvak (executive producer only)
Kraft Suspense Theatre (writer only)
Madigan (executive producer only)
McCoy (executive producer/creator only)
The Name of the Game
Telefeatures
The Big Ripoff (and director/writer)
Cutter (and writer)
The Greatest Gift
Ransom for a Dead Man (and writer)
The Return of the World's Greatest Detective (and director/writer)
HARMON, MATT (associate producer)
Special
A Special Act of Love
HARNELL, JOE (composer)
Series
The Bionic Woman
The Incredible Hulk
HARNELL, JOSEPH see HARNELL, JOE
HAROLD ROBBINS CO. (production company)
Series
Harold Robbins' "The Survivors"
HARPER, JESSICA (actress)
Series
Little Women
HARPER, RON (actor)
Series
The Jean Arthur Show
HARRINGTON, CURTIS (director)
Series
Harold Robbins' "The Survivors"
HARRINGTON, PAT (actor)
Series
The Last Convertible
Telefeatures
Benny and Barney: Las Vegas Undercover
Let's Switch

Savage
HARRIS, GENE (art director)
Telefeature
The Aquarians
HARRIS, HARRY (director)
Series
The D. A.
HARRIS, JULIE (actress)
Series
The Family Holvak
Telefeature
The Greatest Gift
HARRIS, KAREN (story editor)
Series
The Incredible Hulk
HARRIS, RICHARD (actor)
Special
The Snow Goose
HARRIS, ROBERT (producer)
Series
Baretta
HARRIS, THOMAS (creator)
Series
Fay
HARRISON, GREGORY (actor)
Series
Centennial
HARRISON, JOAN (producer with Alfred Hitchcock's Shamley Productions, Inc.)
Series
The Alfred Hitchcock Hour
Alfred Hitchcock Presents
Startime
HARRISON, REX (actor)
Specials
The Adventures of Don Quixote
Short Stories of Love (host only)
HARROLD, KATHRYN (actress)
Series
Women in White
HART, CAROLE (producer)
Telefeature
It Happened One Christmas
HART, HARVEY (director)
Series
Columbo
Court Martial
Harold Robbins' "The Survivors"
The Name of the Game
HARTMAN, DAVID (actor)
Series
The Doctors
Lucas Tanner
The Virginian
Telefeatures

I Love a Mystery
Lucas Tanner
San Francisco International Airport
You'll Never See Me Again
HARTMAN, PAUL (actor)
Series
Pride of the Family
HARTZBAND, MORRIS, A. S. C. (director of photography)
Telefeature
The Borgia Stick
HARVE BENNETT PRODUCTIONS (production company [see also Silverton Productions, Inc., Bennett's other production company])
Series
The Bionic Woman
Gemini Man
The Invisible Man
The Six Million Dollar Man
Telefeatures
Gemini Man
Heat Wave
Houston, We've Got a Problem
HASHIMOTO, RICHARD (1st assistant director)
Series
The Hardy Boys Mysteries
HASKELL, JIM(MIE) (composer)
Series
The Misadventures of Sheriff Lobo
Telefeature
Just a Little Inconvenience
HASKELL, PETER (actor)
Telefeatures
The Jordan Chance
The Suicide Club
Special
The Man Who Came to Dinner
HASSBINDER, MARK (art director)
Telefeature
The 3,000 Mile Chase
HATCH, RICHARD (actor)
Series
Battlestar: Galactica
HAUSER, ROBERT (director of photography)
Series
McMillan and Wife
HAVINGA, NICK (director)
Telefeatures
A Little Bit Like Murder
Murder Works Overtime
HAWN, JACK (writer)
Series

Adam-12
HAYDEN, JEFFREY (director)
Series
Alias Smith and Jones
The Doctors
HAYDN, RICHARD (actor)
Telefeature
Charlie Chan
HAYERS, SIDNEY (director)
Series
The Seekers
HAYES, ALFRED (writer)
Series
The Alfred Hitchcock Hour
Telefeature
The Smugglers
HAYES, BUFORD F. (film editor)
Series
Evening in Byzantium
The Hardy Boys Mysteries
The Rockford Files
HAYES, HELEN (actress)
Series
The Snoop Sisters
Telefeature
The Snoop Sisters
HAYES, PATTI (casting director)
Series
Battlestar: Galactica
BJ and the Bear
The Eddie Capra Mysteries
The Misadventures of Sheriff Lobo
HAYES, STEVIE (writer)
Series
The Seekers
HAYNES, LLOYD (actor)
Series
79 Park Avenue
HAYWARD, LOUIS (actor)
Series
Harold Robbins' "The Survivors"
HEAD, EDITH (costume designer)
Telefeatures
Little Women
The Screaming Woman
Sunshine Christmas
HEATH, LAURENCE (writer)
Series
Seventh Avenue
HECKART, EILEEN (actress)
Telefeatures
Sunshine Christmas
The Victim
HECKART, JAMES T. (film editor)
Series
Wheels
HEDISON, DAVID (actor)
Telefeature
The Art of Crime
HEFFRON, DICK see HEFFRON, RICHARD T.
HEFFRON, RICHARD T. (director)
Series
Banacek
The Lawyers
Telefeatures
The California Kid
Do You Take This Stranger
The Rockford Files
Toma
HEILBRON, MEDORA (associate producer)
Series
Buck Rogers in the 25th Century
HEILPERN, STEVE (associate producer with Roy Huggins Productions)
Series
Alias Smith and Jones
The Lawyers (producer only)
Run for Your Life (assistant to the producer only)
Telefeatures
Do You Take This Stranger
Drive Hard, Drive Fast
The Whole World Is Watching
The Young Country
HEILVEIL, ELAYNE (actress)
Series
Fay (theme lyricist only)
Telefeatures
A Cry for Help
The House of Evil
Pilot
If I Had a Million
HEINDORF, RAY (composer)
Series
O'Hara, U.S. Treasury
Telefeature
O'Hara, United States Treasury
HEMAN, ROGER H., JR. (sound mixer)
Series
The Name of the Game
HENDRA, TONY (theme lyricist)
Series
Delta House
HENDRY, MARSH (film editor)
Special
The Red Pony
HENERSON, JAMES (writer)
Series

The Hardy Boys Mysteries
HENMAN, RAY (director of
    photography)
  Special
  The Snow Goose
HENREID, PAUL (director)
  Series
  Alfred Hitchcock Presents
  Harold Robbins' "The Survivors"
  The Man and the City
  Thriller
  Telefeature
  The Failing of Raymond (actor
    only)
HENRY, GREGG (actor)
  Series
  Rich Man, Poor Man--Book
    II
HENSLEY, PAMELA (actress)
  Series
  Kingston: Confidential
  Telefeature
  Kingston: The Power Play
HERBERT, FREDERICK (music
    supervisor)
  Series
  Alfred Hitchcock Presents
  Startime
HERMAN, MATTHEW N. (producer)
  Telefeature
  Murder Works Overtime
HERRERA, ANTHONY (actor)
  Telefeature
  Mandrake
HERRMANN, BERNARD (composer)
  Series
  Bob Hope Presents the Chrysler
    Theatre
  Convoy
  Telefeature
  Companions in Nightmare
HERSHEY, BARBARA (actress)
  Telefeature
  Just a Little Inconvenience
HESSLER, GORDON (director)
  Series
  The Alfred Hitchcock Hour
    (associate producer only)
  Beggarman, Thief
  Bob Hope Presents the Chrysler
    Theatre (producer only)
  Convoy (producer only)
  The Night Stalker
  Run for Your Life (producer
    only)

Telefeatures
A Cry in the Wilderness
Hitchhike!
Scream, Pretty Peggy
Skyway to Death
HEWITT, LEE (creator)
  Series
  Holmes and Yoyo
HEYDAY PRODUCTIONS (Leonard
    B. Stern's production company)
  Series
  Holmes and Yoyo
  Lanigan's Rabbi
  Operation Petticoat
  Rosetti and Ryan
  Telefeatures
  Lanigan's Rabbi
  Operation Petticoat
  Rosetti and Ryan: Men Who
    Love Women
  Pilots
  Car Wash
  Snafu
  Three Times Daley
  Special
  Funny Business
HEYES, DOUGLAS (director/writer)
  Series
  Aspen
  Baretta (director only)
  Bob Hope Presents the Chrysler
    Theatre (director only)
  Captains and the Kings
  City of Angels (director only)
  McCloud
  Rod Serling's Night Gallery
  Thriller
  Telefeatures
  Drive Hard, Drive Fast (director only)
  The Lonely Profession
HICKMAN, DWAYNE (actor)
  Telefeature
  Don't Push, I'll Charge When
    I'm Ready
HIECKE, CARL (vice-president
    and production manager of
    Revue Productions, Inc. in
    the late 1950s)
HIKEN, NAT (producer/writer)
  Special
  The Slowest Gun in the West
HILDYARD, JACK (director of
    photography)
  Telefeature
  Mousey
HILL, ARTHUR (actor)
  Series

Owen Marshall, Counselor at
   Law
Telefeatures
The Other Man
Owen Marshall, Counselor at
   Law
Vanished
HILL, BILL (producer)
Series
Court Martial
HILLER, ARTHUR (director)
Series
Thriller
HILLERMAN, JOHN (actor)
Telefeatures
Ellery Queen
The Invasion of Johnson
   County
The Law
HI-LOS, THE (vocalists)
Series
The Rosemary Clooney Show
HINDLE, PAT (actor)
Series
Kingston: Confidential
HIRSCH, JAMES G. (producer)
Series
The Incredible Hulk (and
   writer)
Kingston: Confidential
HIRSCH, JUDD (actor)
Series
Delvecchio
The Law
Telefeatures
The Keegans
The Law
HIRSCHMAN, HERBERT (executive
   producer)
Series
The Doctors
The Men from Shiloh (and
   director)
HIRSON, ROGER (writer)
Special
My Secret Mother
HITCHCOCK, ALFRED (producer
   and head of Shamley Pro-
   ductions, Inc.)
Series
Alcoa Premiere/Premiere
The Alfred Hitchcock Hour
   (host/executive producer/
   director only)
Alfred Hitchcock Presents
   (host/executive producer/
   director only)
Startime (and director)

Suspicion (and director)
HITCHENS, DOLORES (writer)
Series
Thriller
HODGES, KENNETH, B.S.C. (di-
   rector of photography)
Series
Court Martial
HOFFBERG, SY (director of photog-
   raphy)
Series
The Hardy Boys Mysteries
Marcus Welby, M.D.
Telefeatures
BJ and the Bear
Kingston: The Power Play
McNaughton's Daughter
HOFFE, ARTHUR (writer)
Telefeatures
Scream, Pretty Peggy
HOFFMAN, BUD (film editor)
Series
The Sixth Sense
Telefeatures
A Cry in the Wilderness
Man on the Outside
Skyway to Death
HOFFMAN, MORRIE (set decora-
   tor)
Series
Delvecchio
The Seekers
HOGAN, JACK (actor)
Series
Sierra
HOGAN, JIM (unit manager)
Series
Banacek
HOLBROOK, HAL (actor)
Series
The Senator
Telefeatures
A Clear and Present Danger
That Certain Summer
The Whole World Is Watching
HOLCOMB, ROD (director)
Series
Quincy, M.E.
The Six Million Dollar Man
   (associate producer only)
Telefeatures
Captain America
HOLDRIDGE, LEE (composer)
Series
The Family Holvak
Gemini Man
Hec Ramsey
Sara

Sierra
Telefeatures
Pine Canyon Is Burning
The Rangers
Skyway to Death
Sunshine
HOLE, BILL (assistant director)
Series
The Sixth Sense
HOLGATE, FRANK (director of photography)
Telefeature
BJ and the Bear
HOLLIMAN, EARL (actor)
Series
The Wide Country
Telefeatures
Alias Smith and Jones
Trapped
HOLLOWAY, JEAN (writer)
Series
The Men from Shiloh
Telefeature
Tom Sawyer
HOLLOWAY, STANLEY (actor)
Telefeature
Run a Crooked Mile
HOLM, CELESTE (actress)
Series
Captains and the Kings
HOLMES, RALPH (production designer)
Telefeatures
Night Life
The Nightmare Step
A Prowler in the Heart
The Suicide Club
Special
A Special Act of Love
HOLT, NAT (executive producer)
Series
The Overland Trail
Shotgun Slade
The Tall Man
HOLT, ROBERT I. (writer)
Series
Adam-12
HOOTEN, PETER (actor)
Telefeature
Dr. Strange
HOPE, BOB (actor and head of Hope Productions and Hovue Productions)
Series
Bob Hope Presents the Chrysler Theatre (host only)
Special
The Jack Benny Special

HOPE PRODUCTIONS (Bob Hope's production company [see also Hovue Productions, Hope's other production company])
Series
Bob Hope Presents the Chrysler Theatre
HOPKINS, ANTHONY (actor)
Telefeature
Dark Victory
HOPKINS, BO (actor)
Series
Aspen
Beggarman, Thief
The Rockford Files
Telefeature
The Invasion of Johnson County
HOPKINS, GEORGE (set decorator)
Telefeature
All My Darling Daughters
HOPKINS, KENYON (composer)
Telefeature
The Borgia Stick
HOPPER, JERRY (director)
Series
Tales of Wells Fargo
Westinghouse Playhouse Starring Nanette Fabray and Wendell Corey
HOPPER, RICHARD (costume designer)
Series
The Man and the City
McCloud
The Psychiatrist
Telefeature
The Hound of the Baskervilles
HORN, LEONARD (producer)
Series
It Takes a Thief
HORNSTEIN, MARTY (assistant director)
Telefeatures
The Other Man
The Whole World Is Watching
The Young Country (unit manager only)
HORWITZ, HOWIE (producer)
Series
Banacek
Baretta
Telefeatures
The California Kid
A Cry for Help
Evil Roy Slade (executive producer only)
The Questor Tapes
Pilot

360 / Index

Stranded
HOTCHNER, A. E. (writer)
  Series
  General Electric Theatre
HOUSE, ROBERT B. (director of photography)
  Series
  Hec Ramsey
HOUSE, RUSSELL (producer)
  Series
  Bob Hope Presents the Chrysler Theatre
HOUSEMAN, JOHN (actor)
  Series
  Aspen
  Captains and the Kings
  The Last Convertible
  Pilot
  Hazard's People
HOUSTON, JAMES D. (writer with partner Jeanne Wakatsuki Houston)
  Telefeature
  Farewell to Manzanar
HOUSTON, JEANNE WAKATSUKI (writer with partner James D. Houston)
  Telefeature
  Farewell to Manzanar
HOVIS, LARRY (actor)
  Telefeature
  Sex and the Married Woman
HOVUE PRODUCTIONS (production company formed by Hope Productions and Revue Productions, Inc.)
  Series
  Bob Hope Presents the Chrysler Theatre
HOWARD, CLINT (actor)
  Special
  The Red Pony
HOWARD, MATTHEW (writer)
  Series
  Alias Smith and Jones
  Rod Serling's Night Gallery
  Telefeatures
  Alias Smith and Jones
  Do You Take This Stranger
  Drive Hard, Drive Fast
HOWARD, VOLNEY, III (film editor)
  Telefeature
  Lanigan's Rabbi
  Special
  Funny Business (associate producer only)
HOWES, SALLY ANN (actress)

  Telefeatures
  Female Artillery
  The Hound of the Baskervilles
HUBBARD, DAVID (actor)
  Series
  Harris and Company
HUBBELL ROBINSON PRODUCTIONS, INC. (production company)
  Series
  87th Precinct
  Startime
  Thriller
HUBLEY, SEASON (actress)
  Series
  Loose Change
HUDDLESTON, DAVID (actor)
  Series
  Once an Eagle
  Tenafly
  Telefeatures
  Brock's Last Case
  Heat Wave
  The Oregon Trail
  The Priest Killer
  Sarge: The Badge or the Cross
  Tenafly
HUDSON, ROCK (actor)
  Series
  McMillan
  McMillan and Wife
  Wheels
  Telefeature
  Once Upon a Dead Man
HUERTA, ARMANDE (2nd assistant director)
  Series
  The Rebels
HUFFMAN, DAVID (actor)
  Series
  Captains and the Kings
  Testimony of Two Men
  Telefeatures
  Amelia Earhart
  The Gun
HUGGINS, BRET (writer)
  Series
  The Lawyers
HUGGINS, ROY (executive producer, head of Roy Huggins-Public Arts Productions and vice-president of Revue Productions, Inc. and Universal Television in the 1960s)
  Series
  Alias Smith and Jones
  Captains and Kings
  City of Angels (creator/writer

only)
Cool Million
Kraft Suspense Theatre (executive in charge of production only)
The Lawyers
The Outsider (and creator)
The Rockford Files (creator only)
Run for Your Life (and creator)
Toma
The Virginian (producer only)
Wheels
Telefeatures
Any Second Now
The Challengers (producer only)
Do You Take This Stranger
Drive Hard, Drive Fast
How to Steal an Airplane
The Invasion of Johnson County (producer only)
The Jordan Chance (producer only)
The Outsider (producer/writer only)
Sam Hill: Who Killed the Mysterious Mr. Foster?
Set This Town on Fire
The Sound of Anger (producer/writer only)
The Story of Pretty Boy Floyd
This Is the West That Was
The 3,000 Mile Chase (and writer)
Toma
The Whole World Is Watching
The Young Country (producer/director/writer only)
Pilots
Hazard's People (producer only)
The Sweet Life
HUGHES, BARNARD (actor)
Telefeatures
The Borgia Stick
Guilty or Innocent: The Sam Sheppard Murder Case
The UFO Incident
HUGO, MICHAEL (director of photography)
Series
The Bastard
HUGO, VICTORIA (set decorator)
Series
Centennial
HULSEY, JAMES (art director)
Special
The Red Pony
HUME, EDWARD (writer)
Series
Toma (creator only)
Telefeatures
The Harness
Toma
HUNT, GRADY (costume designer)
Series
Banacek
Columbo
Ironside
The Name of the Game
Rod Serling's Night Gallery
Telefeatures
Any Second Now
Banacek
Escape to Mindanao
Ironside
Istanbul Express
The Outsider
See the Man Run
The Smugglers
A Very Missing Person
What's a Nice Girl Like You...?
HUNT, PETER H. (director)
Series
Ellery Queen
HUNTER, KIM (actress)
Telefeatures
Dial: Hot Line
Ellery Queen
HUNTER, TAB (actor)
Telefeature
San Francisco International Airport
HUNTINGTON, LEE, A.C.E. (film editor)
Series
Frontier Circus
The Virginian
HURST, RALPH (set decorator)
Telefeatures
Family Flight
That Certain Summer
HUSKY, RICK (producer)
Series
What Really Happened to the Class of '65?
Telefeature
Mandrake (and writer)
HUSSEY, OLIVIA (actress)
Series
The Bastard
HUSSEY, RUTH (actress)
Telefeature
My Darling Daughters' Anniversary
HUSTON, JOHN (actor)

Series
The Rhinemann Exchange
HUTTON, JIM (actor)
Series
Ellery Queen
Telefeature
Ellery Queen
HUTTON, LAUREN (actress)
Series
The Rhinemann Exchange
HYDE-WHITE, WILFRID (actor)
Series
Buck Rogers in the 25th Century
The Rebels
Telefeatures
Fear No Evil
Ritual of Evil
Run a Crooked Mile
The Sunshine Patriot
HYLAND, DIANA (actress)
Telefeature
Ritual of Evil

IBBETSON, ARTHUR (director of photography)
Telefeature
Frankenstein: The True Story
INDEPENDENT TELEVISION CORPORATION (production company)
Series
Court Martial
INGALLS, DON (writer)
Series
Adam-12
Kingston: Confidential (producer only)
Matt Lincoln (creator only)
The Sixth Sense
Telefeature
Captain America
INGE, WILLIAM (writer)
Series
General Electric Theatre
INGSTER, BORIS (producer)
Series
Cimarron City
IRVING, JULES (producer)
Series
Loose Change (executive producer/director only)
Telefeatures
The Art of Crime
Dark Victory
The Jordan Chance (director only)

Pilots
The Detective: Bull in a China Shop (and director)
The Two-Five (director only)
IRVING, RICHARD (executive producer and vice-president of Revue Productions, Inc. and Universal Television in the 1960s)
Series
Columbo (executive in charge of production only)
Court Martial
Frontier Circus (director only)
Laredo
McCloud (executive in charge of production only)
McMillan and Wife (executive in charge of production only)
The Name of the Game
San Francisco International Airport
Seventh Avenue (producer/director only)
The Virginian
What Really Happened to the Class of '65 (and producer)
Telefeatures
The Adventures of Nick Carter
The Art of Crime (and director)
Breakout (producer/director only)
Cutter (and director)
Dark Victory
Exo-Man (and director)
The Hound of the Baskervilles
Istanbul Express (producer/director only)
Prescription: Murder (producer/director only)
Ransom for a Dead Man (and director)
The Six Million Dollar Man (producer/director only)
Trapped
ISAACS, BUD S. (film editor)
Series
The Munsters
Telefeature
The Storyteller
ISHERWOOD, CHRISTOPHER (writer)
Telefeature
Frankenstein: The True Story
ISRAEL, CHARLES E. (writer)
Series
Loose Change
Matt Lincoln

The Psychiatrist
Telefeature
The Dark Secret of Harvest
  Home
ITO, ROBERT (actor)
Series
Quincy, M. E.
IVAN TORS PRODUCTIONS (production company)
Telefeature
The Aquarians
IVANO, PAUL (director of photography)
Series
General Electric Theatre
IVERSON, BETTE (hair stylist)
Special
The Red Pony
IVES, BURL (actor)
Series
Captains and the Kings
The Lawyers
Telefeatures
The Sound of Anger
The Whole World Is Watching

J & M PRODUCTIONS (production company of Jack Benny and his wife, Mary Livingstone)
Series
Checkmate
Holiday Lodge
The Jack Benny Show
J. B. PRODUCTIONS (Jack Benny's production company)
Special
The Jack Benny Special
JACK CHERTOK TV, INC. (production company)
Series
Johnny Midnight
JACKER, CORINNE (writer)
Series
Loose Change
JACKMAN, FRED (director of photography)
Series
Quincy, M. E.
JACKSON, ANDREW, A. S. C. (director of photography)
Series
Dragnet 1967-1970
Laredo
The Rockford Files
Telefeatures
Charlie Cobb: Nice Night for
  a Hanging
Lanigan's Rabbi
San Francisco International Airport
Special
The Red Pony
JACKSON, FELIX (producer)
Series
Cimarron City
JACOBS, RONALD (production executive)
Series
Fay
JACOBY, SCOTT (actor)
Series
79 Park Avenue
Telefeature
That Certain Summer
JAECKEL, RICHARD (actor)
Series
Centennial
Frontier Circus
Telefeatures
The Deadly Dream
Partners in Crime
Special
The Red Pony
JAFFEE, SAM (actor)
Telefeatures
Night Gallery
Sam Hill: Who Killed the Mysterious Mr. Foster?
JAGGER, DEAN (actor)
Telefeature
The Lonely Profession
JAMES, JOHN THOMAS (writer)
Series
Alias Smith and Jones
The Lawyers
Run for Your Life
Toma
Telefeatures
The Challengers
Drive Hard, Drive Fast
The Jordan Chance
The Rockford Files
Set This Town on Fire
JAMESON, JERRY (director)
Telefeatures
The Elevator
Heat Wave
The Invasion of Johnson County
JAMISON, MARSHALL (producer)
Series
General Electric Theatre
JANSSEN, DAVID (actor)
Series
Centennial (and narrator)

364 / Index

O'Hara, U.S. Treasury
  Telefeatures
    The Longest Night
    O'Hara, United States Treasury
JEFFERIES, JOHN D. (art director)
  Pilot
    The Gypsy Warriors
JEFFRIES, JOHN J. (art director)
  Telefeatures
    The Jordan Chance
    The Night Rider
    Operation Petticoat
JEFFRIES, WALTER M. (art director)
  Telefeature
    Killing Stone
JENEVEIN, WALT (sound effects editor)
  Series
    The Rockford Files
JENKINS, GORDON (composer)
  Series
    Rosetti and Ryan
  Pilot
    Stranded
JENNINGS, JOSEPH J. (art director)
  Series
    Captains and the Kings
JENS, SALOME (actress)
  Telefeature
    The House of Evil
JILLSON, ROBERT (art director)
  Telefeature
    Heat Wave
JOBE, BILL (costume designer)
  Series
    Testimony of Two Men
  Telefeature
    The Dark Secret of Harvest Home
JOHN WILDER PRODUCTIONS (production company)
  Series
    Centennial
JOHNSON, BEN (actor)
  Telefeature
    Runaway!
  Special
    The Red Pony
JOHNSON, BRUCE (producer)
  Series
    Sierra
  Telefeature
    Let's Switch
JOHNSON, CHAS. FLOYD (producer/associate producer)
  Series
    The Rockford Files
JOHNSON, DON (actor)
  Telefeature
    Amateur Night at the Dixie Bar and Grill
  Pilot
    The Two-Five
JOHNSON, HOWARD E. (art director)
  Series
    The Man and the City
    Marcus Welby, M.D.
    Matt Lincoln
    Owen Marshall, Counselor at Law
    PAris 7000
    Wagon Train
  Telefeatures
    Any Second Now
    The Chadwick Family
    The City
    Fear No Evil
    The Hound of the Baskervilles
    A Howling in the Woods
    Kingston: The Power Play
    Little Women
    McNaughton's Daughter
    My Darling Daughters' Anniversary
    Night Gallery
    The Sunshine Patriot
JOHNSON, J.J. (composer)
  Series
    The Six Million Dollar Man
JOHNSON, JANET LOUISE (actress)
  Series
    The Hardy Boys Mysteries
JOHNSON, JERRY (director)
  Series
    The Six Million Dollar Man
JOHNSON, KENNETH (director/writer)
  Series
    The Bionic Woman (supervising producer/producer/creator only)
    Cliff Hangers
    Griff
    The Incredible Hulk (and executive producer/developer)
    The Six Million Dollar Man (producer/writer only)
  Telefeature
    The Incredible Hulk (and producer)
JOHNSON, LAMONT (director)
  Series

The Name of the Game
Telefeatures
Deadlock!
The Execution of Private
  Slovik
My Sweet Charlie
That Certain Summer
JOHNSON, MICHAEL F. (composer)
Series
Leave It to Beaver
JOHNSON, RUSSELL (actor)
Telefeatures
Aloha Means Goodbye
Beg, Borrow ... or Steal
The Movie Murderer
Vanished
You Lie So Deep, My Love
Special
The Man from Independence
JOHNSON, VAN (actor)
Series
Black Beauty
Rich Man, Poor Man
Telefeatures
The Doomsday Flight
San Francisco International
  Airport
JOHNSTON, DALE (special effects
  creator)
Series
The Six Million Dollar Man
JOLLEY, NORMAN (producer)
Series
Cimarron City
Ironside (and writer/story
  editor)
O'Hara, U.S. Treasury (story
  consultant only)
Riverboat (and director/writer)
Wagon Train (writer only)
JOLLEY, STAN (art director)
Series
O'Hara, U.S. Treasury
JONES, DEAN (actor)
Telefeature
The Great Man's Whiskers
JONES, HENRY (actor)
Series
Channing
Mrs. Columbo
Telefeatures
Hitched
The Movie Murderer
Something for a Lonely Man
Tail Gunner Joe
JONES, J.J. (director of photography)

Series
Black Beauty
Once an Eagle
Telefeatures
Aloha Means Goodbye
A Cry in the Wilderness
Houston, We've Got a Problem
The Man with the Power
Skyway to Death
The Story of Pretty Boy Floyd
JONES, JAMES EARL (actor)
Telefeature
The UFO Incident
Special
The Cay
JONES, JOHN J. see JONES,
  J.J.
JONES, QUINCY (composer)
Series
Ironside
Telefeature
Ironside
JONES, ROBERT (1st assistant
  director)
Series
The Rockford Files
JONES, SHIRLEY (actress)
Series
Evening in Byzantium
Shirley
Telefeatures
The Family Nobody Wanted
Silent Night, Lonely Night
JORDAN, GLENN (director)
Telefeatures
A Prowler in the Heart
Sunshine Christmas
JORDAN, JAMES CARROLL (actor)
Series
Rich Man, Poor Man--Book II
JORDAN, RICHARD (actor)
Series
Captains and the Kings
JORY, VICTOR (actor)
Telefeature
Perilous Voyage
JOSEPH, ROBERT L. (writer)
Telefeature
Companions in Nightmare
JOURDAN, LOUIS (actor)
Telefeatures
Fear No Evil
Ritual of Evil
Run a Crooked Mile
JOYCE, BERNADETTE (associate
  producer)
Series
The Rebels

The Seekers
JOYCE, MICHAEL (director of photography)
  Telefeature
  The Victim
JUGGERNAUT, INC. (Dale Robertson's production company)
  Series
  Tales of Wells Fargo
JULIEN, MAX (actor)
  Telefeature
  Deadlock!

KTLA-TV (Los Angeles TV station studio used for taping of "ABC Wide World of Entertainment"/"Wide World Mystery" telefeatures)
KADISH, BEN (producer)
  Series
  The Hardy Boys Mysteries
KADISON, ELLIS (writer)
  Series
  Harold Robbins' "The Survivors"
KAGEY, BOB (film editor)
  Series
  Columbo
  Delta House
  McCloud
  O'Hara, U.S. Treasury
  Telefeature
  McCloud: Who Killed Miss U.S.A.?
KAHN, DAVE see KAHN, DAVID
KAHN, DAVID (composer)
  Series
  Centennial (music editor only)
  Mickey Spillane's Mike Hammer
KALISH, RON (sound effects editor)
  Series
  Kojak
KALLIS, STANLEY (producer)
  Series
  Faraday and Company
  Jigsaw
  Telefeatures
  The Adventures of Nick Carter
  Beg, Borrow ... or Steal
  The Hound of the Baskervilles
  Jigsaw
KANDEL, STEPHEN (writer)
  Series
  It Takes a Thief

Switch (and story editor)
  Telefeature
  Winchester 73
KANE, JOE (director)
  Series
  Laramie
KANE, JOEL (associate producer/writer)
  Series
  The John Forsythe Show
KANTER, HAL (producer)
  Series
  Bob Hope Presents the Chrysler Theatre
KANTOR, LEONARD (writer)
  Series
  The Sixth Sense
KAPLAN, BORIS D. (producer)
  Series
  87th Precinct
KAPLAN, ELLIOT (composer)
  Series
  Griff
  Telefeatures
  Bridger
  Man on the Outside
  You Lie So Deep, My Love
KAPLAN, SOL (composer)
  Telefeature
  Winchester 73
KAPRALL, BO (producer)
  Pilot
  The Bay City Amusement Company
KAPROFF, DANA (composer)
  Series
  Ellery Queen
  Once an Eagle
  Telefeature
  Exo-Man
KARLOFF, BORIS (host)
  Series
  Thriller
KARP, DAVID (writer)
  Series
  Alcoa Premiere/Premiere
KARPF, ELINOR (writer with partner Stephen Karpf)
  Series
  Captains and the Kings
  Telefeatures
  A Cry in the Wilderness
  Marriage: Year One
KARPF, STEPHEN (writer with partner Elinor Karpf)
  Series
  Captains and the Kings
  Telefeatures

A Cry in the Wilderness
Marriage: Year One (and producer)
KASHA, LAWRENCE (producer)
Special
Applause
KASZNAR, KURT (actor)
Telefeatures
It Takes a Thief
Once Upon a Dead Man
The Smugglers
The Snoop Sisters
KATKOV, NORMAN (writer)
Series
Harold Robbins' "The Survivors"
KATZ, SIDNEY, A.C.E. (film editor)
Series
Kojak
Telefeature
The Borgia Stick
KATZIN, LEE H. (director)
Series
The Bastard
McMillan and Wife
KAUFMAN, JOHN, JR. (film editor)
Series
The Psychiatrist
The Rebels
Telefeatures
The Astronaut
The Failing of Raymond
Female Artillery
The Log of the Black Pearl
The Rangers
The Return of the World's Greatest Detective
The Victim
Pilot
The Two-Five
KAUFMAN, LEONARD B. (producer)
Series
O'Hara, U.S. Treasury
Telefeature
O'Hara, United States Treasury
KAYDEN, WILLIAM (producer)
Telefeature
The Family Nobody Wanted
KAYRO PRODUCTIONS, INC. (a.k.a. Kayro, Inc. and Kayro Enterprises, Inc. [production company of Joe Connelly and Bob Mosher])
Series

Bringing Up Buddy
Calvin and the Colonel
Ichabod and Me
Pistols 'n' Petticoats
KAYRO-VUE PRODUCTIONS, INC. (production company formed by Joe Connelly and Bob Mosher's Kayro Productions, Inc. and Revue Productions, Inc.)
Series
The Munsters
KEAN, JOHN K. (sound mixer)
Series
The Deputy
The Man and the City
The Night Stalker
Owen Marshall, Counselor at Law
KEARN, JOHN (sound mixer)
Series
Columbo
KEARNEY, GENE R. (writer)
Series
Kojak (producer only)
Rod Serling's Night Gallery
Telefeatures
Charlie Chan
Crime Club
How I Spent My Summer Vacation
KEATING, JOHNNY (composer)
Series
The Jean Arthur Show
KEATS, STEPHEN (actor)
Series
Seventh Avenue
KEENER, JOE (sound mixer)
Telefeature
The Longest Hundred Miles
KEITH, BRIAN (actor)
Series
Centennial
The Crusader
The Seekers
KELLAWAY, ROGER (composer)
Telefeature
The Psychiatrist: God Bless the Children
KELLERMAN, SALLY (actress)
Series
Centennial
KELLEY, RICHARD A. (director of photography)
Series
The Psychiatrist
KELLOGG, RAY (associate producer)

Special
The Red Pony
KELLUM, TERRY (sound mixer)
Series
Owen Marshall, Counselor at Law
KELLY, BRIAN (actor)
Telefeatures
Berlin Affair
Drive Hard, Drive Fast
KELLY, GENE (actor)
Series
Going My Way
KELLY, SEAN (theme lyricist)
Series
Delta House
KEMP, JEREMY (actor)
Series
The Rhinemann Exchange
KENNEDY, ARTHUR (actor)
Telefeature
The Movie Murderer
Special
The Man from Independence
KENNEDY, BURT (director)
Series
The Rhinemann Exchange
KENNEDY, GEORGE (actor)
Series
Sarge
Telefeatures
A Cry in the Wilderness
The Priest Killer
Sarge: The Badge or the Cross
See How They Run
KENNEY, WILLIAM J. (casting director)
Series
Quincy, M. E.
KENNY, BILL (art director)
Telefeature
Jigsaw
KENNY, JOSEPH E. (unit manager)
Series
McCloud
Telefeature
McCloud: Who Killed Miss U.S.A.?
KERAMIDAS, HARRY (film editor)
Series
The Hardy Boys Mysteries
KERR, JOHN (actor)
Series
Arrest and Trial
Telefeature

The Longest Night
KERRY PRODUCTIONS (production company)
Series
Going My Way
KERWIN, BRIAN (actor)
Series
The Misadventures of Sheriff Lobo
KERWIN, LANCE (actor)
Series
The Family Holvak
Telefeatures
Amelia Earhart
The Greatest Gift
KESSLER, BRUCE (director)
Series
Adam-12
Baretta
The Night Stalker
KETCHUM, DAVID (writer)
Telefeature
The Elevator
KIBBEE, ROLAND (producer)
Series
The Bob Cummings Show (creator only)
Columbo (executive producer only)
The Deputy (creator only)
The Family Holvak (executive producer only)
It Takes a Thief (creator/writer only)
Madigan (and writer)
McCoy (executive producer/creator only)
Telefeatures
The Big Ripoff (and writer)
Brock's Last Case
It Takes a Thief (writer only)
Now You See It, Now You Don't (and writer)
The Return of the World's Greatest Detective (and writer)
KIBBIE, DAN (writer)
Series
The Bionic Woman
KIDD, DAVID (writer)
Telefeature
The Birdmen
KIDDER, MARGOT (actress)
Telefeature
The Suicide Club
KIEBACH, HANS JURGEN (art director)
Telefeature
Berlin Affair

KIEL, RICHARD (actor)
Telefeature
Now You See It, Now You Don't
KILEY, RICHARD (actor)
Telefeatures
Jigsaw
Night Gallery
KIMBALL, RUSSELL (art director)
Series
Broadside
General Electric Theatre
McHale's Navy
Telefeatures
Dragnet 1966
Prescription: Murder
KIMBLE, ROBERT L., A.C.E. (film editor)
Series
Columbo
Telefeatures
The Big Ripoff
The Bravos
The Deadly Dream
Don't Push, I'll Charge When I'm Ready
McCloud: Who Killed Miss U.S.A.?
The Other Man
The Priest Killer
The Questor Tapes
Sarge: The Badge or the Cross
Tenafly
The Whole World Is Watching
KINBERG, JUD (executive producer)
Series
Quincy, M.E.
KING, CHARLES (casting director)
Series
The Six Million Dollar Man
KING, PAUL (writer)
Telefeature
Operation Petticoat
KING, PERRY (actor)
Series
Aspen
Captains and the Kings
The Last Convertible
KINON, RICHARD (director)
Series
Fay
KINOSHITA, ROBERT (production designer)
Telefeature

Farewell to Manzanar
KINOY, ERNEST (writer)
Series
Alcoa Premiere/Premiere
KIPNESS, JOSEPH (producer)
Special
Applause
KIRGO, GEORGE (developer)
Series
Get Christie Love!
KIRSCH, ROBERT (executive story consultant)
Series
Bob Hope Presents the Chrysler Theatre
KIRSCHNER, JACK (film editor)
Series
Jigsaw
KISER, TERRY (actor)
Telefeature
Benny and Barney: Las Vegas Undercover
KITT, EARTHA (actress)
Telefeature
Lieutenant Schuster's Wife
KJELLIN, ALF (director)
Series
The Alfred Hitchcock Hour
Columbo
The Family Holvak
Sara
The Sixth Sense
Telefeature
The Deadly Dream
KLATE, SEYMOUR (art director)
Series
Centennial
Columbo
The Incredible Hulk
Mrs. Columbo
Telefeature
Scott Free
KLEIN, JORDAN (director of photography)
Telefeature
The Aquarians
KLEISER, RANDAL (director)
Series
Marcus Welby, M.D.
KLEMPERER, WERNER (actor)
Series
The Rhinemann Exchange
KLINE, BENJAMIN H., A.S.C. (director of photography)
Series
Alcoa Premiere/Premiere
Bachelor Father
Bob Hope Presents the Chrysler

370 / Index

    Theatre
    Dragnet 1967-1970
    Frontier Circus
    McHale's Navy
    The Name of the Game
    Wagon Train
    Telefeatures
    Istanbul Express
    The Manhunter
    Something for a Lonely Man
KLINE, HENRY (unit manager)
    Series
    The Virginian
KLUGMAN, JACK (actor)
    Series
    Harris Against the World
    Quincy, M.E.
    Telefeature
    Fame Is the Name of the Game
KLUGMAN, MAURICE (associate producer)
    Series
    Quincy, M.E.
KNEUBUHL, JOHN (writer)
    Telefeature
    The Sunshine Patriot
KNIGHT, SHIRLEY (actress)
    Telefeatures
    The Outsider
    Shadow Over Elveron
KNIPE, RAY (video tape editor)
    Special
    Hamlet
KNOPF, CHRISTOPHER (writer)
    Telefeature
    The Bravos
KNOTTS, DON (actor)
    Telefeature
    I Love a Mystery
    Special
    The Man Who Came to Dinner
KNOWLES, PATRICK (actor)
    Telefeature
    The D.A.: Murder One
KNUDSTEN, FREDRIC (film editor)
    Telefeature
    Mandrake
KNUDTSON, FRED (film editor)
    Telefeature
    This Is the West That Was
KOENIG, WALTER (actor)
    Telefeature
    The Questor Tapes
KOENIG, WILLIAM (associate producer)
    Series

    The Name of the Game
KOLB, KEN (writer)
    Series
    General Electric Theatre
    Ironside
KOLBE, WINRICH (associate producer)
    Series
    McCloud
KORTNER, PETER (producer)
    Series
    General Electric Theatre
    The John Forsythe Show
KORTY, JOHN (producer/director/writer)
    Telefeature
    Farewell to Manzanar
KOWALSKI, BERNARD L. (director)
    Series
    Baretta (and executive producer)
    Columbo
KOZOLL, MICHAEL (writer)
    Series
    The Night Stalker
    Richie Brockelman, Private Eye
KRAIKE, MICHAEL (producer)
    Series
    The Deputy
KRAMER, KARL (president of Revue Productions, Inc. in the late 1950s)
KRASNER, MILTON R., A.S.C. (director of photography)
    Series
    McMillan and Wife
KRASNY, PAUL (director)
    Series
    Centennial
    Quincy, M.E.
    Telefeatures
    The Adventures of Nick Carter
    The D.A.: Conspiracy to Kill
    The Islander
KRINSKI, SANDY (writer)
    Special
    Mother of the Bride
KRONMAN, HARRY (writer)
    Series
    Harold Robbins' "The Survivors"
KRUMHOLZ, CHESTER (writer)
    Series
    Kojak (and producer)
    Telefeatures
    Captain America
    Deadlock!
    Once Upon a Dead Man
    Shadow Over Elveron

Trial Run
KRUSCHEN, JACK (actor)
   Telefeature
   The Log of the Black Pearl
KUENSTLE, CHARLES R. (writer)
   Telefeatures
   The Astronaut
   Death Race
KUKOFF, BERNIE (writer)
   Telefeature
   Lieutenant Schuster's Wife
KULIK, BUZZ (director primarily for Groverton Productions, Ltd.)
   Series
   Owen Marshall, Counselor at Law
   Telefeatures
   Owen Marshall, Counselor at Law
   Vanished
   Specials
   The Man Who Came to Dinner
   A Man Whose Name Was John
KUNKEL, SHERMAN (director of photography)
   Series
   Baretta
KURI, JOHN (set decorator)
   Special
   The Red Pony

LADD, DIANE (actress)
   Series
   Black Beauty
LAEMMLE, NINA (executive story consultant)
   Series
   Marcus Welby, M.D.
LaHENDRO, BOB (director)
   Pilot
   Off the Wall
LAI, FRANCIS (composer)
   Telefeature
   Berlin Affair
LAIDMAN, HARVEY (director)
   Series
   The Incredible Hulk
LAINE, FRANKIE (theme vocalist)
   Series
   The Misadventures of Sheriff Lobo
LAIRD, JACK (producer)
   Series
   Bob Hope Presents the Chrysler Theatre

Channing
Doctors' Hospital
Kojak (supervising producer only)
The Protectors (executive producer only)
Rod Serling's Night Gallery
Switch
Testimony of Two Men
What Really Happened to the Class of '65?
   Telefeatures
   Charlie Chan
   The Dark Secret of Harvest Home
   Destiny of a Spy
   Hauser's Memory
   How I Spent My Summer Vacation
   The Movie Murderer
   One of Our Own (and writer)
   Perilous Voyage
   See How They Run
   Shadow Over Elveron
   Trial Run
LAKIN, RITA (writer)
   Telefeature
   Death Takes a Holiday
LAMAS, FERNANDO (actor)
   Telefeature
   The Lonely Profession
LAMORISSE, ALBERT (producer/director/writer)
   Series
   General Electric Theatre
LAMPEL, MILLARD (writer)
   Series
   McCloud
   Wheels
LAMPERT, ZOHRA (actress)
   Series
   Black Beauty
   Doctors' Hospital
   Telefeature
   One of Our Own
LANCHESTER, ELSA (actress)
   Series
   The John Forsythe Show
LANDAU, MARTIN (actor)
   Telefeature
   Savage
LANDAU, RICHARD (producer)
   Series
   San Francisco International Airport (story editor only)
   The Six Million Dollar Man
LANDE, NATHANIEL (producer/director)

Telefeature
Don't Push, I'll Charge When I'm Ready
LANDON, MICHAEL (director/writer)
Telefeature
Killing Stone
LANDRES, DANNY (film editor)
Series
Arrest and Trial
General Electric Theatre
The Virginian
LANFIELD, SIDNEY (director)
Series
Ichabod and Me
LANG, DAVID (writer)
Series
The Tall Man
LANG, JENNINGS (vice-president of Universal Television in the 1960s and executive in charge of production for "Revlon Theatre")
LANG, MICHAEL (composer)
Telefeatures
Night Life
The Nightmare Step
A Prowler in the Heart
The Suicide Club
LANG, RICHARD (director)
Telefeature
Dr. Scorpion
LANGE, HOPE (actress)
Telefeature
That Certain Summer
Pilot
Hazard's People
LANSBURY, BRUCE (executive producer and head of Bruce Lansbury Productions, Ltd.)
Series
Buck Rogers in the 25th Century
LANSFORD, WILLIAM DOUGLAS (writer)
Series
Ironside
LANSING, ROBERT (actor)
Series
87th Precinct
Telefeatures
The Astronaut
Crime Club
LAPENIEKS, VILIS (director of photography)
Series
Captains and the Kings
Kojak

Toma
Telefeatures
Deadlock!
That Certain Summer
Toma
The Young Country
LARCH, JOHN (actor)
Series
Arrest and Trial
Convoy
LARKIN, JOHN (producer)
Series
M Squad
LARNER, STEVAN (director of photography)
Telefeatures
The Greatest Gift
Guilty or Innocent: The Sam Sheppard Murder Case
The Gun
The Keegans
Let's Switch
LARRECQ, HENRY (art director)
Series
Tammy
Telefeatures
Breakout
How I Spent My Summer Vacation
The Manhunter
San Francisco International Airport
Something for a Lonely Man
LARROQUETTE, JOHN (actor)
Series
Baa Baa Black Sheep
Black Sheep Squadron
Rich Man, Poor Man
LARSEN, WILLIAM (production supervisor)
Series
General Electric Theatre
LARSON, CHARLES (writer)
Series
Centennial
LARSON, GLEN A. (executive producer and head of Glen A. Larson Productions)
Series
Alias Smith and Jones (producer/creator/writer only)
Battlestar: Galactica (and creator/writer/theme composer)
BJ and the Bear (and creator/writer/theme composer)
Buck Rogers in the 25th Century (developer/theme composer

only)
Evening in Byzantium (and writer)
Galactica 1980 (and theme composer)
The Hardy Boys Mysteries (and developer/director/writer/theme composer)
It Takes a Thief (producer/associate producer only)
McCloud (and producer/writer)
The Misadventures of Sheriff Lobo (and theme composer/lyricist)
The Nancy Drew Mysteries (and writer/theme composer)
Quincy, M.E. (and creator/theme composer)
Switch (and creator/theme composer)
Telefeatures
Alias Smith and Jones (producer/writer only)
Benny and Barney: Las Vegas Undercover (producer/writer only)
BJ and the Bear (and writer/composer)
The Islander (producer/writer only)
Switch (producer/writer only)
LASKO, EDWARD J. (writer)
Series
Matt Lincoln
The Outsider
LASKY, GIL (writer)
Series
The Virginian
LAST, SIMON (writer)
Telefeature
Charlie Chan
LATHAM, LOUISE (actress)
Series
Sara
Telefeatures
Amateur Night at the Dixie Bar and Grill
The Book of Murder
The Harness
McNaughton's Daughter
The Priest Killer
Savage
Stonestreet: Who Killed the Centerfold Model?
LATIMER PRODUCTIONS (production company)
Series
M Squad

LAVA, WILLIAM (composer)
Telefeature
O'Hara, United States Treasury
LAVEN, ARNOLD (director)
Series
Richie Brockelman, Private Eye
Special
Short Stories of Love
LAVERY, EMMET (writer)
Series
Going My Way
LAWFORD, PETER (actor)
Telefeatures
Ellery Queen: Don't Look Behind You
How I Spent My Summer Vacation
LAWRENCE, ANTHONY (writer)
Series
The Sixth Sense (and creator/executive story consultant)
Tales of Wells Fargo
Pilot
Stranded
LAWRENCE, STEPHEN (composer)
Telefeature
It Happened One Christmas
LAZAN, STANLEY M. (director of photography)
Telefeature
Once Upon a Dead Man
LEACHMAN, CLORIS (actress)
Telefeatures
Hitchhike!
It Happened One Christmas
Silent Night, Lonely Night
Pilot
Pete 'n' Tillie
LEACOCK, PHILIP (director)
Telefeatures
The Birdmen
The Great Man's Whiskers
LEADER, TONY (director)
Series
The Virginian
LEAF, MAURY (composer)
Series
State Trooper
LEANDER, MIKE (composer)
Telefeature
Run a Crooked Mile
LEAR, NORMAN (creator)
Series
The Deputy
LEARMAN, RICHARD (director)
Series
Marcus Welby, M.D.

LEAVITT, SAM, A.S.C. (director of photography)
Series
Banacek
Telefeatures
Banacek
Evil Roy Slade
The Longest Night
The Screaming Woman
Pilot
If I Had a Million
LECAP, RUSS (art director)
Telefeature
The Longest Hundred Miles
LEE, ANNA (actress)
Telefeatures
My Darling Daughters' Anniversary
The Night Rider
LEE, MICHELE (actress)
Series
American Flyer (hostess only)
Telefeature
Dark Victory
LEE, RUTA (actress)
Telefeatures
A Howling in the Woods
Indict and Convict
LEE, STAN (creator)
Series
The Incredible Hulk (consultant only)
Telefeature
Dr. Strange
LEEDS, HOWARD (film editor)
Series
Alcoa Premiere/Premiere (writer only)
Telefeature
Exo-Man
LEEDS, ROBERT (film editor)
Series
The Night Stalker
Telefeature
Mobile Two
Pilot
Hazard's People
LEEWOOD, JACK (producer)
Telefeatures
Escape to Mindanao
The Longest Hundred Miles
LEFCOURT, PETER (writer)
Telefeature
Let's Switch
LEFFERTS, GEORGE (producer)
Series
Bob Hope Presents the Chrysler Theatre (writer only)
Telefeature
The Harness
LEGRAND, MICHEL (composer)
Special
The Adventures of Don Quixote
LEHMAN, AL (costume designer)
Series
Buck Rogers in the 25th Century
Galactica 1980
LEIBMAN, RON (actor)
Telefeature
The Art of Crime
LEICESTER, JAMES (film editor)
Series
Rod Serling's Night Gallery
LEIGH, JANET (actress)
Telefeature
The Deadly Dream
LEIGHTON, JIM (associate producer/writer)
Series
It's a Man's World
LEIGHTON, MARGARET (actress)
Telefeature
Frankenstein: The True Story
Special
Hamlet
LEIGHTON, TED (writer)
Telefeature
Ellery Queen: Don't Look Behind You
LEIMANIS, JOHN (art director)
Series
The Misadventures of Sheriff Lobo
Switch
LeMAIRE, GEORGE (producer)
Special
Hamlet
LENARD, MELVYN (composer)
Series
Leave It to Beaver
Mickey Spillane's Mike Hammer
Tales of Wells Fargo
Wagon Train
LENZ, RICK (actor)
Series
Hec Ramsey
LEON, HENNIE (writer)
Telefeature
The Longest Hundred Miles
LEONETTI, MATTHEW F. (director of photography)
Telefeature
The Elevator
LESLIE, BETHEL (writer)
Series
The Virginian

LESTER, LARRY (film editor)
  Series
  Aspen
  Captains and the Kings
  Columbo
  Matt Lincoln
  Mrs. Columbo
  Wheels
  Telefeatures
  The City
  The Jordan Chance
  The 3,000 Mile Chase
  Trapped
LESTER, SELIG (writer)
  Series
  Kraft Suspense Theatre
LEVI, ALAN J. (director)
  Series
  The Bionic Woman
  The Immigrants
  The Invisible Man
  The Six Million Dollar Man
  Telefeature
  Gemini Man
LEVINSON, DAVID (producer)
  Series
  The Doctors (executive producer only)
  Hernandez: Houston P.D. (executive producer only)
  Mrs. Columbo
  Sarge
  The Senator
  Sons and Daughters (executive producer/writer only)
  The Virginian
  Telefeatures
  A Case of Rape (executive producer only)
  Force Five (and writer)
  The Priest Killer
  Ritual of Evil
  Sarah T.--Portrait of a Teenage Alcoholic
  Senior Year
  Pilot
  If I Had a Million (executive producer only)
LEVINSON, RICHARD (writer and head of Fairmount/Foxcroft Productions with partner William Link)
  Series
  Columbo (and creator)
  Ellery Queen (executive producer only)
  The Name of the Game
  The Psychiatrist (creator only)

Tenafly (executive producer/creator only)
  Telefeatures
  Charlie Cobb: Nice Night for a Hanging (executive producer only)
  A Cry for Help (executive producer only)
  Ellery Queen (and producer)
  The Execution of Private Slovik (and executive producer)
  The Gun (and producer)
  Istanbul Express
  The Judge and Jake Wyler (and producer)
  McCloud: Who Killed Miss U.S.A.?
  My Sweet Charlie (and producer)
  Partners in Crime (executive producer only)
  Prescription: Murder
  The Psychiatrist: God Bless the Children
  Ransom for a Dead Man
  Run a Crooked Mile
  Sam Hill: Who Killed the Mysterious Mr. Foster?
  Savage (and executive producer)
  The Storyteller (and producer)
  Tenafly (and executive producer)
  That Certain Summer (and producer)
  Trial Run
  Two on a Bench (and producer)
  The Whole World Is Watching
LEVITT, GENE (director)
  Series
  Alias Smith and Jones
  Cool Million (and producer/writer)
  The Outsider (producer only)
  Telefeatures
  Alias Smith and Jones
  Any Second Now (and producer/writer)
  Cool Million
  Run a Crooked Mile (and writer)
LEVITT, RUBY R. (set decorator)
  Telefeature
  Vanished
LEVY, DAVID (executive producer/creator)
  Series
  Sarge
  Telefeature
  Sarge: The Badge or the Cross (producer only)
LEVY, I. ROBERT (film editor)

376 / Index

Series
The Rockford Files
LEWIN, ALBERT E. (writer)
  Series
  Alfred Hitchcock Presents
LEWIN, ROBERT (producer)
  Series
  Baretta
  McMillan and Wife (executive story consultant only)
LEWIS, AL (actor)
  Series
  The Munsters
LEWIS, ANDY (writer)
  Series
  Kraft Suspense Theatre
  The Virginian
LEWIS, DAVID P. (writer)
  Series
  Tenafly
LEWIS, EDWARD (executive producer and, with partner Jane Wyman, head of Lewman Limited)
  Series
  Fireside Theatre/Jane Wyman's Fireside Theatre
  The Jane Wyman Theatre
  Lux Playhouse
  Schlitz Playhouse of Stars
LEWIS, HAROLD (sound mixer)
  Telefeatures
  The Big Ripoff
  Kingston: The Power Play
LEWIS, MONICA (actress)
  Series
  Shotgun Slade
LEWIS, RICHARD (executive producer and vice-president of Revue Productions, Inc. and Universal Television in the 1960s)
  Series
  Alcoa Premiere/Premiere
  Cimarron City
  The Crusader
  M Squad
  Suspicion (producer only)
  Whispering Smith
  Telefeatures
  The Borgia Stick (producer only)
LEWIS, RICHARD (art director)
  Pilot
  The Two-Five
LEWIS, ROBERT MICHAEL (director)
  Series

The Invisible Man
  Telefeatures
  The Alpha Caper
  The Astronaut
  Guilty or Innocent: The Sam Sheppard Murder Case
  The Invisible Man
  Money to Burn
LEWMAN LIMITED (a.k.a. Lewman, Inc.--production company of Edward Lewis and Jane Wyman)
  Series
  Fireside Theatre/Jane Wyman's Fireside Theatre
  The Jane Wyman Theatre
  Lux Playhouse
  Schlitz Playhouse of Stars
LEYTES, JOSEF (director)
  Series
  Harold Robbins' "The Survivors"
LIBERTI, JOHN (2nd assistant director)
  Series
  BJ and the Bear
LICHTWARDT, SUSAN (associate producer)
  Series
  Centennial
LINCOLN COUNTY PRODUCTION COMPANY (production company)
  Series
  The Tall Man
LINDEN, HAL (actor)
  Series
  Mr. Inside/Mr. Outside
LINDHEIM, RICHARD (co-producer/writer)
  Series
  BJ and the Bear
LINDON, LIONEL, A.S.C. (director of photography)
  Series
  Destry
  Kraft Suspense Theatre
  The Munsters
  Rod Serling's Night Gallery
  The Tall Man
  Thriller
  Telefeatures
  Do You Take This Stranger
  The Movie Murderer
  Ransom for a Dead Man
  Ritual of Evil
  See How They Run
  Vanished
LINK, WILLIAM (writer and head

of Fairmount/Foxcroft Productions with partner Richard Levinson [see Levinson, Richard for Link's credits])
LINVILLE, LARRY (actor)
Telefeature
Vanished
LIPTON, PEGGY (actress)
Series
The John Forsythe Show
LITTLE, CLEAVON (actor)
Telefeature
Money to Burn
LITWACK, SYD(NEY Z.) (art director)
Series
Jigsaw
Telefeatures
Female Artillery
Lucas Tanner
Sarge: The Badge or the Cross
You'll Never See Me Again
LIVINGSTON, BARRY (actor)
Series
Sons and Daughters
Telefeatures
The Elevator
Senior Year
LIVINGSTON, HAROLD (writer)
Telefeature
Escape to Mindanao
LIVINGSTON, STANLEY (actor)
Telefeature
Sarge: The Badge or the Cross
LLEWELLYN, RUSSELL (unit manager)
Special
A Special Act of Love
LLOYD, INNES (executive producer)
Special
The Snow Goose
LLOYD, JOHN J. (art director)
Series
Alfred Hitchcock Presents
Checkmate
The Doctors
Emergency!
General Electric Theatre
It's a Man's World
Kojak
Owen Marshall, Counselor at Law
The Senator
Startime
The Tall Man
Telefeatures
The Alpha Caper
Chase
A Clear and Present Danger
Do You Take This Stranger
Emergency!
Fame Is the Name of the Game
Family Flight
I Love a Mystery
Istanbul Express
It Happened One Christmas
The Longest Night
The Marcus-Nelson Murders
Once Upon a Dead Man
The Other Man
Ransom for a Dead Man
Short Walk to Daylight
Vanished
LLOYD, JOHN ROBERT (art director)
Series
General Electric Theatre
LLOYD, NORMAN (producer)
Series
The Alfred Hitchcock Hour
Alfred Hitchcock Presents (associate producer only)
The Name of the Game
Telefeatures
The Bravos
Companions in Nightmare (and director)
The Dark Secret of Harvest Home (actor only)
The Smugglers (and director)
What's a Nice Girl Like You...?
LoBIANCO, TONY (actor)
Series
The Duke (director only)
Mr. Inside/Mr. Outside
LOCKE, SANDRA (actress)
Special
My Secret Mother
LOCKHART, JUNE (actress)
Series
Loose Change
LODGE, BILL (makeup artist)
Special
The Snow Goose
LOFTIN, CAREY (stunt coordinator)
Telefeature
Killdozer
LOGGIA, ROBERT (actor)
Telefeatures
Mallory: Circumstantial Evidence
Scott Free

LOLLIER, GEORGE (unit manager)
  Telefeature
  Ritual of Evil
LOMOND, BRITT (1st assistant
    director)
  Series
  Battlestar: Galactica
LONDON, JERRY (director)
  Series
  Delvecchio
  Evening in Byzantium
  Kojak
  Marcus Welby, M.D.
  The Six Million Dollar Man
  Wheels
  Telefeatures
  Killdozer
  McNaughton's Daughter
LONDON, JULIE (actress)
  Series
  Emergency!
  Telefeature
  Emergency!
LONGET, CLAUDINE (actress/
    vocalist)
  Telefeature
  How to Steal an Airplane
LOO, RICHARD (actor)
  Telefeature
  Marcus Welby, M.D.
LORD, JACK (actor)
  Telefeature
  The Doomsday Flight
LORD, STEPHEN (writer)
  Series
  Banacek
  Madigan
  The Night Stalker
LOSSEE, FRANK (unit manager)
  Series
  The Doctors
  The Sixth Sense
LOTITO, LEO, JR. (makeup
    artist)
  Series
  Alfred Hitchcock Presents
LOUDERMILK, SHERMAN (art
    director)
  Series
  Centennial
  House Calls
  Telefeature
  Love Is Not Enough
LOURIE, EUGENE (art director)
  Telefeature
  Death Takes a Holiday
LOVE, BESSIE (actress)
  Telefeature
  Mousey
LOVER, PETER (floor manager)
  Special
  The Man Who Came to Dinner
LOVETT, ROBERT O. (sound
    mixer)
  Series
  Kojak
LOWRY, CHUCK (2nd assistant director)
  Series
  Battlestar: Galactica
LOY, MYRNA (actress)
  Telefeatures
  The Couple Takes a Wife
  Death Takes a Holiday
  The Elevator
  Indict and Convict
LUCAS, JOHN MEREDYTH (director)
  Series
  Rod Serling's Night Gallery
LUCKINBILL, LAURENCE (actor)
  Special
  A Special Act of Love
LUDSKI, ARCHIE, G.B.F.E. (film
    editor)
  Telefeature
  Destiny of a Spy
LUDWIG, JERROLD (writer)
  Telefeatures
  The Log of the Black Pearl
  The Man with the Power (film
    editor only)
LUFF, FRED (art director)
  Series
  Buck Rogers in the 25th Century
LUPINO, IDA (director)
  Series
  Alfred Hitchcock Presents
  General Electric Theatre
  Thriller (and writer)
  Telefeatures
  Female Artillery (actress only)
  I Love a Mystery (actress only)
LUSK, SKIP (film editor)
  Series
  Black Beauty
  The Rebels
LUTHARDT, ROBERT (art director)
  Series
  Toma
  Telefeatures
  Drive Hard, Drive Fast
  The Lonely Profession
  My Sweet Charlie
  The Rockford Files
  Set This Town on Fire

The Whole World Is Watching
LYNCH, WILLIAM (sound mixer)
Series
Leave It to Beaver
Westinghouse Playhouse Starring Nanette Fabray and Wendell Corey
LYNDON, BARRE (writer)
Series
Thriller
LYNLEY, CAROL (actress)
Telefeatures
The Elevator
The Smugglers
LYON, EARLE (producer)
Series
Tales of Wells Fargo
LYON, SUE (actress)
Telefeature
Don't Push, I'll Charge When I'm Ready
LYONS, RICHARD E. (producer)
Telefeatures
Something for a Lonely Man
Stranger on the Run
Winchester 73

MCA DISCOVISION (video disc system developed by MCA, Inc. and Magnavision)
McADAM, MICHAEL R., A.C.E. (film editor)
Series
General Electric Theatre
Marcus Welby, M.D.
Telefeature
The Bravos
McADAMS, JAMES (DUFF) (producer)
Series
The Eddie Capra Mysteries
Ironside (and associate producer)
Kojak (and supervising producer)
Mrs. Columbo (supervising producer only)
The Road West
Switch (supervising producer only)
The Virginian
Telefeatures
Crime Club
The Intruders
Pilot
If I Had a Million
McCALLUM, DAVID (actor)

Series
Colditz
The Invisible Man
Telefeatures
Escape from Colditz
Frankenstein: The True Story
Hauser's Memory
The Invisible Man
McCARTHY, JOHN (set decorator)
Series
Alcoa Premiere/Premiere
Columbo
Dragnet 1967-1970
Ellery Queen
General Electric Theatre
The John Forsythe Show
Laramie
The Lawyers
Leave It to Beaver
The Man and the City
Marcus Welby, M.D.
McHale's Navy
The Name of the Game
Tales of Wells Fargo
Telefeatures
Any Second Now
The Intruders
Istanbul Express
The Lonely Profession
Night Gallery
Now You See It, Now You Don't
The Other Man
The Outsider
Prescription: Murder
Silent Night, Lonely Night
The Smugglers
Stranger on the Run
The Sunshine Patriot
Winchester 73
McCARTHY, KEVIN (actor)
Series
Harold Robbins' "The Survivors"
Telefeature
Exo-Man
McCARTHY, LESLIE (set decorator)
Series
Galactica 1980
The Misadventures of Sheriff Lobo
McCLELLAND, CHUCK (film editor)
Series
McCloud
Once an Eagle
Telefeatures
The Desperate Miles
Family Flight
The Family Nobody Wanted

The Invasion of Johnson County
The Man with the Power
The Specialists
The Story of Pretty Boy Floyd
McCLOSKEY, LEIGH J. (actor)
  Series
  Rich Man, Poor Man
McCLURE, DOUG (actor)
  Series
  Checkmate
  The Men from Shiloh
  The Overland Trail
  The Rebels
  The Virginian
  Telefeatures
  The Birdmen
  Death Race
  It Takes a Thief
  The Judge and Jake Wyler
  The Longest Hundred Miles
McCORD, KENT (actor)
  Series
  Adam-12
  Galactica 1980
  Telefeatures
  Beg, Borrow ... or Steal
  Breakout
  Emergency!
  The Outsider
  Pine Canyon Is Burning
  Shadow Over Elveron
McCORMACK, JOHN T. (art director)
  Telefeatures
  The Challengers
  Deadlock!
  Indict and Convict
  That Certain Summer
McCOY, JAMES LEE (makeup artist)
  Special
  A Man Whose Name Was John
McDEVITT, RUTH (actress)
  Series
  The Night Stalker
  Pistols 'n' Petticoats
  Telefeatures
  The Couple Takes a Wife
  Man on the Outside
  A Prowler in the Heart
  Skyway to Death
  Pilot
  If I Had a Million
MacDONALD, JOHN D. (writer)
  Series
  Run for Your Life
  Thriller
McDONALD, JOHN R. (sound mixer)
  Series
  Quincy, M.E.
MacDONALD, NEIL (film editor)
  Series
  Quincy, M.E.
MACDONNELL, NORMAN (executive producer)
  Series
  The Men from Shiloh
  The Road West
  The Virginian
McDOUGALL, DON (director)
  Series
  The Doctors
  Ironside
  Kingston: Confidential
  The Night Stalker
  The Virginian
  Telefeatures
  The Aquarians
  Escape to Mindanao
MacDOUGALL, JOANNE C. (set decorator)
  Series
  Buck Rogers in the 25th Century
MacDOUGALL, RANALD (producer/writer)
  Series
  Westinghouse Playhouse Starring Nanette Fabray and Wendell Corey (writer only)
  Telefeatures
  Fame Is the Name of the Game
  Magic Carpet
McDOWALL, RODDY (actor)
  Series
  The Immigrants
  The Rhinemann Exchange
  Telefeatures
  The Elevator
  Night Gallery
  What's a Nice Girl Like You...?
McEACHIN, JAMES (actor)
  Series
  Tenafly
  Telefeature
  The Alpha Caper
  The D.A.: Conspiracy to Kill
  Deadlock!
  The Judge and Jake Wyler
  The Neon Ceiling
  Short Walk to Daylight
  Tenafly
  That Certain Summer
McEVEETY, BERNARD (director)
  Series
  Centennial

McEVEETY, VINCENT (director)
  Series
  The Road West
McGAVIN, DARREN (actor)
  Series
  Mickey Spillane's Mike Hammer
  The Night Stalker
  The Outsider
  Riverboat
  Telefeatures
  Berlin Affair
  The Challengers
  The Outsider
  The Six Million Dollar Man
McGIVER, JOHN (actor)
  Series
  Mr. Terrific
  Telefeatures
  The Great Man's Whiskers
  Sam Hill: Who Killed the
    Mysterious Mr. Foster?
  Tom Sawyer
McGOOHAN, PATRICK (director)
  Series
  Columbo
McGOWAN, GEORGE (director)
  Series
  Run for Your Life
McGRATH, FRANK (actor)
  Series
  Tammy
McGREEVEY, JOHN (writer)
  Series
  It's a Man's World
  Specials
  A Man Whose Name Was John
  The Woman I Love
McGUIRE, BIFF (actor)
  Telefeature
  Kingston: The Power Play
McGUIRE, DOROTHY (actress)
  Series
  Little Women
  Rich Man, Poor Man
  Telefeature
  Little Women
MACHADO, ROBERT (art director)
  Telefeature
  River of Mystery
McHATTIE, STEPHEN (actor)
  Series
  Centennial
McINTIRE, JOHN (actor)
  Series
  Aspen
  Shirley
  The Virginian

  Wagon Train
  Telefeature
  Linda
McINTYRE, ANDREW J. (director of photography)
  Telefeature
  Fear No Evil
MACK, MARK (casting director)
  Series
  Galactica 1980
McKAY, HARPER (composer)
  Series
  Jigsaw
MacKENZIE, JACK, A.S.C. (director of photography)
  Series
  Ichabod and Me
  Leave It to Beaver
MACKICHAN, ROBERT (art director)
  Series
  The Name of the Game
  Telefeature
  Trial Run
MacKILLOP, ED (writer)
  Telefeature
  Killdozer
McLAGLEN, ANDREW (director)
  Telefeature
  The Log of the Black Pearl
McLAIRD, ARTHUR E. (associate producer)
  Series
  The Six Million Dollar Man
McLAUGHLIN, WILLIAM (set decorator)
  Series
  Columbo
McLEAN, DODIE (casting director)
  Series
  The Rockford Files
MacLEOD, GAVIN (actor)
  Series
  McHale's Navy
MacLEOD, MURRAY (composer)
  Telefeature
  Evil Roy Slade
McMULLEN, TOM (sound effects editor)
  Series
  The Hardy Boys Mysteries
  The Misadventures of Sheriff Lobo
MacMURRAY, FRED (actor)
  Telefeature
  The Chadwick Family
McNAIR, BARBARA (actress)
  Telefeature

The Lonely Profession
McNAUGHTON, MORRIE (music editor)
Series
The Rockford Files
MACNEE, PATRICK (actor)
Series
Evening in Byzantium
Special
The Woman I Love
McNEELY, JERRY (writer)
Series
Owen Marshall, Counselor at Law (and executive story consultant)
Telefeatures
Lucas Tanner (and producer)
Owen Marshall, Counselor at Law
McNEELY, JOHN (creator)
Series
Owen Marshall, Counselor at Law
McNICHOL, JIMMY (actor)
Pilot
Stranded
McPHERSON, JOHN (director of photography)
Series
The Incredible Hulk
McSWEENEY, JACK see McSWEENEY, JOHN
McSWEENEY, JOHN, A.C.E. (film editor)
Series
McMillan and Wife
Telefeature
Tom Sawyer
MAGRO, ANTHONY (sound effects editor)
Series
The Eddie Capra Mysteries
MAHARIS, GEORGE (actor)
Series
Rich Man, Poor Man
Telefeatures
Escape to Mindanao
The Victim
MAJORS, LEE (actor and head of Fawcett-Majors Productions)
Series
The Men from Shiloh
Owen Marshall, Counselor at Law
The Six Million Dollar Man
Telefeatures
Just a Little Inconvenience

(and executive producer)
The Six Million Dollar Man
MAKO (actor)
Telefeature
Farewell to Manzanar
MALONE, DOROTHY (actress)
Series
Rich Man, Poor Man
MALOOF, MIKE (technical director)
Telefeature
Night Life
MANAHAN, BOB (casting director)
Series
Mrs. Columbo
MANCINI, HENRY (composer)
Series
The Invisible Man
Kingston: Confidential
NBC Sunday Mystery Movie (theme only)
MANDL, FRED (director of photography)
Series
O'Hara, U.S. Treasury
Telefeatures
Tom Sawyer
Trapped
MANETTI, LARRY (actor)
Series
Baa Baa Black Sheep
Black Sheep Squadron
The Duke
MANKIEWICZ, DON M. (writer)
Series
Ironside
Lanigan's Rabbi (producer only)
Rosetti and Ryan (supervising producer only)
Telefeatures
Ironside
Lanigan's Rabbi
Marcus Welby, M.D.
Rosetti and Ryan: Men Who Love Women
Sarge: The Badge or the Cross
MANKOFSKY, ISIDORE (director of photography)
Series
Aspen
Captains and the Kings
Testimony of Two Men
MANN, ABBY (executive producer)
Series
Kojak (and creator)
Telefeatures
The Greatest Gift (writer only)
The Marcus-Nelson Murders

(and writer)
MANSBRIDGE, MARK (art director)
Series
Centennial
MANSFIELD, DUNCAN (film editor)
Series
Startime
MANTOOTH, RANDOLPH (actor)
Series
Emergency!
Emergency Plus Four
Operation Petticoat
The Seekers
Testimony of Two Men
Telefeatures
The Bravos
Emergency!
Vanished
MANZA, RALPH (actor)
Series
Banacek
Telefeatures
Banacek
The Smugglers
MARCELLINO, NICK (makeup artist)
Special
A Man Whose Name Was John
MARCH, ALEX (director)
Series
Rosetti and Ryan
MARCH, COLIN (sound mixer)
Special
The Snow Goose
MARDEN, RICHARD (film editor)
Telefeature
Frankenstein: The True Story
MARGOLIN, JANET (actress)
Series
Fay (theme lyricist only)
Lanigan's Rabbi
Telefeatures
Family Flight
Lanigan's Rabbi
MARGOLIN, STUART (actor)
Series
The Hardy Boys Mysteries (director only)
The Rockford Files
Sara (director only)
Telefeatures
The California Kid
Evil Roy Slade (composer only)
The Intruders
It Takes a Thief
Lanigan's Rabbi
Perilous Voyage
The Rockford Files
This Is the West That Was
MARGULIES, MICHAEL (director of photography)
Series
Evening in Byzantium
Jigsaw
Telefeatures
Dark Victory
Death Takes a Holiday
Jigsaw
The Law
Live Again, Die Again
The Questor Tapes
MARGULIES, MIKE see MARGULIES, MICHAEL
MARGULIES, WILLIAM, A.S.C. (director of photography)
Series
Emergency!
It Takes a Thief
McHale's Navy
The Men from Shiloh
PAris 7000
Rod Serling's Night Gallery
Telefeatures
Companions in Nightmare
The Doomsday Flight
Ellery Queen: Don't Look Behind You
The Judge and Jake Wyler
Marriage: Year One
Night Gallery
Shadow Over Elveron
A Very Missing Person
MARK VII LIMITED (Jack Webb's production company)
Series
Adam-12
Chase
The D.A.
Dragnet 1967-1970
Emergency!
Emergency Plus Four
Escape
Mobile One
O'Hara, U.S. Treasury
Sierra
Telefeatures
Chase
The D.A.: Conspiracy to Kill
The D.A.: Murder One
Dragnet 1966
The Log of the Black Pearl
Mobile Two
O'Hara, United States Treasury

The Specialists
MARKEY, ENID (actress)
  Series
  Bringing Up Buddy
MARKHAM, MONTE (actor)
  Telefeatures
  The Astronaut
  Death Takes a Holiday
  Ellery Queen
MARKLE, FLETCHER (producer/director)
  Series
  Thriller
MARKO, ZEKIAL (writer)
  Series
  Toma
MARKOWITZ, ROBERT (director)
  Telefeature
  The Storyteller
MARKS, ALAN (film editor)
  Series
  Switch
  Telefeature
  The Incredible Hulk
MARKS, BEAU (2nd assistant director)
  Series
  Centennial
MARKS, DEAN (1st assistant director)
  Series
  The Rebels
MARKS, SHERMAN (director)
  Series
  General Electric Theatre
MARKUS, JERRY (2nd assistant director)
  Series
  Delta House
MARQUETTE, JACQUES R. (director of photography)
  Series
  Centennial
  The Senator
  Wheels
  Telefeatures
  The Impatient Heart
  The Priest Killer
  Sarge: The Badge or the Cross
  Scott Free
MARS, KENNETH (actor)
  Pilot
  If I Had a Million
MARSHALL, DAVID (art director)
  Series
  The Incredible Hulk
  Telefeatures

Gemini Man
Just a Little Inconvenience
  Pilot
  Stranded
MARSHALL, E. G. (actor)
  Series
  The Doctors
  Telefeatures
  The City
  A Clear and Present Danger
  Ellery Queen: Don't Look Behind You
  Money to Burn
  Vanished
MARSHALL, GARY (producer/writer)
  Telefeature
  Evil Roy Slade
MARSHALL, GEORGE (director)
  Series
  Hec Ramsey
MARSHALL, JACK (composer)
  Series
  The Deputy
  It's a Man's World
  The Munsters
  Telefeature
  Something for a Lonely Man
MARSHALL, PENNY (actress)
  Telefeatures
  The Couple Takes a Wife
  Let's Switch
MARSHALL, STEVE (assistant director)
  Telefeature
  McCloud: Who Killed Miss U.S.A.?
MARSZALLEK, MICHAEL (director of photography)
  Telefeature
  Berlin Affair
MARTA, JACK A. (director of photography)
  Series
  The Name of the Game
  Telefeatures
  Any Second Now
  The Birdmen
  The Challengers
  Chase
  The City
  The Deadly Dream
  Dial: Hot Line
  Duel
  Emergency!
  How to Steal an Airplane
  A Howling in the Woods
  Partners in Crime

Silent Night, Lonely Night
MARTELL, DARRYL (costume designer)
Series
Baretta
The Misadventures of Sheriff Lobo
MARTIN, BILL (film editor)
Telefeature
It Happened One Christmas
MARTIN, DEAN (actor)
Special
The Jack Benny Special
MARTIN, PAMELA SUE (actress)
Series
The Hardy Boys Mysteries
The Nancy Drew Mysteries
MARTIN, ROSS (actor)
Series
The Seekers
Telefeatures
Charlie Chan
Skyway to Death
MARTIN, STROTHER (actor)
Telefeature
One of Our Own
MARTINELLI, ENZO A., A.S.C. (director of photography)
Series
Griff
The Hardy Boys Mysteries
The Man and the City
79 Park Avenue
The Six Million Dollar Man
The Sixth Sense
The Virginian
Telefeatures
The Alpha Caper
The Bravos
Dr. Strange
Exo-Man
Female Artillery
Gemini Man
Heat Wave
The Invisible Man
The Jordan Chance
Mobile Two
Money to Burn
Pilot
The Gypsy Warriors
MARTINELLI, JOHN A. (film editor)
Telefeature
Target Risk
MARTINELLI, TONY, A.C.E. (film editor)
Series
Alcoa Premiere/Premiere

It Takes a Thief
Owen Marshall, Counselor at Law
PAris 7000
Telefeatures
The D.A.: Murder One
It Takes a Thief
Wings of Fire
MARTINELLI, VINCENT A. (director of photography)
Series
The Seekers
Telefeature
Mandrake
MARTINEZ, A (actor)
Series
Centennial
Telefeatures
Exo-Man
Mallory: Circumstantial Evidence
MARTINEZ, RON (assistant director)
Series
Baretta
McCloud
MARTINSON, LESLIE H. (director)
Telefeatures
The Challengers
How to Steal an Airplane
MARUM, WOLFGANG E. (1st assistant director)
Series
The Incredible Hulk
MARVIN, LEE (actor)
Series
M Squad
MASCOLO, JOSEPH (actor)
Telefeature
Stonestreet: Who Killed the Centerfold Model?
MASETTA, MARTY (producer/director)
Series
Don Adams' Screen Test
MASON, JAMES (actor/narrator)
Telefeature
Frankenstein: The True Story
MASON, LORNA (assistant producer)
Special
Hamlet
MASON, MARYLYN (actress)
Telefeature
That Certain Summer
MASON, PAUL (producer)
Series
Arrest and Trial (writer only)

Get Christie Love!
McMillan and Wife
San Francisco International
  Airport (and writer)
Telefeatures
The California Kid (executive
  producer only)
The Longest Hundred Miles
  (writer only)
Once Upon a Dead Man
Savage
MASSELINK, BEN (writer)
Series
It's a Man's World
MASSEY, RAYMOND (actor)
Telefeatures
All My Darling Daughters
My Darling Daughters' Anniversary
MATHERS, JERRY (actor)
Series
Leave It to Beaver
MATHESON, MURRAY (actor)
Series
Banacek
Telefeatures
Banacek
Lieutenant Schuster's Wife
Tail Gunner Joe
Special
The Woman I Love
MATHESON, RICHARD (writer)
Series
Thriller
Telefeature
Duel
MATHESON, TIM (actor)
Series
The Virginian
Telefeatures
Hitched
Lock, Stock and Barrel
Night Life
Owen Marshall, Counselor at
  Law
MATHEWS, KERWIN (actor)
Telefeature
Death Takes a Holiday
MATLOVSKY, SAMUEL (composer)
Telefeature
Wings of Fire
MATTY SIMMONS-IVAN REITMAN PRODUCTIONS (production company)
Series
Delta House
MATZ, PETER (composer)

Series
Rosetti and Ryan
Telefeature
Rosetti and Ryan: Men Who
  Love Women
MAUNDER, WAYNE (actor)
Series
Chase
MAUTINO, F. BUD (director of
  photography)
Series
Adam-12
Telefeatures
The Couple Takes a Wife
The Specialists
MAY, BILL(Y) (composer)
Series
Emergency!
Telefeatures
The Specialists
Tail Gunner Joe
MAY, BO (associate producer)
Series
The Psychiatrist
MAY, HARRY J. (director of
  photography)
Telefeature
Lock, Stock and Barrel
MAY, JACK C. (sound effects
  editor)
Series
Mrs. Columbo
MAYBERRY, RUSS (director)
Series
Baa Baa Black Sheep
Griff
Ironside
Kojak
McCloud
The Men from Shiloh
The Rebels
The Rockford Files
Seventh Avenue
The Six Million Dollar Man
Telefeatures
Stonestreet: Who Killed the
  Centerfold Model?
The 3,000 Mile Chase
A Very Missing Person
MAYER, ALEXANDER A. (art director)
Series
Alcoa Premiere/Premiere
The Bob Cummings Show
It Takes a Thief
The John Forsythe Show
Laramie
Leave It to Beaver

Index / 387

McCloud
McHale's Navy
San Francisco International
   Airport
Tales of Wells Fargo
Telefeatures
Benny and Barney: Las Vegas
   Undercover
Companions in Nightmare
Ellery Queen: Don't Look Behind You
Evil Roy Slade
The Harness
The Invasion of Johnson County
The Judge and Jake Wyler
The Neon Ceiling
Shadow Over Elveron
The Sound of Anger
What's a Nice Girl Like
   You...?
MAYER, GERALD (director)
Series
O'Hara, U.S. Treasury
MAYER, JERRY (producer)
Series
Fay
MAYER, ROBERT (music editor)
Series
The Eddie Capra Mysteries
Kojak
Mrs. Columbo
MAYSVILLE CORPORATION, THE
   (production company)
Series
The Rosemary Clooney Show
MAZZOLA, LEONARD (set
   decorator)
Series
The Sixth Sense
MEADE, TERRY K. (director
   of photography)
Series
Black Beauty
Telefeatures
The California Kid
A Case of Rape
Death Race (and producer)
Killdozer
Short Walk to Daylight
Stonestreet: Who Killed the
   Centerfold Model?
The Storyteller
MEADOWS, JAYNE (actress)
Telefeature
Now You See It, Now You
   Don't
Sex and the Married Woman
MEDFORD, DON (director)

Series
Baretta
City of Angels
MEEHAN, JOHN (art director)
Series
General Electric Theatre
Ichabod and Me
Leave It to Beaver
Startime
Westinghouse Playhouse Starring
   Nanette Fabray and Wendell
   Corey
MEEKER, RALPH (actor)
Telefeature
You'll Never See Me Again
MELADRE COMPANY (production
   company)
Series
Riverboat
MELLE, GIL (composer)
Series
The Night Stalker
The Psychiatrist
Rod Serling's Night Gallery
   (theme only)
The Six Million Dollar Man
Tenafly
Telefeatures
The Art of Crime
A Cry for Help
Frankenstein: The True Story
Hitchhike!
The Judge and Jake Wyler
Killdozer
Lieutenant Schuster's Wife
My Sweet Charlie
Partners in Crime
Perilous Voyage
The Questor Tapes
Savage
The Six Million Dollar Man
Tenafly
That Certain Summer
Trapped
The Victim
MELVOIN, MICHAEL (composer)
Series
Aspen
MENDENHALL, WILLIAM (director
   of photography)
Telefeatures
The Return of the World's Greatest Detective
Richie Brockelman, Private Eye
Rosetti and Ryan: Men Who
   Love Women
MENTEER, DAVID (1st assistant
   director)

Series
The Rockford Files
MENZIES, HEATHER (actress)
Telefeatures
Captain America
The Keegans
Tail Gunner Joe
MENZIES, JAMES (story editor)
Series
The Hardy Boys Mysteries
It's a Man's World
MERANDE, DORO (actor)
Series
Bringing Up Buddy
MEREDITH, BURGESS (actor)
Telefeatures
Lock, Stock and Barrel
Tail Gunner Joe
MERRICK, MAHLON (composer)
Series
The Jack Benny Show
MERRILL, DINA (actress)
Telefeatures
Family Flight
Kingston: The Power Play
The Lonely Profession
The Sunshine Patriot
MERRILL, MARY (costume designer)
Telefeature
The Borgia Stick
MESSENGER, GARY L. (producer)
Telefeature
Trapped
MESSINGER, MICHAEL (1st assistant director)
Series
The Hardy Boys Mysteries
METCALFE, MELVIN M., SR. (sound mixer)
Telefeatures
The D.A.: Conspiracy to Kill
Do You Take This Stranger
How I Spent My Summer Vacation
My Sweet Charlie
The Other Man
That Certain Summer
The Whole World Is Watching
METRANO, ART (actor)
Series
Amy Prentiss
METTY, RUSSELL, A.S.C. (director of photography)
Series
Broadside
Delvecchio
Telefeatures

Brock's Last Case
The Harness
Lock, Stock and Barrel
Mallory: Circumstantial Evidence
Marcus Welby, M.D.
METZ, REXFORD (director of photography)
Telefeatures
The Invasion of Johnson County
The Tribe
The UFO Incident
METZGER, DOUG (2nd assistant director)
Series
Galactica 1980
MEYER, RICHARD C. (film editor)
Series
Faraday and Company
MICHAELJOHN, WALTER (writer)
Series
Harold Robbins' "The Survivors"
MICHAELS, MICKEY S. (set decorator)
Series
The Doctors
Emergency!
Telefeature
The D.A.: Conspiracy to Kill
MICHAELS, RICHARD (director)
Series
Once an Eagle
Telefeature
Charlie Cobb: Nice Night for a Hanging
MIGGINS, JERRY (set decorator)
Series
The Name of the Game
The Senator
MILE, GEORGE (set decorator)
Series
Startime
MILES, VERA (actress)
Telefeatures
A Howling in the Woods
Jigsaw
Live Again, Die Again
McNaughton's Daughter
Owen Marshall, Counselor at Law
Runaway!
MILLAND, RAY (actor)
Series
Markham
Meet Mr. McNulty
The Ray Milland Show
Rich Man, Poor Man
Seventh Avenue

Testimony of Two Men
Thriller (director only)
Telefeature
Ellery Queen
MILLARD, OSCAR (writer)
Series
Alcoa Premiere /Premiere
Telefeature
Perilous Voyage
MILLER, ALAN J. (executive in charge of production at Revue Productions, Inc. in the early 1960s)
Series
Bob Hope Presents the Chrysler Theatre (executive producer only)
MILLER, BURTON (costume designer)
Series
Columbo
It Takes a Thief
McCloud
McMillan and Wife
The Name of the Game
San Francisco International Airport
The Six Million Dollar Man
Telefeatures
The Adventures of Nick Carter
Companions in Nightmare
Lieutenant Schuster's Wife
Night Gallery
Prescription: Murder
Shadow Over Elveron
The Sound of Anger
The Sunshine Patriot
Trial Run
Wings of Fire
MILLER, HERMAN (creator)
Series
McCloud
MILLER, JAMES M. (writer, usually with partner Jennifer Miller)
Series
Testimony of Two Men
Telefeatures
The Dark Secret of Harvest Home
Mobile Two
MILLER, JENNIFER (writer, usually with partner James M. Miller)
Series
Loose Change
Testimony of Two Men
Telefeatures
The Dark Secret of Harvest Home
MILLER, JIM (producer)
Series
What Really Happened to the Class of '65
MILLER, MITCH (conductor/vocalist/host)
Series
Sing Along with Mitch
MILLER, ROBERT (sound mixer)
Series
McCloud
MILLER, ROBERT ELLIS (director)
Series
Alcoa Premiere /Premiere
MILLER, SIDNEY (director)
Series
Tammy
MILLER, STEPHEN (story editor)
Series
The Misadventures of Sheriff Lobo
MILLER, WINSTON (producer)
Series
87th Precinct
Ironside
The Virginian
Telefeatures
The Aquarians
Female Artillery
Indict and Convict (and writer)
The Longest Hundred Miles (writer only)
MILLIGAN, SPENCER (actor)
Telefeature
The Keegans
MILLS, DONNA (actress)
Telefeature
Live Again, Die Again
MILLS, JULIET (actress)
Series
Once an Eagle
Telefeatures
Alone with Terror
The Challengers
Special
Short Stories of Love
MILNER, MARTIN (actor)
Series
Adam-12
Black Beauty
The Last Convertible
The Seekers
Telefeatures
Emergency!
Runaway!
MILO, GEORGE (set decorator)

Telefeature
The Smugglers
MILTON, RICHARD LAWRENCE
 (director)
Series
Marcus Welby, M.D.
MIMIEUX, YVETTE (actress)
Telefeature
Death Takes a Holiday
MINEO, SAL (actor)
Telefeatures
The Challengers
How to Steal an Airplane
Stranger on the Run
MIRISCH, ANDREW (associate
 producer)
Series
The Hardy Boys Mysteries
MITCHELL, CAMERON (actor)
Series
The Bastard
Black Beauty
Testimony of Two Men
Telefeatures
Cutter
Hitchhike!
MITCHELL, DON (actor)
Series
Ironside
Telefeatures
Ironside
The Priest Killer
Short Walk to Daylight
MITCHELL, JOE (set decorator)
Series
The Incredible Hulk
MITCHELL, PHIL (sound mixer)
Series
Adam-12
MITCHELL, ROBERT (writer)
Telefeature
Any Second Now
MIZZY, VIC (composer)
Telefeature
A Very Missing Person
MOCKRIDGE, CYRIL (theme
 composer)
Series
Laramie
MODER, RICHARD (director)
Series
Kingston: Confidential
The Six Million Dollar Man
MOESSINGER, DAVID (writer)
Series
Kraft Suspense Theatre
The Man and the City
Quincy, M.E. (and director)

Telefeature
Mobile Two (and director)
MOLINARO, AL (actor)
Telefeature
Rosetti and Ryan: Men Who
 Love Women
MONT PRODUCTIONS (George
 Montgomery's production
 company)
Series
Cimarron City
MONTAGNE, EDWARD J. (executive
 producer and vice-president
 of Revue Productions, Inc.
 and Universal Television in
 the 1960s)
Series
Broadside (and director)
McHale's Navy (and director)
The Tall Man
Telefeatures
Ellery Queen: Don't Look Be-
 hind You
Short Walk to Daylight (producer/
 writer only)
A Very Missing Person (producer
 only)
MONTALBAN, RICARDO (actor)
Series
McNaughton's Daughter
Telefeatures
The Aquarians
The Longest Hundred Miles
McNaughton's Daughter
Sarge: The Badge or the Cross
MONTEJANO, LOU (art director)
Series
Centennial
The Incredible Hulk
Telefeature
Captain America
MONTENARO, A.C. (set decorator)
Series
Adam-12
Telefeature
The Oregon Trail
Pilot
Stranded
MONTENARO, ANTHONY see
 MONTENARO, A.C.
MONTGOMERY, BELINDA J.
 (actress)
Telefeatures
The Bravos
The D.A.: Conspiracy to Kill
Lock, Stock and Barrel
Ritual of Evil
MONTGOMERY, ELIZABETH

(actress)
Telefeatures
A Case of Rape
Dark Victory
The Victim
MONTGOMERY, GEORGE (actor/
  narrator and head of Mont
  Productions)
Series
Cimarron City
MONTGOMERY, LEE H(ARCOURT)
  (actor)
Telefeatures
A Cry in the Wilderness
Female Artillery
The Harness
Man on the Outside
Runaway!
MOODY, RON (actor)
Series
Nobody's Perfect
MOONEY, HAL (music supervisor)
Series
Adam-12
Banacek
City of Angels
Columbo
Cool Million
Don Adams' Screen Test
Ellery Queen
Emergency!
The Family Holvak
Hec Ramsey
The Incredible Hulk
Lanigan's Rabbi
Madigan
McCloud
McCoy
McMillan
McMillan and Wife
McNaughton's Daughter
Mr. Inside/Mr. Outside
The Night Stalker
The Psychiatrist
The Rockford Files
Sara
Sarge
The Six Million Dollar Man
The Snoop Sisters
Sunshine
Switch
Toma
Telefeatures
Brock's Last Case
A Case of Rape (composer only)
The Chadwick Family (composer
  only)
The Execution of Private
  Slovik (composer only)
The Longest Night (composer
  only)
Mallory: Circumstantial Evidence
My Darling Daughters' Anniversary (composer only)
One of Our Own (composer only)
Runaway! (composer only)
The Storyteller (composer only)
Tom Sawyer (composer only)
The Tribe (composer only)
MOORE, MARY TYLER (actress)
Telefeature
Run a Crooked Mile
MOOREHEAD, AGNES (actress)
Telefeatures
Frankenstein: The True Story
Marriage: Year One
Special
Short Stories of Love
MORENO, GARY (set decorator)
Series
The Rockford Files
MOREY, KEN (costume designer)
Special
The Snow Goose
MORGAN, CHRISTOPHER (producer)
Series
Quincy, M.E.
MORGAN, HARRY (actor)
Series
Adam-12 (director only)
The Bastard
The D.A.
Dragnet 1967-1970
Hec Ramsey
Telefeatures
Dragnet 1966
Ellery Queen: Don't Look Behind You
Exo-Man
MORGAN, JAYE P. (actress)
Series
Fay (theme vocalist only)
Telefeature
The Adventures of Nick Carter
MORGAN, RICHARD NEIL (writer)
Series
Adam-12
MORGAN, RONALD (director of
  photography)
Series
Faraday and Company
MORHEIM, LOU (producer)
Series
Ironside (and writer)
Telefeatures

A Cry in the Wilderness
Scream, Pretty Peggy
Skyway to Death
MORIARTY, DAVID H. (sound mixer)
Series
The Name of the Game
Owen Marshall, Counselor at Law
The Psychiatrist
Rod Serling's Night Gallery
Wagon Train
Telefeatures
Dial: Hot Line
Owen Marshall, Counselor at Law
Sarge: The Badge or the Cross
Silent Night, Lonely Night
Stranger on the Run
Pilot
If I Had a Million
MORITA, PAT (actor)
Telefeature
A Very Missing Person
MOROSS, JEROME (theme composer)
Series
Wagon Train
MORPICS (production company)
Series
Bob Hope Presents the Chrysler Theatre
MORRIS, FRANK (composer)
Series
Ichabod and Me
MORRIS, GREGG (actor)
Telefeature
The Doomsday Flight
MORRIS, STANLEY (art director)
Special
The Snow Goose
MORRISS, FRANK E. (film editor)
Series
It Takes a Thief
Telefeatures
Brock's Last Case
Charlie Chan
A Cry for Help
Duel
The Execution of Private Slovik
The Gun
The Harness
Hauser's Memory
Hitched
The Law

The Movie Murderer
Switch
MORROW, VIC (actor)
Series
Captains and the Kings
The Last Convertible
The Seekers
Telefeatures
The California Kid
The Man with the Power
River of Mystery
Tom Sawyer
MORSE, HOLLINGSWORTH (director)
Series
Adam-12
The D.A.
Marcus Welby, M.D.
McHale's Navy
MORSE, SID (writer)
Series
The D.A.
MORWOOD, WILLIAM (associate producer)
Series
General Electric Theatre
MOSER, JAMES E. (creator)
Series
Doctors' Hospital
O'Hara, U.S. Treasury
Telefeature
O'Hara, United States Treasury (executive producer/writer only)
MOSHER, BILL, A.C.E. (film editor)
Series
The Man and the City
Telefeature
The Hound of the Baskervilles
MOSHER, BOB (producer and, with partner Joe Connelly, head of Kayro Productions and Kayro-Vue Productions)
Series
Bringing Up Buddy (and creator)
Calvin and the Colonel
Ichabod and Me (executive producer/writer only)
Leave It to Beaver (and creator/writer)
The Munsters (and writer)
MOSTEL, JOSH (actor)
Series
Delta House
MOTOWN CORPORATION (production company)
Telefeature

Amateur Night at the Dixie
  Bar and Grill
MOXEY, JOHN LLEWELLYN
  (director)
  Series
  The Name of the Game
  Run for Your Life
  Telefeature
  San Francisco International
    Airport
MULCAHY, MAC (set decorator)
  Series
  Alfred Hitchcock Presents
MULDAUR, DIANA (actress)
  Series
  Black Beauty
  Harold Robbins' "The Sur-
    vivors"
  McCloud
  Telefeatures
  Pine Canyon Is Burning
  McCloud: Who Killed Miss
    U.S.A.?
  Special
  A Special Act of Love
MULGREW, KATE (actress)
  Series
  Mrs. Columbo
MULLIGAN, BERT (producer)
  Series
  Bob Hope Presents the Chrysler
    Theatre
MUMY, BILL (actor)
  Series
  Sunshine
  Telefeatures
  The Rockford Files
  Sunshine
  Sunshine Christmas
MURDOCK, PERRY (set decorator)
  Series
  It's a Man's World
  Telefeatures
  Istanbul Express
  Night Gallery
  A Very Missing Person
MURPHY, AUDIE (actor)
  Series
  Whispering Smith
MURPHY, BEN (actor)
  Series
  Alias Smith and Jones
  Gemini Man
  Griff
  The Name of the Game
  Telefeatures
  Alias Smith and Jones
  Bridger

Gemini Man
Heat Wave
Runaway!
This Is the West That Was
MURPHY, MICHAEL S. (film edi-
  tor)
  Series
  The Bastard
  Black Beauty
  Telefeature
  BJ and the Bear
MURPHY, MIKI (film editor)
  Telefeature
  Captain America
MURRAY, DON (actor)
  Telefeatures
  The Borgia Stick
  The Intruders
MURRAY, LYN (composer)
  Series
  The Alfred Hitchcock Hour
  Alfred Hitchcock Presents
  Dragnet 1967-1970
  General Electric Theatre
  Telefeatures
  Don't Push, I'll Charge When
    I'm Ready
  Dragnet 1966
  Escape to Mindanao
  Magic Carpet
  Now You See It, Now You Don't
  The Smugglers
MUSANTE, JANE (writer, with
  partner Tony Musante)
  Series
  Toma
MUSANTE, TONY (actor)
  Series
  Toma (and writer with partner
    Jane Musante)
  Telefeatures
  The Desperate Miles
  Toma
MUSCATE, LOUIS (2nd assistant
  director)
  Series
  The Hardy Boys Mysteries

NAPIER, CHARLES (actor)
  Series
  The Oregon Trail
NARITA, HIRO (director of photog-
  raphy)
  Telefeature
  Farewell to Manzanar
NARITA, RICHARD (actor)
  Telefeature

Exo-Man
NASOX, PHILIP (hair stylist)
Telefeature
The Borgia Stick
NATWICK, MILDRED (actress)
Series
Little Women
The Snoop Sisters
Telefeatures
Money to Burn
The Snoop Sisters
NAUGHTON, JAMES (actor)
Series
Faraday and Company
NEAL, PATRICIA (actress)
Series
The Bastard
Telefeature
Tail Gunner Joe
NEALE, L. FORD (writer)
Series
The Night Stalker
NEGRIN, SOL, A.S.C. (director of photography)
Series
Kojak
McCloud
NEICSON, JAMES (director)
Series
General Electric Theatre
NEILSON, JAMES (director)
Telefeature
Tom Sawyer
NELSON, BARRY (actor)
Telefeature
The Borgia Stick
NELSON, CHRISTOPHER (film editor)
Series
Captains and the Kings
Telefeatures
Dr. Strange
The Night Rider
Pilot
The Gypsy Warriors
NELSON, DICK (writer)
Series
Alias Smith and Jones
The Lawyers
Telefeatures
The Challengers
Kingston: The Power Play
The Sound of Anger
NELSON, ED (actor)
Telefeatures
Banacek
Houston, We've Got a Problem
Linda

A Little Game
Runaway!
The Screaming Woman
Tenafly
NELSON, GARY (director)
Series
Faraday and Company
The Partners
NELSON, GENE (director)
Series
Escape
Get Christie Love!
McNaughton's Daughter
NELSON, OLIVER (composer)
Series
Chase
Columbo
Ironside
Matt Lincoln
The Six Million Dollar Man
Telefeatures
The Alpha Caper
Chase
Dial: Hot Line
I Love a Mystery
Istanbul Express
Money to Burn
NELSON, PETER (developer)
Series
Get Christie Love!
NELSON, RICHARD (writer)
Series
The Name of the Game
NELSON, RICK (writer)
Telefeature
Houston, We've Got a Problem
NESBITT, CATHLEEN (actress)
Special
The Mask of Love
NETTLETON, LOIS (actress)
Series
Centennial
Telefeature
Any Second Now
NEUFELD, JOHN (writer)
Telefeature
You Lie So Deep, My Love
NEUFELD, SIGMUND, JR. (director)
Series
Buck Rogers in the 25th Century
City of Angels
The Invisible Man
Kojak
Switch
Telefeature
Crime Club (film editor only)
Pilot

If I Had a Million (film editor only)
NEUMAN, E. JACK (producer)
　Telefeature
　　Berlin Affair
NEWBERRY, NORMAN R. (art director)
　Series
　　The Six Million Dollar Man
　Telefeature
　　Lanigan's Rabbi
NEWBERRY, WILLIAM (art director)
　Telefeatures
　　Maneater
　　The Tribe
NEWELL, PATRICK (actor)
　Telefeature
　　Destiny of a Spy
NEWHOUSE, DAVID (film editor)
　Telefeature
　　Live Again, Die Again
NEWLAND, JOHN (director)
　Series
　　Bachelor Father
　　The Family Holvak
　　Harold Robbins' "The Survivors"
　　The Sixth Sense
　　Thriller
NEWMAN, ARTHUR (unit manager)
　Telefeature
　　A Clear and Present Danger
NEWMAN, BARRY (actor)
　Telefeature
　　Sex and the Married Woman
NEWMAR, JULIE (actress)
　Telefeatures
　　McCloud: Who Killed Miss U.S.A. ?
　　A Very Missing Person
NICHOLL, DON (producer)
　Series
　　Kingston: Confidential
NICHOLSON, GEORGE JAY (film editor)
　Telefeature
　　See How They Run
NICKOLAUS, JOHN M., A.S.C. (director of photography)
　Series
　　The Misadventures of Sheriff Lobo
NICOL, ALEX (director)
　Series
　　The D.A.
　　The Law
NIELSEN, LESLIE (actor)
　Series
　　The Protectors
　Telefeatures
　　The Aquarians
　　Charlie Chan
　　Companions in Nightmare
　　Deadlock!
　　Hauser's Memory
　　It Takes a Thief
　　See How They Run
　　Shadow Over Elveron
　　Trial Run
NIMOY, LEONARD (actor)
　Telefeature
　　The Alpha Caper
　Special
　　Short Stories of Love
NOBLE, TRISHA (actress)
　Series
　　Testimony of Two Men
NODELLA, BURT (associate producer)
　Telefeature
　　Dragnet 1966
NOLAN, KATHLEEN (actress)
　Series
　　Broadside
　　The Immigrants
　　Testimony of Two Men
NOLAN, LLOYD (actor)
　Series
　　Special Agent 7
　Telefeature
　　Wings of Fire
NOLAN, TOMMY (actor)
　Series
　　Buckskin
NOLTE, NICK (actor)
　Series
　　Rich Man, Poor Man
　Telefeature
　　The California Kid
NORELL, MICHAEL (writer)
　Telefeature
　　Sex and the Married Woman
NORTH, ALEX (composer)
　Series
　　Bob Hope Presents the Chrysler Theatre (theme only)
　　The Man and the City
　　Rich Man, Poor Man
　　Rich Man, Poor Man--Book II
NORTH, SHEREE (actress)
　Series
　　Women in White
　Telefeatures
　　Amateur Night at the Dixie Bar and Grill

Maneater
Vanished
NORTON, CHARLES (1st assistant director)
Series
Delta House
NOURI, MICHAEL (actor)
Series
Cliffhangers
The Last Convertible
NOVACK, SHELLY (actor)
Telefeatures
The Desperate Miles
The Intruders
McCloud: Who Killed Miss U.S.A. ?
NOVELLO, JAY (actor)
Series
McHale's Navy
Telefeature
Night Life
NOWNES, JAMES (film editor)
Series
Adam-12
NYBY, CHRIS, III (director)
Telefeatures
Pine Canyon Is Burning
The Rangers
NYBY, CHRISTIAN (director)
Series
Emergency!
Escape
Kingston: Confidential

OAKLAND, SIMON (actor)
Series
Baa Baa Black Sheep
Black Sheep Squadron
Evening in Byzantium
The Night Stalker
Toma
Telefeature
Toma
OATES, WARREN (actor)
Series
Black Beauty
Telefeatures
The Movie Murderer
Something for a Lonely Man
O'BRIAN, HUGH (actor)
Series
The Seekers
Telefeature
Benny and Barney: Las Vegas Undercover
O'BRIEN, EDMOND (actor)
Series
Johnny Midnight
Telefeatures
The Doomsday Flight
The Intruders
Jigsaw
The Outsider
River of Mystery
What's a Nice Girl Like You...?
O'BRIEN, LIAM (writer)
Special
Short Stories of Love
O'BRIEN, MARGARET (actress)
Series
Testimony of Two Men
O'BRIEN, PAT (actor)
Telefeature
The Adventures of Nick Carter
OBZINA, MARTIN (art director)
Series
Alcoa Premiere/Premiere
The Deputy
General Electric Theatre
Wagon Train
O'CONNELL, DAVID J. (producer with Groverton Productions, Ltd., originally head of the Universal Television Editorial Department)
Series
Battlestar: Galactica
Buck Rogers in the 25th Century
It's a Man's World (supervising editor only)
Lanigan's Rabbi
Leave It to Beaver (editorial supervisor only)
Marcus Welby, M.D.
McHale's Navy (editorial supervisor only)
Operation Petticoat
The Tall Man (editorial supervisor only)
Wagon Train (editorial supervisor only)
Westinghouse Playhouse Starring Nanette Fabray and Wendell Corey (editorial supervisor only)
Telefeatures
All My Darling Daughters
The Chadwick Family
Cool Million
Kingston: The Power Play
Marcus Welby, M.D.
McNaughton's Daughter
My Darling Daughters' Anniversary

Operation: Petticoat
Stonestreet: Who Killed the Centerfold Model? (executive producer only)
Vanished
You'll Never See Me Again
Specials
A Man Whose Name Was John
The Woman I Love
O'CONNOR, CARROLL (actor)
Telefeature
Fear No Evil
O'CONNOR, FRANK (executive producer for "Bell System Family Theatre" and "Hallmark Hall of Fame")
Specials
The Cay
The Snow Goose (producer only)
The Man Who Came to Dinner
O'CONNOR, GLYNNIS (actress)
Series
Black Beauty
Sons and Daughters
Telefeature
Senior Year
ODEN PRODUCTIONS, INC. (production company)
Telefeature
Brock's Last Case
OHANIAN, GEORGE, A.C.E. (film editor)
Series
The Incredible Hulk
McMillan and Wife
San Francisco International Airport
O'HANLON, GEORGE, JR. (actor)
Series
The Nancy Drew Mysteries
O'HARA, MAUREEN (actress)
Special
The Red Pony
O'KEEFE, DENNIS (host)
Series
Suspicion
O'KEEFE, MICHAEL (actor)
Telefeature
The Dark Secret of Harvest Home
O'LAUGHLIN, GERALD S. (actor)
Series
Wheels
Telefeature
The D.A.: Murder One
OLIANSKY, JOEL (writer)
Series

Delvecchio
Sarge
The Senator
Telefeatures
The Law
Mallory: Circumstantial Evidence
The Priest Killer
OLIVER, GORDON (producer)
Series
Bob Hope Presents the Chrysler Theatre (executive in charge of production only)
Harold Robbins' "The Survivors"
It Takes a Thief (executive producer only)
OLIVER, SUSAN (actress)
Telefeature
Do You Take This Stranger
OLSON, GERALD T. (2nd assistant director)
Series
Buck Rogers in the 25th Century
OLSON, JAMES (actor)
Telefeatures
The Family Nobody Wanted
Man on the Outside
Special
Legend in Granite
OMNIBUS PRODUCTIONS (production company)
Special
The Red Pony
O'NEAL, PATRICK (actor)
Telefeatures
Companions in Nightmare
Cool Million
O'NEILL, ROBERT F. (producer)
Series
Evening in Byzantium
Gemini Man
Griff (production executive only)
The Invisible Man
The Name of the Game (associate producer only)
The Sixth Sense (associate producer only)
Wheels
Telefeatures
Double Indemnity
Gemini Man
Live Again, Die Again
Maneater
Target Risk
ONOFRIO, MIKE (director)
Special
Alone with Terror
OPPENHEIMER, ALAN (actor)

398 / Index

Series
The Six Million Dollar Man
Telefeature
Murder Works Overtime
OPPENHEIMER, JESS (producer/ director)
Series
Bob Hope Presents the Chrysler Theatre
ORBISON, JACK (assistant director)
Series
General Electric Theatre
ORINGER, BARRY (writer)
Series
Doctors' Hospital (executive story editor only)
Telefeature
The Deadly Dream
ORLAND, JOHN (associate producer)
Telefeature
San Francisco International Airport
ORTIZ-GIL, LEON (film editor)
Series
Battlestar: Galactica
OSMOND, KEN (actor)
Series
Leave It to Beaver
OSTER, EMIL (director of photography)
Series
Escape
Telefeatures
Family Flight
The Six Million Dollar Man
Tenafly
OVERLAND PRODUCTIONS (production company)
Series
Tales of Wells Fargo
OWEN, RON (writer)
Telefeature
The Book of Murder

PACKARD, ELTON (writer)
Series
Alcoa Premiere/Premiere
PAGE, GERALDINE (actress)
Telefeature
Live Again, Die Again
PAICH, MARTY (composer)
Series
Ironside
PAIGE, JANIS (actress)
Series
Lanigan's Rabbi
Telefeature
Lanigan's Rabbi
PALEY, IRVING (producer)
Series
Pistols 'n' Petticoats
PALMER, ARNOLD (host)
Series
Challenge Golf
PALMER, GENE (film editor)
Series
Wagon Train
Telefeature
Marcus Welby, M.D.
PANAVISION (manufacturers of lenses and Panaflex camera used in the production of "Columbo")
PAPEZ, LOYD S. (art director)
Series
The Bastard
Black Beauty
Centennial
Evening in Byzantium
Seventh Avenue
79 Park Avenue
Tales of Wells Fargo
Telefeatures
The Big Ripoff
Bridger
The Deadly Dream
The Intruders
Ironside
Lieutenant Schuster's Wife
Now You See It, Now You Don't
Runaway!
The Smugglers
PARIS, JERRY (director)
Telefeatures
The Couple Takes a Wife
Evil Roy Slade
Two on a Bench
What's a Nice Girl Like You...?
PARKER, ARTHUR JEPH (set decorator)
Telefeature
The Hound of the Baskervilles
PARKER, BILL (film editor)
Series
Centennial
Galactica 1980
Telefeature
The Rangers
PARKER, DON (sound mixer)
Telefeature
Tail Gunner Joe
PARKER, EDWARD M. (set

decorator)
Series
Delta House
PARKER, ELEANOR (actress)
Series
The Bastard
Telefeature
Vanished
PARKINS, BARBARA (actress)
Series
Captains and the Kings
Testimony of Two Men
PARKS, MICHAEL (actor)
Telefeatures
Perilous Voyage
The Story of Pretty Boy Floyd
Stranger on the Run
PARRIOTT, JAMES D. (producer)
Series
The Bionic Woman (and writer)
The Incredible Hulk
PARSONS, ESTELLE (actress)
Telefeature
The UFO Incident
PATHE (color film laboratory which processed the prints for "Bob Hope Presents the Chrysler Theatre")
PATRICK, GEORGE (art director)
Series
Bachelor Father
General Electric Theatre
Marcus Welby, M.D.
Telefeatures
Marcus Welby, M.D.
Owen Marshall, Counselor at Law
Perilous Voyage
PATTISON, JERRY (sound mixer)
Telefeatures
The Nightmare Step
A Prowler in the Heart
The Suicide Club
PAUL, ROD (producer)
Telefeature
Lanigan's Rabbi
PAULL, LAWRENCE G. (art director)
Telefeatures
The Storyteller
Tail Gunner Joe
PAULSON, TONY (writer)
Series
Wagon Train
PAXTON, JOHN (writer)
Telefeature
The Great Man's Whiskers
PAYNE, JAMES (set decorator)

Telefeatures
The Adventures of Nick Carter
The Victim
PAYNE, JOHN (actor/executive producer and head of Window Productions)
Series
The Restless Gun
PEACOCK, JOHN (writer)
Telefeature
Mousey
PEARCE, KEN (film editor)
Special
The Snow Goose
PEARLBERG, IRV (writer)
Series
Alias Smith and Jones
The Doctors
PEEPLES, SAMUEL A. (producer/writer)
Series
Frontier Circus (and creator/story editor)
The Overland Trail
The Tall Man (and creator)
PELIKAN, LISA (actress)
Series
The Last Convertible
PELLETIER, LOUIS (writer)
Series
General Electric Theatre
PENN, LEO (director)
Series
The Bionic Woman
Doctors' Hospital
Ironside
Lucas Tanner
Marcus Welby, M.D.
Owen Marshall, Counselor at Law
Switch
Testimony of Two Men
Telefeature
The Dark Secret of Harvest Home
PENNER, JOHN (camera operator)
Series
Delvecchio
PEPPARD, GEORGE (actor)
Series
Banacek
Doctors' Hospital
Telefeatures
Banacek
The Bravos
Guilty or Innocent: The Sam Sheppard Murder Case
One of Our Own

PERKINSON, COLERIDGE-
    TAYLOR (composer)
  Telefeature
  Love Is Not Enough
PERRIN, SAM (writer)
  Series
  The Jack Benny Show
PERRINE, VALERIE (actress)
  Telefeature
  The Couple Takes a Wife
  Pilot
  Lady Luck
PERRY, ROGER (actor)
  Series
  Arrest and Trial
  Telefeature
  The D.A.: Conspiracy to Kill
PERSKY, BILL (producer/writer
    with partner Sam Denoff)
  Special
  The Man Who Came to Dinner
PERSOFF, NEHEMIAH (actor)
  Series
  The Rebels
  Telefeatures
  Escape to Mindanao
  Killing Stone
  Lieutenant Schuster's Wife
PETERMAN, DONALD (director
    of photography)
  Series
  The Night Stalker
PETERS, BERNADETTE (actress)
  Telefeature
  The Islander
PETERSON, MARK (costume de-
    signer)
  Series
  Battlestar: Galactica
PETRIE, DANIEL (director)
  Series
  Hec Ramsey
  The Man and the City
  Telefeatures
  The City
  A Howling in the Woods
  Mousey
  Silent Night, Lonely Night
PETTERSON, MARY (casting di-
    rector)
  Series
  Centennial
PETTET, JOANNA (actress)
  Series
  Captains and the Kings
  Telefeatures
  A Cry in the Wilderness
  The Desperate Miles

Sex and the Married Woman
PETTUS, KEN (writer)
  Series
  Baa Baa Black Sheep
  Faraday and Company (and cre-
    ator)
  Telefeature
  The Adventures of Nick Carter
PEVNEY, JOSEPH (director)
  Series
  Adam-12
  Going My Way
  The Hardy Boys Mysteries
  Johnny Staccato
  Lanigan's Rabbi
  Mobile One
  Telefeature
  My Darling Daughters' Anniver-
    sary
PEYSER, JOHN (producer)
  Series
  Switch
  Telefeature
  BJ and the Bear
PEYSER, PENNY (actress)
  Telefeature
  BJ and the Bear
PFLUG, JoANN (actress)
  Series
  Operation Petticoat
PHILBROOK, JAMES (actor)
  Series
  The Investigators
PHILLIPS, LEE (director)
  Series
  Harold Robbins' "The Survivors"
PHILLIPEE, ROBERT (makeup art-
    ist)
  Telefeature
  The Borgia Stick
PHILLIPS, ALEX, JR. (director of
    photography)
  Series
  The Rhinemann Exchange
PHILLIPS, BILL (supervising pro-
    ducer)
  Telefeature
  The Night Rider
PHILLIPS, FRANK V., A.S.C. (di-
    rector of photography)
  Telefeature
  The Dark Secret of Harvest Home
  Special
  The Red Pony
PHILLIPS, MICHELLE (actress)
  Series
  Aspen
  Telefeature

The California Kid
PHILLIPS, STU (composer, primarily for Glen A. Larson Productions)
Series
Battlestar: Galactica
Evening in Byzantium
Galactica 1980
The Hardy Boys Mysteries
McCloud
The Nancy Drew Mysteries
Quincy, M.E.
The Six Million Dollar Man
Switch
Telefeatures
Benny and Barney: Las Vegas Undercover
The Islander
Switch
PHILLIPS, WILLIAM F. (producer)
Series
Baretta (associate producer only)
Telefeature
Richie Brockelman, Private Eye
PHINNET, FOSTER H. (assistant director)
Series
Banacek
PHINNEY, DAVID G. (associate producer with Glen A. Larson Productions)
Series
Battlestar: Galactica
Buck Rogers in the 25th Century
PICKENS, SLIM (actor)
Telefeatures
The Devil and Miss Sarah Hitched
Sam Hill: Who Killed the Mysterious Mr. Foster?
PIDGEON, WALTER (actor)
Telefeatures
How I Spent My Summer Vacation
Live Again, Die Again
The Screaming Woman
You Lie So Deep, My Love
PIERSON, FRANK A. (director)
Telefeature
The Neon Ceiling
PINCUS, BERNARD F. (sound effects editor)
Series
The Incredible Hulk
PINGITORE, CARL (associate producer with Roy Huggins-Public Arts Productions)
Series
The Name of the Game (film editor only)
Run for Your Life (film editor only)
Telefeatures
Death Race (film editor only)
Drive Hard, Drive Fast
How to Steal an Airplane
The Marcus-Nelson Murders (film editor only)
The Outsider (film editor only)
Perilous Voyage (film editor only)
The Sound of Anger (film editor only)
The Whole World Is Watching (film editor only)
The Young Country
PIPER, THOM (sound mixer)
Telefeature
The Doomsday Flight
PIPERNO, LUCIANO (unit manager)
Series
Madigan
PIROSH, ROBERT (writer)
Series
The Hardy Boys Mysteries
PITTACK, ROBERT W. (director of photography)
Series
General Electric Theatre
PLANTE, EDWARD R. (director of photography)
Series
Baa Baa Black Sheep
Black Sheep Squadron
PLATT, ED (actor)
Telefeature
The Snoop Sisters
PLAYDON, PAUL (producer)
Series
Banacek (executive story consultant only)
The Night Stalker
Switch (and writer)
Telefeature
Beg, Borrow ... or Steal (writer only)
PLAYER, GARY (host)
Series
Challenge Golf
PLEASENCE, DONALD (actor)
Series
The Bastard
Centennial
PLESHETTE, SUZANNE (actress)
Telefeatures

Richie Brockelman, Private
  Eye
Wings of Fire
PLUMB, EVE (actress)
 Series
 Little Women
 Telefeature
 Little Women
POGANY, GABOR (director of
  photography)
 Telefeature
 Cool Million
POGOSTIN, S. LEE (writer)
 Series
 Bob Hope Presents the Chrysler
  Theatre (and director)
 Telefeature
 The UFO Incident
POINTER, PRISCILLA (actress)
 Telefeatures
 The Big Ripoff
 Death Takes a Holiday
 The Failing of Raymond
 The Keegans
 The 3,000 Mile Chase
POLAIRE, HAL (2nd unit director)
 Telefeature
 Istanbul Express
POLAND, CLIFFORD (director of
  photography)
 Telefeature
 The Aquarians
POLITO, EUGENE see POLITO,
  GENE
POLITO, GENE (director of
  photography)
 Series
 Alias Smith and Jones
 The Lawyers
 Telefeatures
 Drive Hard, Drive Fast
 My Sweet Charlie
 Sam Hill: Who Killed the
  Mysterious Mr. Foster?
 Set This Town on Fire
 The Sound of Anger
POLIZZI, JOSEPH (writer)
 Series
 Delvecchio (and creator)
 Kojak
 Telefeature
 Mallory: Circumstantial Evidence
 Pilot
 The Two-Five
POLLACK, SYDNEY (director)
 Series

Bob Hope Presents the Chrysler
  Theatre
POLLINI, JOE (assistant director)
 Series
 Madigan
POLSKY, ABE (writer)
 Series
 The Virginian
PORTALUPI, PIETRO (director of
  photography)
 Series
 The Name of the Game
 Telefeature
 Magic Carpet
PORTER, JAMES T. (sound mixer)
 Telefeatures
 Deadlock!
 Night Gallery
 Trial Run
 Wings of Fire
POST, MIKE (composer with partner Pete Carpenter [see Carpenter, Pete for Post's credits])
POST, TED (director)
 Series
 Alcoa Premiere/Premiere
 Startime
 Thriller
 Telefeature
 The Bravos
POSTER, STEVE (director of photography)
 Telefeature
 The Night Rider
POTTER, GEORGE R. (film editor)
 Series
 Battlestar: Galactica
 Buck Rogers in the 25th Century
 Pilot
 The Gypsy Warriors
POTTS, CLIFF (actor)
 Series
 Little Women
 Once an Eagle
 Telefeatures
 A Case of Rape
 Little Women
 Live Again, Die Again
 Magic Carpet
 San Francisco International Airport
POWELL, DICK (writer)
 Series
 Switch
POWELL, LARRY (1st assistant
  director)
 Series

Baretta
The Eddie Capra Mysteries
POWERS, MALA (actress)
Series
The Man and the City
POWERS, STEFANIE (actress)
Telefeatures
Ellery Queen: Don't Look Behind You
Skyway to Death
PREECE, MICHAEL (director)
Series
The Bionic Woman
PRELUTSKY, BURT (creator/writer)
Series
Faraday and Company
PRENTISS, PAULA (actress)
Telefeature
The Couple Takes a Wife
PRESNELL, ROBERT, JR. (writer)
Series
Banacek
Telefeatures
All My Darling Daughters
Ritual of Evil
PRESSMAN, LAWRENCE (actor)
Series
Rich Man, Poor Man
Telefeatures
Murder by Proxy
The Snoop Sisters
PRICE, FRANK (producer who took over Sidney Sheinberg's job of president of Universal Television in the early 1970s--he resigned in 1978)
Series
Alias Smith and Jones (executive in charge of production only)
Convoy (executive producer/creator only)
Frontier Circus (associate producer only)
Ironside (executive producer only)
It Takes a Thief
Matt Lincoln (executive producer only)
The Men from Shiloh (production supervisor only)
The Sixth Sense (executive in charge of production only)
The Tall Man (and associate producer)
The Virginian
Telefeatures

Alias Smith and Jones (executive producer only)
The City
The Doomsday Flight
I Love a Mystery
It Takes a Thief
San Francisco International Airport (executive producer only)
PRICE, ROGER (writer)
Pilot
Koska and His Family
PRICE, VINCENT (actor)
Telefeature
What's a Nice Girl Like You...?
PRIESTLEY, JACK (director of photography)
Series
Madigan
Seventh Avenue
Telefeatures
The Art of Crime
Cutter
PRIGMORE, JAMES (composer)
Telefeature
Evil Roy Slade
PRINCE, BOB see PRINCE, ROBERT
PRINCE, ROBERT (composer)
Series
Alias Smith and Jones
The Doctors
Rod Serling's Night Gallery
Telefeatures
Charlie Chan
Cool Million
A Cry in the Wilderness
The Desperate Miles
A Little Game
Scream, Pretty Peggy
What's a Nice Girl Like You...?
PRINCE, WILLIAM (actor)
Series
Aspen
Captains and the Kings
The Rhinemann Exchange
PRINE, ANDREW (actor)
Series
The Road West
The Wide Country
Telefeature
Tail Gunner Joe
PRINGLE, JOAN (actress)
Telefeature
Double Indemnity
PRIOR, FRED (music editor)
Series

The Hardy Boys Mysteries
The Rebels
PROCKTER, BERNARD (producer and head of Prockter Television Enterprises)
Series
The Man Behind the Badge
PROCKTER TELEVISION ENTERPRISES (production company)
Series
The Man Behind the Badge
PROCTER & GAMBLE PRODUCTIONS (production company)
Series
Shirley
PUBLIC ARTS PRODUCTIONS see ROY HUGGINS-PUBLIC ARTS PRODUCTIONS
PURCELL, LEE (actress)
Telefeature
Murder Works Overtime
PURL, LINDA (actress)
Series
Testimony of Two Men
Telefeature
The Oregon Trail
PYLE, DENVER (actor)
Series
Tammy

QUAID, DENNIS (actor)
Telefeature
Amateur Night at the Dixie Bar and Grill
QUAYLE, ANTHONY (actor)
Telefeature
Destiny of a Spy
QUIGORA, ALEX (color consultant)
Series
Laramie
The Virginian
QUINE, RICHARD (director)
Series
Columbo
Telefeature
The Specialists
QUINLAN, KATHLEEN (actress)
Telefeature
Lucas Tanner
QUINN, ANTHONY (actor)
Series
The Man and the City
Telefeature
The City

R. B. PRODUCTIONS (Raymond Burr's production company)
Series
Kingston: Confidential
Telefeatures
The Jordan Chance
Kingston: The Power Play
Mallory: Circumstantial Evidence
RABJOHN, RICHARD E. (associate producer)
Series
Quincy, M. E.
RADNEY, ZANE (unit production manager)
Series
The Rockford Files
Special
A Special Act of Love (assistant director only)
RAFFIN, DEBORAH (actress)
Series
The Last Convertible
RAFKIN, ALAN (director)
Telefeature
Let's Switch
RAGIN, JOHN S. (actor)
Series
Quincy, M. E.
Sons and Daughters
Telefeatures
The Islander
Senior Year
The Whole World Is Watching
RAINES, CRISTINA (actress)
Series
Centennial
Loose Change
Telefeature
Sunshine
RAINEY, FORD (actor)
Series
The Bionic Woman
Captains and the Kings
Telefeatures
The D. A.: Murder One
A Howling in the Woods
Linda
My Sweet Charlie
The Story of Pretty Boy Floyd
RAKOFF, ALVIN (director)
Special
The Adventures of Don Quixote
RALSTON, GILBERT A. (writer)
Series
O'Hara, U. S. Treasury
RAMBO, DACK (actor)
Series

Sword of Justice
RAMTEX CORPORATION (visual
    effects creators)
Series
Buck Rogers in the 25th Century
RAMUS, AL (writer)
Telefeature
Don't Push, I'll Charge When
    I'm Ready
RANDOLPH, JOHN (writer)
Series
Adam-12
RANDOLPH, LOUIS (writer)
Telefeatures
A Case of Rape (and producer)
Guilty or Innocent: The Sam
    Sheppard Murder Case
RANNEY, GENE E. (film editor)
Series
McCloud
Wheels
RAPF, MATTHEW (executive
    producer)
Series
Doctors' Hospital
Kojak (and supervising producer)
Switch
Telefeatures
Crime Club
The Marcus-Nelson Murders
    (producer only)
One of Our Own
RAPPAPORT, JOHN (producer/
    creator/writer)
Pilot
Three Times Daley
RATH, EARL (director of photography)
Series
The Name of the Game
Telefeature
This Is the West That Was
RAWLINS, DAVID ERIC (film
    editor)
Telefeatures
Any Second Now
The Outsider
RAWLINS, PHIL (director)
Series
Adam-12
RAY, ALDO (actor)
Telefeature
Deadlock!
RAY, ALEJANDRO (actor)
Telefeature
Money to Burn

RAYE, MARTHA (actress)
Series
McMillan
RAYNOR, WILLIAM (writer)
Series
McHale's Navy
REAGAN, RONALD (host/program
    supervisor)
Series
General Electric Theatre
REDD, JAMES S. (set decorator)
Series
Marcus Welby, M.D.
The Name of the Game
Startime
Telefeatures
The Intruders
Now You See It, Now You Don't
Prescription: Murder
Silent Night, Lonely Night
REDGRAVE, LYNN (actress)
Series
Beggarman, Thief
Centennial
House Calls
REDGRAVE, SIR MICHAEL (actor)
Special
Hamlet
REDMAN, ANTHONY (film editor)
Series
The Rhinemann Exchange
Telefeature
Amateur Night at the Dixie Bar
    and Grill
Pilot
Hazard's People
REDMAN, TONY see REDMOND,
    ANTHONY
REED, ROBERT (actor)
Series
Rich Man, Poor Man
The Seekers
Telefeatures
The City
Lanigan's Rabbi
REED, WAYNE (costume designer)
Series
The Rebels
REEVES, JIM (video engineer)
Special
Hamlet
REGAS, JACK (choreographer)
Special
The Jack Benny Special
REICH, JOE see REICH, JOSEPH
    Z.
REICH, JOSEPH Z. (casting director)

Series
Delta House
The Hardy Boys Mysteries
Quincy, M.E.
REID, KENNETH A. (art director)
Series
McMillan and Wife
Telefeature
The Snoop Sisters
REISMAN, DEL (writer)
Series
Banacek
The Man and the City (executive story consultant only)
REISMAN, PHILIP H., JR. (writer)
Telefeatures
Murder Works Overtime
Short Walk to Daylight
The Suicide Club
A Very Missing Person
REISNER, ALLEN (director)
Series
Captains and the Kings
Going My Way
Ironside
Matt Lincoln
Owen Marshall, Counselor at Law
REITH, JOSEPH (set decorator)
Series
Marcus Welby, M.D.
Telefeatures
The Astronaut
The Other Man
REITMAN, IVAN (composer)
Series
Delta House
REMICK, LEE (actress)
Series
Wheels
Special
The Man Who Came to Dinner
RENNAHAN, RAY, A.S.C. (director of photography)
Series
The John Forsythe Show
Laramie
Leave It to Beaver
Westinghouse Playhouse Starring Nanette Fabray and Wendell Corey
Telefeatures
I Love a Mystery
Prescription: Murder
RENNE, GEORGE (art director)
Series

BJ and the Bear
Emergency!
Telefeatures
Pine Canyon Is Burning
Switch
RENNE, RICHARD (art director)
Series
The Immigrants
REPUBLIC STUDIOS (motion picture studio rented by Revue Productions, Inc. in the 1950s--located at 4024 North Radford Avenue in North Hollywood, California, it is today the CBS Studio Center)
RESCHER, GAYNE (director of photography)
Series
Sons and Daughters
Telefeatures
Crime Club
Sarah T.--Portrait of a Teenage Alcoholic
REUNE, GEORGE (art director)
Telefeatures
The Man with the Power
Rosetti and Ryan: Men Who Love Women
REYNOLDS, BURT (actor)
Series
Riverboat
RHODES, HARI (actor)
Series
The Protectors
Telefeature
Deadlock!
RHODES, LEAH (costume designer)
Telefeature
Dial: Hot Line
RHODES, MICHAEL (producer)
Series
Delvecchio
Ellery Queen
Loose Change
RICE, JEFF (creator)
Series
The Night Stalker
RICH, DAVID LOWELL (director)
Series
Bob Hope Presents the Chrysler Theatre (and producer)
Laredo
Marcus Welby, M.D.
Owen Marshall, Counselor at Law
Telefeatures
All My Darling Daughters
Aloha Means Goodbye (and

executive producer)
Beg, Borrow ... or Steal
Berlin Affair
The Borgia Stick
Bridger (and producer)
Brock's Last Case
The Chadwick Family
Death Race
The Judge and Jake Wyler
Lieutenant Schuster's Wife
Little Women
Marcus Welby, M.D.
Runaway! (and producer)
See How They Run
Set This Town on Fire (and producer)
Wings of Fire (and producer)
You Lie So Deep, My Love (and producer)
RICH, TED (associate producer)
Series
McMillan and Wife
Pilot
Koska and His Family (producer/film editor only)
RICHARD LEWIS PRODUCTIONS (production company)
Series
The Crusader
RICHARDS, LLOYD (director)
Telefeatures
The Book of Murder
Don't Push, I'll Charge When I'm Ready (associate producer only)
RICHARDS, ROBERT K., A.C.E. (film editor)
Series
Adam-12
The Incredible Hulk
RICHARDSON, JAMES G. (actor)
Series
Sierra
RICHARDSON, RALPH (actor)
Telefeature
Frankenstein: The True Story
RIDDLE, NELSON (composer)
Series
City of Angels
The D.A.
Emergency!
Mobile One
The Rosemary Clooney Show (and conductor)
Seventh Avenue
79 Park Avenue
Telefeatures

Emergency!
Mobile Two
RIESNER, DEAN (writer)
Series
The Man and the City (creator only)
Rich Man, Poor Man
Telefeatures
Aloha Means Goodbye
The Intruders
The Keegans
Stranger on the Run
Vanished
RIGGINS, CLAUDE (sound mixer)
Series
The Incredible Hulk
RIOPELLE, JERRY (composer)
Telefeature
Evil Roy Slade
RITCHIE, MICHAEL (director)
Telefeatures
The Outsider
The Sound of Anger
RIVERA, CHITA (actress)
Telefeature
The Marcus-Nelson Murders
ROARKE, ADAM (actor)
Telefeature
The Keegans
ROBBIE, SEYMOUR (director)
Series
Ellery Queen
The Night Stalker
ROBERTS, DONALD (assistant director)
Telefeature
A Clear and Present Danger
ROBERTS, DORIS (actress)
Telefeature
It Happened One Christmas
ROBERTS, LOIS (actress)
Series
Broadside
ROBERTS, PERNELL (actor)
Series
Captains and the Kings
Centennial
The Immigrants
Telefeatures
The Adventures of Nick Carter
The Bravos
Charlie Cobb: Nice Night for a Hanging
The Night Rider
San Francisco International Airport
ROBERTS, RACHEL (actress)
Telefeature

Destiny of a Spy
ROBERTS, ROBBE (film editor)
  Telefeature
  It Happened One Christmas
ROBERTS, TED (music editor)
  Series
  Galactica 1980
ROBERTS, TONY (actor)
  Series
  Rosetti and Ryan
  Telefeature
  Rosetti and Ryan: Men Who Love Women
  Pilot
  Snafu
ROBERTSON, CLIFF (actor)
  Telefeature
  The Sunshine Patriot
ROBERTSON, DALE (actor)
  Series
  Tales of Wells Fargo
ROBERTSON, JERRY (producer)
  Series
  The Man Behind the Badge
ROBINSON, BERNARD (production designer)
  Telefeatures
  Destiny of a Spy
  Run a Crooked Mile (art director only)
ROBINSON, EARL (composer)
  Telefeature
  The Great Man's Whiskers
ROBINSON, HUBBELL (executive producer and head of Hubbell Robinson Productions, Inc.)
  Series
  87th Precinct
  Startime
  Thriller
ROBINSON, STANLEY L. (producer)
  Telefeature
  Love Is Not Enough
ROCCO, ALEX (actor)
  Series
  79 Park Avenue
ROCHE, EUGENE (actor)
  Telefeature
  Crime Club
ROCHE, MARIE (makeup artist)
  Special
  Hamlet
RODDENBERRY, GENE (executive producer/writer)
  Telefeature
  The Questor Tapes

RODEN, PETER (art director)
  Special
  Hamlet
RODGERS, MARK (writer)
  Series
  Jigsaw (executive story consultant only)
  The Name of the Game
  Telefeature
  Savage
RODMAN, HOWARD (writer)
  Series
  The Man and the City (creator only)
  Telefeatures
  The City
  Exo-Man
RODRIGUES, PERCY (actor)
  Telefeature
  The Night Rider
ROGERS, JAMES F. (sound mixer)
  Series
  Galactica 1980
  Quincy, M.E.
ROGERS, SHORTY (composer)
  Telefeature
  Breakout
ROGERS, WAYNE (actor)
  Series
  City of Angels
  House Calls (and director)
  Telefeature
  It Happened One Christmas
ROGOSIN, JOEL (producer)
  Series
  The Doctors (and writer)
  Ironside (and executive producer)
  Kraft Suspense Theatre (associate producer only)
  The Virginian (and director)
  Telefeatures
  The Desperate Miles (executive producer/writer only)
  The Sunshine Patriot (and writer)
ROHRS, GEORGE R. (film editor)
  Telefeature
  Dr. Scorpion
ROLEY, SUTTON (director)
  Series
  The Sixth Sense
ROLFE, SAM H. (writer)
  Series
  Delvecchio (and creator)
  Telefeatures
  Rosetti and Ryan: Men Who Love Women
  This Is the West That Was
ROMAN, JOSEPH (actor)

Series
Quincy, M. E.
ROMANIS, GEORGE (composer)
Series
McNaughton's Daughter
Telefeatures
The Family Nobody Wanted
Live Again, Die Again
Maneater
ROMERO, CESAR (actor)
Telefeature
Don't Push, I'll Charge When I'm Ready
RONCOM FILMS (production company)
Series
Run for Your Life
RONCOM PRODUCTIONS, INC. (production company)
Series
Court Martial
Kraft Suspense Theatre
RONDEAU, CHARLES R. (director)
Series
Gemini Man
RONDELL, RONNIE (assistant director)
Series
Alfred Hitchcock Presents
ROOK, JOHN (lighting director)
Special
Hamlet
ROONEY, MICKEY (actor)
Telefeature
Evil Roy Slade
ROSE, DAVID (composer)
Telefeatures
The Birdmen
The Devil and Miss Sarah
Killing Stone
ROSE, SI (producer)
Series
Broadside
McHale's Navy (and associate producer/script consultant)
Operation Petticoat
ROSEN, ARNIE (producer/writer)
Pilot
Snafu
ROSEN, MILT (writer)
Series
Baa Baa Black Sheep
Black Sheep Squadron (creative consultant only)
ROSEN, MILTON (composer)
Telefeature
Death Race

ROSEN, NEIL (producer/writer)
Pilot
Off the Wall
ROSENBERG, FRANK P. (executive producer)
Series
Arrest and Trial
Kraft Suspense Theatre
ROSENBERG, META (executive producer with Cherokee Productions)
Series
The Rockford Files
Telefeature
Scott Free
ROSENBERG, PHILIP (production designer)
Series
Seventh Avenue
ROSENBERG, STUART (director)
Telefeature
Fame Is the Name of the Game
ROSENBLOOM, RICHARD (producer)
Special
Applause
ROSENMAN, LEONARD (composer)
Series
Holmes and Yoyo
Marcus Welby, M. D.
The Men from Shiloh
The Road West (theme only)
The Virginian
Telefeatures
Any Second Now
The Bravos
Kingston: The Power Play
Lanigan's Rabbi
Marcus Welby, M. D.
Shadow Over Elveron
Stranger on the Run
Vanished
ROSENTHAL, LAURENCE (composer)
Telefeature
The Log of the Black Pearl
ROSENZWEIG, BARNEY (producer)
Series
Sons and Daughters
ROSS, ARTHUR (writer)
Telefeatures
The Desperate Miles
Love Is Not Enough
ROSS, KATHARINE (actress)
Telefeature
The Longest Hundred Miles
ROSS, MARION (actress)
Telefeature

Any Second Now
Special
The Slowest Gun in the West
ROSSON, EDWARD (director of
  photography)
Telefeatures
The Neon Ceiling
Sunshine Christmas
ROTH, RON (producer)
Series
Bob Hope Presents the Chrysler
  Theatre (and associate pro-
  ducer)
Telefeature
The Manhunter
ROWAN, DAN (host)
Series
American Flyer
ROWE, ARTHUR (producer/writer)
Series
The Bionic Woman
ROWLANDS, GENA (actress)
Series
87th Precinct
ROY HUGGINS-PUBLIC ARTS
  PRODUCTIONS (production
  company)
Series
Aspen
Baretta
City of Angels
The Lawyers
The Outsider
The Protectors
The Rockford Files
Run for Your Life
Toma
Telefeatures
The Challengers
Do You Take This Stranger
How to Steal an Airplane
The Invasion of Johnson
  County
The Jordan Chance
The Outsider
The Rockford Files
Sam Hill: Who Killed the
  Mysterious Mr. Foster?
Set This Town on Fire
The Sound of Anger
The Story of Pretty Boy Floyd
Target Risk
This Is the West That Was
The 3,000 Mile Chase
Toma
The Whole World Is Watching
The Young Country
Pilots

Hazard's People
The Sweet Life
RUBEN, ALBERT (writer)
Telefeature
River of Mystery
RUBICHAN, JOHN (associate pro-
  ducer)
Series
Checkmate
RUBIN, EDWARD (associate pro-
  ducer)
Series
The Bob Cummings Show
RUBIN, MANN (writer)
Series
Quincy, M.E.
Telefeature
See the Man Run
RUBIN, STANLEY (producer)
Series
Channing
General Electric Theatre (and
  executive producer/writer)
The Man and the City
RUBINSTEIN, JOHN (actor)
Telefeatures
A Howling in the Woods
The Psychiatrist: God Bless
  the Children
RUCKER, DENNIS (actor)
Series
Get Christie Love!
RUDLEY, SARETT (writer)
Pilot
The Detective: Bull in a China
  Shop
RUGOLO, PETE (composer, pri-
  marily with Roy Huggins-
  Public Arts Productions)
Series
Ichabod and Me
The Invisible Man
Kingston: Confidential
The Outside
Run for Your Life
Thriller
Telefeatures
The Challengers
Do You Take This Stranger
Drive Hard, Drive Fast
How to Steal an Airplane
The Jordan Chance
The Lonely Profession
The Outsider
Sam Hill: Who Killed the
  Mysterious Mr. Foster?
Set This Town on Fire
The Sound of Anger

The Story of Pretty Boy Floyd
Toma
The Whole World Is Watching
The Young Country
RULE, BERT, G. B. F. E. (film editor)
Telefeature
Run a Crooked Mile
RULE, JANICE (actress)
Telefeatures
The Devil and Miss Sarah
Trial Run
RUSKIN, COBY (director)
Series
Alcoa Premiere/Premiere
RUSSELL, A. J. (writer)
Telefeatures
The Borgia Stick
A Clear and Present Danger
RUSSELL, BOBBY (lyricist/vocalist)
Telefeature
The City
RUSSELL, CONRAD (director of photography)
Series
Startime
RUSSELL, GORDON (writer)
Series
Kraft Suspense Theatre
RUSSELL, JOHN (actor)
Series
Soldiers of Fortune
RUSSELL, JOHN L., A. S. C. (director of photography)
Series
Alfred Hitchcock Presents
Bob Hope Presents the Chrysler Theatre
General Electric Theatre
McHale's Navy
Telefeature
Now You See It, Now You Don't
RUSSELL, WILLIAM A. (sound mixer)
Series
The Name of the Game
Startime
RUSSELL THACHER-WALTER SELTZER PRODUCTIONS (production company)
Special
The Cay
RUTHERFORD, CHARLES (set decorator)
Series
Baretta

RYAN, MITCHELL (actor)
Series
Chase
Telefeature
Chase
RYDER, ALFRED (actor)
Telefeatures
The D. A.: Murder One
Indict and Convict
The Specialists

SABAT, JAMES T. (sound mixer)
Series
Kojak
SABATINI, DANILO (production manager)
Series
It Takes a Thief
SACKHEIM, WILLIAM (producer)
Series
Delvecchio (executive producer only)
Once an Eagle (executive producer only)
The Protectors (creator only)
The Senator (executive consultant only)
Telefeatures
A Clear and Present Danger
Deadlock! (and writer)
Dial: Hot Line
The Harness
The Impatient Heart (and writer)
The Law (and writer)
Mallory: Circumstantial Evidence
The Neon Ceiling
Night Gallery
SACRIPANTI, LUCIANO (sound mixer)
Series
The Name of the Game
SAGAL, BORIS (director)
Series
Alfred Hitchcock Presents
Ironside
Madigan
Mrs. Columbo
Rich Man, Poor Man
Telefeatures
A Case of Rape
The D. A.: Murder One
Destiny of a Spy
The Failing of Raymond
The Greatest Gift
The Harness
Hitched

Indict and Convict
Mallory: Circumstantial Evidence
Man on the Outside
The Movie Murderer
Night Gallery
The Oregon Trail
SAINT JAMES, SUSAN (actress)
　Series
　McMillan and Wife
　The Name of the Game
　Telefeatures
　Alias Smith and Jones
　Fame Is the Name of the Game
　It Takes a Thief
　Magic Carpet
　Once Upon a Dead Man
　Scott Free
ST. JOHN, JILL (actress)
　Telefeatures
　Fame Is the Name of the Game
　How I Spent My Summer Vacation
SALES, SOUPY (actor)
　Telefeature
　Don't Push, I'll Charge When I'm Ready
SALINGER, CONRAD (composer)
　Series
　Bachelor Father
　General Electric Theatre
　Startime
SALKOWITZ, SY (writer)
　Series
　Alias Smith and Jones
　The Doctors
　Ironside
　The Virginian
SALTER, HANS (composer)
　Series
　Laramie
　The Virginian
　Wagon Train
SAMUELSON, PAUL (1st assistant director)
　Series
　Quincy, M. E.
SAND, PAUL (actor)
　Pilot
　Lady Luck
SANDEFUR, B. W. (supervising producer)
　Series
　The Hardy Boys Mysteries (and writer)
　The Nancy Drew Mysteries
SANDERS, DENNIS (director)
　Series
　Alcoa Premiere/Premiere
SANDLER, BURNS & MARMER (production company)
　Telefeature
　Charlie Chan
SANDRICH, JAY (director)
　Pilot
　Three Times Daley
SANFORD, DONALD S. (writer)
　Series
　Thriller
SANFORD, ISABEL (actress)
　Telefeature
　The Great Man's Whiskers
SANGSTER, JIMMY (writer)
　Telefeatures
　Maneater
　Scream, Pretty Peggy
SANTORO, GEORGE J. (executive producer)
　Series
　Banacek (executive in charge of production only)
　Ironside (supervising executive only)
　Telefeatures
　Farewell to Manzanar
　Sex and the Married Woman
SANTOS, JOE (actor)
　Series
　The Rockford Files
　Telefeature
　The Rockford Files
SAPINSLEY, ALVIN (writer)
　Series
　Bob Hope Presents the Chrysler Theatre
SARAFIAN, RICHARD (director)
　Telefeature
　One of Our Own
SARGENT, ALVIN (writer)
　Telefeature
　The Impatient Heart
SARGENT, DICK (actor)
　Series
　Broadside
SARGENT, JOSEPH (director)
　Telefeatures
　The Marcus-Nelson Murders
　Sunshine
　The Sunshine Patriot
SARIEGO, RALPH (assistant director)
　Series
　Columbo (unit manager only)
　The Psychiatrist
　Rod Serling's Night Gallery
SARRAZIN, MICHAEL (actor)

Telefeatures
The Doomsday Flight
Frankenstein: The True Story
SARTOR, DICK (sound mixer)
Telefeature
Night Life
SARV, FRANK (sound mixer)
Series
Startime
SATLOF, RON(ALD GILBERT)
 (supervising producer)
Series
McCloud
Telefeature
Benny and Barney: Las Vegas
 Undercover (director only)
SAUNDERS, HERMAN S. (producer)
Series
Adam-12 (and executive producer)
Telefeature
Houston, We've Got a Problem
SAVALAS, GEORGE (actor)
Series
Kojak
Telefeature
The Marcus-Nelson Murders
SAVALAS, TELLY (actor)
Series
Kojak (and director)
Telefeature
The Marcus-Nelson Murders
SAVORY, GERALD (producer)
Special
The Adventures of Don Quixote
SAXON, JOHN (actor)
Series
The Doctors
The Immigrants
Once an Eagle
79 Park Avenue
Telefeatures
The Doomsday Flight
The Intruders
Istanbul Express
It Takes a Thief
Linda
Winchester 73
SCHAAL, RICHARD (actor)
Telefeature
Let's Switch
SCHAEFER, GEORGE (producer)
Series
Alcoa Premiere/Premiere
Telefeature
Amelia Earhart (director only)
SCHAFER, NATALIE (actress)

Series
Harold Robbins' "The Survivors"
SCHALLERT, WILLIAM (actor)
Series
The Hardy Boys Mysteries
Little Women
The Nancy Drew Mysteries
Telefeatures
Little Women
Tail Gunner Joe
SCHEERER, ROBERT (director)
Telefeature
Target Risk
SCHEFF, MICHAEL (executive in
 charge of production)
Special
A Special Act of Love
SCHENCK, AUBREY (producer)
Telefeature
The Alpha Caper
SCHERMER, JAMES (producer)
Series
Chase
SCHERMER, JULES (producer)
Series
The Virginian
SCHICKEL, RICHARD (producer/
 director/writer)
Special
Funny Business
SCHIFRIN, LALO (composer)
Series
The Partners
The Sixth Sense (theme only)
Telefeatures
The Aquarians
The Doomsday Flight
Guilty or Innocent: The Sam
 Sheppard Murder Case
How I Spent My Summer Vacation
See How They Run
SCHILLER, WILTON (writer/
 executive script consultant)
Series
The Six Million Dollar Man
SCHILZ, TED (unit manager)
Series
The Six Million Dollar Man
SCHLOEMP, PETRUS (director
 of photography)
Telefeature
Hauser's Memory
SCHMIDT, ELLEN (art director)
Telefeature
Hauser's Memory
SCHNEIDER, ANDREW (story
 editor)

Series
The Incredible Hulk
SCHNEIDER, MARGARET (writer with partner Paul Schneider)
Series
Marcus Welby, M.D.
Owen Marshall, Counselor at Law
The Six Million Dollar Man
SCHNEIDER, PAUL (writer with partner Margaret Schneider)
Series
Owen Marshall, Counselor at Law
The Six Million Dollar Man
SCHOENBERG, IRVING (film editor)
Series
Tales of Wells Fargo
SCHOENFELD, RALPH (film editor)
Series
Centennial
SCHOENGARTH, JACK W. (film editor)
Series
The Incredible Hulk
The Six Million Dollar Man
Telefeature
The Incredible Hulk
SCHREIBER, TAFT (president of Revue Productions, Inc. and Universal Television in the 1960s)
SCHREYER, JOHN F. (film editor)
Series
Loose Change
Telefeatures
Hitchhike!
Maneater
Trapped
SCHUCK, JOHN (actor)
Series
Holmes and Yoyo
McMillan and Wife
Turnabout
Telefeature
Once Upon a Dead Man
Pilot
If I Had a Million
SCHULBERG, BUDD (writer)
Series
General Electric Theatre
SCHULTZ, BARBARA (producer of the "ABC Wide World of Entertainment"/"Wide World Mystery" telefeatures and executive producer of the "ABC Afternoon Playbreak"/"ABC Matinee Today" specials)
Telefeatures
The Book of Murder
Death Is a Bad Trip
The House of Evil
A Little Bit Like Murder
Murder Works Overtime (executive producer only)
Night Life
The Nightmare Step
A Prowler in the Heart
The Suicide Club
Specials
Alone with Terror
The Mask of Love
My Secret Mother
SCHUMACHER, JOEL (director/writer)
Telefeature
Amateur Night at the Dixie Bar and Grill
SCHUMANN, WALTER (theme composer)
Series
Dragnet 1967-1970
SCHWARTZ, ELROY (writer)
Series
The Six Million Dollar Man
Telefeatures
The Alpha Caper
Money to Burn
SCHWARTZ, HOWARD R. (director of photography)
Series
Rich Man, Poor Man
Telefeatures
Ellery Queen
The Incredible Hulk
One of Our Own
SCHWARTZ, NANCY LYNN (writer)
Series
Wheels
SCHWARZ, EARL (sound mixer)
Telefeature
The Movie Murderer
SCHWEITZER, S. S. (writer)
Telefeature
A Clear and Present Danger
SCOPPETTONE, SANDRA (writer)
Telefeature
A Little Bit Like Murder
SCOTT, ADRIAN (producer)
Telefeature
The Great Man's Whiskers
SCOTT, BRENDA (actress)

Series
The Road West
SCOTT, DEBRALEE (actress)
Series
Sons and Daughters
Telefeature
Senior Year
SCOTT, GEOFFREY (actor)
Series
Cliffhangers
SCOTT, GORDON (film editor)
Telefeature
Sunshine Christmas
SCOTT, JACQUELINE (actress)
Telefeature
Duel
SCOTT, KAY (theme composer/lyricist)
Telefeature
Stranger on the Run
SCOTT, TOM (composer)
Series
Aspen
SEARLS, HANK (writer)
Series
Wheels
SEBERG, JEAN (actress)
Telefeature
Mousey
SEGAL, ALEX (director)
Series
Alcoa Premiere/Premiere (and producer)
Rich Man, Poor Man--Book II
SEGALL, BERNARDO (composer)
Series
Columbo
SEITER, ROBERT (film editor)
Series
Leave It to Beaver
SELANDER, LES(LEY) (director)
Series
Laramie
The Tall Man
SELBY, DAVID (actor)
Telefeature
The Night Rider
SELF, EDWIN (producer with Mark VII Limited)
Series
Emergency!
The Rangers
SELLECK, TOM (actor)
Telefeature
The Movie Murderer
Pilots
Boston and Kilbride

The Gypsy Warriors
SELTZER, WALTER (producer)
Special
The Cay
SENDRY, RICHARD (composer)
Series
Laramie
Riverboat
Wagon Train
SENENSKY, RALPH (director)
Series
The Family Holvak
Matt Lincoln
Telefeature
The Family Nobody Wanted
SENTER, JACK (production designer)
Series
Centennial
SERAFIAN, ENZO (director of photography)
Series
It Takes a Thief
SERLING, ROD (writer)
Series
Bob Hope Presents the Chrysler Theatre
Rod Serling's Night Gallery (and host/narrator/creator)
Telefeatures
The Doomsday Flight
Night Gallery
SEVEN, JOHNNY (actor)
Series
Amy Prentiss
SEYMOUR, JANE (actress)
Series
Captains and the Kings
Telefeatures
Benny and Barney: Las Vegas Undercover
Frankenstein: The True Story
SGARRO, NICHOLAS (director)
Telefeature
The Man with the Power
SHAGAN, STEVE (producer)
Telefeature
River of Mystery
SHAMLEY PRODUCTIONS, INC. (Alfred Hitchcock's production company, named after the town of Shamley Green in England where he lived for many years)
Series
The Alfred Hitchcock Hour
Alfred Hitchcock Presents
Startime

Suspicion
SHANE, MAXWELL (producer)
  Series
  Checkmate
  Thriller (director only)
SHANER, JOHN (writer)
  Telefeature
  Don't Push, I'll Charge When I'm Ready
SHAPIRO, ESTHER (writer with partner Richard Shapiro)
  Telefeature
  Sarah T.--Portrait of a Teenage Alcoholic
SHAPIRO, RICHARD (writer with partner Esther Shapiro)
  Telefeature
  Sarah T.--Portrait of a Teenage Alcoholic
SHARP, MEL (writer)
  Series
  The Bob Cummings Show
SHARPLESS, DON (sound mixer)
  Series
  Escape
SHATNER, WILLIAM (actor)
  Series
  The Bastard
  Testimony of Two Men
  Telefeatures
  The Hound of the Baskervilles
  Indict and Convict
  Little Women
  Owen Marshall, Counselor at Law
  Perilous Voyage
  Vanished
SHAW, DAVID (writer)
  Series
  Quincy, M.E. (executive story consultant only)
  Telefeatures
  The Judge and Jake Wyler
  Partners in Crime
SHAW, LOU (writer)
  Series
  Alcoa Premiere/Premiere (with partner Peggy Shaw)
  The Nancy Drew Mysteries
  Quincy, M.E. (producer/creator only)
SHAW, PEGGY (writer with partner Lou Shaw)
  Series
  Alcoa Premiere/Premiere
SHAWN, DICK (actor)
  Telefeature
  Evil Roy Slade

SHAYNE, ALAN (creator)
  Series
  The Snoop Sisters
SHEAR, BARRY (director)
  Series
  Alias Smith and Jones
  City of Angels
  Telefeatures
  Ellery Queen: Don't Look Behind You
  Short Walk to Daylight
SHEARER, HANNAH L. (producer with partners Gian R. Grimaldi and Gino Grimaldi)
  Series
  The Immigrants
  The Rebels
  The Seekers
  Telefeature
  Pine Canyon Is Burning
  Pilot
  The Two-Five
SHEEN, MARTIN (actor)
  Telefeatures
  The California Kid
  The Execution of Private Slovik
  A Prowler in the Heart
  The Story of Pretty Boy Floyd
  That Certain Summer
SHEINBERG, SIDNEY (president of MCA, Inc. since the early 1970s--former president of Universal Television)
SHELDON, JAMES (director)
  Series
  Ellery Queen
  McMillan
  Owen Marshall, Counselor at Law
SHELLEY, BRUCE (writer)
  Telefeature
  The Elevator
SHER, JACK (writer)
  Series
  Holmes and Yoyo (creator only)
  Telefeature
  Female Artillery
SHERIDAN, ANN (actress)
  Series
  Pistols 'n' Petticoats
SHERMAN, BOBBY (actor)
  Telefeature
  Skyway to Death
SHERMAN, JILL (story editor)
  Series
  The Incredible Hulk
SHERMAN, ROGER, JR. (camera operator)

Series
The Senator
SHERMAN, VINCENT (director)
Series
Baretta
Doctors' Hospital
The Family Holvak
SHIFMAN, MILTON, A.C.E.
  (film editor)
Series
Arrest and Trial
Owen Marshall, Counselor at
  Law
Telefeature
Breakout
SHIGETA, JAMES (actor)
Telefeature
Escape to Mindanao
SHIMODA, YUKI (actor)
Telefeature
Farewell to Manzanar
SHIMOKAWA, GARY (director)
Pilot
The Bay City Amusement
  Company
SHINGLETON, WILFRID (art director)
Telefeature
Frankenstein: The True Story
SHIRE, DAVID (composer)
Series
Lucas Tanner
McCloud
Telefeatures
Amelia Earhart
The Impatient Heart
Lucas Tanner
McCloud: Who Killed Miss
  U.S.A.?
McNaughton's Daughter
The Oregon Trail
The Priest Killer
See the Man Run
The Storyteller
SHIRE, TALIA (actress)
Series
Rich Man, Poor Man
SHOCKLEY, SALLIE (actress)
Telefeature
The Longest Night
Pilot
Lady Luck
SHORES, RICHARD (composer)
Series
Kingston: Confidential
Whispering Smith
SHORR, FREDERICK (producer)
Series

Laredo
The Name of the Game (associate producer only)
SHORR, LESTER, A.S.C. (director of photography)
Series
Delta House
SHORT, CHARLES W. (director of photography)
Series
Centennial
SHOTGUN PRODUCTION CO., THE
  (production company)
Series
Shotgun Slade
SHPETNER, STAN (producer)
Series
The Sixth Sense (and developer)
Telefeatures
The Devil and Miss Sarah
The Deadly Dream
See the Man Run
SHUGRUE, ROBERT F. (film editor)
Series
The Bastard
Centennial
Owen Marshall, Counselor at
  Law
Seventh Avenue
79 Park Avenue
Testimony of Two Men
Telefeatures
The Adventures of Nick Carter
Beg, Borrow ... or Steal
The Birdmen
The California Kid
The D.A.: Conspiracy to Kill
The Dark Secret of Harvest
  Home
The Doomsday Flight
Gemini Man
Guilty or Innocent: The Sam
  Sheppard Murder Case
Houston, We've Got a Problem
A Howling in the Woods
I Love a Mystery
Indict and Convict
The Invisible Man
The Longest Night
Mallory: Circumstantial Evidence
The Neon Ceiling
Owen Marshall, Counselor at
  Law
Partners in Crime
The Psychiatrist: God Bless the
  Children

The Screaming Woman
Something for a Lonely Man
Stonestreet: Who Killed the
 Centerfold Model?
The Tribe
Pilot
Stranded
SHUKEN, LEO (composer)
Series
The Virginian
Whispering Smith
SHULER, LAUREN (producer)
Telefeature
Amateur Night at the Dixie
 Bar and Grill
SHULL, RICHARD B. (actor)
Series
Holmes and Yoyo
SHULMAN, MAX (creator)
Series
House Calls
SHUSTER, FRANK (actor with
 partner Johnny Wayne)
Series
Holiday Lodge
Wayne and Shuster Take an
 Affectionate Look at...
 (host only)
SICKNER, WILLIAM A., A.S.C.
 (director of photography)
Series
Leave It to Beaver
SIDARIS, ANDY (director)
Series
The Nancy Drew Mysteries
SIDARIS, ARLENE (producer/
 co-producer)
Series
The Hardy Boys Mysteries
The Nancy Drew Mysteries
SIEGEL, DON(ALD) (director)
Series
Convoy (and producer)
Destry
Telefeature
Stranger on the Run
SIEGEL, LIONEL E. (writer)
Series
The Doctors (story editor
 only)
San Francisco International
 Airport
79 Park Avenue
The Six Million Dollar Man
 (and executive producer/
 supervising producer/
 executive story consultant)
Telefeature

Exo-Man (producer only)
Pilot
If I Had a Million
SILLIPHANT, STIRLING (writer)
Series
General Electric Theatre
Telefeature
Wings of Fire
SILVA, HENRY (actor)
Telefeature
Drive Hard, Drive Fast
SILVER, SUSAN (writer)
Telefeature
The Couple Takes a Wife
SILVERA, FRANK (actor)
Telefeature
Perilous Voyage
SILVERS, PHIL (actor)
Special
The Slowest Gun in the West
SILVERSTEIN, ELLIOT (director)
Series
Checkmate
SILVERTON PRODUCTIONS, INC.
 (Harve Bennett's production
 company [see also Harve
 Bennett Productions, Ben-
 nett's other production com-
 pany])
Series
The Six Million Dollar Man
Telefeatures
The Alpha Caper
The Invisible Man
Money to Burn
You'll Never See Me Again
SIMON, MAYO (writer)
Series
General Electric Theatre
SIMMONS, JEAN (actress)
Series
Beggarman, Thief
SIMMONS, MATTY (executive pro-
 ducer and head of Matty
 Simmons-Ivan Reitman Pro-
 ductions)
Series
Delta House
SIMMONS, MICHAEL (theme vocal-
 ist)
Series
Delta House
SIMMONS, RICHARD ALAN (pro-
 ducer)
Series
Columbo
Mrs. Columbo (executive pro-
 ducer/developer/writer only)

Telefeatures
Berlin Affair (writer only)
Fear No Evil (and writer)
Hitched (and writer)
Lock, Stock and Barrel (and writer)
SIMMS, JAY (writer)
Series
Thriller
SIMONDS, WALTER M. (art director)
Telefeatures
The Gun
Man on the Outside
Senior Year
This Is the West That Was
Two on a Bench
SIMOUN, HENRI (writer)
Telefeatures
A Clear and Present Danger
Exo-Man
The Neon Ceiling
The Six Million Dollar Man
SIMS, JERRY (director of photography)
Series
Adam-12
SINGER, ALEX(ANDER) (director)
Series
Bob Hope Presents the Chrysler Theatre
The Lawyers
Lucas Tanner
The Outsider
SINGER, MARC (actor)
Series
79 Park Avenue
SIPES, DONALD (replaced Frank Price as president of Universal Television in 1978)
SISTIAM, JOE (producer)
Series
Markham
SKALA, LILIA (actress)
Telefeature
Ironside
SKERRITT, TOM (actor)
Telefeature
The Birdmen
SLATE, JEREMY (actor)
Telefeature
Wings of Fire
SLATE, LANE (writer)
Series
Ironside
Mrs. Columbo
Telefeatures
Tail Gunner Joe

The Tribe
SLESAR, HENRY (writer)
Series
The Alfred Hitchcock Hour
The Name of the Game
SLOAN, MICHAEL (supervising producer, primarily with Glen A. Larson Productions)
Series
BJ and the Bear (executive producer/writer only)
Evening in Byzantium (and writer)
The Hardy Boys Mysteries (and writer)
Sword of Justice
SMALL, BERNARD J. (film editor)
Telefeatures
Just a Little Inconvenience
Tail Gunner Joe
SMALL, BUDD (film editor)
Series
The Name of the Game
Telefeatures
The Devil and Miss Sarah
How to Steal an Airplane
The Islander
The Judge and Jake Wyler
San Francisco International Airport
Silent Night, Lonely Night
The Six Million Dollar Man
Sunshine
The Sunshine Patriot
Switch
SMALL, EDGAR (producer with Arena Productions, Inc.)
Telefeature
The Psychiatrist: God Bless the Children
SMIGHT, JACK (director)
Series
The Alfred Hitchcock Hour
Banacek
Kraft Suspense Threatre
Telefeatures
Banacek
Double Indemnity
Frankenstein: The True Story
The Longest Night
Partners in Crime
The Screaming Woman
Special
The Man from Independence
SMITH, CLIVE (sound effects editor)
Series
Quincy, M.E.

420 / Index

SMITH, CRAIG (art director)
  Series
  General Electric Theatre
SMITH, DICK T. (art director)
  Telefeature
  The Greatest Gift
SMITH, FRANK T. (art director)
  Telefeature
  The Invisible Man
SMITH, GEORGE SHELDON (writer)
  Series
  Banacek
SMITH, HARKNESS, A.S.C. (director of photography)
  Series
  Owen Marshall, Counselor at Law
  Telefeature
  Beg, Borrow ... or Steal
SMITH, JACLYN (actress)
  Telefeature
  Switch
SMITH, JERRY (sound mixer)
  Series
  Columbo
SMITH, JOHN (actor)
  Series
  Cimarron City
  Laramie
SMITH, MARTIN (writer)
  Telefeature
  The Art of Crime
SMITH, PHILIP (set decorator)
  Series
  Kojak
SMITH, REID (actor)
  Telefeature
  Chase
SMITH, ROBERT E. (art director)
  Series
  Alias Smith and Jones
  The Lawyers
  Telefeatures
  Duel
  Sam Hill: Who Killed the Mysterious Mr. Foster?
SMITH, S. MARK (producer)
  Series
  General Electric Theatre
  Suspicion (executive producer only)
SMITH, WARREN (assistant director)
  Series
  Adam-12
  Alias Smith and Jones

SMITH, WAYNE (production and special effects consultant)
  Series
  Battlestar: Galactica
  Buck Rogers in the 25th Century (miniature effects creator only)
SMITHERS, WILLIAM (actor)
  Telefeature
  The Neon Ceiling
SMOTHERS, DICK (actor)
  Special
  The Jack Benny Special
SMOTHERS, TOM (actor)
  Special
  The Jack Benny Special
SNODGRESS, CARRIE (actress)
  Telefeatures
  The Impatient Heart
  Silent Night, Lonely Night
  The Whole World Is Watching
SNOW, MARK (composer)
  Series
  Gemini Man
SNYDER, ALLAN (makeup artist)
  Special
  The Red Pony
SNYDER, DON (costume designer)
  Series
  The Misadventures of Sheriff Lobo
SOBIESKI, CAROL (writer)
  Telefeatures
  Amelia Earhart
  Dial: Hot Line
  A Little Game
  The Neon Ceiling
  Sunshine
SOLANO, ROSALIO (director of photography)
  Special
  The Cay
SOLOMON, BRUCE (actor)
  Series
  Lanigan's Rabbi
SOLOW, HERBERT F. (producer)
  Telefeatures
  Heat Wave (and writer)
  Killdozer
SOMERS, EDWIN J. (sound mixer)
  Series
  Centennial
SOMERSET, PATRICK (sound effects editor)
  Series
  The Incredible Hulk
SOMMARS, JULIE (actress)
  Telefeatures

The Harness
How to Steal an Airplane
Special
Short Stories of Love
SOMMERS, ED (sound mixer)
 Telefeature
 It Takes a Thief
SOREL, LOUISE (actress)
 Series
 Harold Robbins' "The Survivors"
 Telefeatures
 Charlie Chan
 The Nightmare Step
 One of Our Own
 Perilous Voyage
 River of Mystery
SOTHERN, ANN (actress)
 Series
 Captains and the Kings
 Telefeatures
 The Great Man's Whiskers
 The Outsider
SOUL, DAVID (actor)
 Series
 Owen Marshall, Counselor at Law
SOUTH, LEONARD J. (director of photography)
 Telefeatures
 Hitchhike!
 Linda
 Scream, Pretty Peggy
 You Lie So Deep, My Love
 Special
 The Man from Independence
SOWARDS, JACK B. (writer)
 Series
 The Lawyers
SPARKS, ROBERT (producer)
 Series
 Bachelor Father
SPECTOR, DAVID (writer)
 Telefeature
 Skyway to Death
SPECTOR, MAUDE (casting director)
 Special
 The Man Who Came to Dinner
SPENCER, HERBERT (theme composer)
 Series
 Tammy
SPIELBERG, DAVID (actor)
 Series
 Wheels
 Telefeatures
 Force Five

The Storyteller
The 3,000 Mile Chase
SPIELBERG, STEVEN (director)
 Series
 Columbo
 The Name of the Game
 The Psychiatrist
 Telefeatures
 Duel
 Savage
SPIES, ADRIAN (writer)
 Series
 The Protectors
 Telefeatures
 The Failing of Raymond
 Hauser's Memory
SPILLANE, MICKEY (creator)
 Series
 Mickey Spillane's Mike Hammer
SPINNER, ANTHONY (executive producer)
 Series
 Baretta
SPRADLIN, G. D. (actor)
 Telefeatures
 Dial: Hot Line
 The Oregon Trail
 Sam Hill: Who Killed the Mysterious Mr. Foster?
SPRAGUE, RICHARD M. (film editor)
 Series
 Destry
 The Name of the Game
 Telefeatures
 Aloha Means Goodbye
 A Clear and Present Danger
 The D.A.: Conspiracy to Kill
 Evil Roy Slade
 The Marcus-Nelson Murders
 The Six Million Dollar Man
 Sunshine
 A Very Missing Person
 What's a Nice Girl Like You...?
SPRINGSTEEN, R. G. (director)
 Series
 Tales of Wells Fargo
STACK, ROBERT (actor)
 Series
 The Name of the Game
STACY, JAMES (actor)
 Telefeature
 Just a Little Inconvenience
STACY, JOHN (sound effects editor)
 Series
 Aspen

STACY PRODUCTIONS (Don
    Adams' production company)
  Series
  Don Adams' Screen Test
STAGE COACH PRODUCTIONS
    (production company)
  Series
  The Overland Trail
STAMSOE, FRED (actor)
  Series
  Adam-12
STANFORD, DON (writer)
  Series
  Alcoa Premiere/Premiere
STANLEY, JERRY (producer)
  Series
  Adam-12
  Escape
STANLEY, LEE (writer)
  Series
  Banacek
STANLEY, PAUL (director)
  Series
  Laredo
  Rich Man, Poor Man--Book II
  Telefeature
  River of Mystery
STANNARD, ROY (art director)
  Telefeature
  Mousey
STAPLETON, JEAN (actress)
  Telefeature
  Tail Gunner Joe
STARK, WILLIAM (associate
    producer)
  Series
  Adam-12
  Dragnet 1967-1970
  Emergency!
  O'Hara, U.S. Treasury
  Telefeatures
  Emergency!
  The Log of the Black Pearl
    (producer only)
STARK, WILLIAM (film editor)
  Series
  The Six Million Dollar Man
STEBEL, SIDNEY (writer)
  Telefeature
  Perilous Voyage
STEFANO, JOSEPH (writer)
  Series
  Startime
  Telefeatures
  Aloha Means Goodbye
  Live Again, Die Again
STEFFENSEN, ROY (art director)
  Series
  The Hardy Boys Mysteries
STEIN, JULES CAESAR (president
    and later chairman of the
    board of MCA, Inc. which
    he founded as Music Corpor-
    ation of America in 1924 with
    partner William R. Goodhart,
    Jr.)
STEINBERG, NORMAN (executive
    producer)
  Pilots
  The Bay City Amusement Com-
    pany (and director)
  Roosevelt and Truman (and cre-
    ator/writer)
STEINER, FRED (composer)
  Series
  Hec Ramsey
  Telefeatures
  Family Flight
  Heat Wave
STEINER, MAX (composer)
  Series
  The Virginian
STEINHAUER, ROBERT B. (unit
    production manager)
  Series
  The Incredible Hulk
STEINMAN, JIM (theme composer)
  Series
  Delta House
STELL, AARON (film editor)
  Telefeature
  The Couple Takes a Wife
STENGLER, MACK, A.S.C. (direc-
    tor of photography)
  Series
  Leave It to Beaver
STEPHEN, JOHN MORLEY (direc-
    tor of photography)
  Series
  Alias Smith and Jones
  McCloud
  Telefeatures
  Alias Smith and Jones
  Switch
STEPHEN J. CANNELL PRODUC-
    TIONS (production company)
  Series
  Baa Baa Black Sheep
  Black Sheep Squadron
  The Duke
  Telefeatures
  Dr. Scorpion
  The Night Rider
  Pilots
  Boston and Kilbride
  The Gypsy Warriors

STEPHENS, LARAINE (actress)
Series
Women in White
STEPHENS, ROD (film editor)
Series
79 Park Avenue
STEPHENSON, RON (casting director)
Series
The Incredible Hulk
STERLING, ROBERT (actor)
Series
Ichabod and Me
STERLING, TISHA (actress)
Telefeature
Death Is a Bad Trip
STERN, GEORGE (vice-president of Revue Productions, Inc. in the late 1950s)
STERN, LEONARD B. (executive producer with Talent Associates/Norton Simon, Inc. and later his own company, Heyday Productions)
Series
Faraday and Company (and creator/writer)
Holmes and Yoyo (and director)
Lanigan's Rabbi (and director)
McMillan
McMillan and Wife (and creator)
Operation Petticoat
Rosetti and Ryan
The Snoop Sisters
Telefeatures
Brock's Last Case
Lanigan's Rabbi
Once Upon a Dead Man (and director/writer)
Operation: Petticoat (and writer)
Rosetti and Ryan: Men Who Love Women
The Snoop Sisters (and director/writer)
Pilots
Car Wash
Koska and His Family (and writer)
Snafu (and writer)
Three Times Daley
Special
Funny Business
STERN, SANDY (writer)
Series
The Doctors
STERN, STEPHEN (director)
Series
The Hardy Boys Mysteries
Quincy, M. E.
STERN, STEVE see STERN, STEPHEN
STEVENS, ANDREW (actor)
Series
The Bastard
Beggarman, Thief
Once an Eagle
The Oregon Trail
The Rebels
Telefeature
The Oregon Trail
STEVENS, CRAIG (actor)
Series
The Invisible Man
Telefeatures
The Elevator
McCloud: Who Killed Miss U.S.A. ?
STEVENS, INGER (actress)
Telefeature
The Borgia Stick
STEVENS, LESLIE (producer)
Series
Battlestar: Galactica
Bob Hope Presents the Chrysler Theatre (writer only)
Gemini Man
The Invisible Man (and director)
It Takes a Thief (director/writer only)
McCloud (executive producer only)
The Men from Shiloh (executive producer/writer only)
The Name of the Game (and writer)
Telefeatures
The Aquarians (writer only)
Gemini Man (writer only)
I Love a Mystery (director/writer only)
It Takes a Thief (director/writer only)
McCloud: Who Killed Miss U.S.A. ?
Stonestreet: Who Killed the Centerfold Model? (and writer)
STEVENS, MORTON (composer)
Series
87th Precinct
Tales of Wells Fargo
Wheels
Telefeature
Mandrake

STEVENS, ROBERT (director)
Series
Alfred Hitchcock Presents
Bob Hope Presents the Chrysler Theatre
STEVENS, ROD (film editor)
Series
The Rhinemann Exchange
STEVENS, STELLA (actress)
Telefeatures
Charlie Cobb: Nice Night for a Hanging
The Jordan Chance
Linda
STEVENSON, PARKER (actor)
Series
The Hardy Boys Mysteries
STEWART, DOUGLAS (film editor)
Series
The Alfred Hitchcock Hour
The Psychiatrist (director only)
Rich Man, Poor Man
The Senator
Telefeatures
Companions in Nightmare
A Cry for Help
Ellery Queen
The Greatest Gift
How I Spent My Summer Vacation
Man on the Outside
Marriage: Year One
One of Our Own
Ritual of Evil
Runaway!
The Smugglers
Trial Run
The Victim
Special
The Cay
STEWART, RANDY (actor)
Series
Biff Baker, U.S.A.
STOCKWELL, DEAN (actor)
Telefeatures
The Adventures of Nick Carter
The Failing of Raymond
STOCKWELL, GUY (actor)
Telefeature
The Sound of Anger
STONE, EZRA (director)
Series
The Munsters
Tammy
STONE, JOE (writer)
Telefeature
Operation: Petticoat

STONE, JOSEPH J. (set decorator)
Series
Alias Smith and Jones
BJ and the Bear
Columbo
McCloud
The Name of the Game
PAris 7000
Rich Man, Poor Man
San Francisco International Airport
Telefeatures
Bridger
Night Gallery
STORCH, LARRY (actor)
Telefeature
The Couple Takes a Wife
STORDAHL, AXEL (composer)
Series
McHale's Navy
Westinghouse Playhouse Starring Nanette Fabray and Wendell Corey
STO-REV CO. (production company)
Series
McHale's Navy
STOTTER, MICHAEL (associate producer)
Series
Delta House
STRAND, ROBERT (sound mixer)
Series
Alias Smith and Jones
STRANGIS, SAM (producer)
Series
The Six Million Dollar Man
Telefeature
Aloha Means Goodbye
STRASBERG, SUSAN (actress)
Series
Beggarman, Thief
The Immigrants
Toma
Telefeatures
Hauser's Memory
Marcus Welby, M.D.
Toma
STRATTON, W. K. (actor)
Series
Baa Baa Black Sheep
Black Sheep Squadron
STRAUMER, E. CHARLES (director of photography)
Series
The Name of the Game
Telefeatures
The Other Man
The Whole World Is Watching

STRAUSS, PETER (actor)
  Series
  Rich Man, Poor Man
  Rich Man, Poor Man--Book II
STRENGE, WALTER, A.S.C.
  (director of photography)
  Series
  Marcus Welby, M.D.
  Owen Marshall, Counselor at Law
  Wagon Train
  Telefeatures
  All My Darling Daughters
  The Chadwick Family
  Dragnet 1966
  My Darling Daughters' Anniversary
  Owen Marshall, Counselor at Law
  You'll Never See Me Again
STRICKLAND, GAIL (actress)
  Telefeature
  Ellery Queen
STRIMPELL, STEPHEN (actor)
  Series
  Mr. Terrific
STROMBERG, HUNT, JR. (producer)
  Telefeature
  Frankenstein: The True Story
STRONG, LARRY (film editor)
  Telefeatures
  Love Is Not Enough
  Scream, Pretty Peggy
STROUD, DON (actor)
  Series
  Mrs. Columbo
  Telefeatures
  The D.A.: Conspiracy to Kill
  The Deadly Dream
  The Elevator
  The Nightmare Step
  Something for a Lonely Man
STROUSE, CHARLES (composer/lyricist)
  Special
  Applause
STRUTHERS, SALLY (actress)
  Telefeature
  Aloha Means Goodbye
STUART, WILLIAM L. (writer)
  Telefeature
  You Lie So Deep, My Love
STUBBS, JACK (unit manager)
  Series
  Sons and Daughters

STURGEON, THEODORE (writer)
  Telefeature
  Killdozer
STURGES, MICHAEL (1st assistant director)
  Series
  The Misadventures of Sheriff Lobo
STURTEVANT, JOHN (set decorator)
  Series
  Adam-12
  Dragnet 1967-1970
  Telefeature
  The Couple Takes a Wife
STYLER, BURT (writer)
  Series
  Alfred Hitchcock Presents
SUESS, MAURIE M. (unit manager)
  Series
  Columbo
SULLIVAN, BARRY (actor)
  Series
  The Bastard
  The Immigrants
  Rich Man, Poor Man--Book II
  The Road West
  The Tall Man
  Telefeatures
  Night Gallery
  Savage
SULLIVAN, DON (set decorator)
  Series
  McMillan and Wife
  Telefeature
  The Screaming Woman
SULLIVAN, SUSAN (actress)
  Telefeature
  The Incredible Hulk
SULTAN, ARNE (executive producer with Heyday Productions)
  Series
  Holmes and Yoyo (producer only)
  The Partners (and writer)
  Pilot
  Car Wash
SUMAGALLI, FRANCO (art director)
  Series
  The Name of the Game
SUTHERLAND, DONALD (actor)
  Telefeature
  The Sunshine Patriot
SVENSON, BO (actor)
  Telefeatures
  The Bravos

Hitched
Target Risk
You'll Never See Me Again
SWACKHAMER, E. W. (director)
  Series
  The Nancy Drew Mysteries
  Once an Eagle
  Quincy, M. E.
  Switch
SWAIN, JACK (director of photography)
  Telefeature
  Force Five
SWANSON, MARY (set decorator)
  Series
  Switch
SWANTON, HAROLD (writer)
  Series
  General Electric Theatre
  The Wide Country
SWEET, DOLPH (actor)
  Series
  When the Whistle Blows
SWEET, KEN (sound effects editor)
  Series
  Quincy, M. E.
SWERLING, JO, JR. (producer with Roy Huggins-Public Arts Productions)
  Series
  Alias Smith and Jones (associate executive producer only)
  Aspen
  Baretta (executive producer only)
  Captains and the Kings
  City of Angels (executive producer only)
  Cool Million
  87th Precinct (coordinator only)
  Kraft Suspense Theatre (associate producer only)
  The Lawyers
  Run for Your Life
  Toma (associate executive producer only)
  Telefeatures
  Do You Take This Stranger
  Drive Hard, Drive Fast
  How to Steal an Airplane
  The Invasion of Johnson County (executive producer only)
  The Jordan Chance
  The Lonely Profession
  The Rockford Files (executive producer only)
  Sam Hill: Who Killed the Mysterious Mr. Foster?
  The Story of Pretty Boy Floyd
  Target Risk (executive producer only)
  This Is the West That Was
  The 3,000 Mile Chase
  Toma
  The Whole World Is Watching
  Pilot
  Hazard's People (executive producer only)
SWIFT, LELA (director)
  Special
  My Secret Mother
SYLOS, RALPH (set decorator)
  Series
  Leave It to Beaver
  Tales of Wells Fargo
  Wagon Train
  Telefeature
  The Sunshine Patriot
SYLVESTER, WILLIAM (actor)
  Series
  Little Women
SZWARC, JEANNOT (director)
  Series
  Ironside (associate producer only)
  The Six Million Dollar Man
  Toma
  Telefeatures
  Crime Club
  You'll Never See Me Again
  Pilot
  Hazard's People

TABORI, KRISTOFFER (actor)
  Series
  Black Beauty
  Seventh Avenue
  Telefeatures
  Brave New World
  Family Flight
TAIT, ABE (writer)
  Series
  The Virginian
TALBOT, NITA (actress)
  Telefeatures
  The Movie Murderer
  The Rockford Files
  Sex and the Married Woman
TALENT ASSOCIATES-NORTON SIMON, INC. (production company founded by David Susskind which merged with

the Norton Simon Corporation
--its principal TV producer
was Leonard B. Stern)
Series
Faraday and Company
McMillan
McMillan and Wife
The Snoop Sisters
Telefeatures
Brock's Last Case
Once Upon a Dead Man
The Snoop Sisters
TALLMAN, FRANK (aerial photography director)
Telefeatures
Amelia Earhart
Family Flight
TALLMANTZ AVIATION (aerial photography company)
Telefeature
Family Flight
TAMM, DANIEL (actor)
Series
Black Beauty
TANCHUCK, NATHANIEL (writer)
Series
The Doctors
TAPER, BERNARD (actor)
Telefeature
The Movie Murderer
TAPP, WILLIAM (set decorator)
Series
The Deputy
TARLOFF, ERIK (writer)
Series
House Calls
TARTAGLIA, JOHN ANDREW (composer)
Series
Alias Smith and Jones
Sword of Justice
Telefeature
The Adventures of Nick Carter
TAYBACK, VIC (actor)
Series
Griff
Telefeatures
The Alpha Caper
Dark Victory
Partners in Crime
TAYLOR, DON (director)
Series
Mobile One
Telefeatures
The Manhunter
Something for a Lonely Man
TAYLOR, JERRY (film editor)
Telefeature

Killing Stone
TAYLOR, JUDD (director)
Series
Sara
TAYLOR, RAY (unit manager)
Series
Aspen
Columbo (and assistant director)
TAYLOR, ROD (actor)
Series
The Oregon Trail
Telefeatures
Family Flight
The Oregon Trail
TAYLOR, SAMUEL (writer)
Series
General Electric Theatre
TECHNICOLOR (color film processing laboratory which has been Universal Television's exclusive lab since the late 1960s)
TEKTRONIX (supplier of test and display equipment to the series "Battlestar: Galactica")
TELFORD, FRANK (producer)
Series
Destry
Gemini Man
Kraft Suspense Theatre
Owen Marshall: Counselor at Law (writer only)
The Wide Country
TERRELL, DEAN (video engineer)
Telefeature
Night Life
Special
A Special Act of Love
TERRILL, HOWARD see TERRILL, J. HOWARD
TERRILL, J. HOWARD (film editor)
Series
Emergency!
Telefeatures
The Desperate Miles
The Intruders
TERRY, JACK (assistant director)
Telefeature
The D.A.: Conspiracy to Kill
TERRY-THOMAS (actor)
Telefeature
I Love a Mystery
TEWKSBURY, PETER (producer/director/writer)
Series
Alcoa Premiere/Premiere
It's a Man's World (and creator)
THACHER, RUSSELL (producer/

writer)
Special
The Cay
THACKERY, BUD, A. S. C. (Ellis F. Thackery) (director of photography)
Series
Emergency!
Ironside
Kraft Suspense Theatre
Tales of Wells Fargo
Whispering Smith
Telefeatures
Bridger
How I Spent My Summer Vacation
Lieutenant Schuster's Wife
The Outsider
Perilous Voyage
Runaway!
Stranger on the Run
Winchester 73
Wings of Fire
THACKERY, ELLIS F. see THACKERY, BUD
THACKERY, FRANK (director of photography)
Series
Battlestar: Galactica
The Immigrants
The Rebels
Telefeatures
Operation: Petticoat
Pine Canyon Is Burning
Pilot
The Two-Five
THAXTER, PHYLLIS (actress)
Telefeature
The Longest Night
THINNES, ROY (actor)
Series
The Psychiatrist
Telefeatures
Death Race
The Manhunter
The Other Man
The Psychiatrist: God Bless the Children
THOMAS, DANNY (executive producer)
Series
Fay
Special
The Jack Benny Special (actor only)
THOMAS, LOWELL (actor)
Telefeature
Amelia Earhart

THOMAS, MARLO (actress/producer)
Telefeature
It Happened One Christmas
THOMAS, SCOTT (actor)
Telefeature
Crime Club
THOMAS, TONY (producer/associate producer)
Series
Fay
THOMERSON, TIMOTHY (actor)
Telefeature
Benny and Barney: Las Vegas Undercover
THOMPSON, CHARLES S. (set decorator)
Series
The Name of the Game
The Psychiatrist
Telefeatures
The Failing of Raymond
Sarge: The Badge or the Cross
THOMPSON, ERNEST (actor)
Series
Sierra
THOMPSON, PETER J. (executive producer)
Series
Quincy, M. E.
THOMPSON, ROBERT C. (producer)
Telefeature
Lanigan's Rabbi
THOMPSON, ROBERT E. (writer)
Series
Jigsaw (creator only)
The Name of the Game
Run for Your Life
Telefeatures
Brave New World
A Case of Rape
Deadlock!
The Hound of the Baskervilles
Jigsaw
THOR, JEROME (actor)
Telefeature
O'Hara, United States Treasury
THORPE, JERRY (director)
Telefeatures
Dial: Hot Line
Lock, Stock and Barrel
THRONE, MALACHI (actor)
Series
It Takes a Thief
Telefeatures
The Doomsday Flight
It Takes a Thief
TIBBLES, GEORGE (writer)

Series
Tammy
TIGHE, KEVIN (actor)
Series
Emergency!
Emergency Plus Four (voice only)
The Rebels
Telefeature
Emergency!
TIPTON, GEORGE ALICESON (theme composer)
Series
Fay
TISDALE, JIM (writer)
Series
The Incredible Hulk
TOKAR, NORMAN (director)
Series
Leave It to Beaver
TOKATYAN, LEON (writer)
Telefeature
The Harness
TOLKIN, MICHAEL (story editor)
Series
Delta House
TOLKIN, STEPHEN (story editor)
Series
Delta House
TOMA, DAVID (production consultant)
Series
Toma
TOMS, DON (production manager)
Telefeatures
Destiny of a Spy
Run a Crooked Mile
TONE, FRANCHOT (actor)
Telefeatures
See How They Run
Shadow Over Elveron
TONG, SAMMEE (actor)
Series
Bachelor Father
TOP GUN PRODUCTIONS (production company)
Series
The Deputy
TORDJMANN, FABIEN (film editor)
Series
Griff
Telefeature
Killdozer
TORRES, GABRIEL (director of photography)
Telefeature
The Log of the Black Pearl

TORS, IVAN (producer/writer and head of Ivan Tors Productions)
Telefeature
The Aquarians
TOSI, MARIO (director of photography)
Telefeatures
Man on the Outside
The Marcus-Nelson Murders
TOTTEN, ROBERT (director/writer)
Special
The Red Pony
TOTTER, AUDREY (actress)
Series
Cimarron City
Telefeature
The Outsider
TOWNES, HARRY (actor)
Telefeature
The Specialists
TOZZI, GIORGIO (actor)
Series
Captains and the Kings
Telefeature
One of Our Own
TRA-NAN PRODUCTIONS (production company)
Special
The Slowest Gun in the West
TRENT, WILLIAM (sound editor)
Telefeature
Run a Crooked Mile
TREVEY, KEN (writer)
Telefeature
McNaughton's Daughter
TRICKER, GEORGE (producer/writer)
Pilot
Off the Wall
TROUP, BOBBY (actor)
Series
Emergency!
The Rebels
Telefeatures
Dragnet 1966
Emergency!
TRUEBLOOD, GUERDON (writer associated with producer R. A. Cinader)
Series
Adam-12
The Bastard
Telefeature
Family Flight
TRUMBO, CHRISTOPHER (writer)
Series
Ironside
TRUMPER, JOHN (film editor)

Telefeature
Mousey
TRYON, TOM (actor)
Telefeature
Winchester 73
TUCH, FRED T. (art director)
Series
Galactica 1980
TUCKER, FORREST (actor)
Series
Black Beauty
Once an Eagle
The Rebels
Telefeature
Alias Smith and Jones
TUCKER, TANYA (actress)
Series
The Rebels
Telefeature
Amateur Night at the Dixie Bar and Grill
TULLY, TOM (actor)
Telefeature
Any Second Now
TUNTKE, WILLIAM H. (art Director)
Series
The Eddie Capra Mysteries
Griff
Kojak
The Rhinemann Exchange
The Sixth Sense
Testimony of Two Men
Wheels
Telefeatures
Amelia Earhart
Dark Victory
Dr. Strange
Sunshine Christmas
A Very Missing Person
TURLEY, JACK (writer)
Series
Tales of Wells Fargo
TURNER, ARNOLD F. (associate producer)
Series
The Six Million Dollar Man
Telefeature
The Alpha Caper
TURNER, LANA (actress)
Series
Harold Robbins' "The Survivors"
TURNER, LLOYD (executive story consultant)
Series
The Misadventures of Sheriff Lobo
TYLER, WALTER (art director)

Telefeature
The Execution of Private Slovik
TYSON, CICELY (actress)
Telefeature
Marriage: Year One

UDOFF, YALE M. (writer)
Series
Harold Robbins' "The Survivors"
Telefeature
Hitchhike!
UGGAMS, LESLIE (vocalist)
Series
Sing Along with Mitch
ULLMAN, DAN (associate producer)
Series
Jigsaw (writer only)
Laramie
UNI-BET PRODUCTIONS (production company)
Series
Tammy
UNIVERSAL HARTLAND (miniatures and special effects photography company owned by Universal Studios)
Series
Galactica 1980
UNIVERSAL TITLE (Universal Studios' in-house title and optical effects photography company)
UNSON, DALE (writer with partner Katherine Unson)
Series
Leave It to Beaver
UNSON, KATHERINE (writer with partner Dale Unson)
Series
Leave It to Beaver
URECAL, MINERVA (actress)
Series
Meet Mr. McNulty
URICH, ROBERT (actor)
Telefeatures
Killdozer
The Specialists

VACCARO, BRENDA (actress)
Series
Sara
Telefeatures
The Big Ripoff
Sunshine
What's a Nice Girl Like You...?

VALENTINO, JEAN (sound
    mixer)
  Series
  Switch
VALLARIO, LAWRENCE J.
    (film editor)
  Series
  Aspen
  Captains and the Kings
  Telefeature
  The 3,000 Mile Chase
VAN ARK, JOAN (actress)
  Series
  Testimony of Two Men
  Telefeature
  The Judge and Jake Wyler
VANCE, LEIGH (executive pro-
    ducer)
  Series
  Baretta
  Switch (producer only)
VAN CLEEF, LEE (actor)
  Special
  The Slowest Gun in the West
VAN DYKE, BARRY (actor)
  Series
  Galactica 1980
VAN PATTEN, DICK (actor)
  Series
  The Partners
VAN PATTEN, JOYCE (actress)
  Telefeatures
  The Book of Murder
  Let's Switch
VAN PATTEN, VINCENT (actor)
  Telefeatures
  The Bravos
  Dial: Hot Line
VAN RUNKLE, THEADORA
    (costume designer)
  Special
  The Woman I Love
VAN SCOYK, ROBERT (writer)
  Series
  Banacek (and story consultant)
  The Doctors
  Ellery Queen (story editor
    only)
  Hernandez: Houston P.D.
  The Virginian (and associate
    producer)
  Telefeatures
  Night Life
  The Priest Killer
  Pilot
  If I Had a Million
VARELA, MIGDIA (writer)
  Series

  The Incredible Hulk
VAUGHN, JUANITA (writer)
  Series
  Going My Way
VAUGHN, ROBERT (actor)
  Series
  Captains and the Kings
  Centennial
  The Rebels
  Telefeature
  The Islander
  Special
  The Man from Independence
VERNON, JOHN R. (actor)
  Series
  Delta House
VERTUE, BERYL (executive pro-
    ducer)
  Telefeature
  Mousey
VICTOR, DAVID (executive pro-
    ducer and head of Groverton
    Productions, Ltd.)
  Series
  Griff
  Kingston: Confidential
  Little Women
  Lucas Tanner
  The Man and the City
  Marcus Welby, M.D. (and cre-
    ator)
  McNaughton's Daughter
  The Name of the Game (producer
    only)
  Owen Marshall, Counselor at
    Law (and creator/writer)
  Women in White
  Telefeatures
  All My Darling Daughters
  The Bravos
  The Chadwick Family (and writ-
    er)
  Double Indemnity
  The Family Nobody Wanted
  Indict and Convict
  Kingston: The Power Play (and
    writer)
  Little Women
  Live Again, Die Again
  Lucas Tanner
  Man on the Outside
  Marcus Welby, M.D. (and writ-
    er)
  McNaughton's Daughter (and
    writer)
  My Darling Daughters' Anniver-
    sary
  Owen Marshall, Counselor at

Law (and writer)
Vanished
Pilot
Stranded (and writer)
Specials
Legend in Granite
The Man from Independence
A Man Whose Name Was John
The Woman I Love
VIGODA, ABE (actor)
Telefeatures
The Story of Pretty Boy Floyd
Toma
VILLAR, ROBERT (2nd assistant director)
Series
Mrs. Columbo
Quincy, M.E.
VILS, OPAL (costume designer)
Series
The Rebels
VINCENT, JAN-MICHAEL (actor)
Series
Harold Robbins' "The Survivors"
VINCENT EDWARDS PRODUCTIONS, INC. (production company)
Series
Matt Lincoln
VISUAL COMPUTING CORPORATION (main title designers)
Series
Rod Serling's Night Gallery
VITALE, CARL (producer)
Series
Adam-12 (associate producer only)
The Oregon Trail
VLAHOS, JOHN (writer)
Telefeature
Silent Night, Lonely Night
VOGEL, VIRGIL W. (director)
Series
Centennial
The Overland Trail
Wagon Train
VOIGTLANDER, TED (director of photography)
Telefeatures
Amelia Earhart
Killing Stone
VON GLYTTOV, BRIENNE (costume designer)
Series
The Hardy Boys Mysteries
The Incredible Hulk
Mrs. Columbo

VON ZELL, HARRY (actor)
Telefeature
Ellery Queen
VON ZERNECK, FRANK (producer)
Telefeature
The Desperate Miles
VOWELL, DAVID H. (story editor)
Series
Adam-12
VREELAND, RUSSELL (unit manager)
Series
Switch

WADE, HARKER (unit production manager)
Series
Battlestar: Galactica
Buck Rogers in the 25th Century
McCloud
Telefeatures
Dial: Hot Line (assistant director only)
Silent Night, Lonely Night (assistant director only)
WADSWORTH, JACK B. (music supervisor)
Series
Leave It to Beaver
WAGNER, LINDSAY (actress)
Series
The Bionic Woman
Telefeature
The Rockford Files
WAGNER, ROBERT (actor)
Series
Colditz
It Takes a Thief
Switch
Telefeatures
Escape from Colditz
How I Spent My Summer Vacation
It Takes a Thief
Switch
WAHRMAN, DICK R. (sound effects editor)
Series
Battlestar: Galactica
Buck Rogers in the 25th Century
Galactica 1980
WAINWRIGHT, JAMES (actor)
Series
Jigsaw
Telefeatures
Bridger
Jigsaw

Index / 433

Killdozer
  Once Upon a Dead Man
WAITE, RALPH (actor)
  Telefeature
  The Borgia Stick
WAITE, RIC (director of photography)
  Series
  Captains and the Kings
  Telefeatures
  Amateur Night at the Dixie Bar and Grill
  Tail Gunner Joe
WALBERG, GARY (actor)
  Series
  Quincy, M. E.
  Telefeature
  Man on the Outside
WALDEN, ROBERT (actor)
  Series
  Centennial
  The Doctors
  Telefeature
  The Marcus-Nelson Murders
WALDEN, SUSAN (actress)
  Series
  Little Women
WALDO, CHARLES (costume designer)
  Series
  Aspen
  The Doctors
  The Eddie Capra Mysteries
  The Lawyers
  Rich Man, Poor Man
  The Rockford Files
  Telefeatures
  All My Darling Daughters
  Brock's Last Case
  The Lonely Profession
  My Sweet Charlie
  Silent Night, Lonely Night
  Vanished
WALKER, CLINT (actor)
  Series
  Centennial
  Telefeature
  Killdozer
WALKER, DAVID (assistant to the producer)
  Special
  Hamlet
WALKER, NANCY (actress)
  Series
  McMillan and Wife
WALLACE, ART (writer)
  Special
  Alone with Terror

WALLACE, TREVOR (writer)
  Telefeatures
  Run a Crooked Mile
  Tom Sawyer (producer only)
WALLACH, ELI (actor)
  Series
  Seventh Avenue
  Telefeature
  Indict and Convict
WALLDER, GEORGE (graphic designer)
  Special
  Hamlet
WALOWITZ, MARVIN (sound effects editor)
  Series
  Baretta
WALSTON, RAY (actor)
  Series
  Cliffhangers
WALTER, JESSICA (actress)
  Series
  Amy Prentiss
  Wheels
  Telefeature
  Dr. Strange
WALTERS, JAMES M. (SR.) (set decorator)
  Series
  Tales of Wells Fargo
  The Virginian
  Telefeatures
  Any Second Now
  A Little Game
  The Lonely Profession
  Winchester 73
WALTERS, JAMES M., JR. (unit production manager)
  Series
  Emergency!
  It Takes a Thief
  The Psychiatrist
  The Senator
WALTERS, JIMMY see WALTERS, JAMES M., JR.
WARD, JIM (special effects creator)
  Special
  The Snow Goose
WARD, JOHN (director)
  Series
  Baretta
WARDEN, JACK (actor)
  Telefeatures
  Lieutenant Schuster's Wife
  What's a Nice Girl Like You...?
WARE, CLYDE (director/writer)

Telefeature
The Story of Pretty Boy Floyd
WARNER, KENT (costume designer)
Series
Delta House
The Rockford Files
WARREN, CHARLES MARQUIS (producer)
Series
The Virginian
WARREN, HARRY (theme composer)
Series
Tales of Wells Fargo
WARREN, JACK see WARREN, JOHN F.
WARREN, JOHN F., A.S.C. (director of photography)
Series
Alcoa Premiere/Premiere
Going My Way
Startime
Telefeatures
Fame Is the Name of the Game
The Great Man's Whiskers
Ironside
The Smugglers
WARREN, LESLEY ANN (actress)
Series
79 Park Avenue
WASSERMAN, LEW R. (became president of MCA in 1946 and was later appointed chairman of the board of MCA, Inc.)
WATERS, ED (supervising producer)
Series
Baretta
The Sixth Sense (story editor only)
WATSON, DEBBIE (actress)
Series
Karen
Tammy
WATSON, MILLS (actor)
Series
The Misadventures of Sheriff Lobo
Telefeatures
BJ and the Bear
The Story of Pretty Boy Floyd
WATTS, RICHARD (film editor)
Telefeature
McNaughton's Daughter
WATTS, ROBERT, A.C.E. (film editor)
Series
Banacek
Centennial
Marcus Welby, M.D.
The Name of the Game
Run for Your Life
Telefeatures
Banacek
The City
The Dark Secret of Harvest Home
The Lonely Profession
Sex and the Married Woman
Vanished
The Young Country
WATTS, ROY (associate producer)
Series
BJ and the Bear
WAXMAN, FRANZ (composer)
Telefeature
The Longest Hundred Miles
WAXMAN, SAM E., A.C.E. (film editor)
Series
Adam-12
The Bob Cummings Show
Broadside
The D.A.
Madigan
Marcus Welby, M.D.
McHale's Navy
Telefeatures
Ellery Queen: Don't Look Behind You
My Darling Daughters' Anniversary
Short Walk to Daylight
WAYNE, DAVID (actor)
Series
Black Beauty
Ellery Queen
House Calls
Loose Change
Once an Eagle
Telefeature
Ellery Queen
WAYNE, JOHNNY (actor with partner Frank Shuster)
Series
Holiday Lodge
Wayne and Shuster Take an Affectionate Look at... (host only)
WEATHERLY, JIM (theme composer)
Telefeature
Just a Little Inconvenience

WEAVER, DENNIS (actor)
　Series
　　Centennial
　　McCloud
　　Telefeatures
　　　Duel
　　　Female Artillery
　　　The Great Man's Whiskers
　　　The Islander
　　　McCloud: Who Killed Miss
　　　　U.S.A. ?
WEAVER, FRITZ (actor)
　Telefeatures
　　Berlin Affair
　　The Book of Murder
　　The Snoop Sisters
WEBB, DON (set decorator)
　Series
　　Sons and Daughters
WEBB, GEORGE (art director)
　Series
　　Banacek
　　McCloud
　Telefeatures
　　Alias Smith and Jones
　　The Astronaut
　　Banacek
　　Beg, Borrow ... or Steal
　　A Case of Rape
　　The D.A.: Murder One
　　Dial: Hot Line
　　Ellery Queen
　　The Great Man's Whiskers
　　Linda
　　Live Again, Die Again
　　Sunshine
　　Trapped
　Special
　　The Man from Independence
WEBB, JACK (executive producer and head of Mark VII Limited)
　Series
　　Adam-12 (and creator/director/writer)
　　The D.A.
　　Dragnet 1967-1970 (and actor/producer/creator/director)
　　Emergency!
　　Escape (narrator only)
　　Hec Ramsey
　　Mobile One
　　O'Hara, U.S. Treasury (and creator)
　Telefeatures
　　Chase (producer/director only)
　　Dragnet 1966 (actor/producer/director only)
　　Emergency! (and director)
　　The Log of the Black Pearl
　　Mobile Two
　　O'Hara, United States Treasury (and director)
　　The Rangers
WEBB, TRACY (production assistant)
　Series
　　Adam-12
WEBBER, ROBERT (actor)
　Series
　　79 Park Avenue
　Telefeatures
　　Cutter
　　Double Indemnity
　　Hauser's Memory
　　The Movie Murderer
WEBSTER, NORMAN (sound mixer)
　Series
　　The Rebels
WEINER, CELIA L. (music editor)
　Series
　　The Incredible Hulk
WEINGART, MARK (writer)
　Series
　　Going My Way
　　Heat Wave
WEINGARTEN, ARTHUR (writer)
　Series
　　The Six Million Dollar Man
WEIS, DON (director)
　Series
　　Alfred Hitchcock Presents
　　The Bob Cummings Show
　　Harold Robbins' "The Survivors"
　　Ironside
　　It Takes a Thief
　　Kingston: Confidential
　　The Night Stalker
　Telefeatures
　　The Longest Hundred Miles
　　Now You See It, Now You Don't
WELLES, ORSON (actor)
　Telefeature
　　It Happened One Christmas
　Special
　　The Man Who Came to Dinner
WENDKOS, PAUL (director)
　Series
　　79 Park Avenue (and producer)
　Telefeatures
　　Fear No Evil
　　A Little Game
　Special
　　The Woman I Love
WENDLEY, RICHARD (writer)
　Series

436 / Index

The Virginian
WESSON, DICK (producer)
  Series
  The John Forsythe Show (and director)
  Tammy
WEST, ELLIOT (writer)
  Telefeature
  Berlin Affair
WEST, JESSAMYN (writer)
  Series
  General Electric Theatre
WEST, RED (actor)
  Series
  Baa Baa Black Sheep
  Black Sheep Squadron
  The Duke
WESTMAN, JAMES A. (assistant director)
  Series
  McCloud
  Telefeature
  Drive Hard, Drive Fast
WESTMORE, BUD (makeup artist)
  Series
  Adam-12
  The Doctors
  Dragnet 1967-1970
  Ironside
  The John Forsythe Show
  The Lawyers
  McCloud
  The Men from Shiloh
  The Name of the Game
  The Psychiatrist
  Rod Serling's Night Gallery
  San Francisco International Airport
  The Virginian
  Telefeatures
  Any Second Now
  A Clear and Present Danger
  Companions in Nightmare
  The D.A.: Conspiracy to Kill
  The Doomsday Flight
  Dragnet 1966
  How I Spent My Summer Vacation
  Istanbul Express
  The Lonely Profession
  McCloud: Who Killed Miss U.S.A.?
  The Movie Murderer
  My Sweet Charlie
  Night Gallery
  Now You See It, Now You Don't

The Outsider
Prescription: Murder
Ritual of Evil
Shadow Over Elveron
Silent Night, Lonely Night
The Smugglers
Something for a Lonely Man
The Sound of Anger
Stranger on the Run
The Sunshine Patriot
Trial Run
Vanished
Winchester 73
Wings of Fire
WESTWARD PRODUCTIONS (production company)
  Telefeature
  Magic Carpet
WEVERKA, ROBERT (writer)
  Telefeature
  Perilous Voyage
WHEELER, HUGH (writer)
  Telefeature
  The Snoop Sisters
WHISPERING SMITH COMPANY, THE (production company)
  Series
  Whispering Smith
WHITE, BETTY (actress)
  Telefeature
  Vanished
WHITE, JOAN (hair stylist)
  Telefeature
  Destiny of a Spy
WHITE, PHYLLIS (writer with partner Robert White)
  Series
  The Doctors
  The Name of the Game
WHITE, ROBERT (writer with partner Phyllis White)
  Series
  The Doctors
  The Name of the Game
WHITE, ROY (technical director)
  Telefeatures
  The Nightmare Step
  A Prowler in the Heart
  The Suicide Club
WHITING, LEONARD (actor)
  Telefeature
  Frankenstein: The True Story
WHITLOCK, ALBERT J. (special photographic effects creator)
  Series
  McMillan and Wife
  Telefeatures
  The Hound of the Baskervilles

Index / 437

Killdozer
The Questor Tapes
Short Walk to Daylight
Vanished
WHITMORE, HUGH (writer)
  Special
  The Adventures of Don Quixote
WHITMORE, JAMES, JR. (actor)
  Series
  Baa Baa Black Sheep
  Black Sheep Squadron
  Pilots
  Boston and Kilbride
  The Gypsy Warriors
WHITMORE, STANFORD (writer)
  Telefeatures
  The D.A.: Conspiracy to Kill
  Destiny of a Spy
  McCloud: Who Killed Miss U.S.A.?
  The Movie Murderer
WHITTAKER, GEORGE R. (costume designer)
  Series
  The Hardy Boys Mysteries
  Switch
WIARD, WILLIAM (director)
  Series
  The Eddie Capra Mysteries
  The Rockford Files
  Sara
  Telefeature
  Scott Free
WICKES, MARY (actress)
  Special
  The Man Who Came to Dinner
WIDMARK, RICHARD (actor)
  Series
  Madigan
  Telefeatures
  Brock's Last Case
  Vanished
WILDER, JOHN (executive producer and head of John Wilder Productions)
  Series
  The Bastard
  Centennial (and writer)
  Harold Robbins' "The Survivors" (writer only)
  PAris 7000 (producer/writer only)
WILDER, MILES (writer)
  Series
  McHale's Navy
WILDER, YVONNE (actress)
  Series
  Operation Petticoat
WILKINSON, FRANK H. (sound mixer)
  Series
  The Doctors
  Owen Marshall, Counselor at Law
  Telefeatures
  The Intruders
  The Outsider
WILLENS, SHEL (writer)
  Series
  The Duke
WILLIAMS, ANDY CHUBBY (writer)
  Telefeature
  Let's Switch
WILLIAMS, BILL (actor)
  Series
  The Adventures of Kit Carson
WILLIAMS, EDWARD W., A.C.E. (film editor)
  Series
  The Alfred Hitchcock Hour
  Alfred Hitchcock Presents
  The Immigrants
  Startime
  Switch
  Telefeatures
  Fame Is the Name of the Game
  Ironside
  Mandrake
  Now You See It, Now You Don't
  The Snoop Sisters
WILLIAMS, J. JERRY (film editor)
  Telefeatures
  The Elevator
  Heat Wave
  The Questor Tapes
  Special
  The Man from Independence
WILLIAMS, JERRY see WILLIAMS, J. JERRY
WILLIAMS, JOHN(NY) (composer)
  Series
  Alcoa Premiere/Premiere
  Bachelor Father
  Checkmate
  Kraft Suspense Threatre (theme only)
  Tales of Wells Fargo
  Telefeature
  The Screaming Woman
WILLIAMS, KENNETH J. (director of photography)
  Series
  The Six Million Dollar Man
WILLIAMS, KENNY (assistant

director)
Series
Columbo (unit manager only)
PAris 7000
Telefeatures
Do You Take This Stranger
Fear No Evil
WILLIAMS, PAT(RICK) (composer)
Telefeatures
The Failing of Raymond
Hitched
Lock, Stock and Barrel
The Man with the Power
San Francisco International Airport
Short Walk to Daylight
Stonestreet: Who Killed the Centerfold Model?
WILLIAMS, TOM (producer/associate producer/assistant to the producer with Mark VII Limited)
Series
Adam-12
WILLINGHAM, WILLARD (producer)
Series
Whispering Smith
WILLS, CHILL (actor)
Series
Frontier Circus
WILSON, ANTHONY (writer)
Series
Banacek (creator only)
Telefeature
Banacek
WILSON, DAVID (lyricist)
Telefeature
The Harness
WILSON, DON (actor/announcer)
Series
The Jack Benny Show
WILSON, EDMUND (composer)
Series
The Crusader
WILSON, STANLEY (music supervisor)
Series
Adam-12
Alcoa Premiere/Premiere
The Alfred Hitchcock Hour
Alfred Hitchcock Presents (composer only)
Bachelor Father
Broadside
Buckskin (composer only)
Checkmate
The Deputy

Destry
The Doctors
Dragnet 1967-1970
Frontier Circus
It Takes a Thief
The John Forsythe Show
Johnny Midnight
Johnny Staccato
Laramie
Laredo
M Squad
Markham
McHale's Navy
The Munsters
The Name of the Game
The Outsider
PAris 7000
Pistols 'n' Petticoats
The Protectors
The Restless Gun
Rich Man, Poor Man--Book II
The Road West
Run for Your Life
Startime
State Trooper
Tales of Wells Fargo
Tammy
The Virginian
Wagon Train
Westinghouse Playhouse Starring Nanette Fabray and Wendell Corey
Whispering Smith (composer only)
The Wide Country
Telefeatures
Deadlock! (composer only)
Istanbul Express
McCloud: Who Killed Miss U.S.A.?
The Movie Murderer
Now You See It, Now You Don't
The Other Man (composer only)
The Outsider
Stranger on the Run
The Sunshine Patriot (composer only)
Trial Run (composer only)
WILSON, TERRY (associate producer)
Series
The Oregon Trail
WINANT, ETHEL (associate producer)
Series
General Electric Theatre
WINCELBERG, SHIMON (writer)
Series

Hec Ramsey
WINDOM, WILLIAM (actor)
Series
Seventh Avenue
Telefeatures
Bridger
Guilty or Innocent: The Sam
  Sheppard Murder Case
Marriage: Year One
Prescription: Murder
Richie Brockelman, Private
  Eye
WINDOW PRODUCTIONS, INC.
  (John Payne's production
  company)
Series
The Restless Gun
WINDUST, BRETAIGNE (director)
Series
Alfred Hitchcock Presents
Startime
WINGO, ROBERT (set decorator)
Series
The Incredible Hulk
WINSTON, ROY (director)
Series
McMillan and Wife
WINTER, GARY B. (associate
  producer)
Series
Battlestar: Galactica
The Misadventures of Sheriff
  Lobo
Wheels
WINTERS, JONATHAN (actor)
Telefeature
Now You See It, Now You
  Don't
WINTERS, SHELLEY (actress)
Telefeature
The Adventures of Nick Carter
WISEMAN, JOSEPH (actor)
Telefeatures
The Outsider
The Suicide Club
Pilot
If I Had a Million
WITT, PAUL JUNGER (producer)
Series
Fay
WITTRIDGE, J. R., A. C. E.
  (film editor)
Series
The Jack Benny Show
WOLF, HARRY L., A. S. C.
  (director of photography)
Series
Baretta

Columbo
Loose Change
Telefeatures
The Devil and Miss Sarah
The Hound of the Baskervilles
Lucas Tanner
The Snoop Sisters
Two on a Bench
What's a Nice Girl Like
  You...?
WOLF, HENRY (director of photog-
  raphy)
Telefeature
A Little Game
WOLFBERG, LEE (producer)
Series
The Partners
WOLFE, WES (sound effects editor)
Series
Delta House
The Rebels
WOLPER, DAVID L. (executive
  producer and head of Wolper
  Productions)
Series
Get Christie Love!
WOLPER PRODUCTIONS (produc-
  tion company)
Series
Get Christie Love!
WOLPERT, ROLAND (writer)
Series
The Protectors (creator only)
Telefeature
Deadlock!
WOLTERSTORFF, ROBERT (story
  editor)
Series
The Misadventures of Sheriff
  Lobo
WOOD, BRICE (main title designer)
Series
The Psychiatrist
WOOD, NATALIE (actress)
Series
Pride of the Family
WOOD, PETER (director)
Special
Hamlet
WOOD, PRESTON (writer primarily
  for Mark VII Limited)
Series
Adam-12
Emergency!
The Senator
Sierra
Telefeatures
The Rangers

The Specialists
WOOD, WILLIAM (writer)
　Series
　　Bob Hope Presents the Chrysler Theatre
　Telefeature
　　You'll Never See Me Again
WOOD, YVONNE (costume designer)
　Series
　　BJ and the Bear
　　The Family Holvak
　　Quincy, M.E.
　Special
　　The Red Pony
WOODCOCK, JOHN M. (film editor)
　Telefeature
　　Lieutenant Schuster's Wife
WOODFIELD, WILLIAM READ (producer/writer)
　Series
　　San Francisco International Airport (creator only)
　Telefeature
　　San Francisco International Airport
WOODS, HERBERT D. (music editor)
　Series
　　Baretta
　　Battlestar: Galactica
　　Buck Rogers in the 25th Century (and composer)
WOODVILLE, KATE (actress)
　Telefeatures
　　Fear No Evil
　　The Marcus-Nelson Murders
WOOLEY, PETER M. (art director)
　Telefeatures
　　Crime Club
　　The UFO Incident
WOOLF, JACK (director of photography)
　Series
　　The Hardy Boys Mysteries
　　Matt Lincoln
　Telefeatures
　　The Desperate Miles
　　The Family Nobody Wanted
　　The Oregon Trail
　　Senior Year
WOOLSEY, RALPH, A.S.C. (director of photography)
　Series
　　It Takes a Thief
　　The Name of the Game

Telefeatures
　　It Takes a Thief
　　The Lonely Profession
WORLEY, JO ANNE (actress)
　Telefeature
　　What's a Nice Girl Like You...?
WORSLEY, WALLACE (unit manager)
　Series
　　Madigan
WRAY, FAY (actress)
　Series
　　Pride of the Family
WRAY, RICHARD G., A.C.E. (film editor)
　Series
　　Arrest and Trial
　　Alfred Hitchcock Presents
　　Bachelor Father
　　The Deputy (editorial supervisor only)
　　The John Forsythe Show
　　Leave It to Beaver (editorial supervisor only)
　　Marcus Welby, M.D.
　　The Name of the Game
　　Startime (editorial supervisor only)
　　Tales of Wells Fargo
　　The Tall Man (editorial supervisor only)
　　Whispering Smith (editorial supervisor only)
　Telefeatures
　　All My Darling Daughters
　　The Chadwick Family
　　Escape to Mindanao
　　Istanbul Express
　　Kingston: The Power Play
　　The Longest Hundred Miles
　　Magic Carpet
　　Prescription: Murder
　　River of Mystery
　　Stranger on the Run
　　Winchester 73
　　You'll Never See Me Again
WRIGHT, BEN (actor)
　Series
　　The Rhinemann Exchange
　Telefeatures
　　Marcus Welby, M.D.
　　My Darling Daughters' Anniversary
WRIGHT, GILBERT (writer)
　Telefeature
　　A Cry in the Wilderness
WRIGHT, HERBERT (writer)

Pilot
If I Had a Million
WRIGHT, THERESA (actress)
Telefeature
The Elevator
WRIGHT, TOM (gallery paintings artist)
Series
Rod Serling's Night Gallery
WRYE, DONALD (director)
Telefeature
It Happened One Christmas
WYATT, JANE (actress)
Telefeatures
Amelia Earhart
See How They Run
Tom Sawyer
You'll Never See Me Again
WYCOFF, ROBERT H. (director of photography)
Series
Tammy
Telefeature
The Rangers
WYLIE, PHILIP (writer)
Series
The Name of the Game
WYMAN, JANE (actress and, with partner Edward Lewis, head of Lewman Limited)
Series
Fireside Theatre/Jane Wyman's Fireside Theatre
The Jane Wyman Theatre
Telefeature
The Failing of Raymond
WYNN, KEENAN (actor)
Series
The Bastard
Telefeatures
Sex and the Married Woman
Target Risk
WYNTER, DANA (actress)
Telefeatures
Any Second Now
Companions in Nightmare
Owen Marshall, Counselor at Law
The Questor Tapes

YARBROUGH, JEAN (director)
Series
Adam-12
YATES, WILLIAM ROBERT (writer)
Series
Harold Robbins' "The Survivors"
YELLEN, SHERMAN (writer)
Telefeature
A Prowler in the Heart
Special
The Mask of Love
YORK, DICK (actor)
Series
Going My Way
YORK, ROBERT see URICH, ROBERT
YOUNG, AIDA (producer)
Telefeature
Mousey
YOUNG, COLLIER (producer)
Series
Ironside (and executive producer/creator)
Telefeature
Ironside (and writer)
YOUNG, DAVID (film editor)
Telefeature
Heat Wave
YOUNG, GIG (actor)
Telefeatures
Companions in Nightmare
The Neon Ceiling
YOUNG, ROBERT (actor)
Series
Little Women
Marcus Welby, M.D.
Telefeatures
All My Darling Daughters
Little Women
Marcus Welby, M.D.
My Darling Daughters' Anniversary
Vanished
YOUNG, ROBERT MALCOLM (writer)
Series
Marcus Welby, M.D.
YULIN, HARRIS (actor)
Telefeatures
The Greatest Gift
The Night Rider
Special
The Mask of Love
YUST, LARRY (director)
Series
Testimony of Two Men

ZABKA, STAN (2nd assistant director)
Series
The Eddie Capra Mysteries
The Rebels

ZARCOFF, MORT (associate
  producer)
 Series
 It Takes a Thief
 The Road West
 Switch
ZERBE, ANTHONY (actor)
 Series
 Centennial
 Once an Eagle
 Telefeatures
 The Hound of the Baskervilles
 The Priest Killer
ZERBE, L. RALPH (sound
  mixer)
 Series
 McCloud
ZIEGMAN, JERRY (writer)
 Series
 Centennial
ZILLIOX, ROBERT L. (set
  decorator)
 Series
 The Rockford Files
ZIMMER, DOLPH M. (assistant
  director)
 Series
 Leave It to Beaver
ZSIGMOND, VILMOS (director
  of photography)
 Series
 The Protectors
ZUNIGA, ALBERT J. (film
  editor)
 Series
 The Doctors
 The Immigrants
 Telefeatures
 The Alpha Caper
 Female Artillery
 Let's Switch
 Pine Canyon Is Burning

JEB H. PERRY, free-lance writer and media historian, was born in New Haven, Connecticut, and has worked as a production coordinator at Center Stage in Baltimore, Maryland, and on the staff of WHCN Radio and the Concert Network in Hartford, Connecticut. Mr. Perry is the author of three books for Scarecrow Press: Variety Obits: An Index to Obituaries in "Variety," 1905-1978 (1980), Universal Television: The Studio and Its Programs, 1950-1980 (1983) and Screen Gems: A History of Columbia Pictures Television (in preparation). A programmer and consultant for many film retrospectives at the Atheneum Cinema in Hartford, Connecticut, Mr. Perry has also worked at the Hartford Stage Company, done commercials for The National Lampoon, designed the lighting for Max Morath's "The Ragtime Years" at the University of Hartford, done photo research for Walter Kerr and contributed material to Classic Images and American Film. Mr. Perry has studied percussion at the Hartt School of Music and his other interests include literature, popular music, swimming, and horseback riding. Mr. Perry is the grandson of industrialist Henry E. Perry and a cousin of writer Bliss Perry.

ROY HUGGINS entered television as a producer at Warner Bros. in the mid-1950s. There he was responsible for creating and/or producing such classic series as Cheyenne, Colt .45, Maverick, and 77 Sunset Strip. In 1962, Mr. Huggins moved to Universal Television (where he was also a corporate vice-president) and produced and/or created such acclaimed series as The Virginian, Run for Your Life, The Bold Ones, Toma, Baretta, Captains and the Kings, The Rockford Files, and City of Angels. In 1960, while attending the University of California at Los Angeles as a candidate for a Ph.D., Mr. Huggins created The Fugitive, sold it to ABC, and contracted with QM Productions to produce it. The last episode of The Fugitive remains one of the highest-rated programs in the history of television. Mr. Huggins joined Columbia Pictures Television as Executive Producer in January 1983.